SACRED WRITINGS

JUDAISM

CHRISTIANITY

ISLAM

CONFUCIANISM

HINDUISM

&

BUDDHISM

EDITED BY
JAROSLAV PELIKAN

SACRED WRITINGS

VOLUME 2

CHRISTIANITY:
THE APOCRYPHA
AND
THE NEW TESTAMENT

SACRED WRITINGS

CHRISTIANITY:
THE APOCRYPHA
AND
THE NEW TESTAMENT

FROM *THE REVISED ENGLISH BIBLE*

QUALITY PAPERBACK BOOK CLUB
NEW YORK

CONTENTS

CONTENTS

ABBREVIATIONS AND NOTES

An explanation of terms, names of ancient versions, etc., as used in footnotes to the text.

Aq.	Aquila	*Jas*	James
Aram.	Aramaic	*Jer.*	Jeremiah
Bel & Snake	Daniel, Bel, and the Snake	*Josh.*	Joshua
ch(s).	chapter(s)	*Judg.*	Judges
Chr.	Chronicles	*Kgs.*	Kings
Col.	Colossians	*Lam.*	Lamentations
Cor.	Corinthians	*Lat.*	Latin
cp.	compare	*Lev.*	Leviticus
Dan.	Daniel	*lit.*	literally
Deut.	Deuteronomy	*L. of Jer.*	Letter of Jeremiah
Eccles.	Ecclesiastes	*Luc.*	Lucian
Ecclus	Ecclesiasticus	*Macc.*	Maccabees
Eph.	Ephesians	*Mal.*	Malachi
Esd.	Esdras	*Matt.*	Matthew
Exod.	Exodus	*Mic.*	Micah
Ezek.	Ezekiel	*mng*	meaning
Gal.	Galatians	*MS(S)*	manuscript(s)
Gen.	Genesis	*Neh.*	Nehemiah
Gk	Greek	*Num.*	Numbers
Hab.	Habakkuk	*Obad.*	Obadiah
Hag.	Haggai	*or*	indicates an alternative interpretation
Heb.	Hebrew (in references to texts, normally the Massoretic Text)	*Pet.*	Peter
		Phil.	Philippians
		Philem.	Philemon
Hos.	Hosea	*poss.*	possible
Isa.	Isaiah	*prob.*	probable

Pr. of Az.	Prayer of Azariah	*S. of S.*	Song of Songs
Pr. of Man.	Prayer of Manasseh	*S. of Three*	Song of the Three
Prov.	Proverbs	*Sus.*	Daniel and Susanna
Ps(s).	Psalm(s)	*Symm.*	Symmachus
rdg	reading	*Targ.*	Targum
Rest of Esth.	Rest of Esther	*Theod.*	Theodotion
Rev.	Revelation	*Thess.*	Thessalonians
Rom.	Romans	*Tim.*	Timothy
Sam.	Samuel	*Vs(s).*	Version(s)
Samar.	Samaritan Pentateuch	*Wisd.*	Wisdom
Scroll	text derived from the Dead Sea Scrolls	*Zech.*	Zechariah
		Zeph.	Zephaniah

[ ] In keywords, square brackets enclose words that are included for clarity of reference, but are not themselves the subject of the note.

INTRODUCTION

a. The Apocrypha

Title. This volume of *Sacred Writings* contains two collections of Sacred Books that appear only in Christian Bibles. The first section of this volume, The Apocrypha, appears in some Christian Bibles as an addendum to the books that appear in volume 1, The Tanakh, which in Christian Bibles bears the identification "Old Testament." The standing of the books included under this category is a highly ambiguous one. That ambiguity, moreover, attends the status of these books throughout their history, as the various names of the collection suggest. "Apocrypha" means "things that are hidden." As the editors of the Apocrypha for the Revised Standard Version of the Bible have summarized the problem, "Some have suggested that the books were 'hidden' or withdrawn from common use because they were deemed to contain mysterious or esoteric lore. . . . Others have suggested that the term was employed by those who held that such books deserved to be 'hidden' because they were spurious or heretical." Another term for them has been "deuterocanonical," indicating that even where they are accepted, they occupy a secondary position in the canon of Christian Scriptures (see "Canon" below). With the titles and in the order in which they appear here, the Apocrypha are: The First Book of Esdras; The Second Book of Esdras; Tobit; Judith; The Rest of the Chapters of the Book of Esther; The Wisdom of Solomon; Ecclesiasticus or The Wisdom of Jesus Son of Sirach; Baruch; A Letter of Jeremiah; The Prayer of Azariah and The Song of the Three; Daniel and Susanna; Daniel, Bel, and the Snake; The Prayer of Manasseh; The First Book of the Maccabees; The Second Book of the Maccabees.

Composition and Authorship. Although these books, in their literary form and style, form a miscellany of Jewish religious literature, there is one characteristic that they have in common, a characteristic that also serves to define their position in the history of the Jewish and the Christian Bibles, that is, their relative lateness. They are not only second in rank to the canonical books of the Tanakh/ Old Testament, they are also written after most or all of them. As the title indicates, The Rest of the Chapters of the Book of Esther appeared as an addendum to the canonical Esther; The Prayer of Azariah and The Song of the Three, Daniel and Susanna, and Daniel, Bel, and the Snake were similarly addenda to the canonical Daniel. Although they stand as separate books unto themselves, The Wisdom of Solomon and Ecclesiasticus or the Wisdom of Jesus Son of Sirach are collections of sayings and proverbs that have important affinities and continuity with the canonical books of Proverbs and Ecclesiastes. The Books of the Maccabees and I Esdras, on the other hand, approach the historiography of the canonical books of Samuel, Kings, and Chronicles. II Esdras harks back to the apocalyptic tradition of the canonical Ezekiel and Daniel, and it anticipates the apocalypticism of the Book of Revelation in the New Testament. As most introductions to the Apocrypha point out, the one genre of the Tanakh that is missing here is the prophetic. I Maccabees (9:27) acknowledges that these books come from a time in the history of Israel when "prophets ceased to appear among them."

Language and Text. The differences of scholarly opinion about the original language of the several books of the Apocrypha befit their heterogeneity. Some of them were written in Hebrew or Aramaic (Tobit, Judith, Ecclesiasticus or The Wisdom of Jesus Son of Sirach, Baruch, I Maccabees), whereas others were written in Greek (The Rest of the Chapters of the Book of Esther, The Wisdom of Solomon, II Maccabees). In the case of several of them (I Esdras; A Letter of Jeremiah; The Prayer of Azariah and The Song of the Three; Daniel and Susanna; Daniel, Bel, and the Snake; The Prayer of Manasseh) scholars have found it impossible to decide with any certainty the question of the original language. II Esdras, for example, exists as a Latin translation of an original that seems to have been composed partly in Greek and partly in Hebrew or Aramaic. Except for some Hebrew and Aramaic versions that have been discovered over the past century or so, the Apocrypha survive chiefly as part of the Septuagint, and it is also from that Greek text that they have been translated.

Canon and Authority. The most prominent feature of these books historically, and the one that binds them together, is their dubious canonicity and authority. It does appear anachronistic to speak of a "canon" in connection with the Septuagint; for in it, as well as in the Dead Sea Scrolls discovered in the twentieth century, books that were later to be defined as "canonical" appear alongside others that were not, with no obvious differentiation among them. The eventual canonization of the Tanakh by the Jewish community excluded these dubious books while ultimately including some about which there had been question. But it is a measure of the rapid and all but total alienation between the Jewish and the Christian communities that very few Christians after the end of the first century of the Common Era could read Hebrew, so that effectively the Septuagint became "the Christian Tanakh"; its readings (and misreadings) and its "canon" prevailed in the Church. Doubts remained, the strongest doubts being, significantly, those of Christian scholars like Jerome (d. 420 C.E.), who did know Hebrew and who did have associations with Jewish scholarship. Those doubts found a powerful echo in the Protestant Reformers, whose emphasis on the authoritativeness of the original Hebrew and Greek texts of the Bible, inspired by Renaissance humanism, carried over also to the Hebrew canon. It was in response to Protestant criticism that the Roman Catholic Council of Trent in 1546, and then the Eastern Orthodox Synod of Jerusalem in 1672, for the first time made most of the books of the Apocrypha an official part of the Christian canon of the Old Testament.

Traditional Interpretation. The Christian interpretation of the Apocrypha, like the interpretation of the "rest" of the Old Testament, has been decisively affected by the tradition of prophecy and fulfillment. According to this tradition, the history of the New Testament and the subsequent history of the Church are the divine performance of that which had been promised before the coming of Christ. Conversely, the rejection of their canonicity by Protestant Christians caused them to be neglected not only by believers in the pew, but by scholars, and even to be omitted altogether from most printings of the English Bible. From both sides, the sharp antitheses of the Reformation period have softened in recent decades, as the inclusion of the Apocrypha in both the Revised Standard Version and the Revised English Bible indicates.

Translations and This Translation. In a real sense, it is to the accident of translation that many of the books of the Apocrypha owe their very survival, for the Greek Septuagint and then the Latin Vulgate have been responsible for their preservation and circulation. In spite of their rejection of the canonicity and authority of these books, moreover, the biblical translators of the Reformation era did include them in their editions, usually with some warning that they were not worthy of being put on the same level with the canonical Scriptures. (See below, under "The New Testament," for the origins of the translation being included here.)

b. The New Testament

Title. The New Testament is well-nigh universal as the title for the specifically Christian portion of the Scriptures, although such titles as "New Law" also appear in some languages. The word "testament" means "covenant," and is so used in older English translations of the words of Jesus that were the first to be written down (1 Cor. 11:25): "This cup is the new testament in my blood." But the title seems not to have been used about a book—or, again, more precisely a collection of books—until a body of normative Christian writings was placed alongside the body of writings inherited from Judaism. Together these formed a Christian Scripture, made up of the records of the two covenants of God as these had been distinguished by the apostle Paul (2 Cor. 3:6), the "Old Testament" and the "New Testament." Similarly, the word "gospel," meaning "good news," referred first to a message and only later to the fourfold book with which the New Testament opens. The title "scripture," when it appears in the New Testament, obviously refers in most instances only to the "Old Testament," there being no "New Testament" in existence yet; but once there was a Christian Bible with two Testaments, terms like "scripture" and "word of God" came to be applied to this Bible in its entirety.

Composition and Authorship. The oldest and the most numerous books of the New Testament are the letters of the apostle Paul, which traditionally are thirteen in number: Romans, I Corinthians, II Corinthians, Galatians, Ephesians, Philippians, Colossians, I Thessalonians, II Thessalonians, I Timothy, II Timothy, Titus, Philemon. They are addressed to specific congregations or individuals and usually were written in response to very specific needs and occasions. Distinguished from these as "general letters" or "catholic epistles" are those seven, bearing the names of other leaders of the early church, that were not addressed so specifically: James, I Peter, II Peter, I John, II John, III John, Jude. The "Letter to Hebrews," as it is labeled here, has neither a title nor a writer's name as part of its text, but it received that designation because of its method of argumentation on the basis of an extensive use of the Jewish Scriptures. The four Gospels—or rather, the one Gospel in its four renderings—likewise have no writer's names, but they have traditionally been attributed to Matthew (one of the original twelve disciples of Jesus), John Mark (a disciple of the apostle Peter), Luke ("the doctor" mentioned in Col. 4:14), and John (also one of the twelve). As the account of the life and teachings of Jesus, whom Christian faith identifies as the Messiah or Christ of God and thus as the "founder" in a unique sense (see chapter 10 of *On Searching the Scriptures*), the Gospels have pride of place within the New Testament. The Acts of the Apostles is a continuation, by the same writer, of the narrative in the Gospel of Luke. The Revelation of John, traditionally ascribed to the writer of the Fourth Gospel and the three epistles bearing that name, is a Christian apocalypse in the succession of Ezekiel, Daniel, and The Second Book of Esdras.

Language and Text. Although there has been a persistent scholarly rumor about Aramaic originals, particularly for the Gospel of Matthew, the New Testament was written in Greek—not the classical Greek of Plato and Sophocles but the everyday Greek of the Mediterranean world, hence called Koine, meaning "common." Several of the writers of the New Testament, notably Paul, were themselves of Jewish origin; some of the traditions, oral and perhaps written, upon which various of them drew were Aramaic; and most of them knew and used the Septuagint translation of the Old Testament. For all of these reasons, much of the Greek of the New Testament has the strong flavor of translation about it. History has handed down to us none of the original manuscripts of the books of the New Testament, but it has preserved literally thousands of copies in manuscript, together with early quotations from the New Testament and early translations of it. The net result of this process of transmission is a welter of variant readings that, it seems safe to say, is unmatched in the history of Western literature. Coping with these textual variants, the most important of which are reflected in the footnotes of our edition, has been the task of many generations of scholars and scribes, and has helped to develop the science of textual criticism, which has in turn been applied to the editing of the works of other writers, ancient and modern.

Canon and Authority. Already in the later books of the New Testament there are some indications that the letters of Paul and the sayings of Jesus were being preserved, copied, and circulated as "scripture," but in the absence of a centralized legislative body there appears to have been great variety and a form of local option in the use of such collections. It was, at least in part, the challenge of other writings purporting to be on the same level that provoked from the leaders of the Church some of the earliest compilations of lists of authoritative "apostolic" books. Many of the books now included were on all of those lists; some books, such as Hebrews, James, and Revelation, were in doubt, whereas some that eventually did not qualify, such as the First Letter of Clement and the Letter of Barnabas, did appear in some collections and do appear in some New Testament manuscripts. As authoritative scripture, the New Testament took its place alongside the "Old," but the writings of such Christian leaders as Irenaeus of Lyons at the end of the second century indicate that the process by which its authority acquired universal recognition was part of an evolution in which the authority of the bishop and the authority of tradition were linked to the authority of the Bible.

Traditional Interpretation. That definition of the authority of the New Testament has also decisively shaped its traditional interpretation, through the circular argument that the creedal and liturgical tradition of the Church was based on the New Testament but that the New Testament was to be interpreted in such a way as to harmonize with the creedal and liturgical tradition of the Church. Because the first part of this argument carried the force that the authority of Scripture was supreme though it was not the sole authority, the interpretation of the Bible has always held a special place in the life and thought, the preaching and worship, of the Christian community. Throughout Christian history, when voices of renewal and reform have been heard, they have come in the name of the original revelation contained in the New Testament, even though their interpretation of it was novel or revolutionary.

Translations and This Translation. The New Testament has been translated into almost two thousand languages, and into some of these many times. Coming as they did at crucial points in the history of their languages, many of these translations have shaped the vocabulary and style of succeeding generations. They have also repeatedly become archaic, with the result that new versions have continued to appear. The English-speaking world has been particularly rich in producing these versions, among which the Authorized ("King James") Version of 1611 has long occupied a position of special honor, even for those who no longer find its language completely intelligible. The translation of the New Testament (and that of the Apocrypha) in these *Sacred Writings* is taken from the Revised English Bible, which appeared in 1989 as a far-reaching revision of the New English Bible, whose New Testament was originally published in 1961. The Revised English Bible was a cooperative venture involving several denominations and many scholars. One of the reasons for its success is that when the scholars had finished their work, the translations were vetted by a group of literary advisers, who tested them for style and idiom.

Jaroslav Pelikan

THE APOCRYPHA

THE FIRST BOOK OF
ESDRAS

The reign of Josiah

1 JOSIAH celebrated the Passover to his Lord at Jerusalem, and the Passover victims were sacrificed on the fourteenth day of the first month. ² He installed the priests, duly robed in their vestments, in the temple of the Lord according to the order of daily service. ³ He commanded the Levites, who served the temple in Israel, to purify themselves for the Lord, before placing the sacred Ark in the Lord's house, which King Solomon son of David built. ⁴ Josiah said to them, 'You shall not carry it about on your shoulders any longer. Now you are to serve the Lord your God and minister to his people Israel: prepare yourselves, family by family and clan by clan, ⁵ in the manner prescribed by King David of Israel and provided for so magnificently by his son Solomon. Stand in the holy place according to your family groups, you Levites who are in divisions to act for your brother Israelites. ⁶ Sacrifice the Passover victims, and prepare the sacrifices for your kinsmen. Keep the Passover according to the command given by the Lord to Moses.'

⁷ For those who were present Josiah contributed thirty thousand lambs and kids and three thousand calves; they were given from the king's own resources to the people and to the priests and Levites in fulfilment of his promise. ⁸ The temple wardens, Chelkias, Zacharias, and Esyelus, gave the priests two thousand six hundred sheep and three hundred calves for the Passover. ⁹ Jechonias, Samaeas, his brother Nathanael, Sabias, Ochielus, and Joram, high-ranking officers in the army, gave the Levites five thousand sheep and seven hundred calves for the Passover.

¹⁰ This was the procedure: the priests and the Levites, bearing the unleavened bread, stood in all their splendour by clans ¹¹ and by family groups before the people, to make offerings to the Lord as is laid down in the book of Moses. This took place in the morning. ¹² The Passover victims were roasted over the fire in the prescribed way and the sacrifices boiled with fragrant herbs in the bronze vessels and cauldrons; ¹³ then portions were carried round to the whole assembly. After that the Levites made preparations for themselves and for their kinsmen, the priests of Aaron's line. ¹⁴ It was because the priests were engaged until nightfall in offering up the fat portions that the Levites made the preparations both for themselves and for their kinsmen, the priests of Aaron's line. ¹⁵ The temple singers, the sons of Asaph, were in their places according to the ordinances of David, and Asaph, Zacharias, and Eddinous of the royal court; ¹⁶ and the door-keepers were at each gateway. There was no need for any of them to leave their posts, for their kinsmen, the Levites, made the preparations for them.

¹⁷ Everything for the sacrifice to the Lord was completed that day: the celebration of the Passover ¹⁸ and the offering of the sacrifices on the Lord's altar, according to King Josiah's orders. ¹⁹ Israelites who were present at that time kept the Passover and the feast of Unleavened Bread for seven days. ²⁰ No Passover like it had been celebrated in Israel since the time of the prophet Samuel; ²¹ none of the kings of Israel had kept such a Passover as was kept by Josiah, with the priests, Levites, and men of Judah, and all the Israelites who happened to be resident in Jerusalem. ²² It was in the eighteenth year of Josiah's reign that this Passover was celebrated.

²³ Josiah was deeply pious and his deeds were upright in the sight of his Lord. ²⁴ The events of his reign are to be found among earlier records, records of sin and rebellion against the Lord graver than anything perpetrated by any other nation or kingdom, and of offences against him which brought down his judgement on Israel.

²⁵ Some time after Josiah's act of worship had taken place, it happened that Pharaoh king of Egypt was advancing to

open hostilities at Carchemish on the Euphrates. When Josiah marched out to confront him, ²⁶ the Egyptian king sent him this message: 'What do you want with me, king of Judah? ²⁷ It is not against you that the Lord God has sent me to fight; my campaign is on the Euphrates. On this occasion the Lord is with me. He is with me, speeding me on my way. Stand aside, and do not oppose the Lord.' ²⁸ Josiah did not return to his chariot but set out to give battle, disregarding the words of the prophet Jeremiah, the spokesman of the Lord. ²⁹ When he joined battle in the plain of Megiddo, Pharaoh's captains swept down on King Josiah. ³⁰ 'I am badly wounded,' the king said to his servants; 'take me out of the battle.' They took him out of the line at once, ³¹ and when he had been put into his second chariot, he was brought back to Jerusalem. There he died and was buried in the ancestral tomb.

³² Throughout Judah there was mourning for Josiah, and the prophet Jeremiah made lament for him. The lamentation for Josiah has been observed by the chief men and their wives from that day to this: an edict was issued to all the people of Israel that this should be done for all time. ³³ These things are recorded in the annals of the kings of Judah; every deed of Josiah's which won him fame and showed his understanding of the law of the Lord, both what he did earlier and what is told of him here, is related in the book of the kings of Israel and Judah.

Exile and return

³⁴ His fellow-countrymen took Jeconiah son of Josiah and made him king in succession to his father. He was twenty-three years old, ³⁵ and he reigned over Judah and Jerusalem for three months. Then the king of Egypt deposed him, ³⁶ fined the nation a hundred talents of silver and one talent of gold, ³⁷ and replaced him by his brother Joakim as king of Judah and Jerusalem. ³⁸ Joakim imprisoned the leading men and had his brother Zarius arrested and brought back from Egypt.

³⁹ Joakim was twenty-five years old when he became king of Judah and Jerusalem. He did what was wrong in the eyes of the Lord, ⁴⁰ and King Nebuchad-

nezzar of Babylon marched against him, put him in bronze fetters, and took him away to Babylon. ⁴¹ Nebuchadnezzar also seized some of the sacred vessels of the Lord; he carried them off and placed them in his own temple at Babylon. ⁴² The stories about Joakim, his depraved and impious conduct, are recorded in the chronicles of the kings.

⁴³ He was succeeded by his son Joakim, who was eighteen years old when he came to the throne. ⁴⁴ He reigned in Jerusalem for three months and ten days, and he too did what was wrong in the eyes of the Lord. ⁴⁵ A year later Nebuchadnezzar sent and had him brought to Babylon together with the sacred vessels of the Lord, ⁴⁶ and he made Zedekiah king of Judah and Jerusalem.

Zedekiah was twenty-one years old, and he reigned for eleven years. ⁴⁷ He did what was wrong in the eyes of the Lord and disregarded the advice of the prophet Jeremiah, the spokesman of the Lord. ⁴⁸ King Nebuchadnezzar had made him swear by the Lord an oath of allegiance, but he renounced his oath and rebelled. He was stubborn and obstinate, and broke the commandments of the Lord God of Israel.

⁴⁹ The leaders of both people and priests committed many impious and lawless acts. They outdid even the heathen in their abominable practices, and defiled the Lord's temple which had been consecrated in Jerusalem. ⁵⁰ The God of their fathers sent his messenger to reclaim them, because he wished to spare them and his dwelling-place. ⁵¹ But they held his messengers in derision: they were scoffing at his prophets on the very day when the Lord spoke. ⁵² At last his anger was so roused against his people on account of their impieties that he ordered the Chaldaean kings to attack them. ⁵³ The Lord handed them all over to their enemies, who put their young men to the sword around the holy temple, and spared neither young man nor maiden, neither the old nor the infant. ⁵⁴ All the sacred vessels of the Lord, large and small, the furnishings of the Ark of the Lord, and the royal treasures were taken as spoil to Babylon. ⁵⁵ The Lord's house was burnt down, the walls of Jerusalem razed to the

1:54 **the furnishings of the Ark**: *in other MSS the treasure chests.*

ground, its towers set ablaze, [56] and all its splendours brought to ruin. Nebuchadnezzar transported to Babylon those who escaped the sword, [57] and they remained slaves to him and his sons until his empire fell to the Persians. This fulfilled the word of the Lord spoken by Jeremiah [58] that, until the land should have run the full term of its sabbaths, it should keep sabbath all the time of its desolation till the end of the seventy years.

2 IN the first year of King Cyrus of Persia the Lord, to fulfil his word spoken through Jeremiah, [2] moved the heart of the king so that throughout his kingdom the following proclamation was made and at the same time issued in writing:

[3] The decree of King Cyrus of Persia.

The Lord of Israel, the Most High Lord, has made me king of the world [4] and has charged me to build him a house at Jerusalem in Judaea. [5] Whoever among you, therefore, belongs to his people, may his Lord be with him! Let him go up to Jerusalem in Judaea and build the house of the Lord of Israel, the Lord who dwells in Jerusalem. [6] Throughout the country let assistance be given to each man by his neighbours with gold and silver [7] and other gifts, with horses and pack-animals, together with anything else set aside as votive offerings for the temple of the Lord in Jerusalem.

[8] Then the heads of the families of the tribes of Judah and Benjamin came forward, along with the priests, the Levites, and all who had been prompted by the Lord to go up and build his house in Jerusalem. [9] Their neighbours assisted with gifts of every kind, silver and gold, horses and pack-animals. Many were also moved to help with votive offerings in great quantity. [10] Moreover, the sacred vessels of the Lord which Nebuchadnezzar had removed from Jerusalem and placed in the temple of his idols were brought out by King Cyrus of Persia [11] and given into the charge of Mithradates his treasurer, [12] by whom they were handed over to Sanabassar, governor of Judaea. [13] Here is the list of them: a thousand gold cups, a thousand silver cups, twenty-nine silver censers, thirty gold bowls, two

thousand four hundred and ten silver bowls, and a thousand other articles. [14] In all, five thousand four hundred and sixty-nine gold and silver vessels were sent back, [15] and they were brought by Sanabassar to Jerusalem from Babylon along with the exiles.

[16] But when Artaxerxes was king of Persia, Belemus, Mithradates, Tabellius, Rathymus, Beeltethmus, Semellius the secretary, and their colleagues in office in Samaria and elsewhere, wrote the king the following letter denouncing the inhabitants of Judaea and Jerusalem:

[17] To our Sovereign Lord Artaxerxes your servants Rathymus the Recorder, Semellius the Secretary, the other members of their council, and the magistrates in Coele-Syria and Phoenicia.

[18] Be it known to your majesty that the Jews who left you to come up here have arrived in Jerusalem, and are rebuilding that rebellious and wicked city, repairing its streets and walls and laying the foundation of a temple. [19] Once this city is rebuilt and the walls are completed, they will never submit to paying tribute but will even rebel against your royal house. [20] Since work on the temple is in hand, we have thought it well not to overlook such an important matter [21] but to bring it to your majesty's attention, in order that, if it please your majesty, search may be made in the records left by your predecessors. [22] You will discover in the archives references to these matters; you will learn that this has been a rebellious city, a source of trouble to kings and cities. [23] From earliest times it has been a centre of armed resistance by the Jews, and for that reason it was laid in ruins. [24] Therefore we now submit to your majesty that, if this city be rebuilt and its walls rise again, you will be denied access to Coele-Syria and Phoenicia.

[25] The king sent this reply:

To Rathymus the Recorder, Beeltethmus, Semellius the Secretary, and their colleagues in office in Samaria, Syria, and Phoenicia.

[26] Having read the letter you sent me, I ordered search to be made, and that city, it was discovered, has a long history of opposition to the royal house,

27 and its inhabitants have been given to rebellion and war. There have been powerful and ruthless kings ruling in Jerusalem who have exercised authority over Coele-Syria and Phoenicia and laid them under tribute. 28 I therefore command that the men of whom you write be prevented from rebuilding the city, and that measures be taken to enforce this order 29 and to check the spread of an evil likely to be troublesome to our royal house.

30 On receipt of the letter from King Artaxerxes, Rathymus, Semellius the secretary, and their colleagues hurried to Jerusalem with cavalry and a large body of other troops and stopped the builders. Work on the temple at Jerusalem remained at a standstill until the second year of the reign of King Darius of Persia.

A debate at the Persian court

3 KING Darius gave a great banquet for all his retainers, for all the members of his household, all the chief men of Media and Persia, 2 along with the whole body of satraps, commanders, and governors of his empire in the hundred and twenty-seven satrapies from India to Ethiopia. 3 After eating and drinking as much as they wanted, they withdrew. King Darius retired to his bedchamber, where he lay down and fell fast asleep.

4 Then the three young men of the king's personal bodyguard said among themselves: 5 'Let each of us name the thing he judges to be strongest, and to the one whose opinion appears wisest let King Darius give rich gifts and prizes: 6 he shall be robed in purple, drink from gold cups, and sleep on a golden bed; he shall have a chariot with gold-studded bridles, and a turban of fine linen, and a chain around his neck. 7 His wisdom shall give him the right to sit next to the king and to bear the title Kinsman of Darius.' 8 Each then put his opinion in writing, affixed his seal, and placed it under the king's pillow. 9 'When the king wakes,' they said, 'the writing will be given him, and the king and the three chief men of Persia shall judge whose opinion is wisest; the award will be made to that man on the evidence of what he has written.'

10 One wrote, 'Wine is strongest.' 11 The second wrote, 'The king is strongest.' 12 The third wrote, 'Women are strongest, but truth conquers all.' 13 When the king awoke, he was handed what they had written. Having read it 14 he summoned all the chief men of Persia and Media, satraps, commanders, governors, and chief officers, 15 and took his seat in the council-chamber. What each of the three had written was then read out before them. 16 'Call the young men,' said the king, 'and let them explain their opinions.' They were summoned and, on coming in, 17 were asked to clarify what they had written.

The first, who spoke about the strength of wine, began: 18 'Sirs, how true it is that wine is strongest! It bemuses the wits of all who drink it: 19 king and orphan, slave and free, poor and rich, on them all it has the same effect. 20 It turns all thoughts to revelry and mirth; it brings forgetfulness of grief and debt. 21 It makes everyone feel rich; it cares nothing for king or satrap, but sets all men talking in millions. 22 When they are in their cups, they forget to be friendly to friends and relations, and before long are drawing their swords; 23 and when they awake after their wine, they cannot remember what they have done. 24 Sirs, is not wine the strongest, seeing that it makes men behave in this way?' With that he ended his speech.

4 Then the second, he who spoke of the strength of the king, began: 2 'Sirs, is not man the strongest, man who subdues land and sea and everything in them? 3 But the strongest of men is the king; he is their lord and master, and they obey whatever command he gives them. 4 If he bids them make war on one another, they do so; if he dispatches them against his enemies, they march off and make their way over mountains and walls and towers. 5 They kill and are killed, but they never disobey the king's command. If they are victorious they bring everything, spoil and all else, to the king. 6 Again, take those who do not serve as soldiers or go to war, but work the land: they sow and reap, and lay the harvest before the king. They compel each other to pay him their tribute. 7 Though he is no more than one man, if he orders them to kill, they kill; if he orders them to release, they release. He

3:3 **and fell fast asleep:** *prob. rdg ; Gk* sleepless.

orders them ⁸ to smite and they beat, to demolish and they demolish, to build and they build, ⁹ to cut down and they cut down, to plant and they plant. ¹⁰ People and troops all obey him. Further, while he himself is at table, whether he eats, drinks, or goes to sleep, ¹¹ they stand in attendance round him and none can leave and see to his own affairs; in nothing whatever do they disobey. ¹² Sirs, surely the king must be the strongest, when he commands such obedience!' With that he ended.

¹³ The third, he who spoke about women and truth, was Zerubbabel; he began: ¹⁴ 'Sirs, it is true that the king is great, that men are many, and that wine is strong, but who rules over them? Who is the master? Women, surely! ¹⁵ The king and all his people, lords over land and sea, were born of women, ¹⁶ and from them they came. Women brought up the men who planted the vineyards which yield the wine. ¹⁷ They make the clothes men wear and they bring honour to men; without women men could not exist.

¹⁸ 'If men have amassed gold and silver and all manner of beautiful things, and then see a woman with a lovely face and figure, ¹⁹ they leave it all to gape and stare at her with open mouth, and every one of them will prefer her above gold and silver or any thing of beauty. ²⁰ A man will abandon his father who brought him up, abandon even his country, and become one with his wife. ²¹ To the end of his days he stays with her, forgetful of father, mother, and country. ²² Here is the proof that women are your masters: do you not toil and sweat and then bring all you earn and give it to your wives? ²³ A man will take his sword and sally forth to plunder and steal, to sail on sea and river; ²⁴ he confronts lions, he goes about in the dark; and when he has stolen and robbed and looted, he brings the spoil home to his beloved.

²⁵ 'A man loves his wife above father or mother. ²⁶ For women's sakes many men have been driven out of their minds, many have become slaves, ²⁷ many have perished or come to grief or taken to evil ways. ²⁸ Now do you believe me? Certainly the king wields great authority; no country dare lift a finger against him. ²⁹ Yet I watched him with Apame, his favourite concubine, daughter of the cel-ebrated Bartacus. She was sitting on the king's right, ³⁰ and she took the diadem off his head and put it on her own. She was slapping his face with her left hand, ³¹ and all the king did was gape at her open-mouthed. When she laughed at him he laughed; when she was cross with him he coaxed her to make it up with him. ³² Sirs, if women do as well as this, how can their strength be denied?' ³³ The king and the chief men looked at one another.

Zerubbabel then went on to speak about truth: ³⁴ 'Sirs, we have seen that women are strong. The earth is vast, the sky is lofty, yet the sun, swift in its course, moves through the circle of the sky and speeds home in a single day. ³⁵ How great is the sun which can do this! But truth too is great; it is stronger than all else. ³⁶ The whole earth calls on truth, and the sky praises her; all created things shake and tremble. With her there is no injustice. ³⁷ There is injustice in wine, and in kings, and in women, injustice in all men and in all their works, whatever they may be. There is no truth in them, and in their injustice they shall perish. ³⁸ But truth abides and remains strong for ever; she lives and is sovereign for ever and ever.

³⁹ 'There is no favouritism with her, no partiality; rather she exacts justice from everyone who is wicked or unjust. All approve what she does; ⁴⁰ in her judgements there is no injustice. Hers are strength and royalty, the authority and majesty of all ages. Praise be to the God of truth!'

⁴¹ As Zerubbabel finished speaking, all the people shouted, 'Great is truth: truth is strongest!' ⁴² Then the king said to him, 'Ask what you will, even beyond what is laid down in the terms, and we shall grant it you. You have been proved to be the wisest, and you shall sit next to me and be called my Kinsman.' ⁴³ Zerubbabel answered, 'Remember, O king, the vow you made on the day when you came to the throne: you promised to rebuild Jerusalem ⁴⁴ and to send back all the vessels taken from there. Cyrus had set them aside, for when he vowed to destroy Babylon, at the same time he vowed to restore these vessels. ⁴⁵ You also made a vow to rebuild the temple, burnt by the Edomites when Judaea had been ravaged by the Chaldaeans. ⁴⁶ This is the favour I now beg of you, my lord king, this the

magnanimous gesture I request: that you should perform the vow made by you to the King of heaven.'

⁴⁷ King Darius stood up, embraced him, and wrote letters on his behalf, instructing all the treasurers, governors, commanders, and satraps to give safe conduct to him and to all those going up with him to rebuild Jerusalem. ⁴⁸ He wrote also to all the governors in Coele-Syria and Phoenicia and to those in Lebanon ordering them to transport cedar-wood from Lebanon to Jerusalem and help Zerubbabel build the city. ⁴⁹ He gave all Jews going up from his kingdom to Judaea a written assurance of their liberties: no one in authority, whether satrap, governor, or treasurer, was to molest them in their homes. ⁵⁰ All land which they might acquire was to be exempt from taxation, and the Edomites were to surrender the villages they had seized from the Jews. ⁵¹ Each year twenty talents were to be contributed to the building of the temple until it was completed, ⁵² and a further ten talents annually for the seventeen whole-offerings to be sacrificed every day on the altar in accordance with their law. ⁵³⁻⁵⁴ All who were going from Babylonia to build the city were to enjoy freedom, they and their descendants after them. The king gave orders in writing that all the priests going there should also receive maintenance and the vestments in which they would officiate; ⁵⁵ that the Levites too should receive maintenance, until that day when the temple should be completed and Jerusalem rebuilt; ⁵⁶ and that all who guarded the city should be given land and pay. ⁵⁷ He sent back from Babylon the vessels which Cyrus had set aside. He reaffirmed all that Cyrus had commanded, and gave orders that everything should be restored to Jerusalem.

⁵⁸ When the young man, Zerubbabel, went out, he turned to face the direction of Jerusalem, and looking heavenwards praised the King of heaven, saying:

⁵⁹ 'From you come victory and wisdom; yours is the glory, and I am your servant.

⁶⁰ All praise to you, for you have given me wisdom;

to you, Lord of our fathers, I ascribe praise.'

⁶¹ He took the letters and set out for Babylon. There his fellow-Jews, on receiving his report, ⁶² praised the God of their fathers who had given them leave and liberty ⁶³ to go up and rebuild Jerusalem and the temple which bore his name; and they feasted for seven days with music and rejoicing.

The returned Israelites

5 AFTER this the heads of families, tribe by tribe, were chosen to go up to Jerusalem with their wives, their sons and daughters, their male and female slaves, and their pack-animals. ² Darius dispatched a thousand horsemen to escort them safely there, with a band of drums and flutes, ³ to which all their kinsmen danced. So he sent them off with their escort.

⁴ These are the names of the men who went up to Jerusalem, arranged according to their families and tribes and their allotted duties: ⁵ the priests, sons of Phineas son of Aaron, with Jeshua son of Josedek, son of Saraeas, and Joakim son of Zerubbabel, son of Salathiel, of the house of David of the line of Phares of the tribe of Judah; ⁶ it was Zerubbabel who spoke wise words before King Darius of Persia. This was in the second year of his reign, in Nisan the first month.

⁷ These are the men from Judaea who returned from captivity and exile, those whom King Nebuchadnezzar of Babylon had taken to Babylon. ⁸ Each of them returned to his own town, whether to Jerusalem or elsewhere in Judaea. They were led by Zerubbabel and Jeshua, Nehemiah, Zaraeas, Resaeas, Enenius, Mardochaeus, Beelsarus, Aspharasus, Reelias, Roimus, and Baana.

⁹ The number of those of the nation who returned with their leaders was: the line of Phoros two thousand one hundred and seventy-two; the line of Saphat four hundred and seventy-two; ¹⁰ the line of Ares seven hundred and fifty-six; ¹¹ the line of Phaath-moab, belonging to the line of Jeshua and Joab, two thousand eight hundred and twelve; ¹² the line of Olamus one thousand two hundred and fifty-four; the line of Zathui nine hundred and forty-five; the line of Chorbe seven hundred and five; the line of Banei six hundred and forty-eight; ¹³ the line of Bebae six hundred and twenty-three; the line of Argai one thousand three hundred and

twenty-two; [14] the line of Adonikam six hundred and sixty-seven; the line of Bagoi two thousand and sixty-six; the line of Adinus four hundred and fifty-four; [15] the line of Ater son of Hezekias ninety-two; the line of Keilan and Azetas sixty-seven; the line of Azurus four hundred and thirty-two; [16] the line of Annias one hundred and one; the line of Arom and the line of Bassa three hundred and twenty-three; the line of Arsiphurith one hundred and twelve; [17] the line of Baeterus three thousand and five. The men of Bethlomon one hundred and twenty-three; [18] the men of Netophae fifty-five; the men of Anathoth one hundred and fifty-eight; the men of Bethasmoth forty-two; [19] the men of Cariathiarius twenty-five; the men of Caphira and Beroth seven hundred and forty-three; [20] the Chadiasans and Ammidaeans four hundred and twenty-two; the men of Kirama and Gabbes six hundred and twenty-one; [21] the men of Macalon one hundred and twenty-two; the men of Betolio fifty-two; the line of Niphis one hundred and fifty-six; [22] the line of Calamolalus and Onus seven hundred and twenty-five; the line of Jerechus three hundred and forty-five; [23] the line of Sanaas three thousand three hundred and thirty.

[24] The priests: the line of Jeddu son of Jeshua, belonging to the line of Anasib, nine hundred and seventy-two; the line of Emmeruth one thousand and fifty-two; [25] the line of Phassurus one thousand two hundred and forty-seven; the line of Charme one thousand and seventeen.

[26] The Levites: the line of Joshua, Cadmielus, Bannus, and Sudius seventy-four.

[27] The temple singers: the line of Asaph one hundred and forty-eight.

[28] The door-keepers: the line of Salum, of Atar, of Tolman, of Dacubi, of Ateta, of Sabi, in all one hundred and thirty-nine.

[29] The temple servitors: the line of Esau, of Asipha, of Taboth, of Keras, of Soua, of Phaleas, of Labana, of Aggaba, [30] of Acud, of Uta, of Ketab, of Gaba, of Subai, of Anan, of Cathua, of Geddur, [31] of Jairus, of Desan, of Noeba, of Chaseba, of Gazera, of Ozius, of Phinoe, of Asara, of Basthae, of Asana, of Maani, of Naphisi, of Acum, of Achipha, of Asur, of Pharakim, of Baaloth, [32] of Meedda, of Coutha, of Charea, of Barchue, of Serar, of Thomi, of Nasith, of Atepha. [33] The descendants of Solomon's servants: the line of Asapphioth, of Pharida, of Je-eli, of Lozon, of Isdael, of Saphythi, [34] of Agia, of Phacareth, of Sabie, of Sarothie, of Masias, of Gas, of Addus, of Subas, of Apherra, of Barodis, of Saphat, of Allon. [35] The temple servitors and the descendants of Solomon's servants amounted to three hundred and seventy-two in all.

[36] The following, who returned from Thermeleth and Thelsas with their leaders Chara, Athalar, and Alar, [37] were unable to prove by their families and descent that they were Israelites: the line of Dalan, the son of Tuban, and the line of Necodan amounting to six hundred and fifty-two.

[38] From among the priests the claimants to the priesthood whose record could not be traced: the lines of Obdia, of Accos, and of Joddus who married Augia, one of the daughters of Pharzellaeus, and took his name. [39] When search was made for the record of their descent in the register it could not be traced, and so they were debarred from officiating. [40] Nehemiah the governor forbade them to partake of the sacred food until there should be a high priest wearing the breastpiece of Revelation and Truth.

[41] They were in all: Israelites from twelve years old, not counting slaves male and female, forty-two thousand three hundred and sixty; [42] their slaves seven thousand three hundred and thirty-seven; musicians and singers two hundred and forty-five. [43] Their camels numbered four hundred and thirty-five, their horses seven thousand and thirty-six, their mules two hundred and forty-five, and their donkeys five thousand five hundred and twenty-five.

[44] On their arrival at the temple of God in Jerusalem, certain of the heads of the families took a vow to put forth their best efforts to rebuild the house on its original site, [45] and to give to the sacred treasury one thousand minas of gold and five thousand minas of silver for the fabric and one hundred vestments for priests.

[46] The priests, the Levites, and some of the people stayed in Jerusalem and its neighbourhood, while the temple

---

5:40 **the governor:** *prob. mng* (*cp.* Ezra 2: 63); Gk and Attharias.

musicians, the door-keepers, and all the rest of the Israelites lived in their villages.

⁴⁷ WHEN it was the seventh month and the Israelites were settled in their homes, they came together with one accord in the broad square of the first gateway toward the east. ⁴⁸ Jeshua son of Josedek and his fellow-priests, and Zerubbabel son of Salathiel and his colleagues set to work and made ready the altar of the God of Israel, ⁴⁹ in order to offer on it whole-offerings as prescribed in the book of Moses, the man of God. ⁵⁰ Other peoples of the land joined them, and they succeeded in setting up the altar on the original site; for in general the peoples in the land were hostile and too strong for them. Then they offered to the Lord sacrifices at the proper time and whole-offerings morning and evening. ⁵¹ They celebrated the feast of Tabernacles as decreed in the law, with the appropriate sacrifices each day, ⁵² and thereafter the regular offerings, and sacrifices on sabbaths, at new moons, and on all solemn feasts. ⁵³ From the new moon of the seventh month, whoever had made a vow to God offered sacrifices to him, although the temple of God was not yet built. ⁵⁴⁻⁵⁵ Money was given to the stone-masons and carpenters; the Sidonians and Tyrians were supplied with food and drink, and with carts to bring cedar trees from the Lebanon, floating them down as rafts to the roadstead at Joppa. This was done on the written instructions of King Cyrus of Persia.

⁵⁶ In the second month of the second year, Zerubbabel son of Salathiel came to the temple of God in Jerusalem and began the work. There were with him Jeshua son of Josedek, their kinsmen, the levitical priests, and all who had returned to Jerusalem from captivity; ⁵⁷ and they laid the foundation of the temple of God. This was at the new moon, in the second month of the second year after the return to Judaea and Jerusalem. ⁵⁸ Levites who were aged twenty and upwards were appointed to supervise the works of the Lord. Jeshua, his sons and his kinsmen, his brother Cadoel, the sons of Jeshua Emadabun, and the sons of Joda son of Iliadun with their sons and kinsmen, all the Levites who were supervising co-operated in the work on the house of God.

While the builders built the Lord's temple, ⁵⁹ the priests in their vestments with musical instruments and trumpets, and the Levites the sons of Asaph with their cymbals, took their places ⁶⁰ singing to the Lord and praising him in the manner prescribed by King David of Israel. ⁶¹ They sang psalms in praise of the Lord, 'for his goodness and glory towards all Israel endures for ever'. ⁶² The people all sounded their trumpets and raised a great shout, and they sang to the Lord as the building rose.

⁶³ But those of the priests, Levites, and heads of families who were old enough to have seen the former house came to the building of this house with cries of lamentation. ⁶⁴ Though many were shouting and sounding the trumpets loudly for joy—⁶⁵ so loudly as to be heard from afar—the people could not hear the trumpets for the noise of lamentation. ⁶⁶ The enemies of Judah and Benjamin heard the sound of the trumpets and came to see what it meant. ⁶⁷ When they found the returned exiles rebuilding the temple for the Lord God of Israel, ⁶⁸ they approached Zerubbabel and Jeshua and the heads of the families. 'We will build with you,' they said, ⁶⁹ 'for like you we obey your Lord and have sacrificed to him ever since the days of King Asbasareth of Assyria who brought us here.' ⁷⁰ Zerubbabel, Jeshua, and the heads of the Israelite families replied: 'It is not for you to build the house for the Lord our God; ⁷¹ we alone shall build for the Lord of Israel, as King Cyrus of Persia commanded us.' ⁷² But the peoples of the land harassed and blockaded the men of Judaea, and interrupted the building. ⁷³ By their plots, agitations, and riots they prevented its completion during the lifetime of King Cyrus. All building was held up for two years until Darius became king.

The temple rebuilt

6 IN the second year of the reign of Darius, the prophets Haggai and Zechariah son of Addo prophesied to the Jews in Judaea and Jerusalem, rebuking them in the name of the Lord God of Israel. ² Then Zerubbabel son of Salathiel and Jeshua son of Josedek, with the prophets of the Lord at their side to help them, began at once to rebuild the Lord's house

5:72 **harassed**: *prob. rdg*; *Gk obscure.*

in Jerusalem. [3] Immediately Sisinnes, the governor-general of Syria and Phoenicia, together with Sathrabuzanes and their colleagues, came to them and asked, [4] 'Who has given you authority to rebuild this house, to put on the roof and complete the whole work? Who are the builders engaged on this?' [5] But thanks to the Lord who protected the returned exiles, the elders of the Jews [6] were not prevented from building until such time as Darius should be informed and instructions issued.

[7] Here is a copy of the letter sent to Darius by Sisinnes, the governor-general of Syria and Phoenicia, with Sathrabuzanes and their colleagues the authorities in Syria and Phoenicia:

To King Darius.
Greeting.
[8] Be these matters fully known to our lord the king: we went to the province of Judaea and to Jerusalem, its city, and there we found the elders of the Jews returned from exile [9] building a great new house for their Lord with costly hewn stone and with beams set in the walls. [10] This work was carried on with all speed and the undertaking was making rapid headway under their direction; it was being executed in great splendour and with the utmost care. [11] We then enquired of these elders by whose authority they were building this house and laying such foundations. [12] We questioned them so that we could write and inform you who their leaders were, and we asked for a list of those in charge. [13] Their reply to us was: 'We are servants of the Lord who made heaven and earth. [14] This house was built and completed many years ago by a great and powerful king of Israel. [15] But when our fathers by their sin provoked the heavenly Lord of Israel to anger, he delivered them into the power of the Chaldaean monarch, King Nebuchadnezzar of Babylon. [16] The house was demolished and set on fire, and the people carried away captive to Babylon. [17] 'But King Cyrus in the first year of his reign over Babylonia issued a decree that the house should be rebuilt. [18] He brought out again from the temple in Babylon the sacred vessels of gold and silver which Nebuchadnezzar had taken from the house at Jerusalem and set up in his own temple, and he handed them over to Zerubbabel and Sanabassar the governor, [19] with orders to take them all and restore them to the temple at Jerusalem, and to rebuild this temple of the Lord on its original site. [20] Then Sanabassar came and laid the foundations of the house of the Lord in Jerusalem; and from that time until now the rebuilding has continued and is still not completed.'

[21] Now, therefore, if it please your majesty, let search be made in the Babylonian royal archives, [22] and if it is found that the building of the Lord's house in Jerusalem was done with the approval of King Cyrus, and if our lord the king should so decide, let directions be issued to us on this matter.

[23] King Darius ordered search to be made in the archives deposited in Babylonia, and there was found in the citadel at Ecbatana in the province of Media a scroll containing the following memorandum:

[24] In the first year of his reign King Cyrus gave orders for the rebuilding of the Lord's house at Jerusalem, where they sacrifice with perpetual fire. [25] Its height was to be sixty cubits and its breadth sixty cubits, with three courses of hewn stone to one of new local timber, the cost to be defrayed from the royal treasury. [26] The sacred .vessels, both gold and silver, which Nebuchadnezzar carried away from the house of the Lord at Jerusalem and brought to Babylon, were to be restored to the house in Jerusalem and placed where they had been in former times.

[27] Then Darius instructed Sisinnes, the governor-general of Syria and Phoenicia, with Sathrabuzanes, their colleagues, and the governors in office in Syria and Phoenicia, that they should see to it that the place was left unmolested and that the Lord's servant, Zerubbabel, governor of Judaea, and the elders of the Jews should be free to rebuild the house of the Lord on its original site. [28] 'I have also issued instructions', he went on, 'that it should be completely rebuilt, and that every effort be made to co-operate with the returned exiles in Judaea until the house of the Lord is finished. [29] From the tribute

of Coele-Syria and Phoenicia a sufficient grant, payable to Zerubbabel the governor, is to be given to these men for sacrifices to the Lord, for bulls, rams, and lambs. ³⁰ Similarly wheat, salt, wine, and olive oil as the priests in Jerusalem require to meet the needs of each day are to be provided regularly every year without question. ³¹ Let all this be expended in order that sacrifices and libations may be offered to the Most High God and intercession made for the king and his children.'

³² Darius further decreed: 'If anyone contravenes or fails to observe anything written herein, let a beam be taken from his own house and let him be hanged on it, and his property shall be forfeit to the king. ³³ May the Lord himself, therefore, whose name is invoked in this temple, utterly destroy any king or people who lifts a finger to delay the work or damage the Lord's house in Jerusalem. ³⁴ I, Darius, the king, have directed that these decrees shall be strictly obeyed.'

7 Then, in compliance with the orders of King Darius, Sisinnes, governor-general of Coele-Syria and Phoenicia, with Sathrabuzanes and their colleagues, ² carefully supervised the sacred works, co-operating with the elders of the Jews and the temple officers. ³ Good progress was made with the sacred works, as the result of the prophecies of Haggai and Zechariah, ⁴ and they were finished as commanded by the Lord God of Israel and with the approval of Cyrus and Darius; ⁵ and the house was completed on the twenty-third of the month of Adar in the sixth year of King Darius.

⁶ The Israelites, priests, Levites, and the rest of the former exiles who had joined them carried out the directions in the book of Moses. ⁷ At the rededication of the temple of the Lord they offered one hundred bulls, two hundred rams, four hundred lambs, ⁸ and as a purification-offering for all Israel twelve he-goats corresponding to the number of the patriarchs of Israel. ⁹ The priests and the Levites robed in their vestments stood family by family to preside over the services of the Lord God of Israel according to the book of Moses, while the door-keepers were stationed at every gateway.

¹⁰ On the fourteenth day of the first month the Israelites who had returned from exile celebrated the Passover. The priests and the Levites were purified together; ¹¹ not all the returned exiles were purified with the priests, but the Levites were. ¹² They sacrificed the Passover victims for all the returned exiles, for their kinsmen the priests, and for themselves. ¹³ They were eaten by the Israelites who had returned from exile, and by all who had held aloof from the abominations of the peoples of the land and remained faithful to the Lord. ¹⁴ They celebrated the feast of Unleavened Bread for seven days, rejoicing before the Lord, ¹⁵ because he had changed the policy of the Assyrian king towards them so that he supported them in their work for the Lord God of Israel.

Ezra in Jerusalem

8 It was after these events, when Artaxerxes was king of Persia, that Ezra came. He was the son of Saraeas son of Ezerias, son of Chelkias, son of Salemus, ² son of Zadok, son of Ahitub, son of Amarias, son of Ezias, son of Mareroth, son of Zaraeas, son of Savia, son of Bocca, son of Abishua, son of Phineas, son of Eleazar, son of Aaron the chief priest. ³ Ezra had come up from Babylon. He was a scribe expert in the law of Moses that had been given by the God of Israel. ⁴ The king held him in high regard and looked with favour on all the requests he made.

⁵ He was accompanied to Jerusalem by a number of Israelites, priests, Levites, temple singers, door-keepers, and temple servitors ⁶ in the fifth month of the seventh year of Artaxerxes' reign. They left Babylon at the new moon in the first month and reached Jerusalem at the new moon in the fifth month, for the Lord gave them a good journey. ⁷ Ezra's knowledge of the law of the Lord and the commandments was full and exact, so that he was able to instruct all Israel in all the ordinances and judgements.

⁸ The following is a copy of the mandate from King Artaxerxes to Ezra the priest, doctor of the law of the Lord:

⁹ King Artaxerxes to Ezra the priest, doctor of the law of the Lord.

7:8 **purification-offering:** *or* sin-offering. 7:11 **not all … but:** *prob. rdg; Gk obscure; some witnesses omit* not. 8:2 **son of Mareroth … Savia:** *some MSS omit.*

Greeting.

[10] I have graciously decided, and now command, that throughout our kingdom any of the Jewish nation and of the priests and Levites who so desire, may go with you to Jerusalem. [11] I and my council of seven Friends have decreed that all who so choose may accompany you. [12] They are to consider the situation in Judaea and Jerusalem with regard to the law of the Lord. [13] They shall convey to Jerusalem for Israel's Lord the gifts which I and my Friends have vowed, together with all the gold and silver in Babylonia that may be found to belong to the Lord, [14] and the gifts provided by the nation for the temple of their Lord at Jerusalem. Let the gold and silver be expended on the purchase of bulls, rams, lambs, and the like, [15] so that sacrifices may be offered on the altar of their Lord in Jerusalem. [16] In whatever ways you and your colleagues may wish to use the gold and silver, let it be done in accordance with the will of your God. [17] You are to deliver the sacred vessels of the Lord which have been handed over for the service of the temple of your God in Jerusalem.

[18] Any other expenses you may incur for the needs of the temple of your God you shall defray from the royal treasury.

[19] I, Artaxerxes the king, hereby direct the treasurers of Syria and Phoenicia to supply exactly to Ezra the priest, doctor of the law of the Most High God, whatever he may request [20] up to one hundred talents of silver, and similarly up to one hundred sacks of wheat and one hundred casks of wine, and salt without limit. [21] Let all the requirements of God's law be diligently fulfilled in honour of the Most High God; otherwise wrath may befall the realm of the king and his sons. [22] You are also informed that no tribute or other impost is to be exacted from the priests, the Levites, the temple singers, the door-keepers, the temple servitors, or the lay officers of this temple; no one is authorized to impose any levy on them.

[23] Under the wise guidance of God you, Ezra, are to appoint judges and magistrates throughout Syria and Phoenicia to administer justice for all who acknowledge the law of your God; you must instruct those who do not know it. [24] Whoever transgresses the law of your God or the law of the king shall be duly punished, whether he be put to death or sentenced to a fine or imprisonment.

[25] Then Ezra the scribe said, 'Blessed is the Lord and he alone! He put this into the king's mind, to glorify his house in Jerusalem, [26] and has singled me out for honour in the eyes of the king and his counsellors, all his Friends and courtiers. [27] 'Encouraged by the help of the Lord my God, I gathered men of Israel to go up with me. [28] These are the leaders according to families and divisions who went up with me from Babylon in the reign of King Artaxerxes: [29] from the line of Phineas, Gershom; from the line of Ithamar, Gamael; from the line of David, Attus son of Sechenias; [30] from the line of Phoros, Zacharias and with him a hundred and fifty men according to the register; [31] from the line of Phaath-moab, Eliaonias son of Zaraeas and with him two hundred men; [32] from the line of Zathoe, Sechenias son of Jezelus and with him three hundred men; from the line of Adin, Obeth son of Jonathan and with him two hundred and fifty men; [33] from the line of Elam, Jessias son of Gotholias and with him seventy men; [34] from the line of Saphatias, Zaraeas son of Michael and with him seventy men; [35] from the line of Joab, Abadias son of Jezelus and with him two hundred and twelve men; [36] from the line of Banias, Salimoth son of Josaphias and with him a hundred and sixty men; [37] from the line of Babi, Zacharias son of Bebae and with him twenty-eight men; [38] from the line of Astath, Joannes son of Hacatan and with him a hundred and ten men; [39] last came those from the line of Adonikam, by name Eliphalatus, Jeuel, and Samaeas, and with them seventy men; [40] from the line of Bago, Uthi son of Istalcurus and with him seventy men.

[41] 'I assembled them by the river Theras, and we encamped there for three days. I checked them, [42] and finding no one there who was a priest or a Levite, [43] I sent to Eleazar, Iduelus, Maasmas, [44] Elnathan, Samaeas, Joribus, Nathan, Ennatas, Zacharias, and Mosollamus, who

were prominent and discerning men, [45] and instructed them to go to Addaeus, the head of the treasury in the district. [46] I told them to speak with Addaeus and his colleagues and fellow-treasurers, asking that men should be sent to us to officiate in the house of our Lord. [47] Under the providence of our Lord they sent us discerning men from the line of Mooli son of Levi, son of Israel, Asebebias and his sons and brothers, eighteen men in all, [48] and Asebias and Annunus and his brother Hosaeas. Those of the line of Chanunaeus and their sons amounted to twenty men; [49] and those of the temple servitors whom David and the leading men appointed for the service of the Levites amounted to two hundred and twenty. A register of all those names was compiled.

[50] 'I made a vow there that the young men should fast before our Lord and ask from him a prosperous journey for ourselves, our children who accompanied us, and our pack-animals. [51] I was ashamed to apply to the king for an escort of infantry and cavalry to protect us against our enemies, [52] for we had told him that the might of our Lord would ensure a successful outcome for those who looked to him. [53] So once more we laid all these things before our Lord in prayer and found him gracious.

[54] 'Then I set apart twelve men from among the chiefs of the priestly families, Sarabias and Asamias and with them ten of their kinsmen. [55] I weighed out for them the silver and gold, and the sacred vessels for the house of our Lord which had been presented by the king, by his counsellors and courtiers, and by all Israel. [56] After weighing it, I handed over to them six hundred and fifty talents of silver, and silver vessels weighing a hundred talents, a hundred talents of gold, [57] and twenty gold dishes, and twelve vessels made of bronze so fine that it gleamed like gold. [58] I said, "Just as you are consecrated to the Lord, so too are the vessels; the silver and the gold are vowed to the Lord, the Lord of our fathers. [59] Guard them with all vigilance until you hand them over at Jerusalem, in the priests' rooms in the house of our Lord, to the chiefs of the priestly and levitical families and to the leaders of the clans of Israel." [60] The priests and the Levites who had custody of the silver, the

gold, and the vessels which had been in Jerusalem brought them to the temple of the Lord.

[61] 'On the twelfth day of the first month we struck camp at the river Theras and, under the powerful protection afforded by our Lord, who saved us from every enemy attack on the way, we reached Jerusalem. [62] On our fourth day there, the silver and gold were weighed and handed over in the house of our Lord to the priest Marmathi son of Uri, [63] with whom was Eleazar son of Phineas; present with them were the Levites Josabdus son of Jeshua and Moeth son of Sabannus. Everything was counted and weighed, [64] and every weight recorded then and there.

[65] 'Those who had returned from captivity offered sacrifices to the Lord, the God of Israel: twelve bulls for all Israel, with ninety-six rams [66] and seventy-two lambs, and also twelve goats for a shared-offering, the whole as a sacrifice to the Lord. [67] They delivered the king's orders to the royal treasurers and the governors of Coele-Syria and Phoenicia, thereby adding lustre to the nation and the temple of the Lord.

[68] 'ONCE this business was concluded, the leaders came to me and said: [69] "The people of Israel, including even the rulers, priests, and Levites, have not kept themselves apart from the alien population of the land with all their unclean practices, that is to say the Canaanites, Hittites, Perizzites, Jebusites, Moabites, Egyptians, and Edomites. [70] Both they and their sons have intermarried with the women of these peoples, so that the holy race has become mixed with the alien population of the land. From the very beginning, the leaders and principal men have shared in this violation of the law."

[71] 'At this news I rent my clothes and sacred vestment, I tore my hair and beard and sat appalled and grieving. [72] All who were moved by the word of the Lord of Israel gathered round me, and I sat grief-stricken over this failure to observe the law; and I sat in grief until the evening sacrifice. [73] Then with my clothes and sacred vestment torn I rose from my fast and, kneeling down, held out my hands in supplication to the Lord. [74] "O Lord," I said, "I am covered with shame and

confusion in your presence. [75] Our sins tower above us and our offences have reached high heaven [76] ever since the time of our forefathers; and today we are as deep in sin as ever. [77] Because of our sins and the sins of our forefathers, we, together with our brothers, our kings, and our priests, have been given into the power of the earthly rulers to be killed, taken captive, pillaged, and humiliated, down to this very day. [78] Yet even now, Lord, how great is your mercy! For we still have a root and a name in this your holy place. [79] Our light has been rekindled in the house of our Lord, and we have been given sustenance in the time of our enslavement. [80] Even when we were slaves we were not forsaken by our Lord, but he secured for us the favour of the kings of Persia: they have provided our sustenance [81] and added lustre to the temple of our Lord and restored the ruins of Zion, establishing us securely in Judaea and Jerusalem.

[82] '"Now, Lord, in the face of this, what are we to say? For we have broken your commandments given through your servants the prophets. You said: [83] 'The land which you are going to occupy is a land defiled with the pollution of its heathen population; they have filled it with their impure ways. [84] Now therefore do not marry your daughters to their sons or take their daughters for your sons; [85] nor must you ever seek to be at peace with them. Only thus will you be strong and enjoy the good things of the land, and hand it on as an everlasting possession to your descendants.' [86] It is our evil deeds and great sins which have brought all our misfortunes on us. Although you, Lord, have lightened the burden of our sins [87] and given us firm roots in the land, yet we have fallen away again and broken your law by sharing in the impurity of the peoples of this land. [88] But you were not so angry with us as to destroy us, root, stock, and name. [89] O Lord of Israel, you are just; for we today are a root that is left. [90] In all our sin we are here before you; because of it we can no longer stand in your presence.'''

[91] While Ezra was praying and making confession, prostrate in tears before the temple, there gathered round him a vast throng from Jerusalem, men, women, and children, and there was widespread lamentation among the crowd. [92] One of the Israelites, Jechonias son of Jehiel, spoke up and said to Ezra: 'We have sinned against the Lord in taking foreign wives from the peoples of the land; yet there is still hope for Israel. [93] In this matter let us promise on oath to the Lord to get rid of our wives of foreign race together with their children, [94] in keeping with your judgement and the judgement of all who are obedient to the law of the Lord. [95] Get up and see to it; the matter is in your hands. Take strong action and we are with you!' [96] Ezra stood up and put the chiefs of the priestly and levitical families of all Israel on oath to act in this way.

9 Ezra then left the forecourt of the temple and went to the room of the priest Joanan grandson of Eliasib, [2] and there he stayed, eating no bread and drinking no water, for he was still mourning over the people's flagrant violations of the law. [3] A proclamation was issued throughout Judaea and Jerusalem that all the returned exiles were to assemble at Jerusalem. [4] If any failed to arrive within two or three days, as decided by the elders in office, they were to have their cattle confiscated for temple use and would themselves be excluded from the community of the exiles.

[5] Three days later—it was the twentieth day of the ninth month—the men of Judah and Benjamin had assembled in Jerusalem, [6] where they all sat together in the broad space before the temple, shivering because winter had set in. [7] Ezra stood up and addressed them: 'In marrying foreign women you have broken the law and added to Israel's guilt. [8] Now acknowledge the majesty of the Lord God of our fathers: [9] do his will and cut yourselves off from the peoples of the land and from your foreign wives.'

[10] The whole company assented loudly, 'We will do as you say! [11] But', they added, 'our numbers are great; it is the rainy season and we cannot stay out in the open. Besides, this is not the work of one or two days only, for the offence is rife amongst us. [12] Let the leaders of the community remain here, and let all members of our settlements who have foreign wives present themselves at a stated time [13] accompanied by the elders and judges for each place, until the Lord's anger at what has been done is averted from us.'

¹⁴ Jonathan son of Azael and Hezekias son of Thocanus took charge on these terms, and Mosollamus, Levi, and Sabbataeus were their assessors.

¹⁵ The returned exiles duly put all this into effect. ¹⁶ Ezra the priest selected, each by name, certain men, chiefs of their clans. They met in session to investigate the matter at the new moon in the tenth month, ¹⁷ and by the new moon of the first month the affair of the men who had taken foreign wives was brought to a conclusion.

¹⁸ Among the priests, some of those who had come together were found to have married foreign women: ¹⁹ namely Mathelas, Eleazar, Joribus, and Joadanus of the line of Jeshua son of Josedek and his brothers. ²⁰ They pledged themselves to dismiss their wives and to offer rams in expiation of their offence. ²¹ Of the line of Emmer: Ananias, Zabdaeus, Manes, Samaeus, Jereel, and Azarias; ²² of the line of Phaesus: Elionas, Massias, Ishmael, Nathanael, Okidelus, and Saloas. ²³ Of the Levites: Jozabadus, Semis, Colius (this is Calitas), Phathaeus, Judah, and Jonas. ²⁴ Of the temple singers: Eliasibus, Bacchurus. ²⁵ Of the door-keepers: Sallumus and Tolbanes.

²⁶ Of the people of Israel there were, of the line of Phoros: Jermas, Jeddias, Melchias, Maelus, Eleazar, Asibias, and Bannaeas. ²⁷ Of the line of Ela: Matthanias, Zacharias, Jezrielus, Oabdius, Jeremoth, and Aedias. ²⁸ Of the line of Zamoth: Eliadas, Eliasimus, Othonias, Jarimoth, Sabathus, and Zardaeas. ²⁹ Of the line of Bebae: Joannes, Ananias, Ozabadus, and Emathis. ³⁰ Of the line of Mani: Olamus, Mamuchus, Jedaeus, Jasubus, Asaelus, and Jeremoth. ³¹ Of the line of Addi: Naathus, Moossias, Laccunus, Naidus, Matthanias, Sesthel, Balnuus, and Manasseas. ³² Of the line of Annas: Elionas, Asaeas, Melchias, Sabbaeas, and Simon Chosomaeus. ³³ Of the line of Asom: Altannaeus, Mattathias, Bannaeus, Eliphalat, Manasses, and Semi. ³⁴ Of the line of Baani: Jeremias, Momdis, Ismaerus, Juel, Mandae, Paedias, Anos, Carabasion, Enasibus, Mamnitanaemus, Eliasis, Bannus, Eliali, Somis, Selemias, and Nathanias. Of the line of Ezora: Sessis, Ezril, Azael, Samatus, Zambris, and Josephus. ³⁵ Of the line of Nooma: Mazitias, Zabadaeas, Edaes, Juel, and Banaeas. ³⁶ All these had married foreign women, whom they now dismissed together with their children.

³⁷ THE priests and Levites, with such Israelites as were in Jerusalem and its neighbourhood, settled down there. On the new moon of the seventh month, the other Israelites being now in their settlements, ³⁸ the entire company assembled with one accord in the broad space in front of the east gateway of the temple precinct ³⁹ and asked Ezra, priest and doctor of the law, to bring the law of Moses given by the Lord God of Israel. ⁴⁰ At the new moon of the seventh month Ezra the high priest brought the law to the whole assembly, both men and women, and to all the priests, for them to hear it. ⁴¹ From daybreak until noon he read aloud from it in the square in front of the temple gateway, in the presence of both men and women, and all the company listened attentively to the law.

⁴² Ezra, priest and doctor of the law, stood on the wooden platform which had been made for this purpose. ⁴³ Beside him stood Mattathias, Sammus, Ananias, Azarias, Urias, Hezekias, and Baalsamus on his right, ⁴⁴ and on his left Phaldaeus, Misael, Melchias, Lothasubus, Nabarias, and Zacharias. ⁴⁵ Then in front of the whole assembly, for he was seated in a prominent place where everyone could see him, Ezra took up the book of the law, ⁴⁶ and when he opened it they all stood. Ezra praised the Lord God, the Most High God of Hosts, the Almighty, ⁴⁷ and all the people cried 'Amen, Amen.' They raised their hands and prostrated themselves in worship before the Lord. ⁴⁸ Jeshua, Annus, Sarabias, Jadinus, Jacubus, Sabbataeas, Autaeas, Maeannas, Calitas, Azarias, Jozabdus, Ananias, and Phiathas, the Levites, taught the law of the Lord. They read the law of the Lord to the people, at the same time instilling into their minds the sense of what was read.

⁴⁹ The governor said to them all, to Ezra, high priest and doctor of the law, and to the Levites who taught the people: ⁵⁰ 'This day is holy to the Lord.' All were weeping as they listened to the law. ⁵¹ 'Go, therefore,' he continued, 'feast yourselves

9:49 **The governor**: *cp.* 5:40; *Gk* Attharates.

14

on rich food and sweet drinks, and send a share to those who have none, ⁵² for the day is holy to the Lord. Let there be no sadness, for the Lord will give you glory.' ⁵³ The Levites enjoined the people: 'This day is holy; let there be no sadness.' ⁵⁴ So

they all went away to eat and drink and make merry, and to distribute shares to those who had none. They held a great celebration, ⁵⁵ because the teaching given them had been instilled into their minds. So they held their assembly.

THE SECOND BOOK OF
ESDRAS

Israel's rejection and glory to come

1 THE second book of the prophet Ezra son of Seraiah, son of Azariah, son of Hilkiah, son of Shallum, son of Zadok, son of Ahitub, ² son of Ahijah, son of Phinehas, son of Eli, son of Amariah, son of Aziah, son of Marimoth, son of Arna, son of Uzzi, son of Borith, son of Abishua, son of Phinehas, son of Eleazar, ³ son of Aaron, of the tribe of Levi.

I, EZRA, was a captive in Media during the reign of King Artaxerxes of Persia ⁴ when this word of the Lord came to me: ⁵ Go to my people and proclaim their crimes; tell their children how they have sinned against me, and let them tell their children's children. ⁶ My people have sinned even more than their fathers, for they have forgotten me and sacrificed to alien gods. ⁷ Was it not I who brought them out of Egypt, out of the land where they were slaves? And yet they have aroused my anger and spurned my warnings.

⁸ But it is for you, Ezra, to tear out your hair and to let every calamity loose on those who have disobeyed my law. My people are beyond correction. ⁹ How much longer can I tolerate a people on whom I have lavished such great benefits? ¹⁰ Many are the kings I have overthrown for their sake; I struck down Pharaoh along with his court and his whole army. ¹¹ Every nation that stood in their way I destroyed; in the east I routed the peoples of two provinces, Tyre and Sidon, and killed all Israel's enemies.

¹² Say to them, 'These are the words of the Lord: ¹³ Was it not I who brought you through the sea, and made for you safe roads where no road had been? I gave you

Moses as your leader, and Aaron as your priest; ¹⁴ I provided you with light from a pillar of fire; I performed great miracles among you. And yet you have forgotten me, says the Lord.

¹⁵⁻¹⁶ 'These are the words of the Lord Almighty: The quails were a sign to you; I gave you a camp for your protection. Instead of celebrating the victory when I destroyed your enemies, all you did there was to grumble and complain, and from that day to this your complaints have never ceased. ¹⁷ Have you forgotten what benefits I conferred on you? When you were hungry and thirsty on your journey through the wilderness, you cried out: ¹⁸ "Why have you led us into this wilderness to kill us? Better for us to be slaves to the Egyptians than to perish here in this wilderness!" ¹⁹ Grieved at your complaints, I gave you manna for food; it was the bread of angels you were eating. ²⁰ When you were thirsty, I split open the rock, and water flowed out in plenty. Against the summer heat I provided you with the shade of leafy trees. ²¹ I expelled those who opposed you, the Canaanites, Perizzites, and Philistines, and distributed their fertile lands among you. What more could I do for you? says the Lord.

²² 'These are the words of the Lord Almighty: When you were in the wilderness, suffering thirst by the stream of bitter water and cursing me, ²³ I did not bring fire down on you for your blasphemy; instead I cast a log into the stream and made the water sweet. ²⁴ Jacob, what am I to do with you? You have refused to obey me, Judah! I shall turn to other nations and give them my name, and they will keep my statutes. ²⁵ Because you have forsaken me, I shall forsake

you; when you implore me for mercy, I shall show you none; [26] when you pray to me, I shall not listen. You have stained your hands with blood; you hasten hotfoot to commit murder. [27] It is not that you have forsaken me: you have forsaken yourselves, says the Lord.

[28] 'These are the words of the Lord Almighty: Have I not pleaded with you as a father with his sons, as a mother with her daughters, or as a nursemaid with her children, [29] that you should be my people and I should be your God, that you should be my sons and I should be your father? [30] I gathered you as a hen gathers her brood under her wings. But now, what am I to do with you? I shall cast you out from my presence. [31] When you offer me sacrifice, I shall turn from you, for I have rejected your feasts, your new moons, and your circumcisions. [32] I sent my servants the prophets to you, but you took them and killed them and mutilated their bodies. For their murder I shall call you to account, says the Lord.

[33] 'These are the words of the Lord Almighty: Your house is forsaken. I shall toss you away like straw before the wind. [34] Your children will have no posterity, because like you they have ignored my commandments and done what I have condemned. [35] I shall hand over your homes to a people yet to come: a people who will trust me, though they have not known me; who will do my bidding, though I gave them no signs; [36] who never saw the prophets, and yet will keep in mind what the prophets taught of old. [37] I vow that this people yet to come shall have my favour; their little ones will jump for joy, and though they themselves have not seen me with their eyes, they will perceive by the spirit and believe what I have said.'

[38] Now, father Ezra, look with pride at the nation coming from the east. [39] The leaders I shall give them are Abraham, Isaac, and Jacob, Hosea and Amos, Micah and Joel, Obadiah and Jonah, [40] Nahum, Habakkuk, and Zephaniah, Haggai and Zechariah, and Malachi, who is also called the Lord's messenger.

2 These are the words of the Lord: I brought that people out of slavery and gave them commandments through my servants the prophets; but they shut their ears to the prophets, and allowed my precepts to become a dead letter. [2] The mother who bore them says: 'Go, my children; I am widowed and forsaken. [3] With joy I brought you up, but with mourning and sorrow I have lost you, because you have sinned against the Lord God and done what I have condemned. [4] But now, what can I do for you, widowed and forsaken as I am? Go, my children, ask the Lord for mercy.' [5] I call upon you, father Ezra, to add your testimony to hers that her children have refused to keep my covenant; [6] and let your words bring confusion on them. May their mother be despoiled, and may they themselves have no posterity. [7] Let them be dispersed among the nations and let their name vanish from the earth, because they have spurned my covenant.

[8] Woe to you, Assyria, you harbourer of sinners! Remember, you evil nation, what I did to Sodom and Gomorrah: [9] their land lies buried under masses of pitch and heaps of ashes. So shall I deal with those who have disobeyed me, says the Lord Almighty.

[10] These are the words of the Lord to Ezra: Tell my people that I shall give to them the kingdom of Jerusalem, which once I offered to Israel. [11] I shall also withdraw the splendour of my presence from Israel, and the home that was to be theirs for ever I shall give to my people. [12] The tree of life will spread its fragrance over them; they will neither toil nor grow weary. [13] Ask, and you will receive; pray that your short time of waiting may be cut shorter still. Even now the kingdom is ready for you; be vigilant! [14] I summon heaven and earth to witness: I have cancelled the evil and brought the good into being; for I am the Living One, says the Lord.

[15] Mother, keep your children close to you. Rear them with gladness, as a dove rears her nestlings; teach them to walk without stumbling. You are my chosen one, says the Lord. [16] I shall raise up the dead from their resting-places and bring them out of their tombs, for I have acknowledged that they bear my name. [17] There is nothing to fear, mother of many children, for I have chosen you, says the Lord. [18] I shall send my servants Isaiah and Jeremiah to help you. As they prophesied, I have set you apart to be my people. I

have made ready for you twelve trees laden with different kinds of fruit, ¹⁹ twelve fountains flowing with milk and honey, and seven great mountains covered with roses and lilies. There I shall fill your children with joy. ²⁰ Champion the widow, defend the cause of the fatherless, give to the poor, protect the orphan, provide clothing for those who have none; ²¹ care for the weak and the helpless, and do not mock at the cripple; watch over the disabled, and bring the blind to the vision of my radiance. ²² Keep both old and young safe within your walls.

²³ When you find the dead unburied, mark them with the sign and commit them to the tomb; and then, when I cause the dead to rise, I shall give you the chief place. ²⁴ Be calm, my people; your time of rest will come. ²⁵ Be a good nursemaid to your children, and teach them to walk without stumbling. ²⁶ Of servants whom I have given you, not one will be lost; I shall look for them from among your number. ²⁷ Do not be anxious when the time of trouble and hardship comes; others will lament and be sad, but you will have happiness and plenty. ²⁸ Though you become the envy of the nations, they will be powerless against you, says the Lord.

²⁹ My power will protect you, and save your children from hell. ³⁰ Be joyful, mother, you and your children, for I shall come to your rescue. ³¹ Remember your children who sleep in the grave; I shall bring them up from the depths of the earth, and show mercy to them; for I am merciful, says the Lord Almighty. ³² Keep your children close to you until I come; proclaim my mercy to them, for my grace which flows from gushing springs will never run dry.

³³ I, Ezra, received on Mount Horeb a commission from the Lord to go to Israel; but when I came to them, they spurned me and rejected the Lord's command. ³⁴ Therefore I say to you Gentiles, who hear and understand: 'Look forward to the coming of your shepherd; he who is to come at the end of the world is close at hand, and he will give you everlasting rest. ³⁵ Be ready to receive the rewards of the kingdom, for light perpetual will shine on you throughout all time. ³⁶ Flee from

the shadow of this world, and receive the joy and splendour that await you. I bear witness openly to my Saviour. ³⁷ It is he whom the Lord has appointed; receive him and be joyful, giving thanks to the One who has called you to the heavenly realms. ³⁸ Arise, stand up and see the whole company of those who bear the Lord's mark and sit at his banquet. ³⁹ They have moved out of the shadow of this world and have received shining robes from the Lord. ⁴⁰ Take your full number, O Zion, and close the roll of those arrayed in white who have faithfully kept the law of the Lord. ⁴¹ The number of your children whom you so long desired is now complete. Pray that the Lord's kingdom may come, so that your people, whom he called when the world began, may be set apart as his own.'

⁴² I, Ezra, saw on Mount Zion a throng too vast to count, all singing hymns of praise to the Lord. ⁴³ In the middle stood a young man. He was very tall, taller than any of the others, and was setting a crown on the head of each one of them; he towered above them all. Enthralled at the sight, ⁴⁴ I asked the angel, 'My lord, who are these?' ⁴⁵ He replied, 'They are those who have laid aside their mortal dress and put on the immortal, those who acknowledged the name of God. Now they are being given crowns and palms.' ⁴⁶ I asked again, 'Who is the young man setting the crowns on their heads and giving them the palms?' ⁴⁷ The angel replied, 'He is the Son of God, whom they acknowledged in this mortal life.' I began to praise those who had stood so valiantly for the Lord's name. ⁴⁸ Then the angel said to me: 'Go and tell my people the many great and wonderful acts of the Lord God that you have seen.'

Ezra's first vision

3 IN the thirtieth year after the fall of Jerusalem, I, Salathiel (who am also Ezra), was in Babylon. Lying on my bed I was troubled and my mind filled with perplexity ² as I reflected on the desolation of Zion and the prosperity of those who lived in Babylon. ³ I was deeply disturbed in spirit, and full of fear I addressed the Most High. ⁴ 'My Master and Lord,' I said, 'was it not you alone who in the beginning spoke the word that formed the world? At your command the dust

[5] brought forth Adam. His body was lifeless; yours were the hands that had moulded it, and you breathed the breath of life into it and he became a living person. [6] You led him into paradise, which you yourself had planted before the earth came into being. [7] You gave him your one commandment to obey; and when he disobeyed it, you made both him and his descendants subject to death.

'From him there sprang nations and tribes, peoples and families, too numerous to count. [8] Each nation went its own way, sinning against you and treating you with scorn, and you did not stop them. [9] Then, in course of time, you brought the flood upon the inhabitants of the earth and destroyed them. [10] The same fate came upon all: death upon Adam, and the flood upon that generation. [11] But one man, Noah, you spared, together with his household and all the righteous descended from him.

[12] 'The population of the earth expanded; families and peoples increased, nation upon nation. But once again they began to sin, more wickedly than those before them. [13] When they sinned, you chose for yourself one of them; Abraham was his name. [14] Him you loved, and to him alone, secretly at dead of night, you disclosed how the world would end. [15] You made an everlasting covenant with him and promised never to abandon his descendants. [16] You gave him Isaac, and to Isaac you gave Jacob and Esau; of these you chose Jacob for yourself, and he grew to be a great nation; but Esau you rejected.

[17] 'You rescued Jacob's descendants from Egypt and led them to Mount Sinai. [18] There you made the heavens bow down, shook the earth, moved the world; you made the depths shudder and convulsed the whole creation. [19] Your glory passed through the four gates of fire and earthquake, wind and frost, in order to give the commandments of the law to the Israelites, the race of Jacob. [20] But you did not take away their evil heart and thus enable your law to bear fruit in them; [21] for the first man, Adam, burdened as he was with an evil heart, sinned and was overcome, and not only he but all who were descended from him. [22] So the weakness became inveterate, and although your law was in your people's hearts, a rooted wickedness was there too; thus the good came to nothing, and what was evil persisted.

[23] 'Years went by, and when the time came you raised up for yourself a servant, whose name was David. [24] You instructed him to build the city that bears your name and to offer to you there in sacrifice what was already your own. [25] This was done for many years, until the inhabitants of the city went astray, [26] behaving just like Adam and all his line; for they had the same evil heart. [27] And so you handed over your city into the power of your enemies.

[28] 'I had thought that perhaps those in Babylon lead better lives, and that is why Zion is in subjection. [29] But when I arrived here, I saw wickedness beyond reckoning, and with my own eyes I have seen evildoers in great numbers these thirty years. My heart sank [30] because I observed how you tolerate sinners and spare the godless, how you have destroyed your own people but preserved your enemies. You have given no indication [31] to anyone how your ways are to be understood. Is Babylon more virtuous than Zion? [32] Has any nation except Israel ever known you? What tribes have put their trust in your covenants as have the tribes of Jacob? [33] But they have seen no reward, no fruit for their labours. I have travelled far and wide among the nations and have seen how they prosper, heedless though they are of your commandments. [34] Now weigh our sins in the balance, therefore, against the sins of the rest of the world, and it will be clear which way the scale tips. [35] Has there ever been a time when the inhabitants of the earth did not sin against you? Has any nation ever kept your commandments like Israel? [36] You may indeed find a few individuals here and there who have done so, but nowhere a whole nation.'

4 Uriel, the angel who was sent to me, replied: [2] 'You are completely at a loss to understand this world; can you then expect to understand the way of the Most High?' [3] 'Yes, my lord,' I said.

'I have been sent', he continued, 'to propound to you three of the ways of this world, to give you three illustrations; [4] if you can explain to me any one of them, I shall show to you the way that you long to see and teach you why the heart is evil.'

⁵'Speak on, my lord,' I said. 'Come then, weigh me a pound of fire,' he said, 'or measure me a bushel of wind, or call back for me a day that has passed.'

⁶'How can you ask me to do that, something no man on earth can do?' I replied. ⁷Then said he, 'Suppose I had asked you, "How many dwellings are there in the heart of the sea? Or how many streams to feed the depths? Or how many paths above the vault of heaven? Or where are the ways out of the grave, or the roads into paradise?" ⁸You might have retorted, "I have not been down into the deep, I have not yet descended into the grave, or ever ascended into heaven." ⁹But, as it is, I have asked you only about fire, about wind, and about yesterday, things bound up with your experience and essential to your life; and yet you have failed to give me an answer. ¹⁰If then', he went on, 'you cannot understand things you have grown up with, ¹¹how can you with your limited mind grasp the way of the Most High? A man corrupted by the corrupt world can never know the way of the incorruptible.'

¹²At those words I fell prostrate, exclaiming: 'Better never to have come into existence than be born into a world of evil and suffering we cannot explain!' ¹³He replied, 'I went out into a wood, and the trees of the forest were devising a plot. ¹⁴They said, "Come, let us make war on the sea, force it to retreat, and so win ground for more woods." ¹⁵The waves of the sea had a similar plan: they said, "Come, let us attack and conquer the trees of the forest, and annex their territory." ¹⁶The plan made by the trees came to nothing, for fire broke out and burnt them up. ¹⁷So too the plot of the waves came to nothing, for the sand remained firm and blocked their way. ¹⁸If you had to judge between the two, which would you pronounce right, and which wrong?'

¹⁹'Both were wrong,' I answered; 'their plans were folly, for the land is assigned to the trees, and to the sea is allotted a place for its waves.'

²⁰'Yes,' he replied, 'you have judged rightly. Why then have you not done so with your own question? ²¹Just as the land belongs to the trees and the sea to the waves, so dwellers on earth can understand earthly things and nothing beyond; only he who lives above the heavens can understand the things high above the heavens.'

²²'But, my lord, please tell me,' I asked, 'why have I been given the faculty of understanding? ²³My question is not about the distant heavens, but about what happens every day before our eyes. Why has Israel been made a byword among the Gentiles? Why has the people you loved been put at the mercy of godless nations? Why has the law of our fathers been brought to nothing, and the written covenants made a dead letter? ²⁴We pass from the world like a flight of locusts, our life is but a vapour, and we are not worth the Lord's pity. ²⁵What then will he do for us who bear his name? Those are my questions.'

²⁶He answered: 'If you survive, you will see; if you live long enough, you will marvel. For this present age is passing away; ²⁷it is full of sorrow and weakness, too full to grasp what is promised in due time for the godly. ²⁸The evil about which you ask me has been sown, but the time for reaping is not yet. ²⁹Until the crop of evil has been reaped as well as sown, until the ground where it was sown has vanished, there will be no room for the field where the good is sown. ³⁰A grain of the evil seed was sown in the heart of Adam from the first; how much godlessness has it produced already! How much more will it produce before the harvest! ³¹Reckon this up: if one grain of evil seed has produced so great a crop of godlessness, ³²how vast a harvest will there be when seeds beyond number have been sown!'

³³I asked, 'But when? How long have we to wait? Why are our lives short and miserable?' ³⁴He replied, 'Do not be in a greater hurry than the Most High himself. You are in a hurry for yourself alone; the Exalted One for many. ³⁵Are not these the very questions asked by the righteous in the storehouse of souls: "How long must we stay here? When will the harvest begin, the time when we get our reward?" ³⁶And the answer they got from the archangel Jeremiel was: "As soon as the tally of those like yourselves is

---

4:21 **he who lives:** *or* those who live.   4:26 **if you live ... marvel:** *so one Vs.; Lat.* live, you will often marvel.

complete. God has weighed the world in a balance, ³⁷ he has measured and numbered the ages; he will move nothing, alter nothing, until the appointed measure is reached.'''

³⁸ 'But, my master and lord,' I replied, 'we are all of us sinners through and through. ³⁹ Can it be because of us, because of the sins of mankind, that the harvest and the reward of the just are delayed?' ⁴⁰ 'Go,' he said, 'ask a pregnant woman whether she can keep the child in her womb any longer once the nine months are up.' ⁴¹ 'No, my lord, she cannot,' I said. He went on: 'The storehouses of souls in the world below are like the womb: ⁴² as a woman in labour is impatient to reach the end of the birth-pains, so they are impatient to give back all the souls entrusted to them since time began. ⁴³ Then you will be shown all you wish to see.'

⁴⁴ I said, 'If I have found favour with you and if it is possible for you to tell and for me to understand, ⁴⁵ disclose to me one thing more: which is the longer—the future still to come, or the past that has gone by? ⁴⁶ What is past I know, but not what is still to be.' ⁴⁷ He said: 'Come, stand at my right hand, and I shall explain the vision you will see.'

⁴⁸ I stood watching, and there passed before my eyes a blazing fire; when the flames had disappeared, there was still smoke left. ⁴⁹ After that a dark rain-cloud passed before me; there was a heavy storm, and when it had gone over, there were still some raindrops left. ⁵⁰ 'Reflect on this,' said the angel. 'As the shower of rain filled a far greater space than the drops of water, and the fire more than the smoke, in the same way the past far exceeds the future in length; what remains is but raindrops and smoke.'

⁵¹ 'Pray tell me,' I said, 'do you think that I shall live to see those days? Or in whose lifetime will they come?' ⁵² 'If you ask me what signs will herald them,' he replied, 'I can tell you in part. But the length of your own life I am not commissioned to tell you; of that I know nothing.

5 'But to speak of the signs: a time is coming when the earth's inhabitants will be seized with great panic. The way of truth will be hidden from sight, and the land will be barren of faith. ² Wickedness will increase beyond anything you yourself see or have ever heard of. ³ The country you now observe ruling the world will become a trackless desert, lying waste before men's eyes. ⁴ After the third period (if the Most High grants you a long enough life) you will see universal disorder. The sun will suddenly begin to shine at night, and the moon by day. ⁵ Trees will drip blood, stones will speak, nations will be in confusion, and the courses of the stars will be changed. ⁶ A king unwelcome to the earth's inhabitants will bear rule. The birds will all fly away, ⁷ the Dead Sea will cast up fish, and at night a voice will sound, unknown to the many but heard by all. ⁸ Chasms will open in many places and spurt out incessant flames. Wild beasts will range far from their haunts, menstruous women will give birth to monsters, ⁹ freshwater springs will run with brine, and everywhere friends will make war on one another. Then understanding will be hidden, and reason withdraw within her chamber. ¹⁰ Many will seek her, but not find her; the earth will overflow with wickedness and vice. ¹¹ One country will ask another, "Has justice, justice in action, ever passed your way?" and the answer will be "No!" ¹² In those days men will hope, but hope in vain; they will strive, but meet with no success.

¹³ 'Those are the signs I am allowed to tell you. But turn once more to prayer, continue to weep and fast for seven days; then again you will hear of greater signs than those.'

¹⁴ I awoke with a start, trembling in every limb; my spirits faltered, and I was near to fainting. ¹⁵ But the angel who had come and talked to me held me and put strength into me, and raised me to my feet.

¹⁶ The next night Phaltiel, leader of the people, came to me and asked: 'Where have you been, and why that sad look? ¹⁷ Have you forgotten that Israel in exile has been entrusted to your care? ¹⁸ Rouse yourself; eat some food. Do not abandon us like a shepherd abandoning his flock to savage wolves.' ¹⁹ I replied: 'Leave me, and do not come near me for the next seven days; after that you may return.' On hearing this he went away.

5:7 **Dead Sea:** *or* sea of Sodom.

Ezra's second vision

²⁰ FOR seven days I fasted with tears and lamentations, as commanded by the angel Uriel. ²¹ At the end of the seven days my mind was again deeply disturbed, ²² but I recovered the power of thought and began once more to address the Most High.

²³ 'My Master and Lord,' I said, 'out of all the forests on earth and all their trees, you have chosen one vine; ²⁴ from all the lands in the whole world you have chosen one plot; and out of all the flowers in the world you have chosen one lily. ²⁵ From all the depths of the sea you have filled one river for yourself, and of all the cities ever built you have set apart Zion as your own. ²⁶ From all the birds that were created you have named for yourself one dove, and from all the animals that were fashioned you have taken one sheep. ²⁷ Out of all the countless nations, you have adopted one for your own, and to this chosen people you have given a law approved above all others. ²⁸ Why then, Lord, have you put this one people at the mercy of so many? Why have you humiliated this one stock more than all others, and dispersed your own people far and wide? ²⁹ Those who reject your promises have trampled on the people who put their trust in your covenants. ³⁰ If you are so deeply displeased with your people, yours should be the hand that punishes them.'

³¹ When I had finished speaking, there was sent to me the angel who had visited me that earlier night. ³² 'Listen to me,' he said, 'and I shall instruct you; attend carefully, and I shall tell you more.' ³³ 'Speak on, my lord,' I replied.

He began: 'You are in great sorrow of heart for Israel's sake. Do you love Israel more than Israel's Maker does?' ³⁴ 'No, my lord,' I answered, 'but sorrow has compelled me to speak; my heart is tortured every hour as I strive to understand the ways of the Most High and to fathom even part of his judgement.'

³⁵ 'You cannot,' he said to me. 'Why not, my lord?' I asked. 'Why then was I born? Why could not my mother's womb have been my grave? Then I should never have seen Jacob's trials and the utter exhaustion of Israel's people.'

³⁶ He said, 'Count me the days that are not yet come, collect the scattered raindrops for me, make the withered flowers bloom again, ³⁷ unlock for me the storehouses and let loose the winds shut up there, or give visible form to a voice—then I shall answer your question about the trials of Israel.'

³⁸ 'My master and lord,' I argued, 'how can there be anyone with such knowledge except the One whose dwelling is not among men? ³⁹ I am only a fool; how can I answer your questions?'

⁴⁰ 'Just as you cannot do any of the things I have put to you,' he replied, 'so you will not be able to find out my judgement or the ultimate purpose of the love I have promised to my people.'

⁴¹ 'But surely,' I objected, 'your promise, lord, is for those who are alive at the end. What is to be the fate of those who lived before us, or of ourselves, or of those who come after us?'

⁴² He said, 'I shall compare my judgement to a circle: the latest will not be too late, nor the earliest too early.'

⁴³ To this I replied, 'Could you not have made all men, past, present, and future, at one and the same time? Then you could have held your assize with less delay.'

⁴⁴ His answer to me was: 'Creation may not proceed faster than the Creator, nor could the world support at the same time all those created to live in it.'

⁴⁵ 'My lord,' I pointed out, 'you have just told me that you will at one and the same time restore to life every creature you ever made; how can that be? If all of them are to be alive at the same time and the world is to support them all then, it could support all of them together now.'

⁴⁶ He replied, 'Think of a woman's womb: say to a woman, "If you give birth to ten children, why do you do so at intervals? Why not give birth to ten at one and the same time?"' ⁴⁷ 'No,' I said, 'that would be impossible; the births must take place at intervals.' ⁴⁸ 'True,' he answered; 'and I have made the earth's womb to bring forth at intervals those conceived in it. ⁴⁹ An infant cannot give birth, nor can a woman who is too old; and I have made the same rule for the world I have created.'

⁵⁰ I continued my questioning. 'Since you have now opened the way for me,' I said, 'may I ask: is our mother that you

---

5:41 **your promise:** *so one Vs.; Lat. obscure.*

21

speak of still young, or is she already approaching old age?' ⁵¹ He replied, 'For an answer, ask any mother; ⁵² ask why the children she has borne later are not like those born earlier, but smaller. ⁵³ She will tell you that those who were born in the vigour of her youth are very different from those born in her old age, when her womb is beginning to fail. ⁵⁴ Think of it, then, like this: if you are smaller than those born before you, ⁵⁵ and those who follow you are smaller still, the reason is that creation is growing old and losing the strength of its youth.'

⁵⁶ I said, 'If I have found favour with you, my lord, show me through whom you will judge your creation.' ¹ He said to me, 'When the earth began, the gates of the world were not yet standing in place; no winds gathered and blew, ² no thunder pealed, no lightning flashed; the foundations of paradise were not yet laid, ³ nor were its fair flowers there to see; the powers that move the stars were not established, nor the countless hosts of angels assembled, ⁴ nor the vast tracts of air lifted up on high; the divisions of the firmaments had not received their names. Zion had not yet been chosen as God's own footstool; ⁵ the present age had not been planned; the schemes of its sinners had not yet been outlawed, nor had God's seal yet been set on those who have laid up a treasure of faithfulness. ⁶ Then it was that I had my thought, and the whole world was created through me and through me alone; in the same way, through me and through me alone the end will be.'

⁷ 'Tell me', I responded, 'about the interval that divides the ages. When will the first age end and the next begin?' ⁸ He said, 'The interval will be no bigger than that between Abraham and Abraham; for Jacob and Esau were his descendants, and Jacob's hand was grasping Esau's heel at the moment of their birth. ⁹ Esau's heel represents the end of the first age, and Jacob's hand the beginning of the next, ¹⁰ for the beginning of a man is his hand, and the end of a man is his heel; between the heel and the hand, Ezra, do not look for any interval.'

¹¹ 'My master and lord,' I said, 'if I have found favour with you, ¹² make known to me the last of your signs, of which

you showed me some part that former night.'

¹³ 'Rise to your feet', he replied, 'and you will hear a voice, loud and resonant. ¹⁴⁻¹⁵ Do not be frightened if the place where you are standing shakes at the sound; it speaks of the end, and the earth's foundations will understand ¹⁶ that it is talking of them. They will tremble and shake, for they know that at the end they must be transformed.' ¹⁷ At this I stood up and listened. A voice began to speak, and the sound of it was like the sound of a mighty torrent. ¹⁸ The voice said: 'The time draws near when I shall come to judge earth's inhabitants, ¹⁹ the time when I shall enquire into the wickedness of wrongdoers, the time when Zion's humiliation will be over, ²⁰ the time when a seal will be set on the age about to pass away. Then I shall perform these signs: the books will be opened out against the vault of heaven, and all will see my judgement at the same moment. ²¹ Children only one year old will be able to talk, and pregnant women will give birth prematurely at three and four months to babes who will survive and dance about. ²² Fields that were sown will suddenly prove unsown, and barns that were full will suddenly be found empty. ²³ A loud trumpet-blast will sound, striking sudden terror into all who hear it. ²⁴ At that time friends will make war on friends as though on foes; the earth and its inhabitants will be terrified. Running streams will stand still, and for three hours cease to flow.

²⁵ 'Whoever is left after all I have foretold will be saved and see the salvation that I bring and the end of this world of mine. ²⁶ They will see the men who were taken up into heaven without ever tasting death. Then will earth's inhabitants have a change of heart and come to a better mind. ²⁷ Wickedness will be blotted out and deceit destroyed, ²⁸ but faithfulness will flourish, corruption be overcome, and truth, so long unfruitful, will be revealed.'

²⁹ While the voice was speaking, the ground where I stood gradually moved to and fro. ³⁰ Then the angel said to me, 'These are the revelations I have brought you this night. ³¹ If once again you pray and fast for seven days, then I shall return

to tell you even greater things. ³² For be sure your voice has been heard by the Most High; the Mighty God has seen your integrity and the chastity you have observed all your life. ³³ That is why he has sent me to you with all these revelations, and with this message: Be confident, and have no fear! ³⁴ Do not rush too hurriedly into unprofitable thoughts about the past; then you will not act hastily when the last age comes.'

Ezra's third vision

³⁵ AFTER that I wept once more and I fasted for seven days as I did previously, thus completing the three weeks enjoined on me. ³⁶ On the eighth night I was again troubled in mind, and began to address the Most High. ³⁷ With spirit truly aflame and in agony of mind ³⁸ I said: 'O Lord, at the beginning of creation you spoke the word. On the first day you said, "Let there be heaven and earth!" and your word accomplished its work. ³⁹ At that time a wind was blowing, and there was encircling darkness with silence everywhere; there was as yet no sound of human voice. ⁴⁰ Then you commanded a ray of light to be brought out of your treasure-chambers, to make your works visible from that time onwards.

⁴¹ 'On the second day you created the angel of the firmament, and commanded him to make a barrier dividing the waters, so that one part of them should withdraw upwards and the other remain beneath.

⁴² 'On the third day you ordered the waters to collect in a seventh part of the earth; the other six parts you made into dry land, and from it kept some to be sown and tilled for your service. ⁴³ Your word went forth, and at once the work was done. ⁴⁴ In an instant there appeared a vast profusion of fruits of every kind and taste that can be desired, with flowers of colours unsurpassed and scents mysterious in their fragrance. These were made on the third day.

⁴⁵ 'On the fourth day by your command were created the splendour of the sun, the light of the moon, and the stars in their appointed places; ⁴⁶ and you ordered them to be at the service of mankind, whom you were about to create.

⁴⁷ 'On the fifth day you commanded the seventh part, where the water was collected, to bring forth living things, birds and fishes. At your command, ⁴⁸ the dumb, lifeless water brought forth living creatures, and gave the nations cause to tell of your wonderful acts. ⁴⁹ Then you set apart two creatures: to one you gave the name Behemoth and to the other Leviathan. ⁵⁰ You put them in separate places, for the seventh part where the water was collected was not large enough to hold them both. ⁵¹ You assigned to Behemoth as his territory a part of the land which was made dry on the third day, a country of a thousand hills; ⁵² to Leviathan you gave the seventh part, the water. You have kept them to be food for whom you will and when you will.

⁵³ 'On the sixth day you ordered the earth to bring forth for you cattle, wild beasts, and creeping things. ⁵⁴ To crown your work you created Adam, and gave him lordship over everything you had made. It is from Adam that we, your chosen people, are all descended.

⁵⁵ 'I have recited the whole story of the creation, O Lord, because you have said that it was for our sake you made this first world, ⁵⁶ and that the rest of the nations descended from Adam are nothing, no better than spittle and, for all their numbers, no more than a drop from a bucket. ⁵⁷ And yet, O Lord, those nations which count for nothing are today ruling over us and trampling us down. ⁵⁸ We, your people, have been put into their power—your people, whom you have called your firstborn, your only son, your champion, and your best beloved. ⁵⁹ Now if the world was made for us, why may we not take possession of our inheritance? How much longer must this go on?'

The angel instructs Ezra

7 WHEN I had finished speaking, there was sent to me the same angel as on the previous nights. ² He addressed me, 'Rise to your feet, Ezra, and listen to the message I have brought you.' ³ 'Speak on, my lord,' I replied.

He said: 'Imagine a sea set in a vast open space and spreading far and wide, ⁴ but the entrance to it narrow like the gorge of a river. ⁵ If anyone wishes to reach this sea, whether to set eyes on it or to gain control of it, how can he arrive at

6:31 **greater things**: *Lat. adds* by day.   6:41 **angel**: *lit.* spirit. **firmament**: *or* vault of heaven.

23

its broad, open waters without passing through the narrow gorge? ⁶Or again, imagine a city built in a plain, a city full of every good thing, ⁷but the entrance to it narrow and steep, with fire to the right and deep water to the left. ⁸Between the fire and the water there is only one path, and that wide enough for but one person at a time. ⁹If someone has been given this city as a legacy, how can he take possession of his inheritance except by passing through this dangerous approach?' ¹⁰I agreed: 'That is the only way, my lord.'

The angel said: 'Such is the lot of Israel. ¹¹It was for Israel that I made the world, and when Adam transgressed my decrees the creation came under judgement. ¹²The entrances to the present world were made narrow, painful, and arduous, few and evil, full of perils and grinding hardship. ¹³But the entrances to the greater world are broad and safe, and lead to immortality. ¹⁴Everyone must therefore enter this narrow and futile existence; otherwise they can never attain the blessings in store. ¹⁵Then why are you so disquieted and perturbed, Ezra, at the thought that you are mortal and must die? ¹⁶Why have you not turned your mind from the present to the future?'

¹⁷'My master and lord,' I replied, 'in your law you have laid it down that the just shall inherit these blessings, but the ungodly shall perish. ¹⁸The just, therefore, can endure this narrow life and look for the spacious life hereafter; but those who have lived a wicked life will have gone through the narrows without ever reaching the open spaces.'

¹⁹He said: 'You are not a better judge than God, nor wiser than the Most High. ²⁰Better that many now living should perish, than that the law which God has set before them should be despised! ²¹God has given clear instructions to all when they come into this world, telling them how to attain life and how to avoid punishment. ²²But the ungodly have refused to obey him; they have adopted their own futile devices ²³and made deceit and wickedness their goal; they have even denied the existence of the Most High and ignored his ways. ²⁴They have

rejected his law and repudiated his promises; they have neither put faith in his decrees nor done what he commands. ²⁵Therefore, Ezra, it is emptiness for the empty, fullness for the full!

²⁶'Listen! The time will come when the signs I have foretold will be seen; the city which is now invisible will appear and the country now hidden be revealed. ²⁷Everyone who has been delivered from the calamities I have foretold will see for himself the wonderful things I shall do. ²⁸My son the Messiah will appear with his companions, bringing four hundred years of joy to all who survive. ²⁹At the end of that time my son the Messiah will die, and so will all mankind who draw breath. ³⁰Then the world will return to its original silence for seven days as at the beginning of creation; no one will be left alive. ³¹After seven days the age which is not yet awake will be aroused, and the age which is corruptible will cease to be. ³²The earth will give up those who sleep in it, and the dust those who rest there in silence; and the storehouses will give back the souls entrusted to them. ³³The Most High will be seen on the judgement-seat, and there will be an end of all pity and patience. ³⁴Judgement alone will remain, truth will stand firm, and faithfulness be strong. ³⁵The work of each man will come forward and its recompense be made known; good deeds will awake and wicked deeds will not be allowed to sleep. ⁽³⁶⁾The place of torment will appear, and over against it the place of rest; the furnace of hell will be displayed, and on the opposite side the paradise of joy.

⁽³⁷⁾'Then the Most High will say to the nations that have been raised from the dead: "Look and understand who it is you have denied and refused to serve, whose commandments you have despised. ⁽³⁸⁾Look on this side, and on that: here are joy and rest, there fire and torments." That is how he will speak to them on the day of judgement.

⁽³⁹⁾'That day will be without sun, moon, or stars; ⁽⁴⁰⁾without cloud, thunder, or lightning; wind, water, or air; darkness, evening, or morning; ⁽⁴¹⁾without summer, spring, or winter; without

7:26 *the city ... invisible: so some Vss.; Lat.* the city, the bride which is now seen.   7:28 *the Messiah: so some Vss.; Lat.* Jesus.   7:(36–105) *This passage, missing from the text of the Authorized (King James) Version, but found in ancient witnesses, has been restored.*

heat, frost, or cold; without hail, rain, or dew; (42) without noonday, night, or dawn; without brightness, light, or brilliance. There will be only the radiant glory of the Most High, by which all will see what lies before them. (43) That day will last for a week of years, as it were. (44) Such is the order that I have decreed for the judgement; but only to you have I given this revelation.'

(45) I replied: 'My lord, I repeat what I said before: "How blest are the living who obey your decrees!" (46) But as for those for whom I have been praying, has there ever lived a man who has not sinned, who has never transgressed your covenant? (47) I see now that only to the few will the next world bring joy, while to the many it will bring torment. (48) For an evil heart has grown strong in us; it has estranged us from God's decrees, brought us into corruption and the paths of death, opened up to us the way to ruin, and carried us far away from life. This it has done, not merely to a few, but to almost all who have been created.'

(49) The angel replied: 'Listen to me and I shall instruct and correct you yet further. (50) The Most High has made not one world but two, and for this reason: (51) there are, as you say, not many who are just, but only a few, whereas the wicked are very numerous; well then, listen to the explanation. (52) Suppose you had a very few precious stones; would you add to their number by putting common lead and clay among them?' (53) 'No, my lord,' I said, 'no one would do that.' (54) 'Look at it also in this way,' he continued: 'enquire of the earth, ask her humbly, and she will give you the answer. (55) Say to her, "You produce gold, silver, and copper, iron, lead, and clay. (56) There is more silver than gold, more copper than silver, more iron than copper, more lead than iron, more clay than lead." (57) Then judge for yourself which things are valuable and desirable—those which are plentiful, or those which are rare.' (58) 'My master and lord,' I said, 'what is plentiful is cheaper; the more rare is the more valuable.' (59) He replied, 'Consider then what follows from that: the owner of what is hard to get has more cause to be pleased than the owner of

what is plentiful. (60) In the same way, when I fulfil my promise to the creation, I shall have joy in the few who are saved, because it is they who have made my glory prevail now, and through them my name has been made known. (61) I shall not grieve for the many who are lost, for even now they are no more than a vapour; they are like flame or smoke—they catch fire, blaze up, and then die out.'

(62) I said: 'Mother Earth, if the human mind, like the rest of creation, is but a product of the dust, why did you bring it forth? (63) It would have been better if the very dust had never come into being, for then the mind would never have been produced. (64) But, as it is, our mind grows up with us and we are tortured by it, for we realize we are doomed to die. (65) What sorrow for mankind; what happiness for the wild beasts! What sorrow for every mother's son; what joy for the cattle and flocks! (66) How much better their lot than ours! They have no judgement to expect, no knowledge of torment, no knowledge of salvation promised them after death. (67) What good to us is the promise of a future life if it is to be nothing but torture? (68) For everyone alive is burdened and defiled with wickedness, sinful through and through. (69) Would it not have been better for us if there had been no judgement awaiting us after death?'

(70) The angel replied: 'When the Most High was making the world and Adam and his descendants, he first of all planned the judgement and what goes with it. (71) Your own words, when you said that man's mind grows up with him, will give you the answer. (72) It was in spite of having a mind that the people of this world sinned, and that is why torment awaits them: they received the commandments, but did not keep them; they accepted the law, then violated it. (73) What defence will they be able to make at the judgement, what answer at the last day? (74) How patient the Most High has been with the inhabitants of this world, and for how long!—not for their own sake, but for the sake of the destined age to be.'

(75) 'If I have found favour with you, my lord,' I said, 'make this also plain to me: at

---

7:(48) from ... decrees: *lit.* from these.

death, when each one of us gives back his soul, shall we be kept in peace until the time when you begin to create your new world, or does our torment begin at once?' [76] 'That too I will explain to you,' he replied. 'Do not, however, include yourself among those who have despised my law, nor count yourself with those who are to be tormented. [77] You after all have a treasure of good works stored up with the Most High, though you will not be shown it until the last days. [78] But now to speak of death: when the Most High has pronounced final sentence for a person to die, the spirit leaves the body to return to the One who first gave it, that it may render adoration to the glory of the Most High. [79] As for those who have scornfully rejected the ways of the Most High, who have spurned his law, and who hate the godfearing, [80] their spirits enter no settled abode, but from then on must wander in torment, endless grief, and sorrow. And this for seven reasons. [81] First, they have held in contempt the law of the Most High. [82] Secondly, they have lost their chance of making a full repentance and so gaining life. [83] Thirdly, they can see the reward in store for those who have trusted the covenants of the Most High. [84] Fourthly, they begin to think of the torment that awaits them at the end. [85] Fifthly, they see that angels are guarding the abode of the other souls in undisturbed peace. [86] Sixthly, they see that they are soon to enter into torment. [87] The seventh cause for grief, the greatest cause of all, is this: at the sight of the Most High in his glory they break down in shame, waste away in remorse, and shrivel with fear, remembering how they sinned against him in their lifetime and how they are soon to be brought before him for judgement on the last day.

[88] 'As for those who have kept to the ways of the Most High, this is what is appointed for them when their time comes to leave their mortal bodies. [89] During their stay on earth they served the Most High in spite of great hardship and constant danger, and kept to the last letter the law given them by the Lawgiver. [90] Therefore the decision is this: [91] they shall rejoice greatly to see the glory of God, who will receive them as his own, and they shall enter into rest through seven appointed stages. [92] The first stage is their victory in the long struggle against their innate impulse to evil, so that it did not lead them astray from life into death. [93] The second is to see the souls of the wicked wandering endlessly and the punishment awaiting them. [94] The third is seeing the good report given of them by their Maker, that while they were alive they kept the law entrusted to them. [95] The fourth is to understand the rest which they are now to share in the storehouses, guarded by angels in undisturbed peace, and the glory awaiting them in the next age. [96] The fifth is the contrast between the corruptible world from which they have joyfully escaped and the future life that is to be their possession, between the cramped, arduous existence from which they have been set free and the spacious life which will soon be theirs to delight in for ever and ever. [97] The sixth will be the revelation that they are to shine like stars, never to fade or die, with faces radiant as the sun. [98] The seventh stage, the greatest of them all, will be the confident and joyful assurance which will be theirs, free from all fear and shame, as they press forward to see face to face the One whom they served in their lifetime, and from whom they are now to receive their reward in glory.

[99] 'What I have here set forth is the appointed destiny for the souls of the just; the torments I spoke of before are what the rebellious are to suffer!'

[100] I asked him: 'When souls are separated from their bodies, will they be given the opportunity to see what you have described to me?' [101] 'They will be allowed seven days,' he replied; 'for seven days they will be permitted to see the things I have told you, and after that they will join the other souls in their abodes.'

[102] 'If I have found favour with you, my lord,' I said, 'tell me one thing more: on the day of judgement will the just be able to plead for the wicked, or by prayer win pardon for them from the Most High? [103] Can fathers do so for their sons, or sons for their parents? Can brothers pray for brothers, relatives and friends for their nearest and dearest?'

7:(103) **friends**: *so some Vss.; Lat.* the faithful.

(104) 'Since you have found favour with me,' the angel replied, 'this too I will tell you. The day of judgement is decisive and sets its seal on the truth for all to see. In the present age a father cannot send his son in his place, nor a son his father, nor a master his slave, nor a man his best friend, to be ill for him, or sleep, or eat, or be cured for him. (105) In like manner no one shall ever ask pardon for another; every individual will be held responsible for his own wickedness or goodness when that day comes.'

36 (106) To this I replied: 'But how is it, then, that we read of intercessions in scripture? First, there is Abraham, who prayed for the people of Sodom; then Moses, who prayed for our ancestors when they sinned in the wilderness. 37 (107) Next, there is Joshua, who prayed for the Israelites in the time of Achan, 38 (108) as did Samuel in the time of Saul, David on account of the plague, and Solomon for those present at the dedication. 39 (109) Elijah prayed for rain for the people, and he prayed for one who had died, that he might be brought back to life. 40 (110) Hezekiah prayed for the nation in the time of Sennacherib; and there are many more besides. 41 (111) If, then, in an age when corruption had spread and wickedness increased, the just made entreaty for the wicked, why cannot it be the same on the day of judgement?'

42 (112) The answer he gave me was: 'The present world is not the end, and the glory of God does not stay in it continually. That is why the strong have prayed for the weak. 43 (113) But the day of judgement will be the end of the present world and the beginning of the eternal world to come, a world in which corruption will have disappeared, 44 (114) all excess will be abolished and unbelief eliminated, in which justice will be full-grown, and truth will have risen like the sun. 45 (115) On the day of judgement, therefore, there can be no mercy for those who have lost their case, no reversal for those who have won.'

46 (116) I replied, 'But this is my point, my first point and my last: how much better it would have been if the earth had never produced Adam at all, or, once it had done so, if he had been restrained from sinning! 47 (117) For what good does it do any of us to live in misery now and have nothing but punishment to expect after death? 48 (118) O Adam, what have you done? Though the sin was yours, the fall was not yours alone; it was ours also, the fall of all your descendants. 49 (119) What good is the promise of immortality to us, when we have committed mortal sins? 50 (120) What good is the hope of eternity, in the wretched and futile state to which we have come; 51 (121) or the prospect of dwelling in health and security, when we have lived such wicked lives? 52 (122) You say that the glory of the Most High will guard those who have led pure lives; but what help is that to us who have walked in the most wicked ways? 53 (123) What good is the revelation to us of paradise and its imperishable fruit, the source of perfect satisfaction and healing? For we shall never enter it, 54 (124) since we have made depravity our home. 55 (125) You say that those who have practised self-discipline will shine with faces brighter than the stars; but what good is that to us whose faces are darker than night? 56 (126) During a lifetime of iniquity we have never given a thought to the sufferings in store for us after death.'

57 (127) The angel replied, 'This is the thought for every man on earth to keep in mind during the battle of life: 58 (128) if he is defeated, he must accept the sufferings you have mentioned, but if he is victorious, the rewards I have been describing will be his. 59 (129) That was the way which Moses in his time urged the people to take, when he said, "Choose life and live!" 60 (130) But they believed neither him, nor the prophets after him, no, nor me when I spoke to them. 61 (131) There will be no sorrow over their damnation; but there will be joy for the salvation of those who have believed.'

62 (132) 'My lord,' I said, 'I know that the Most High is now called compassionate, because he has compassion on those yet unborn; 63 (133) and merciful, because he shows mercy to those who repent and live by his law; 64 (134) and patient, because he shows patience to those who have sinned, his own creatures as they are; 65 (135) and Benefactor, because he would rather give

---

7:37 Achan: *Lat.* Achar.

than demand; [66(136)] and rich in forgiveness, because again and again he forgives sinners, past, present, and to come. [67(137)] Without his continued forgiveness there could be no hope of life for the world and its inhabitants. [68(138)] He is called generous, because without his generosity in releasing sinners from their sins, not one ten-thousandth part of mankind could hope to be given life; [69(139)] and he is also called Judge, for unless he grants pardon to those who have been created by his word, and blots out their countless offences, [70(140)] only a very few of the entire human race would, I suppose, be spared.'

8 The angel said to me, 'The Most High has made this world for many, the next world for but a few. [2] Let me give you an illustration, Ezra: enquire of the earth, and it will tell you that it can produce an abundance of clay for making earthenware, but very little gold-dust. It is the same with the present world: [3] many have been created, but only a few will be saved.'

Ezra's prayer and the answer

[4] I said: 'My soul, drink deep of understanding and eat your fill of wisdom! [5] Without your consent you came here, and against your will you depart; only a brief span of life is given you.

[6] 'O Lord above, if I may be allowed to approach you in prayer, implant a seed in our hearts and minds, and make it grow until it bears fruit, so that fallen man may obtain life. [7] For you alone are God, and by your hands we are all shaped in one mould, as your word declares. [8] The body moulded in the womb receives from you life and limbs; that which you create is kept safe amid fire and water, and for nine months the body moulded by you bears what you have created in it. [9] Both the womb which holds safely and that which is safely held will be kept safe only because you keep them so. And after the womb has delivered up what was created in it, [10] then, at your command, from the breasts the human body itself supplies milk, the fruit of the breasts. [11] For a certain time what has been made is nourished in that way; and afterwards in your mercy it is still cared for. [12] You bring it up to know your justice, train it in your law, and correct it by your wisdom. [13] It is

your creature and you made it; you can put it to death or give it life, as you please. [14] But if you should lightly destroy what was fashioned by your command with so much labour, to what purpose was it created?

[15] 'And now let me say this: about mankind at large, you know best; but it is for your own people that I grieve, [16] for your inheritance that I mourn; my sorrow is for Israel, my distress for the descendants of Jacob. [17] For them and for myself, therefore, I shall address my prayer to you, since I perceive how low we have fallen, we who dwell in the land; [18] and I have heard how quickly your judgement will follow. [19] Hear, then, what I have to say, and consider the prayer which I make to you.'

This is the prayer offered by Ezra, before he was taken up to heaven: [20] 'O Lord, you inhabit eternity, to you the sky and the highest heavens belong; [21] your throne is beyond imagining, your glory past conceiving; you are attended by the host of angels, trembling [22] as they turn themselves into wind or fire at your bidding; your word is true, your declarations are constant, your commands mighty and terrible; [23] your glance dries up the depths, your anger melts the mountains, and your truth stands for ever: [24] hear, O Lord, the prayer of your servant, listen to my petition and attend to my words, for you it is who have fashioned me. [25] While I live, I must speak; while I have understanding, I must respond.

[26] 'Do not look upon the offences of your people, but rather look on those who have served you faithfully. [27] Pay heed not to the godless and their practices, but to those who have observed your covenant and suffered for it. [28] Do not think of those who all their lives have been untrue to you, but remember those who of their own will have acknowledged the fear due to you. [29] Do not destroy those who have lived like animals, but take account of those who have borne shining witness to your law. [30] Do not be angry with those considered worse than beasts, but show love to those who have put unfailing trust in your glory. [31] We and our fathers have lived evil lives, yet it is on account of us sinners that you are called merciful; [32] for if it is your desire to have mercy on us,

sinners who have no just deeds to our credit, then indeed you will be called merciful. [33] The reward which will be given to the just, who have many good works stored up with you, will be no more than their own deeds have earned.

[34] 'What is man that you should be angry with him? Or the race of mortals that you should treat them so harshly? [35] The truth is, no one was ever born who did not sin, no one alive is innocent of offence. [36] Indeed, it is through your mercy shown towards those with no fund of good deeds to their name that your justice and kindness will be made known.'

[37] In reply to me the angel said: 'Some part of what you have said is correct, and it will be as you say. [38] You may be sure that I shall not give thought to sinners, to their creation, death, judgement, or damnation; [39] but I shall have joy in the creation of the just, in their pilgrimage through this world, their salvation, and their final reward. [40] So I have said, and so it is. [41] The farmer sows many seeds in the ground and plants many plants, but not all the seeds come up safely in due season, nor do all the plants strike root. It is the same in the world of men: not all who are sown will be saved.'

[42] To that I replied: 'If I have found favour with you, let me speak. [43] The farmer's seed may not come up, because you did not give it rain at the right time, or it may rot because of too much rain; [44] but man, who was fashioned by your hands and called your image because he is made like you, and for whose sake you formed everything, will you really compare him with seed sown by a farmer? [45] Do not be angry with us, Lord; but spare your people and show them pity, for it is your own creation you will be pitying.'

[46] He answered: 'The present is for those now alive, the future for those yet to come. [47] It is not possible for you to love my creation with a love greater than mine—far from it! But never again rank yourself among the unjust, as so often you have done. [48] Yet the Most High approves [49] of the proper modesty you have shown; you have not sought great glory by including yourself among the godly. [50] In the last days the inhabitants of the world will be punished for their arrogant lives by prolonged suffering. [51] But you should direct your thoughts to your-self and look to the glory awaiting those like you. [52] For all of you paradise lies open, the tree of life is planted, the age to come stands prepared, and rich abundance is in store; the city is already built, rest from toil is assured, goodness and wisdom are brought to perfection. [53] From you the root of evil has been cut off; for you disease is at an end and death abolished, hell is gone, and the corruption of the grave blotted out. [54] All sorrows are at an end, and the treasure of immortality has been finally revealed.

[55] 'Ask no more questions, therefore, about the many who are lost; [56] for when they were given freedom they used it to despise the Most High, to treat his law with contempt and abandon his ways. [57] What is more, they trampled on the godly. [58] "There is no God," they said to themselves, knowing full well that they must die. [59] Yours, then, will be the joys I have predicted, theirs the thirst and torments already prepared. It is not that the Most High has wanted any man to be destroyed, [60] but that those he created have themselves brought dishonour on their Creator's name, and shown ingratitude to the One who had put life within their reach. [61] That is why my judgement is now close at hand, [62] but I have not made this known to all—only to you and a few like you.'

[63] 'My lord,' I said, 'you have now revealed to me the many signs which you are to perform in the last days; but you have not shown me when that will be.'

9 The angel answered: 'Keep a careful check; when you see that some of the signs predicted have already passed, [2] then you will understand that the time has come for the Most High to begin to judge the world he created. [3] When the world becomes the scene of earthquakes, insurrections, plots among the nations, unstable government, and panic among rulers, [4] then you will recognize these as the events foretold by the Most High since first the world began. [5] Just as everything that is done on earth has its beginning and end clearly marked, [6] so it is with the times which the Most High has determined: the beginning is marked by portents and miracles, the end by manifestations of power.

[7] 'All who come safely through and escape destruction, thanks to their good

deeds or the faith they have shown, [8] will survive the dangers I have foretold and witness the salvation I shall bring to my land, the territory I have set apart from all eternity as my own. [9] Then those who have neglected my ways will be taken by surprise; their utter contempt for my ways will bring them lasting torment. [10] All who in their lifetime failed to acknowledge me in spite of the benefits I brought them, [11] all who disdained my law while freedom still was theirs, who scornfully dismissed the idea of penitence while the way was still open—[12] all these must learn the truth through torments after death. [13] Do not be curious any more, Ezra, to know how the godless will be tormented, but only how and when the just will be saved; the world is theirs and for their sake it exists.'

[14] I answered, [15] 'I repeat what I have said again and again: the lost outnumber the saved [16] as a wave exceeds a drop of water.'

[17] The angel replied: 'The seed to be sown depends on the soil, the colour depends on the flower, the product on the craftsman, and the harvest on the farmer. There was a time [18] before the world had been created for men to live in, and I was planning it for the sake of those who now exist. No one then disputed my plan, [19] for no one existed. I supplied this world with unfailing food and a law not to be questioned; but those whom I created turned to corrupt ways of life. [20] I looked at my world and there it lay spoilt, at my earth and it was in danger from men's wicked plans. [21] I saw this and I was hard put to it to spare any at all; but I saved for myself one grape out of a cluster, one tree out of a large forest. [22] So then let it be: destruction for the many who were born in vain, and salvation for my grape and my tree, which have cost me such labour to bring to perfection.

[23] 'You, however, must wait seven days more, Ezra. Do not fast this time, [24] but go to a flowery field where no house stands, and eat only what grows there; taste no meat or wine, [25] and pray to the Most High the whole time. I shall then come and talk with you.'

Ezra's fourth vision

[26] I WENT out, as the angel told me, to a field called Ardat. There I sat among the flowers; my food was what grew in the field, and I ate to my heart's content. [27] As I lay on the grass at the end of the seven days, I was troubled again in mind with all the same perplexities. [28] I broke my silence and addressed the Most High: [29] 'Lord, you showed yourself to our fathers in the wilderness at the time of the exodus from Egypt, when they were travelling through a barren waste where no one ever trod, [30] and you said, "Hear me, Israel, listen to my words, you descendants of Jacob: [31] this is my law, which I am sowing among you to bear fruit and to bring you everlasting glory." [32] But our fathers, though they received the law, did not observe it; they disobeyed its commandments. Not that the fruit of the law perished—that was impossible, for it was yours; [33] rather, those who received it perished, because they failed to keep safe the seed that had been sown in them. [34] Now the usual way of things is that when seed is put into the earth, or a ship on the sea, or food or drink into a jar, then if the seed, or the ship, [35] or the contents of the jar should be destroyed, what held or contained them does not perish along with them. But with us sinners it is different: [36] destruction will come upon us, the recipients of the law, and upon our hearts, the vessel that held the law. [37] The law itself is not destroyed; it survives in all its glory.'

[38] While turning over these things in my mind, I looked round and on my right I saw a woman in great distress, mourning and lamenting loudly; her dress was torn, and she had ashes on her head. [39] Breaking off my meditations, I turned to her [40] and asked: 'Why are you weeping? What is troubling you?' [41] 'Sir,' she replied, 'please leave me to my tears and my grief, for great is my bitterness of heart and great my affliction.' [42] 'Tell me', I said, 'what has happened.' [43] 'Sir, I was barren and childless throughout thirty years of marriage,' she replied; [44] 'every hour of every day during those thirty years, night and day alike, I prayed to the Most High. [45] Then after thirty years God answered my prayer and had mercy on my affliction; he took note of my sorrow and granted me a son. What joy he brought to my husband and myself and to all our neighbours! What praise we gave to the Mighty God! [46] I took great pains

over his upbringing, [47] and when he grew up I chose a wife for him and held a wedding feast.

10 'But when my son entered the bridal chamber, he fell down dead. [2] We put out all the lights, and my neighbours all came to comfort me; I controlled my feelings till the evening of the following day. [3] When everyone had stopped urging me to take comfort and control myself, I rose and stole away in the night, and came here, as you see, to this field. [4] I have made up my mind never to return to the city; I shall stay here, neither eating nor drinking, but mourning and fasting all the time until I die.'

[5] At that I abandoned the reflections which occupied my mind and spoke sternly to the woman: [6] 'You are the most foolish of women,' I said; 'are you blind to the mourning and sufferings of our nation? [7] It is for the anguish and affliction of Zion, the mother of us all, that you should mourn with such poignancy; [8] you should share in our common mourning and anguish. But your anguish is for your one son. [9] Ask the earth and she will tell you that she must mourn for the countless thousands who come to birth upon her. [10] In the beginning all sprang from her, and there are more still to come; yet almost all her children go to perdition, and vast numbers of them are wiped out. [11] Who, then, has the better right to be mourning—the earth, which has lost such vast numbers, or you, whose sorrow is for one only? [12] You may say to me, "But my lamentation is different from that of the earth; I have lost the fruit of my womb, which I brought to birth in pain and travail, [13] whereas it is only in the course of nature that the vast numbers now alive on earth should depart as they came." [14] My answer is: at the cost of pain you have been a mother, but in the same way the earth has always been the mother of mankind, bearing fruit to earth's Creator.

[15] 'Now, therefore, keep your sorrow to yourself, and bear your misfortunes bravely. [16] If you will accept God's decree as just, then in due time you will receive your son again and win an honoured name among women. [17] Go back, therefore, into the city to your husband.'

[18] 'No,' she replied, 'I will not. I will never go back; I shall die here.'

[19] But I continued to argue with her. [20] 'Do not do that,' I urged; 'let yourself be persuaded because of Zion's misfortunes, and take comfort from the sorrow of Jerusalem. [21] You see how our sanctuary has been laid waste, our altar demolished, our temple destroyed. [22] Our harps are unstrung, our hymns silenced, our shouts of joy cut short; the light of the sacred lamp has been extinguished, and the Ark of our covenant has been plundered; the holy vessels are defiled, and the name which God has conferred on us is disgraced; our leading men have been treated with violence, our priests burnt alive, and the Levites taken into captivity; our virgins have been ravished and our wives violated, our godfearing men carried off, and our children left abandoned; our young men have been enslaved, and our strong warriors reduced to impotence. [23] Worst of all, Zion, once sealed with God's own seal, has forfeited its glory and been delivered into the hands of those who hate us. [24] Then throw off your own heavy grief, and lay aside all your sorrows; may the Mighty God restore you to his favour, may the Most High give you rest and peace after your troubles!'

[25] Suddenly, as I was still speaking to the woman, I saw her face begin to shine brightly. Her countenance flashed like lightning, and I shrank from her in fear, and wondered what this meant. [26] All at once she uttered a great cry of terror that shook the earth. [27] I looked up and saw no longer a woman but a city, built on massive foundations. I was terrified and cried aloud, [28] 'Where is the angel Uriel who came to me before? It is his doing that I have reached this state of panic, that my end is to be bodily corruption, and my prayers are met by reproach.'

[29] I was still speaking when there appeared the angel who had come previously. When he saw me [30] lying unconscious, in a dead faint, he grasped me by my right hand, put strength into me, and raised me to my feet. [31] 'What is the matter?' he asked. 'Why are you overcome? What has so disturbed you and troubled your mind?' [32] 'You abandoned me,' I replied. 'I did as you told me: I came out to the fields; and what I have seen

here and can still see is beyond my power to explain.'

³³ 'Stand up like a man,' he said, 'and I shall enlighten you.'

³⁴ 'Speak on, my lord,' I replied; 'only do not abandon me and leave me to die to no purpose. ³⁵ I have seen and heard things beyond my knowledge and understanding—³⁶ unless this is all an illusion and a dream. ³⁷ My lord, explain this state, I beg you.'

³⁸ 'Listen to me,' replied the angel, 'while I expound the things that terrify you; for the Most High has revealed many secrets to you. ³⁹ He has seen your upright life, your unceasing grief for your people, and your deep mourning over Zion.

⁴⁰ 'Here, then, is the meaning of the vision. ⁴¹ A little while ago you saw a woman mourning and tried to console her; ⁴² now you no longer see that woman, but a complete city has appeared to you. ⁴³ She told you about losing her son, and this is the explanation. ⁴⁴ The woman you saw is Zion, which you now see as a city complete with its buildings. ⁴⁵ She told you she was childless for thirty years; that was because three thousand years passed before any sacrifices were offered in Zion. ⁴⁶ But then, after the three thousand years, Solomon built the city and offered the sacrifices; that was when the childless woman bore a son. ⁴⁷ She took great trouble, she said, over his upbringing; that was the period when Jerusalem was inhabited. ⁴⁸ She told you of the loss she suffered, how her son had died on the day he entered his bridal chamber; that was the destruction which has overtaken Jerusalem. ⁴⁹ Such then was the vision you saw—the woman mourning for her son—and you tried to comfort her in her sufferings; this was the revelation you had to receive. ⁵⁰ Seeing the sincerity of your grief and how you feel for her with all your heart, the Most High is now showing you her radiant glory and her surpassing beauty. ⁵¹ That was why I told you to stay in a field where no house has been built, ⁵² for I knew that the Most High intended to send you this revelation. ⁵³ I told you to come to this field, where no foundation had been laid for any building, ⁵⁴ because in the place where the city of the Most High was to be

revealed no building made by man could stand.

⁵⁵ 'Have no fear, then, and set your mind at rest; go into the city, and see the great buildings in all their splendour, so far as your eyes have power to see them. ⁵⁶ After that you will hear as much as your ears have power to hear. ⁵⁷ You are more blessed than most, and few have such a name with the Most High as you have. ⁵⁸ Stay here till tomorrow night, ⁵⁹ when the Most High will show you in dreams and visions what he will do to earth's inhabitants in the last days.' So, as I had been told, I slept there that night and the next.

Ezra's fifth vision

11 ON the second night I had a vision in my sleep: there, rising out of the sea, appeared an eagle with twelve wings and three heads. ² I saw it spread its wings over the whole earth; and all the winds of heaven blew upon it and clouds gathered about it. ³ Out of its wings I saw opposing wings sprout, which proved to be only small and stunted. ⁴ Its heads lay still; even the middle head, which was bigger than the others, lay still between them. ⁵ As I watched, the eagle rose on its wings to establish itself as ruler over the earth and its inhabitants. ⁶ I saw it bring into subjection everything under heaven; it encountered no protest at all from any creature on earth. ⁷ I saw the eagle stand erect on its talons and address its wings: ⁸ 'Do not all wake together,' it said; 'sleep each of you in your place and wake up in your turn; ⁹ the heads are to be kept till the last.' ¹⁰ I saw that the sound was coming not from its heads but from the middle of its body. ¹¹ I counted the opposing wings: there were eight of them.

¹² As I watched, one of the wings on its right side rose and became ruler over the whole earth. ¹³ After a time its reign came to an end, and it disappeared, leaving no trace. Then the next arose and established its rule, holding sway for a long time. ¹⁴ When its reign was coming to an end and it was about to disappear like the first, ¹⁵ a voice could be heard addressing it: ¹⁶ 'You have held the world in your grasp; now listen to my message before your time comes to disappear. ¹⁷ None of your

11:2 **clouds**: *so some Vss.; Lat. omits.*

successors will achieve a reign as long as yours, or even half as long.' ¹⁸ Then the third wing arose, exercised power for a time like its predecessors, and like them disappeared. ¹⁹ In the same way all the wings came to power one after the other, and in turn each disappeared.

²⁰ As time went on, I saw the little wings on the right side also raise themselves up to seize power. Some achieved this, and at once passed from sight, ²¹ while others arose but never attained to power. ²² At this point I noticed that two of the little wings were, like the twelve large ones, no longer to be seen; ²³ nothing was left on the eagle's body except the three motionless heads and six little wings. ²⁴ As I watched, two of the six little wings separated from the rest and stationed themselves under the head on the right. The other four remained where they were, ²⁵ and I saw them planning to rise up and seize power. ²⁶ One rose, but disappeared immediately; ²⁷ so too did the second, vanishing even more quickly than the first. ²⁸ I saw the last two planning to make themselves the rulers; ²⁹ but while they were still plotting, suddenly one of the heads woke from sleep, the one in the middle, the biggest of the three. ³⁰ I saw how it joined with the other two heads, ³¹ and along with them turned and devoured the two little wings which were planning to become rulers. ³² This head got the whole earth into its grasp, establishing an oppressive regime over all its inhabitants and a world-wide kingdom mightier than any of the wings had governed. ³³ But after that I saw the middle head vanish as suddenly as the wings had done. ³⁴ There were two heads left, and they also made themselves rulers over the earth and its inhabitants; ³⁵ but, as I watched, the head on the right devoured the head on the left.

³⁶ Then I heard a voice saying to me: 'Look carefully at what you see in front of you.' ³⁷ I looked, and saw what seemed to be a lion roused out of the forest and roaring as it came. I heard it address the eagle in a human voice. ³⁸ 'Listen, you, to what I tell you!' it said. 'The Most High says: ³⁹ Are you not the sole survivor of the four beasts to which I gave the rule over my world, intending through them to bring to an end the times I fixed? ⁴⁰⁻⁴¹ You are the fourth beast to come,

and you have conquered all who went before, dominating the whole world and holding it in the grip of fear and harsh oppression. You have lived long in the world, governing it with deceit and with no regard for truth. ⁴² You have trodden underfoot the gentle and injured the peaceful, hating the truthful and loving liars; you have destroyed the homes of the prosperous, and razed to the ground the walls of those who had done you no harm. ⁴³ Your insolence is known to the Most High, your pride to the Mighty One. ⁴⁴ The Most High has surveyed the periods he has fixed: they are now at an end, and his ages have reached their completion. ⁴⁵ Therefore, eagle, you must now disappear and be seen no more, you and your terrible great wings, your villainous small wings, your cruel heads, your grim talons, and your whole worthless carcass. ⁴⁶ Then all the earth will be refreshed and relieved by being freed from your violence, and will look forward in hope to the judgement and mercy of its Creator.'

12 While the lion was still addressing the eagle, I looked ² and saw the one remaining head disappear, and the two wings which had gone over to it arose and set themselves up as rulers. But their reign was short and troubled, ³ and when I looked they were already vanishing. Then the eagle's whole body burst into flames, filling the earth with terror.

So great was my agitation and alarm that I awoke. I said to myself: ⁴ 'See the result of the attempt to discover the ways of the Most High! ⁵ I am weary of mind and utterly exhausted; the terrors I have experienced this night have bereft me of the last vestige of strength. ⁶ I shall now pray, therefore, to the Most High to be given strength to the end.' ⁷ I said: 'My Master and Lord, if I have found favour with you and am esteemed more just than most men, and if it is true that my prayers have reached your presence, ⁸ then give me strength. Reveal to me, my Lord, the precise interpretation of this terrifying vision, and set my soul fully at ease, ⁹ for you have already judged me worthy to be shown the end of the present age.'

¹⁰ The angel answered: 'Here is the interpretation of your vision. ¹¹ The eagle you saw rising out of the sea represents the fourth kingdom in the vision seen by your brother Daniel. ¹² But he was not

given the interpretation which I am now giving you or have already given you. ¹³ The days are coming when the earth will be under an empire more terrible than any before. ¹⁴ It will be ruled by twelve kings, one after another, ¹⁵ the second to come to the throne having the longest reign of all the twelve. ¹⁶ That is the meaning of the twelve wings you saw.

¹⁷ 'As for the voice which you heard speaking from the middle of the eagle's body, and not from its heads, this is what it means: ¹⁸ after this second king's reign, great conflicts will arise, which will bring the empire into danger of collapse; yet it will not collapse then, but will be restored to its original power.

¹⁹ 'As for the eight lesser wings which you saw growing from the eagle's wings, this is what they mean: ²⁰ the empire will come under eight kings whose reigns will be brief and transient; ²¹ two of them will come and go just before the middle of the period, four will be kept back until shortly before its end, and two will be left until the end itself.

²² 'As for the three heads which you saw sleeping, this is what they mean: ²³ in the last years of the empire, the Most High will bring to the throne three kings, who will restore much of its strength, and rule over the earth ²⁴ and its inhabitants more oppressively than any who preceded them. They are called the eagle's heads, ²⁵ because they will bring to a head and consummate its long series of wicked deeds. ²⁶ As for the greatest head, which you saw disappear, it signifies one of the kings; he will die in his bed, but in agony. ²⁷ The two that survived will be destroyed by the sword; ²⁸ one of them will fall victim to the sword of the other, who will himself fall by the sword in the last days.

²⁹ 'As for the two little wings that went over to the head on the right side, ³⁰ this is what they mean: they are the ones whom the Most High has reserved until the last days, and their reign, as you saw, was short and troubled.

³¹ 'As for the lion which you saw coming out of the forest, roused from sleep and roaring, and which you heard addressing the eagle, taxing it with its wicked deeds and words, ³² he is the Messiah whom the Most High has kept back until the end of the days; he will arise from the stock of David and will come and address those rulers, taxing them openly with their sins, their crimes, and their defiance. ³³ First, he will bring them alive to judgement; then, after convicting them, he will destroy them. ³⁴ But he will be merciful to the rest of my people, all who have survived in my land; he will set them free and give them joy, until the final day of judgement comes, about which I told you at the beginning.

³⁵ 'That is the vision you saw, and that its meaning. ³⁶ It is the secret of the Most High, of which no one except yourself has proved worthy to be told. ³⁷ You must therefore write in a book all you have seen, and deposit it in a hiding-place. ³⁸ You must also disclose these secrets to those of your people whom you know to be wise enough to understand them and to keep them safe. ³⁹ However, you must stay here for seven days more, to receive whatever revelation the Most High thinks fit to send you.' Then the angel left me.

⁴⁰ When all the people heard that seven days had passed and I had not yet returned to the city, both high and low assembled and came to me and asked: ⁴¹ 'What wrong or what injury have we done you, that you have abandoned us for good and settled in this place? ⁴² Out of all the prophets you are the only one left to us. You are like the last cluster in a vineyard, like a lamp in a dark place, or a safe harbour for a ship in a storm. ⁴³ Have we not suffered enough already? ⁴⁴ If you abandon us, we had far better have perished in the fire that destroyed Zion. ⁴⁵ We are no better than those who died there.' And they wept aloud.

⁴⁶ 'Take courage, Israel,' I answered them; 'lay aside your grief, house of Jacob. ⁴⁷ The Most High bears you in mind, the Mighty God has not forgotten you for ever. ⁴⁸ I have not abandoned you, nor shall I leave you; I came here to pray for Zion in her desolation, and to beg for mercy for our sanctuary now fallen so low. ⁴⁹ Go to your homes for the present, every one of you, and in a few days' time I shall come back to you.'

⁵⁰ So the people returned to the city as I

12:23 **who ... rule:** *so some Vss.; Lat.* and he will restore ... and they will rule.   12:32 **of the days ... address:** *so one Vs.; Lat. defective.*

34

told them, [51] while I remained in the field. As commanded by the angel I stayed there for seven days, eating nothing but what grew in the field, and living on that for the whole of the time.

Ezra's sixth vision

13 THE seven days passed; and the following night I had a dream. [2] In my dream, a wind arose from the sea and set all its waves in turmoil. [3] As I watched, the wind brought a figure like that of a man out of the depths, and he flew with the clouds of heaven. Wherever he turned his face, everything he looked at trembled, [4] and wherever the sound of his voice reached, everyone who heard it melted as wax at the touch of fire.

[5] Next I saw a countless host of men gathering from the four winds of heaven to vanquish the man who had come up out of the sea. [6] I saw that the man hewed out for himself a great mountain, and flew on to it. [7] Though I tried to see from what region or place the mountain had been taken, I could not. [8] Then I saw that all who had gathered to fight against the man were greatly afraid, and yet they dared to fight. [9] When he saw the hordes advancing to the attack, he did not so much as lift a finger against them. He had no spear in his hand, no weapon at all; [10] only, as I watched, he poured out what appeared to be a stream of fire from his mouth, a breath of flame from his lips with a storm of sparks from his tongue. [11] These, the stream of fire, the breath of flame, and the great storm, combined into one mass which fell on the host prepared for battle, and burnt them all up. Of that enormous multitude suddenly nothing was to be discerned but dust and ashes and a reek of smoke. I was astounded at the sight.

[12] After that, I saw the man come down from the mountain and summon to himself a different, a peaceful company. [13] He was joined by great numbers of men, some with joy on their faces, others with sorrow, some coming from captivity, and some bringing others to him as an offering. I woke up overcome by terror, and I prayed to the Most High: [14] 'O Lord, from first to last you have revealed those wonders to me, and judged me worthy to have my prayers answered. [15] Now show me the meaning of this dream also. [16] How terrible it will be, to my thinking, for all who survive to those days, but how much worse for those who do not! [17] Those who do not survive will have the sorrow [18] of knowing what the last days have in store, yet without attaining it. [19] Those who do survive are to be pitied for the terrible dangers and many trials which those visions show they will have to face. [20] But perhaps after all it is better to endure the dangers and reach the goal than to vanish from the world like a cloud and never see what will happen at the last.'

[21] 'Yes,' he replied, 'I shall disclose the meaning of the vision, and tell you what you ask. [22] To your question about those who survive, the answer is this: [23] the very person from whom danger will then come will protect those exposed to the danger if they have good deeds and faith laid up to their credit with God Most Mighty. [24] You may rest assured that those who survive are more blessed than those who have died.

[25] 'This is what the vision means: the man you saw coming up from the heart of the sea [26] is he whom the Most High has held in readiness during many ages; through him he will deliver the world he has made, and he will determine the destiny of those who survive. [27] As for the breath of flame, the fire, and the storm you saw issuing from the mouth of the man, [28] so that without spear or any other weapon in his hand he crushed the onslaught of the hordes advancing to fight against him, the meaning is this: [29] the day is near when the Most High will start bringing deliverance to those on earth. [30] Its panic-stricken inhabitants [31] will plot hostilities against one another, city against city, region against region, nation against nation, kingdom against kingdom. [32] When that happens, and all the signs that I have shown you take place, then my son will be revealed, he whom you saw as a man coming up out of the sea. [33] At the sound of his voice all nations will leave their own territories and their separate wars, [34] and unite as you saw in your vision in one large host past counting, all intent on overpowering him.

13:3 **the wind ... depths:** *so other Vss.; Lat. defective.*   13:26 **him:** *so one Vs.; Lat. himself.*

35 When he takes his stand on the summit of Mount Zion, 36 then Zion, completed and fully built, will come and appear before all people, corresponding to the mountain which you saw hewn out, though not by human hands. 37 My son will convict of their godless deeds the nations that confront him; this will accord with the storm you saw. 38 He will reproach them to their face with their evil plotting and the torments they are soon to undergo; this is symbolized by the flame. And he will destroy them without effort by means of the law—and that is like the fire.

39 'You saw him assemble a company which was different and peaceful. 40 They are the ten tribes that were taken into exile in the days of King Hoshea, whom King Shalmaneser of Assyria made captive. Carrying them off beyond the river Euphrates, he deported them to a foreign country. 41 But then they resolved to leave behind the gentile population and go to a more distant region never yet inhabited, 42 and there at least to be obedient to their laws, which in their own country they had failed to keep. 43 As they passed through the narrow passages of the Euphrates, 44 the Most High performed miracles for them, halting the flow of the river until they had crossed over. 45 Their long journey through that region called Arzareth took a year and a half. 46 They have lived there ever since, until this final age. Now they are on their way back, 47 and once more the Most High is halting the river to let them cross.

'That is the meaning of the peaceful company you saw assembled. 48 With them too are the survivors of your own people, all who are found inside my sacred borders. 49 When the time comes, therefore, for him to destroy the assembled nations, he will protect those of your people who are left, 50 and then display to them countless portents.'

51 'My master and lord,' I said, 'explain to me why the man I saw came up out of the heart of the sea.' 52 He replied: 'It is beyond the power of anyone to explore the deep sea and discover what is in it; in the same way no one on earth can set eyes on my son and those who accompany him until the appointed day. 53 Such then is the meaning of your vision. This revelation has been given to you, and to you

alone, 54 because you have laid aside your own affairs, and devoted yourself entirely to mine and to the study of my law. 55 You have taken wisdom as your guide in life, and you have called understanding your mother. 56 That is why I have given this revelation to you: there is a reward for you with the Most High. In three more days' time I shall speak with you again, and tell you of momentous and wonderful things.'

57 So I went away to the field, glorifying and praising the Most High for the wonders he performed from time to time 58 and for his providential control of the passing ages and what happens in them. There I remained for three days.

Ezra's seventh vision

14 On the third day I was sitting under an oak tree, when there came a voice from a bush in front of me: 'Ezra, Ezra!' it called. 2 'Here I am, Lord,' I answered, rising to my feet. 3 The voice went on: 'When my people was in slavery in Egypt, I revealed myself in the bush and spoke to Moses, 4 sending him to lead Israel out of Egypt. I brought him to Mount Sinai, where for many days I kept him with me. 5 I explained many wonderful things to him, showing him the secrets of the ages and the end of time, and I instructed him 6 what to make public and what to keep hidden. 7 To you also I now say: 8 Store up in your mind the signs I have shown you, the visions you have seen, and the interpretations you have heard. 9 You are about to be taken away from the world of men, and thereafter you will remain with my son and with those like you until the end of time. 10 The world has lost its youth, and time is growing old; 11 for the whole of time is in twelve divisions, of which nine divisions and half the tenth are already past; 12 so there remain only two and a half. 13 Now, therefore, set your house in order; admonish your nation, and give comfort to those of them who are lowly. Then take your leave of this corruptible life; 14 let go your earthly cares, and throw off your human burdens; shed your weak nature, 15 and put on one side the anxieties that vex you; then make haste to depart from this world of time. 16 However great the evils you have witnessed, there are worse to come. 17 As this ageing world grows

ever more feeble, the more will evils increase for its inhabitants. [18] Truth will move farther away, and falsehood draw nearer. The eagle you saw in your vision is already on the wing.'

[19] 'Lord, if I may speak in your presence,' I replied, [20] 'I am to depart, by your command, after admonishing those of my people who are now alive; but who will give a warning to those born hereafter? The world is shrouded in darkness and its inhabitants are without light. [21] Because your law was destroyed in the fire, no one can know what you have done or intend to do. [22] If, then, I have found favour with you, send into me your holy spirit, and I shall put in writing the whole story of the world from the very beginning, everything that was contained in your law, so that all may have the possibility of finding the right path, and, if they so choose, of obtaining life in the last days.'

[23] 'Go,' he answered, 'call the people together, and tell them not to look for you for forty days. [24] Prepare a large number of writing tablets, and bring with you Seraiah and Dabri, Shelemiah, Ethan, and Asiel, five men all trained to write quickly. [25] On your return here, I shall light in your mind a lamp of understanding which will not go out until you have finished what you are to write. [26] When it is complete, some of it you must make public; the rest you must give to wise men to keep hidden. Tomorrow at this time you shall begin writing.'

[27] I went as I was ordered, called together all the people, and said: [28] 'Israel, listen to what I say. [29] At first our ancestors lived as aliens in Egypt; from there they were rescued [30] and given the law which imparts life. But they disobeyed it, and you have followed their example. [31] You were given a land of your own, the land of Zion; but, like your ancestors, you sinned and abandoned the ways laid down for you by the Most High. [32] Being a just judge, he took back in due time what he had given you. [33] Now you are here, and your fellow-countrymen are still farther away. [34] If, therefore, you direct your understanding and instruct your minds, you will be kept safe in life and meet with mercy after death. [35] For after death will come the judgement: we shall be restored

to life, and then the names of the just will be known and the deeds of the godless exposed. [36] But no one must come near me now or look for me during the next forty days.'

[37] As instructed I took the five men with me, and we went out to the field and stayed there. [38] On the next day I heard a voice calling to me: 'Ezra, open your mouth and drink what I give you.' [39] I opened my mouth, and was handed a cup full of what seemed like water, except that its colour was the colour of fire. [40] I took it and drank, and, as soon as I had done so, understanding welled up in my mind, and wisdom increased within me. My memory remained fully active, [41] and I began to speak and went on without stopping. [42] The Most High gave understanding to the five men, who took turns at writing down what was said, using characters which they had not known before. They continued at work throughout the forty days, writing all day, and taking food only at night. [43] But as for me, I spoke all through the day, and even at night I did not break off. [44] In the forty days, ninety-four books were written down. [45] At the end of the time the Most High said to me: 'Make public the twenty-four books you wrote first; they are to be read by everyone, whether worthy to do so or not. [46] But the last seventy books are to be kept back, and given to none but the wise among your people; [47] they contain a stream of understanding, a fountain of wisdom, a flood of knowledge.' [48] And this I did.

Prophecies and warnings

15 PROCLAIM to my people the words of prophecy which I give you to speak, says the Lord; [2] have them written down, for they are trustworthy and true. [3] Do not be afraid of plots against you, and do not be troubled by the unbelief of your opponents; [4] for everyone who does not believe will die because of his unbelief.

[5] Beware! says the Lord; I am letting loose over the earth terrible evils, sword and famine, death and destruction, [6] because evil men have spread their wickedness the whole world over, and it is filled to overflowing with their deeds of violence. [7] Therefore the Lord declares: [8] I

15:4 **because ... unbelief:** *or* in his unbelief.

shall no longer keep silent about their godless acts, nor shall I tolerate their wicked practices. See how the blood of innocent victims cries to me for vengeance, and the souls of the just never cease to plead with me! ⁹ I shall most surely avenge them, says the Lord, and give ear to the plea of all the innocent blood that has been shed. ¹⁰ My people are being led like sheep to the slaughter. I shall allow them to remain in Egypt no longer, ¹¹ but shall rescue them with a strong hand and an outstretched arm; I shall strike the Egyptians with plagues, as I did once before, and bring ruin on their whole land. ¹² Shaken to its very foundations, how Egypt will mourn when scourged and chastised by plagues from the Lord! ¹³ How workers on the land will mourn when seed fails to grow and their trees are devastated by blight and hail and terrible storm! ¹⁴ Woe to the world and its inhabitants: ¹⁵ the sword that will destroy them is not far distant! With blade unsheathed, nation will rise against nation. ¹⁶ Stable government will be at an end; as one faction prevails over another, they will in their day of power care nothing for king or magnate. ¹⁷ Anyone wishing to visit a city will find himself unable to do so, ¹⁸ for rival ambitions will have reduced cities to chaos, demolishing houses and inspiring widespread fear. ¹⁹ Sword in hand, a man will attack his neighbour's house and plunder his possessions; when he is driven by famine and grinding misery, no pity will restrain him.

²⁰ See how I summon all the kings of the earth, God says, from the sunrise and the south wind, from the east and the south, to turn and repay what has been given to them. ²¹ I shall do to them as they are doing to my chosen ones even to the present day; I shall pay them back in their own coin.

These are the words of the Lord God: ²² I shall show sinners no pity; the sword will not spare those murderers who stain the ground with innocent blood. ²³ The Lord's anger has burst out in flame, scorching the earth to its foundations and consuming sinners like burning straw. ²⁴ Woe to sinners who flout my commands! says the Lord; ²⁵ I shall show them no mercy. Away from me, you rebels! Do not pollute my sanctuary with your presence. ²⁶ The Lord well knows all

who offend against him, and has consigned them to death and destruction. ²⁷ Already calamities have spread over the world, and there is no escape for you; God will refuse to rescue you, because you have sinned against him.

²⁸ How terrible is the vision that comes from the east! ²⁹ Hordes of dragons from Arabia will sally forth with countless chariots, and from the first day of their advance their hissing is borne across the land, so that all who hear them will tremble in fear. ³⁰ The Carmanians, beside themselves with fury, will rush like wild boars out of a thicket, advancing in full force to do battle with them; they will devastate whole tracts of Assyria with their tusks. ³¹ But then the dragons will summon up their native fury and prove the stronger. Massing all their forces, they will fall on the Carmanians with overwhelming might ³² until, routed and their power silenced, the Carmanians turn to flight. ³³ Their way will be blocked by a lurking enemy from Assyria, and when one of them is killed, terror and trembling will spread in their army and confusion among their kings.

³⁴ See the clouds stretching from east and north to south! Full of fury and tempest, their appearance is hideous. ³⁵ They will clash together, letting loose a vast storm over the land; blood, shed by the sword, will reach as high as a horse's belly, ³⁶ a man's thigh, or a camel's hock. ³⁷ There will be terror and trembling throughout the world; those who see the fury rage will shudder, stricken with panic. ³⁸ Then vast storm-clouds will approach from south and north, and others from the west. ³⁹ But the winds from the east will be stronger still, and will hold in check the raging cloud and its leader; and the storm which was bent on destruction will be fiercely driven back to the south and west by the winds from the east. ⁴⁰ Huge clouds, mighty and full of fury, will pile up and ravage the whole land and its inhabitants, and a terrible storm will sweep over all that is high and exalted, ⁴¹ with fire and hail and flying swords and a deluge of water which will flood all the plains and rivers. ⁴² They will flatten to the ground cities and walls, mountains and hills, trees in the woods and crops in the fields. ⁴³ They will force their way to Babylon, and destroy her; ⁴⁴ for they will

encompass her when they get there, and let loose a storm in all its fury. The dust and smoke will reach the sky, and all the neighbouring cities will mourn over her. [45] Any who survive in her will be enslaved by her destroyers.

[46] And you, Asia, who have shared in the beauty and the glory of Babylon, [47] woe to you, miserable wretch! Like her you have dressed up your daughters as whores, to attract for your glorification the lovers who have always lusted for you. [48] You have imitated all the practices and schemes of that vile harlot. Therefore God says: [49] I shall unleash calamities on you—widowhood and poverty, famine, sword, and pestilence, to bring devastation to your homes with violence and death. [50] When the scorching heat bears down upon you, your strength and splendour will wither like a flower. [51] You will become a poor, weak woman, bruised, beaten, and wounded, unable any more to receive your wealthy lovers. [52] I should not be so fierce with you, says the Lord, [53] if you had not always killed my chosen ones, gloating over the blows you struck and hurling your drunken taunts at their corpses.

[54] Paint your face; beautify yourself! [55] The prostitute's hire shall be yours; you will get what you have earned. [56] What you do to my chosen people, God will do to you, says the Lord; he will consign you to a terrible fate. [57] Your children will perish from hunger, you will fall by the sword, your cities will be reduced to rubble, and all your people will fall on the field of battle. [58] Those who are on the mountains will be dying of hunger: their hunger and thirst will drive them to gnaw their own flesh and drink their own blood. [59] You will be foremost in misery; and there will be more still to come. [60] As the victors go past on their way home from the sack of Babylon, they will reduce your peaceful city to dust, destroy a great part of your territory, and bring much of your splendour to an end. [61] They will destroy you—you will be stubble to their fire. [62] They will completely devour you and your cities, your land and your mountains, and will burn down all your woodlands and your fruit trees. [63] They will carry off your sons as captives and plunder your possessions; not a trace will be left of your splendid beauty.

16 Woe to you, Babylon and Asia! Woe to you, Egypt and Syria! [2] Put on sackcloth and hair shirt and raise a cry of lamentation over your people, for destruction is close at hand. [3] The sword is let loose against you, and who will turn it aside? [4] Fire is let loose upon you, and who will extinguish it? [5] Calamities have been let loose against you, and who is to avert them? [6] Can anyone drive off a hungry lion in the forest, or put out a fire among stubble once it has begun to blaze? [7] Can anyone ward off an arrow shot by a strong archer? [8] When the Lord God sends calamities, who can avert them? [9] When his anger bursts into flame, who can extinguish it? [10] When the lightning flashes, who will not tremble? When it thunders, who will not quake with dread? [11] When the Lord threatens, is there anyone who will not be crushed to the ground at his approach? [12] The earth is shaken to its very foundations, and the sea is churned up from the depths; its waves and all the fish are in turmoil before the presence of the Lord and the majesty of his power. [13] Strong is his arm that bends the bow, and sharp the arrows he shoots; once they are on their way, nothing will stop them until they reach the ends of the earth. [14] Calamities are let loose, and will not turn back before they fetch up on earth. [15] The fire is alight and will not be put out until it has consumed earth's foundations. [16] An arrow shot by a powerful archer does not turn back; no more will the calamities let loose against the earth be recalled.

[17] Alas, alas for me! Who will rescue me in those days? [18] At the onset of troubles, many will groan; at the onset of famine, many will die; at the onset of wars, empires will tremble; at the onset of bad times, all will be filled with terror. What will men do in the face of calamity? [19] Famine, plague, suffering, and hardship are scourges sent to teach them better ways; [20] but even so, they will not abandon their crimes or always keep the scourging in mind. [21] A time will come when food is so cheap that people will imagine peace and prosperity have arrived; but at that very moment the earth will become a hotbed of disasters—sword, famine, and anarchy. [22] Most of the inhabitants will die in the famine, while those who survive will be destroyed by the

sword. [23] The dead will be thrown out like dung, and there will be no one to give them the last rites. The forsaken land will go to waste, and its cities to ruin; [24] no one will be left to cultivate the ground. [25] Trees will bear their fruits, but who will pick them? [26] Grapes will ripen, but who will tread them? There will be vast desolation everywhere. [27] A man will long to see a human face or hear a human voice, [28] for out of a whole city, only ten will survive, and in the countryside, only two will be left, hiding in the forest or in holes in the rocks. [29] As in an olive grove three or four olives might be left on each tree, [30] or as in a vineyard a few grapes might be overlooked by the sharp-eyed pickers, [31] so also in those days three or four will be overlooked by those who with sword in hand are searching the houses. [32] The forsaken land will go to waste and its fields be overrun with briars; thorns will grow over all the roads and paths, because there are no sheep to tread them. [33] Maidens will live in mourning with none to marry them; women will mourn because they have no husbands; their daughters will mourn because they have no one to support them. [34] The young men who should have been bridegrooms will have been killed in the war, and the men who were married will have been wiped out by the famine.

[35] BUT you servants of the Lord, listen and learn. [36] This is the word of the Lord; take it to heart, and do not doubt what he says: [37] Calamities are close at hand, and will not be delayed. [38] When a woman is in the ninth month of her pregnancy and the moment of her child's birth is drawing near, there are two or three hours in which her womb suffers pangs of agony, and then the child comes from the womb without any further delay; [39] similarly, calamities will not defer their coming on the earth, and the world will groan under the pangs that beset it.

[40] My people, listen to my words; get ready for battle, and when the calamities surround you, behave as though you were strangers on earth. [41] The seller must expect to have to run for his life, the buyer to lose what he buys; [42] the merchant must expect to make no profit, the builder never to live in the house he builds. [43] The sower must not expect to reap, nor should he who prunes the vine expect to harvest the grapes. [44] Those who marry must not look for children; the unmarried must think of themselves as widowed. [45] For all who labour, labour in vain. [46] Their fruits will be gathered by foreigners, who will plunder their goods, pull down their houses, and take their sons captive, because only for captivity and famine will they bear children. [47] Any who make money do so only to have it plundered. The more care they lavish on their cities, houses, and property, and on their own persons, [48] the fiercer will be my indignation against their sins, says the Lord. [49] Like the indignation of a virtuous woman towards a prostitute, [50] so will be the indignation of justice towards wickedness decked out in finery; she will accuse her to her face, when the champion arrives to expose every sin on earth. [51] Therefore, do not imitate wickedness or her deeds; [52] in a very short time she will be swept away from the earth, and the reign of justice over us will begin.

[53] Let not the sinner deny that he has sinned; he will only bring burning coals on his own head if he says, 'I have committed no sin against the majesty of God.' [54] Everything that men do is known to the Lord; he knows their plans, their schemes, their inmost thoughts. [55] He said, 'Let the earth be made,' and it was made; 'Let the heavens be made,' and they were made. [56] The stars were fixed in their places by his word, and he knows the number of the stars. [57] He looks into the depths with their treasures; he has measured the sea and everything it contains. [58] By his word he confined the sea within the bounds of the waters and suspended the land above the water. [59] He spread out the sky like a vault, and fixed it firmly over the waters. [60] He provided springs in the desert, and pools on the mountaintops as the source of rivers flowing down to water the earth. [61] He created man, and put a heart in the middle of his body; he gave him breath, life, understanding, [62] and the very spirit of Almighty God who created all things and searches out secrets in secret places. [63] He knows well your plans and your inmost thoughts. Woe to sinners who try to conceal their sins! [64] The Lord will scrutinize all their deeds; he will call you all to account. [65] You will be covered with

confusion, when your sins are brought into the open and your wicked deeds stand up to accuse you on that day. ⁶⁶ What can you do? How will you hide your sins in the presence of God and his angels? ⁶⁷ God is the judge; fear him! Abandon your sins, and have done with your wicked deeds for ever! Then God will set you free from all distress.

⁶⁸ Fierce flames are being kindled to consume you. A great horde will descend on you; they will seize some of you and compel you to eat food sacrificed to idols. ⁶⁹ Those who give in to them will be derided, taunted, and humiliated. ⁷⁰ In place after place and throughout the neighbouring cities there will be a violent attack on those who fear the Lord. ⁷¹ Their enemies will be like maniacs, plundering and destroying without mercy all who still fear the Lord, ⁷² destroying and plundering their possessions, and ejecting them from their homes. ⁷³ Then it will be seen that my chosen ones have stood the test like gold in the assayer's fire.

⁷⁴ Listen, you whom I have chosen, says the Lord: the days of harsh suffering are close at hand, but I shall rescue you from them. ⁷⁵ Have done with fears and doubts! God is your guide. ⁷⁶ As followers of my commandments and instructions, says the Lord God, you must not let your sins weigh you down or your wicked deeds gain the ascendancy. ⁷⁷ Woe to those who are entangled in their sins and overrun with their wicked deeds! They are like a field where the path is entwined with bushes and brambles and there is no way through; ⁷⁸ it is separated off in readiness for destruction by fire.

TOBIT

Tobit in exile

1 THIS is the story of Tobit son of Tobiel, son of Hananiel, son of Aduel, son of Gabael, son of Raphael, son of Raguel, of the family of Asiel, of the tribe of Naphtali. [2] In the time of King Shalmaneser of Assyria he was taken captive from Thisbe which is south of Kedesh-naphtali in Upper Galilee above Hazor, beyond the road to the west, north of Peor.

[3] I, TOBIT, have made truth and righteousness my lifelong guide. I did many acts of charity to my kinsmen, those of my nation who had gone with me into captivity at Nineveh in Assyria. [4] While I was quite young in my own country, Israel, the whole tribe of Naphtali my ancestor broke away from the dynasty of David and from Jerusalem, the city chosen out of all the tribes of Israel as the one place of sacrifice; it was there that God's dwelling-place, the temple, had been consecrated, built to last for all generations. [5] My kinsmen, the whole house of my ancestor Naphtali, sacrificed on the mountains of Galilee to the image of a bull-calf which King Jeroboam of Israel had set up in Dan. [6] At the festivals I, and I alone, made the frequent journey to Jerusalem prescribed as an eternal commandment for all Israel. I would hurry off to Jerusalem with the firstfruits of crops and herds, the tithes of the cattle, and the first shearings of the sheep; these I gave to the priests of Aaron's line for the altar, [7] while the tithe of wine, grain, olive oil, pomegranates, and other fruits I gave to the Levites ministering at Jerusalem. The second tithe for the six years I turned into money and brought it year by year to Jerusalem for distribution [8] among the orphans and widows and among the converts who had attached themselves to Israel. Every third year when I brought it and gave it to them, we held a feast in accordance with the command prescribed in the law of Moses and the instructions enjoined by Deborah the mother of Hananiel our grandfather; for on the death of my father I had been left an orphan.

[9] When I grew up, I took a wife from our kindred and had by her a son whom I called Tobias. [10] After the deportation to Assyria in which I was taken captive and came to Nineveh, everyone of my family and nation ate gentile food; [11] but I myself scrupulously avoided doing so. [12] And since I was wholeheartedly mindful of my God, [13] the Most High endowed me with a presence which won me the favour of Shalmaneser, and I became his buyer of supplies. [14] During his lifetime I used to travel to Media and buy for him there, and I deposited bags of money to the value of ten talents of silver with my kinsman Gabael son of Gabri in Media. [15] When Shalmaneser died and was succeeded by his son Sennacherib, the roads to Media passed out of Assyrian control and I could no longer make the journey.

[16] In the days of Shalmaneser, I had done many acts of charity to my fellow-countrymen: I would share my food with the hungry [17] and provide clothing for those who had none, and if I saw the dead body of anyone of my people thrown outside the wall of Nineveh, I gave it burial. [18] I buried all those who fell victim to Sennacherib after his headlong retreat from Judaea, when the King of heaven brought judgement on him for his blasphemies. In his rage Sennacherib killed many of the Israelites, but I stole their bodies away and buried them, and when search was made for them by Sennacherib they were not to be found. [19] One of the Ninevites disclosed to the king that it was I who had been giving burial to his victims and that I had gone into hiding. When I learnt that the king knew about me and was seeking my life, I was alarmed and made my escape. [20] All that I possessed was seized and confiscated for the royal treasury; I was left with nothing but Anna my wife and my son Tobias. [21] However, less than forty days afterwards the king was murdered by two of

---

1:2 **Shalmaneser**: *Gk* Enemessaros.

his sons, and when they sought refuge in the mountains of Ararat, his son Esarhaddon succeeded to the throne. He appointed Ahikar, my brother Anael's son, to oversee all the revenues of his kingdom, with control of the entire administration. ²² Then Ahikar interceded on my behalf and I came back to Nineveh; he had been chief cupbearer, keeper of the signet, comptroller, and treasurer when Sennacherib was king of Assyria, and Esarhaddon confirmed him in office. Ahikar was a relative of mine; he was my nephew.

Misfortune strikes Tobit and Sarah

2 During the reign of Esarhaddon, I returned to my house, and my wife Anna and my son Tobias were restored to me. At our festival of Pentecost, that is the feast of Weeks, a fine meal was prepared for me and I took my place. ² The table being laid and food in plenty put before me, I said to Tobias: 'My son, go out and, if you find among our people captive here in Nineveh some poor man who is wholeheartedly mindful of God, bring him back to share my meal. I shall wait for you, son, till you return.' ³ Tobias went to look for a poor man of our people, but came straight back and cried, 'Father!' 'Yes, my son?' I replied. 'Father,' he answered, 'one of our nation has been murdered! His body is lying in the market-place; he has just been strangled.' ⁴ I jumped up and left my meal untasted. I took the body from the square and put it in one of the outbuildings until sunset when I could bury it; ⁵ then I went indoors, duly bathed myself, and ate my food in sorrow. ⁶ I recalled the words of the prophet Amos in the passage about Bethel:

Your festivals shall be turned into
    mourning,
and all your songs into lamentation,

and I wept. ⁷ When the sun had gone down, I went and dug a grave and buried the body. ⁸ My neighbours jeered. 'Is he no longer afraid?' they said. 'He ran away last time, when they were hunting for him to put him to death for this very offence; and here he is again burying the dead!' ⁹ That night, after bathing myself, I went into my courtyard and lay down to sleep by the courtyard wall, leaving my face uncovered because of the heat. ¹⁰ I did not know that there were sparrows in the wall above me, and their droppings fell, still warm, right into my eyes and produced white patches. I went to the doctors to be cured, but the more they treated me with their ointments, the more my eyes became blinded by the white patches, until I lost my sight. I was blind for four years; my kinsmen all grieved for me, and for two years Ahikar looked after me, until he moved to Elymais.

¹¹ At that time Anna my wife used to earn money by women's work, spinning and weaving, ¹² and her employers would pay her when she took them what she had done. One day, the seventh of Dystrus, after she had cut off the piece she had woven and delivered it, they not only paid her wages in full, but also gave her a kid from their herd of goats to take home. ¹³ When my wife came into the house to me, the kid began to bleat, and I called out to her: 'Where does that kid come from? I hope it was not stolen? Return it to its owners; we have no right to eat anything stolen.' ¹⁴ But she assured me: 'It was given me as a present, over and above my wages.' I did not believe her and insisted that she return it, and I blushed with shame for what she had done. Her rejoinder was: 'So much for all your acts of charity and all your good works! Everyone can now see what you are really like.'

3 In deep distress I groaned and wept aloud, and as I groaned I prayed: ² 'O Lord, you are just and all your acts are just; in all your ways you are merciful and true; you are the Judge of the world. ³ Now bear me in mind, Lord, and look upon me. Do not punish me for the sins and errors which I and my fathers have committed. ⁴ We have sinned against you and disobeyed your commandments, and you have given us up to the despoiler, to captivity and death, until we have become a proverb and a byword; we are taunted by all the nations among whom you have scattered us. ⁵ I acknowledge the justice of your many judgements, the due penalty for our sins, for we have not carried out your commandments or lived in true obedience before you. ⁶ And now deal with me as you will. Command that

2:6 **songs:** *so one Vs.* (*cp. Amos* 8: 10)*; Gk ways.*

my life be taken away from me so that I may be removed from the face of the earth and turned to dust. I would be better dead than alive, for I have had to listen to taunts I have not deserved and my grief is great. Lord, command that I be released from this misery; let me go to the eternal resting-place. Do not turn your face from me, Lord; I had rather die than live in such misery, listening to such taunts.'

⁷ On the same day it happened that Sarah, the daughter of Raguel who lived at Ecbatana in Media, also had to listen to taunts, from one of her father's servant-girls. ⁸ Sarah had been given in marriage to seven husbands and, before the marriages could be duly consummated, each one of them had been killed by the evil demon Asmodaeus. The servant said to her: 'It is you who kill your husbands! You have already been given in marriage to seven, and you have not borne the name of any one of them. ⁹ Why punish us because they are dead? Go and join your husbands. I hope we never see son or daughter of yours!'

¹⁰ Deeply distressed at that, she went in tears to the roof-chamber of her father's house, meaning to hang herself. But she had second thoughts and said to herself: 'Perhaps they will taunt my father and say, "You had one dear daughter and she hanged herself because of her troubles," and so I shall bring my aged father in sorrow to his grave. No, I will not hang myself; it would be better to beg the Lord to let me die and not live on to hear such reproaches.' ¹¹ Thereupon she spread out her hands towards the window in prayer saying: 'Praise be to you, merciful God, praise to your name for evermore; let all your creation praise you for ever! ¹² And now I lift up my eyes and look to you. ¹³ Command that I be removed from the earth, never again to hear such taunts.

¹⁴ 'You know, Lord, that I am a virgin, guiltless of intercourse with any man; ¹⁵ I have not dishonoured my name or my father's name in the land of my exile. I am my father's only child; he has no other to be his heir, nor has he any near kinsman or relative who might marry me and for whom I should stay alive. Already seven husbands of mine have died; what have I to live for any longer? But if it is not your will, Lord, to let me die, have regard to me in your mercy and spare me those taunts.'

¹⁶ At that very moment the prayers of both were heard in the glorious presence of God, ¹⁷ and Raphael was sent to cure the two of them: Tobit by removing the white patches from his eyes so that he might see God's light again, and Sarah daughter of Raguel by giving her in marriage to Tobias son of Tobit and by setting her free from the evil demon Asmodaeus, for it was the destiny of Tobias and of no other suitor to possess her. At the moment when Tobit went back into his house from the courtyard, Sarah came down from her father's roof-chamber.

Tobias's journey

4 THAT same day Tobit remembered the money he had deposited with Gabael at Rages in Media, ² and he said to himself, 'I have asked for death; before I die I ought to send for my son Tobias and explain to him about this money.' ³ So he sent for Tobias and, when he came, said to him: 'When I die, give me decent burial. Honour your mother, and do not abandon her as long as she lives; do what will please her, and never grieve her heart in any way. ⁴ Remember, my son, all the hazards she faced for your sake while you were in her womb. When she dies, bury her beside me in the same grave.

⁵ 'Keep the Lord in mind every day of your life, my son, and never deliberately do what is wrong or violate his commandments. As long as you live do what is right, and avoid evil ways; ⁶ for an honest life leads to success in any undertaking, and to all who do right the Lord will give good counsel.

⁷ 'Distribute alms from what you possess and never with a grudging eye. Do not turn your face away from any poor man, and God will not turn away his face from you. ⁸ Let your almsgiving match your means. If you have little, do not be ashamed to give the little you can afford; ⁹ you will be laying up sound insurance against the day of adversity. ¹⁰ Almsgiving preserves the giver from death and keeps him from going down into darkness. ¹¹ All who give alms are making an offering acceptable to the Most High.

¹² 'Be on your guard, my son, against fornication; and above all choose your wife from the race of your ancestors. Do not take a foreign wife, one not of your

father's tribe, for we are descendants of the prophets. My son, remember that back to the earliest days our ancestors, Noah, Abraham, Isaac, Jacob, all chose wives from their kindred. They were blessed in their children, and their descendants will possess the land. [13] So you too, my son, must love your kindred; do not be too proud to take a wife from among the women of your own nation. Such pride breeds ruin and disorder, and the waster declines into poverty; waste is the mother of starvation.

[14] 'Pay any man who works for you his wages that same day; let no one wait for his money. If you serve God, you will be repaid. Be circumspect, my son, in all that you do, and in all your behaviour be true to your upbringing. [15] Do to no one what you yourself would hate. Do not drink to excess or let drunkenness become a habit. [16] Share your food with the hungry, your clothes with those who have none. Whatever you have beyond your own needs, distribute in alms, and do not give with a grudging look. [17] Pour out your wine and offer your bread on the tombs of the righteous; but give nothing to sinners. [18] Seek advice from every sensible person; do not despise any advice that may be of use. [19] Praise the Lord God at all times and ask him to guide your steps; then all you do and all you plan will be crowned with success. The heathen lack such guidance; it is the Lord himself who gives all good things and who humbles whomsoever he chooses to the lowly grave. Now remember those injunctions, my son; let them never be effaced from your mind.

[20] 'And now, my son, I should tell you that I have ten talents of silver on deposit with Gabael son of Gabri at Rages in Media. [21] Do not be anxious because we have become poor; there is great wealth awaiting you, if only you fear God and avoid all wickedness and do what is good in the sight of the Lord your God.'

5 Tobias said: 'I will do all that you have told me, father. [2] But how shall I be able to recover this money from Gabael, since he does not know me and I do not know him? What proof of identity shall I give him to make him trust me and give me the money? Besides, I do not know the roads which would get me to Media.' [3] To this Tobit replied: 'He gave me his note of hand, and I divided it in two and we took one part each. I kept one half of it and put half with the money. It is all of twenty years since I deposited that money! Now, my son, find someone reliable to go with you, and we shall pay him his wages up to the time of your return; then go and recover the money from Gabael.'

[4] Tobias went out to look for someone who knew the way and would accompany him to Media, and found himself face to face with the angel Raphael. [5] Not knowing he was an angel of God, he questioned him: 'Where do you come from, young man?' 'I am an Israelite,' he replied, 'one of your fellow-countrymen, and I have come here to find work.' Tobias asked, 'Do you know the road to Media?' [6] 'Yes,' he said, 'I have been there many times; I am familiar with all the routes, I know them well. I have frequently travelled into Media and used to stay with Gabael our fellow-countryman who lives there in Rages. It is two full days' journey to Rages from Ecbatana; for Rages is situated in the hills, and Ecbatana lies in the middle of the plain.' [7] Tobias said: 'Wait for me, young man, while I go in and tell my father. I need you to go with me and I shall pay you for it.' [8] 'Very well, I shall wait,' he answered, 'only do not be long.'

Tobias went in and told his father. 'I have found a fellow-Israelite to accompany me,' he said. His father replied, 'Call him in; I must find out the man's family and tribe and make sure, my son, that he will be a trustworthy companion for you.'

[9] Tobias went out and called him: 'Young man, my father is asking for you.' When he entered, Tobit greeted him first. To Raphael's reply, 'May all be well with you!' Tobit retorted: 'How can anything be well with me any more? I am now blind; I cannot see the light of heaven, but lie in darkness like the dead who can no longer see the light. Though still alive, I am as good as dead. I hear voices, but I cannot see those speaking.' Raphael answered: 'Take heart; in God's design your cure is at hand. Take heart!' Tobit went on: 'My son Tobias wishes to travel to Media. Can you go with him as his guide?

5:6 in **Rages**: *so one Vs. (cp. 4: 1); Gk in Ecbatana.*

45

I shall pay you, my friend.' 'Yes,' he said, 'I can go with him. I know all the roads, for I have often been to Media. I have travelled over all the plains and mountains there and am familiar with the whole way.' [10] Tobit said to him, 'Tell me, my friend, what family and tribe do you belong to?' [11] He asked, 'Why do you need to know my tribe?' Tobit said, 'I wish to know whose son you are, my friend, and what your name is.' [12] 'I am Azarias,' he replied, 'son of the older Ananias, one of your kinsmen.'

[13] Tobit said to him: 'Welcome, may all be well with you! Do not be angry with me, my friend, for wanting to know all about you and your parentage. You are, as it turns out, a kinsman and a man of good and honourable family. I knew Ananias and Nathan, the two sons of the older Semelias. They used to go with me to Jerusalem and worship with me there; they were never led into error. Your kinsmen are worthy men; you come of a sound stock. You are indeed welcome.' [14] And he added: 'I shall pay you a drachma a day and allow you the same expenses as my son. [15] Accompany him, and I shall give you something over and above your wage.' [16] Raphael agreed: 'I shall go with him. Never fear; we shall travel there and back without mishap, for the road is not dangerous.' Tobit said to him, 'God bless you, my friend!' He called his son and said: 'My son, get ready what you need for the journey and go with your kinsman. May God in heaven preserve you both on your journey there, and restore you to me safe and sound. May his angel safely escort you both, my son.' Before setting out Tobias kissed his father and mother, and Tobit wished him a safe journey.

[17] Then his mother burst into tears. 'Why must you send my boy away?' she said to Tobit. 'Is he not the staff on which we lean? Do we not depend on him at every turn? [18] Why the haste to lay out money for money? For the sake of our boy write it off! [19] Let us be content to live the life appointed for us by the Lord.' [20] 'Do not worry,' replied Tobit, 'our son will go safely and come back safely, and you will see him with your own eyes on the day of his return. Do not worry or be anxious about them, my dear. [21] A good angel will go with him; his journey will prosper and he will come back without mishap.' [22] At that she stopped weeping.

6 THE youth and the angel left the house together; the dog followed Tobias out and accompanied them. They travelled until night overtook them, and then camped by the river Tigris. [2] Tobias went down to bathe his feet in the river, and a huge fish leapt out of the water and tried to swallow his foot. He cried out, [3] and the angel said to him, 'Seize the fish and hold it fast.' So Tobias caught hold of it and dragged it up on the bank. [4] The angel said: 'Split open the fish and take out its gall, heart, and liver; keep them by you, but throw the guts away; the gall, heart, and liver can be used as remedies.' [5] Tobias split the fish open, and put its gall, heart, and liver on one side. He broiled and ate part of the fish; the rest he salted and kept.

They continued the journey together, and when they came near to Media [6] the youth asked the angel: 'Azarias, my friend, what remedy is there in the fish's heart and liver and in its gall?' [7] He replied: 'You can use the heart and liver as a fumigation for any man or woman attacked by a demon or evil spirit; the attack will cease, and it will give no further trouble. [8] The gall is for anointing a person's eyes when white patches have spread over them; after one has blown on the patches, the eyes will recover.'

[9] When he had entered Media and was already approaching Ecbatana, [10] Raphael said to the youth, 'Tobias, my friend.' 'Yes?' he replied. Raphael said: 'We must stay tonight with Raguel, who is a relative of yours. He has a daughter named Sarah, but no other children, neither sons nor daughters. [11] You as her next of kin have the right to marry her and inherit her father's property. [12] The girl is sensible, brave, and very beautiful indeed, and her father is an honourable man.' He went on: 'It is your right to marry her. Be guided by me, my friend; I shall speak to her father this very night and ask him to promise us the girl as your bride, and on our return from Rages we shall celebrate her marriage. I know that Raguel cannot withhold her from you or betroth her to another without incurring the death penalty according to the decree in the book of Moses; and he is aware that

his daughter belongs by right to you rather than to any other man. Now be guided by me, my friend; we shall talk about the girl tonight and betroth her to you, and when we return from Rages we shall take her back with us to your home.'

¹³ At this Tobias protested: 'Azarias, my friend, I have heard she has already been given to seven husbands who died in the bridal chamber; the very night they went into the bridal chamber to her they died. ¹⁴ A demon kills them, I have been told. And now it is my turn to be afraid; he does her no harm, because he loves her, but he kills any man who tries to come near her. I am my father's only child, and I fear that, were I to die, grief for me would bring my father and mother to their grave; and they have no other son to bury them.'

¹⁵ Raphael said: 'But have you forgotten your father's instructions? He told you to take a wife from your father's kindred. Now be guided by me, my friend: marry Sarah, and do not worry about the demon. I am sure that this night she will be given to you as your wife. ¹⁶ When you enter the bridal chamber, take some of the fish's liver and its heart, and put them on the burning incense. The smell will spread, ¹⁷ and when it reaches the demon he will make off, never to be seen near her any more. When you are about to go to bed with her, both of you must first stand up and pray, beseeching the Lord of heaven to grant you mercy and protection. Have no fear; she was destined for you before the world was made. You will rescue her and she will go with you. I have no doubt you will have children by her and they will be very dear to you. Now do not worry!' When Tobias heard what Raphael said, and learnt that Sarah was his kinswoman and of his father's house, he was filled with love for her and set his heart on her.

Tobias weds Sarah

7 As THEY entered Ecbatana Tobias said, 'Azarias, my friend, take me straight to our kinsman Raguel.' So he took him to Raguel's house, where they found him sitting by the courtyard gate. They greeted him first, and he replied, 'Greetings to you, my friends. You are

indeed welcome.' When he brought them into his house, ² he said to Edna his wife, 'Is not this young man like my kinsman Tobit? ³ Edna questioned them, 'Friends, where do you come from?' 'We belong to the tribe of Naphtali, now in captivity at Nineveh,' they answered. ⁴ 'Do you know our kinsman Tobit?' she asked, and they replied, 'Yes, we do.' 'Is he well?' she said. ⁵ 'He is alive and well,' they answered, and Tobias added, 'He is my father.' ⁶ Raguel jumped up and, with tears in his eyes, he kissed him. ⁷ 'God bless you, my boy,' he said, 'son of a good and upright father. But what a calamity that so just and charitable a man has lost his sight!' He embraced Tobias his kinsman and wept; ⁸ Edna his wife and their daughter Sarah also wept for Tobit.

Raguel slaughtered a ram from the flock and entertained them royally. They bathed and then, after washing their hands, took their places for the meal. Tobias said to Raphael, 'Azarias, my friend, ask Raguel to give me Sarah my kinswoman.' ⁹ Raguel overheard this and said to the young man: 'Eat and drink tonight, and enjoy yourself. ¹⁰ There is no one but yourself who should have my daughter Sarah; indeed I ought not to give her to anyone else, since you are my nearest kinsman. However, I must reveal the truth to you, my son: ¹¹ I have given her in marriage to seven of our kinsmen, and they all died on their wedding night. My son, eat and drink now, and may the Lord deal kindly with you both.' Tobias answered, 'I shall not eat again or drink until you have disposed of this business of mine.' ¹² Raguel said to him, 'I shall do so: I give her to you in accordance with the decree in the book of Moses, and Heaven itself has decreed that she shall be yours. Take your kinswoman; from now on you belong to her and she to you, from today she is yours for ever. May all go well with you both this night, my son; may the Lord of heaven grant you mercy and peace.'

¹³ Raguel called for Sarah and, when she came, he took her by the hand and gave her to Tobias with these words: 'Receive my daughter as your wedded wife in accordance with the law, the decree written in the book of Moses; keep her and take her safely home to your

6:17 **be very dear to you:** *lit.* be like brothers to you.

47

father. And may the God of heaven grant you prosperity and peace.' ¹⁴ Then he sent for her mother and told her to fetch a roll of papyrus, and he wrote out and put his seal on a marriage contract giving Sarah to Tobias as his wife according to this decree. ¹⁵ After that they began to eat and drink.

¹⁶ Raguel called his wife and said, 'My dear, get the other bedroom ready and take her in there.' ¹⁷ Edna went and prepared the room as he had told her, and brought Sarah into it. She wept over her, and then drying her tears said: ¹⁸ 'Take heart, dear daughter; the Lord of heaven give you gladness instead of sorrow. Take heart, daughter!' Then she went out.

8 When they had finished eating and drinking and were ready for bed, the young man was escorted to the bedroom. ² Tobias recalled what Raphael told him; he removed the fish's liver and heart from the bag in which he had them, and put them on the burning incense. ³ The smell from the fish kept the demon away, and he made off into Upper Egypt. Raphael followed him there and promptly bound him hand and foot.

⁴ After they were left alone and the door was shut, Tobias got up from the bed, saying to Sarah, 'Rise, my love; let us pray and beseech our Lord to show us mercy and keep us in safety.' ⁵ She got up, and they began to pray that they might be kept safe. Tobias said: 'We praise you, God of our fathers, we praise your name for ever and ever. Let the heavens and all your creation praise you for ever. ⁶ You made Adam and also Eve his wife, who was to be his partner and support; and those two were the parents of the human race. This was your word: "It is not good for the man to be alone; let us provide a partner suited to him." ⁷ So now I take this my beloved to wife, not out of lust but in true marriage. Grant that she and I may find mercy and grow old together.' ⁸ They both said 'Amen, Amen,' ⁹ and they slept through the night.

Raguel rose and summoned his servants, and they went out and dug a grave, ¹⁰ for he thought, 'Tobias may be dead, and then we shall have to face scorn and taunts.' ¹¹ When they had finished digging the grave, Raguel went into the house and called his wife: ¹² 'Send one of the servant-girls', he said, 'to go in and see whether he is alive; for if he is dead, let us bury him so that no one may know.' ¹³ They lit a lamp, opened the door, and sent a servant in; and she found them sound asleep together. ¹⁴ She came out and told them, 'He is alive and has come to no harm.'

¹⁵ Then Raguel praised the God of heaven: 'All praise to you, O God, all perfect praise! Let men praise you throughout the ages. ¹⁶ Praise to you for the joy you have given me: the thing I feared has not happened, but you have shown us your great mercy. ¹⁷ Praise to you for the mercy you have shown to these two, these only children. Lord, show them mercy, keep them safe, and grant them a long life of happiness and affection.' ¹⁸ And he ordered his servants to fill in the grave before dawn came.

¹⁹ Telling his wife to bake a great batch of bread, he went to the herd and brought two oxen and four rams and ordered his servants to get them ready; so they set about the preparations. ²⁰ Then calling Tobias he said: 'You shall not stir from here for two weeks. Stay; eat and drink with us, and cheer my daughter's heart after all her suffering. ²¹ Here and now take half of all I possess, and may you have a safe journey back to your father; the other half will come to you both when I and my wife die. Be reassured, my son, I am your father and Edna is your mother; now and always we are as close to you as we are to your wife. You have nothing to fear, my son.'

9 Tobias sent for Raphael and said: ² 'Azarias, my friend, take four servants and two camels with you, and go to Rages. Make your way to Gabael's house, give him the note of hand and collect the money; then bring him with you to the wedding feast. ³⁻⁴ My father, as you know, will be counting the days, and if I am even one day late it will distress him. Yet you see what Raguel has sworn, and I cannot go against his oath.' ⁵ So Raphael went with the four servants and two camels to Rages in Media and stayed the night with Gabael. He delivered the note of hand and informed him that Tobit's son Tobias had taken a wife and was inviting him to the wedding feast. At once Gabael counted out to him the bags with their seals intact, and they put them together. ⁶ They all made an early start and came to the wedding. Entering Raguel's house they found Tobias at the feast, and he jumped up and greeted Gabael. With tears in his eyes Gabael blessed him and said: 'Good and worthy son of a worthy father, that just and charitable man, may the Lord give Heaven's blessing to you, your wife, and your parents-in-law. Praise be to God, for I have seen my cousin Tobias, the very likeness of his father.'

Tobias's homecoming

10 DAY by day Tobit was keeping count of the time Tobias would take for his journey there and for his journey back. When the time was up and his son had not made his appearance, [2] Tobit said: 'Perhaps he has been detained there? Or perhaps Gabael is dead and there is no one to give him the money?' [3] And he grew anxious. [4] Anna his wife said: 'My child has perished. He is no longer in the land of the living.' She began to weep, lamenting for her son: [5] 'O my child, the light of my eyes, why did I let you go?' [6] Tobit said to her: 'Hush! Do not worry, my dear; he is all right. Something has happened there to distract them. The man who went with him is one of our kinsmen and can be trusted. My dear, do not grieve for him; he will soon be back.' [7] 'Hush yourself!' she retorted. 'Do not try to deceive me. My child has perished.' Each day she would rush out to keep watch on the road her son had taken, and would listen to no one; and when she came indoors at sunset she was unable to sleep, but lamented and wept the whole night long.

After the two weeks of wedding celebrations which Raguel had sworn to hold for his daughter came to an end, Tobias approached him. 'Let me be on my way,' he said, 'for I am sure that my parents are thinking they will never see me again. I beg you, father, let me go home now to my father Tobit. I have already told you how I left him.' [8] Raguel replied: 'Stay, my son, stay with me, and I shall send messengers to your father to explain matters to him.' [9] But Tobias insisted: 'No, please let me go home to my father.' [10] Then without more ado Raguel handed over to Tobias Sarah his bride along with half of all that he possessed, male and female slaves, cattle and sheep, donkeys and camels, clothes, money, and house-

hold goods. [11] He bade them farewell. Embracing Tobias he said: 'Goodbye, my son, goodbye; a safe journey to you! May the Lord of heaven prosper you and Sarah your wife; and may I live to see your children.' [12] To his daughter Sarah he said: 'Honour your husband's father and mother; they are now your parents as much as if you were their own child. Go in peace, my daughter; as long as I live I hope to hear nothing but good news of you.' After bidding them both goodbye, he sent them on their way. Edna said to Tobias: 'My very dear cousin, may the Lord bring you safely home, you and my daughter Sarah, and may I live long enough to see your children. In the sight of the Lord I entrust my daughter to your keeping; do nothing to cause her distress throughout your life. Go in peace, my son. From now on I am your mother and Sarah is your beloved wife. May we all be blessed with prosperity to the end of our days!' She kissed them both goodbye and let them go.

11 Tobias parted from Raguel in good health and spirits, praising the Lord of heaven and earth, the King of all, for the success of his journey. He gave his blessing to Raguel and Edna his wife, saying, 'It is the Lord's command that I should honour you all your days.'

[2] When they reached Caserin close to Nineveh, Raphael said: 'You know how your father was when we left him. [3] Let us hurry on ahead of your wife and see that the house is ready before the others arrive'; [4] and as the two of them went on together he added, 'Bring the fish-gall in your hand.' The dog went with the angel and Tobias, following at their heels.

[5] Anna sat watching the road by which her son would return. [6] She caught sight of him coming and exclaimed to his father, 'Here he comes—your son and the man who went with him!' [7] Before Tobias reached his father's house Raphael said: 'I know for certain that his eyes will be opened. [8] Spread the fish-gall on them; this remedy will make the white patches shrink and peel off. Your father will get his sight back and see the light of day.' [9] Anna ran forward, flung her arms round her son, and said to him: 'Now that I have seen you again, my child, I am ready to die.' And she wept.

[10] As Tobit rose to his feet and came

stumbling out through the courtyard gate, [11] Tobias went up to him with the fish-gall in his hand. He blew into his father's eyes and then, taking him by the arm and saying, 'Do not be alarmed, father,' [12] he applied the remedy carefully [13] and with both hands peeled off the patches from the corners of Tobit's eyes. Tobit threw his arms round him [14] and burst into tears. 'I can see you, my son, the light of my eyes!' he cried. 'Praise be to God, and praise to his great name and to all his holy angels. May his great name rest on us. Praised be all the angels for ever and ever. [15] He laid his scourge on me, and now, look, I see my son Tobias!'

Tobias went inside, rejoicing and praising God with all his might. He told his father about the success of his journey and the recovery of the money, and how he had married Raguel's daughter Sarah. 'She is on her way,' he said, 'quite close to the city gate.' [16] Tobit went out joyfully to meet his daughter-in-law at the gate, praising God as he went. At the sight of him passing through the city in full vigour and walking without anyone to guide his steps, the people of Nineveh were amazed; [17] and Tobit gave thanks to God before them all for his mercy in opening his eyes.

When he met Sarah, the wife of his son Tobias, he blessed her and said to her: 'Come in, daughter, welcome! Praise to God who has brought you to us. Blessings on your father and mother, and on my son Tobias, and blessings on you, my daughter. Come into your home, and may health, blessings, and joy be yours; come in, my daughter.' For all the Jews in Nineveh it was a day of joy, [18] and Ahikar and Nadab, Tobit's cousins, came to share his happiness. The joyful celebrations went on for a week, and many were the presents given to them.

12 After the wedding celebrations were over, Tobit sent for Tobias. 'My son,' he said, 'when you pay the man who went with you, see that you give him something extra, over and above his wages.' [2] Tobias asked: 'How much shall I pay him, father? It would not hurt to give him half the money he and I brought back. [3] He has kept me safe, cured my wife, helped me bring the money, and

healed you. How much extra shall I pay him?' [4] Tobit replied, 'It would be right, my son, for him to be given half of all that he has brought with him.' [5] So Tobias called him and said, 'Half of all that you have brought with you is to be yours for your wages; take it, and may you fare well.'

[6] Then Raphael called them both aside and said to them: 'Praise God, and in the presence of all living creatures thank him for the good he has done you, so that they may sing hymns of praise to his name. Proclaim to all the world what God has done; pay him honour and give him willing thanks. [7] A king's secret ought to be kept, but the works of God should be publicly acknowledged. Acknowledge them, therefore, and pay him honour. Do good, and no evil will befall you. [8] Better prayer with sincerity, and almsgiving with righteousness, than wealth with wickedness. Better give alms than hoard up gold. [9] Almsgiving preserves from death and wipes out every sin. Givers of alms will enjoy long life; [10] but sinners and wrongdoers are their own enemies.

[11] 'I will tell you the whole truth, hiding nothing from you. I have already made it clear to you that while a king's secret ought to be kept, the works of God should be glorified in public. [12] Now Tobit, when you and Sarah prayed, it was I who brought your prayers to be remembered in the glorious presence of the Lord. [13] So too when you buried the dead: that day when without hesitation you got up from your meal to go and bury the dead man, I was sent to test you. [14] At the same time God sent me to cure both you and Sarah your daughter-in-law. [15] I am Raphael, one of the seven angels who stand in attendance on the Lord and enter his glorious presence.'

[16] Both of them were deeply shaken and prostrated themselves in fear. [17] But he said to them: 'Do not be afraid, peace be with you; praise God for ever. [18] It is no thanks to me that I have been with you; it was the will of God. To him all your life long sing hymns of praise. [19] Take note that I ate no food; what you saw was an apparition. [20] And now praise the Lord, give thanks to God here on earth; I am about to ascend to him who sent me.

12:8 sincerity: *or, in some texts,* fasting.

Write down everything that has happened to you.' ²¹ He then ascended and, when they rose to their feet, was no longer to be seen. ²² They sang hymns of praise to God, giving him thanks for the great deeds he had done when an angel of God appeared to them.

Tobit's thanksgiving and last words

13 In the fullness of his joy Tobit wrote this prayer:

Praise to the ever-living God and to his kingdom.
² He both punishes and shows mercy;
he brings men down to the grave below,
and he brings them up from the great destruction;
nothing can escape his power.

³ Israelites, give him thanks in the sight of the nations,
for, having scattered you among them,
⁴ he has shown you his greatness there.
In the sight of every living creature exalt him,
for he is our Lord and our God,
our Father and God for ever.

⁵ Though for your wickedness he will punish you,
yet he will show mercy to you all,
wherever you may be dispersed among the nations.
⁶ When you turn to him with all your heart and soul
and act in loyal obedience to him,
then he will turn to you;
he will hide his face from you no longer.
Consider now what he has done for you,
and with full voice give him thanks;
praise the righteous Lord
and exalt the eternal King.

In the land of my exile I give thanks to him
and declare his might and greatness to a sinful nation.
Sinners, turn and do what is right in his eyes;
who knows, he may yet welcome you and show mercy.
⁷ I shall exalt my God

and rejoice in the King of heaven.
⁸ Let all men tell of his majesty
and in Jerusalem give him thanks.

⁹ O Jerusalem, Holy City,
he will punish you for what your sons have done,
but he will have mercy once more on the righteous.
¹⁰ Give thanks to the Lord for his goodness
and praise to the eternal King.
Your sanctuary will be rebuilt for you with rejoicing.
May he give happiness to all your exiles
and cherish for all generations those in distress.

¹¹ Your radiance will shine to the ends of the earth.
Many nations will come to you from afar,
to your holy name from every corner of the earth,
bearing gifts in their hands for the King of heaven.
In you endless generations will utter their joy;
the name of the chosen city will endure for ever and ever.
¹² Accursed will be all who speak harshly to you,
all who wreak destruction, pulling down your walls,
overthrowing your towers, and burning your houses;
but for ever blessed will be those who rebuild you.
¹³ Come then, be joyful for the righteous,
for they will all be gathered together and will praise the eternal Lord.
¹⁴ How happy will they be who love you
and happy those who rejoice in your prosperity,
happy those who grieve for you in all your afflictions!
They will rejoice over you
and behold all your joy for ever.

¹⁵ My soul, praise the Lord, the great King,
¹⁶ for Jerusalem will be built again
to be his dwelling-place for all time.
How happy I shall be when the remnant of my descendants

see your splendour and give thanks
   to the King of heaven!
The gates of Jerusalem will be built of
   sapphire and emerald,
and all the walls of costly stones.
The towers of Jerusalem will be built
   of gold,
   their battlements of the finest gold.
[17] The streets of Jerusalem will be
   paved
   with garnets and jewels of Ophir.
[18] Jerusalem's gates will sing hymns of
   joy
and all the houses in her will say,
   'Alleluia! Praise to the God of
   Israel!'
In you, O Jerusalem, his holy name
   will be praised for ever and ever.

14 So ended Tobit's thanksgiving. He died peacefully at the age of a hundred and twelve, and was buried in Nineveh with all honour. [2] He was sixty-two years old when his eyes were damaged, and after he recovered his sight he lived in prosperity, doing acts of charity and never ceasing to praise God and to proclaim his majesty.

[3] When he was dying, he sent for his son Tobias and gave him these instructions: 'My son, you must take your children [4] and be off to Media with all haste, for I believe God's word spoken against Nineveh by Nahum. It will all come true; everything will happen to Asshur and Nineveh that was spoken by the prophets of Israel who were sent by God. Not a word of it will fall short; all will take place in due time. It will be safer in Media than in Assyria or Babylon. I know, I am convinced, that all God's words will be fulfilled. It will be so: not one of them will fail. Our countrymen who live in Israel will all be scattered and carried off into captivity out of that good land. The whole of Israel's territory with Samaria and Jerusalem will lie waste; and for a time the house of God will be in mourning, burnt to the ground.

[5] 'But God will have mercy on them again and bring them back to the land of Israel. They will rebuild the house of God, yet not as it was at first, not until the time of fulfilment comes. Then they will all return from their captivity and rebuild Jerusalem in splendour; then indeed God's house will be built in her as the prophets of Israel foretold. [6] All the nations in the whole world will be converted to the true worship of God; they will renounce the idols which led them astray into error, [7] and will praise the eternal God in righteousness. All the Israelites who survive at that time and are firm in their loyalty to God will be brought together; they will come to Jerusalem to take possession of the land of Abraham and will live there securely for ever. Those who love God in sincerity will rejoice; sinners and wrongdoers will disappear from the earth.

[8] 'My children, I give you this command: serve God in truth and do what is pleasing to him. [9] Teach your children to do what is right and give alms, to be mindful of God and praise his name sincerely at all times and with all their strength.

[10] 'Now, my son, you must leave Nineveh; do not stay here. Once you have laid your mother in the grave beside me, do not spend another night within the city boundaries, for I observe that the place is full of wickedness and shameless dishonesty. My son, think what Nadab did to Ahikar who brought him up: he forced him to hide in a living grave. Ahikar survived to see God requite the disgrace brought on him; he came out into the light of day, but Nadab passed into everlasting darkness for his attempt to kill Ahikar. Because he gave alms, Ahikar escaped from the deadly trap Nadab set for him, and it was Nadab who fell into the trap and was destroyed. [11] See what comes of almsgiving, my children; and see what comes of wickedness—death. But now my strength is failing.' They laid him on his bed and he died, and he was given honourable burial.

[12] When his mother died, Tobias buried her beside his father; then he and his wife and children went to Media, where they settled at Ecbatana with his father-in-law Raguel. [13] He honoured and cared for his wife's parents in their old age. He buried them at Ecbatana in Media, and he inherited the estate of Raguel as well as that of his father Tobit. [14] At the age of a hundred and seventeen he died, greatly

14:10 **he gave alms:** *prob. rdg; Gk* I gave alms.

respected. [15] Tobias lived long enough to hear of the destruction of Nineveh by King Ahasuerus of Media and to see the prisoners of war brought from there into Media. He praised God for all that he had done to the inhabitants of Nineveh and Asshur; before he died he rejoiced over the fate of Nineveh, and he praised the Lord God who lives for ever and ever. Amen.

JUDITH

The Assyrian campaign

1 In the twelfth year of the reign of Nebuchadnezzar, who ruled the Assyrians from his great city of Nineveh, Arphaxad was ruling the Medes from Ecbatana. [2] Arphaxad encircled Ecbatana with a wall built of hewn stones, each four and a half feet thick and nine feet long. He made the wall a hundred and five feet high and seventy-five feet thick, [3] and at the city gates he set up towers a hundred and fifty feet high with foundations ninety feet thick; [4] the gates themselves he made a hundred and five feet high, and he made them sixty feet wide to allow his army to march out in full force with the infantry in formation. [5] It was in those days, then, that King Nebuchadnezzar waged war against King Arphaxad in the great plain on the borders of Ragau. [6] All the inhabitants of the hill-country, all who lived along the Euphrates, the Tigris, and the Hydaspes, and, on the plain, King Arioch of Elam, these rallied to Nebuchadnezzar; and many tribes of the Chelodites joined forces with them.

[7] King Nebuchadnezzar of Assyria sent a summons to all the inhabitants of Persia, and to all who lived in the west: the inhabitants of Cilicia and Damascus, Lebanon and Antilebanon, all who lived along the coast, [8] the peoples in Carmel and Gilead, Upper Galilee, and the great plain of Esdraelon, [9] all who were in Samaria and its towns, and those to the west of the Jordan as far as Jerusalem, Betane, Chelus, Kadesh, and the wadi of Egypt, those who lived in Tahpanhes, Rameses, and the whole land of Goshen [10] as far as Tanis and Memphis, and all the inhabitants of Egypt as far as the borders of Ethiopia. [11] But the king's summons was flouted by the entire region, and they did not join him for the campaign. They were not afraid of him; they regarded him as a mere man and, treating his envoys with contempt, they sent them back empty-handed.

[12] This roused Nebuchadnezzar to fury against the whole region; he swore by his throne and kingdom to exact vengeance from all the territories of Cilicia, Damascus, and Syria, and to put their inhabitants to the sword, along with the Moabites, the Ammonites, the people throughout Judaea, and everyone in Egypt, the whole region within the limits of the two seas. [13] In the seventeenth year of his reign he marshalled his forces against King Arphaxad and defeated him in battle, with the complete rout of his army, all his cavalry and chariots. [14] He occupied his towns, and advancing on Ecbatana he captured its towers, looted the bazaars, and reduced its splendour to abject ruin. [15] He caught Arphaxad in the mountains of Ragau and ran him through with his spear, and so made an end of him. [16] Then he and his combined forces, an immense host of warriors, went back with the spoil to Nineveh, where for four months he relaxed and feasted with his army.

2 In the eighteenth year, on the twenty-second day of the first month, there was a conference in King Nebuchadnezzar's palace about implementing his threat of vengeance on the whole region. [2] Calling together all his officers and nobles, the king laid before them his secret plan for the region and declared his determination to put an end to the disaffection. [3] It was resolved by them that everyone who had not obeyed the king's summons should die.

[4] When his plans were completed, King Nebuchadnezzar of Assyria summoned his commander-in-chief Holophernes,

---

1:15 **made an end of him:** *prob. rdg; Gk adds* up to that day.

who was second only to himself, and said, ⁵ 'This is the decree of the Great King, lord of all the earth: Directly you leave my presence, you are to take under your command an army of seasoned troops, a hundred and twenty thousand infantry with a force of twelve thousand cavalry, ⁶ and march against all the peoples of the west who have dared to disobey the order I issued. ⁷ Bid them have earth and water ready in token of submission, for I am coming to vent my wrath on them. Every corner of their land will be overrun by my army, and I shall give them up to be plundered by my troops; ⁸ their wounded will fill the ravines and wadis, and every river will be choked with their dead; ⁹ and I shall send them into captivity to the ends of the earth. ¹⁰ Go, and occupy all their territory for me. If they submit, hold them for me until the time comes to punish them. ¹¹ But to those who resist show no mercy; throughout the whole region give them up to be slaughtered and plundered. ¹² By my life and royal power I have spoken and shall act accordingly. ¹³ You are to obey these orders to the letter; see that you discharge them exactly as I your sovereign have commanded you, and do so without delay!'

¹⁴ Withdrawing from the royal presence, Holophernes summoned all the marshals, generals, and officers of the Assyrian army. ¹⁵ He mustered, as the king had commanded, a hundred and twenty thousand infantry and twelve thousand mounted archers, all picked men, ¹⁶ and marshalled them in the regular battle order of a great army. ¹⁷ He took an immense number of camels, donkeys, and mules for the baggage, innumerable sheep, oxen, and goats for provisions, ¹⁸ ample rations for every man, as well as a great quantity of gold and silver from the royal palace. ¹⁹ With his whole army he set off in advance of King Nebuchadnezzar to overrun the entire region to the west with his chariots, cavalry, and picked infantry. ²⁰ Accompanying them went a motley host like a swarm of locusts, countless as the dust of the earth.

²¹ From Nineveh they marched for three days towards the plain of Bectileth, and encamped over against Bectileth near the mountain to the north of Upper Cilicia. ²² From there Holophernes pushed on into the hill-country with his whole army—infantry, cavalry, and chariots. ²³ He devastated Put and Lud, and plundered all the people of Rassis, and the Ishmaelites on the edge of the desert south of the land of the Cheleans. ²⁴ Then following the Euphrates he traversed Mesopotamia and destroyed every fortified town along the wadi Abron as far as the sea. ²⁵ He occupied the territory of Cilicia, cutting down any who resisted. He marched south to the borders of Japheth which fronts Arabia. ²⁶ He encircled the Midianites, set their encampments on fire, and plundered their sheepfolds. ²⁷ He went down into the plain of Damascus at the time of the wheat harvest, and set fire to the crops; he slaughtered the flocks and herds, sacked the towns, laid waste the countryside, and put all the young men to the sword.

²⁸ Fear and dread of him assailed the inhabitants of the coast at Sidon and Tyre, and the people of Sur and Okina, and of Jemnaan; terror seized the populations of Azotus and Ascalon. **3** ¹ They sent envoys to sue for peace. ² 'We, the servants of the Great King, Nebuchadnezzar, lie prostrate before you,' they said; 'do with us as you please. ³ Our homesteads, all our territory and wheatfields, our flocks and herds with every sheepfold in our encampments, all are yours to deal with as you will. ⁴ Our towns along with their inhabitants are yours to enslave; come and dispose of them as you think fit.'

⁵ When the envoys brought this message to Holophernes, ⁶ he went down with his army to the coast, where he established garrisons in all the fortified towns, and, at the same time, took from them picked men to serve as auxiliaries. ⁷ Both there and throughout the surrounding country he was welcomed with garlands and dancing and the sound of tambourines. ⁸ He demolished all their sanctuaries and cut down their sacred groves, for his commission was to destroy all the gods of the land, so that Nebuchadnezzar alone should be worshipped by every nation, and he alone be invoked as a god by men of every tongue and tribe.

⁹ Holophernes then advanced towards Esdraelon, near Dothan, which faces the

2:24 **following:** _or_ crossing.　　3:8 **sanctuaries:** _so one Vs.; Gk_ borders.

Judaean ridge, [10] and encamped between Geba and Scythopolis, where he remained for a whole month to collect whatever supplies were needed for his army.

Israelite resistance

4 A FULL report of the measures undertaken by Holophernes, King Nebuchadnezzar's commander-in-chief, how he had despoiled all the temples of the nations and razed them to the ground, reached the ears of the Israelites living in Judaea. [2] His approach filled them with terror, and they trembled for the fate of Jerusalem and the sanctuary of the Lord their God. [3] They had just returned from captivity, and only recently had all the people been reunited in Judaea, and the sacred vessels, the altar, and the temple been sanctified after their desecration. [4] Accordingly they sent out a warning to the whole of Samaria, Cona, Beth-horon, Belmain and Jericho, Choba and Aesora, and the valley of Salem; [5] the tops of all the high hills were occupied, the hill villages fortified, and stores of food from the newly harvested fields laid up in preparation for war. [6] Joakim, high priest in Jerusalem at that time, wrote to the people of Bethulia and Bethomesthaim, which is opposite Esdraelon facing the plain near Dothan, [7] directing them to hold the passes into the hill-country, because they gave access to Judaea; as the approaches were wide enough for only two men at most, it was easy to prevent the passage of an invader.

[8] The Israelites complied with the orders issued by Joakim the high priest and by the senate of all Israel in Jerusalem. [9] They all cried to God with great fervour, fasting and humbling themselves; [10] they put on sackcloth—they, their wives and children, their livestock, and every resident foreigner, hired labourer, and slave. [11] In Jerusalem the Israelites, men, women, and children, all prostrated themselves in front of the sanctuary, and, with ashes on their heads, spread out their sackcloth before the Lord. They draped the altar in sackcloth, [12] and with one voice they fervently implored the God of Israel not to allow their infants to be captured, their wives carried off, their ancestral cities destroyed, and the temple desecrated and dishonoured, so giving the heathen cause for gloating. [13] The Lord heard their prayer and took pity on their distress.

For many days the entire population of Judaea and Jerusalem fasted before the temple of the Lord Almighty. [14] Joakim the high priest and the priests who stood in the presence of the Lord, and all who served him, wore sackcloth when they offered the regular whole-offering and the votive and freewill-offerings of the people; [15] they put ashes on their turbans, and they cried with all their might to the Lord to look favourably on the whole house of Israel.

5 When it was reported to Holophernes that the Israelites had prepared for war by closing the passes through the hill-country, fortifying all the heights, and putting obstructions in the plains, [2] his anger knew no bounds. He summoned all the rulers of Moab and the Ammonite generals, and all the governors of the coastal region. [3] 'Tell me, you Canaanites,' he demanded, 'what people is this that lives in the hill-country? What are their cities? How large is their army, and wherein lies their power and strength? Who has set up as king at the head of their forces? [4] Of all the people of the west, why do they alone disdain to come to meet me?'

[5] Achior, the commander of the Ammonites, replied: 'My lord, if you will allow your servant to speak, I shall give you the true facts about this people that lives close at hand in the hill-country; no lie will pass your servant's lips. [6] They are descended from the Chaldaeans; [7] and at one time they settled in Mesopotamia, because they refused to worship the gods their fathers had worshipped in Chaldaea. [8] They abandoned the ways of their ancestors and worshipped the God of heaven, the God whom they acknowledge today. When they were driven from the presence of their fathers' gods, they fled to Mesopotamia and lived there for a long time. [9] Commanded by their God to leave their new home and move to Canaan, they settled there and acquired great wealth in gold and silver, and livestock in plenty.

[10] 'Because of a famine which spread throughout Canaan, they went down to Egypt, where they lived as long as they found food. While there, they multiplied so greatly that their numbers were past counting, [11] and the king of Egypt took

precautionary action by setting them to labour at brickmaking and by reducing them to slavery. [12] They cried to their God, and he inflicted incurable plagues on the whole of Egypt. When the Egyptians expelled them, [13] their God dried up the Red Sea for them [14] and led them towards Sinai and Kadesh-barnea. They drove out all the inhabitants of the wilderness [15] and settled in the land of the Amorites, and by force of arms exterminated the whole population of Heshbon. Then they crossed the Jordan and took possession of the entire hill-country, [16] driving out the Canaanites, the Perizzites, the Jebusites, the Shechemites, and all the Girgashites; and there they lived for a long time.

[17] 'As long as they did not sin against their God, they prospered, for they had the support of a God who hates wickedness. [18] When, however, they strayed from the path he had marked out for them, they suffered heavy losses in many wars; they were carried captive to a foreign country, the sanctuary of their God was razed to the ground, and their towns were seized by enemies. [19] But now that they have turned again to their God, they have come back from the lands to which they had been dispersed; they have occupied Jerusalem, the site of their holy place, and have settled in the hill-country, which lay uninhabited. [20] Now, my sovereign lord, if these people have fallen into the error of sinning against their God, and if we find that in so doing they have put themselves at a disadvantage, then we can go up and attack them. [21] But if these people have not violated their law, then let my lord leave them alone, for fear that the God they serve should defend and protect them, and we become the laughing-stock of the whole world.'

[22] When Achior finished speaking there were protests from all who stood round the tent. Holophernes' officers, together with the people from the coastal region and from Moab, demanded that Achior be hacked to pieces. [23] 'We are not going to be scared of the Israelites,' they said, 'a people incapable of putting a force of any strength in the field. [24] Let us march into the hill-country, Lord Holophernes; your great army will swallow them whole.'

6 When the uproar among the men surrounding the council had died down, Holophernes, the Assyrian commander-in-chief, addressed Achior in front of all the assembled foreigners: [2] 'And who are you, Achior, you and your Ephraimite mercenaries, to play the prophet in our presence as you have done today, telling us not to make war against this people, Israel, because their God will protect them? What god is there besides Nebuchadnezzar? [3] When he exerts his power he will wipe them off the face of the earth; their God will assuredly not come to their rescue. We who serve Nebuchadnezzar shall strike them down as if they were but one man. They will not be able to withstand the weight of our cavalry; [4] we shall overwhelm them. Their mountains will be drenched with their blood, and the plains filled with their dead. They cannot stand against us; they will perish without trace. So says King Nebuchadnezzar, lord of all the earth; he has spoken, and his words are no empty threat.

[5] 'As for you, Achior, you Ammonite mercenary, this is treasonable talk. You shall not see my face again from this day until I have taken vengeance on that brood of fugitives from Egypt; [6] but when I come back my warriors will run you through with sword and spear and add you to their victims. [7] My men will now take you away to the hill-country and leave you in one of the towns in the passes; [8] you will be allowed to live until you share their fate. [9] If you are so confident that these places will not fall into our hands, you need not look downcast. I have spoken, and not a single word of mine will go unfulfilled.'

[10] Holophernes ordered the slaves standing by in the tent to seize Achior, escort him to Bethulia, and hand him over to the Israelites. [11] So laying hold of him they took him outside the camp into the plain, and from there up into the hill-country, until they arrived at the springs below Bethulia. [12] The moment the men of Bethulia sighted them, they picked up their weapons and sallied forth from the town to the top of the hill, and the slingers all pelted the enemy with stones to prevent them from coming up. [13] But they slipped through under cover of the hill, bound Achior and left him lying there at the foot, and then returned to their master.

[14] When the Israelites came down from the town and found Achior, they untied

him and took him into Bethulia, where they brought him before the town magistrates [15] then in office, Ozias son of Mica, of the tribe of Simeon, and Chabris son of Gothoniel, and Charmis son of Melchiel. [16] The magistrates summoned the elders of the town, and all the young men and women also came running to the assembly. When Achior had been put in the centre of the crowd, Ozias questioned him as to what had happened. [17] He answered by telling them everything that had taken place in Holophernes' council, what he himself had said in the presence of the Assyrian commanders, and how Holophernes had boasted of what he would do to Israel. [18] At this the people prostrated themselves in worship and cried out to God: [19] 'O Lord, God of heaven, consider their arrogance; have pity on us and our nation in our humiliation; show favour this day to your own people.' [20] Then they reassured Achior and commended him warmly. [21] Ozias brought him from the assembly to his own house, where he gave a feast for the elders; and all night long they invoked the help of the God of Israel.

7 THE next day Holophernes gave orders to his whole army together with all his allies to strike camp and march on Bethulia, to seize the passes up into the hill-country, and engage the Israelites in battle. [2] The entire force moved off, an army of a hundred and seventy thousand infantry and twelve thousand cavalry, not counting the baggage train of the infantry, an immense host. [3] They encamped in the valley near Bethulia, beside the spring; and their camp extended in breadth towards Dothan as far as Belbaim, and in length from Bethulia to Cyamon which faces Esdraelon. [4] The Israelites viewed the enemy's numbers with great alarm. 'These men will devour the whole country,' they said to one another; 'neither the high mountains nor the valleys, nor yet the hills, will ever be able to support the burden of them.' [5] Each man stood to arms; they lit beacons on their towers and remained on guard throughout the night. [6] On the following day Holophernes led out all his cavalry in full view of the Israelites in Bethulia. [7] He reconnoitred the approaches to the town and in the course of his tour seized the springs which were its water supply; he stationed detachments of soldiers to picket them, before returning to his main force.

[8] The rulers of Esau's descendants and the Moabite leaders, along with the commanders of the coastal region, made a joint approach to him. [9] 'Be pleased to listen to our proposal,' they said, 'so that no disaster may befall the army of our lord. [10] These Israelites rely, not on their spears, but on the height of the mountains where they live, for it is no easy task to assault those mountain peaks. [11] Therefore, Lord Holophernes, avoid a pitched battle with them, and not one of your men will be lost. [12] Remain in the camp and keep all your soldiers in their quarters; but permit us, my lord, to take possession of the spring at the foot of the hill, [13] for that is where the whole population of Bethulia draws its water. When they are dying of thirst they will surrender the town. Meanwhile, we and our troops shall scale the neighbouring hills and make our camp there to see that not a man escapes from the place. [14] They and their wives and children will waste away with famine; even before the sword reaches them, the streets will be strewn with their corpses. [15] So you will make them pay dearly for rebelling against you and refusing to receive you peaceably.'

[16] Their plan met with the approval of Holophernes and his entire staff, and he gave orders for it to be carried out. [17] A Moabite force, along with five thousand Assyrians, moved camp into the valley, where they seized the springs which were the Israelites' water supply. [18] Esau's descendants and the Ammonites went up into the hill-country and pitched camp opposite Dothan, and they sent a detachment south-east in the direction of Egrebel, which is near Chus by the wadi Mochmur. The rest of the Assyrian army, a vast host, made their camp on the plain; they filled the entire countryside, forming, with their tents and baggage train, an immense encampment.

[19] The Israelites cried to the Lord their God. They were encircled by their enemies; there was no way of escape, and

7:17 **Moabite**: *so Old Lat.;* Gk Ammonite.

their courage failed. ²⁰ For thirty-four days the whole Assyrian army, infantry, chariots, and cavalry, kept them blockaded. The people of Bethulia came to the end of their household supplies of water, ²¹ and the cisterns too were running dry; drinking water was so strictly rationed that there was never a day when their needs were satisfied. ²² Infants were listless, women and young men, faint with thirst, collapsed in the streets and gateways from sheer exhaustion.

²³ The people—young men, women, and children—all gathered round Ozias and the magistrates of the town, protesting loudly and saying in the presence of the elders: ²⁴ 'May God judge between us, for you have done us a great wrong in not suing for terms from the Assyrians. ²⁵ Now we have no one to help us; God has sold us into their power, and they will find us struck down, all dead of thirst. ²⁶ Surrender to them even now; let Holophernes' people and his army sack the whole town. ²⁷ It is better for us to be carried off by them, for even as slaves we shall at least be alive, and we shall not have to watch our little ones dying before our eyes, the women and children at their last gasp. ²⁸ We call heaven and earth to witness against you, we call our God, the Lord of our fathers, who is punishing us for our sins and the sins of our fathers. We pray that he may not let our forebodings come true this day.' ²⁹ The whole assembly broke into a chorus of lamentation and cried loudly to the Lord God.

³⁰ Ozias said to them, 'Courage, my friends! Let us hold out for five more days; by that time the Lord our God will again show us his mercy, for he will not abandon us for ever. ³¹ But if by the end of that time no help has reached us, I shall do what you ask.' ³² He dismissed the men, each to his post, and they went off to the walls and towers of the town; the women and children were sent to their homes. And throughout the town there was deep dejection.

Judith and Holophernes

8 NEWS of what was happening reached Judith, daughter of Merari who was the son of Ox, son of Joseph, son of Oziel, son of Helkias, son of Ananias, son of Gideon, son of Raphaim, son of Ahitob, son of Elias, son of Chelkias, son of Eliab, son of Nathanael, son of Salamiel, son of Sarasadae, son of Israel. ² Her husband Manasses, who belonged to the same tribe and clan as she did, had died during the barley harvest. ³ While he was out in the fields supervising the binding of the sheaves, he suffered sunstroke; he took to his bed and died in Bethulia his native town and was buried beside his ancestors in the field between Dothan and Balamon. ⁴ For three years and four months Judith had lived in her house as a widow; ⁵ she had a shelter erected on the roof, and she put on sackcloth and always wore mourning. ⁶ After she became a widow she used to fast every day except sabbath eve, the sabbath itself, the eve of the new moon, the day of the new moon, and the Israelite feasts and days of public rejoicing. ⁷ She was beautiful and very attractive. Manasses had left her gold and silver, slaves and slave-girls, livestock and land, and she lived on her property. ⁸ No one had a word to say against her, for she was a deeply religious woman.

⁹ When Judith heard how the people, demoralized by the shortage of water, had made shameful demands on Ozias the magistrate, and how he had given them his oath to surrender the town to the Assyrians at the end of five days, ¹⁰ she sent her maid who had charge of everything she owned to ask Ozias, Chabris, and Charmis, the elders of the town, to come and see her.

¹¹ On their arrival she said: 'Listen to me, magistrates of Bethulia. It was wrong of you to speak as you did to the people today, binding yourselves and God in a solemn contract to surrender the town to our enemies unless the Lord sends relief within so many days. ¹² Who are you to put God to the test at a time like this, and to usurp his role in human affairs? ¹³ It is the Lord Almighty you are now putting to the proof! Will you never understand? ¹⁴ You are unable to plumb the depths of the human heart or grasp the way the mind works; how then can you fathom the Maker of mortal beings? How can you know God's mind and understand his thought? No, my friends, do not provoke the anger of the Lord our God. ¹⁵ For even if he does not choose to help us within the five days, he has the power to shield us at any time he pleases, or equally he can let us be destroyed by our enemies. ¹⁶ It is not

for you to impose conditions on the Lord our God, because God will neither yield to threats nor be bargained with like a mere mortal. [17] So while we wait for the deliverance which is his to give, let us appeal to him for help. If he sees fit, he will hear us.

[18] 'At the present day there is not one of our tribes or clans, districts or towns, that worships man-made gods, or has done so within living memory. This did take place in days gone by, [19] and that was why our forefathers were abandoned to slaughter and pillage, and great was their downfall at the hand of the enemy. [20] We, however, acknowledge no god but the Lord, and so have confidence that he will not spurn us or any of our nation. [21] If we should lose Bethulia, then all Judaea will be lost; the temple will be sacked, and God will hold us responsible for its desecration. [22] The slaughter and deportation of our fellow-countrymen and the devastation of our ancestral land will bring his judgement on our heads, wherever among the Gentiles we become slaves. Our masters will regard us with disgust and contempt. [23] There will be no happy ending to our servitude, no return to favour; the Lord our God will use it to dishonour us.

[24] 'My friends, let us now set an example to our fellow-countrymen, for their lives depend on us, and with us rests the fate of the temple, its precincts, and the altar. [25] Despite our peril let us give thanks to the Lord our God, for he is putting us to the test as he did our forefathers. [26] Remember how he dealt with Abraham, and how he tested Isaac, and what happened to Jacob in Syrian Mesopotamia while he was working as a shepherd for his uncle Laban. [27] The Lord is subjecting us to the same fiery ordeal by which he tested their loyalty, not taking vengeance on us: it is as a warning that he scourges his worshippers.'

[28] Ozias replied, 'You have spoken from the wisdom of your heart, and what you say no one can deny. [29] This is not the first time you have given proof of your wisdom; throughout your life we have all recognized your good sense and sound judgement. [30] But the people were desperate with thirst, and drove us to make this promise and bind ourselves by an oath we may not break. [31] You are a devout woman; pray for us now and ask the Lord to send the rain to fill our cisterns, and then we shall be faint no more.'

[32] 'Listen to me,' said Judith. 'I am going to do something which will be remembered among our countrymen for all generations. [33] Be at the gate tonight; I shall go out with my maid and, before the day on which you have promised to surrender the town to our enemies, the Lord will deliver Israel by my hand. [34] But do not question me about my plan; I shall tell you nothing until I have accomplished what I mean to do.' [35] Ozias and the magistrates said to her, 'Go with our blessing, and may you have the guidance of the Lord God as you take vengeance on our enemies.' [36] They then left her roof-shelter and returned to their posts.

9 Judith prostrated herself; she put ashes on her head and uncovered the sackcloth she was wearing, and at the moment when the evening incense was being offered in the house of God at Jerusalem, she raised her voice and cried to the Lord: [2] 'Lord, the God of my forefather Simeon, you put a sword in Simeon's hand for him to take vengeance on those foreigners who had stripped off a virgin's veil to defile her, uncovered her thighs to shame her, and violated her womb to dishonour her. Though you said, "Such a thing shall not be done," yet they did so. [3] That was why you gave up their rulers to be slain, and the bed they had disgraced with their treachery to be stained with blood; beneath your stroke both slaves and princes fell, even princes upon their thrones. [4] You gave their wives as booty, and their daughters as captives, and all the spoils to be apportioned among your beloved sons, who, aflame with zeal for your cause and aghast at the pollution of their blood, called on you for help. God, my God, hear also a widow's prayer. [5] All that happened then, and all that happened before and after, was your work. What is now and what is yet to be, you have planned; and what you have planned has come to pass. [6] The things you have foreordained present themselves and say, "We are here." All your ways are prepared beforehand: your judgement rests on foreknowledge.

[7] 'Here are the Assyrians massed in force, exultant in their horses and riders, boasting of the might of their infantry, confident in shield and javelin, bow and

sling. They do not know that you are the Lord who stamps out wars; the Lord is your name. [8] Overthrow their strength by your power and crush their might in your anger, for their aim is to desecrate your temple, to defile the dwelling-place of your glorious name, and to lay low the horns of your altar with the sword. [9] See how arrogant they are! Bring down your wrath on their heads, and give to me, widow though I am, the strength to achieve my end. [10] Use the guile of my words to strike them down, the slave with the ruler, the ruler with the servant; shatter their pride by a woman's hand. [11] Your might lies not in numbers nor your sovereign power in strong men, but you are the God of the humble, the help of the poor, the support of the weak, the protector of the despairing, the deliverer of those who have lost all hope. [12] God of my forefather, God of Israel's heritage, Lord of heaven and earth, Creator of the waters, King of all your creation, hear my prayer! [13] Grant that my deceiving words may wound and bruise those who harbour cruel designs against your covenant and against your temple, the summit of Zion, and the home and possession of your children. [14] May your whole nation, every tribe, be made aware that you are God, God of all power and might, and that you and you alone are Israel's shield.'

10 When Judith had ended this prayer to the God of Israel, [2] she rose from where she had been lying prostrate, called her maid, and went down into the house in which she spent her sabbaths and days of festival. [3] She removed the sackcloth she was wearing and laid aside her widow's dress. After bathing, she anointed herself with rich perfume. She arranged her hair elaborately, tied it with a ribbon, and arrayed herself in her gayest clothes, those she used to wear while her husband Manasses was still alive. [4] She put sandals on her feet and adorned herself with anklets, bracelets and rings, her ear-rings, and all her ornaments, and made herself very attractive, to catch the eye of any man who saw her. [5] She gave her maid a skin of wine and a flask of oil; she filled a bag with roasted grain, cakes of dried figs, and loaves of fine bread, packed up her utensils, and gave it all to her maid to carry. [6] From the house they made their way

to the town gate of Bethulia, where they found Ozias standing with Chabris and Charmis, the elders of the town. [7] When they beheld Judith transformed in appearance and quite differently dressed, they marvelled at her beauty and said to her, [8] 'The God of our fathers grant that you meet with favour and accomplish what you are undertaking, so that Israel may triumph and Jerusalem be exalted!' Judith bowed in worship to God [9] and then said, 'Give the order for the gate to be opened for me, and I shall go and carry out all we have spoken of.' They ordered the young men to do as she asked, [10] and when the gate was opened Judith went out, accompanied by her maid. The men of the town gazed after her until she had gone down the hillside and along the valley, where they lost sight of her.

[11] As the two women were making their way straight down the valley, they were confronted by an Assyrian outpost [12] who stopped Judith and questioned her: 'What is your nationality? Where have you come from, and where are you going?' 'I am a Hebrew,' she replied; 'but I am running away from my people, because they are about to fall into your hands and become your prey. [13] I am on my way to Holophernes, your commander-in-chief, with accurate information for him: I shall show him a route by which he can gain control of the entire hill-country without one of you suffering injury or worse.'

[14] The men listened to her story, looking at her face and marvelling at her beauty. [15] 'By coming down at once to see our master you have saved your life,' they said. 'You must go to his tent straight away; some of us will escort you and hand you over. [16] When you are in his presence, do not be afraid; just tell him what you have told us, and he will treat you well.' [17] They detailed a hundred of their number to accompany her and her maid, and the two women were conducted to Holophernes' tent.

[18] As the news of her coming spread from tent to tent, men ran from all parts of the camp and gathered in a circle round her as she stood outside Holophernes' tent waiting for him to be told about her. [19] Admiration for her beauty led them to feel admiration for all Israelites; they said to each other, 'Who could despise a

nation whose women are like these? We had better not leave a man of them alive, for if they get away they will be able to outwit the whole world.'

²⁰ Holophernes' bodyguard and all his attendants came out and escorted her into the tent, ²¹ where he was resting on his bed under a mosquito-net of purple interwoven with gold, emeralds, and precious stones. ²² When Judith was announced he came out to the front part of the tent, with silver lamps carried before him. ²³ She entered his presence, and he and his attendants all marvelled at the beauty of her face. She prostrated herself and did obeisance to him, but his slaves raised her up.

11 'Do not be alarmed, madam,' said Holophernes; 'there is no cause for fear. I have never injured anyone who chose to serve Nebuchadnezzar, king of all the earth. ² I should never have raised my spear against your people in the hill-country had they not insulted me; they have brought it on themselves. ³ Now tell me why you have run away from them and joined us. You have saved your life by coming. Be reassured! You are in no danger, this night or at any time; ⁴ no one will harm you. On the contrary, you will enjoy the benefits that are accorded to the subjects of my master, King Nebuchadnezzar.'

⁵ Judith replied, 'My lord, grant your slave a hearing and listen to what I have to say to you. The information I am giving you tonight is the truth. ⁶ If you follow my advice, through you God will accomplish a great thing, and my lord will not fail to attain his ends: ⁷ I swear this by the life of Nebuchadnezzar, king of all the earth, and by the living might of him who sent you to bring order to all creatures. Thanks to you and to your power, not only do men serve him, but wild animals, cattle, and birds will live at the disposal of Nebuchadnezzar and his whole house. ⁸ We have heard how wise and clever you are; you are known throughout the world as a man of ability who has no peer in all the empire, a man of powerful intellect and amazing skill in the arts of war.

⁹ 'Now, we have heard about the speech that Achior made in your council; the men of Bethulia rescued him and he told them everything he had said in your presence. ¹⁰ Do not disregard his words, my sovereign lord, but give them full weight. They are true: no punishment ever befalls our race nor does the sword subdue them, except when they sin against their God. ¹¹ And yet, my lord, you are not to be thwarted and cheated of success; they are doomed to die, and sin has them in its power, for whenever they do wrong they arouse their God's anger. ¹² Since they have run out of food and their water supply is desperately low, they have decided to lay hands on their cattle, proposing to eat all the things that God by his laws has strictly prohibited; ¹³ they have resolved to use up the firstfruits of the grain and the tithes of wine and oil, although these are dedicated and reserved for the priests who stand in attendance before our God in Jerusalem, and no layman may so much as touch them. ¹⁴ They have sent to Jerusalem for permission from the senate, because even the people there have done this. ¹⁵ As soon as ever the word comes and they act on it, that same day they will be given up to you to be destroyed.

¹⁶ 'When I learnt all this, my lord, I left them and made my escape; the things that God has sent me to do with you will be the wonder of the whole world, wherever men hear about them. ¹⁷ For I, your servant, am a godfearing woman: day and night I worship the God of heaven. I shall stay with you now, my lord, and each night I shall go out into the valley and pray to God, and when they have committed their sins he will tell me. ¹⁸ Immediately I bring you word, you may go out at the head of your army; you will meet with no resistance. ¹⁹ I shall guide you across Judaea until you reach Jerusalem, and I shall set up your throne in the heart of the city. You will drive them like sheep that have lost their shepherd, and not a dog will so much as growl at you. I have been given foreknowledge of this; it has been revealed to me, and I have been sent to announce it to you.'

²⁰ Judith's words delighted Holophernes and all those in attendance on him and, amazed at her wisdom, ²¹ they declared, 'From one end of the earth to the other there is not a woman to compare with her for beauty of face or shrewdness of speech.' ²² Holophernes assured her, 'Your God has done well in sending you

out from your people, to bring strength to us and destruction to those who have insulted my lord! ²³ Your looks are striking and your words are wise. Do as you have promised, and your God shall be my god, and you shall live in King Nebuchadnezzar's palace and be renowned throughout the whole world.'

12 Holophernes then told them to bring her in where his silver was set out, and gave orders for a meal to be served to her from his own food and wine. ² But Judith said, 'I must not eat of it for fear I should be breaking our law. What I have brought will be sufficient for my needs.' ³ 'But', asked Holophernes, 'where can we get you a fresh supply of the same kind if you use up all you have with you? There is no one from your people here among us.' ⁴ Judith replied, 'As sure as you live, my lord, I shall not finish what I have with me before God accomplishes by my hand what he has purposed.'

⁵ Holophernes' attendants conducted her to a tent, and she slept until midnight. Shortly before the dawn watch she rose ⁶ and sent this request to Holophernes: 'May it please my lord to give orders for me to be allowed to go out and pray.' ⁷ Holophernes ordered his bodyguard not to prevent her. She stayed in the camp for three days, going out each night into the valley of Bethulia and bathing in the spring at the camp. ⁸ When she came up out of the water she would pray the Lord, the God of Israel, to prosper her undertaking to restore his people. ⁹ Then she returned to the camp purified, and remained in the tent until she took her evening meal.

¹⁰ On the fourth day Holophernes gave a banquet for his personal servants only; none of the army officers were invited. ¹¹ He said to Bagoas, the eunuch in charge of all his personal affairs: 'Go to the Hebrew woman who is in your care, and persuade her to join us at our feast. ¹² We shall lose face if we let such a woman go without enjoying her favours; if we do not win her, she will laugh us to scorn.' ¹³ Bagoas withdrew from Holophernes' presence and went in to Judith. 'Now, my fair one,' he said, 'do not be bashful; come along to my master and give yourself the honour of his company. Drink with us and enjoy yourself, and behave today like one of the Assyrian women in attendance at Nebuchadnezzar's palace.' ¹⁴ 'Who am I to refuse my lord?' answered Judith. 'I am eager to do whatever pleases him, and it will be something to boast of till my dying day.' ¹⁵ She proceeded to dress herself up, putting on all her feminine finery. Her maid went ahead of her, and spread on the ground in front of Holophernes the fleeces which Bagoas had provided for her daily use, so that she might recline on them while eating.

¹⁶ As Judith came in and took her place, Holophernes was beside himself with desire for her. He trembled with passion and was filled with an ardent longing to possess her; indeed ever since he first set eyes on her he had been seeking an opportunity to seduce her. ¹⁷ He said to her, 'Drink, and join in our merriment.' ¹⁸ 'Certainly I shall, my lord,' replied Judith, 'for today is the greatest day of my life.' ¹⁹ Then she took what her servant had prepared, and ate and drank in his presence. ²⁰ Holophernes was entranced with her, and he drank a great deal of wine, more than he had ever drunk on any single day in his whole life.

13 When it grew late, Holophernes' servants made haste to withdraw, and Bagoas closed the tent from outside, shutting out the attendants from his master's presence, and they went off to their beds; the banquet had lasted so long that they were all exhausted. ² Judith was now alone in the tent, with Holophernes lying sprawled on his bed, dead drunk. ³ Judith had told her maid to stand outside the sleeping apartment and wait for her to go out as she did on other days; she had said that she would be going out to pray, and had explained this to Bagoas also.

⁴ When all had left and not a soul remained, Judith stood beside Holophernes' bed and prayed silently: 'O Lord, God of all power, look favourably now on what I am doing to bring glory to Jerusalem, ⁵ for this is the moment to come to the aid of your heritage and to prosper my plan for crushing the enemies who have attacked us.' ⁶ She went to the bed-rail beside Holophernes' head, reached down his sword, ⁷ and drawing close to the bed she gripped him by the hair. 'Now give me strength, O Lord, God of Israel,' she said, ⁸ and struck at his neck twice with all her might and cut off his head. ⁹ She rolled

the body off the bed and removed the mosquito-net from its posts; quickly she came out and gave Holophernes' head to her maid, ¹⁰ who put it in the food-bag. Then the two of them went out together as they always did when they went to pray. They passed through the camp, and went round the valley and up the hill to Bethulia till they approached its gates.
¹¹ From a distance Judith called to the guards: 'Open up! Open the gate! God, our God, is with us, still showing his strength in Israel and his might against our enemies. Today he has shown it!' ¹² When the townspeople heard her voice, they hurried down to the gate and summoned the elders of the town. ¹³ Everyone, high and low, came running, hardly able to believe that Judith had returned. They opened the gate, and welcomed in the two women. Then, kindling a fire to give light, they gathered round them. ¹⁴ Judith raised her voice: 'Praise God! O praise him!' she cried. 'Give praise to God who has not withdrawn his mercy from the house of Israel, but has crushed our enemies by my hand this very night!' ¹⁵ She took the head from the bag and showed it to them. 'Look!' she said. 'The head of Holophernes, the Assyrian commander-in-chief! And here is the net under which he lay drunk! The Lord has struck him down by a woman's hand! ¹⁶ And I swear by the Lord who has brought me safely along the way I have travelled, that, though my face lured him to his destruction, he committed no sin with me, and my honour is unblemished.'
¹⁷ The people were all astounded at what she had done; and bowing in worship to God, they spoke with one voice: 'Praise be to you, our God, who has this day humiliated the enemies of your people!' ¹⁸ Ozias addressed Judith: 'Daughter, the blessing of God Most High rests on you more than on any other woman on earth; praise be to the Lord God who created heaven and earth; under his guidance you struck off the head of the leader of our enemies. ¹⁹ As long as men commemorate the power of God, the sure hope which inspired you will never fade from their minds. ²⁰ May God make your deed redound to your honour for ever, and may he shower blessings on you! You risked your life for our nation when it was faced with humili-

ation. Boldly you went to meet the disaster that threatened us, and firmly you held to God's straight road.' All the people responded, 'Amen, Amen.'

The triumph of Israel

14 JUDITH said to them: 'Listen to me, my friends; take this head and hang it out on the battlements. ² Then at daybreak, as soon as the sun rises, let every able-bodied man among you arm himself; march out of the town with a leader before you, as if you were going down to the plain to attack the Assyrian outpost, but do not go down. ³ The men there will pick up their weapons and make for the camp to rouse their commanders, who will rush to Holophernes' tent. When he is not to be found, panic will seize them and they will flee from you; ⁴ pursue them, you and all who live within Israel's borders, and cut them down in their tracks. ⁵ But first of all, summon Achior the Ammonite to me, so that he may see for himself and identify the man who treated Israel with contempt and sent him to us as if to his death.'
⁶ Achior was summoned from Ozias's house. He came, and when he saw Holophernes' head held by one of the men among the assembled people, he fell down in a faint. ⁷ After they revived him, he threw himself at Judith's feet and did obeisance to her. 'Your praises will be sung in every home in Judah and among all nations,' he declared; 'they will tremble when they hear your name. ⁸ And now tell me what you have done during these days.' So while the people listened, Judith told him everything from the day she left until that very moment. ⁹ As she ended her story, the people raised a shout of acclamation, making the town resound with their cheers. ¹⁰ Achior, realizing all that the God of Israel had done, believed wholeheartedly in him; he was circumcised, and admitted as a member of the community of Israel, as his descendants are to this day.
¹¹ At dawn they hung Holophernes' head on the wall; then every man took up his weapons, and they marched out in companies towards the approaches to the town. ¹² The moment the Assyrians set eyes on them, they passed word to their leaders, who went to the commanders, captains, and all the other officers. ¹³ They

presented themselves at Holophernes' tent and said to his steward: 'Wake our master! These slaves have had the audacity to come down and offer battle. They are asking to be utterly wiped out.' ¹⁴ Bagoas went in and knocked at the screen of the inner tent, supposing that Holophernes was sleeping with Judith. ¹⁵ When there was no reply, he drew aside the screen, entered the sleeping apartment, and found the dead body sprawled over a footstool, with the head gone. ¹⁶ He gave a great cry, wailing and groaning aloud, and tearing his clothes. ¹⁷ He went into the tent which Judith had occupied, and not finding her there he burst out, shouting to the troops, ¹⁸ 'The slaves have fooled us. One Hebrew woman has brought shame on King Nebuchadnezzar's house. Look! Holophernes is lying on the ground, headless!' ¹⁹ At his words the officers of the Assyrian army were appalled and tore their clothes, and the camp rang with their shouting and wild cries.

15 When news of those events spread to the men in the camp, they were thrown into confusion. ² Terrified and panic-stricken and making no attempt to keep together, they streamed out as if by a common impulse, seeking to escape by any and every path across the plain and the hill-country, ³ while those who were encamped in the hills around Bethulia also took to flight. Thereupon all the fighting men of Israel poured out in pursuit. ⁴ Ozias sent messengers to Bethomesthaim, Choba, and Chola, and throughout the whole territory of Israel, to report what had happened and to encourage all to attack and destroy the enemy. ⁵ At this every man in Israel joined in the onslaught, cutting down the fugitives the whole way to Choba. So also the men from Jerusalem and the entire hill-country rallied in support, for word had reached them of what had happened to the enemy camp. The men of Gilead and Galilee outflanked the Assyrians and inflicted heavy losses on them, pressing on beyond Damascus and its surrounding district. ⁶ The rest of the inhabitants of Bethulia fell on the Assyrian camp and made themselves rich with the spoils. ⁷ When the Israelites returned from the slaughter, they helped themselves to what remained; there was a huge quan-

tity, and the villages and hamlets in the hill-country and in the plain secured booty in plenty.

⁸ Joakim the high priest and the senate of Israel came from Jerusalem to see for themselves the great things the Lord had done for his people, and to greet Judith in person. ⁹ When they came into her presence, they all with one accord praised her: 'You are the glory of Jerusalem, the great pride of Israel, the great boast of our people! ¹⁰ With your own hand you have done all this, bestowing these benefits on Israel, and God has shown his approval. Blessings on you from the Lord Almighty, for all time to come!' And the people responded, 'Amen.'

¹¹ The looting of the camp went on for thirty days. Judith was given Holophernes' tent, with all his silver, and his couches, bowls, and furniture. She loaded her mule, then got her wagons ready and piled the goods on them. ¹² The Israelite women all came flocking to see her; they sang her praises, and some performed a dance in her honour. She took garlanded wands and distributed them among the women who accompanied her, ¹³ and she and those who were with her crowned themselves with olive leaves. Then, at the head of the people, she led the women in the dance; the men of Israel, in full armour, followed, all wearing garlands on their heads and singing hymns.

16 In the presence of all Israel, Judith began this hymn of praise and thanksgiving, which was echoed by the people:

² 'Strike up a song to my God with
   tambourines;
sing to the Lord with cymbals;
raise a psalm of praise to him;
honour him and invoke his name.
³ The Lord is a God who stamps out
   wars;
he has brought me safe from my
   pursuers;
he has stationed his camp among his
   people.

⁴ 'The Assyrian came from the
   mountains of the north;
his armies came in such myriads
that his troops choked the valleys,
the cavalry covered the hills.

⁵ He threatened to set my whole land
　on fire,
to put my young men to the sword
and dash my infants to the ground,
to take my children as booty, my
　maidens as spoil.
⁶ 'The Lord Almighty has thwarted
　them by a woman's hand.
⁷ It was no young man that brought
　their champion low;
no Titan struck him down,
no tall giant set upon him;
but Judith, Merari's daughter,
　disarmed him by her beauty.
⁸ To raise up the afflicted in Israel
she laid aside her widow's dress;
she anointed her face with perfume,
bound her hair with a ribbon,
and chose a linen gown to beguile
　him.
⁹ Her sandal entranced his eye,
her beauty took his heart captive—
and the sword cut through his neck!

¹⁰ 'The Persians shuddered at her
　daring,
the Medes were daunted by her
　boldness.
¹¹ Then my lowly ones shouted in
　triumph
and the enemy were dismayed;
my weak ones shouted
and the enemy cowered in fear;
they raised their voices and the
　enemy took to flight.
¹² The sons of maidservants ran them
　through,
wounding them like runaway slaves;
they were destroyed by the army of
　my Lord.
¹³ 'I will sing a new hymn to my God:
O Lord, you are great and glorious,
you are marvellous in your strength,
　invincible.
¹⁴ Let your whole creation serve you;
for you spoke, and all things came to
　be;
you sent out your spirit, and it gave
　them form;
none can oppose your word.
¹⁵ Mountains will shake to their depths
　like water,

rocks melt like wax at your
　presence;
but you still show compassion
to those who fear you.
¹⁶ All sacrifices with their fragrance are
　but a small thing,
all the fat for whole-offerings is of no
　significance to you;
but he who fears the Lord is great
　always.
¹⁷ Woe to the nations which attack my
　people!
The Lord Almighty will punish them
　on the day of judgement;
he will consign their bodies to fire
　and worms;
in pain they will weep for ever.'

¹⁸ They went to worship God at Jerusalem, and as soon as the people were purified, they presented their whole-offerings, freewill-offerings, and gifts. ¹⁹ Judith dedicated to God all Holophernes' possessions which the people had given to her; the net, which she herself had taken from the sleeping apartment, she gave to God as a votive offering. ²⁰ For three months the people continued their celebrations before the temple at Jerusalem; and Judith remained with them.

²¹ At the end of that time they all returned to their own homes. Judith went back to Bethulia, where she lived on her estate, and throughout her lifetime was renowned in the whole country. ²² Though she had many suitors, she remained a widow all her days after her husband Manasses died and was gathered to his fathers. ²³ Her fame continued to increase, and she lived on in her husband's house until she was a hundred and five years old. She gave her maid her liberty. She died in Bethulia and was laid in the burial cave beside her husband Manasses, ²⁴ and Israel observed mourning for seven days. Before her death she divided her property among all those who were most closely related to her husband, and among her own nearest relations. ²⁵ No one dared to threaten the Israelites again in Judith's lifetime, or indeed for a long time after her death.

THE REST OF THE CHAPTERS
OF THE BOOK OF
ESTHER
WHICH ARE FOUND NEITHER IN THE HEBREW
NOR IN THE SYRIAC

NOTE. The portions of the Book of Esther commonly included in the Apocrypha are extracts from the Greek version of the book, which differs substantially from the Hebrew text (translated in *The Revised English Bible: Old Testament*). In order that they may be read in their original sequence, the whole of the Greek version is here translated, those portions which are not normally printed in the Apocrypha being enclosed in square brackets, with the chapter and verse numbers in italic figures. The order followed is that of the Greek text, but the chapter and verse numbers are made to conform to those of the Authorized Version. Proper names are given in the form in which they occur in the Greek version.

11 [² IN the second year of the reign of Artaxerxes the Great King, on the first day of the month of Nisan, Mardochaeus son of Jairus, son of Semeius, son of Kisaeus, of the tribe of Benjamin, had a dream. ³ Mardochaeus, who was in the royal service at court, was a Jew living in the city of Susa and a man of high standing; ⁴ he was one of the exiles, a descendant of those whom King Nebuchadnezzar of Babylon had carried away from Jerusalem with King Jechonias of Judah. This was his dream: ⁵ first came din and tumult, peals of thunder and an earthquake, turmoil on the earth. ⁶ Then two great dragons appeared, each poised to grapple with the other. They gave a mighty roar, ⁷ and every nation was roused by it to prepare for war and fight against the righteous nation. ⁸ It was a day of darkness and gloom, distress and anguish, oppression and great turmoil on the earth. ⁹ The whole righteous nation, dreading the evils in store, was troubled and prepared for death. ¹⁰ They cried aloud to God, and in answer there came as though from a little spring a great river brimming with water. ¹¹ As the sun rose it grew light; the humble were exalted and they devoured those of high degree. ¹² After this dream, in which he saw what God had resolved to do, Mardochaeus woke; he pondered over the dream until nightfall, trying in every way to understand it.

12 Once, while Mardochaeus was taking his rest in the royal courtyard with Gabatha and Tharra, the two eunuchs in the king's service who were on guard in the courtyard, ² he overheard them deep in discussion. He listened carefully to discover what was on their minds, and found they were plotting violence against King Artaxerxes. He denounced them to the king, ³ who had the two eunuchs interrogated; on their confessing, they were led away to execution. ⁴ The king wrote an account of this affair to have it on record; Mardochaeus also wrote an account of it. ⁵ The king gave him an appointment at court, and rewarded him for his services. ⁶ But Haman son of Hamadathus, a Bugaean, who enjoyed the royal favour, looked for a chance to harm Mardochaeus and his people because of the king's two eunuchs.]

A Jewess becomes queen in Persia

1 [THOSE events happened in the days of Artaxerxes, that Artaxerxes who ruled from India to Ethiopia, a hundred and twenty-seven provinces, ² at the time when he had taken his seat on the royal throne in the city of Susa. ³ In the third year of his reign he gave a reception for the king's Friends and for others of various races, the Persian and Median nobles, and the leading provincial governors. ⁴ Afterwards he put on display to them the wealth of his kingdom and the dazzling splendour of his riches for a hundred and eighty days. ⁵ When these days of feasting were over, the king held a banquet for all the people of various races present in the city of Susa; it lasted six days and took place in the palace court, ⁶which was decorated with white curtains of linen and cotton stretched on cords of purple, and these were attached to blocks of gold and silver resting on stone and marble columns. There were gold and silver couches placed on a pavement of malachite, marble, and mother-of-pearl, and there were coverings of transparent weave elaborately embroidered with roses arranged in a circle. ⁷The cups were of gold and silver, and on display was a miniature cup made from a ruby worth thirty thousand talents. The wine, which was from the king's own cellar, was abundant and sweet. ⁸The drinking was according to no fixed rule, for the king had laid down that all the palace stewards should respect his wishes and those of the guests. ⁹Queen Astin gave a banquet for the women inside King Artaxerxes' palace.

¹⁰On the seventh day, when he was feeling merry, the king ordered Haman, Mazan, Tharra, Borazes, Zatholtha, Abataza, and Tharaba, the seven eunuchs who were in attendance on the king's person, ¹¹to bring the queen into his presence, so that he might place the royal diadem on her head and display her beauty to the officers and people of various races; for she was indeed a beautiful woman. ¹²But Queen Astin refused to obey and accompany the eunuchs. This incensed the king and his anger flared up. ¹³He said to his courtiers, 'You hear how Astin spoke. Give your ruling and judgement in the matter.' ¹⁴Harkesaeus, Sarathaeus, and Malesear, the nobles of Persia and Media who were closest to the king and occupied the seats of honour by him, approached ¹⁵and made known to him what, according to the law, should be done to Queen Astin for disobeying the royal command conveyed to her by the eunuchs.

¹⁶Muchaeus made this reply to the king and the nobles: 'Queen Astin has done wrong, not to the king alone, but also to all the nobles and officers of the king.' ¹⁷(For he had repeated to them what the queen had said and how she had defied the king.) ¹⁸'Just as she defied King Artaxerxes, so now the nobles of Persia and Media will find that all the great ladies are emboldened to treat their husbands with disrespect, when they hear what she

said to the king. ¹⁹If it please your majesty, let a royal decree be issued once and for all, and let it be inscribed among the laws of the Medes and Persians, that Astin shall not come in again to the king; and let your majesty give her place as queen to another who is more worthy of it than she. ²⁰Let whatever law the king makes be proclaimed throughout the kingdom, and so all women, rich and poor alike, will give honour to their husbands.' ²¹The advice pleased the king and the princes, and the king did as Muchaeus had proposed. ²²Dispatches were sent to all the provinces of the kingdom, to every province in its own language, in order that each man should be treated with deference in his own house.

2 Some time later, when the anger of King Artaxerxes had died down, he called Astin to mind, remembering what she had done and how he had given judgement against her. ²So the king's attendants said: 'Let there be sought out for your majesty beautiful young virgins; ³let your majesty appoint commissioners in every province of your kingdom to select these beautiful virgins and bring them to the women's quarters in the city of Susa. Have them placed under the care of the king's eunuch who has charge of the women, and let them be provided with cosmetics and everything else they need. ⁴The girl who is most acceptable to the king shall become queen in place of Astin.' The advice pleased the king, and he acted on it.

⁵In the city of Susa there lived a Jew named Mardochaeus son of Jairus, son of Semeius, son of Kisaeus, of the tribe of Benjamin; ⁶he had been taken into exile from Jerusalem when it was captured by King Nebuchadnezzar of Babylon. ⁷He had a foster-child named Esther, the daughter of his father's brother Aminadab; and after the death of her parents he had brought her up, intending to make her his wife. She was a beautiful girl. ⁸When the king's edict was proclaimed and many girls were brought to Susa to be committed to the care of Gai, who had charge of the women, Esther too was entrusted to him. ⁹He found her pleasing and she received his special favour: he promptly supplied her with cosmetics and with her allowance of food, and also with

seven maids assigned to her from the king's palace. She and her maids were accorded favourable treatment in the women's quarters.

[10] Esther had not disclosed her race or country, because Mardochaeus had forbidden her to do so. [11] Every day Mardochaeus would walk past the forecourt of the women's quarters to keep an eye on what was happening to Esther.

[12] The full period of preparation before a girl went to the king was twelve months: six months' treatment with oil of myrrh, and six months' with perfumes and cosmetics. At the end of this the girl went to the king. [13] She was handed to the person appointed and accompanied him from the women's quarters to the king's palace. [14] She entered the palace in the evening and returned in the morning to another part of the women's quarters, to be under the care of Gai, the king's eunuch in charge of the women. She did not go again to the king unless summoned by name.

[15] When the time came for Esther, the daughter of Aminadab, uncle of Mardochaeus, to go to the king, she neglected none of the instructions given her by the king's eunuch in charge of the women. Esther charmed all who saw her, [16] and when she went to King Artaxerxes in the twelfth month, that is, the month of Adar, in the seventh year of his reign, [17] the king fell in love with her. He treated her with greater favour than all the rest of the virgins, and put the queen's diadem on her head. [18] Then, to celebrate his marriage with Esther, the king gave a banquet lasting seven days for all the king's Friends and the officers. He also granted a remission of taxation to all the subjects of his kingdom.

Mardochaeus and Haman

[19] MARDOCHAEUS was in attendance in the court. [20] On his instructions Esther had not disclosed her country; she was to fear God and keep the commandments, as she used to do when she was with him. So Esther made no change in her rule of life.

[21] Two of the king's eunuchs, officers of the bodyguard, were offended at the advancement of Mardochaeus and plotted to murder King Artaxerxes. [22] This became known to Mardochaeus, who told Esther, and she revealed the plot to the king. [23] The king interrogated the two eunuchs and had them hanged, and he ordered that the service Mardochaeus had rendered should be recorded to his honour in the royal archives.

3 It was after those events that King Artaxerxes promoted Haman, son of Hamadathus, a Bugaean, advancing him and giving him precedence above all the king's Friends. [2] Everyone at court did obeisance to Haman, for so the king had commanded it should be done; but Mardochaeus did not do obeisance. [3] The courtiers said, 'Mardochaeus, why do you flout his majesty's command?' [4] They challenged him day after day, and when he refused to listen they informed Haman that Mardochaeus was defying the king's order. Mardochaeus had told them he was a Jew. [5] Haman was furious when he learnt that Mardochaeus was not doing obeisance to him, and [6] he plotted to exterminate all the Jews throughout the kingdom.

[7] In the twelfth year of Artaxerxes' reign Haman made an order for lots to be cast, taking the days and months one by one, to decide on a day for the destruction of Mardochaeus's whole race. The lot fell on the thirteenth day of the month of Adar.

[8] Then Haman said to King Artaxerxes: 'Dispersed among the nations throughout your whole kingdom, there is one whose laws are different from those of every other nation. They flout your majesty's laws, and it is not in your majesty's interest to tolerate them. [9] If it please you, sire, let an order be issued for their destruction; and I shall make over to the royal treasury the sum of ten thousand talents of silver.' [10] The king drew off his signet ring and, handing it to Haman to seal the decree against the Jews, [11] he said, 'Keep the money, and deal with the people as you think fit.'

[12] On the thirteenth day of the first month the king's secretaries were summoned, and in accordance with Haman's instructions they wrote in the name of King Artaxerxes to his army commanders and governors of every province from India to Ethiopia; there were a hundred

[3:7] **thirteenth**: *so some witnesses (cp. [8:12]); other witnesses read* fourteenth.

and twenty-seven provinces in all, and each was addressed in its own language. *13* Dispatches were sent by courier throughout the kingdom of Artaxerxes ordering the extermination of the Jewish race, on a given day of the twelfth month, Adar; and their goods were to be treated as spoil.]

13 This is a copy of the letter:

Artaxerxes the Great King to the Governors of the one hundred and twenty-seven provinces from India to Ethiopia and to their regional officials. *2* As ruler over many nations and master of the whole world, it is my will—not in the arrogance of power, but because my rule is equitable and mild—to ensure for my subjects a life permanently free from disturbance, to make my kingdom quiet and safe for travel to its farthest limits, and to restore the peace that all men desire. *3* I have enquired of my counsellors how this object might be achieved. Among us Haman is eminent for sound judgement, one whose worth is proved by his constant goodwill and steadfast loyalty, and who has gained the honour of the second place at our court. *4* He has represented to us that dispersed among all the races of the world is a disaffected people, opposed in its laws to every nation, and continually ignoring the royal ordinances, so that our perfected plans for the unified administration of the empire cannot be accomplished. *5* We understand that this nation stands quite alone in its continual hostility to the human race, that it evades the laws by its strange manner of life, and in disloyalty to our government commits the most grave offences, thus undermining the stability of our kingdom. *6* Accordingly we have given orders that all those who are designated to you in the indictments drawn up by Haman our vicegerent and second father shall, with their wives and children, be utterly destroyed by their enemies' swords without mercy or pity, on the thirteenth day of Adar, the twelfth month of the present year.

7 Therefore these persons, who have long been disaffected, shall in a single day meet a violent end, so that our government may henceforth be stable and untroubled.

3 *14* [Copies of the dispatch were posted up in every province, and all the peoples were ordered to be ready for that day. *15* The matter was expedited also in Susa. The king and Haman caroused together, but in the city of Susa confusion reigned.

4 When Mardochaeus learnt of all that had been done, he tore his clothes, put on sackcloth, and sprinkled himself with ashes. He rushed out through the city square, crying loudly: 'A nation that has committed no crime is being destroyed.' *2* He went right up to the palace gate, and there he halted, because no one wearing sackcloth and ashes was allowed to enter the courtyard. *3* In every province where the king's decree was posted up, there was a great cry of mourning and lamentation among the Jews, and they put on sackcloth and ashes. *4* When the queen's maids and eunuchs came in and told her, she was distraught at what she heard. She sent clothes for Mardochaeus and urged him to put off his sackcloth, but he refused. *5* Esther then summoned Hachrathaeus, the eunuch who waited upon her, and sent him to Mardochaeus to obtain accurate information for her. *7* Mardochaeus told him all that had happened, and how Haman had promised the king to pay ten thousand talents into the treasury to bring about the destruction of the Jews. *8* He also gave him a copy of the written decree for their destruction which had been posted up in Susa, that he might show it to Esther; and he told him to bid her go to the king to implore his favour and intercede for her people. 'Say to her,' he added, '"Do not forget your humble origins and your upbringing in my house. Because Haman, who stands next to the king, has spoken against us and demanded our death, call on the Lord, and then speak to the king on our behalf and save our lives."' *9* When Hachrathaeus came in and told Esther all Mardochaeus had said, *10* she bade him take back this

---

13: 6 **thirteenth**: *prob. rdg*; *Gk* fourteenth; *see note on* [3: 7].   [4: 5] **information for her**: *some witnesses add* *6* So he went out to Mardochaeus in the square opposite the city gate.

message: [11] 'Every nation in the kingdom knows that there is no hope for any person, man or woman, who enters the king's presence in the inner court without being summoned; only one to whom the king holds out the gold sceptre is spared. Further, I have not been summoned to go to the king these thirty days.' [12] When Hachrathaeus delivered Esther's message, [13] Mardochaeus sent this reply: 'Do not imagine, Esther, that of all the Jews in the kingdom you alone will be safe. [14] If you remain silent at such a time as this, relief and deliverance for the Jews will come from another quarter, but you and your father's family will perish. And who knows whether it is not for a time like this that you have become queen?' [15] Esther gave the messenger this answer to take back to Mardochaeus: [16] 'Go and assemble the Jews that are in Susa and hold a fast for me; for three days, night and day, take neither food nor drink, and I and my maids shall also fast. After that, in defiance of the law, I shall go to the king, even if it costs me my life.' [17] Mardochaeus then went away and did everything Esther had bidden him.]

13 [8] CALLING to mind all that the Lord had done, Mardochaeus uttered this prayer. [9] 'O Lord, Lord and King, Ruler over all, for the whole creation is under your authority, and when it is your will to save Israel there is none who can oppose you: [10] you made heaven and earth and every wonderful thing under heaven; [11] you are Lord of all, and there is none who can resist you, the Lord. [12] You know all things; you know, Lord, that it was not from insolence or arrogance or vainglory that I refused to bow before this proud Haman, [13] for to save Israel I would gladly have kissed the soles of his feet! [14] But I acted in this way so as not to hold a man in greater honour than God; I shall not bow before any but you, my Lord, and it is not from arrogance that I refuse this homage. [15] Now, O Lord, God and King, God of Abraham, spare your people, for our enemies are bent on bringing us to ruin, and they have set their hearts upon the destruction of your chosen people, yours from the beginning. [16] Do not disregard your own possession which you ransomed and brought out of Egypt for yourself. [17] Hear my prayer, and have mercy on your heritage; turn our mourning into feasting, that we may live to sing of your name, O Lord. Do not put to silence the lips that give you praise.' [18] The Israelites cried aloud with all their might, for death stared them in the face.

The triumph of the Jews

14 QUEEN Esther, in the grip of mortal anxiety, sought refuge in the Lord. [2] She took off her royal robes and put on the garb of distress and mourning. Instead of rich perfumes she strewed ashes and dirt over her head; she abased her body, and every part that she had delighted to adorn she covered with her dishevelled hair. [3] Then she prayed to the Lord God of Israel.

'O my Lord, you alone are our King; come to my help who am alone and have no other helper but you, [4] for I am taking my life in my hands. [5] From my earliest days I have been taught by my father's family and tribe that you, Lord, chose Israel out of all the nations, and from all who went before them you chose our fathers as an everlasting possession, and you have performed for them whatever you promised. [6] But now we have sinned against you, and you have handed us over to our enemies [7] because we paid honour to their gods. O Lord, you are just. [8] Yet even now our enemies are not content that we are in bitter servitude; they have taken a vow [9] to annul the decree you have proclaimed and to destroy Israel, your possession, silencing those who praise you, extinguishing the glory of your house and the flame on your altar. [10] They would give the heathen cause to sing the praises of their worthless gods, and would have a mortal king held in everlasting honour.

[11] 'Do not yield your sceptre, Lord, to gods that have no real existence; let not our enemies mock at our ruin, but turn their plot against them, and make an example of the man who planned it. [12] Be mindful of us, Lord; reveal yourself in the time of our distress, and give me courage, O King of gods, Sovereign over every power. [13] Put the right words into my mouth when I enter this lion's den,

14:1 **in ... anxiety:** *or* caught up in this deadly struggle.

and divert his hatred to him who is our enemy, so that there may be an end of him and his associates. [14] 'By your power save us, and help me who am alone and have no one but you, Lord. [15] You know all things; you know that I hate the splendour of the heathen; I abhor the bed of the uncircumcised or of any Gentile. [16] You know in what straits I am: I loathe that symbol of pride, the headdress that I wear when I show myself in public, I loathe it as one loathes a filthy rag and in private never wear it. [17] I, your servant, have not eaten at Haman's table, nor have I graced a banquet of the king nor touched the wine of his drink-offerings. [18] From the day of my preferment until now I have known no joy except in you, Lord God of Abraham. [19] O God, the all-prevailing, give heed to the cry of those driven to despair: deliver us from the power of the wicked, and rescue me from what I dread.'

15 On the third day, after ending her prayers, Esther put off the clothes she had worn while she worshipped, and arrayed herself in her robes of state. [2] When she was attired in all her splendour and had invoked the all-seeing God, her preserver, she took her two maids with her; [3] on one she leaned for support, as befitted a fine lady, [4] while the other followed, bearing her train. [5] She was radiant and in the height of her beauty; her face was as cheerful as it was lovely, but her heart was constricted with fear. [6] She passed through all the doors until she stood in the royal presence. The king was seated on his throne in the full array of his majesty, all gold and precious stones, an awe-inspiring figure. [7] He looked up, his face aglow with regal dignity, and regarded her with towering anger. The queen sank down, changing colour and fainting, and she swooned on the shoulder of the maid who went before her. [8] But the king's mood was changed by God to one of gentleness. In deep concern he started up from his throne and held her in his arms until she came to herself. He soothed her with reassuring words: [9] 'Esther, what is it? Have no fear of me, your loving husband; [10] you shall not die,

for our order is only for our subjects. You may approach.' [11] The king raised his gold sceptre and touched her neck; [12] then he kissed her and said, 'You may speak to me.' [13] She answered, 'My lord, I saw you like an angel of God; I was awestruck at your glorious appearance. [14] Your countenance is so full of grace, my lord, that I look in wonder.' [15] But while she was speaking she sank down fainting; [16] the king was distressed, and his attendants all tried to reassure her.

5 [3] [THE king said, 'What is your wish, Esther? Whatever you request, up to half my kingdom, shall be given you.' [4] 'This is a festive day for me,' she answered; 'if it please your majesty, will you come, and Haman with you, to a banquet I am preparing today?' [5] The king gave orders for Haman to be brought with all speed to meet Esther's wishes; and they both went to the banquet to which she had invited them. [6] Over the wine the king said to her, 'What is it, Queen Esther? Whatever you request shall be yours.' [7] She said, 'This is my petition and request: [8] if I have found favour with your majesty, will your majesty and Haman come again tomorrow to the banquet that I shall prepare for you both? Tomorrow I shall do as I have done today.'

[9] Although Haman left the royal presence overjoyed and in the best of spirits, as soon as he saw Mardochaeus the Jew in the king's court he was furious. [10] When he arrived home, he sent for his friends and for Zosara, his wife, [11] and held forth to them about his wealth and the honours with which the king had invested him, and how he had advanced him to the chief position in the kingdom. [12] 'The queen', Haman went on, 'had no one but myself come with the king to her banquet; and I am invited tomorrow. [13] Yet all this gives me no satisfaction so long as I see that Jew Mardochaeus at court.' [14] His wife Zosara and his friends said to him: 'Have a gallows set up, seventy-five feet high, and in the morning propose to the king that Mardochaeus be hanged on it. Then you can go with the king to the banquet and enjoy yourself.' This advice seemed good to Haman, and the gallows was made ready.

[5:14] **seventy-five feet:** *lit.* fifty cubits.

6 THAT night the Lord prevented the king from sleeping, so he ordered his secretary to bring the court chronicle and read it to him. ²In it he found recorded an entry concerning Mardochaeus, how he had furnished information for the king about the two royal eunuchs on guard who had plotted to assassinate Artaxerxes. ³When the king asked, 'What honour or favour did we confer on Mardochaeus?' his attendants said, 'You have not done anything for him.' ⁴While the king was enquiring about Mardochaeus's service to him, Haman appeared in the courtyard. 'Who is in the court?' said the king. As Haman had just then entered to propose to the king that Mardochaeus should be hanged on the gallows he had prepared, ⁵the king's servants replied, 'Haman is standing there in the court.' 'Let him enter!' commanded the king. ⁶Then he asked him, 'What shall I do for the man I wish to honour?' Haman thought, 'Whom other than myself would the king wish to honour?' ⁷So he answered, 'For the man whom the king wishes to honour? ⁸Let the king's attendants bring a robe of fine linen which the king himself has worn, and a horse on which the king rides. ⁹Let both be handed over to one of the king's most noble Friends, and let him invest the man whom the king loves and mount him on the horse, and let him proclaim through the city square: "This shall be done for any man whom the king honours."' ¹⁰The king said to Haman, 'Well spoken! Do this for Mardochaeus the Jew who serves in the courtyard. Let nothing be omitted of what you have proposed.' ¹¹Haman took the robe and the horse; he invested Mardochaeus, mounted him on horseback, and went through the city square proclaiming: 'See what is done for any man whom the king wishes to honour.'

¹²Mardochaeus then returned to the courtyard, while Haman hurried off home in grief with his head veiled. ¹³When he told his wife Zosara and his friends what had happened to him, the response he got was: 'If you have begun to be humiliated before Mardochaeus, and he is a Jew, your downfall is certain; you cannot get the better of him, because the living God is on his side.'

¹⁴While they were still talking, the eunuchs arrived and Haman was hurried off to the banquet Esther had prepared.

7 So the king and Haman went to the queen's banquet, ²and on that second day, over the wine, the king said, 'What is it, Queen Esther? What is your petition? What is your request? You shall have it, up to half my kingdom.' ³She answered: 'If I have found favour with your majesty, my petition and request is that my own life and the lives of my people be spared. ⁴For we have been sold, I and my people, to be destroyed, plundered, and enslaved, we and our children, male and female—or so I have heard. Our adversary brings discredit on the king's court.' ⁵The king demanded, 'Who is he that has dared to do such a thing?' ⁶She answered, 'An enemy, this wicked Haman!' Haman stood dumbfounded before the king and queen. ⁷The king rose from the banquet and went into the garden, while Haman began to plead with the queen, for he saw that things looked very black for him. ⁸When the king returned from the garden, Haman in his entreaties had flung himself across the queen's couch. The king exclaimed, 'What! You even assault the queen in my own palace?' At those words Haman turned away in despair. ⁹Bugathan, one of the eunuchs, said to the king, 'There is actually a gallows seventy-five feet high, standing in Haman's grounds; he prepared it for Mardochaeus, the man who reported the plot against your majesty.' 'Let Haman be hanged on it!' said the king. ¹⁰Haman was hanged on the gallows that had been prepared for Mardochaeus, and the king's anger subsided.

8 The same day King Artaxerxes gave Esther all that had belonged to Haman, the adversary of the Jews, and Mardochaeus was summoned to the king's presence, for Esther had revealed his relationship to her. ²The king took off his signet ring, which he had taken back from Haman, and gave it to Mardochaeus. Esther put Mardochaeus in charge of all Haman's property.

³Once again Esther addressed the king, falling at his feet and imploring him to thwart the wickedness of Haman and all he had devised against the Jews. ⁴The king extended his gold sceptre to her, and she rose and stood before the king. ⁵'If it pleases you,' she said, 'and if I have found

favour, let a writ be issued to recall the dispatches sent by Haman in pursuance of his plan to destroy the Jews in your kingdom. *6* For how can I bear to witness the ill-treatment of my people? How can I bear to survive the destruction of my kindred?' *7* The king replied: 'What more do you want? To please you I have given you the whole of Haman's property, and hanged him on the gallows because he threatened the lives of the Jews. *8* Now you may issue a writ in my name, in whatever terms you think fit, and seal it with my signet; no order written at the king's direction and sealed with his signet can be gainsaid.'

9 On the twenty-third day of the first month, Nisan, in the same year, the secretaries were summoned; and the Jews were informed in writing of the instructions given to the administrators and chief governors in the hundred and twenty-seven provinces from India to Ethiopia, to each province in its own language. *10* The writ was drawn up in the king's name and sealed with his signet, and dispatches were sent by courier. *11* By these dispatches permission was granted to the Jews in every city to observe their own laws and to defend themselves, and to deal as they wished with their opponents and enemies, *12* throughout the kingdom of Artaxerxes, in one day, the thirteenth of Adar, the twelfth month.]

16 THE following is a copy of the letter:

From Artaxerxes the Great King to the Governors of the one hundred and twenty-seven provinces from India to Ethiopia, and to our loyal subjects. Greeting.

2 Many who have been repeatedly honoured by the bountiful goodness of their benefactors have grown arrogant, *3* and not only attempt to injure our subjects but, unable to keep their insolence within bounds, even plot mischief against those same benefactors. *4* Not content with destroying gratitude among men, they are so carried away by the presumption of those who are strangers to good breeding that they even suppose they will escape the avenging justice of the all-seeing God. *5* Often, when the king's business has been entrusted to those he counts his

friends, they have, by their plausibility, made those in supreme authority partners in the shedding of innocent blood and involved them in irreparable misfortunes, *6* for their malevolence with its misleading sophistries has imposed upon the sincere goodwill of their rulers. *7* The evil brought about by those who wield power unworthily you can observe, not only in the accounts handed down to us from the past, but also in your familiar experience, *8* and the lesson can be applied to the future. Thus we shall ensure the peace and stability of the realm for the benefit of all; *9* we shall make no changes but shall always decide such matters as come to our notice with firmness and equity.

10 Now Haman son of Hamadathus, a Macedonian, an alien in fact with no Persian blood and not a trace of our kindly nature, was accepted by us *11* and enjoyed so fully the benevolence which we extend to every nation that he was given the title of Father and used to receive obeisance from everyone as second only to our royal throne. *12* But this man in his unbridled arrogance schemed to deprive us of our kingdom and our life; *13* by deceitfulness and tortuous cunning he sought to bring about the destruction of Mardochaeus, our constant benefactor who had saved our life, and of Esther, our blameless consort, together with their whole nation. *14* He thought, by these means, to catch us without support and transfer to the Macedonians the sovereignty now held by the Persians.

15 We find, however, that the Jews whom this double-dyed villain had consigned to extinction are no evildoers; on the contrary, they order their lives by the most just of laws *16* and are children of the living God, the Most High and Most Mighty, who for us as for our ancestors has maintained the kingdom in excellent order. *17* You will, therefore, disregard the letters sent by Haman son of Hamadathus, *18* because he, the contriver of all this, has been hanged at the gate of Susa, he and his whole household, for God who controls all things brought on him speedily the punishment he deserved.

19 Copies of this letter are to be posted

up in all public places. The Jews are to live under their own laws, [20] and be given every assistance so that on the very same day, the thirteenth day of Adar, the twelfth month, they may avenge themselves on their assailants in the time of oppression. [21] God, who has all things in his power, has made that a day of joy, not of ruin, for his chosen people.

[22] Therefore you also must keep it with all good cheer, as a notable day among your feasts of commemoration, [23] so that henceforth it may be a standing symbol of deliverance to us and our loyal Persians, but a reminder of destruction to those who plot against us. [24] Any city or country whatsoever which does not act upon these orders will incur our wrath and be destroyed with fire and sword. Not only will no man set foot in it, but it will also be shunned by beast and bird for all time.

8 [13] [Let copies be posted up prominently throughout the kingdom, so that all the Jews may be prepared for that day, to fight against their enemies.

[14] MOUNTED couriers set out post-haste to do what the king commanded; and the decree was published also in Susa.

[15] When Mardochaeus went out in a royal robe, wearing a gold crown and a turban of fine linen dyed purple, the people in Susa rejoiced to see him. [16] For the Jews all was light and gladness [17] in every city and province, wherever the decree was posted up; there was joy and gladness for them, feasting and merrymaking. And many of the Gentiles were circumcised and professed Judaism, because of fear of the Jews.

9 ON the thirteenth day of Adar, the twelfth month, the decree drawn up by the king arrived. That same day the enemies of the Jews perished, [2] for in their fear none offered resistance. [3] The leading provincial governors, the princes, and the royal secretaries paid honour to the Jews out of fear of Mardochaeus, [4] for they had received the king's decree that his name should be honoured throughout the kingdom. [5] In the capital itself the Jews slaughtered five hundred men, [7] in-

cluding Pharsanestan, Delphon, Phasga, [8] Pharadatha, Barsa, Sarbach, [9] Marmasima, Ruphaeus, Arsaeus, and Zabuthaeus, [10] the ten sons of Haman son of Hamadathus, the Bugaean and enemy of the Jews; and they took plunder.

[11] When the number of those killed in Susa was reported to the king that day, [12] he said to Esther, 'In the city of Susa the Jews have killed five hundred men; what do you suppose they have done in the surrounding country? Whatever further request you have, it shall be granted.' [13] Esther replied, 'Let the Jews be permitted to do the same tomorrow, and hang up the bodies of Haman's ten sons.' [14] He allowed this to be done, and he handed over the bodies of Haman's ten sons to the Jews of the city to be hung up. [15] The Jews in Susa assembled on the fourteenth day of Adar also, and killed three hundred men, but they took no plunder.

[16] The rest of the Jews throughout the kingdom rallied in self-defence, and so had respite from their enemies, for they slaughtered fifteen thousand on the thirteenth of Adar, but they took no plunder. [17] On the fourteenth of the month they rested, and made it a day of rest, with rejoicing and merrymaking. [18] The Jews in the city of Susa had assembled also on the fourteenth day; they did not rest on that day, but they kept the fifteenth with rejoicing and merrymaking. [19] That is why Jews who are dispersed over the remoter parts observe the fourteenth of Adar as a holiday with merrymaking, sending presents of food to one another; but those who live in the principal cities keep the fifteenth of Adar as a holiday, for merrymaking and sending presents of food to one another.

The festival of Purim founded
[20] MARDOCHAEUS put these things on record in a book and sent it to the Jews in Artaxerxes' kingdom, both near and far, [21] requiring them to establish these holidays, and to observe the fourteenth and fifteenth of Adar, [22] because these were the days on which the Jews had respite from their enemies; and they were to observe the whole month of Adar, in which came the change from sorrow to joy and from a time of mourning to

[9:4] **the kingdom:** *some witnesses add from the Heb.* [5] The Jews put their enemies to the sword. There was great slaughter and destruction, and they worked their will on those who hated them.

holiday, as days for weddings and merry-making, days for sending presents of food to friends and to the poor. ²³ The Jews welcomed the account which Mardochaeus wrote: ²⁴ how Haman son of Hamadathus, the Macedonian, fought against them, how he made a decree and cast lots with intent to destroy them, ²⁵ how he came before the king with a proposal to hang Mardochaeus, how all the evils which he had plotted against the Jews recoiled upon him, and how he and his sons were hanged. ²⁶ This is why these days were named Purim, because in the Jews' language it means 'Lots'. Because of all that was written in this letter, because of all that they had experienced, and all that had happened and been done, ²⁷ the Jews gladly undertook, on behalf of themselves, their descendants, and those who should join them, to observe these days without fail; ²⁸ they were to be days of commemoration, duly celebrated generation after generation in every city, family, and province; further, these days of Purim were to be observed for all time, and the commemoration was never to cease throughout all ages.

²⁹ Queen Esther daughter of Aminadab, and Mardochaeus the Jew, recorded in writing all that they had done, and confirmed the letter about Purim; ^{30–31} they had made themselves responsible for this decision and staked their life upon the plan. ³² Esther established it for all time by her decree, and it was put on record.

10 The king made decrees for his kingdom over land and sea. ² His strength and courage, his wealth and the splendour of his kingdom, are recorded in the book of the kings of the Persians and Medes. ³ Mardochaeus was viceroy for King Artaxerxes; he was a great man in the kingdom and honoured by the Jews. His way of life won him the affection of his whole nation.]

10 ⁴ MARDOCHAEUS said, 'This is God's doing, ⁵ for I have been reminded of the dream I had about these matters; every one of the visions I saw has been fulfilled. ⁶ There was the little spring which became a river, and there was light and sun and abundant water: the river is Esther, whom the king married and made queen; ⁷ the two dragons are Haman and myself; ⁸ the nations are those who combined to blot out all memory of the Jews; ⁹ my nation is Israel, which cried out to God and was delivered. The Lord has delivered his people, he has rescued us from all these evils. God performed great signs and portents, such as have never occurred among the nations. ¹⁰ He prepared two lots, one for the people of God and one for all the nations; ¹¹ then came the hour and the time for these two lots to be cast, the judgement by God upon all the nations; ¹² he remembered his people and gave the verdict for his heritage.

¹³ 'So they are to keep these days in the month of Adar, the fourteenth and fifteenth of that month, by assembling with joy and gladness before God from one generation of his people Israel to another for ever.'

11 ¹ IN the fourth year of the reign of Ptolemy and Cleopatra, Dositheus, who declared he was a levitical priest, and Ptolemaeus his son, brought the foregoing letter about Purim; according to their declaration it was authentic and had been translated by Lysimachus son of Ptolemaeus, a resident in Jerusalem.

[9:27] observe ... days: *prob. rdg; cp. Heb.*

THE
WISDOM
OF SOLOMON

Wisdom and human destiny

1 Love justice, you rulers of the earth; set your mind upon the Lord in the right way, and seek him in singleness of heart; ² for he is to be found by those who trust him without question, and he makes himself known to those who never doubt him. ³ Dishonest thinking cuts people off from God, and if fools take liberties with his power he shows them up for what they are. ⁴ Wisdom will not enter a shifty soul, nor make her home in a body that is mortgaged to sin. ⁵ This holy spirit of discipline will shun falsehood; she cannot stay in the presence of unreason, and will withdraw at the approach of injustice.

⁶ The spirit of wisdom is kindly towards mortals, but she will not hold a blasphemer blameless for his words, because God, who sees clearly into his heart and hears every word he speaks, is a witness of his inmost being. ⁷ For the spirit of the Lord fills the whole earth, and that which holds all things together knows well everything that is said. ⁸ Hence no one can utter injustice and not be found out, nor will justice overlook him when she passes sentence. ⁹ The devices of a godless person will be brought to account, and a report of his words will come before the Lord as proof of his iniquity; ¹⁰ no muttered syllable escapes that vigilant ear. ¹¹ Beware, then, of futile grumbling, and avoid all bitter talk; for even a secret whisper will not go unheeded, and a lying tongue brings destruction on its owner.

¹² Do not court death by a crooked life; do not draw disaster on yourselves by your own actions. ¹³ For God did not make death, and takes no pleasure in the destruction of any living thing; ¹⁴ he created all things that they might have being. The creative forces of the world make for life; there is no deadly poison in them. Death has no sovereignty on earth, ¹⁵ for justice is immortal; ¹⁶ but the godless by their deeds and words have asked death for his company. Thinking him their friend and

pining for him, they have made a pact with him because they are fit members of his party.

2 They said to themselves in their deluded way: 'Our life is short and full of trouble, and when a person comes to the end there is no remedy; no one has been known to return from the grave. ² By mere chance were we born, and afterwards we shall be as though we had never existed, for the breath in our nostrils is but a wisp of smoke; our reason is a mere spark kept alive by the beating of our hearts, ³ and when that goes out, our body will turn to ashes and the breath of our life disperse like empty air. ⁴ With the passing of time our names will be forgotten, and no one will remember anything we did. Our life will vanish like the last vestige of a cloud; and as a mist is chased away by the sun's rays and overborne by its heat, so too will life be dispersed. ⁵ A fleeting shadow—such is our life, and there is no postponement of our end. Man's fate is sealed: no one returns.

⁶ 'Come then, let us enjoy the good things while we can and, with all the eagerness of youth, make full use of the creation. ⁷ Let us have costly wines and perfumes to our heart's content, and let no flower of spring escape us. ⁸ Let us crown ourselves with rosebuds before they wither. ⁹ Let none of us fail to share in the good things that are ours; let us leave behind on every side traces of our revelry. This is the life for us, this our birthright.

¹⁰ 'Down with the poor and honest man! Let us show no mercy to the widow, no reverence to the grey hairs of old age. ¹¹ For us let might be right! Weakness is proved to be good for nothing. ¹² Let us set a trap for the just man; he stands in our way, a check to us at every turn; he girds at us as breakers of the law, and calls us traitors to our upbringing. ¹³ He knows God, so he says; he styles himself "child of the Lord". ¹⁴ He is a living condemnation

2:13 **child**: *or* servant.

76

of all our way of thinking. [15] The very sight of him is an affliction to us, because his life is not like other people's, and the paths he follows are quite different. [16] He rejects us like base coin, and avoids us and our ways as if we were filth; he says that the just die happy, and boasts that God is his father. [17] Let us test the truth of his claim, let us see what will happen to him in the end; [18] for if the just man is God's son, God will stretch out a hand to him and save him from the clutches of his enemies. [19] Insult and torture are the means to put him to the test, to measure his forbearance and learn how long his patience lasts. [20] Let us condemn him to a shameful death, for, if what he says is true, he will have a protector.'

[21] So they argued, and how wrong they were! Blinded by their own malevolence, [22] they failed to understand God's hidden plan; they never expected that holiness of life would have its recompense, never thought that innocence would have its reward. [23] But God created man imperishable, and made him the image of his own eternal self; [24] it was the devil's spite that brought death into the world, and the experience of it is reserved for those who take his side.

3 But the souls of the just are in God's hand; no torment will touch them. [2] In the eyes of the foolish they seemed to be dead; their departure was reckoned as defeat, [3] and their going from us as disaster. But they are at peace, [4] for though in the sight of men they may suffer punishment, they have a sure hope of immortality; [5] and after a little chastisement they will receive great blessings, because God has tested them and found them worthy to be his. [6] He put them to the proof like gold in a crucible, and found them acceptable like an offering burnt whole on the altar. [7] In the hour of their judgement they will shine in glory, and will sweep over the world like sparks through stubble. [8] They will be judges and rulers over nations and peoples, and the Lord will be their King for ever. [9] Those who have put their trust in him will understand that he is true, and the faithful will attend upon him in love; they are his chosen, and grace and mercy will be theirs.

[10] But the godless will meet with the punishment their evil thoughts deserve, because they took no heed of justice and rebelled against the Lord. [11] Wretched indeed is he who thinks nothing of wisdom and discipline; the hopes of such people are void, their labours unprofitable, their actions futile; [12] their wives are wanton, their children depraved, [13] their parenthood is under a curse. But blessed is the childless woman if she is innocent, if she has never slept with a man in sin; at the great assize of souls she will find a fruitfulness of her own. [14] Blessed also is the eunuch, if he has never done anything against the law and never harboured a wicked thought against the Lord; in return for his faith he will receive special favour, and a place in the Lord's temple to delight his heart the more. [15] Honest work bears glorious fruit, and wisdom grows from roots that are imperishable. [16] But the children of adultery are like fruit that never ripens; they have sprung from a union forbidden by the law and will come to nothing. [17] Even if they attain length of life, they will be held of no account, and at the end their old age will be without honour. [18] If they die young, they will have no hope, no consolation in the day of judgement; [19] the unjust generation has a harsh fate in store.

4 It is better to be childless, provided one is virtuous; for virtue held in remembrance is a kind of immortality, because it wins recognition from God, and also from mankind; [2] they follow the good person's example while it is with them, and when it is gone they mourn its loss. Through all time virtue makes its triumphal progress, crowned with victory in the contest for prizes that nothing can tarnish. [3] But the swarming progeny of the godless will come to no good; none of their bastard offshoots will strike deep root or take firm hold. [4] For a time their branches may flourish, but as they have no sure footing they will be shaken by the wind, and uprooted by the violence of the gales. [5] Their boughs will be snapped off half grown, and their fruit will be worthless, unripe, uneatable, and fit for nothing. [6] Children engendered in unlawful union are living evidence of their parents' sin when God brings them to account.

[7] But the just person, even one who dies an untimely death, will be at rest. [8] It is not length of life and number of years which bring the honour due to age; [9] if people have understanding, they have

grey hairs enough, and an unblemished life is the true ripeness of age. ¹⁰ There was once such a man who pleased God, and God accepted him and took him while still living from among sinners. ¹¹ He was snatched away before his mind could be perverted by wickedness or his soul deceived by falsehood ¹² (because evil is like witchcraft: it dims the radiance of good, and the waywardness of desire unsettles an innocent mind); ¹³ in a short time he came to the perfection of a full span of years. ¹⁴ His soul was pleasing to the Lord, who removed him early from a wicked world. ¹⁵ People see this but give it no thought; they do not lay to heart the truth, that those whom God has chosen enjoy his grace and mercy, and that he comes to the help of his holy people.

¹⁶ Even after his death the just person will shame the godless who are still alive; youth come quickly to perfection will shame the person who has grown old in sin. ¹⁷ The godless will see the end of the wise person, without understanding what the Lord had purposed for him and why he took him into safe keeping; ¹⁸ they will see it and make light of him, but it is they whom the Lord will laugh to scorn. In death their bodies will be dishonoured, and among the dead they will be an object of lasting contempt; ¹⁹ for he will fling them speechless to the ground, shake them from their foundations, and leave them barren as a desert; they will be in anguish, and all memory of them will perish. ²⁰ So, on the day of reckoning for their sins, they will come cringing, convicted to their face by their own lawless actions.

5 Then the just man will take his stand, full of assurance, to confront those who oppressed him and made light of his sufferings; ² at the sight of him there will be terror and confusion, and they will be astounded at his unforeseen deliverance. ³ Remorseful, groaning and gasping for breath, they will say among themselves: 'Was not this the man who was once our butt, a target for our contempt? ⁴ Fools that we were, we held his way of life to be madness and his end dishonourable. ⁵ To think he is now counted one of the sons of God and assigned a place of his own among God's people! ⁶ How far we strayed from the way of truth! The lamp of justice never gave us light, the sun never

rose on us. ⁷ We roamed to our heart's content along the paths of wickedness and ruin, wandering through trackless deserts and ignoring the Lord's highway. ⁸ What good has pride been to us? What can we show for all our vaunted wealth? ⁹ All those things have passed like a shadow, like a messenger galloping by; ¹⁰ like a ship that cleaves the surging sea and, when she has passed, not a trace is to be found, no wake from her keel in the waves; ¹¹ or as when a bird flies through the air, there is no sign of her passage, but with the stroke of her pinions she lashes the insubstantial breeze and parts it with the whirr and the rush of her beating wings, and so she passes through it, and thereafter it bears no mark of her assault; ¹² or as when a shaft is shot at a target, the air is parted and instantly closes up again and no one can tell where the arrow passed. ¹³ So too with us, as soon as we were born we ceased to be; we had no token of virtue to show, and in our wickedness we frittered our lives away.' ¹⁴ The hope of the godless is like down flying on the wind, like spindrift swept before a storm, like smoke which the wind whirls away, transient like the memory of a guest who stayed but one day.

¹⁵ But the just live for ever; their reward is in the Lord's keeping, and the Most High has them in his care. ¹⁶ Therefore royal splendour will be theirs, and a fair diadem from the Lord himself; he will protect them with his right hand and shield them with his arm. ¹⁷ He will array himself from head to foot with the armour of his wrath, and make all creation his weapon against his enemies. ¹⁸ With the cuirass of justice on his breast, and on his head the helmet of inflexible judgement, ¹⁹ he will take holiness for his invincible shield ²⁰ and sharpen his relentless anger for a sword; and his whole world will join him in the fight against his frenzied foes. ²¹ The bolts of his lightning will fly straight upon the mark, they will leap upon the target as if his bow in the clouds were drawn in its full arc, ²² and the artillery of his resentment will let fly a fury of hail. The waters of the sea will rage over them, and the rivers wash them relentlessly away; ²³ a great tempest will arise against them, and scatter them like chaff before a whirlwind. So lawlessness will make the whole world desolate, and

evildoing will overturn the thrones of princes.

In praise of wisdom

6 HEAR then, you kings, take this to heart; lords of the wide world, learn this lesson; [2] give ear, you rulers of the multitude, who take pride in the myriads of your people. [3] Your authority was bestowed on you by the Lord, your power comes from the Most High. He will probe your actions and scrutinize your intentions. [4] Though you are servants appointed by the King, you have not been upright judges; you have not maintained the law or guided your steps by the will of God. [5] Swiftly and terribly he will descend on you, for judgement falls relentlessly on those in high places. [6] The lowest may find pity and forgiveness, but those in power will be called powerfully to account; [7] for he who is Master of all is obsequious to none, and shows no deference to greatness. Small and great alike are of his making, and all are under his providence equally; [8] but it is for those who wield authority that he reserves the sternest inquisition. [9] To you, then, who have absolute power I speak, in hope that you may learn wisdom and not go astray; [10] those who in holiness have kept a holy course will be accounted holy, and those who have learnt that lesson will be able to make their defence. [11] Therefore be eager to hear me; long for my teaching, and you will learn.

[12] Wisdom shines brightly and never fades; she is readily discerned by those who love her, and by those who seek her she is found. [13] She is quick to make herself known to all who desire knowledge of her; [14] he who rises early in search of her will not grow weary in the quest, for he will find her seated at his door. [15] To meditate on her is prudence in its perfect shape, and to be vigilant in her cause is the short way to freedom from care; [16] she herself searches far and wide for those who are worthy of her, and on their daily path she appears to them with kindly intent, meeting them half-way in all their purposes. [17] The true beginning of wisdom is the desire to learn, and a concern for learning means love towards her; [18] the love of her means the keeping of her laws; to keep her laws is a warrant of immortality; [19] and immortality brings a person near to God. [20] Thus desire for wisdom leads to a kingdom. [21] If, therefore, you value your thrones and your sceptres, you rulers of the nations, you must honour wisdom so that you may reign for ever.

[22] What wisdom is, and how she came into being, I shall tell you; I shall not conceal her mysteries from you. I shall trace out her course from her first beginnings, and bring the knowledge of her into the light of day; I shall not leave the truth untold. [23] Pale envy will not travel in my company, for the spiteful will have no share in wisdom. [24] Wise men in plenty are the world's salvation, and a prudent king is the sheet-anchor of his people. [25] Therefore learn what I have to teach you, and it will be for your good.

7 I too am a mortal like everyone else, descended from the first man, who was made of dust, [2] and in my mother's womb I was wrought into flesh during a ten-month space, compacted in blood from the seed of her husband and the pleasure that accompanies sleep. [3] When I was born, I breathed the common air and was laid on the earth that all mortals tread; and the first sound I uttered, as all do, was a cry; [4] they wrapped me up and nursed me and cared for me. [5] No king begins life in any other way; [6] for all come into life by a single path, and by a single path they go out again.

[7] Therefore I prayed, and prudence was given me; I called for help, and there came to me a spirit of wisdom. [8] I valued her above sceptre and throne, and reckoned riches as nothing beside her; [9] I counted no precious stone her equal, because compared with her all the gold in the world is but a handful of sand, and silver worth no more than clay. [10] I loved her more than health and beauty; I preferred her to the light of day, for her radiance is unsleeping. [11] So all good things together came to me with her, and in her hands was wealth past counting. [12] Everything was mine to enjoy, for all follow where wisdom leads; yet I was in ignorance that she is the source of them all. [13] What I learnt with pure intention I now share ungrudgingly, nor do I hoard for myself the wealth that comes from her. [14] She is an inexhaustible treasure for mortals, and those who profit by it become God's friends, commended to him by the gifts they derive from her instruction.

15 God grant that I may speak according to his will, and that my own thoughts may be worthy of his gifts, for even wisdom is under God's direction and he corrects the wise; 16 we and our words, prudence and knowledge and craftsmanship, all are in his hand. 17 He it was who gave me true understanding of things as they are: a knowledge of the structure of the world and the operation of the elements; 18 the beginning and end of epochs and their middle course; the alternating solstices and changing seasons; 19 the cycles of the years and the constellations; 20 the nature of living creatures and behaviour of wild beasts; the violent force of winds and human thought; the varieties of plants and the virtues of roots. 21 I learnt it all, hidden or manifest, 22 for I was taught by wisdom, by her whose skill made all things.

In wisdom there is a spirit intelligent and holy, unique in its kind yet made up of many parts, subtle, free-moving, lucid, spotless, clear, neither harmed nor harming, loving what is good, eager, unhampered, beneficent, 23 kindly towards mortals, steadfast, unerring, untouched by care, all-powerful, all-surveying, and permeating every intelligent, pure, and most subtle spirit. 24 For wisdom moves more easily than motion itself; she is so pure she pervades and permeates all things. 25 Like a fine mist she rises from the power of God, a clear effluence from the glory of the Almighty; so nothing defiled can enter into her by stealth. 26 She is the radiance that streams from everlasting light, the flawless mirror of the active power of God, and the image of his goodness. 27 She is but one, yet can do all things; herself unchanging, she makes all things new; age after age she enters into holy souls, and makes them friends of God and prophets, 28 for nothing is acceptable to God but the person who makes his home with wisdom. 29 She is more beautiful than the sun, and surpasses every constellation. Compared with the light of day, she is found to excel, 30 for day gives place to night,

8 but against wisdom no evil can prevail. 1 She spans the world in power from end to end, and gently orders all things.

Solomon and wisdom

2 WISDOM I loved; I sought her out when I was young and longed to win her for my bride; I was in love with her beauty. 3 She adds lustre to her noble birth, because it is given her to live with God; the Lord of all things has accepted her. 4 She is initiated into the knowledge that belongs to God, and she chooses what his works are to be. 5 If riches are a possession to be desired in life, what is richer than wisdom, the active cause of all things? 6 If prudence shows itself in action, who more than wisdom is the artificer of all that is? 7 If someone loves uprightness, the fruits of wisdom's labours are the virtues; temperance and prudence, justice and fortitude, these are her teaching, and life can offer nothing of more value than these. 8 If someone longs, perhaps, for great experience, she knows the past, she can infer what is yet to come; she understands the subtleties of argument and the solving of hard questions; she can read signs and portents and foretell what the different times and seasons will bring about.

9 So I determined to take her home to live with me, knowing that she would be my counsellor in prosperity and my comfort in anxiety and grief. 10 Through her, I thought, I shall win fame in the eyes of the people and honour among older men, young though I am. 11 When I sit in judgement, I shall prove myself acute, and the great will admire me; 12 when I say nothing, they will wait for me to speak; when I speak, they will attend and, though I talk at some length, they will lay a finger to their lips and listen. 13 Through her I shall have immortality and leave an undying memory to those who come after me. 14 I shall govern peoples, and nations will become subject to me. 15 Tyrants, however dread, will be afraid when they hear of me; among my own people I shall show myself a good king, and on the battlefield a brave one. 16 When I come home, I shall find rest with her; for there is no bitterness in her company, no pain in life with her, only gladness and joy.

17 I turned this over in my mind, and I perceived that there is immortality in kinship with wisdom, 18 and in her friendship there is pure delight; that in doing her work is wealth inexhaustible, to

---

7:26 the radiance ... from: *or* the reflection of.

be taught in her school gives understanding, and an honourable name is won by converse with her. So I went about in search of some way to win her for my own. ¹⁹As a child I was born to excellence, and a noble soul fell to my lot; ²⁰ or rather, I myself was noble, and I entered into an undefiled body; ²¹ but I saw that there was no way to gain possession of her except by gift of God—and it was itself a mark of understanding to know from whom that gift must come. So I pleaded with the Lord, and from the depths of my

9 heart I prayed to him in these words: ¹ God of our forefathers, merciful Lord, who made all things by your word, ² and in your wisdom fashioned man to have sovereignty over your whole creation, ³ and to be steward of the world in holiness and righteousness, and to administer justice with an upright heart: ⁴ give me wisdom, who sits beside your throne, and do not refuse me a place among your servants. ⁵ I am your slave, your slave-girl's son, weak and with but a short time to live, too feeble to understand justice and law; ⁶ for let someone be never so perfect in the eyes of his fellows, if the wisdom that comes from you is wanting, he will be of no account. ⁷ You chose me to be king of your own people and judge of your sons and daughters; ⁸ you told me to build a temple on your sacred mountain and an altar in the city which is your dwelling-place, a copy of the sacred tabernacle prepared by you from the beginning. ⁹ With you is wisdom, who is familiar with your works and was present when you created the universe, who is aware of what is acceptable to you and in keeping with your commandments. ¹⁰ Send her forth from your holy heaven, and from your glorious throne bid her come down, so that she may labour at my side and I may learn what is pleasing to you. ¹¹ She knows and understands all things; she will guide me prudently in whatever I do, and guard me with her glory. ¹² So my life's work will be acceptable, and I shall judge your people justly, and be worthy of my father's throne.

¹³ How can any human being learn what is God's plan? Who can apprehend what is the will of the Lord? ¹⁴ The reasoning of mortals is uncertain, and our plans are fallible, ¹⁵ because a perishable

body weighs down the soul, and its frame of clay burdens the mind already so full of care. ¹⁶ With difficulty we guess even at things on earth, and laboriously find out what lies within our reach; but who has ever traced out what is in heaven? ¹⁷ Who ever came to know your purposes, unless you had given him wisdom and sent your holy spirit from heaven on high? ¹⁸ Thus it was that those on earth were set on the right path, and mortals were taught what pleases you; thus were they kept safe by wisdom.

Wisdom in Israel's history

10 WISDOM it was who kept guard over the first father of the human race, created alone as he was; after he had sinned she saved him ² and gave him the strength to rule over all things. ³ It was because a wicked man forsook her in his anger that he murdered his brother in a fit of rage, and so destroyed himself. ⁴ Through his fault the earth was overwhelmed by a flood, and again wisdom came to the rescue, teaching the one good man to pilot his plain wooden hulk. ⁵ When heathen nations leagued in wickedness were thrown into confusion, she it was who recognized one good man and kept him blameless in God's sight, giving him strength to resist his pity for his child. ⁶ She saved a good man when the godless were being destroyed, and he escaped the fire that rained down on the Five Cities, ⁷ cities whose wickedness is still attested by a smoking waste, by plants whose fruit can never ripen, and by a pillar of salt standing there as a memorial of a disbelieving soul. ⁸ They ignored wisdom and suffered for it, losing the power to recognize what is good and leaving for mankind a monument to their folly, such that their enormities can never be forgotten. ⁹ But wisdom brought her servants safely out of their troubles. ¹⁰ When a good man was a fugitive from his brother's anger, she it was who guided him on straight paths; she gave him a vision of God's kingdom and a knowledge of holy things; she prospered his labours and made his toil fruitful. ¹¹ When others in their rapacity sought to exploit him, she stood by him and made him rich. ¹² She kept him safe from his enemies, and preserved him from treacherous attacks; after his hard struggle she gave him victory, and taught him that godliness is the mightiest power of all. [13] It was she who refused to desert a good man when he was sold into slavery; she preserved him from sin and went down into the dungeon with him, [14] nor did she leave him when he was in chains until she had brought him a kingdom's sceptre with authority over his persecutors; she gave the lie to his accusers, and bestowed on him undying fame.

[15] It was wisdom who rescued a god-fearing people, a blameless race, from a nation of oppressors; [16] she inspired a servant of the Lord, and with his signs and wonders he defied formidable kings. [17] She rewarded the labours of a godfearing people, she guided them on a miraculous journey, and became a covering for them by day and a blaze of stars by night. [18] She brought them over the Red Sea, leading them through its deep waters; [19] but their enemies she engulfed, and cast them up again out of the fathomless deep. [20] So the good despoiled the ungodly; they sang the glories of your holy name, O Lord, and with one accord praised your power, their champion; [21] for wisdom enabled the dumb to speak, and made the tongues of infants eloquent.

11 Wisdom, working through a holy prophet, gave them success in all they did. [2] They made their way across an unpeopled desert and pitched camp in untrodden wastes; [3] they stood firm against their enemies, and fought off hostile assaults. [4] When they were thirsty they cried to you, and water to slake their thirst was given them out of the hard stone of a rocky cliff. [5] The selfsame means by which their oppressors had been punished were used to help them in their hour of need: [6] those others found their river no unfailing stream of water, but putrid and befouled with blood, [7] a punishment for their order that all the infants should be killed; to these, however, when they had lost hope, you gave abundant water. [8] So, from the thirst they then endured, they learnt how you had punished their enemies; [9] when they themselves were put to the test, though chastisement was tempered with mercy, they understood the tortures of the godless who were sentenced in anger. [10] Your own people you subjected to an ordeal, disciplining them like a father, but those others you put

to the torture like a stern king passing sentence. [11] Whether at home or abroad, they were equally in distress, [12] for double misery had come upon them, and they groaned as they recalled the past. [13] When they heard that the means of their own punishment had been used to benefit your people, they saw your hand in it, Lord. [14] The man who long ago had been abandoned and exposed, whom they had rejected with contumely, became in the event the object of their wonder and admiration; their thirst was such as the godly never knew.

[15] In return for the foolish imagination of those wicked people, which deluded them into worshipping reptiles incapable of reason, and mere vermin, you sent upon them in your vengeance mindless swarms [16] to teach them that the instruments of someone's sin are the instruments of his punishment. [17] For your almighty hand, which created the world out of formless matter, was not without other resource: it could have let loose on those wicked people a horde of bears or ravening lions [18] or unknown ferocious monsters newly created, breathing out blasts of fire, or roaring and belching smoke, or flashing terrible sparks like lightning from their eyes, [19] beasts with power not only to exterminate them by the wounds they inflicted, but by their mere appearance to kill them with fright. [20] Even without these, a single breath would have sufficed to lay them low, with justice in pursuit and the breath of your power to blow them away; but you have set all things in order by measure and number and weight.

[21] Great strength is yours to exert at any moment, and the power of your arm no one can resist, [22] for in your sight the whole world is like a grain that just tips the scale or like a drop of dew alighting on the ground at dawn. [23] But you are merciful to all because you can do all things; you overlook people's sins in order to bring them to repentance; [24] for all existing things are dear to you and you hate nothing that you have created—why else would you have made it? [25] How could anything have continued in existence, had it not been your will? How could it have endured unless called into being by you? [26] You spare all things because they are yours, O Lord, who love all that lives;

12 ¹ for your imperishable breath is in every one of them. ² For this reason you correct offenders little by little, disciplining them and reminding them of their sins, in order that they may abandon their evil ways and put their trust in you, Lord. ³ There were the ancient inhabitants of your holy land: ⁴ you hated them for their loathsome practices, their sorcery and unholy rites, ⁵ their pitiless killing of children, their cannibal feasts of human flesh and blood; ⁶ they were initiates of a secret ritual in which parents slaughtered their defenceless children. Therefore it was your will to destroy them at the hands of our forefathers, ⁷ so that the land which is of all lands most precious in your eyes might receive in God's children settlers worthy of it. ⁸ And yet you spared them because they too were human beings, and you sent hornets as the advance guard of your army to exterminate them by stages. ⁹ It was well within your power to have the godly overwhelm the godless in a pitched battle, or to wipe them out in an instant by fearsome beasts or with one relentless word. ¹⁰ But instead you carried out the sentence by stages to give them room for repentance, knowing well enough that they came of evil stock, that their wickedness was innate, and that their way of thinking would not change to the end of time, ¹¹ for there was a curse on their race from the beginning.

Nor was it out of deference to anyone else that you gave them an amnesty for their misdeeds, ¹² for no one can say 'What have you done?' Who can challenge your verdict? Who can bring a charge against you for destroying nations which were of your own making? Who can appear against you in court to plead the cause of the guilty? ¹³ For there is no other god but you; all the world is your concern, and there is none to whom you must prove the justice of your sentence. ¹⁴ There is no king or other ruler who can outface you on behalf of those whom you have punished. ¹⁵ But you are just and you order all things justly, counting it alien to your power to condemn anyone to undeserved punishment. ¹⁶ For your strength is the source of justice, and it is because you are Master of all that you are lenient to all. ¹⁷ You show your strength when people doubt whether your power is absolute; it is when they know it and yet are insolent that you punish them. ¹⁸ But you, with strength at your command, judge in mercy and rule us in great forbearance; for the power is yours to exercise whenever you choose.

¹⁹ By acts like these you taught your people that he who is just must also be kind-hearted, and you have filled your children with hope by the offer of repentance for their sins. ²⁰ If you used such care and such indulgence even in punishing your children's enemies who deserved to die, granting them time and opportunity to win free of their wickedness, ²¹ with what discrimination you passed judgement on your people, to whose forefathers you gave sworn covenants full of the promise of good! ²² So we are chastened by you, but you scourge our enemies ten thousand times more, so that we may lay your goodness to heart when we sit in judgement, and may hope for mercy when we ourselves are judged. ²³ This is why the wicked who had lived their lives in heedless folly were tormented by you with their own abominations. ²⁴ They had strayed far down the paths of error, taking for gods the most despised and hideous creatures; they were deluded like thoughtless infants. ²⁵ And so, as though they were children who had not learnt reason, you imposed on them a sentence that made them ridiculous; ²⁶ but those who are not disciplined by such derisive correction will experience the full weight of divine judgement. ²⁷ They were indignant at their own sufferings, but, finding themselves chastised through the very creatures they had deemed to be gods, they recognized that the true God was he whom they had formerly refused to know. For this reason the full rigour of condemnation overtook them.

Indictment of idolatry

13 WHAT born fools were all who lived in ignorance of God! From the good things before their eyes they could not learn to know him who is, and failed to recognize the artificer though they observed his handiwork! ² Fire, wind, swift air, the circle of the starry signs, rushing water, or the great lights in heaven that rule the world—these they accounted gods. ³ If it was through delight in the beauty of these things that people supposed them gods, they ought to have understood how much better is the Lord and Master of them all; for it was by the prime author of all beauty they were created. [4] If it was through astonishment at their power and influence, people should have learnt from these how much more powerful is he who made them. [5] For the greatness and beauty of created things give us a corresponding idea of their Creator. [6] Yet these people are not greatly to be blamed, for when they go astray they may be seeking God and really wishing to find him. [7] Passing their lives among his works and making a close study of them, they are persuaded by appearances because of the beauty of what they see. [8] Yet even so they do not deserve to be excused, [9] for with enough understanding to speculate about the universe, why did they not sooner discover its Lord and Master?

[10] The really degraded ones are those whose hopes are set on lifeless things, who give the title of gods to the work of human hands, to gold and silver fashioned by art into images of living creatures, or to a useless stone carved by a craftsman long ago. [11] Suppose some skilled worker in wood fells with his saw a convenient tree and deftly strips off all the bark, then works it up elegantly into some household vessel suitable for everyday use; [12] and the bits left over from his work he uses to cook his food, and then eats his fill. [13] But among what is left over there is one useless piece, crooked and full of knots, and this he takes and carves to occupy his idle moments. He shapes it with leisurely skill into the image of a human being, [14] or else he gives it the form of some worthless creature, smearing it over with vermilion and raddling its surface with red paint, so that every flaw in it is daubed over. [15] Then he makes a suitable shrine for it and fixes it on the wall, securing it with nails. [16] It is he who has to take the precautions on its behalf to save it from falling, for he well knows that it cannot fend for itself: it needs help, for it is only an image. [17] Yet he prays to it about his possessions and his wife and children, and feels no shame in addressing this inanimate object; [18] for health he

appeals to a thing that is weak, for life he prays to a thing that is dead, for aid he asks help from something utterly incapable, for a prosperous journey from something that cannot put one foot before the other; [19] where earnings or business or success in handicraft are in question he asks effectual help from a thing whose hands are entirely ineffectual.

14 Again, the man who gets ready for a voyage and plans to set his course through the wild waves invokes a piece of wood more fragile than the ship which is to carry him. [2] Desire for gain invented the ship, and the shipwright with his skill built it; [3] but your providence, Father, is the pilot, for you have given it a pathway through the sea and a safe course among the waves, [4] showing that you can save from every danger, so that even the inexpert can put to sea. [5] It is your will that the things made by your wisdom should not lie unused; and therefore people entrust their lives even to the frailest spar, and passing through the billows on a mere raft come safe to land. [6] So in the beginning, when the proud race of giants was being brought to an end, the hope of mankind escaped on a raft and, piloted by your hand, bequeathed to the world a new breed of people. [7] While a blessing is on the wood through which right prevails, [8] the wooden idol made by human hands is accursed, and so is its maker—he because he made it, and the perishable thing because it was called a god. [9] Equally hateful to God are the godless and their ungodliness; [10] the doer and the deed will both be punished. [11] Therefore retribution will fall on the idols of the heathen, because although part of God's creation they have been made into an abomination, to make people stumble and to catch the feet of the foolish. [12] The devising of idols is the beginning of immorality; they are an invention which has blighted human life. [13] They did not exist from the beginning, nor will they be with us for ever; [14] superstition brought them into the world, and for good reason a speedy end is in store for them.

[15] Some father, overwhelmed with untimely grief for the child suddenly taken from him, made an image of his child and

---

14:2 **and the shipwright … built it:** *other witnesses read* and wisdom was the shipwright who built it.

honoured thenceforth as a god what was once a dead human being, handing on to his household the observance of rites and ceremonies. [16] Then this impious custom, established by the passage of time, was observed as law. Or again, graven images came to be worshipped at the command of despotic princes. [17] When people could not do honour to such a prince before his face because he lived too far away, they made a likeness of that distant face, and produced a visible image of the king they sought to honour, in order that by their zeal they might gratify the absent prince as though he were present. [18] Then the cult grows in fervour as those to whom the king is unknown are spurred on by ambitious craftsmen. [19] In his desire, it may be, to please the monarch, a craftsman skilfully distorts the likeness into an ideal form, [20] and the common people, beguiled by the beauty of the workmanship, take for an object of worship him whom lately they honoured as a man. [21] So this becomes a snare in the life of a people: enslaved by mischance or misgovernment, they confer on stocks and stones the name that none may share.

[22] Then, not content with crass error in their knowledge of God, people live in the constant warfare of ignorance and call this monstrous evil peace. [23] They perform ritual killing of children and secret ceremonies and the frenzied orgies of unnatural cults; [24] the purity of life and marriage is abandoned; and a man treacherously murders a neighbour or by corrupting his wife breaks his heart. [25] All is chaos—bloody murder, theft and fraud, corruption, treachery, riot, perjury, [26] honest folk driven to distraction; ingratitude, depravity, sexual perversion, breakdown of marriage, adultery, debauchery. [27] For the worship of idols, whose names it is wrong even to mention, is the beginning, the cause, and the end of every evil. [28] People either indulge themselves to the point of madness, or pass off lies as prophecies, or live dishonest lives, or break their oath without scruple. [29] They perjure themselves and expect no harm because the idols they trust in are lifeless. [30] But judgement will overtake them on two counts: both because in their devotion to idols they have thought wrongly about God, and also because in their contempt for religion they have deliberately perjured themselves. [31] It is not any power in what they swear by, but the nemesis of sin, that ever pursues the transgressions of the wicked.

15 But you, our God, are kind and true and patient, a merciful ruler of all that is. [2] Even if we sin, we are yours, since we acknowledge your power. But because we know that we are accounted yours we shall not sin. [3] To know you is the whole of righteousness, and to acknowledge your power is the root of immortality. [4] We have not been led astray by the perverted inventions of human skill or the barren labour of painters, by some gaudily coloured shape, [5] the sight of which arouses in fools a passionate desire for an image without life or breath. [6] They are in love with evil and do not deserve anything better to trust in, those who make such evil things, those who hanker after them, and those who worship them.

[7] A potter laboriously kneading the soft clay shapes every vessel for our use. Out of the selfsame clay he fashions without distinction the pots that are to serve for clean uses and the opposite; and what the purpose of each one is to be, the moulder of the clay decides. [8] Then with ill-directed toil he makes a false god out of the same clay, this man who not long before was himself fashioned out of earth and soon returns to the place whence he was taken, when the living soul that was lent to him must be returned on demand. [9] His concern is not that he must one day fall sick or that his span of life is short; but he must vie with goldsmiths and silversmiths and emulate the workers in bronze, and he thinks it does him credit to contrive fakes. [10] His heart is ashes, his hope worth less than common earth, and his life cheaper than clay, [11] because he did not recognize by whom he himself was moulded, or who it was that inspired him with an active soul and breathed into him the breath of life. [12] No, he reckons this life of ours a game, and our existence a market where money can be made: 'By fair means or foul', he says, 'one must get a living.' [13] But this maker of fragile pots and idols from the same earthy stuff knows better than anyone that he is doing wrong.

[14] The greatest fools of all, and worse

than infantile, were the enemies and oppressors of your people, ¹⁵for they supposed all their heathen idols to be gods, although they have eyes that cannot see, nostrils that cannot draw breath, ears that cannot hear, fingers that cannot feel, and feet that are useless for walking; ¹⁶for it was a man who made them, one drawing borrowed breath who gave them their shape. But no human being has the power to shape a god in his own likeness: ¹⁷he is only mortal, but what he makes with his impious hands is dead. So he is better than the objects of his worship, for at least he is alive—they never can be. ¹⁸Moreover, these people worship animals, the most revolting animals. Compared with the rest of the brute creation, their divinities are the least intelligent. ¹⁹Even as animals they are without a trace of beauty which might make them desirable. When God approved and blessed his work, they were left out.

Israel and the Egyptians

16 For that reason it was fitting that the oppressors were chastised by creatures like these: they were tormented by swarms of vermin. ²They were punished; but your own people you treated with kindness, sending quails for them to eat, a novel food to satisfy their hunger. ³Your purpose was that whereas those others, hungry as they were, should turn in loathing even from essential food because the creatures sent against them were so repulsive, your people, after a short spell of scarcity, should partake of novel delicacies. ⁴It was right that the scarcity falling on the oppressors should be inexorable, and that your people should learn by brief experience how their enemies were tortured.

⁵Even when fierce and venomous snakes attacked your people and the bites of writhing serpents were spreading death, your anger did not continue to the bitter end. ⁶Their short-lived trouble was sent them as a lesson, and they were given a symbol of salvation to remind them of the requirements of your law. ⁷Anyone turning towards it was saved, not by what he looked at but by you, the saviour of all. ⁸In this way also you convinced our enemies that you are the deliverer from every evil. ⁹Those others died from the bites of locusts and flies, and no remedy to save their lives was found, because they deserved to be punished by such creatures.

¹⁰But your people did not succumb to the fangs of snakes, however poisonous, because your mercy came to their aid and healed them. ¹¹It was to remind them of your decrees that they were bitten, and they were quickly healed for fear they might fall into deep forgetfulness and become unresponsive to your kindness. ¹²It was neither herb nor poultice that cured them, but your all-healing word, O Lord. ¹³You have the power of life and death, you bring a person down to the gates of death and you bring him up again. ¹⁴In his wickedness a human being may kill, but he cannot bring back the breath of life that has gone or release a soul that death has arrested. ¹⁵But from your hand there is no escape; ¹⁶for the godless who refused to acknowledge you were scourged by your mighty arm, they were pursued by unwonted storms of rain and hail falling in relentless torrents, and were utterly destroyed by fire. ¹⁷Strangest of all, in water, that quenches everything, the fire burned more fiercely; creation itself fights to defend the righteous. ¹⁸At one time the flame was moderated, so that it should not burn up the living creatures inflicted on the godless, who were to learn from this that it was by God's judgement they were pursued; ¹⁹at another time it blazed even in water with more than the natural power of fire, to destroy the produce of a sinful land.

²⁰In contrast to this your own people were given angels' food. You sent to them from heaven, without labour on their part, bread ready to eat, rich in every kind of delight and suited to every taste. ²¹The sustenance you supplied showed the sweetness of your disposition towards your children, and the bread, serving the appetite of every person who ate it, was transformed into what each wished. ²²Though like snow and ice, yet it resisted fire and did not melt, to teach them that whereas their enemies' crops had been destroyed by fire blazing in the hail and flashing through the teeming rain, ²³that same fire had now forgotten its own power, in order that the godly might be fed.

²⁴For creation, serving you its Maker,

strains to punish the unrighteous and relaxes into benevolence towards those who put their trust in you. ²⁵ It was so at that time too: it adapted itself endlessly in the service of your universal bounty, according to the desire of your suppliants. ²⁶ So your people, whom you, Lord, have loved, were to learn that it is not by the growing of crops that mankind is nourished, but it is by your word that those who trust in you are sustained. ²⁷ That substance, which fire did not destroy, simply melted away when warmed by the sun's first rays, ²⁸ to teach us that we must rise before the sun to give you thanks and pray to you as daylight dawns. ²⁹ The hope of the ungrateful will melt like wintry hoar-frost, and drain away like water that runs to waste.

17 Great are your judgements and hard to expound; and this was why uninstructed souls went astray. ² The heathen imagined that they could lord it over your holy nation, but, prisoners of darkness and captives of unending night, they themselves lay immured each under his own roof, fugitives from eternal providence. ³ Thinking that their secret sins might escape detection beneath a dark pall of oblivion, they lay in disorder, dreadfully afraid, terrified by apparitions. ⁴ Not even the dark corner that hid them offered refuge from fear, but loud, unnerving noises resounded about them, and phantoms with faces grim and downcast passed before their eyes. ⁵ No fire, however intense, was strong enough to give them light, nor were the brilliant, flaming stars adequate to pierce that hideous darkness. ⁶ There shone on them only a terrifying blaze of no human making, and in their panic they thought the real world even worse than the sight their imagination conjured up. ⁷ The tricks of the sorcerer's art failed, and their boasted wisdom was exposed and put to shame; ⁸ for those who professed to drive out fear and trouble from sick souls were themselves sick with dread that made them ridiculous. ⁹ Even if there was nothing frightful to terrify them, yet having once been scared by the advance of the vermin and the hissing of the serpents, ¹⁰ they collapsed in terror, even refusing to look upon the air from which there could be no escape. ¹¹ For wickedness proves a cowardly thing when con-

demned by an inner witness, and in the grip of conscience gives way to forebodings of disaster. ¹² Fear is nothing but an abandonment of the aid that reason affords; ¹³ and hope, defeated by this inward weakness, capitulates in ignorance of the cause by which the torment comes.

¹⁴ So all that night, which really had no power over them because it came upon them from the powerless depths of hell, they slept the same haunted sleep, ¹⁵ now harried by portentous spectres, now paralysed by the treachery of their own souls; sudden and unforeseen, fear came upon them. ¹⁶ Thus someone would fall down wherever he was and be held captive, locked in a prison that had no bars. ¹⁷ Farmer or shepherd or a labourer toiling out in the wilderness, he was overtaken, and awaited the inescapable doom; the same chain of darkness bound all alike. ¹⁸ The whispering breeze, the sweet melody of birds in spreading branches, the steady noise of rushing water, ¹⁹ the headlong crash of rocks falling, the racing of creatures as they bound along unseen, the roar of savage wild beasts, or an echo reverberating from hollows in the hills—all these sounds paralysed them with fear. ²⁰ The whole world was bathed in the bright light of day, and went about its tasks unimpeded; ²¹ those people alone were overspread with heavy night, fit image of the darkness that awaited them. But heavier than the darkness was the burden each was to himself.

18 For your holy ones, however, there shone a very great light. Their enemies, hearing their voices but not seeing them, counted them happy because they had not suffered as they themselves had; ² they thanked them for their forbearance under provocation, and begged as a favour that they should part company. ³ In place of the darkness you provided a pillar of fire to be the guide of their uncharted journey, a sun that would not scorch them on that glorious expedition. ⁴ Their enemies did indeed deserve to lose the light of day and be imprisoned in darkness, for they had kept in durance your people, through whom the imperishable light of the law was to be given to the world.

⁵ They planned to kill the new-born infants among your holy people but,

when one babe had been exposed and rescued, you deprived them of their children in requital, and drowned them all together in the swelling waves. ⁶ Of that night our forefathers were given warning in advance, so that, having sure knowledge, they might be heartened by the promises which they trusted. ⁷ Your people were looking for the deliverance of the godly and the destruction of their enemies; ⁸ for you used the same means to punish our assailants and to make us glorious when we heard your call. ⁹ The devout children of a virtuous race were offering sacrifices in secret, and covenanted with one accord to keep the law of God and to share alike in the same benefits and the same dangers; already they were singing their ancestral sacred songs of praise.

¹⁰ In discordant contrast there came a clamour from their enemies, as piteous lamentation for their children spread abroad. ¹¹ Master and slave were punished together with the same penalty; king and commoner suffered the selfsame fate. ¹² All alike had dead past counting, struck down by one common form of death; there were not even enough living to bury the dead; at one stroke the most precious of their offspring had perished. ¹³ Relying on their magic arts, they had scouted all warnings; but when they saw the destruction of their firstborn, they acknowledged that your people have God as their Father.

¹⁴ All things were lying in peace and silence, and night in her swift course was half spent, ¹⁵ when your all-powerful word leapt from your royal throne in heaven into the midst of that doomed land like a relentless warrior, ¹⁶ bearing the sharp sword of your inflexible decree; with his head touching the heavens and his feet on earth he stood and spread death everywhere. ¹⁷ Then all at once nightmare phantoms appalled the godless, and fears unlooked-for beset them; ¹⁸ flinging themselves half dead to the ground, one here, another there, they made clear why they were dying; ¹⁹ for the dreams that tormented them had taught them before they died, so that they should not perish still ignorant of why they suffered.

²⁰ The godly also had a taste of death when large numbers were struck down in the wilderness. But the divine wrath did not long continue, ²¹ for a blameless man was quick to be their champion, bearing the weapons of his priestly ministry, prayer and the incense that propitiates; he withstood the divine anger and set a limit to the disaster, thus showing that he was indeed your servant. ²² He overcame the anger neither by bodily strength nor by force of arms; but by words he subdued the avenger, appealing to the sworn covenants made with our forefathers. ²³ The dead were already fallen in heaps when he interposed himself and drove back the divine wrath, barring its line of attack on those still alive. ²⁴ On his long-skirted robe the whole world was represented; the glories of the fathers were engraved on his four rows of precious stones; and your majesty was on the diadem upon his head. ²⁵ To these the destroyer yielded, for they made him afraid. It was only a taste of the wrath, but it was enough.

19 But the godless were assailed by pitiless anger to the very end, for God knew their future also: ² how after allowing your people to go, and even urging their departure, they would have a change of heart and set out in pursuit. ³ While they were still mourning, still lamenting at the graves of their dead, they rushed into another foolish decision, and pursued as runaways those whom they had entreated to leave. ⁴ For a well-deserved fate was drawing them on to this conclusion and made them forget what had happened, so that they might suffer the torments still needed to complete their punishment, ⁵ and so that your people might achieve an incredible journey but their enemies meet a strange death.

⁶ The whole creation, with all its elements, was refashioned in subservience to your commands, in order that your servants might be preserved unscathed. ⁷ They gazed at the cloud that overshadowed the camp, at dry land emerging where before was only water, at an open road leading out of the Red Sea, and a grassy plain in place of stormy waves, ⁸ across which the whole nation passed under the protection of your hand, after witnessing amazing portents. ⁹ They were

18:22 **anger:** *prob. rdg; Gk* crowd.

like horses at pasture, like skipping lambs, as they praised you, O Lord, by whom they were rescued. ¹⁰ They still remembered their life in a foreign land: how instead of cattle the earth bred lice, and instead of fish the river disgorged swarms of frogs; ¹¹ and how, at a later stage, they had seen a new sort of bird when, driven by appetite, they had begged for delicacies to eat, ¹² and for their relief quails came up from the sea.

¹³ On the sinners, however, punishment came, heralded by violent thunderbolts. They suffered justly for their own wickedness, because their hatred of strangers was on a new level of bitterness. ¹⁴ While others there had been who refused to welcome strangers when they came to them, these made slaves of guests who were their benefactors. ¹⁵ There will indeed be a judgement for those whose reception of foreigners was hostile; ¹⁶ but these, after a festal welcome, oppressed with hard labour men who had earlier shared their rights. ¹⁷ They were struck with blindness also, like the men at the door of the one good man, when yawning darkness fell upon them and each went groping for his own doorway.

¹⁸ As the strings of a harp can make various tunes with different names though each string retains its own pitch, so the elements combined among themselves in different ways, as can be accurately inferred from the observation of what happened. ¹⁹ Land animals took to the water and creatures that swim migrated to dry land; ²⁰ fire retained its normal power even in water, and water forgot its fire-quenching properties. ²¹ Flames on the other hand failed to consume the flesh of perishable creatures that walked in them, and the substance of heavenly food, like ice and prone to melt, no longer melted.

²² In everything, O Lord, you have made your people great and glorious, and in every time and place you have been their unfailing helper.

ECCLESIASTICUS

OR THE WISDOM OF JESUS SON OF SIRACH

Preface

A LEGACY of great value has come down to us through the law, the prophets, and the writers who followed in their steps, and Israel deserves recognition for its traditions of learning and wisdom. It is the duty of those who study the scriptures not only to become expert themselves, but also to use their scholarship for the benefit of the world outside through both the spoken and the written word. For that reason my grandfather Jesus, who had applied himself diligently to the study of the law, the prophets, and the other writings of our ancestors, and had gained a considerable proficiency in them, was moved to compile a book of his own on the themes of learning and wisdom, in order that, with this further help, scholars might make greater progress in their studies by living as the law directs.

You are asked, then, to read with sympathetic attention, and to make allowances wherever you think that, in spite of all the devoted work that has been put into the translation, some of the expressions I have used are inadequate. For what is said in Hebrew does not have the same force when translated into another tongue. Not only the present work, but even the law itself, as well as the prophets and the other writings, are not a little different when spoken in the original.

When I came to Egypt and settled there in the thirty-eighth year of the reign of King Euergetes, I found much scope for giving instruction; and I thought it very necessary to spend some energy and labour on the translation of this book. Ever since then I have applied my skill night and day to complete it, and to publish it for the use of those who have made their home in a foreign land, and wish to study and so train themselves to live according to the law.

The ways of wisdom

1 ALL wisdom is from the Lord;
she dwells with him for ever.
2 Who can count the sands of the sea,
the raindrops, or the days of
unending time?
3 Who can measure the height of the
sky,
the breadth of the earth, or the depth
of the abyss?
4 Wisdom was first of all created
things;
intelligent purpose has existed from
the beginning.
6 To whom has the root of wisdom
been revealed?
Who has understanding of her
subtlety?
8 One alone is wise, the Lord most
terrible,
seated upon his throne.
9 It is he who created her, beheld and
measured her,
and infused her into all his works.
10 To everyone he has given her in
some degree,
but without stint to those who love
him.

11 THE fear of the Lord brings honour
and pride,
cheerfulness and a garland of joy.
12 The fear of the Lord gladdens the
heart;
it brings cheerfulness and joy and
long life.
13 Whoever fears the Lord, it will be
well with him at the last,
and on the day of his death blessings
will be his.
14 The beginning of wisdom is the fear
of the Lord;
she is created with the faithful in
their mother's womb,
15 she has built an everlasting home
among mortals,

1 : 3 **of the abyss**: *prob. rdg ; Gk adds* or wisdom.   1 : 4 **from the beginning**: *some witnesses add* ⁵ The fountain of wisdom is God's word on high, and her ways are eternal commandments.   1 : 6 **of her subtlety**: *some witnesses add* ⁷ Who has discovered all that wisdom knows, or understood her wealth of experience?

and with their descendants she will keep faith.

¹⁶ The full measure of wisdom is the fear of the Lord;
she gives to mortals deep draughts of her wine.

¹⁷ She fills her home with all that the heart can desire,
and her storehouses with her produce.

¹⁸ Wisdom's garland is the fear of the Lord,
flowering with peace and perfect health.

¹⁹ She showers down knowledge and discernment,
and bestows high honour on those who hold fast to her.

²⁰ Wisdom is rooted in the fear of the Lord,
and long life grows on her branches.

²² Unjust rage can never be excused;
when anger tips the scale it is a person's downfall.

²³ Until the right moment comes, he who is patient restrains himself,
and afterwards cheerfulness breaks through again;

²⁴ until the right moment he keeps his thoughts to himself,
and later his good sense is on everyone's lips.

²⁵ In wisdom's treasure house are wise proverbs,
but godliness is detestable to a sinner.

²⁶ If you long for wisdom, keep the commandments,
and the Lord will give it you without stint.

²⁷ The fear of the Lord is wisdom and instruction;
fidelity and gentleness are his delight.

²⁸ Do not disregard the fear of the Lord or approach him without sincerity.

²⁹ Do not act a part before the eyes of the world;
keep guard over your lips.

³⁰ Never be arrogant, or you will fall and bring disgrace on yourself;
the Lord will reveal your secrets and humble you before the assembly,

because what prompted you was not the fear of the Lord:
guile filled your heart.

2 My son, if you aspire to be a servant of the Lord,
prepare yourself for testing.

² Set a straight course and keep to it,
and do not be dismayed in the face of adversity.

³ Hold fast to him and never let go,
if you would end your days in prosperity.

⁴ Bear every hardship that is sent you,
and whenever humiliation comes, be patient;

⁵ for gold is assayed in the fire,
and the chosen ones in the furnace of humiliation.

⁶ Trust him and he will help you;
steer a straight course and fix your hope on him.

⁷ You that fear the Lord, wait for his mercy;
do not stray, for fear you will fall.

⁸ You that fear the Lord, trust in him,
and you will not be baulked of your reward.

⁹ You that fear the Lord, hope for prosperity
and lasting joy and favour.

¹⁰ Consider the past generations and see:
was anyone who trusted the Lord ever disappointed?
Was anyone who stood firm in the fear of him ever abandoned?
Did he ever ignore anyone who called to him?

¹¹ For the Lord is compassionate and merciful;
he forgives sins and saves in time of trouble.

¹² Woe to faint hearts and nerveless hands
and to the sinner who leads a double life!

¹³ Woe to the feeble-hearted! They have no faith,
and therefore will go unprotected.

¹⁴ Woe to you who have given up the struggle!
What will you do at the Lord's coming?

1:20 **on her branches:** *some witnesses add* ²¹ The fear of the Lord drives away sins, and wherever it dwells it averts his anger.   1:30 **because ... the Lord:** *or* because you had no concern for the fear of the Lord.

15 Those who fear the Lord never
      disobey his words,
   and all who love him keep to his
      ways.
16 Those who fear the Lord try to do his
      will,
   and all who love him steep
      themselves in the law.
17 Those who fear the Lord will always
      be ready;
   they humble themselves before him
      and say,
18 'Let us fall into the Lord's hands, not
      into the hands of men,'
   for his majesty is equalled by his
      mercy.

3 CHILDREN, listen to me, for I am
      your father;
   do what I tell you, that you may be
      safe.
2 The Lord has given the father
      honour in his children's eyes
   and confirmed a mother's rights in
      the eyes of her sons.
3 Respect for a father atones for sins;
4 to honour your mother is like laying
      up treasure.
5 He who respects his father will be
      made happy by children,
   and when he prays, he will be heard.
6 He who honours his father will have
      a long life,
   and he who obeys the Lord gives
      comfort to his mother;
7 he submits to his parents as though
      he were their servant.

8 Honour your father by deed and
      word,
   so that you may receive his blessing;
9 for a father's blessing strengthens his
      children's houses,
   but a mother's curse uproots their
      foundations.
10 Never seek honour at the cost of
      discredit to your father;
   how can his discredit bring honour
      to you?
11 A man gets honour from his father's
      honour;
   a mother's dishonour is disgrace to
      her children.
12 My son, look after your father in his
      old age,

and as long as he lives do nothing to
      grieve him.
13 Even if his mind fails, make
      allowances
   and do not despise him because you
      are in your prime.
14 If you support your father it will
      never be forgotten
   and will stand to your credit against
      your sins;
15 when you are in trouble, it will be
      remembered in your favour,
   and your sins will melt away like
      frost in sunshine.
16 To leave your father in the lurch is
      like blasphemy;
   to curse your mother is to provoke
      your Creator's wrath.

17 My son, in all you do be unassuming,
   and those whom the Lord approves
      will love you.
18 The greater you are, the humbler
      must you be,
   and the Lord will show you favour;
20 for his power is great,
   yet he reveals his secrets to the
      humble.
21 Do not pry into things too hard for
      you
   or investigate what is beyond your
      reach.
22 Meditate on what the Lord has
      commanded;
   what he has kept hidden need not
      concern you.
23 Do not busy yourself with matters
      that are beyond you;
   even what has been shown you is
      above the grasp of mortals.
24 Many have been led astray by their
      theorizing,
   and evil imaginings have impaired
      their judgements.
26 Stubbornness will come to a bad end,
   and he who flirts with danger will
      lose his life.
27 Stubbornness brings a load of
      troubles;
   the sinner piles sin on sin.
28 When calamity befalls the arrogant,
      there is no cure;
   wickedness is too deeply rooted in
      them.

3:18 **show you favour:** *some witnesses add* 19 Many are high and illustrious, but he reveals his secrets to the
humble.   3:24 **their judgements:** *some witnesses add* 25 Without the apple of the eye, light is lacking;
without knowledge, wisdom is lacking.

²⁹ A sensible person will take a proverb
to heart;
an attentive audience is the desire of
the wise.
³⁰ As water quenches a blazing fire,
so almsgiving atones for sin.
³¹ He who repays a favour is mindful of
his future;
when he is falling, he will have
support at hand.

4 My son, do not cheat a poor
person of his livelihood
or keep him waiting with hungry
eyes.
² Do not tantalize one who is starving
or drive him to desperation in his
need.
³ If someone is desperate, do not add
to his troubles
or keep him waiting for the charity
he asks.
⁴ Do not reject the appeal of someone
in distress
or turn your back on the poor;
⁵ when one begs for alms, do not look
the other way,
so giving him cause to curse you,
⁶ for if he curses you in his bitterness,
his Creator will hear his prayer.
⁷ Make yourself popular in the
assembly,
and show deference to the great.
⁸ When anyone who is poor speaks to
you, give him your attention
and answer his greeting courteously.
⁹ Rescue the downtrodden from the
oppressor
and be firm when giving a verdict.
¹⁰ Be as a father to the fatherless
and like a husband to their mother;
then the Most High will call you his
son,
and greater than a mother's love will
be his love for you.

¹¹ WISDOM raises her sons to greatness
and gives help to those who seek her.
¹² To love her is to love life;
those who rise early to greet her will
be filled with joy.
¹³ He who holds fast to her will gain
honour;
the Lord's blessing rests on the house
she enters.
¹⁴ To serve her is to serve the Holy One,
and the Lord loves those who love
her.
¹⁵ He who is obedient to her will give
true judgement,
and, because he listens to her, his
home will be secure.
¹⁶ If he trusts her, he will possess her
and bequeath her to his descendants.
¹⁷ At first she will lead him by tortuous
ways,
filling him with craven fears.
Her discipline will be a torment to
him,
and her decrees a hard test,
until he trusts her with all his heart;
¹⁸ then she will come straight back to
him,
bringing gladness and revealing to
him her secrets.
¹⁹ But if he strays, she will abandon him
and leave him to his fate.

²⁰ BE on your guard at all times and
beware of evil;
do not be over-modest in your own
cause,
²¹ for there is a modesty that leads to
sin,
as well as a modesty that brings
honour and favour.
²² Do not be untrue to yourself in
deference to another,
or diffident to your own undoing.
²³ Never remain silent when a word
might put things right,
and do not hide your wisdom,
²⁴ for it is by the spoken word that
wisdom is known,
and learning finds expression in
speech.
²⁵ Do not argue against the truth,
but have a proper sense of your own
ignorance.
²⁶ Never be ashamed to admit your
mistakes,
and do not try to swim against the
current.
²⁷ Do not let yourself be a doormat to a
fool
or curry favour with the powerful.
²⁸ Fight to the death for truth,
and the Lord God will fight on your
side.
²⁹ Do not be forward in your speech
while slack and feeble in deeds.

4:13 **she:** *or* he.

93

30 Do not play the lion in your home
   or swagger among your servants.
31 Do not keep your hand wide open to
   receive,
   but closed when it is time to repay.

5 Do not rely on your money
   and say, 'This makes me self-
   sufficient.'
2 Do not yield to every impulse you
   can gratify
   or follow the desires of your heart.
3 Do not say, 'I have no master';
   the Lord, you may be sure, will call
   you to account.
4 Do not say, 'I sinned, yet nothing
   happened to me';
   it is only that the Lord is very
   patient.
5 Do not be so confident of pardon
   that you pile up sin on sin;
6 do not say, 'His compassion is so
   great
   he will pardon my sins, however
   many.'
   To him belong both mercy and
   anger,
   and sinners feel the weight of his
   retribution.
7 Turn back to the Lord without delay,
   and do not defer action from one day
   to the next;
   for the Lord's anger can suddenly
   pour out,
   and at the time of reckoning you will
   perish.
8 Do not rely on ill-gotten gains,
   for they will not avail on the day of
   calamity.

Wisdom in human relations
9 Do NOT winnow in every wind
   or walk along every path:
   this is the mark of duplicity.
10 Stand firmly by what you know,
   and be consistent in what you say.
11 Be quick to listen,
   but over your answer take time.
12 Give an answer if you know what to
   say,
   but if not, hold your tongue.
13 Through speaking come both honour
   and dishonour,
   and the tongue can be its owner's
   downfall.
14 Do not get a name for tale-bearing

or lay traps with your tongue,
   for, as there is shame in store for the
   thief,
   so there is harsh censure for
   duplicity.
15 Avoid all faults, both great and
   small.

6 Do not change from a friend into
   an enemy,
   for a bad name earns shame and
   disgrace:
   this is the mark of duplicity.

2 Never let violent passions rouse you;
   they will tear you apart like a bull,
3 they will devour your foliage, destroy
   your fruit,
   and leave you a withered tree.
4 Evil passion ruins anyone who
   harbours it,
   and gives his enemies cause to gloat
   over him.
5 Pleasant words win many friends,
   and affable talk makes acquaintance
   easy.
6 Live at peace with everyone:
   accept advice, however, from but one
   in a thousand.
7 When you make a friend, begin by
   testing him,
   and be in no hurry to give him your
   trust.
8 Some friends are loyal when it suits
   them
   but desert you in time of trouble.
9 Some friends turn into enemies
   and shame you by making the
   quarrel public.
10 Another may sit at your table
   but in time of trouble is nowhere to
   be found;
11 when you are prosperous, he is your
   second self
   and talks familiarly with your
   servants,
12 but if you come down in the world,
   he turns against you
   and you will not see his face again.
13 Hold your enemies at a distance,
   and keep a wary eye on your friends.

14 A faithful friend is a secure shelter;
   whoever finds one, finds a treasure.
15 A faithful friend is beyond price;
   there is no measure of his worth.
16 A faithful friend is an elixir of life,

6:2 they ... bull: *prob. mng; Gk obscure.*

94

found only by those who fear the
Lord.
¹⁷ Whoever fears the Lord directs his
friendship aright,
for he treats a neighbour as himself.
¹⁸ My son, seek wisdom's instruction
while you are young,
and you will still find her when your
hair turns white.
¹⁹ Come to her like a farmer who
ploughs and sows;
then wait for the good fruits she
supplies.
If you cultivate her, you will labour
for a little while,
but soon you will be enjoying the
harvest.
²⁰ How harsh she seems to the
uninstructed!
The fool cannot abide her;
²¹ like a boulder she tests and strains
his strength,
and he is not slow to let her drop.
²² Wisdom well deserves her name;
she is not accessible to many.

²³ Listen, my son: accept my opinion
and do not reject my advice.
²⁴ Put your feet in wisdom's fetters
and your neck into her collar.
²⁵ Stoop to carry her on your shoulders
and do not chafe at her bonds.
²⁶ Come to her wholeheartedly,
and with all your might keep to her
ways.
²⁷ Follow her track, and she will make
herself known;
once you have grasped her, do not
let her go.
²⁸ In the end you will find the
refreshment she offers;
she will transform herself for you
into joy:
²⁹ her fetters will become your strong
defence
and her collar a splendid robe.
³⁰ Her yoke is a golden ornament
and her bonds a violet cord;
³¹ you will put her on like a splendid
robe
and wear her like a garland of joy.

³² If it is your wish, my son, you will be
instructed;
if you give your mind to it, you will
become clever;

³³ if you are content to listen, you will
learn;
if you are attentive, you will grow
wise.
³⁴ When you stand among the
assembled elders,
see who is wise and stick close by
him.
³⁵ Listen gladly to every godly
conversation;
let no wise maxim escape you.
³⁶ If you discover anyone who is wise,
rise early to visit him;
let your feet wear out his doorstep.
³⁷ Ponder the decrees of the Lord
and study his commandments at all
times.
He will instruct your mind,
and your desire for wisdom shall be
met.

7 Do no evil, and no evil will befall
you;
² keep clear of wrong, and it will avoid
you.
³ Do not sow in the furrows of
injustice,
for fear of reaping a sevenfold crop.

⁴ Do not ask the Lord for high office
or the king for preferment.
⁵ Do not pose as righteous before the
Lord
or act the sage in the king's
presence.
⁶ Do not aspire to be a judge;
you may lack the strength to root
out injustice,
or you may be intimidated by rank
and so compromise your integrity.
⁷ Do not commit an offence against the
community
and so incur a public disgrace.
⁸ Do not pile up sin on sin,
for just one is enough to make you
guilty.
⁹ Do not say, 'All my gifts to God will
be taken into account;
when I make an offering to the Most
High he will accept it.'
¹⁰ Do not grow weary of praying
or neglect almsgiving.
¹¹ Never laugh at anyone in his bitter
humiliation,
for there is One who both humbles
and exalts.

6:30 **Her yoke:** *so Heb.; Gk* Upon her.

12 Do not plot to deceive your brother
   or do the like to your friend.
13 Refuse ever to tell a lie;
   it is a habit from which no good
      comes.
14 Do not be loquacious among the
      assembled elders,
   and when you pray do not repeat
      yourself.
15 Do not resent manual labour;
   work on the land was ordained by
      the Most High.
16 Do not enlist in the ranks of sinners;
   remember that retribution will not
      tarry.
17 Humble yourself to the uttermost,
   for the doom of the ungodly is fire
      and worms.

18 Do not part with a friend for gain,
   or a true brother for all the gold of
      Ophir.
19 Do not miss the chance of a wise and
      good wife;
   her attractions are worth more than
      gold.
20 Do not ill-treat a servant who works
      honestly
   or a hireling whose heart is in his
      work.
21 Regard a good servant with deep
      affection
   and do not withhold his freedom
      from him.
22 Have you cattle? Take care of them,
   and if they bring you profit, do not
      part with them.
23 Have you sons? Discipline them
   and break them in from their earliest
      years.
24 Have you daughters? Keep a close
      watch over them,
   and do not look on them with
      indulgence.
25 Marry off your daughter, and you
      will have done well;
   but give her to a sensible husband.
26 If you have a wife after your own
      heart, do not divorce her;
   but do not trust yourself to one you
      cannot love.
27 Honour your father with all your
      heart
   and do not forget your mother's
      birth-pangs.

28 Remember that your parents brought
      you into the world;
   how can you repay them for all that
      they have done?

29 Reverence the Lord wholeheartedly
   and show respect to his priests.
30 Love your Maker with all your might
   and do not leave his ministers
      without support.
31 Fear the Lord and honour the priest,
   and give them their due as you have
      been commanded:
   the firstfruits, the guilt-offering, and
      the shoulder of the victim,
   the sacred grain-offering, and the
      firstfruits of holy things.

32 Be open-handed also with the poor,
   that your blessedness may be
      complete.
33 Every living being appreciates
      generosity;
   do not withhold kindness even from
      the dead.
34 Do not turn your back on those who
      weep,
   but mourn with those who mourn.
35 Do not hesitate to visit the sick,
   for by such acts you will win
      affection.
36 In whatever you are doing,
   remember the end that awaits you;
   then all your life you will never go
      wrong.

8 Do not pit yourself against the
      great,
   for fear of falling into their power.
2 Do not quarrel with the rich,
   for fear they will outbid you;
   for gold has brought ruin on many
   and has perverted the minds of kings.
3 Do not argue with a garrulous
      person
   and so add fuel to his fire.
4 Never make fun of the ill-mannered,
   or you may hear your ancestors
      insulted.
5 Do not taunt a repentant sinner;
   remember that we are all guilty.
6 Despise nobody in his old age;
   some of us are growing old as well.
7 Do not gloat over the death of
      anyone;
   remember we all must die.

7:18 **gain:** *prob. rdg; Gk* a trifle.   7:31 **guilt-offering:** *or* reparation-offering. **sacred grain-offering:** *lit.* sacrifice of consecration.

⁸ Do not neglect the discourse of the
  wise,
  but apply yourself to their maxims;
  from these you will gain instruction
  and learn how to serve the great.
⁹ Attend to the discourse of your
  elders,
  for they themselves learned from
  their fathers;
  they can teach you to understand
  and to have an answer ready when
  you need one.
¹⁰ Do not fan a sinner's embers into a
  blaze,
  for fear of being burnt in the flames.
¹¹ Do not let anyone's insolence bring
  you to your feet;
  he is but waiting to trap you with
  your own words.
¹² Do not lend to someone more
  powerful than yourself,
  or, if you do, write off the loan as a
  loss.
¹³ Do not stand surety beyond your
  means,
  and, when you do stand surety, be
  prepared to pay.
¹⁴ Do not go to law with a judge;
  in deference to his position he will be
  given the verdict.
¹⁵ Do not go on a journey with a
  reckless man,
  for you may find him a burden;
  he will take the way he fancies,
  and through his folly you also will
  come to ruin.
¹⁶ Do not fall out with a hot-tempered
  man
  or travel with him across the desert;
  he thinks nothing of bloodshed,
  and where no help is at hand he will
  set upon you.
¹⁷ Never discuss your plans with a fool,
  for he cannot keep anything to
  himself.
¹⁸ Do nothing private in the presence of
  a stranger;
  you do not know what use he will
  make of it.
¹⁹ Do not tell what is in your mind to
  all comers
  or accept favours from them.

9 Do not be jealous over your dear
  wife;
  what you teach her may cause you
  harm.

² Do not surrender yourself to a
  woman
  for her to trample your strength
  underfoot.
³ Do not go near a loose woman
  or you may fall into her snares.
⁴ Do not keep company with a
  dancing-girl
  or you may be caught by her
  advances.
⁵ Do not stare at a virgin
  or you may be trapped into paying
  damages for her.
⁶ Never surrender yourself to
  prostitutes,
  for fear of losing all you possess.
⁷ Do not gaze about you in the city
  streets
  or wander in its unfrequented areas.
⁸ Do not let your eye linger on a
  comely figure
  or stare at beauty not yours to
  possess.
  Many have been seduced by the
  beauty of a woman;
  it kindles passion like fire.
⁹ Never sit down with another man's
  wife
  or join her in a drinking party,
  for fear of succumbing to her charms
  and slipping into fatal disaster.

¹⁰ Do not desert an old friend;
  a new one is not on a par with him.
  A new friend is like new wine:
  until it has matured, you do not
  enjoy it.
¹¹ Do not envy a bad man his success;
  you do not know what is in store for
  him.
¹² Take no pleasure in the pleasures of
  the ungodly;
  remember that before they die
  punishment will overtake them.
¹³ Keep clear of a man who has power
  to kill,
  and you will not be haunted by the
  fear of death;
  but if you should approach him,
  make no false step
  or you will risk losing your life.
  Be aware that you are moving
  among pitfalls,
  or walking on the battlements of the
  city.
¹⁴ Take the measure of your neighbours
  as best you can,

and accept advice from those who
are wise.
¹⁵ Let your discussion be with
intelligent men
and all your talk about the law of
the Most High.
¹⁶ At table choose the company of good
men
whose pride is in the fear of the Lord.
¹⁷ A craftsman is recognized by the skill
of his hands
and a councillor by his words of
wisdom.
¹⁸ A garrulous person is the terror of
his town,
and one who is unguarded in his
speech is detested.

10 A wise ruler instructs his people
and gives them sound and
orderly government.
² Like ruler, like ministers;
like sovereign, like subjects;
³ a king lacking instruction is his
people's ruin,
but sound judgement in a prince
upholds a city.

The exercise of wisdom
⁴ THE government of the world is in
the hand of the Lord;
at the right time he will find the
right man to rule it.
⁵ In the Lord's hand is all human
success;
it is he who confers honour on the
legislator.
⁶ Do not be angry with your neighbour
for every offence,
and do not resort to acts of insolence.
⁷ Arrogance is hateful in the sight of
God and man,
and injustice is offensive to both.
⁸ Because of injustice, insolence, and
greed,
empire passes from nation to nation.
⁹ What has a mortal to be so proud of?
He is only dust and ashes,
subject even in life to bodily decay.
¹⁰ A long illness mocks the doctor's
skill;
today's king is tomorrow's corpse.
¹¹ When anyone dies, he comes into an
inheritance
of maggots and vermin and worms.

¹² The beginning of pride is to forsake
the Lord,
when the human heart revolts
against its Maker;
¹³ as its beginning is sin,
so persistence in it brings on a deluge
of depravity.
Therefore the Lord inflicts signal
punishments on the proud
and brings them to utter disaster.
¹⁴ The Lord overturns the thrones of
princes
and installs the meek in their place.
¹⁵ The Lord uproots nations
and plants the humble in their place.
¹⁶ The Lord lays waste the territory of
nations,
destroying them to the very
foundations of the earth;
¹⁷ some he shrivels away to nothing,
so that all memory of them vanishes
from the earth.
¹⁸ Pride was not the Creator's design for
man
nor violent anger for those born of
woman.

¹⁹ What creature is worthy of honour?
Man.
What men? Those who fear the Lord.
What creature is worthy of
contempt? Man.
What men? Those who break the
commandments.
²⁰ The members of the family honour
their head;
the Lord honours those who fear him.
²² The convert, the stranger, and the
poor—
their pride is in the fear of the Lord.
²³ It is not right to despise a poor man
whose judgement is sound,
and it is wrong to honour a rich
man who is a sinner.
²⁴ The mighty, the judge, and the
prince win high renown,
but none is as great as he who fears
the Lord.
²⁵ When a wise servant is waited on by
free men,
the sensible person will not protest.

²⁶ Do NOT be too clever to do a day's
work

10:9 **even ... decay**: *prob. mng, based on Heb.; Gk obscure.*   10:20 **fear him**: *some witnesses add* ²¹ Fear the
Lord, and you will be accepted; be obstinate and proud, and you will be rejected.   10:22 **convert**: *so Heb.;*
Gk rich.   10:23 **rich**: *so Syriac; Gk omits.*

or give yourself airs when you have
nothing to live on.

27 It is better to work and have more
than enough
than to be full of conceit on an
empty stomach.

28 My son, be modest, but keep your
self-respect
and value yourself at your true
worth.

29 Who will speak up for anyone who is
his own enemy,
or respect someone who disparages
himself?

30 The poor may be honoured for good
sense,
the rich for wealth.

31 If someone is honoured in poverty,
how much more in wealth!
If he is dishonoured in wealth, how
much more in poverty!

11 Someone poor but wise can hold
his head high
and take his seat among the great.

2 Do not overrate one person for his
good looks
or be repelled by another's
appearance.

3 The bee is small among winged
creatures,
yet her produce takes first place for
sweetness.

4 Do not brag about your fine clothes
or be elated when honours come
your way.
Remember, the Lord can perform
marvels
which are hidden from mortal eyes:

5 many a king has been reduced to
sitting on the ground,
while crowns have gone where least
expected;

6 many a ruler has been stripped of
every honour,
and the eminent have found
themselves at the mercy of others.

7 Do not find fault before examining
the evidence;
think first, and criticize afterwards.

8 Do not answer without first listening,
and do not interrupt while another is
speaking.

9 Never take sides in a quarrel not
your own
or become involved in the disputes of
the wicked.

10 My son, do not engage in too many
transactions;
attempting too much, you will come
to grief;
in pursuit you will not overtake;
in flight you will not escape.

11 One person slaves and toils and
presses on,
and yet falls farther behind.

12 Another is slow and in need of help,
poor in strength, rich only in
poverty;
yet the Lord turns on him a kindly
eye,
lifts him up out of his miserable
plight,

13 and, to the amazement of many,
raises him to dignity.

14 Good fortune and bad, life and death,
poverty and wealth, all are from the
Lord.

17 His gifts to the devout endure;
his approval brings unending
prosperity.

18 Someone may grow rich by stinting
and sparing,
but what does he get for his pains?

19 When he says, 'I have earned my
rest
and now I can live on my savings,'
he does not know how long it will be
before he must die and leave them to
others.

20 Stand by your contract and give your
mind to it;
grow old at your work.

21 Do not envy the wicked their
achievements;
trust the Lord and stick to your job,
for it is very easy for the Lord
to make the poor rich all in a
moment.

22 Piety is rewarded by the Lord's
blessing,
which blossoms in a single hour.

23 Do not say, 'What use am I?
What good can the future hold for
me?'

11:14 **from the Lord**: *some witnesses add* 15 From the Lord come wisdom, understanding, and knowledge of the law, love, and the doing of good works. 16 Error and darkness have been with sinners from their birth, and evil grows old with them who delight in it.

24 And do not say, 'I am self-sufficient;
  nothing can ever go wrong for me.'
25 Hardship is forgotten in time of
  prosperity,
  and prosperity in time of hardship.
26 Even on the day a person dies it is
  easy for the Lord
  to give him what he deserves.
27 An hour's misery wipes out all
  memory of delight,
  and someone's end reveals how he
  has lived.
28 Call no one happy before he dies,
  for not until death is a person known
  for what he is.

29 Do NOT invite all comers into your
  home;
  dishonesty wears many a guise.
30 A proud person's mind is like a decoy
  partridge in its cage,
  or like a spy watching for a false
  step;
31 he waits for a chance to twist good
  into evil
  or to cast blame on praiseworthy
  actions.
32 One spark kindles many coals,
  and a plot laid by a bad man ends in
  bloodshed.
33 Beware of a scoundrel and his evil
  schemes,
  or he may ruin your reputation for
  ever.
34 Admit a stranger to your home and
  he will stir up trouble
  and estrange you from your own
  flesh and blood.

12 If you do a good turn, make
  sure to whom you are
  doing it;
  then you will have credit for your
  kindness.
2 A good turn done to a godfearing
  person will be repaid,
  if not by him, then by the Most High.
3 There is no prosperity for the
  persistent wrongdoer
  or for him who never gives alms.
4 Give to the godfearing, but never
  help the sinner.
5 Keep your good works for the
  humble, not the godless;
  put away your bread, do not give
  him any;
  he will use your gift to get the better
  of you,
  and for every favour you have done
  him
  you will suffer a twofold injury;
6 for the Most High himself hates
  sinners
  and sends the ungodly what they
  deserve.
7 Give to anyone who is good, but
  never help a sinner.

8 Prosperity does not reveal your
  friends,
  nor does adversity conceal your
  enemies.
9 When all goes well with someone his
  enemies are friendly;
  when things go badly even a friend
  will shun him.
10 Never trust an enemy;
  he will turn vicious as surely as
  bronze corrodes.
11 Even if he appears humble and
  cringing,
  keep your distance and be on your
  guard.
  Behave towards him like someone
  who polishes a mirror
  to ensure it does not tarnish.
12 Do not place him by your side,
  or he will trip you up and supplant
  you;
  do not seat him at your right hand,
  or he will thrust you out and take
  your place;
  and in the end you will admit the
  force of my words
  and recall my warning with regret.
13 Who sympathizes with a snake-
  charmer when he is bitten,
  or with those who deal with wild
  animals?
14 So is it with the person who keeps
  bad company
  and is involved in another's
  wickedness.
15 He may stand by you for a while,
  but if your fortunes decline, his
  friendship will not last.

16 An enemy speaks honeyed words,
  but in his heart he plans to topple
  you into the ditch.
  He may have tears in his eyes,
  but given the chance he will not stop
  at bloodshed.
17 If disaster overtakes you, you will
  find him there ahead of you,

and while pretending to help, he will
catch you by the heel.
¹⁸ Then he will wag his head and rub
his hands
and with many a whispered slander
reveal his true colours.

13 Handle pitch and it will make
you dirty;
associate with the arrogant and you
will grow like them.
² Do not lift a weight too heavy for
you,
nor associate with someone greater
and richer than yourself.
How can a jug be friends with a
kettle?
If they knock together, it will be
smashed.
³ A rich person does wrong, and then
adds insult to injury;
a poor person is wronged, and must
apologize into the bargain.
⁴ If you can serve his turn, a rich
person will exploit you,
but if you are in need, he will drop
you.
⁵ If you are in funds, he will be your
constant companion
and without a twinge of remorse
drain you dry.
⁶ He may need you, and then he will
deceive you
and be all smiles and
encouragement,
paying you compliments and asking,
'What can I do for you?'
⁷ embarrassing you with his
hospitality,
until he has drained you two or
three times over;
but he will end up by laughing at
you.
Afterwards, when he sees you, he
will pass you by
and wag his head over you.

⁸ Take care not to be led astray
and humiliated when you are
enjoying yourself.
⁹ If a great man invites you, be slow to
accept,
and he will be the more pressing in
his invitation.

¹⁰ Do not push yourself forward, for
fear of a rebuff,
but do not keep aloof, or you may be
forgotten.
¹¹ Do not presume to converse with him
as an equal,
and put no trust in his effusive
speeches;
the more he speaks, the more he is
testing you,
weighing you up even while he
smiles.
¹² The person who betrays a confidence
is without compunction
and will not spare you injury or
imprisonment.
¹³ Confide in no one and be on your
guard,
for you are walking with disaster.

¹⁵ Every living thing loves its like,
and every person his own sort.
¹⁶ All creatures flock together with their
kind,
and human beings stick close to their
fellows.
¹⁷ What has a wolf in common with a
lamb,
or a sinner with someone who fears
God?
¹⁸ What peace can there be between
hyena and dog,
what peace between rich and poor?
¹⁹ As lions prey on the wild asses of the
desert,
so the rich live off the poor.
²⁰ As humility disgusts the proud,
so the rich are disgusted by the poor.
²¹ If a rich person staggers, he is
steadied by his friends;
a poor one falls, and his friends
promptly disown him.
²² When a rich person slips, many
come to his rescue;
if he says something outrageous,
they make excuses for him.
A poor one makes a slip, and at once
he is criticized;
even if he talks sense, he is not given
a hearing.
²³ A rich person speaks, and all keep
silent;
then they praise his speech to the
skies.

13:13 with disaster: *some witnesses add* When you hear this in your sleep, wake up! ¹⁴ Love the Lord all your
life, and appeal to him to keep you safe.

The exercise of wisdom

A poor one speaks, and they say,
'Who is this?'
and if he stumbles, they push him
farther.

24 WEALTH untainted by sin is good;
poverty brought on by godless
conduct is evil.
25 It is the heart that changes the look
on the face
either for better or for worse.
26 A cheerful face betokens someone in
good heart,
but the invention of proverbs
involves wearisome thought.

14 Happy is the one who has never
let slip a careless word,
who has never felt the sting of
remorse!
2 Happy is the one whose conscience
does not accuse him,
whose hopes have never been
dashed!

3 Meanness and wealth do not go well
together:
what use is money to a miser?
4 He deprives himself only to hoard for
others;
on his possessions someone else will
lead a life of luxury.
5 How can anyone who is hard on
himself be kind to others?
His money brings him no
enjoyment.
6 No one is worse than he who is
grudging to himself:
his niggardliness is its own
retribution.
7 If ever he does good, he does it by
mistake,
and his villainy comes out at the
finish.
8 He is hard who has a grudging eye,
who turns his back on need and
looks the other way.
9 The covetous eye is not satisfied with
its share;
greedy injustice shrivels the soul.
10 Someone with a miserly outlook
begrudges bread
and keeps a bare table.

11 My son, treat yourself well if you can
afford it,
and present worthy sacrifices to the
Lord.
12 Remember that death will not tarry;

the hour of your appointment with
the grave is undisclosed.
13 Before you die, treat your friend well;
reach out as far as you can to help
him.
14 Do not miss a day's enjoyment
or forgo your share of innocent
pleasure.
15 Are you to leave to others all you
have laboured for
and let them draw lots for your hard-
earned wealth?
16 Give and take; pamper yourself;
expect no luxury in the grave.
17 The body wears out like a garment;
for the age-old sentence stands: you
shall die.
18 In the thick foliage of a spreading
tree
some leaves fall and others grow in
their stead;
so too with the generations of flesh
and blood;
one dies and another comes to birth.
19 All human works decay and vanish,
and the worker follows them into
oblivion.

20 HAPPY is he who gives his mind to
wisdom
and meditates on understanding;
21 happy is he who reflects on her ways
and ponders her secrets!
22 Stalk her like a hunter
and lie in wait by her paths.
23 He who peeps in at her window
and listens at her door,
24 who camps beside her house,
driving his tent-peg into her wall,
25 who pitches his tent close by her,
having found a good place to live—
26 that man will put his children under
her shade
and camp beneath her branches;
27 sheltered by her from the heat,
he will dwell in her glory.

15 He who fears the Lord will act
thus,
and if he masters the law, wisdom
will be his.
2 She will come out to meet him like a
mother;
she will receive him like a young
bride.
3 For food she will give him the bread
of understanding
and for drink the water of wisdom.

⁴ He will lean on her and will not fall,
he will rely on her and not be put to
shame.
⁵ She will advance him above his
neighbours
and find words for him when he
speaks in the assembly.
⁶ He will be crowned with joy and
exultation;
lasting renown will be his heritage
from her.
⁷ Fools will never possess wisdom,
nor will sinners catch a glimpse of
her.
⁸ She holds aloof from arrogance;
liars never call her to mind.
⁹ Praise is out of place on the lips of a
sinner,
because it has not come from the
Lord;
¹⁰ for praise is the outward expression
of wisdom,
and the Lord himself prompts it.
¹¹ Do not say, 'The Lord is to blame for
my going astray';
it is for you to avoid what he hates.
¹² Do not say, 'It was he who led me
into error';
he has no use for a sinner.
¹³ The Lord hates every kind of vice;
you cannot love vice and still fear
him.
¹⁴ When in the beginning God created
the human race,
he left them free to take their own
decisions:
¹⁵ if you choose, you can observe the
commandments;
you can keep faith if you are so
minded.
¹⁶ He has set before you fire and
water:
reach out and make your choice.
¹⁷ Mortals are offered life or death:
whichever they prefer will be given
them.
¹⁸ For great is the wisdom of the Lord;
he is mighty in power, all-seeing;
¹⁹ his eyes are on those who fear him;
no human action escapes his notice.
²⁰ He has commanded no one to be
impious;
to none has he given licence to sin.

16 Do NOT set your heart on a large
family of ne'er-do-wells
or think yourself happy in sons who
are godless.
² However many your children, do not
think yourself happy
unless the fear of the Lord is in them.
³ Do not count on their living to be old
or rely on their number,
for one son can be better than a
thousand.
Better indeed to die childless than to
have ungodly children!
⁴ One person of good sense can
establish a city,
but a tribe of lawless people can turn
it into a desert.
⁵ Many such things have I seen with
my own eyes,
and still weightier examples have
come to my ears.
⁶ Where sinners assemble, fire breaks
out;
retribution blazes up when a nation
is disobedient.
⁷ There was no pardon for the giants
of old,
who rebelled in all their strength.
⁸ There was no reprieve for Lot's
adopted home,
abhorrent in its arrogance.
⁹ There was no mercy for the doomed
nation,
exterminated in its sin,
¹⁰ and no mercy for those six hundred
thousand warriors
assembled in stubborn defiance.
¹¹ Even if there were but one stubborn
person,
it would be a miracle for him to
escape punishment,
for mercy and anger belong to the
Lord:
he shows his power now in
forgiveness, now in overflowing
anger.
¹² His mercy is great, but great also his
condemnation;
he judges each by what he has done.
¹³ He does not let the wrongdoer escape
with his plunder
or try the patience of the godly too
long.
¹⁴ He gives scope freely to his mercy,

16:14 **his deeds**: *some witnesses add* ¹⁵ The Lord made Pharaoh too stubborn to acknowledge him, so that his
deeds might be published to the world. ¹⁶ He displays his mercy to the whole creation, and has assigned his light
and his darkness for human beings.

and everyone is treated according to
his deeds.

¹⁷ Do not say, 'I am hidden from the
Lord;
who is there up above to give a
thought to me?
Among so many I shall not be
noticed;
what am I in the immensity of
creation?'
¹⁸ Heaven itself, the highest heaven,
the abyss, and the earth are shaken
at his coming;
¹⁹ the mountains also and the
foundations of the world
quiver and tremble when he looks
upon them.
²⁰ What mortal mind can grasp this
or comprehend his ways?
²¹ As a squall takes people unawares,
so his works for the most part are
done in secret.
²² 'Who is to declare his acts of justice
or who will wait for them,
their fulfilment being so remote?'
²³ These are the thoughts of a small
mind,
the absurdities of a senseless and
misguided person.

God in creation

²⁴ My son, listen to me and acquire
knowledge;
pay heed to what I say.
²⁵ I will offer you correct instruction
and teach you accurate knowledge.
²⁶ When in the beginning the Lord
created his works
and, after making them, defined their
boundaries,
²⁷ he disposed them in an eternal
order
and fixed their domains for all time.
They do not grow hungry or weary,
or abandon their tasks;
²⁸ one does not jostle another,
nor will they ever disobey his word.
²⁹ Then the Lord looked at the earth
and filled it with his good things.

³⁰ With every kind of living creature he
covered its surface,
and to the earth they must all
return.

17 The Lord created human beings
from the earth
and to it he turns them back again.
² He set a fixed span of life for mortals
and gave them authority over
everything on earth.
³ He clothed them with power like his
own
and made them in his own image.
⁴ He put the fear of them into all
creatures
and granted them lordship over
beasts and birds.
⁶ He fashioned tongues, eyes, and ears
for them,
and gave them minds with which to
think.
⁷ He filled them with understanding
and knowledge
and showed them good and evil.
⁸ He kept watch over their hearts,
to display to them the majesty of his
works.
¹⁰ They will praise his holy name,
proclaiming the grandeur of his
works.
¹¹ He gave them knowledge
and endowed them with the life-
bringing law.
¹² He established with them an
everlasting covenant
and revealed to them his decrees.
¹³ Their eyes saw his glorious majesty,
and their ears heard the glory of his
voice.
¹⁴ He said to them, 'Refrain from all
wrongdoing,'
and he taught each his duty towards
his neighbour.
¹⁵ Their conduct lies open before him at
all times,
never hidden from his sight.
¹⁷ For every nation he appointed a
ruler,
but Israel is the Lord's portion.

17:4 **beasts and birds:** *some witnesses add* ⁵ The Lord gave them the use of the five faculties; as a sixth
gift he assigned to them mind, and as a seventh, reason, the interpreter of those faculties. 17:8 **his
works:** *some witnesses add* ⁹ To them it is given to boast for ever of his marvels. 17:15–17 **his sight
... nation:** *some witnesses read* his sight. ¹⁶ Everyone from his youth tended towards evil; they could not
make themselves hearts of flesh in place of their hearts of stone. ¹⁷ When he dispersed the nations over all
the earth, for every nation. 17:17 **portion:** *some witnesses add* ¹⁸ He rears them with discipline as his
firstborn, imparting to them the light of love and never neglecting them.

19 Whatever they do is as clear as the
sun to him;
his eyes are always on their ways.
20 Their misdeeds are not hidden from
the Lord;
he observes all their sins.
22 Charitable giving he treasures like a
signet ring,
and kindness like the apple of his
eye.
23 In the end he will arise and give the
wicked their deserts,
bringing down retribution on their
heads.
24 Yet he leaves a way open for the
penitent to return to him
and endows the waverer with
strength to endure.
25 Return to the Lord and have done
with sin;
make your prayer in his presence
and lessen your offence.
26 Come back to the Most High,
renounce wrongdoing,
and hate intensely what he abhors.
27 The living give him thanks,
but who will praise the Most High
from the grave?
28 When the dead cease to be, their
gratitude dies with them;
only when alive and well do they
praise the Lord.
29 How great is the Lord's mercy
and his forgiveness to those who
turn to him!
30 Not everything is within human
reach,
for we are not immortal.
31 Is anything brighter than the sun?
Yet it suffers eclipse;
so flesh and blood have evil thoughts.
32 The Lord judges the armies of high
heaven,
and humankind, who are but dust
and ashes.

18 He who lives for ever is the
Creator of the whole universe;
2 the Lord alone will be proved
supreme.
4 To whom is it given to unfold the
story of his works?

Who can fathom his mighty acts?
5 No one can measure his majestic
power,
still less tell the full tale of his
mercies.
6 They can neither be diminished nor
increased,
and the wonders of the Lord cannot
be fathomed.
7 When anyone finishes he is still only
beginning,
and when he stops he will still be at
a loss.
8 What is a human being, and what
use is he?
His good or evil deeds, what do they
signify?
9 His span of life is at the most a
hundred years;
10 compared with unending time, his
few years
are like one drop from the ocean or a
single grain of sand.
11 That is why the Lord is patient with
people;
that is why he lavishes his mercy
upon them.
12 He sees and knows the harsh fate in
store for them,
and therefore gives full play to his
forgiveness.
13 Their compassion is only for their
own kin,
but the Lord's compassion is for all
mankind.
He corrects, disciplines and
teaches,
and brings them back as a shepherd
brings his flock.
14 He has compassion on those who
accept discipline
and are eager to obey his decrees.

Self-discipline

15 Do GOOD, my son, but without
scolding;
do not spoil your generosity with
hurtful words.
16 Does not the dew give respite from
the scorching heat?
So a word can do more than a gift.

17:20 **their sins:** *some witnesses add* 21 The Lord who is gracious and knows of what they are made has neither
rejected nor deserted them, but spared them.   17:32 **The Lord … ashes:** *so Syriac.*   18:2 **proved
supreme:** *some witnesses add* and there is none beside him 3 who can steer the world with a touch of his hand, so
that all things obey his will; as King of the universe, he has power to fix the bounds between what is holy and
what is profane.

17 Does not a kind word count for more
than a rich present?
With someone gracious you will find
both.
18 A graceless fool must always be
taunting,
and a grudging giver makes no eyes
sparkle.

19 Before you speak, learn;
before sickness comes, attend to your
health.
20 Before judgement, examine yourself,
and you will find pardon in your
hour of trial.
21 Before you fall ill, humble yourself;
whenever you sin, show your
penitence.
22 Let nothing hinder the prompt
discharge of your vows;
do not wait until death to be
absolved.
23 Before you make a vow, give it due
thought;
do not be like those who try the
Lord's patience.
24 Think of the wrath you must face in
the hour of death,
when the time of reckoning comes
and he turns away his face.
25 Remember in time of plenty the time
of famine,
poverty and need in your days of
wealth.
26 Between dawn and dusk times may
alter;
before the Lord all change comes
quickly.
27 The wise are always on their guard;
when sin is rife they will beware of
negligence.
28 Everybody with sense makes
acquaintance with wisdom,
and to him who finds her she gives
cause for thankfulness.
29 They who are trained in learning
prove wise themselves
and pour forth apt proverbs.

30 Do not let your passions be your
guide;
keep your lusts under control.
31 If you indulge yourself with all that
passion fancies,
it will give your enemies cause to
gloat over you.
32 Do not revel in great luxury,
or the expense of it may ruin you.

33 Squandering and drunkenness
will leave you with nothing in your
purse.
19 A drunken workman will never
grow rich;
carelessness in small things leads by
degrees to ruin.
2 Wine and women rob the wise of
their wits,
and a frequenter of prostitutes
becomes more and more reckless;
3 decay and worms take possession of
him;
through his recklessness he is
destroyed.

4 To trust anyone hastily shows a
shallow mind,
and to sin is to do oneself an injury.
5 To delight in wickedness is to court
condemnation,
6 but evil loses its hold on him who
hates gossip.
7 Never repeat what you hear,
and you will never be the loser.
8 Tell no tales before friend or foe;
unless silence makes you an
accomplice, never betray a secret.
9 Suppose someone has heard you and
learnt to distrust you,
he will seize a chance to show his
hatred.
10 Have you heard a rumour? Let it die
with you.
Never fear, it will not make you
burst!
11 A fool with a rumour goes through
agony
like a woman in labour.
12 As painful as an arrow through the
thigh
is a rumour in the heart of a fool.
13 Put it to your friend; he may not
have done it,
or if he did, he will know not to do it
again.
14 Put it to your neighbour; he may not
have said it,
or if he did, he will know not to say
it again.
15 Put it to your friend; it will often
turn out to be slander;
so do not believe everything you
hear.
16 Someone may let slip what he does
not intend;
is anyone's tongue free from guilt?

¹⁷ Put your case to your neighbour
before you threaten him,
and let the law of the Most High take
its course.

²⁰ All wisdom is the fear of the Lord
and includes the fulfilling of the law.
²² To know about wickedness is not
wisdom,
nor is there good sense in the advice
of sinners.
²³ There is a cleverness that repels,
and some fools are merely ignorant.
²⁴ Better to lack brains and be
godfearing
than to have great intelligence and
transgress the law.
²⁵ A meticulous cleverness may lead to
injustice,
and crooked means may be used to
uncover the right.
²⁶ A scoundrel may bow his head and
wear mourning,
but at heart be an out-and-out fraud.
²⁷ He hides his face and pretends to be
deaf,
but when no one is looking, he steals
a march on you;
²⁸ and if lack of strength prevents him
from doing wrong,
he will still harm you at the first
opportunity.
²⁹ You can tell a person by his
appearance
and recognize good sense at first
sight.
³⁰ His clothes, the way he laughs,
his gait—these reveal his character.

20 A reproof may be untimely,
and silence may show a man's
good sense.
² How much better to rebuke than to
nurse one's anger!
Confession may save someone from
losing face.
⁴ Like a eunuch longing to ravish a
young girl
is he who resorts to force to secure
right.
⁵ One person is silent, and is reckoned
to be wise;

another chatters, and is detested for it.
⁶ There is the person who is silent, at
a loss for an answer;
another is silent, biding his time.
⁷ The wise are silent until the right
moment,
but a swaggering fool is always
speaking out of turn.
⁸ The garrulous get themselves
detested,
and one who abuses his position
arouses hatred.

⁹ Some find profit in adversity,
while good fortune may turn into
loss.
¹⁰ Sometimes liberality does not benefit
the giver;
sometimes it brings a double return.
¹¹ The quest for honour may lead some
to loss of position,
while others may rise from obscurity
to eminence.
¹² Someone may make a good bargain,
yet pay for it seven times over.
¹³ A wise person endears himself when
he speaks,
but a fool makes himself agreeable to
no purpose.
¹⁴ A gift from a fool will bring you no
profit;
it looks bigger to him than to you.
¹⁵ He gives small gifts accompanied by
long lectures
and opens his mouth as wide as the
town crier.
Today he gives a loan, and tomorrow
demands it back.
Such conduct is detestable!
¹⁶ The fool says, 'I have not one friend
and I get no thanks for my
kindnesses;
those who eat my bread speak ill of
me.'
¹⁷ How everyone will laugh at him—
and how often!

¹⁸ Better a slip on the floor than a slip
of the tongue;
the downfall of the wicked comes just
as suddenly.

19:17 **its course:** *some witnesses add* without giving way to anger. ¹⁸The fear of the Lord is the beginning of acceptance by him, and wisdom wins love from him. ¹⁹The knowledge of the Lord's commandments is discipline for life, and those who do what pleases him pluck the fruit of the tree of immortality. 19:20 **the law:** *some witnesses add* and a knowledge of his omnipotence. ²¹A servant who says to his master, 'I will not do as you wish,' even if he does it later, angers him who feeds him. 20:2 **losing face:** *some witnesses add* ³ How good it is to meet reproof with repentance, and so escape deliberate sin!

¹⁹ An ill-mannered man is like an ill-timed story,
continually on the lips of the ill-bred.
²⁰ A proverb will fall flat when uttered by a fool;
he is sure to bring it out at the wrong moment.
²¹ Poverty may keep someone from doing wrong;
when he goes to rest, conscience will not trouble him.
²² Diffidence may be someone's undoing,
or a foolish appearance may bring him disaster.
²³ Someone may be shamed into making promises to a friend
and needlessly turn him into an enemy.
²⁴ A lie is an ugly blot on anyone's name
and is continually on the lips of the ill-bred.
²⁵ Better be a thief than a habitual liar,
but both will come to a bad end.
²⁶ A lying disposition brings disgrace,
shame that can never be shaken off.

²⁷ He that is wise in discourse advances himself,
and he that has sense is pleasing to the great.
²⁸ He who cultivates his land heaps up a harvest;
he who pleases the great secures pardon for his offence.
²⁹ Hospitality and gifts make the wise blind;
like a gag in the mouth they silence criticism.
³⁰ Hidden wisdom and buried treasure—
what is the use of either?
³¹ Better one who hides his folly than one who hides his wisdom!

21 My son, have you done wrong? Do no more,
and for your past wrongdoing ask pardon.
² Avoid wrong as you would a viper,
for it will bite you if you go near;
its teeth are like a lion's teeth
and can deprive men of their lives.

³ Every breach of the law is a two-edged sword;
the wound it inflicts is incurable.
⁴ Bullying and insolence are destroyers of wealth;
thus a proud man will be bereft of his home.
⁵ The Lord listens to the appeal of the poor,
and his verdict follows promptly.
⁶ To hate reproof is to go the way of sinners,
but whoever fears the Lord will repent wholeheartedly.
⁷ A great talker is known far and wide;
a sensible person is aware of his own failings.
⁸ To build a house with borrowed money
is like gathering the stones for one's own tomb.
⁹ An assembly of the wicked is like a bundle of tow;
they end in flames.
¹⁰ The sinners' road is smoothly paved,
but it leads straight down to the grave.

Folly and indiscretion

¹¹ WHOEVER keeps the law keeps control of his thoughts;
the fear of the Lord has its outcome in wisdom.
¹² He who is not clever cannot be taught,
but there is a cleverness which breeds bitterness.
¹³ The knowledge of the wise is like a river in full flood;
advice from such is like a fountain of life.
¹⁴ A fool's mind is like a broken jug:
it cannot retain anything it learns.
¹⁵ If an instructed man hears a wise saying,
he applauds it and improves on it;
if a dissolute man hears it, he is annoyed
and flings it away out of his sight.
¹⁶ Listening to a fool is like travelling with a heavy pack,
but delight is to be found in learned conversation.

20:31 **his wisdom**: *some witnesses add* ³² Better to seek the Lord with unremitting patience than to drive one's way through life on one's own.

108

17 The assembly welcomes a word from
a wise man
and ponders what he says.
18 To a fool, wisdom is like a derelict
house;
the knowledge of the stupid is a
string of ill-digested sayings.
19 To the ignorant, instruction is like
fetters,
like a manacle on the right wrist.
21 To the wise, instruction is a gold
ornament
like a bracelet on the right arm.
20 A fool guffaws,
but a clever man smiles quietly, if at
all.
22 A fool rushes into a house,
while someone of experience hangs
back politely.
23 A boor peers into a house from the
doorstep,
while a well-bred person stands
outside.
24 It is bad manners to eavesdrop at
doors;
anyone with sense would think it an
intolerable disgrace.
25 The glib only repeat what others
have said,
but the wise weigh every word.
26 Fools speak before they think,
but the wise think before they speak.
27 When the ungodly curses his
adversary,
he is really cursing himself.
28 A tale-bearer blackens his own
character
and gets himself detested throughout
the neighbourhood.

22 A sluggard is like a filthy
stone:
everyone jeers at his disgrace.
2 A sluggard is like a lump of dung:
whoever picks it up shakes it off his
hand.

3 There is shame in being father to an
ill-mannered son,
and the birth of a daughter means
loss.
4 A sensible daughter wins a husband,
but an immodest one is a grief to her
father.

5 A brazen daughter brings shame on
father and husband,
and is despised by both.
6 Unseasonable talk is like music in
time of mourning,
but the lash of wisdom's discipline is
always in season.

7 Teaching a fool is like mending
pottery with paste,
or like rousing a sleeper from heavy
slumber.
8 As well talk with someone dozing as
with a fool;
when you have finished, he will say,
'What was that?'
11 Weep for the dead: he has taken
leave of the light;
weep for the fool: he has taken leave
of his wits.
Weep less bitterly for the dead, for he
is at rest;
but the fool's life is worse than death.
12 Mourning for the dead lasts seven
days;
for an impious fool it lasts all the
days of his life.

13 Do not prolong talk with a fool
or visit one who is stupid.
Beware of him, or you may be in
trouble
and find yourself bespattered when
he shakes himself.
Avoid him, if you are looking for
peace,
and you will not be worn out by his
folly.
14 What is heavier than lead?
What is its name but 'Fool'?
15 Sand, salt, and a lump of iron
are less of a burden than a stupid
person.

16 A tie-beam fixed firmly into a
building
is not shaken loose by an
earthquake;
so a mind kept steadfast by sensible
advice
will not be daunted in a crisis.
17 A mind solidly backed by intelligent
thought
is like stucco decorating a well-
prepared wall.

22:8 **'What was that?'**: *some witnesses add* 9 Children nurtured in a good life do not show the low birth of their parents; 10 but those who run riot, haughty and undisciplined, sully the good name of their family.

¹⁸ As a fence set on a hilltop
will not stand against the wind,
so a mind made timid by foolish
fancies
is not proof against any terror.

¹⁹ Prick the eye and tears will flow;
prick the heart and you will find it
sensitive.
²⁰ Throw a stone at birds and you scare
them away;
taunt a friend and you destroy a
friendship.
²¹ If you have drawn your sword on a
friend,
do not despair; a way back is still
open.
²² If you have quarrelled with a friend,
do not hold aloof, for there can still
be reconciliation.
But taunts, scorn, a secret betrayed,
a stab in the back—
these will make any friend keep his
distance.
²³ Win your neighbour's confidence
while he is poor,
that you may share fully in his
prosperity;
stand by him in time of trouble,
that you may be his partner when he
comes into a fortune.
²⁴ As furnace fumes and smoke precede
the flame,
so insults come before bloodshed.
²⁵ I shall not be ashamed to protect a
friend,
nor shall I turn my back on him;
²⁶ and if on his account harm should
befall me,
everyone who hears of it will beware
of him.

²⁷ O FOR a sentry to guard my mouth
and a seal of discretion to close my
lips,
to prevent them from being my
downfall,
to keep my tongue from causing my
ruin!

23

Lord, Father, and Ruler of my
life,
do not abandon me to the tongue's
control
or allow it to bring about my
downfall.

² O for wisdom's rod to curb my
thoughts
and to discipline my mind,
that my shortcomings may not be
overlooked
or any sin of mine be condoned!
³ Then my errors would not multiply
or my sins increase in number,
humiliating me before my opponents
and giving my enemy cause to gloat.
⁴ Lord, Father, and God of my life,
do not let me wear a supercilious
look.
⁵ Protect me from the onslaught of
desire;
⁶ let neither gluttony nor lust take
hold of me,
and do not give me over to
shamelessness.

⁷ Hear how to discipline the mouth,
my sons;
he that does so will never be caught
out.
⁸ It is by his own words that the
sinner is ensnared;
by his own scurrility and pride he is
tripped.
⁹ Do not accustom your mouth to
oaths
or make a habit of using the Holy
One's name.
¹⁰ As a servant constantly questioned
under the lash
is never free from weals,
so also anyone who has oaths and
the sacred name forever on his lips
will never be clear of guilt.
¹¹ One given to oaths is wicked to the
core;
the rod will never be far from his
house.
If he goes back on his word, he must
bear the blame;
if he wilfully neglects it, he sins twice
over;
if his oath was insincere, punishment
will overtake him
and his house will be filled with
trouble.
¹² There is a kind of speech that is the
counterpart of death;
may it never be found among Jacob's
descendants!

22:18 **a fence:** *or* pebbles.

The godly will keep clear of such
conduct
and will not wallow in sin.

13 Do not make a habit of coarse and
filthy talk,
or you will be bound to say
something sinful.

14 Remember your father and mother
when you take your seat among the
great;
otherwise you may forget yourself in
their presence
and through such habits make a fool
of yourself;
then you will wish you had never
been born,
and curse the day of your birth.

15 Someone addicted to scurrilous talk
will never learn better as long as he
lives.

16 Two KINDS of people add sin to sin,
and a third brings God's wrath on
himself.
Hot lust that blazes like a fire
can never be suppressed till life itself
is quenched.
A man whose whole body is given to
sensuality
never stops till the fire consumes
him.

17 To the profligate every cake is as
sweet as the last,
and he will not leave off until he
dies.

18 The man who strays from his own
bed
says to himself, 'Who can see me?
All around is dark and the walls hide
me;
nobody can see me; why need I
worry?
The Most High will take no note of
my sins.'

19 The eyes of human beings are all he
fears;
he forgets that the eyes of the Lord
are ten thousand times brighter than
the sun,
observing every step that mortals
take
and penetrating to every secret place;

20 before all things were created, they
were known to him,
and so it is since their completion.

21 Such a man will pay the penalty in
the public street,
caught where he least expected it.

22 So too with the woman who is
unfaithful to her husband,
presenting him with an heir by
another man:

23 first, she disobeys the law of the Most
High;
secondly, she commits an offence
against her husband;
thirdly, she has prostituted herself
by bearing bastard children.

24 She shall be brought before the
assembly for judgement,
and the consequences will fall on her
children.

25 Her children will not take root,
nor will fruit grow on her branches.

26 A curse will rest on her memory,
and her shame will never be wiped
out.

27 All who survive her will learn
that nothing is better than the fear of
the Lord,
nothing sweeter than obeying his
commandments.

In praise of wisdom

24 HEAR the praise of wisdom from
her own mouth,
as she speaks with pride among her
people,

2 before the assembly of the Most High
and in the presence of the heavenly
host:

3 'I am the word spoken by the Most
High;
it was I who covered the earth like a
mist.

4 My dwelling-place was in high
heaven;
my throne was in a pillar of cloud.

5 Alone I made a circuit of the sky
and traversed the depths of the abyss.

6 The waves of the sea, the whole
earth,
every people and nation were under
my sway.

7 Among them all I sought where I
might come to rest:
in whose territory was I to settle?

8 Then the Creator of all things laid a
command on me;

23:27 **his commandments:** *some witnesses add* 28 To follow God brings great honour; to win his approval
means length of days.

he who created me decreed where I
should dwell.
He said, "Make your home in Jacob;
enter on your heritage in Israel."
⁹ Before time began he created me,
and until the end of time I shall
endure.
¹⁰ In the sacred tent I ministered in his
presence,
and thus I came to be established in
Zion.
¹¹ He settled me in the city he loved
and gave me authority in Jerusalem.
¹² I took root among the people whom
the Lord had honoured
by choosing them to be his own
portion.

¹³ 'There I grew like a cedar of
Lebanon,
like a cypress on the slopes of
Hermon,
¹⁴ like a date-palm at En-gedi,
like roses at Jericho.
I grew like a fair olive tree in the
vale,
or like a plane tree planted beside the
water.
¹⁵ Like cinnamon or camel-thorn I was
redolent of spices;
like choice myrrh I spread my
fragrance,
like galbanum, aromatic shell, and
gum resin,
like the smoke of frankincense in the
sacred tent.
¹⁶ Like a terebinth I spread out my
branches,
laden with honour and grace.
¹⁷ I put forth graceful shoots like the
vine,
and my blossoms were a harvest of
honour and wealth.

¹⁹ 'Come to me, all you who desire me,
and eat your fill of my fruit.
²⁰ To think of me is sweeter than
honey,
to possess me sweeter than the
honeycomb.
²¹ Whoever feeds on me will hunger
for more;

whoever drinks from me will thirst
for more.
²² To obey me is to be safe from
disgrace;
those who make me their business
will not go astray.'

²³ All this is the book of the covenant of
God Most High,
the law laid on us by Moses,
a possession for the assemblies of
Jacob.
²⁵ It sends out wisdom in full flood like
the river Pishon
or like the Tigris at the time of
firstfruits;
²⁶ it overflows like the Euphrates with
understanding
or like the Jordan at the harvest
season.
²⁷ It pours forth instruction like the Nile,
like the Gihon at the time of vintage.
²⁸ No one has ever known wisdom fully
and from first to last no one has
fathomed her,
²⁹ for her thoughts are vaster than the
ocean,
her purpose more profound than the
great abyss.

³⁰ As for me, I was like a watercourse
leading from a river,
like a conduit into a pleasure garden.
³¹ I said, 'I will water my garden,
soaking its flower beds';
all at once my watercourse became a
river
and my river a sea.
³² I will again make learning shine like
the dawn,
that its light may be seen from afar.
³³ I will again pour out my teaching
like prophecy
and bequeath it to future
generations.
³⁴ Truly, I have not toiled for myself
alone
but for all who seek wisdom.

25 THERE are three sights which
warm my heart
and are beautiful in the eyes of the
Lord and of men:

24:17 **honour and wealth**: *some witnesses add* ¹⁸ I give birth to honourable love, to reverence, knowledge, and
holy hope; all these my eternal progeny I give to God's elect (*prob. mng; Gk obscure*).   24:23 **assemblies of
Jacob**: *some witnesses add* ²⁴ Never fail to be strong in the Lord; hold fast to him, so that he may strengthen you.
The Lord Almighty is God alone, and beside him there is no saviour.   24:25,26,27 **It**: *or* He.
24:27 **pours ... Nile**: *so one Vs.; Gk* makes instruction shine like light.

concord among brothers, amity
among neighbours,
and a man and wife who are
inseparable.
² There are three kinds of men who
arouse my hatred
and disgust me by their manner of
life:
a poor man who boasts, a rich man
who lies,
and an old fool who commits
adultery.

³ If you have not gathered wisdom in
your youth,
will you find it when you are old?
⁴ How well sound judgement befits
grey hairs,
as wise advice does those advanced
in years!
⁵ How well wisdom befits the aged,
and ripe counsel persons of
eminence!
⁶ Long experience is the crown of the
aged,
and their pride is the fear of the Lord.

⁷ I can think of nine men I count
happy,
and I can tell you of a tenth:
a man who delights in his children,
and one who lives to see the
downfall of his enemy.
⁸ Happy the husband of a sensible wife,
the farmer who does not plough with
ox and ass together,
he whose tongue never trips him,
and he who has never had to work
for his inferior!
⁹ Happy the man who has found a
friend,
and the speaker who has an attentive
audience!
¹⁰ How great is he who finds wisdom!
But no greater than he who fears the
Lord.
¹¹ The fear of the Lord excels all other
gifts;
to whom can its possessor be
compared?

Domestic counsels
¹³ ANY wound but a wound in the
heart,

any malice but a woman's!
¹⁴ Any disaster but one caused by hate,
any vengeance but the vengeance of
an enemy!
¹⁵ There is no venom deadlier than a
snake's
and no anger deadlier than a
woman's.

¹⁶ I would sooner live with a lion or a
serpent
than share a house with a malicious
wife.
¹⁷ Her spite changes her expression,
making her look as surly as a bear.
¹⁸ Her husband goes to a neighbour for
his meals
and cannot repress a bitter sigh.

¹⁹ There is nothing so bad as a bad
wife;
may the fate of the wicked overtake
her!
²⁰ It is as easy for an old man to climb
a sand-dune
as for a quiet husband to live with a
garrulous wife.
²¹ Do not be enticed by a woman's
beauty
or set your heart on possessing one
who has wealth.
²² If a man is supported by his wife
he must expect tantrums, effrontery,
and much humiliation.
²³ Depression, downcast looks, and a
broken heart:
these are caused by a worthless wife.
Feeble of hand and weak at the knees
is the man whose wife fails to bring
him happiness.
²⁴ Sin began with a woman,
and because of her we all die.
²⁵ Do not leave a leaky cistern to drip
or allow a worthless wife to say
whatever she likes.
²⁶ If she does not accept your control,
bring the marriage to an end.

26 A good wife makes a happy
husband;
she doubles the length of his life.
² A staunch wife is her husband's joy;
he will live out his days in peace.
³ A good wife is a blessing;

25:8 **the farmer ... together**: *so Heb.; Gk omits.*   25:9 **found a friend**: *so Vss.; Gk* found good sense.
25:11 **be compared**: *some witnesses add* ¹² The fear of the Lord is the source of love for him, and faith is the
source of adherence to him.   25:15 **venom**: *prob. mng.; Gk* head. **a woman's**: *so some Vss.; Gk* an enemy's.
26:3 **blessing**: *lit.* good portion.

she is one of the Lord's gifts to those
who fear him.
4 Rich or poor, they are in good heart,
with always a smile on their faces.
5 Three things there are that alarm
me,
and a fourth I am afraid to face:
scandalmongering in the city, a mob
controlling the assembly,
and false accusation—all harder to
bear than death;
6 but a wife's jealousy of a rival brings
heartache and grief,
and everyone alike feels the lash of
her tongue.
7 A bad wife is a yoke that chafes;
controlling her is like handling a
scorpion.
8 A drunken wife provokes much
anger;
she will not conceal her excesses.
9 A loose woman betrays herself by her
bold looks;
you can tell her by her glance.
10 Keep close watch over a headstrong
daughter;
if she finds you off your guard, she
will take her chance.
11 Beware of her impudent looks
and do not be surprised if she
disobeys you.
12 As a parched traveller with gaping
mouth
drinks from any spring that offers,
she will open her arms to every
embrace
and her quiver to every arrow.
13 A wife's charm is the delight of her
husband,
and her womanly skill puts flesh on
his bones.

14 A silent wife is a gift from the Lord;
her good breeding is more than
money can buy.
15 A modest wife has infinite charm;
no scales can weigh the worth of her
self-control.
16 As beautiful as the sunrise in the
Lord's heavens
is a good wife in a well-ordered home.
17 As bright as the light on the sacred
lampstand
is a beautiful face with a stately
figure.
18 Like a golden pillar on a silver base
is a shapely leg with a firm foot.
28 TWO THINGS grieve my heart,
and a third excites my anger:
a soldier in distress through poverty,
the wise treated with contempt,
and someone deserting right conduct
for wrong—
for such a one the Lord will get
ready the sword.
29 How rare it is for a merchant to keep
clear of wrong
or a shopkeeper to be acquitted of
dishonesty!

27 Many have cheated for gain;
a money-grubber will always
turn a blind eye.
2 As a peg is fixed in the joint between
stones,
so dishonesty squeezes in between
selling and buying.
3 Unless a person holds resolutely to
the fear of the Lord,
his house will soon collapse in ruins.
4 Shake a sieve, and the rubbish
remains;
start an argument, and a man's
faults show up.

26:18 **a firm foot:** *some witnesses add*
19 My son, guard your health in the bloom of your
youth,
and do not waste your vigour on strange
women.
20 Search the whole plain for a fertile plot;
sow your own seed, trusting in your sound
stock.
21 Then the children you leave behind
will prosper, confident in their parentage.
22 A woman of the streets is no better than
spittle;
a married woman is a mortuary for her lovers.
23 A godless woman is a good match for a lawless
husband,
a godly one for a man who fears the Lord.

24 A brazen woman courts disgrace,
but a virtuous daughter is modest even before
her husband.
25 A headstrong woman is a shameless bitch,
but a modest one fears the Lord.
26 A woman who honours her husband is
accounted wise by all,
but if she despises him, all know her as proud
and godless.
A good wife makes a happy husband;
she doubles the length of his life.
27 A strident, garrulous wife is like a trumpet
sounding the charge;
in a home like hers a man lives in the
confusions of war.

5 As the work of a potter is tested in
  the kiln,
so a man is tried in debate.
6 As a tree's fruit reveals the skill of
  the grower,
so the expression of a man's
  thoughts reveals his character.
7 Do not praise a man till you hear
  him in argument,
for that is the test.

8 If justice is what you seek, you will
  succeed
and wear it like a splendid robe.
9 Birds of a feather roost together,
and honesty comes home to those
  who practise it.
10 A lion lies in wait for its prey;
so does sin for those whose conduct
  is evil.

11 The conversation of the godly is
  constantly wise,
but a fool is as changeable as the
  moon.
12 Grudge every minute spent among
  fools,
but linger among the thoughtful.
13 The conversation of fools provokes
  disgust;
to them a life of licence is just a
  joke.
14 The chatter of the profane makes the
  hair stand on end;
when such folk quarrel, others stop
  their ears.
15 The quarrels of the proud lead to
  bloodshed;
their abuse makes sorry hearing.

16 The betrayer of secrets forfeits all
  trust;
he will never find an intimate friend.
17 Love your friend and keep faith with
  him;
but if you betray his secrets, steer
  clear of him,
18 for as one kills an enemy,
so you have killed your neighbour's
  friendship.
19 As a bird that is allowed to fly out of
  your hand,
your neighbour, once lost, will not
  be caught again.
20 He has gone too far for you to
  pursue him;
he has escaped like a gazelle from a
  trap.

21 A wound may be bandaged, an
  insult pardoned,
but the betrayer of secrets has
  renounced all hope.
22 Someone who winks is plotting
  mischief;
those who know him will keep their
  distance.
23 He speaks sweetly enough to your
  face
and admires whatever you say,
but later he will change his tune
and use your own words to trip you.
24 There are many things I hate, but
  him above all;
and the Lord will hate him too.

25 Throw a stone in the air and you
  throw it on your own head;
and a treacherous blow means
  wounds all round.
26 Dig a pit and you will fall into it;
set a trap and you will be caught by
  it.
27 The wrong anyone does recoils on
  him,
and he has no idea where it comes
  from.
28 The arrogant deal in mockery and
  taunts,
but like a lion retribution lies in wait
  for them.
29 Those who rejoice at the downfall of
  the good will be trapped,
and before they die they will be
  consumed with pain.

30 Rage and anger, these also I abhor,
but a sinner has them ready at hand.

28 Whoever acts vengefully will
  face the vengeance of the
  Lord,
who keeps strict account of sins.
2 Forgive your neighbour any wrong
  he has done you;
then, when you pray, your sins will
  be forgiven.
3 If anyone harbours anger against
  another,
can he expect help from the Lord?
4 If he refuses mercy to his fellow,
can he ask forgiveness for his own
  sins?
5 If a mere mortal cherishes rage,
where is he to look for pardon?
6 Think of the end that awaits you,
and have done with hate;

think of mortality and death, and be
true to the commandments;
⁷ think of the commandments, and do
not be enraged at your neighbour;
think of the covenant of the Most
High, and overlook errors.

⁸ To avoid a quarrel is a setback for
sin,
for quarrels are kindled by a hot
temper.
⁹ A sinner sets friends at odds
and spreads enmity where before
there was peace.
¹⁰ The more fuel, the fiercer the blaze;
the more stubborn the defence, the
fiercer the fight.
The greater a person, the greater his
anger;
the more his wealth, the higher his
temper will flare.
¹¹ A hasty dispute kindles a fire;
a hasty quarrel leads to bloodshed.
¹² Blow on a spark to make it glow,
or spit on it to put it out;
both results come from your mouth.

¹³ Curses on tale-bearing and duplicity!
For they have been the ruin of many
who were living peaceably.
¹⁴ A third party's talk has wrecked the
lives of many
and driven them from country to
country;
it has destroyed strong cities
and overthrown the houses of the
great.
¹⁵ A third party's talk has brought
divorce on staunch wives
and deprived them of the fruits of
their industry;
¹⁶ whoever heeds it will never again
find rest
or live in peace of mind.
¹⁷ The lash of a whip raises weals,
but the lash of a tongue will break
bones.
¹⁸ Many have been killed by the edge of
the sword,
but not so many as by the tongue.
¹⁹ Happy are they who are sheltered
from its onslaught,
who have not been exposed to its
fury,
who have not borne its yoke
or been chained with its fetters;
²⁰ for its yoke is of iron,
its fetters are of bronze!

²¹ The death it inflicts is a horrible
death;
better the grave than the tongue!
²² But it has no power over the
godfearing;
they cannot be burnt in its flames.
²³ Rather, those who desert the Lord
fall victim to it;
among them it will blaze up and
never be quenched.
It will launch itself against them like
a lion
and tear them like a leopard.
²⁴ As you enclose your garden with a
thorn hedge,
and as you tie up securely your silver
and gold,
²⁵ so weigh your words and measure
them,
and make for your mouth a door
that locks.
²⁶ Take care you are not tripped by
your tongue
to fall before a waiting enemy.

29 HE who is compassionate lends
to his neighbour;
by giving a helping hand he fulfils
the commandments.
² Lend to your neighbour in his hour
of need;
repay your neighbour punctually.
³ Be as good as your word and keep
faith with him,
and your needs will always be met.
⁴ Many treat a loan as a windfall
and create trouble for those who
helped them.
⁵ Until he gets a loan, a man kisses his
neighbour's hand
and at the sight of his wealth drops
his voice;
when repayment is due, he delays,
pays back only perfunctory promises,
and claims that times are hard.
⁶ If the creditor presses, he will get
back scarcely half,
and will count himself lucky at that;
if he does not press, he has deprived
himself of the money,
and made an enemy into the
bargain.
The debtor will pay him back in
curses and insults,
with dishonour in place of honour.
⁷ Because of such knavery many refuse
to lend,

for fear of being parted from their
money to no purpose.

⁸ Nevertheless be patient with the
penniless,
and do not keep them waiting for
your charity;
⁹ for the commandment's sake help the
poor,
and in their need do not send them
away empty-handed.
¹⁰ Be ready to lose money for a brother
or a friend
rather than leave it to rust away
under a stone.
¹¹ Dispose of your treasure as
commanded by the Most High;
that will benefit you more than gold.
¹² Let almsgiving be the treasure in
your strong-room,
and it will deliver you from every
misfortune;
¹³ better than stout shield or strong
spear,
it will arm you against the enemy.

¹⁴ A good person will stand surety for
his neighbour;
only he who is lost to shame will let
him down.
¹⁵ If someone stands surety for you, do
not forget the favour;
he has staked his very self on your
behalf.
¹⁶ A sinner ruins the property of his
surety,
¹⁷ and one who is ungrateful leaves his
rescuer in the lurch.
¹⁸ Standing surety has overturned the
prosperity of many
and wrecked them like a storm at
sea;
it has driven people of influence into
exile
and set them wandering in foreign
countries.
¹⁹ When a sinner involves himself in
accepting surety,
his pursuit of gain will land him in
lawsuits.
²⁰ So help your neighbour to the best of
your ability,
but beware of becoming too deeply
involved.

²¹ The basis of life is water, bread, and
clothing,
and a home with decent privacy.

²² Better the life of the poor in his own
hut
than a sumptuous banquet in
someone else's house!
²³ Rest content with whatever you
have, be it much or little,
and do not become known for living
on hospitality.
²⁴ It is a miserable life going from house
to house,
keeping your mouth shut because
you are a visitor.
²⁵ Without thanks you play the host
and hand round the drinks,
and into the bargain must listen to
things that rankle:
²⁶ 'Come here, you stranger, and lay
the table;
whatever you have there, hand it to
me.'
²⁷ 'Be off, stranger! Make way for a
more important guest;
my brother has come to stay, and I
need the guest room.'
²⁸ Two things a sensitive person finds
hard to bear:
criticism at home and abuse from a
creditor!

30 A MAN who loves his son will
not spare the rod,
and then in his old age he may have
joy of him.
² He who disciplines his son will find
profit in him
and take pride in him among his
acquaintances.
³ He who educates his son makes his
enemy envious
and will boast of him among friends.
⁴ When the father dies, it is as if he
were still alive,
for he has left behind a copy of
himself.
⁵ During his lifetime he saw and
rejoiced,
and on his deathbed he had no
regrets.
⁶ He has left an heir to take vengeance
on his enemies
and to repay friends for their
kindness.
⁷ A man who coddles his son will
bandage every scratch
and be on tenterhooks at every cry.
⁸ An unbroken horse turns out
stubborn,

and an unchecked son turns out
headstrong.
⁹ Pamper a boy and he will shock you;
join in his games and he will grieve
you.
¹⁰ Do not share his laughter, or you
will share his pain
and end by grinding your teeth.
¹¹ While he is young do not give him
freedom
or overlook his errors.
¹² While he is young break him in,
and beat him soundly while he is still
a child;
otherwise he may grow stubborn and
disobedient
and cause you distress.
¹³ Discipline your son and take pains
with him
or he may affront you by some
disgraceful act.

¹⁴ BETTER to be poor and healthy and fit
than to be rich and racked by
disease.
¹⁵ Health and fitness are better than
any amount of gold,
and vigour of body than boundless
prosperity.
¹⁶ There is no wealth to compare with
bodily health,
no joy to surpass gladness of heart.
¹⁷ Better death than a life of misery,
eternal rest than a long illness.
¹⁸ Delicacies heaped before someone
with no appetite
are like offerings of food placed on a
tomb.
¹⁹ What use is a sacrifice to an idol
which can neither taste nor smell?
So it is with one afflicted by the
Lord:
²⁰ he gazes at the food before him and
groans
as a eunuch groans when he
embraces a virgin.
²¹ Do not abandon yourself to grief
or go out of your way to distress
yourself.
²² A merry heart keeps a person alive,
and joy lengthens his span of days.
²³ Indulge yourself, take comfort,
and banish grief far from you;
for grief has been the death of many
and no advantage ever came of it.
²⁴ Envy and anger shorten life,
and anxiety brings premature old age.

²⁵ He who has a light heart has a good
appetite
and relishes the food he eats.

31 Wakeful nights make the rich
person lose weight,
when the cares of wealth drive sleep
away;
² sleepless worry keeps him wide
awake,
just as serious illness banishes sleep.
³ The rich man toils to amass a
fortune,
and when he relaxes he enjoys every
luxury.
⁴ The poor man toils to make a slender
living,
and when he relaxes he finds himself
in want.

⁵ Passion for gold can never be right;
the pursuit of profit leads astray.
⁶ Because of gold many a one has met
his downfall
and found himself face to face with
ruin.
⁷ Gold is a pitfall to those who make it
their god,
and every fool is ensnared by it.
⁸ Happy are the rich who have
remained blameless
and have not let gold become their
guide!
⁹ Show us such a person, and we will
congratulate him;
he has performed a miracle among
his people.
¹⁰ Has anyone come through this test
unscathed?
Then he has good cause to be proud.
Has anyone had it in his power to
sin and refrained,
to do wrong and not done it?
¹¹ Then he will be confirmed in his
prosperity,
and the assembly will hail him as a
benefactor.

¹² WHEN seated at a grand table
do not smack your lips and exclaim,
'What a feast!'
¹³ Remember, it is a bad thing to have
a greedy eye.
There is no greater evil in creation
than the eye;
for that reason it must shed tears at
every turn.

¹⁴ Do not reach for everything within
    sight,
    or jostle your fellow-guest at the
    dish;
¹⁵ judge his feelings by your own,
    and always behave with
    consideration.
¹⁶ Eat what is set before you, but not
    like a beast;
    do not munch your food and make
    yourself objectionable.
¹⁷ Be the first to stop for good manners'
    sake
    and do not be a glutton, or you will
    give offence.
¹⁸ If you are dining in a large
    company,
    do not reach out your hand before
    others.
¹⁹ A person of good upbringing is
    content with little,
    so when he goes to bed he is not
    short of breath.
²⁰ The moderate eater enjoys healthy
    sleep:
    he rises early, feeling refreshed;
    but sleeplessness, nausea, and colic
    are the lot of the glutton.
²¹ If you cannot avoid overeating at a
    banquet,
    leave the table and find relief by
    vomiting.

²² Listen to me, my son; do not
    disregard me,
    and in the end my words will come
    home to you.
    In all you do avoid extremes,
    and no illness will come your way.
²³ Everyone has a good word for a
    liberal host;
    the evidence of his generosity is
    convincing.
²⁴ The whole town grumbles at a mean
    host,
    and there is sure evidence of his
    meanness.

²⁵ Do not use wine to prove your
    manhood,
    for wine has been the ruin of many.
²⁶ As the furnace tests iron when it is
    being tempered,
    so wine tests character when
    boasters are wrangling.
²⁷ Wine puts life into anyone
    who drinks it in moderation.

What is life to somebody deprived of
    wine?
Was it not created to gladden the
    heart?
²⁸ Wine brings gaiety and high spirits
    if people know when to drink and
    when to stop;
²⁹ but wine in excess makes for bitter
    feelings
    and leads to offence and retaliation.
³⁰ Drunkenness inflames a fool's anger
    to his own hurt;
    it saps his strength and exposes him
    to injury.
³¹ At a banquet do not rebuke your
    fellow-guest
    or make him feel small while he is
    enjoying himself.
    That is no time to upbraid him
    or pester him to pay his debts.

32 ARE you chosen to preside at a
    feast? Do not put on airs;
    mix with the others as one of them.
    Look after them and only then sit
    down yourself;
    discharge your duties before you take
    your place.
² Let the enjoyment of others be your
    pleasure,
    and you will win a garland for good
    manners.
³ When you are old, you are entitled
    to speak,
    but come to the point and do not
    interrupt the music.
⁴ Where entertainment is provided, do
    not keep up a stream of talk;
    it is the wrong moment to show off
    your wisdom.
⁵ Like a garnet set in a gold ring
    is a concert of music at a banquet.
⁶ Like an emerald in a setting of
    gold
    is tuneful music with good wine.
⁷ When you are young, speak if the
    need arises,
    but twice at the most, and only
    when asked.
⁸ Be brief, say much in few words,
    like someone who knows and can
    still hold his tongue.
⁹ In the company of the great do not
    make yourself their equal
    or go on chattering when another is
    speaking.

10 As lightning streaks ahead of
   thunder,
   so esteem goes before a modest
   person.
11 Leave in good time and do not be the
   last to go;
   go straight off home without lingering.
12 There you may amuse yourself to
   your heart's content
   without giving offence by arrogant
   talk.
13 And one thing more: give praise to
   your Maker,
   who has filled your cup with his
   benefits.

14 WHOEVER fears the Lord will accept
   his discipline;
   those diligent in their search for him
   win his approval.
15 Those who study the law will find
   satisfaction therein,
   but the law will prove a stumbling
   block to the insincere.
16 Those who fear the Lord discover his
   will
   and make his decrees shine out like a
   beacon.
17 A sinner does not accept criticism;
   he will find precedents to justify his
   choice.
18 A thoughtful person can always take
   a hint,
   but an arrogant upstart lacks all
   diffidence.
19 Never do anything without due
   thought,
   and once started do not change your
   mind.
20 Do not travel by a road full of
   obstacles
   and stumble along among its
   boulders.
21 Do not be careless on a clear road;
22 watch where you go.
23 Whatever you are doing, keep
   yourself safe,
   for this too is fulfilling the
   commandments.
24 To rely on the law is to heed its
   commandments;
   trust the Lord and suffer no loss.

33 No misfortune ever befalls him
   who fears the Lord:
   in trials he will be rescued time and
   again.

2 A wise person does not hate the law,
   but he who is insincere about it is
   like a skiff in a squall.
3 A sensible person puts his trust in
   the law,
   finding it reliable like the oracle of
   God.

4 If you want a hearing, prepare what
   you have to say;
   marshal your learning, then give
   your answer.
5 The feelings of a fool turn like a
   cartwheel,
   and his thoughts spin like an axle.
6 A sarcastic friend is like a stallion
   which neighs no matter who is on its
   back.

7 Why is one day more important than
   another,
   when every day in the year has its
   light from the sun?
8 It was by the Lord's decision that
   they were distinguished;
   he appointed the various seasons and
   festivals:
9 some days he made high and holy,
   and others he assigned to the
   common run of days.
10 All mankind comes from the
   ground—
   Adam himself was created out of
   earth—
11 yet in his great wisdom the Lord
   distinguished them
   and made them go their various
   ways:
12 some he blessed and lifted high,
   some he hallowed and brought near
   to himself,
   others he cursed and humbled
   and removed from their place.
13 As clay is in the potter's hands
   to be moulded just as he chooses,
   so are human beings in the hands of
   their Maker
   to be dealt with as he decides.
14 Good is the opposite of evil, and life
   of death;
   so the sinner is the opposite of the
   godly.
15 Look at all the works of the Most
   High—
   they are in pairs, one the counterpart
   of the other.

16 I, last of all, kept watch.

I was like a gleaner following the
  grape-pickers,
and by the Lord's blessing I arrived
  in time
to fill my winepress as full as any of
  them.
¹⁷ Note that I did not toil for myself
  alone,
but for all who seek learning.
¹⁸ Listen to me, you dignitaries among
  the people;
you leaders of the assembly, give me
  your attention.

¹⁹ As long as you live, give no one
  power over yourself—
son or wife, brother or friend.
Do not give your possessions to
  another,
in case you change your mind and
  want them back.
²⁰ As long as you have life and breath,
do not let anyone take your place.
²¹ It is better for your children to ask
  help from you
than for you to be dependent on
  them.
²² In all that you do, keep the upper
  hand
and allow no stain on your
  reputation.
²³ Let your life run its full course
and then, at the hour of death,
  distribute your property.

²⁴ Fodder, the stick, and burdens for a
  donkey;
for a servant—bread, discipline, and
  work!
²⁵ Keep your slave at work, if you want
  rest for yourself;
if you let him slack, he will be
  looking for his liberty.
²⁶ The ox is tamed by yoke and
  harness,
the bad servant by rack and torture.
²⁷ Set him to work to keep him from
  being idle,
for idleness is a great teacher of
  mischief.
²⁸ Give him work to do, for that is what
  he is for,
and if he disobeys you, load him with
  fetters.
²⁹ Do not be too exacting towards
  anyone

or do anything contrary to justice.
³⁰ If you have only one servant, treat
  him as you do yourself,
because you bought him at a high
  price.
³¹ If you have only one servant, treat
  him like a brother;
you will need him as much as you
  need yourself.
If you ill-treat him and he takes to
  his heels,
where will you go to look for him?

34 Vain hopes delude the senseless,
and dreams give wings to a
  fool's fancy.
² Paying heed to dreams
is like clutching a shadow or chasing
  the wind.
³ What you see in a dream is nothing
  but a reflection,
the image of a face in a mirror.
⁴ Truth can no more come from
  illusion
than purity can come from impurity.
⁵ Divination, omens, and dreams are
  all futile,
mere fantasies, like those of a woman
  in labour.
⁶ Unless they are sent by intervention
  from the Most High,
pay no attention to them.
⁷ Dreams have led many astray
and disappointed those who built
  their hopes on them.
⁸ The law is perfect without such
  illusions;
wisdom spoken by those faithful to
  the law is complete.

⁹ He who is well travelled knows
  much,
and a person of experience
  understands what he is talking
  about.
¹⁰ He who has little experience knows
  little,
but travel increases a person's
  resources.
¹¹ In the course of my own journeyings
  I have seen much
and understand more than I can put
  into words.
¹² I have often been in deadly danger
but escaped, thanks to the experience
  I had gained.

33:30 **at a high price:** *Gk* with blood.

True piety

13 THOSE who fear the Lord will live,
for their trust is in him who can keep
them safe.
14 Fear the Lord and have nothing else
to fear;
he whose trust is in him will never
be daunted.
15 How happy is he who fears the Lord!
He knows where to look for support.
16 The Lord keeps watch over those
who love him;
he is their strong shield and firm
support,
a shelter from scorching wind and
noonday heat,
a safeguard against stumbling, a help
against falling.
17 He raises the spirits and makes the
eyes sparkle;
he gives healing and life and
blessing.

18 A sacrifice from ill-gotten gains is
tainted,
and the gifts of the wicked win no
approval.
19 The Most High has no pleasure in
the offerings of the godless,
nor do countless sacrifices win his
forgiveness.
20 To offer a sacrifice from the
possessions of the poor
is like killing a son before his father's
eyes.
21 Bread is life to the destitute,
and to deprive them of it is murder.
22 To rob your neighbour of his
livelihood is to kill him,
and he who defrauds a worker of his
wages sheds blood.

23 WHEN one builds and another pulls
down,
what have they gained except hard
work?
24 When one prays and another curses,
which is the Lord to listen to?
25 Bathe after touching a corpse and
then touch it again,
and what have you gained by your
washing?
26 So it is with the one who fasts for his
sins
and goes and repeats his offence;
who will listen to his prayer?
What has he gained by his penance?

35 To keep the law is worth many
offerings;
to heed the commandments is a
shared-offering.
2 A kindness repaid is a grain-offering,
and to give alms is a thank-offering.
3 The way to please the Lord is to keep
clear of evil,
and to keep clear of wrongdoing is to
make atonement.
4 Yet do not appear before the Lord
empty-handed;
5 perform all the sacrifices, for they are
commanded.
6 When the just person brings his
offering of fat to the altar,
its fragrance rises to the presence of
the Most High.
7 The sacrifice of the just is acceptable,
and such a memorial will never be
forgotten.
8 Be generous in your worship of the
Lord
and do not stint the firstfruits of your
labour.
9 Give all your gifts cheerfully,
and with gladness dedicate your
tithe.
10 Give to the Most High as he has
given to you,
as generously as your means allow,
11 for the Lord always repays
and you will be repaid seven times
over.

12 Do not offer him a bribe, for he will
not accept it,
and do not rely on an ill-gotten
sacrifice.
The Lord is a judge
who is no respecter of persons.
13 He has no favourites at the expense
of the poor,
and he listens to the prayer of the
wronged.
14 He never ignores the appeal of the
orphan
or of the widow as she pours out her
complaint.
15 How the tears run down the widow's
cheeks,
and her cries accuse him who caused
them!
16 To be accepted a man must serve the
Lord as he requires,
and then his prayer will reach the
clouds.

¹⁷ The prayer of the humble pierces the
  clouds;
  before it reaches its goal there is no
  comfort for him.
  He does not desist until the Most
  High intervenes,
  giving the just their rights and seeing
  justice done.
¹⁸ The Lord will not be slow,
  neither will he be patient with the
  wicked,
  until he breaks the bones of the
  merciless
  and sends retribution on the
  heathen;
  until he blots out the insolent, one
  and all,
  and shatters the power of the unjust;
¹⁹ until he gives all people their deserts,
  measuring their actions by their
  intentions;
  until he gives his people their rights
  and gladdens them with his mercy.
²⁰ When affliction comes, mercy is as
  timely
  as rain-clouds in a time of drought.

36 Look on us with pity, Lord God
  of all,
² and strike fear into every nation.
³ Lift your hand against the heathen,
  and let them behold your power.
⁴ As they have seen your holiness
  displayed among us,
  so let us see your greatness displayed
  among them.
⁵ Let them learn, as we ourselves have
  learned,
  that there is no god but you, O Lord.
⁶ Renew your signs, repeat your
  miracles,
  win glory for your mighty hand and
  right arm.
⁷ Rouse your anger, pour out your
  wrath,
  to destroy the adversary and wipe
  out the enemy.
⁸ Remember the day you have
  appointed and hasten it,
  and give men cause to recount your
  wonders.
⁹ Let burning wrath devour the
  survivors,
  and let the oppressors of your people
  meet their doom.
¹⁰ Crush the heads of hostile princes
  who say, 'No one counts but us.'

¹¹ Gather all the tribes of Jacob,
  and grant them their inheritance, as
  you did long ago.
¹² Have pity, Lord, on the people called
  by your name,
  on Israel, whom you have named
  your firstborn.
¹³ Show mercy to the city of your
  sanctuary,
  to the city of Jerusalem, your
  dwelling-place.
¹⁴ Fill Zion with the praise of your
  triumph
  and the temple with your glory.
¹⁵ Acknowledge those you created at
  the beginning
  and fulfil the prophecies spoken in
  your name.
¹⁶ Reward those who look to you in
  trust;
  prove your prophets worthy of
  credence.
¹⁷ Listen, O Lord, to the prayer of your
  servants,
  who claim Aaron's blessing on your
  people.
  Let all who live on earth
  acknowledge
  that you are the Lord, the eternal
  God.

Life in society

¹⁸ THE stomach will accept any food,
  but one food is better than another.
¹⁹ As the palate identifies game by its
  taste,
  so the discerning mind detects lies.
²⁰ A warped mind makes trouble,
  but he who has wide experience can
  get his own back.

²¹ A woman will take any man for
  husband,
  but a man may prefer one girl to
  another.
²² A woman's beauty makes a man
  happy,
  and there is nothing he desires more.
²³ If she has a kind and gentle tongue,
  then her husband has no peer among
  men.
²⁴ He who acquires a wife has the
  beginnings of a fortune,
  a helper to match his needs and a
  pillar to give him support.
²⁵ Where there is no hedge, a vineyard
  is plundered;

where there is no wife, a man
  wanders about in misery.
²⁶ Does anyone trust the swift-moving
    bandit
  who swoops on town after town?
  No more will they trust a homeless
    man
  who lodges wherever night overtakes
    him.

37 Every friend says, 'I too am
    your friend';
  but some are friends in name only.
² What a mortal grief it is
  when a dear friend turns into an
    enemy!
³ O propensity to evil, how did you
    creep in
  to cover the earth with treachery?
⁴ A friend may be all smiles when you
    are joyful,
  but turn against you when trouble
    comes.
⁵ Another shares your toil for the sake
    of a meal,
  and yet may shield you against an
    enemy.
⁶ Do not forget a friend in the fight,
  and do not neglect him when
    prosperity comes your way.

⁷ Every counsellor says his advice is
    best,
  but he may have in view his own
    advantage.
⁸ Be on your guard against him who
    proffers advice;
  find out first where his interest lies,
  for his advice will be weighted in his
    own favour.
  He may tip the scales against you;
⁹ he may say, 'Your road is clear,'
  and then stand aside to see what
    befalls you.
¹⁰ Do not consult anyone who regards
    you with suspicion,
  or reveal your intentions to those
    who envy you.
¹¹ Never consult a woman about her
    rival
  or a coward about war,
  a merchant about a bargain
  or a buyer about a sale,
  a grudging person about gratitude
  or a hard-hearted person about a
    kind action,
  an idler about work of any sort,

a seasonal worker about the end of
    the job,
  or a lazy servant about an exacting
    task—
  do not turn to them for any advice.
¹² Rely rather on a godfearing person
  whom you know to be a keeper of
    the commandments,
  one who is with you heart and soul
  and will show you sympathy if you
    have a setback.
¹³ But trust your own judgement also,
  for you have no more reliable
    counsellor.
¹⁴ One's own mind has sometimes a
    way of bringing word
  better than seven watchmen posted
    on a tower.
¹⁵ But above all pray to the Most High
  to guide you on the path of truth.

¹⁶ Every undertaking begins in
    discussion,
  and deliberation precedes every
    action.
¹⁷ The roots of choice are in the heart:
¹⁸ destiny takes four forms,
  good and evil, life and death;
  and always it is the tongue that
    decides the issue.
¹⁹ Someone may be clever enough to
    teach many
  and yet be of no use to himself.
²⁰ A brilliant speaker may make
    enemies
  and end by dying of hunger,
²¹ if the Lord has withheld grace and
    charm
  by depriving him of wisdom.
²² If someone is wise in the conduct of
    his own life,
  his good sense can be trusted when
    he gives advice.
²³ If someone is wise and instructs his
    people,
  then his good sense can be trusted.
²⁴ A wise person will have praise
    heaped on him,
  and all who see him will count him
    happy.
²⁵ Human life can be numbered in days,
  but the days of Israel are countless.
²⁶ A person who is wise will possess the
    confidence of his people,
  and his name will live for ever.

²⁷ My son, test yourself all your life
    long;

note what is bad for you, and do not
indulge in it;
28 for not everything is good for
everyone,
nor do we all enjoy the same things.
29 Do not be greedy for every delicacy
or eat without restraint,
30 for illness is a sure result of
overeating,
and gluttony is next door to nausea.
31 Gluttony has been the death of
many,
but he who is careful prolongs his
life.

38 Value the services of a doctor
for he has his place assigned
him by the Lord.
2 His skill comes from the Most High,
and he is rewarded by kings.
3 The doctor's knowledge gives him
high standing
and wins him the admiration of the
great.
4 The Lord has created remedies from
the earth,
and a sensible man will not disparage
them.
5 Was not water sweetened by a log,
and so the power of the Lord was
revealed?
6 The Lord has imparted knowledge to
mortals,
that by their use of his marvels he
may win praise;
7 by means of them the doctor relieves
pain
8 and from them the pharmacist
compounds his mixture.
There is no limit to the works of the
Lord,
who spreads health over the whole
world.

9 My son, in time of illness do not be
remiss,
but pray to the Lord and he will heal
you.
10 Keep clear of wrongdoing, amend
your ways,
and cleanse your heart from all sin.
11 Bring a fragrant offering and a
memorial sacrifice of flour;
pour oil on the sacrifice; be as lavish
as you can.
12 And the doctor should be called;
keep him by you, for you need him
also.

13 A time may come when your
recovery is in his hands;
14 then he too will pray to the Lord
to grant success in relieving pain
and finding a cure to save the
patient's life.
15 He who sins before his Maker
shows himself arrogant before the
doctor.

16 My son, shed tears for one who has
died;
raise a lament for your grievous loss.
Shroud the body with proper
ceremony
and do not neglect his burial.
17 With bitter weeping and passionate
wailing
make your mourning worthy of
him.
Mourn for a few days and avoid
criticism;
then take comfort in your grief,
18 for grief may lead to death,
and a grieving heart saps the
strength.
19 With the burial, grief should pass;
a life of misery is an affliction to the
heart.
20 Do not abandon yourself to grief;
put it from you and think of your
own end.
21 Never forget: there is no returning;
you cannot help the dead and can
only harm yourself.
22 Remember that his fate will also be
yours:
'Mine today, yours tomorrow.'
23 When the dead is at rest, let his
memory rest too;
be comforted for him as soon as his
spirit departs.

24 A SCHOLAR's wisdom comes of
ample leisure;
to be wise he must be relieved of
other tasks.
25 How can one become wise who
follows the plough,
whose pride is in wielding the goad,
who is absorbed in the task of driving
oxen,
whose talk is all about cattle?
26 He concentrates on ploughing his
furrows,
and toils late to give the heifers their
fodder.

27 So it is with every craftsman and
designer
working both day and night.
Such are those who make engravings
on signets
and patiently vary the design;
they concentrate on making an exact
likeness
and stay up to all hours to finish
their task.
28 So it is with the smith, sitting by his
anvil,
intent on his ironwork.
The fiery vapours shrivel his flesh
as he wrestles in the heat of the
furnace;
the hammer rings in his ears again
and again,
and his eyes are on the pattern he is
copying.
He concentrates on completing the
task
and stays up late to give it a perfect
finish.
29 So it is with the potter, sitting at his
work,
turning the wheel with his feet,
always engrossed in the task
of making up his tally of vessels;
30 he moulds the clay with his arm,
crouching forward to exert his
strength.
He concentrates on finishing the
glazing,
and stays up to clean out the
furnace.

31 All those rely on their hands,
and each is skilful at his own craft.
32 Without them a city would have no
inhabitants;
no settlers or travellers would come
to it.
33 Yet they are not in demand at public
discussions,
nor do they attain to high office in
the assembly.
They do not sit on the judge's bench
or understand the decisions of the
courts.
They cannot expound moral or legal
principles
and are not ready with maxims.
34 But they maintain the fabric of this
world,
and the practice of their craft is their
prayer.

39 How different it is with one who
devotes himself
to reflecting on the law of the Most
High,
who explores all the wisdom of the
past
and occupies himself with the study
of prophecies!
2 He preserves the sayings of the
famous
and penetrates the subtleties of
parables.
3 He explores the hidden meaning of
proverbs
and knows his way among enigmatic
parables.
4 The great avail themselves of his
services,
and he appears in the presence of
rulers.
He travels in foreign countries,
learning at first hand human good
and human evil.
5 He makes a point of rising early
to seek the Lord, his Maker;
he prays to the Most High,
asking pardon for his sins.
6 If it is the will of the mighty Lord,
he will be filled with a spirit of
intelligence;
then he will pour forth wise sayings
of his own
and give thanks to the Lord in
prayer.
7 He is directed in his counsel and
knowledge by the Lord,
whose secrets are his constant study.
8 In his teaching he will reveal his
learning,
and his pride will be in the law of the
Lord's covenant.
9 Many will praise his intelligence,
and it will never be forgotten.
The memory of him will not die,
and his name will live for ever and
ever.
10 The nations will tell of his wisdom,
and the assembled people will sing
his praise.
11 If he lives long, he will leave a name
in a thousand;
when he goes to his long rest, his
reputation is secure.

12 I HAVE still more thoughts to express;
I am as full as the moon at mid-
month.

¹³ Listen to me, my devout sons, and
blossom
like a rose planted by a stream.
¹⁴ Spread your fragrance like
frankincense,
and bloom like a lily.
Scatter your fragrance; lift your
voices in song,
praising the Lord for all he has done.
¹⁵ Ascribe majesty to his name
and give thanks to him with praise,
with harps and the singing of songs.
Let these be your words of
thanksgiving:
¹⁶ 'All that the Lord has done is
excellent;
all that he commands will in due
time take place.'
¹⁷ Let no one ask, 'What is this?' or
'Why is that?'
In due time all such questions will be
answered.

At his bidding the waters stood up
like a heap,
and his word created reservoirs for
them.
¹⁸ When he commands, his will is done,
and no one can thwart his saving
power.
¹⁹ The deeds of all mankind lie plain
before him,
and there is no hiding from his eyes.
²⁰ From the beginning to the end of
time he keeps watch;
nothing is too marvellous or too
difficult for him.
²¹ Let no one ask, 'What is this?' or
'Why is that?'
for everything has been created for
its own purpose.

²² His blessing is like a river in full
flood
which soaks the parched ground.
²³ As surely as he turned fresh water
into brine,
so shall the heathen incur his anger.
²⁴ For the devout his ways are straight;
for the wicked they are full of pitfalls.
²⁵ From the beginning good was created
for the good,
and evil for sinners.
²⁶ The basic necessities of human life
are water, fire, iron, and salt,
flour, honey, and milk,
the juice of the grape, oil, and
clothing—

²⁷ all these are good for the godfearing,
but turn to evil for sinners.
²⁸ There are winds created to be agents
of retribution,
with great whips to give play to their
fury;
on the day of reckoning they exert
their force
and so allay the anger of their
Maker.
²⁹ Fire and hail, famine and pestilence,
all these were created for
retribution;
³⁰ beasts of prey, scorpions, and vipers,
and the avenging sword to destroy
the ungodly.
³¹ They delight in carrying out his
commandments,
always standing ready for his service
on the earth;
and when the time comes, they
never disobey his word.

³² I have been convinced of all this
from the beginning;
I have thought it over and left it in
writing:
³³ all that the Lord has made is good,
and he supplies every need as it
arises.
³⁴ Let no one say, 'This is less good
than that,'
for all things prove good at their
proper time.
³⁵ Come now, sing with full heart and
voice,
and to the name of the Lord give
praise!

40 HARD work is the lot of every
mortal,
and a heavy yoke is laid on the
children of Adam
from the day when they come from
their mothers' womb
until the day of their return to the
earth, the mother of all;
² troubled thoughts and fears are
theirs,
and anxious expectation of the day of
their death.
³ Whether someone sits in royal
splendour on a throne
or lies humbled in dust and ashes,
⁴ whether he wears the purple and a
crown
or is clothed in sackcloth,

5 his life is nothing but anger and
envy,
a troubled and anxious mind,
fear of death, and guilt, and
contention.
Even at night when he goes to bed,
sleep brings fresh confusion to his
mind.
6 There is little or no rest for him;
he is as confused in his sleep as in
the daytime.
Disturbed by nightmares,
he fancies himself a fugitive from the
line of battle;
7 and at the moment when he reaches
safety, he wakes up,
amazed to find his fears groundless.

8 To all living creatures, human and
animal—
and seven times over to sinners—
9 come death and bloodshed,
quarrelling and the sword,
disaster, famine, havoc, and plague.
10 All these were created for the wicked,
on whose account the flood came.
11 All that is of earth returns to earth
again,
and all that is of water finds its way
back to the sea.

12 Bribery and injustice will vanish
completely,
but good faith will stand for ever.
13 Wealth from wickedness will dry up
like a wadi
and die away like a clap of thunder
in a storm;
14 when the torrent rises, rocks are
rolled away;
yet suddenly it ceases for ever.
15 The branches of an impious stock put
out few shoots;
their tainted roots are planted on
sheer rock.
16 The rush that grows on every river
bank
dries up before any other grass.
17 But kindness is a paradise in its
blessings,
and almsgiving lasts for ever.
18 To be employed and to be one's own
master, both are sweet,
but to find a treasure is better still.
19 Offspring and the founding of a city
perpetuate a name,
but better still is a perfect wife.

20 Wine and music gladden the heart,
but better still is the love of wisdom.
21 Flute and harp make pleasant
melody,
but better still is a pleasant voice.
22 The eye likes to look on grace and
beauty,
but better still on the green shoots in
a cornfield.
23 A friend or companion is a welcome
partner,
but better still to be man and wife.
24 Brothers and helpers are a stand-by
in time of trouble,
but better still is almsgiving.
25 Gold and silver make a person stand
firm,
but better still is good advice.
26 Wealth and strength uplift the heart,
but better still is the fear of the Lord.
To fear the Lord is to lack nothing,
never to be in need of support.
27 The fear of the Lord is a paradise in
its blessings;
it affords better protection than high
position.

28 My son, do not live the life of a
beggar;
better die than beg!
29 When someone starts looking to
another's table,
his existence is not worth calling life.
It is demoralizing to live on the food
of another,
and he who is wise and well
disciplined will guard against it.
30 He who has lost all shame speaks as
if begging were sweet,
but in his breast resentment burns.

41 How bitter the thought of you,
O Death,
to anyone at ease among his
possessions,
free from cares, prosperous in all
things,
and still vigorous enough to enjoy a
good meal!
2 How welcome your sentence, O
Death,
to a destitute person whose strength
is failing,
who is worn down by age and
endless anxiety,
resentful and at the end of his
patience!
3 Do not fear death's sentence;

remember those before you and those
coming after.
⁴ This is the Lord's decree for all
mortals;
why try to argue with the will of the
Most High?
Whether life lasts ten years, or a
hundred, or a thousand,
no questions will be asked about it in
the grave.

⁵ What a loathsome brood are the
children of sinners,
brought up in the haunts of the
godless!
⁶ Their inheritance disappears,
and their descendants live in lasting
disgrace.
⁷ A godless father is taunted by his
children
for the disgrace they endure on his
account.
⁸ Woe to you who are impious,
who have abandoned the law of God
Most High!
⁹ When you are born, you are born to
a curse,
and when you die, a curse is your
lot.
¹⁰ All that is of earth returns to earth;
so too the godless go from curse to
destruction.
¹¹ There is grief over the death of the
body,
but sinners have no good name to
survive them.
¹² Take thought for your name: it will
outlive you
longer than thousands of great
hoards of gold.
¹³ The days of a good life are
numbered,
but a good name lasts for all time.

¹⁴ BE true to your upbringing, my
children, and live in peace.
Hidden wisdom and buried
treasure—
what is the use of either?
¹⁵ Better someone who hides his folly
than one who hides his wisdom!

¹⁶ Show deference, then, to my
teaching:
shame is not appropriate on all
occasions,
nor are all things held in high repute
by everyone.

¹⁷ Be ashamed to be detected in
fornication by your parents,
or in lies by a ruler or prince;
¹⁸ in crime by a judge or magistrate,
or in a breach of God's law by the
assembly and people;
in dishonesty by a partner or friend,
¹⁹ or in theft by the neighbourhood.
Be ashamed of breach of oath or
contract.

Be ashamed of leaning your elbow on
the table,
of giving or receiving with ill grace,
²⁰ of refusing to return a greeting,
or of ogling a prostitute.
²¹ Be ashamed of turning away a
relative,
of robbing someone of his rightful
share,
or of eyeing another man's wife.
²² Be ashamed of meddling with his
slave-girl
or of visiting her bed.
Be ashamed of taunting your friends
or following up your charity with a
lecture.
²³ Be ashamed of repeating what you
have heard
and of betraying a confidence.
²⁴ Then you will show a proper sense of
shame
and be popular with everyone.

42 But at other times you must not
be ashamed,
or you will do wrong out of deference
to others.
² Do not be ashamed of the law and
covenant of the Most High,
or of acting justly even if you acquit
the ungodly;
³ of settling an account with a partner
or travelling companion,
or of sharing an inheritance with the
other heirs;
⁴ of using accurate weights and
measures,
or of acquiring possessions, many or
few,
⁵ or of making a profit out of trade;
of frequent disciplining of children,
or of drawing blood from the back of
a worthless servant.
⁶ If your wife is untrustworthy, bolt
your door;
where there are many hands, keep
things under lock and key.

7 When you make a deposit, see it
counted and weighed,
and when you give or receive, have
it all in writing.
8 Do not be ashamed to discipline the
ignorant and foolish,
or a greybeard on trial for
fornication.
You will be showing your sound
upbringing
and win universal approval.

9 A daughter is a secret anxiety to her
father,
and worry about her keeps him
awake at night:
when she is young, for fear she may
grow too old to marry,
and when she is married, for fear her
husband may divorce her;
10 when she is a virgin, for fear she
may be seduced
and become pregnant in her father's
house;
when she has a husband, for fear she
may prove unfaithful,
and after marriage, for fear she may
be barren.
11 Keep close watch over a headstrong
daughter,
or she may give your enemies cause
to gloat,
making you the talk of the town, a
byword among the people,
shaming you in the eyes of the
world.
12 Give her a bedroom without
windows,
a room that does not overlook the
entrance.
Do not let her display her beauty to
any man,
or sit gossiping in the women's
quarters;
13 for out of clothes comes the moth,
and out of woman comes woman's
wickedness.
14 Better a man's wickedness than a
woman's goodness;
it is woman who brings shame and
disgrace.

Wonders of creation
15 Now I SHALL call to mind the works
of the Lord
and describe what I have seen,
his works which by his word were
made.

16 As everything is illumined by the
rays of the sun,
so the works of the Lord are full of
his glory.
17 Even to the angels the Lord has not
given the power
to tell the full tale of the marvels
accomplished by the Lord Almighty,
so that the universe may stand firm
in his glory.
18 He fathoms both the abyss and the
human heart,
he is versed in their intricacies;
for the Most High possesses all
knowledge,
and the signs of the times are under
his eye.
19 He discloses both past and future,
and lays bare the traces of secret
things.
20 No thought escapes his notice,
and not a single word is hidden from
him.
21 He has set in order the masterpieces
of his wisdom,
he who is One from eternity to
eternity;
nothing is added, nothing taken
away,
and he needs none to give him
counsel.
22 How pleasing is all that he has made,
even the smallest spark the eye can
see!
23 His works endure, all of them active
for ever
and all responsive to their several
functions.
24 All things go in pairs, one the
counterpart of the other;
he has made nothing incomplete.
25 One thing supplements the virtues of
another.
Of his glory who can ever see too
much?

43 How splendid is the clear vault
of the sky,
how glorious the spectacle of the
heavens!
2 The sun comes into view proclaiming
as it rises
how marvellous it is, the handiwork
of the Most High.
3 At noon it parches the earth,
and no one can endure its blazing
heat.

⁴ The stoker of a furnace works in the heat,
but three times as hot is the hill-scorching sun.
It breathes out fiery vapours;
the glare of its rays blinds the eyes.
⁵ Great is the Lord, its Creator,
whose word speeds it on its course.

⁶ He made the moon also to serve in its turn,
a perpetual sign to mark the divisions of time.
⁷ From the moon, feast days are reckoned;
it is a light that wanes as it completes its course.
⁸ The moon gives its name to the month;
it waxes marvellously as its phases change,
a beacon to the armies of heaven,
shining in the vault of the sky.

⁹ The stars in their brilliance adorn the heavens,
a glittering array in the heights of the Lord.
¹⁰ At the Holy One's command each stands in its place,
never defaulting at its post.

¹¹ Look at the rainbow and praise its Maker;
it shines with a surpassing beauty,
¹² spanning the heavens with its gleaming arc,
a bow bent by the hands of the Most High.

¹³ His command speeds the snowstorm
and sends the swift lightning to execute his sentence.
¹⁴ To that end the storehouses are opened,
and the clouds fly out like birds.
¹⁵ By his mighty power the clouds are massed
and the hailstones broken small.
¹⁶⁻¹⁷ The thunder of his voice makes the earth writhe,
and on his appearing the hills are shaken.
At his will the south wind blows,
the squall from the north and the hurricane.
He scatters the snowflakes like birds alighting;
they settle like a swarm of locusts.

¹⁸ The eye is dazzled by their beautiful whiteness,
and the mind is entranced as they fall.
¹⁹ He sprinkles hoar-frost on the earth like salt,
and icicles congeal like pointed stakes.
²⁰ A cold blast from the north
and ice freezes hard on the water,
settling on every pool
as though the water were putting on a breastplate.
²¹ He consumes the hills, burns up the wilderness,
and like fire shrivels the grass.
²² Cloudy weather quickly puts all to rights,
and dew brings welcome relief after the scorching heat.

²³ In his design he curbed the deep
and planted islands there.
²⁴ Those who sail the sea have tales of its dangers
which astonish all of us who hear them;
²⁵ in it are strange and wonderful creatures,
all kinds of living things and great sea monsters.
²⁶ By his own action his purpose succeeds,
and by his word all things are held together.

²⁷ However much we say, our words will always fall short;
the end of the matter is: God is all.
²⁸ Where can we find the skill to sing his praises?
For he is greater than all his works.
²⁹ The Lord is terrible and very great;
marvellous is his power.
³⁰ Honour the Lord to the best of your ability,
yet still is he high above all praise.
Summon all your strength to extol him,
and be untiring, for you will always fall short.
³¹ Who has seen him, that he can describe him?
Can anyone praise him as he truly is?
³² We have seen but a small part of his works,
and there remain many mysteries greater still.

³³ The Lord has created all things,
and to the godly he has granted
wisdom.

Heroes of Israel's past

44 LET us now praise famous men,
the fathers of our people in their
generations;
² to them the Lord assigned great
glory,
his majestic greatness from of old.
³ Some held sway over kingdoms
and gained renown by their might.
Others were far-seeing counsellors
who spoke out with prophetic power.
⁴ Some guided the people by their
deliberations
and by their knowledge of the
nation's law,
giving instruction from their fund of
wisdom.
⁵ Some were composers of music;
some were writers of poetry.
⁶ Others were endowed with wealth
and strength,
living at ease in their homes.
⁷ All those won glory in their own
generation
and were the pride of their times.
⁸ Some there are who have left behind
them a name
to be commemorated in story.
⁹ Others are unremembered;
they have perished as though they
had never existed,
as though they had never been
born;
so too it was with their children after
them.
¹⁰ But not so our forefathers, men true
to their faith,
whose virtuous deeds have not been
forgotten.
¹¹ Their prosperity is handed on to their
descendants,
their inheritance to future
generations.
¹² Through them their children are
within the covenants—
the whole race of their descendants.
¹³ Their line will endure for all time;
their glory will never die.
¹⁴ Their bodies are buried in peace
and their name lives for ever.
¹⁵ Nations will tell of their wisdom,
and the assembled people will sing
their praise.

¹⁶ Enoch pleased the Lord and was
taken up to heaven,
an example of repentance to future
ages.
¹⁷ Noah was found perfect and
righteous,
and thus he made amends in the
time of God's wrath;
that was why when the flood came
a remnant survived on the earth.
¹⁸ An everlasting covenant was
established with him,
that never again should all life be
swept away by a flood.
¹⁹ Abraham was the great father of a
host of nations;
no one has ever been found to equal
him in fame.
²⁰ He kept the law of the Most High;
he entered into a covenant with him,
setting the mark of it on his body.
When put to the test he proved
steadfast.
²¹ Therefore the Lord assured him on
oath
that through his descendants nations
should find blessing,
and that his family should be
countless as the dust of the earth
and be exalted as high as the stars;
that their territories should extend
from sea to sea,
from the river to the ends of the
earth.
²² To Isaac, for the sake of Abraham his
father,
he gave the same assurance
of a blessing for all mankind and a
covenant.
²³ He made the blessing rest on the
head of Jacob,
who was confirmed in the blessings
he had received
and was given the land for his
inheritance,
divided into portions
which were allotted to the twelve
tribes.

45 From Jacob's stock the Lord
raised up a man of faith
who won favour in the eyes of all:
Moses of blessed memory, beloved by
God and his people.
² The Lord made him equal in glory to
the angels,

132

giving him power to the terror of his
enemies.

³ He sent sign after sign at his request,
so enhancing his reputation with the
king.
He gave him a commission to his
people
and revealed to him some part of his
glory.

⁴ For his loyalty and humility he
consecrated him,
choosing him above everyone else.

⁵ He let him hear his voice
and brought him into the dark cloud,
where face to face he gave him the
commandments,
law which is the source of life and
knowledge,
so that he might teach his covenant
to Jacob,
his decrees to Israel.

⁶ He raised up Aaron of the tribe of
Levi,
a holy man like his brother.

⁷ He made an everlasting covenant
with him,
conferring on him the priesthood of
the nation.
He honoured and adorned him,
clothing him in splendid vestments,

⁸ robing him in full and proud array.
He gave him the emblems of his
station,
the linen trousers, the mantle, and
the tunic.

⁹ Round his robe he put pomegranates
and a circle of many golden bells
to make music as he walked,
ringing aloud throughout the temple
as a reminder to his people.

¹⁰ He gave him the sacred vestment
adorned with embroidery,
gold and violet and purple;
the oracle of judgement with the
tokens of truth;

¹¹ the scarlet thread spun with a
craftsman's art;
the precious stones, engraved like
signets,
and mounted by the jeweller in a
setting of gold,
with inscriptions to serve as
reminders,
one for each of the tribes of Israel;

¹² the gold diadem upon his turban,
engraved like a signet with 'Holy to
the Lord'.
A proud adornment! A miracle of
art!
What rich decoration to delight the
eyes!

¹³ Before him there had not been such
things of beauty.
Only his family has ever worn them,
throughout the ages only his sons
and his descendants.

¹⁴ Twice each day without fail
they present his sacrifice, a complete
offering.

¹⁵ It was Moses who installed him
and anointed him with sacred oil,
to mark the everlasting covenant
made with him
and with his descendants as long as
the heavens endure,
that he should be the Lord's minister
in the priestly office
and bless his people in his name.

¹⁶ The Lord chose him out of all
mankind
to bring offerings to him,
incense and the fragrance of
memorial sacrifice,
to make expiation for the people.

¹⁷ He entrusted to him his
commandments,
with authority to pronounce legal
decisions,
to teach Jacob his decrees
and enlighten Israel about his law.

¹⁸ Upstarts became envious of him
and conspired against him in the
wilderness:
Dathan and Abiram with their
supporters
and Korah's men inflamed with
anger.

¹⁹ The Lord saw and was displeased;
in the heat of his wrath he destroyed
them;
amid portents he consumed them
with blazing fire.

²⁰ But he added to Aaron's glory
and gave him a heritage
by allotting to the priests the choicest
firstfruits,
thus ensuring that they above all
should have bread in plenty;

45:10 **the oracle ... truth:** *or* the breastpiece of judgement with the Urim and Thummim (*Exod. 28:30*).
45:12 **signet ... Lord:** *cp. Exod. 28:36; lit.* signet of holiness.

21 for they eat the sacrifices of the Lord,
which he gave to Aaron and his
descendants.
22 But Aaron was to have no holding in
the land of his people,
no portion among them was allotted
to him;
the Lord himself is his portion and
holding.
23 Phinehas son of Eleazar ranks third
in renown
for being zealous in reverence
towards the Lord,
and for standing firm with noble
courage
when the people defected;
by so doing he made expiation for
Israel.
24 Therefore a covenant was established
with him,
assuring him charge of the sanctuary
and the people,
conferring on him and on his
descendants
the high-priesthood for ever.

25 As by a covenant with David son of
Jesse of the tribe of Judah
the royal succession should always
pass from father to son,
so the priestly succession was to pass
from Aaron to his descendants.
26 Now praise the Lord who is good
and gives you a crown of glory!
May he grant you a wise mind
to judge his people with justice,
so that their prosperity may never
vanish
and their glory may be passed on to
future generations!

46 Joshua son of Nun was a
mighty warrior
and the successor of Moses in the
prophetic office.
He well deserved his name
as a great saviour of the Lord's
chosen people.
He wrought vengeance on the
enemies who attacked them,
and so put Israel in possession of its
heritage.
2 How glorious he was when with
upraised hand
he brandished his sword against the
city!
3 He was fighting the Lord's battles

and none could oppose him.
4 Was it not through him that the sun
stood still
and made one day as long as two?
5 When the enemy was pressing him
hard on every side,
he called to the Most High, the
Mighty One;
his prayer was answered by the great
Lord,
6 who displayed his power in a storm
of hail.
Joshua overwhelmed the hostile
nation
and crushed his assailants as they
fled down the pass,
that the nations should know the
source of his strength
and learn that he fought under the
eyes of the Lord,
for he followed where the Mighty
One led.

7 In the time of Moses he had proved
his faithfulness,
he and Caleb son of Jephunneh:
they stood their ground against the
assembled Israelites,
restrained the people from sin,
and silenced their wicked grumbling.
8 Out of six hundred thousand
warriors
these two alone survived
to bring the people into their
heritage,
into a land flowing with milk and
honey.
9 The Lord gave Caleb strength,
which even in old age did not fail
him,
and he was able to invade the hill-
country
and win possession of it for his
descendants.
10 Thus all Israel might see
how good it is to follow the Lord.

11 Then there are the judges, name
after famous name;
all of them rejected idolatry
and never turned away from the
Lord—
blessings be on their memory!
12 May their bones send forth new life
from the grave!
May the fame of the honoured dead
be matched by their sons!

13 Samuel was beloved by his Lord.
   As prophet of the Lord he established
      the monarchy
   and anointed rulers over his people.
14 He dispensed justice according to the
      law of the Lord,
   and the Lord kept watch over the
      people of Jacob.
15 By his fidelity he was proved a
      trustworthy prophet;
   his faithfulness to his vision was
      shown by his words.
16 When enemies were pressing him
      hard on every side,
   he called to the mighty Lord,
   offering a sucking-lamb in sacrifice.
17 Then the Lord thundered from
      heaven,
   making his voice heard in a mighty
      sound,
18 and routed the leaders of the enemy,
   all the lords of the Philistines.
19 Before the time came for his eternal
      sleep,
   Samuel called the Lord and his
      anointed to witness:
   'I have never taken anyone's
      property,
   not so much as a pair of shoes';
   and no man brought any charge
      against him.
20 Even after he had gone to his rest he
      prophesied
   and made the king's fate known to
      him,
   lifting up his voice in prophecy from
      the ground
   to wipe out the wickedness of the
      people.

47 After him there arose Nathan
   to prophesy in the reign of
      David.
2 As the choice fat is set aside from the
      sacrifice,
   so David was chosen out of all Israel.
3 He disported himself with lions as
      though they were young goats,
   with bears as though they were
      lambs.
4 While still a youth he killed a giant
   and removed the shame of his
      people,
   when he whirled his sling with its
      stone

and brought down the arrogant
   Goliath;
5 for he called to the Lord Most High,
   who gave strength to his right arm
   to strike that mighty warrior down
6 and win victory for his people.
   So they hailed him as conqueror of
      tens of thousands,
   and sang his praises for the blessings
      bestowed by the Lord.
   When he assumed the glorious
      crown,
7 he fought and subdued enemies on
      every side;
   he crushed the resistance of the
      Philistines,
   whose power remains broken to this
      day.
8 In all he did he gave thanks,
   ascribing glory to the Holy One, the
      Most High;
   with all his heart he sang hymns of
      praise
   to show his love for his Maker.
9 He appointed musicians to stand
      before the altar
   and sing sweet music to the harp.
10 He ordered the festivals with
      dignity
   and fixed for all time the round of
      sacred seasons,
   when the Lord's holy name is praised
   and the sanctuary resounds from
      dawn to dusk.
11 The Lord pardoned his sins
   and endowed him with great power
      for ever:
   by a covenant he gave him the
      kingship
   and a glorious throne in Israel.

12 He was succeeded by a wise son,
      Solomon;
   thanks to David his father, he lived
      in spacious days.
13 He reigned in an age of peace,
   because on every side God gave him
      tranquillity,
   that he might build a house in God's
      honour,
   a sanctuary founded to last for ever.
14 How wise you were, Solomon, in
      your youth,
   full of understanding like a brimming
      river!

46: 18 **the enemy**: *so Heb.; Gk* Tyre.

¹⁵ Your mind embraced the whole
  world,
  and you stored it with proverbs and
  riddles.
¹⁶ Your fame reached distant islands,
  and you were beloved for your
  peaceful reign.
¹⁷ Your songs, your sayings, your
  proverbs,
  and the answers you gave were the
  wonders of the world.
¹⁸ In the name of the Lord God,
  who is known as the God of Israel,
  you amassed gold and silver
  like so much tin and lead.
¹⁹ But you took women to lie at your
  side
  and let them usurp your authority.
²⁰ You stained your reputation
  and tainted your line.
  You brought God's wrath on your
  children
  and there was outrage at your folly,
²¹ because it divided the sovereignty
  and in Ephraim a rebel dynasty came
  to power.
²² But the Lord never ceases to be
  merciful;
  he does not destroy what he himself
  has made;
  he will never wipe out the offspring
  of his chosen servant
  or cut short the line of one who has
  loved him.
  So he granted a remnant to Jacob
  and let a scion of David survive.

²³ When Solomon rested with his
  forefathers,
  he left one of his sons to succeed him,
  a man of weak mind, the fool of the
  nation,
  Rehoboam, whose policy drove the
  people to revolt.
  Jeroboam son of Nebat led Israel into
  sin
  and started Ephraim on its wicked
  course.
²⁴ Their sins increased beyond measure
  until they were driven into exile from
  their native land;
²⁵ they explored every kind of
  wickedness
  until punishment overtook them.

48 Then there arose Elijah, a
  prophet like fire,
  whose word blazed like a torch.

² He brought famine on the people,
  and in his zeal reduced them in
  number.
³ By the word of the Lord he shut up
  the sky,
  and three times he called down fire
  from heaven.
⁴ How glorious you were, Elijah, in
  your miracles!
  Who else can boast such deeds?
⁵ By the word of the Most High
  you raised a corpse from death and
  the grave.
⁶ You sent kings and famous men
  from their sick-beds down to
  destruction.
⁷ You heard a rebuke at Sinai,
  a sentence of doom at Horeb.
⁸ You anointed kings for retribution,
  and a prophet to succeed you.
⁹ You were taken up to heaven in a
  fiery whirlwind,
  in a chariot drawn by horses of
  fire.
¹⁰ Scripture records that you are to
  come at the appointed time
  to allay the divine wrath before it
  erupts in fury,
  to reconcile father and son,
  and to restore the tribes of Jacob.

¹¹ Happy are those who see you,
  happy those who have fallen asleep
  in love!
  (For we also shall certainly live.)

¹² After Elijah had vanished in a
  whirlwind,
  Elisha was filled with his spirit.
  Throughout his life no ruler made
  him tremble,
  no one lorded it over him.
¹³ Nothing was too difficult for him,
  and even in the grave his body kept
  its prophetic power.
¹⁴ In life he worked miracles;
  in death also his deeds were
  marvellous.

¹⁵ Despite all this the people did not
  repent
  or renounce their sins,
  until they were carried off captive
  from their land
  and scattered over the whole world.
  Only a very small nation was left
  under a ruler from the house of
  David;

16 some of them did what was pleasing
     to the Lord,
   but others committed sin upon sin.

17 Hezekiah fortified his city
   and brought water within its walls;
   with tools of iron he cut through
     sheer rock
   and made cisterns for the water.
18 In his reign Sennacherib invaded the
     country,
   and from Lachish sent Rab-shakeh,
   who came with threats against Zion,
   boasting loudly in his arrogance.
19 At this the people were unnerved in
     heart and hand,
   and suffered the anguish of a woman
     in labour;
20 they called to the merciful Lord,
   holding out their hands to him in
     supplication.
   From heaven the Holy One quickly
     answered their prayer:
   he sent Isaiah to the rescue,
21 he struck at the camp of the
     Assyrians
   and his angel destroyed them.
22 For Hezekiah did what was pleasing
     to the Lord
   and held firmly to the ways of David
     his ancestor
   as he was instructed to do by Isaiah,
   the great prophet whose vision could
     be trusted.
23 In his time the sun went back,
   and he added many years to the
     king's life.
24 With inspired power he saw the
     future
   and comforted the mourners in Zion.
25 He revealed what was to be until the
     end of time,
   the secrets of things still to come.

49 The memory of Josiah is
     fragrant as incense
   blended by the perfumer's craft,
   sweet as honey to every palate
   or like music at a banquet.
2 He followed a right course, reforming
     the nation
   and rooting out loathsome and
     lawless practices.
3 He was wholeheartedly loyal to the
     Lord
   and in a lawless age made godliness
     prevail.

4 Except David, Hezekiah, and Josiah,
   all were guilty of wrongdoing,
   for all abandoned the law of the Most
     High.
   So the royal line of Judah came to an
     end;
5 they surrendered their power to
     others
   and their glory to a foreign nation.
6 The chosen city, the city of the
     sanctuary, was set on fire,
   and its streets were left deserted, as
     Jeremiah had foretold.
7 He was maltreated,
   even though he was a prophet
     consecrated from the womb
   to uproot, to damage, and to
     demolish,
   but also to build and to plant.

8 There was revealed to Ezekiel a vision
     of the Glory
   which was enthroned on the chariot
     of the cherubim.
9 The Lord remembered his enemies
     and sent a storm,
   but to those who kept to the right
     path he brought benefits.
10 May the bones of the twelve prophets
     also
   send forth new life from the grave!
   For they put new heart into Jacob,
   and by their confident hope delivered
     the people.

11 How can we tell the greatness of
     Zerubbabel,
   who was like a signet ring on the
     Lord's right hand?
12 Jeshua son of Jozadak was with him,
   and in their day they rebuilt the
     house,
   erecting a temple holy to the Lord,
   destined for eternal glory.
13 Great also is the memory of
     Nehemiah,
   who restored for us the fallen walls,
   who reconstructed their barred gates,
   and built again our ruined homes.

14 No one to equal Enoch has been
     created on earth,
   for from the earth he was taken up
     into heaven.
15 No man has been born to be Joseph's
     peer,
   the ruler of his brothers and the
     support of the people;

over his bones watch was kept.
¹⁶ Shem and Seth were honoured
  among men,
  but Adam holds pre-eminence over
  all creation.

50 Greatest among his brothers
  and the glory of his people
was the high priest Simon son of
  Onias
in whose lifetime the house was
  repaired,
in whose days the temple was
  fortified.
² He laid the foundation for the high
  double wall,
  the high retaining wall of the temple
  precinct.
³ In his day a reservoir was dug,
  a cistern broad as the sea.
⁴ He was concerned to ward off
  disaster from his people
  and made the city strong against
  siege.
⁵ How glorious he was as he processed
  through the temple,
  emerging from behind the veil of the
  sanctuary!
⁶ He was like the morning star
  appearing through a cloud
  or the full moon on festal days;
⁷ like the sun shining on the temple of
  the Most High
  or the light of the rainbow on the
  gleaming clouds;
⁸ like a rose in springtime
  or lilies by a fountain of water;
  like a green shoot upon Lebanon on
  a summer's day
⁹ or frankincense burning in the
  censer;
  like a cup all of beaten gold,
  decorated with every kind of precious
  stone;
¹⁰ like an olive tree laden with fruit
  or a cypress with its summit in the
  clouds.
¹¹ When he assumed his resplendent
  vestments,
  robing himself in full and proud
  array,
  he went up to the holy altar,
  adding lustre to the court of the
  sanctuary.
¹² While he received the sacrificial
  portions from the priests,
  as he stood by the altar hearth

with his brother priests around him
  like a garland,
he was like a young cedar of
  Lebanon
in the midst of encircling palms.
¹³ All the priests of Aaron's line in their
  splendour
stood before the whole assembly of
  Israel,
holding the Lord's offering in their
  hands.
¹⁴ To complete the ceremonies at the
  altar
and adorn the offering of the Most
  High, the Almighty,
¹⁵ he reached out his hand for the cup
  and made the libation from the blood
  of the grape,
  pouring its fragrance at the base of
  the altar
  to the Most High, the King of all.
¹⁶ Then the priests of Aaron's line
  shouted
  and blew their trumpets of beaten
  silver;
  they sounded a mighty fanfare
  as a reminder before the Most High.
¹⁷ At once all the people prostrated
  themselves
  to worship their Lord, the Almighty,
  God Most High.
¹⁸ The choir broke into praise,
  in the full, sweet strains of
  resounding song,
¹⁹ while the people were making their
  petitions
  to the Lord Most High, the Merciful
  One,
  until the liturgy of the Lord was
  finished
  and the ritual complete.
²⁰ Then Simon came down and raised
  his hands
  over the whole congregation of Israel
  to pronounce the Lord's blessing
  and to glory in his name;
²¹ and again they bowed in worship
  to receive the blessing from the Most
  High.

²² Now COME, let us praise the God of
  the universe,
  who everywhere works great
  wonders,
  who from our birth raises us up
  and deals with us in mercy.
²³ May he grant us a joyful heart,

and in our days send Israel lasting
  peace.
²⁴ May he confirm his mercy towards us,
  and in his own good time grant us
    deliverance.

²⁵ Two nations I detest,
  and a third is no nation at all:
²⁶ the inhabitants of Mount Seir, the
    Philistines,
  and the senseless folk that live at
    Shechem.

²⁷ I, Jesus son of Sirach Eleazar, of
    Jerusalem,
  whose mind became a fountain of
    wisdom,
  have provided in this book
  instruction in good sense and
    understanding.
²⁸ Happy the man who occupies himself
    with these things,
  who lays them to heart and becomes
    wise!
²⁹ If he follows them he will be equal to
    anything,
  for the light of the Lord will shine on
    his path.

Epilogue

51 I SHALL give thanks to you,
        Lord and King;
  I shall praise you, God my Saviour.
  I give thanks to you
² because you have been my protector
    and my helper,
  rescuing me from destruction,
  from the trap laid by a slanderous
    tongue
  and from lips that invent lies.
  In the face of my assailants you came
    to my help;
³ in the fullness of your mercy and
    honour you rescued me
  from gnashing teeth waiting to
    devour me,
  from hands that threatened my life,
  from the many troubles I endured,
⁴ from the choking fire enveloping me,
  from flames I had not kindled,
⁵ from the deep recesses of the grave,
  from the foul tongue and the lying
    word—
⁶ a wicked slander spoken in the king's
    presence.
  I came very near to death,

close to the brink of the grave.
⁷ On every side I was surrounded
  and there was no one to help;
  I looked for human aid and there
    was none.
⁸ Then I remembered your mercy,
    Lord,
  what you did in days long past;
  you deliver those who put their trust
    in you
  and free them from the power of
    their enemies.
⁹ From the earth I sent up my prayer,
  begging to be rescued from death.
¹⁰ I cried, 'Lord, you are my Father;
  do not abandon me in time of
    trouble,
  when I am helpless in the face of
    arrogance.
¹¹ I shall praise you continually;
  I shall sing hymns of thanksgiving.'
  My petition was granted,
¹² for you saved me from destruction,
  bringing me out from my desperate
    plight.
  Therefore I shall give you thanks and
    praise;
  I shall bless the name of the Lord.

¹³ WHEN I was still young, before I set
    off on my travels,
  in my prayers I asked openly for
    wisdom.
¹⁴ In the forecourt of the sanctuary I
    laid claim to her,
  and I shall seek her to the end.
¹⁵ From the first blossom to the ripening
    of the grape
  she has been the delight of my heart.
  From my youth my steps have
    followed her without swerving.
¹⁶ I had hardly begun to listen when I
    was rewarded,
  and I gained for myself much
    instruction.
¹⁷ I made progress in my studies;
  all glory to God who gives me
    wisdom!
¹⁸ I determined to practise what I
    learnt;
  I pursued goodness, and shall never
    regret it.
¹⁹ With all my might I strove for
    wisdom
  and was scrupulous in whatever I
    did.

50:26 **Mount Seir:** *cp. Heb.; Gk* the mountain of Samaria.

I spread out my hands to Heaven
above,
deploring my shortcomings;
²⁰ I set my heart on possessing wisdom,
and by keeping myself pure I found
her.
With her I gained understanding
from the first;
therefore I shall never be at a loss.
²¹ Because I passionately yearned to
discover her,
a noble possession was mine:
²² as my reward the Lord gave me
eloquence,
and with it I shall praise him.

²³ You that are uninstructed,
come to me and lodge in the house
of instruction.
²⁴ Why do you still lack these things
and leave your great thirst unslaked?

²⁵ I have made this proclamation:
'Buy wisdom for yourselves without
money.
²⁶ Bend your neck to the yoke
and be ready to accept instruction;
you need not go far to find it.'
²⁷ See for yourselves how little were my
labours
compared with the great refreshment
I have found.
²⁸ Your instruction may cost you a
large amount of silver,
but it will bring you a large return in
gold.
²⁹ May you take delight in the Lord's
mercy
and never be ashamed of praising
him.
³⁰ Do your duty in good time,
and he in his own time will give you
your reward.

51:24 **Why … things:** *prob. rdg; Gk obscure.*

BARUCH

A message to a conquered people

1 This is the book of Baruch son of
Neriah, son of Mahseiah, son of
Zedekiah, son of Hasadiah, son of Hilkiah,
written by him in Babylon, ² on the
seventh day of the month, in the fifth year
after the capture and burning of Jeru-
salem by the Chaldaeans. ³ Baruch read the book aloud to Jeconiah son of Joakim, king of Judah, and to
the whole community assembled to hear
it: ⁴ the nobles, the princes of the royal
blood, the elders, and all the people, high
and low—in short, all who were living in
Babylon by the river Soud. ⁵ Then with
tears and fasting they offered their prayers
before the Lord. ⁶ Each of them got together as much money as he could, ⁷ and
this was sent to Jerusalem, to the high
priest Joakim son of Hilkiah, son of Shallum, and to the other priests and all the
people who were with him there. ⁸ At the
same time, on the tenth day of the month
of Sivan, Baruch took the vessels belonging to the house of the Lord which had
been looted from the temple, and returned
them to the land of Judah. These were the
silver vessels which Zedekiah son of Jo-
siah, king of Judah, had made, ⁹ after King
Nebuchadnezzar of Babylon deported
Jeconiah from Jerusalem and carried him
off to Babylon, along with the rulers,
craftsmen, nobles, and the common
people.
¹⁰ They sent this message: The money
we are sending you is to be used to buy
whole-offerings, sin-offerings, and frankincense, and to provide grain-offerings;
you are to offer them on the altar of the
Lord our God, ¹¹ with prayers for King
Nebuchadnezzar of Babylon and for his
son Belshazzar, that their life may last as
long as the heavens are above the earth.
¹² So the Lord will strengthen us and bring
light to our eyes, and we shall live under
the protection of King Nebuchadnezzar of
Babylon and of Belshazzar his son; we
shall give them service for many a day
and find favour with them. ¹³ Pray also for
us to the Lord our God, because we have
sinned against him, and to this day the
Lord's anger and wrath have not been
averted from us.
¹⁴ You shall read this book we are

1:9 **craftsmen:** *prob. rdg; Gk prisoners.* 1:10 **sin-offerings:** *or purification-offerings.*

sending you, and on the feast day and throughout the festal season make confession in the house of the Lord [15] in these words: The right is on the side of the Lord our God; the shame, now as ever, belongs to us, the men of Judah and the citizens of Jerusalem, [16] to our kings and rulers, our priests and prophets, and to our forefathers. [17] We have sinned against the Lord [18] and disobeyed him; we paid no heed to the voice of the Lord our God and did not conform to the laws he laid down for us. [19] We have been disobedient to the Lord our God from the day he brought our forefathers out of Egypt until now; we have thoughtlessly disregarded his voice. [20] So we find ourselves in the grip of adversity, suffering under the curse which the Lord commanded his servant Moses to pronounce, when he led our forefathers out of Egypt to give us a land flowing with milk and honey, as it still is today. [21] Moreover, we refused to hear the Lord our God speaking in all the words of the prophets he sent us; [22] we went our own way, each to follow the promptings of his wicked heart, to serve other gods, and to do what was evil in the sight of the Lord our God.

2 The Lord has made good the warning he gave about us and about our judges in Israel, about our kings and rulers and the people of Israel and Judah. [2] Under the whole of heaven no such things have been done as were done in Jerusalem; they fulfilled what was foretold in the law of Moses: [3] that we should eat the flesh of our children, one his own son and another his own daughter. [4] The Lord made our nation subject to all the kingdoms round about; to all the peoples among whom he had scattered us our name was a byword, our land a wilderness. [5] Instead of rising high, our nation sank low, because in disregarding his voice we sinned against the Lord our God. [6] The right is on the side of the Lord our God; the shame, now as ever, belongs to us and to our forefathers. [7] All those disasters of which the Lord gave us warning have come upon us; [8] yet we did not entreat the Lord to turn each one of us from the thoughts of his wicked heart. [9] The Lord has kept strict watch and brought the disasters on us. In all that he has done to us he is just; [10] yet we did not heed his warning, nor did we

conform to the laws he laid down for our guidance. [11] Lord God of Israel, who brought your people out of Egypt by a strong hand, with signs and portents, with great power and arm uplifted, winning for yourself a name that lives on to this day, [12] now, Lord our God, we have broken all your commandments by our sin, our godlessness, and our injustice. [13] Turn your anger away from us, for we are left few in number among the heathen where you have scattered us. [14] Listen, Lord, to our prayer and supplication, deliver us for your own sake, and grant us favour with those who have taken us into exile, [15] so that the whole world may know you are the Lord our God, and yours is the name by which Israel and his posterity are called.

[16] Lord, look down from your holy dwelling-place and take thought for us; incline your ear to us, Lord, and hear; [17] open your eyes, Lord, and see. The dead are in their graves, all breath gone from their bodies, and they cannot sing the Lord's praises or applaud his justice; [18] it is the living, mourning their fall from greatness, walking the earth bent and enfeebled, with eyes dimmed and with failing appetite—it is they, Lord, who will sing your praises and applaud your justice.

[19] Not for any righteous deeds of our forefathers and our kings do we lay before you our plea for pity, Lord our God. [20] You have vented on us that anger and wrath of which you warned us through your servants the prophets when you said: [21] 'These are the words of the Lord: Bow your shoulders and serve the king of Babylon, and you will remain in the land that I gave to your fathers; [22] but if you ignore the Lord's command to serve the king of Babylon, [23] then I shall banish from the cities of Judah and from the streets of Jerusalem the sound of joy and gladness, the voices of bridegroom and bride; the whole land will lie waste and abandoned.' [24] When we went against your command to serve the king of Babylon, you made good the warning given through your servants the prophets: the bones of our kings and of our fathers have been brought out from their resting-place, [25] thrown down, and exposed to the scorching heat by day and the frost by night. They died a painful death by

famine, sword, and pestilence. [26] And because of the wickedness of Israel and Judah the house that bears your name has become what it is today.

[27] Yet, Lord our God, you have shown us all your wonted forbearance and all your great mercy. [28] This is as you promised through your servant Moses on the day you commanded him to write down your law in the presence of the Israelites, when you said: [29] 'If you will not heed what I say, this great swarming multitude will be reduced to a mere handful among the heathen where I shall scatter them. [30] I know this stubborn people will not listen to me, but in the land of their exile they will come to their right mind [31] and know that I am the Lord their God. I shall give them a mind to understand and ears to hear. [32] They will praise me in the land of their exile and turn their thoughts to me; [33] recalling how their forefathers sinned against the Lord, they will repent of their stubbornness and their wicked practices. [34] Then I shall bring them again to the land that I swore to give to their forefathers, Abraham, Isaac, and Jacob, and they will rule over it. I shall increase their number: they will never dwindle away. [35] I shall enter into an everlasting covenant with them, that I become their God and they become my people. Never again shall I remove my people Israel from the land I have given them.'

3 Lord Almighty, God of Israel, to you the soul in anguish and the fainting spirit cry out. [2] Hear and have mercy, Lord, for we have sinned against you. [3] You are enthroned for ever; we are for ever passing away. [4] Now Lord Almighty, God of Israel, hear the prayer of the men of Israel and of the sons of those who sinned against you. They did not heed the voice of the Lord their God, and so we are in the grip of adversity. [5] Do not call to mind the misdeeds of our forefathers, but remember at this time your power and your name, [6] for you are the Lord our God, and we shall praise you, Lord. [7] It is for this that you have put into our hearts the fear of you: to make us call on your name. And we shall praise you in our exile, for we have renounced all the wrongdoing of our forefathers who sinned against you. [8] Today we are exiled in the lands where

you have scattered us; you have made us a byword and a curse, to be punished for all the sins of our forefathers, who rebelled against the Lord our God.

[9] Israel, listen to the life-giving
    commandments;
hear, and learn understanding.
[10] Why is it, Israel, that you are in
    your enemies' country,
grown old in a foreign land?
Why have you shared defilement
    with the dead
[11] and been numbered among those
    that lie in the grave?
[12] Because you have forsaken the
    fountain of wisdom!
[13] If only you had walked in God's
    ways,
you would have lived in peace for
    ever.
[14] Where is understanding, where is
    strength,
where is intelligence? Learn that,
and you will know where are length
    of days and life,
where happiness and peace.
[15] Who has discovered wisdom's
    dwelling-place,
who has entered her treasure house?
[16] Where are the rulers of the nations
    now?
Where are those who had lordship
    over earth's wild beasts,
[17] those who made their sport with the
    birds of the air?
Where are the hoarders of silver and
    gold
in which men put their trust,
those whose greed knew no limit?
[18] Where are the silversmiths with their
    patient skill
and the secrets of their craft?
[19] They have vanished, gone down to
    the grave,
and others have arisen to take their
    place.
[20] The light of day dawned on a later
    generation;
they dwelt in the land,
but they did not learn the way of
    knowledge
[21] or discover its paths; they did not lay
    hold of it;
their children went far astray.

3:4 **men**: *prob. rdg; Gk* dead.

²² Wisdom was not heard of in Canaan
    or seen in Teman.
²³ Hagar's descendants who sought for
     knowledge on earth,
    the merchants of Merran and Teman,
    the story-tellers, the seekers after
     understanding,
    not one of them discovered the way
     of wisdom
    or had any recollection of her paths.
²⁴ Israel, how great is God's dwelling-
     place,
    how vast the extent of his domain!
²⁵ Great and boundless it is, lofty and
     immeasurable.
²⁶ There of old the giants were born,
    a famous race, mighty in stature,
     skilled in war.
²⁷ But those were not chosen by God
    or shown the way of knowledge.
²⁸ Their race perished for lack of
     insight;
    they perished in their folly.

²⁹ Has anyone gone up to heaven and
     gained wisdom
    and brought her down from the
     clouds?
³⁰ Has anyone crossed the sea and
     found her,
    or obtained her for fine gold?
³¹ No one can know the path
    or conceive the way that will lead to
     her.
³² Only the omniscient God knows her;
    the mind of God discovered her.
    He who established the earth for all
     time
    filled it with four-footed animals.
³³ He sent forth the light and it went on
     its way;
    he summoned it, and trembling it
     obeyed.
³⁴ The stars shone in their appointed
     places and rejoiced;
    he summoned them, and they
     answered, 'We are ready,'
    and joyfully they shone for their
     Maker.
³⁵ This is he who is our God;
    there is none to compare with him.
³⁶ Every way of knowledge he found
     out
    and gave to Jacob his servant,
    to Israel whom he loved.
³⁷ After that, wisdom appeared on earth
    and lived among men.

4 She is the book of God's
     commandments,
    the law that endures for ever.
    All who hold fast to her will live,
    but those who forsake her will die.
² Return, you people of Jacob, and lay
     hold of her;
    set your course towards the radiance
     of her light.
³ Do not yield up your glory to another
    or your privileges to a foreign nation.
⁴ Happy are we, Israel,
    for we know what is pleasing to God!

⁵ Take heart, my people, who keep
     Israel's name alive.
⁶ You were sold to the heathen, but
     not to be destroyed.
    Because you excited God's wrath
    you were handed over to the foe,
⁷ for you provoked your Maker
    by sacrificing not to God but to
     demons.
⁸ You forgot the eternal God who
     nurtured you;
    you caused sorrow to Jerusalem who
     fostered you.
⁹ She saw how God's wrath had
     befallen you
    and said: Listen, you neighbours of
     Zion;
    God has brought on me great grief,
¹⁰ for I have witnessed the captivity of
     my sons and daughters
    inflicted on them by the Eternal.
¹¹ With joy I brought them up,
    but with tears and mourning I
     watched them go.
¹² Let no one exult over me, a widow,
     forsaken by so many,
    left desolate through the sins of my
     children.
    They turned away from the law of
     God;
¹³ they would not learn his statutes,
    nor would they follow his
     commandments,
    nor let God guide and train them in
     his righteousness.

¹⁴ Come, you neighbours of Zion,
    bear in mind the captivity of my sons
     and daughters
    inflicted on them by the Eternal;
¹⁵ for he let loose on them a nation
     from afar,
    a ruthless nation speaking a strange
     tongue

and with no reverence for the old,
  no pity for the young.
¹⁶ They carried off the widow's beloved
  sons,
  and left her in loneliness, bereft of
  her daughters.
¹⁷ But I, how can I help you?
¹⁸ Only the One who brought the
  disasters on you
  can deliver you from the power of
  your enemies.
¹⁹ Go your way, my children, go,
  for I am left desolate.
²⁰ I have stripped off the robes of
  peaceful days
  and put on the sackcloth of a
  supplicant;
  I shall call to the Eternal as long as I
  live.
²¹ Take heart, my children! Cry out to
  God,
  and he will rescue you from tyranny
  and from the power of your enemies.
²² I set my hope of your deliverance on
  the Eternal;
  the Holy One, your everlasting
  Saviour, has filled me with joy
  for the mercy soon to be granted
  you.
²³ With mourning and tears I watched
  you go,
  but God will give you back to me
  with gladness and joy for ever.
²⁴ As the neighbours of Zion have now
  seen your captivity,
  so they will soon witness God's
  deliverance of you,
  which will come to you with the
  great glory
  and the radiance of the Eternal.
²⁵ My children, endure in patience
  the wrath God has brought on you;
  your enemy has hunted you down,
  but soon you will see him
  destroyed,
  soon put your foot on his neck.
²⁶ My pampered children have trodden
  rough paths,
  driven off like a flock seized by
  raiders.
²⁷ Take heart, my children! Cry out to
  God,
  for he who afflicted you will not
  forget you.
²⁸ Once you were resolved to go astray
  from God;

now with tenfold zeal you must turn
  back and seek him.
²⁹ He who brought the disasters on
  you
  will bring you everlasting joy when
  he delivers you.
³⁰ Take heart, Jerusalem! He who called
  you by name will comfort you.
³¹ Wretched will they be who
  maltreated you
  and gloated over your fall;
³² wretched the cities where your
  children were slaves;
  wretched the city that received your
  sons!
³³ She that rejoiced over your downfall
  and was jubilant at your ruin,
  that same city will grieve at her own
  desolation.
³⁴ I shall strip her of the multitudes that
  were her boast,
  and turn her pride into grief.
³⁵ Fire from the Eternal will be her
  doom for many a day,
  and for a long time to come she will
  be the haunt of demons.
³⁶ Jerusalem, look eastwards and see
  the joy
  that is coming to you from God.
³⁷ They come, the sons from whom you
  parted;
  from east to west they come,
  assembling at the word of the Holy
  One
  and rejoicing in the glory of God.

5 Jerusalem, strip off your garment
  of mourning and affliction,
  and put on for ever the glorious
  majesty, the gift of God.
² Wrap about you his robe of
  righteousness;
  place on your head as a diadem the
  splendour of the Eternal.
³ God will show your radiance to every
  land under heaven;
⁴ from him you will receive for ever
  the name
  Righteous Peace, the Splendour of
  Godliness.

⁵ Arise, Jerusalem, stand on the
  height;
  look eastwards and see your children
  assembled
  from west to east at the word of the
  Holy One,

rejoicing that God has remembered them.
6 They went away from you on foot, led off by their enemies;
but God is bringing them home to you,
borne aloft in glory, as on a royal throne.
7 All the high mountains and everlasting hills
are to be made low as God commanded,

and every ravine is to be filled and levelled,
that Israel may walk securely in the glory of God;
8 and the woods and every fragrant tree
will give Israel shade at God's command.
9 He will lead Israel with joy
by the light of his glory,
in his mercy and his righteousness.

A LETTER OF JEREMIAH

The folly of idolatry

6 A COPY of a letter sent by Jeremiah to the captives who were to be taken to Babylon by the king of the Babylonians; it conveys a message entrusted to him by God.

2 IT is because of the sins you have committed in the sight of God that you are being led away captive to Babylon by Nebuchadnezzar, king of the Babylonians. 3 Once you are in Babylon, your stay there will be long; it will last for many years, up to seven generations; afterwards I will lead you out from there in peace.
4 In Babylon you can now see gods carried on men's shoulders, gods made of silver, gold, and wood, which fill the nations with awe. 5 You must be careful, then, never to become like those foreigners. Do not be overawed by the gods when you see them in the midst of a procession of worshippers, 6 but say in your hearts, 'To you alone, O Lord, is worship due.' 7 For my angel will be with you; your lives will be in his care.
8 The idols are plated with gold and silver. They have tongues fashioned by a craftsman: they are a sham and cannot speak. 9 The people take gold and make crowns for the heads of their gods, as one might for a girl fond of finery. 10 Sometimes the priests filch gold and silver from their gods and spend it on themselves; 11 they will even give some to the temple

prostitutes. They dress up the idols in clothes like human beings, their gods of silver, gold, and wood; 12 but the gods, decked in purple though they are, cannot protect themselves against corrosion and moth. 13 The dust in the temple lies thick upon them, so that their faces have to be wiped clean. 14 Like the ruler of a land, the god holds a sceptre, yet he has no power to put to death anyone who offends him. 15 In his right hand he has a dagger and an axe, yet he is powerless to save himself from war and pillage. 16 Clearly they are not gods; therefore have no fear of them.
17 These gods, sitting in their temples, are of no more use than a broken pot. Their eyes get filled with dust from the feet of those who come in. 18 And just as the court of the guardhouse is barricaded when a traitor awaits execution, so the priests secure their temples with doors and bolts and bars to guard against pillage by robbers. 19 The priests light lamps, more than they need for themselves—yet the idols can see none of them. 20 They are like one of the beams of the temple, but, as men admit, their hearts are eaten out, for creatures crawl from the ground and devour both them and their vestments without their being aware of it. 21 Their faces are blackened by the smoke in the temple. 22 Bats and swallows and birds of all kinds perch on their bodies and heads, and cats do likewise. 23 From all this you may be sure that they are not gods; therefore have no fear of them.

6 : 1 etc. *The chapter and verse numbering is that of the Authorized (King James) Version, in which this forms chapter 6 of Baruch.*

²⁴ Though embellished with gold plating, the idols will not shine unless someone rubs off the tarnish. Even when being cast they felt nothing. ²⁵ They were bought regardless of price, but there is no breath in them. ²⁶ As they lack feet they are carried on men's shoulders, which proclaims to all how worthless they are. ²⁷ Even those who serve them are put to shame because, if ever an idol topples to the ground, it does not get up by itself; nor, if anyone sets it up again, can it move by its own effort; and if it is tilted it cannot straighten itself. To set an offering before them is like setting it before the dead! ²⁸ The sacrifices made to gods are sold by the priests, who spend the proceeds on themselves. Their wives are no better; they take portions of the sacrifices and cure the meat, and give no share to the needy or helpless. ²⁹ These offerings are handled by women who are menstruating or by mothers fresh from childbirth. Be assured by this that they are not gods; have no fear of them.

³⁰ For how can they be called gods, these gods of silver, gold, and wood, when it is women who serve them food? ³¹ In the temples are seated the priests, shaven and shorn, with their clothes rent and their heads uncovered. ³² They shout and howl before these gods of theirs, like mourners at a funeral feast. ³³ The priests clothe their wives and children with vestments they stripped from the gods. ³⁴ Should anyone do the gods either injury or service they are incapable of repaying it. They cannot set up or depose a king; ³⁵ so too they are quite unable to bestow wealth or money. Anyone making a vow to them and failing to honour it will never be called to account. ³⁶ They will never save anyone from death, never rescue the weak from the strong, ³⁷ never restore the sight of the blind, or rescue a person in distress. ³⁸ They neither pity the widow nor befriend the fatherless. ³⁹ They are like blocks from the quarry, these wooden things plated with gold and silver, and all who serve them will be discredited. ⁴⁰ How then can anyone suppose them to be gods or call them so?

Besides, even the Chaldaeans themselves bring these idols of theirs into disrepute; ⁴¹ for when they see a dumb man without the power of articulate speech, they bring him into the temple and ask Bel to give him speech, as if Bel could understand. ⁴² Because they themselves are void of understanding, they do not see the folly of it and abandon their idols. ⁴³ The women sit in the street with cords round them, burning bran for incense; and when one of them has been drawn aside by a passer-by and she has lain with him, she taunts her neighbour, who has not been thought as attractive as herself and whose cord has not been broken. ⁴⁴ Everything to do with these idols is a sham. How then can anyone suppose them to be gods or call them so?

⁴⁵ They are the products of the carpenter and the goldsmith; they can be nothing but what the craftsmen intend them to be. ⁴⁶ Even their makers' lives cannot be prolonged; how then can the things they make be gods? ⁴⁷ It is a disgraceful sham they have bequeathed to posterity. ⁴⁸ If war or disaster overtakes the idols, the priests discuss among themselves where they can hide with their gods. ⁴⁹ How then can anyone fail to see that these are not gods, when they are powerless to save themselves from war or disaster? ⁵⁰ Since they are nothing but wood plated all over with gold and silver, they will in such times be recognized for the shams they are. ⁵¹ To every nation and king it will be evident that these are not gods but the work of human hands, with no divine power in them whatsoever. ⁵² Will anyone still not admit that they are not gods?

⁵³ They cannot set up a king over a country; they cannot provide rain; ⁵⁴ they cannot decide a case or redress an injustice. They are as helpless as crows tossed about in mid-air. ⁵⁵ When fire breaks out in a temple belonging to those wooden gods all gilded and silvered, their priests will run for safety, but the gods will go up in flames like timbers. ⁵⁶ They cannot offer resistance to king or enemy. How then can anyone accept or believe that they are gods?

⁵⁷ They cannot save themselves from thieves and robbers, these wooden gods, plated with gold and silver. ⁵⁸ Any able-bodied person can strip them of their gold

---

6:54 **cannot ... injustice:** *some witnesses read* cannot judge in their own cause, or redress an injustice done them.

and silver and make off with the vestments in which they are arrayed; they can in no way help themselves. ⁵⁹ Better a king who displays his courage than such a sham god, better a household pot that serves its owner's purpose, better even the door of a house that keeps the contents safe, or a wooden pillar in a palace!

⁶⁰ Sun and moon and the stars that shine so brightly are sent to serve a purpose, and they obey. ⁶¹ So too, when the lightning flashes, it is seen far and wide. Likewise the wind blows in every land. ⁶² When God commands the clouds to travel over all the world, they accomplish their task; ⁶³ and fire, when it is sent down from above to consume mountains and forests, carries out his bidding. But idols are not to be compared with any of these, either in appearance or in power. ⁶⁴ It follows they are not to be considered gods or given that name, since they are incapable of pronouncing judgement or of conferring benefits on mankind. ⁶⁵ Being

assured, therefore, that they are not gods, have no fear of them.

⁶⁶ They wield no power over kings, either to curse or to bless; ⁶⁷ and they cannot provide the nations with signs in the heavens, either by shining like the sun or by giving light like the moon. ⁶⁸ Wild beasts are better off; they at least can save themselves by taking cover. ⁶⁹ From first to last there is no evidence that they are gods; so banish all fear of them.

⁷⁰ These wooden gods of theirs, all plated with gold and silver, give no better protection than a scarecrow in a bed of cucumbers. ⁷¹ They are like a thorn bush in a garden, a perch for every bird, or like a corpse cast out in the dark. Such are their wooden gods, with their plating of gold and silver! ⁷² The purple and fine linen rotting on them proves that they are not gods; in the end they will themselves be eaten away, to the disgrace of the land.

⁷³ Better, then, to be upright and have no idols, for such a one will be in no danger of disgrace.

6:72 **fine linen**: *prob. mng;* Gk marble.

THE PRAYER OF AZARIAH AND THE SONG OF THE THREE

AN ADDITION IN THE GREEK VERSION OF DANIEL
BETWEEN 3:23 AND 3:24

THEY walked in the heart of the fire, praising God and blessing the Lord.

The prayer

²AZARIAH stood among the flames and began to pray aloud: ³'Blessed are you and worthy of praise, Lord, the God of our fathers; your name is glorious for ever: ⁴you are just in all you have done to us; all your works are true; your paths are straight, your judgements all true. ⁵Just is the sentence in all that you have brought on us and on Jerusalem, the holy city of our ancestors; true and just the sentence you have passed upon our sins. ⁶For we sinned and broke your law in rebellion against you; ⁷in all we did we sinned. We did not heed your commandments, we did not keep them, we failed to do what you commanded for our good. ⁸So in all the punishments you have sent on us, in all you have done to us, your judgements have been just, ⁹in that you have handed us over to our enemies, detested rebels against your law, and to a wicked king, the vilest in all the world. ¹⁰Now we are reduced to silence: shame and disgrace have befallen your servants and worshippers.

¹¹'For the sake of your honour do not abandon us for ever; do not annul your covenant. ¹²Do not withdraw your mercy from us, for the sake of Abraham your friend, for the sake of Isaac your servant and Israel your holy one. ¹³You promised them that their descendants should be as numerous as the stars in the sky, as the grains of sand on the seashore. ¹⁴Yet, Lord, we have been made the smallest of all nations; for our sins we are today the most abject in the world. ¹⁵Now we have no ruler, no prophet, no leader; there is no whole-offering, no sacrifice, no oblation, no incense, no place to make an offering before you and find mercy. ¹⁶But because we come with contrite heart and humbled spirit, may we be accepted. ¹⁷As though we came with whole-offerings of rams and bullocks and with thousands of fat lambs, let our sacrifice be made before you this day, that we may obey you in everything, for no shame shall come to those who put their trust in you. ¹⁸Now we shall follow you with our whole heart, and in fear seek your presence. ¹⁹Do not put us to shame, but deal with us in your forbearance and in the greatness of your mercy. ²⁰Lord, Worker of wonders, deliver us, and let your name be glorified. May all who harm your servants be brought low; ²¹let them be put to shame, stripped of all power and sovereignty, and may their strength be crushed; ²²let them know that you alone are the Lord God, glorious over all the earth.'

²³THE king's servants who had thrown them into the furnace kept feeding it with naphtha, pitch, tow, and brushwood, ²⁴so that the flames, blazing above it to a height of seventy-five feet, ²⁵leapt out and burnt up those Chaldaeans who were caught near it. ²⁶But the angel of the Lord came down to join Azariah and his companions in the furnace; he scattered the flames ²⁷and made the heart of the furnace as if a moist wind were whistling through. The fire touched them not at all; it neither harmed nor distressed them.

The song

²⁸THEN with one voice the three who were in the furnace praised and glorified and blessed God:

17 **that ... everything:** *poss. mng; Gk obscure.*   24 **seventy-five feet:** *Gk forty-nine cubits.*

²⁹ Blessed are you, Lord, the God of our
     fathers;
   worthy of praise, highly exalted for
     ever.
³⁰ Blessed is your holy and glorious
     name;
   highly to be praised, highly exalted
     for ever.
³¹ Blessed are you, glorious in your
     holy temple;
   most worthy to be glorified in hymns
     for ever.
³² Blessed are you, for, enthroned on
     the cherubim, you behold the
     depths;
   worthy of praise, highly exalted for
     ever.
³³ Blessed are you on your royal
     throne;
   most worthy to be hymned, highly
     exalted for ever.
³⁴ Blessed are you in the vault of
     heaven;
   worthy to be glorified in hymns for
     ever.
³⁵ Let his whole creation bless the Lord,
   sing his praise and exalt him for
     ever.
³⁶ Bless the Lord, you heavens;
   sing his praise and exalt him for
     ever.
³⁷ Bless the Lord, you that are his
     angels;
   sing his praise and exalt him for
     ever.
³⁸ Bless the Lord, all you waters above
     the heavens;
   sing his praise and exalt him for
     ever.
³⁹ Bless the Lord, all you his hosts;
   sing his praise and exalt him for
     ever.
⁴⁰ Bless the Lord, sun and moon;
   sing his praise and exalt him for
     ever.
⁴¹ Bless the Lord, you stars of heaven;
   sing his praise and exalt him for
     ever.
⁴² Bless the Lord, all rain and dew;
   sing his praise and exalt him for
     ever.
⁴³ Bless the Lord, all winds that blow;
   sing his praise and exalt him for
     ever.
⁴⁴ Bless the Lord, fire and heat;

   sing his praise and exalt him for
     ever.
⁴⁵ Bless the Lord, searing blast and
     bitter cold;
   sing his praise and exalt him for
     ever.
⁴⁶ Bless the Lord, sleet and falling
     snow;
   sing his praise and exalt him for
     ever.
⁴⁷ Bless the Lord, you nights and days;
   sing his praise and exalt him for
     ever.
⁴⁸ Bless the Lord, light and darkness;
   sing his praise and exalt him for
     ever.
⁴⁹ Bless the Lord, frost and cold;
   sing his praise and exalt him for
     ever.
⁵⁰ Bless the Lord, rime and snow;
   sing his praise and exalt him for
     ever.
⁵¹ Bless the Lord, lightning and
     clouds;
   sing his praise and exalt him for
     ever.
⁵² Let the earth bless the Lord,
   sing his praise and exalt him for
     ever.
⁵³ Bless the Lord, you mountains and
     hills;
   sing his praise and exalt him for
     ever.
⁵⁴ Bless the Lord, all that grows in the
     earth;
   sing his praise and exalt him for
     ever.
⁵⁵ Bless the Lord, you flowing springs;
   sing his praise and exalt him for
     ever.
⁵⁶ Bless the Lord, you seas and rivers;
   sing his praise and exalt him for
     ever.
⁵⁷ Bless the Lord, you whales and
     everything that moves in the
     waters;
   sing his praise and exalt him for
     ever.
⁵⁸ Bless the Lord, all birds of the air;
   sing his praise and exalt him for
     ever.
⁵⁹ Bless the Lord, you cattle and wild
     beasts;
   sing his praise and exalt him for
     ever.

46 **sleet**: *prob. mng; Gk* dew.

60 Let all mankind bless the Lord,
    sing his praise and exalt him for
    ever.
61 Israel, bless the Lord;
    sing his praise and exalt him for
    ever.
62 Bless the Lord, you that are his
    priests;
    sing his praise and exalt him for
    ever.
63 Bless the Lord, you that are his
    servants;
    sing his praise and exalt him for
    ever.
64 Bless the Lord, spirits and souls of
    the righteous;
    sing his praise and exalt him for
    ever.
65 Bless the Lord, you that are devout
    and humble in heart;
    sing his praise and exalt him for
    ever.

66 Hananiah, Azariah, and Mishael,
    bless the Lord;
    sing his praise and exalt him for
    ever.
    He has rescued us from the grave,
    he has saved us from the power of
    death;
    he has delivered us from the furnace
    of burning flame,
    from the very heart of the fire.
67 Give thanks to the Lord, for he is
    gracious,
    for his mercy endures for ever.
68 All who worship the Lord, bless the
    God of gods,
    sing his praise and give him thanks,
    for his mercy endures for ever.

DANIEL AND SUSANNA

Innocence vindicated

IN Babylon there lived a man named Joakim, 2 who had married Susanna daughter of Hilkiah, a very beautiful and devout woman. 3 Her parents were god-fearing people who had brought up their daughter according to the law of Moses. 4 Joakim was very rich, and his house had adjoining it a fine garden; this was a regular meeting-place for the Jews, because he was the man of greatest distinction among them.

5 Now that year the judges appointed were two of the community's elders; of such the Lord had said, 'Wickedness came forth from Babylon, from elders who were judges and were supposed to guide my people.' 6 These men were constantly at Joakim's house, and everyone who had a case to be tried came to them there.

7 At noon, when the people went away, Susanna would go and walk in her husband's garden. 8 Every day the two elders used to see her entering the garden for her walk, and they were inflamed with lust. 9 Their minds were perverted; their thoughts went astray and were no longer turned to God, and they did not keep in mind the demands of justice. 10 Both were infatuated with her; but they did not disclose to each other what torments they suffered, 11 because they were ashamed to confess they wanted to seduce her. 12 Day after day they watched eagerly for a sight of her.

13 One day, having said, 'Let us go home; it is time to eat,' 14 they left and went off in different directions; but turning back they found themselves face to face, and on questioning each other about this, they admitted their passion. Then they agreed on a time when they might find her alone.

15 While they were watching for an opportune moment, Susanna went into the garden as usual, accompanied only by her two maids; it was very hot, and she felt a desire to bathe in the garden. 16 No one else was there apart from the two elders, who had hidden and were spying on her. 17 She said to the maids, 'Bring me olive oil and unguents, and shut the garden doors so that I may bathe.' 18 They did as she said: they made fast the garden doors and went out by the side entrance for the things they had been told to bring; they did not see the elders, because they were in hiding.

19 As soon as the maids had gone, the two elders got up and ran to Susanna.

150

20 'Look, the garden doors are shut,' they said, 'and no one can see us! We are overcome with desire for you; consent, and yield to us. 21 If you refuse, we shall swear in evidence there was a young man with you and that was why you sent your maids away.' 22 Susanna groaned and said: 'It is a desperate plight I am in! If I do this, the penalty is death; if I do not, you will have me at your mercy. 23 My choice is made: I will not do it! Better to be at your mercy than to sin against the Lord!' 24 With that she called out at the top of her voice, but the two elders shouted her down, 25 and one of them ran and opened the garden door. 26 The household, hearing the uproar in the garden, rushed in through the side entrance to see what had happened to her. 27 When the elders had told their story, the servants were deeply shocked, for no such allegation had ever been made against Susanna.

28 Next day, when the people gathered at her husband Joakim's house, the two elders arrived, intent on their criminal design to have Susanna put to death. 29 In the presence of the people they said, 'Send for Susanna daughter of Hilkiah, Joakim's wife.' She was summoned, 30 and came with her parents and children and all her relatives. 31 Now Susanna was a woman of great beauty and delicate feeling. 32 She was closely veiled, but those scoundrels ordered her to be unveiled so that they might feast their eyes on her beauty. 33 Her family and all who saw her were in tears.

34 Then the two elders stood up before the people and put their hands on her head, 35 she meanwhile looking towards heaven through her tears, for her trust was in the Lord. 36 The elders said: 'As we were walking by ourselves in the garden, this woman came in with her two maids. She shut the garden doors and dismissed her maids, 37 and then a young man, who had been in hiding, came and lay with her. 38 We were in a corner of the garden, and when we saw this wickedness we ran towards them. 39 We saw them in the act, but we could not hold the man; he was too strong for us, he opened the door and got clean away. 40 We seized the woman and asked who the young man was, but she would not tell us. That is our evidence.'

41 Because they were elders of the people and judges, the assembly believed them and condemned her to death. 42 Then raising her voice Susanna cried: 'Eternal God, you know all secrets and foresee all things, 43 you know that their evidence against me is false. And now I am to die, innocent though I am of the charges these wicked men have brought against me.'

44 The Lord heard her cry, 45 and as she was being led off to execution, God inspired a devout young man named Daniel to protest. 46 He shouted out, 'I will not have this woman's blood on my hands.' 47 At this the people all turned towards him and demanded, 'What do you mean?' 48 He stepped forward and said: 'Are you such fools, you Israelites, as to condemn a woman of Israel, without making careful enquiry and finding out the truth? 49 Reopen the trial; the evidence these men have given against her is false.'

50 Everyone hurried back, and the rest of the elders said to Daniel, 'Come, take your place among us and state your case, for God has given you the standing of an elder.' 51 He said, 'Separate these men and keep them at a distance from each other, and I shall examine them.' 52 When they had been separated, Daniel summoned one of them. 'You hardened reprobate,' he began, 'the sins of your past have now come home to you. 53 You have given unjust decisions, condemning the innocent and acquitting the guilty, although the Lord has said, "You must not cause the death of the innocent and guiltless." 54 Now, if you really saw this woman, then tell us, under what tree did you see them together?' He answered, 'Under a clove tree.' 55 Daniel retorted, 'Very good! This lie has cost you your life, for already God's angel has received your sentence from God, and he will cleave you in two.' 56 He ordered him to stand aside, and told them to bring forward the other.

He said to him: 'Spawn of Canaan, no son of Judah, beauty has been your undoing and lust has perverted your heart! 57 So this is how the two of you have been treating the women of Israel, terrifying them into yielding to you! But here is a woman of Judah who would not

---

54 **clove**: *lit.* mastic.　　54–55 **clove … cleave**: *there is a play on words in the Greek.*

submit to your villainy. ⁵⁸ Now tell me, under what tree did you surprise them together?' 'Under a yew tree,' he replied. ⁵⁹ Daniel said to him, 'Very good! This lie has cost you also your life, for the angel of God is waiting sword in hand to hew you down and destroy the pair of you.'

⁶⁰ At that the whole assembly shouted aloud, praising God, the Saviour of those who trust in him. ⁶¹ They turned on the two elders, for out of their own mouths Daniel had convicted them of giving false evidence; ⁶² they dealt with them according to the law of Moses, putting them to death as they in their wickedness had intended to do to their neighbour. So an innocent life was saved that day. ⁶³ Then Hilkiah and his wife gave praise for their daughter Susanna, as did also her husband Joakim and all her relatives, because she was found innocent of a shameful deed.

⁶⁴ From that day forward Daniel was held in great esteem among the people.

58 **yew**: *lit.* oak.   58–59 **yew ... hew**: *there is a play on words in the Greek.*

DANIEL, BEL, AND THE SNAKE

The destruction of Bel

WHEN King Astyages was gathered to his forefathers, he was succeeded on the throne by Cyrus the Persian. ² Daniel was a companion of the king and the most honoured of all the king's Friends.

³ The Babylonians had an idol called Bel, for which every day they provided twelve bushels of fine flour, forty sheep, and fifty gallons of wine. ⁴ The king went daily to bow down to it in worship; but Daniel bowed before his own God. When the king asked him, 'Why do you not bow down to Bel?' ⁵ he replied, 'Because I do not worship man-made idols; I worship the living God who created heaven and earth and is sovereign over all mankind.' ⁶ The king protested, 'How can you think Bel is not a living god? Do you not see how much he eats and drinks each day?' ⁷ Daniel laughed. 'Do not be deceived, your majesty,' he said; 'this Bel of yours is just clay inside and bronze outside, and has never eaten or drunk anything.'

⁸ Angered by this, the king summoned the priests of Bel and said to them, 'If you cannot tell me who it is that consumes these provisions, you shall die; ⁹ but if you can show it is Bel that eats them, then, for blasphemy against Bel, Daniel shall die.' Daniel said to the king, 'Let it be as you propose.' ¹⁰ (There were seventy priests of Bel, and in addition their wives and children.) When the king, along with Daniel, went into the temple of Bel, ¹¹ the priests said, 'We are now leaving; let your majesty set out the food yourself, with the wine you have mixed; then make fast the door and seal it with your signet. ¹² In the morning when you return, if you do not find that Bel has eaten it all, let us be put to death; but if Daniel's charges against us turn out to be false, then let him die.' ¹³ They treated the affair lightly, for beneath the table they had constructed a hidden entrance, by which they used to go in and eat up everything.

¹⁴ After the priests had gone, the king set out the food for Bel; and Daniel ordered his servants to bring ashes and sift them over the whole temple with only the king present. They then left the building, closed the door, sealed it with the royal signet, and went away. ¹⁵ During the night the priests, with their wives and children, came as usual and ate and drank everything.

¹⁶ Next morning the king was up early, and Daniel with him. ¹⁷ The king said, 'Are the seals intact, Daniel?' 'They are intact, your majesty,' he answered. ¹⁸ As soon as the door was opened, the king took one look at the table and cried aloud, 'Great are you, O Bel! In you there is no deception whatsoever.' ¹⁹ But Daniel laughed and held back the king from going in. 'Just look at the floor,' he said, 'and judge whose footprints these are.'

²⁰ The king said, 'I see the footprints of men, women, and children.' In a rage ²¹ he had the priests arrested together with their wives and children, and they showed him the secret door through which it was their custom to go and eat what was on the table. ²² The king then put them to death, and he handed Bel over to Daniel, who destroyed both idol and temple.

The destruction of the snake

²³ THERE was a huge snake which the Babylonians worshipped. ²⁴ The king said to Daniel, 'Bow down to him; you cannot say that this is not a living god.' ²⁵ Daniel answered, 'I shall bow before the Lord my God, for he is a living God. ²⁶ But give me authority, your majesty, and without using sword or staff I shall kill the snake.' 'I grant it,' replied the king. ²⁷ Then Daniel took pitch and fat and hair, boiled them together, and made them into cakes, which he put into the mouth of the snake. The snake swallowed them and burst. Daniel said, 'See what things you people worship!'

²⁸ When they heard of this, the Babylonians in their indignation made common cause against the king. 'The king has turned Jew!' they cried. 'He has pulled down Bel, killed the snake, and put the priests to the sword.' ²⁹ They went to the king. 'Hand Daniel over to us,' they demanded, 'or else we shall kill you and your family.' ³⁰ The king, finding himself thus hard pressed, was compelled to hand him over.

³¹ They threw Daniel into the lion-pit, and he was there for six days. ³² In the pit were seven lions, and every day two slaves and two sheep were fed to them; now, to make sure they would devour Daniel, they were given nothing.

³³ The prophet Habakkuk, who was in Judaea, had made a stew; he broke bread into the bowl, and he was on the way to his field, carrying it to the reapers, ³⁴ when an angel of the Lord said to him, 'Habakkuk, carry that meal you have to Babylon for Daniel, who is in the lion-pit.' ³⁵ 'My lord,' replied Habakkuk, 'I have never been to Babylon, and I do not know where the lion-pit is.' ³⁶ The angel took the prophet by the head, and carrying him by his hair swept him to Babylon with the blast of his breath and set him down above the pit. ³⁷ Habakkuk called out, 'Daniel, Daniel! Take the meal that God has sent you.' ³⁸ Daniel said, 'You do indeed remember me, God; you never abandon those who love you.' ³⁹ He got up and ate; and at once God's angel brought Habakkuk home again.

⁴⁰ On the seventh day the king went to mourn for Daniel, but when he arrived at the pit and looked in, there sat Daniel! ⁴¹ The king cried aloud, 'You are indeed great, Lord, the God of Daniel, and there is no god but you alone.' ⁴² He drew Daniel up, while those men who had plotted to destroy Daniel were flung into the pit, and then and there they were devoured before his eyes.

THE PRAYER OF
MANASSEH

Repentance

ALMIGHTY Lord,
God of our fathers,
of Abraham, Isaac, and Jacob, and of
　　their righteous posterity,
² who made heaven and earth in their
　　manifold array,
³ who fettered the ocean by your word
　　of command,
who closed the abyss

and sealed it with your fearful and
　　glorious name—
⁴ before your power all things quake
　　and tremble.
⁵ The majesty of your glory is more
　　than can be borne;
none can endure the threat of your
　　wrath against sinners.

⁶ Your promised mercy is beyond
　　measure and none can fathom it;

7 for you are Lord Most High,
   compassionate, patient, and of great
      mercy,
   relenting when men suffer for their
      sins.
8 Therefore, Lord God of the
      righteous,
   you appointed repentance not for
      Abraham, Isaac, and Jacob,
   who were righteous and did not sin
      against you,
   but for me, 9 whose sins outnumber
      the sands of the sea.
   My transgressions abound, Lord, my
      transgressions abound,
   and, because of the multitude of my
      wrongdoings,
   I am not worthy to look up and gaze
      at the height of heaven.
10 Bowed down with many an iron
      chain,
   I grieve over my sins and find no
      relief,
   because I have provoked your anger
   and done what is wrong in your
      eyes,

setting up idols and so multiplying
   offences.
11 Now my heart submits to you,
   imploring your great goodness.
12 I have sinned, Lord, I have sinned,
   and I acknowledge my
      transgressions.
13 I beg and beseech you,
   spare me, Lord, spare me;
   destroy me not with my
      transgressions on my head,
   do not be angry with me for ever,
   or store up punishment for me.
   Do not condemn me to the depths of
      the earth,
   for you, Lord, are the God of the
      penitent.
14 You will show your goodness
      towards me,
   for, unworthy as I am, you will save
      me in your great mercy;
15 and I shall praise you continually all
      the days of my life.
   The whole host of heaven sings your
      praise,
   and yours is the glory for ever. Amen.

---

7 **for their sins:** *some witnesses add*
   For out of your great goodness, Lord,
   you have promised repentance and remission
   to those who have sinned against you,
   and in your boundless mercy you have appointed
   repentance for sinners as the way to salvation.

THE FIRST BOOK OF THE
MACCABEES

Background to the Maccabaean revolt

1 ALEXANDER of Macedon, the son of Philip, marched from the land of Kittim, defeated Darius, king of Persia and Media, and seized his throne, being already king of Greece. [2] During the course of many campaigns, in which he captured strongholds and put kings to death, [3] he traversed the earth to its remotest bounds and plundered countless nations. When at last the world lay quiet under his sway, his pride knew no limits; [4] he built up an extremely powerful army and ruled over countries, nations, and princedoms, all of which rendered him tribute.

[5] The time came when Alexander fell ill, and, realizing that he was dying, [6] he summoned his generals, nobles who had been brought up with him from childhood, and divided his empire among them while he was yet alive. [7] At his death he had reigned for twelve years. [8] His generals took over the government, each in his own province, [9] and, when Alexander died, they all assumed royal crowns, and for many years the succession passed to their descendants. They brought untold miseries on the world.

[10] An offshoot of this stock was that impious man, Antiochus Epiphanes, son of King Antiochus. He had been a hostage in Rome before he succeeded to the throne in the year 137 of the Greek era.

[11] At that time there emerged in Israel a group of renegade Jews, who inveigled many by saying, 'We should go and make an agreement with the Gentiles round about; nothing but disaster has been our lot since we cut ourselves off from them.' [12] This proposal was widely approved, [13] and some of the people in their enthusiasm went to the king and received authority to introduce pagan laws and customs. [14] They built a gymnasium in the gentile style at Jerusalem; [15] they removed their marks of circumcision and repudiated the holy covenant; they inter-married with Gentiles and sold themselves to evil.

[16] Once he was firmly established on his throne, Antiochus determined to become king of Egypt and so rule both kingdoms. [17] He invaded Egypt with a powerful force of chariots, elephants, and cavalry, together with a great fleet. [18] When battle was joined, King Ptolemy was routed with heavy loss and took flight. [19] The fortified towns in Egypt were captured and the land pillaged.

[20] On his return from the conquest of Egypt in the year 143 Antiochus marched up with a strong force against Israel and Jerusalem. [21] In his arrogance he entered the temple and carried off the gold altar, the lampstand with all its fittings, [22] the table of the Bread of the Presence, the libation cups and bowls, the gold censers, the curtain, and the garlands. He stripped the gold plating from the front of the temple, [23] seized the silver and gold, the precious vessels, and whatever secret treasures he found, [24] and carried them all away when he left for his own country. He had caused much bloodshed, and he boasted arrogantly of what he had done.

[25] Great was the mourning throughout Israel,
[26] deep the groans of rulers and elders.
Girls and young men languished;
the beauty of our women was disfigured.
[27] Every bridegroom took up the lament;
every bride sat mourning in her bridal chamber.
[28] The land trembled for its inhabitants,
and all the house of Jacob was wrapped in shame.

[29] Two years later, the king sent a governor to put the towns of Judaea under tribute. When he arrived at Jerusalem with a powerful force [30] his language, though friendly, was full of guile, for once

---

1:1 **being ... Greece**: *prob. mng ; Gk obscure.*   1:10 **the year ... era**: *that is* 175 B.C.   1:20 **143**: *that is* 169 B.C.

he had gained the city's confidence he launched a sudden and savage attack. Many of the Israelites were killed, [31] and their city was sacked and set ablaze. On every side the houses and city walls were demolished; [32] the women and children were captured, and the livestock seized.

[33] The City of David was turned into a citadel, enclosed by a high, stout wall with strong towers, [34] and garrisoned by impious foreigners and renegades. Having made themselves secure, [35-36] they laid up a store of arms and provisions, and brought in the plunder they had collected from Jerusalem. They lurked there, a snare and threat to the temple and a perpetual menace to Israel.

[37] They shed innocent blood all round
  the temple;
  they defiled the holy place.
[38] For fear of them the inhabitants of
  Jerusalem fled;
  the city became the abode of aliens,
  and alien herself to her offspring:
  her children forsook her.
[39] Her temple lay desolate as a
  wilderness;
  her festivals were turned to
  mourning,
  her sabbaths to a reproach,
  her honour to contempt.
[40] Her present dishonour was equalled
  only by her past renown,
  and her pride was turned to
  mourning.

[41] The king issued an edict throughout his empire: his subjects were all to become one people [42] and abandon their own customs. Everywhere the nations complied with the royal command, [43] and many in Israel willingly adopted the foreign cult, sacrificing to idols and profaning the sabbath. [44] The king sent agents to Jerusalem and the towns of Judaea with written orders that ways and customs foreign to the country should be introduced. [45] Whole-offerings, sacrifices, and drink-offerings were forbidden in the temple; sabbaths and feast days were to be profaned, [46] the temple and its ministers defiled. [47] Pagan altars, idols, and sacred precincts were to be established, swine and other unclean beasts to be offered in sacrifice. [48] The Jews were to

leave their sons uncircumcised; they had to make themselves in every way abominable, unclean, and profane, [49] and so forget the law and change all their statutes. [50] The penalty for disobeying the royal command was death.

[51] Such were the terms of the edict issued by the king throughout his realm. He appointed superintendents over all the people, and instructed the towns of Judaea to offer sacrifice, town by town. [52] Those of the people who were ready to betray the law all thronged to their side in large numbers. Their wicked conduct throughout the land [53] drove Israel into hiding in every possible place of refuge.

[54] On the fifteenth day of the month of Kislev in the year 145, 'the abomination of desolation' was set up on the altar of the Lord. In the towns throughout Judaea pagan altars were built; [55] incense was offered at the doors of houses and in the streets. [56] Every scroll of the law that was found was torn up and consigned to the flames, [57] and anyone discovered in possession of a Book of the Covenant or conforming to the law was by sentence of the king condemned to die. [58] Thus month after month these wicked men used their power against the Israelites whom they found in their towns. [59] On the twenty-fifth day of each month they offered sacrifice on the pagan altar which was on top of the altar of whole-offering. [60] In accordance with the royal decree, they put to death women who had had their children circumcised; [61] their babies, their families, and those who had performed the circumcisions were hanged by the neck.

[62] Yet many in Israel found strength to resist, taking a determined stand against the eating of any unclean food. [63] They welcomed death and died rather than defile themselves and profane the holy covenant. [64] Israel lay under a reign of terror.

2 It was in those days that a certain Mattathias son of John, son of Symeon, came on the scene. He was a priest of the Joarib family from Jerusalem, now settled at Modin, [2] and he had five sons: John called Gaddis, [3] Simon called Thassis, [4] Judas called Maccabaeus, [5] Eleazar called Avaran, and Jonathan called Apphus.

1:54 **145**: *that is* 167 B.C.

[6] When Mattathias saw the sacrilegious acts committed in Judaea and, above all, in Jerusalem, [7] he said:

> 'Oh! Why was I born to see this,
> the ruin of my people, the ruin of the Holy City,
> to sit by while she was surrendered,
> the holy place given up to foreigners?
> [8] Her temple is like a man robbed of honour;
> [9] its glorious vessels are carried off as spoil.
> Her infants are slain in her streets,
> her young men by the sword of the foe.
> [10] Is there any nation that has not usurped her sovereignty,
> any people that has not taken plunder from her?
> [11] She has been stripped of all her adornment;
> she is no longer free, she is a slave.

[12] 'We see the temple, which is our splendour and glory, laid waste and desecrated by the Gentiles. [13] Why should we go on living?' [14] Mattathias and his sons tore their garments, put on sackcloth, and mourned loud and long.

[15] The king's officers who were enforcing apostasy came to the town of Modin to see that sacrifice was offered. [16] Many Israelites went over to them, but Mattathias and all his sons stood apart. [17] The officers addressed Mattathias: 'You are a leader here, a man of mark and influence in this town, with your sons and brothers at your back. [18] Now you be the first to come forward; carry out the king's decree as all the nations have done, as well as the leading men in Judaea and the people left in Jerusalem. Then you and your sons will be enrolled among the king's Friends; you will all receive high honours, rich rewards of silver and gold, and many further benefits.'

[19] In a ringing voice Mattathias replied: 'Though every nation within the king's dominions obeys and forsakes its ancestral worship, though all have chosen to submit to his commands, [20] yet I and my sons and my brothers will follow the covenant made with our forefathers. [21] Heaven forbid we should ever abandon the law and its statutes! [22] We will not

obey the king's command, nor will we deviate one step from our way of worship.'

[23] As he finished speaking, a Jew came forward in full view of all to offer sacrifice on the pagan altar at Modin, in obedience to the royal decree. [24] The sight aroused the zeal of Mattathias, and, shaking with passion and in a fury of righteous anger, he rushed forward and cut him down on the very altar. [25] At the same time he killed the officer sent by the king to enforce sacrifice, and demolished the pagan altar. [26] So Mattathias showed his fervent zeal for the law, as Phinehas had done when he killed Zimri son of Salu. [27] He shouted for the whole town to hear, 'Follow me, all who are zealous for the law and stand by the covenant!' [28] Then he and his sons took to the hills, leaving behind in the town all they possessed.

[29] At that time many who sought to maintain their religion and law went down to live in the desert, [30] taking their children and their wives and their livestock with them, for their miseries were more than they could bear. [31] Word soon reached the king's officers and the forces stationed in Jerusalem, the city of David, that Israelites who had defied the king's order had gone down into hiding-places in the desert. [32] A large body of soldiers, setting off in pursuit, came upon them, and drew up in battle order ready to attack on the sabbath. [33] 'There is still time,' they shouted; 'come out, do as the king commands, and your lives will be spared.' [34] 'We will not come out,' was the reply; 'we will not obey the king's command to profane the sabbath.' [35] Without more ado the attack was launched, [36] but the Israelites did nothing in reply; they neither hurled stones, nor barricaded their caves. [37] 'Let us all meet death with a clear conscience,' they said; 'we call heaven and earth to witness it is contrary to all justice that you are making away with us.' [38] So on the sabbath they were attacked and massacred, men, women, and children, up to a thousand in all, along with their livestock.

[39] When Mattathias and his friends learnt of it, their grief was very great, [40] and they said to one another, 'If we all do as our brothers have done and refuse to

---

2:10 **usurped her sovereignty**: *or* occupied her palaces.

fight the Gentiles in defence of our lives as well as our laws and customs, then they will soon wipe us off the face of the earth.' [41] That day the decision was taken that if anyone came to fight against them on the sabbath, they would fight back, rather than all perish as their brothers in the caves had done.

[42] They were joined at that time by a group of Hasidaeans, stalwarts of Israel, every one of them a volunteer in the cause of the law; [43] and all who were refugees from the troubles came to swell their numbers and add to their strength. [44] Now that they had an organized force, they turned the fierceness of their wrath on the guilty men and renegades; those who escaped their onslaught took refuge with the Gentiles.

[45] Mattathias and his friends swept through the country, demolishing the pagan altars [46] and forcibly circumcising all the uncircumcised boys found within the frontiers of Israel. [47] They hunted down their arrogant enemies, and the cause prospered in their hands. [48] Thus they came to the defence of the law against the Gentiles and their kings and withheld power from the wicked.

[49] As the time drew near for Mattathias to die, he said to his sons: 'Arrogance now stands secure and gives judgement against us; these are days of calamity and raging fury. [50] Now, my sons, be zealous for the law, and give your lives for the covenant made with your forefathers. [51] If you keep in mind the deeds they did in their generations, great glory and everlasting fame will be yours. [52] Did not Abraham prove faithful under trial, and so win credit as a righteous man? [53] Joseph, hard pressed though he was, kept God's commandment, and he became overlord of Egypt. [54] Phinehas, our forefather, never flagged in his zeal, and his was the covenant of an everlasting priesthood. [55] Joshua kept the law, and he became a judge in Israel. [56] Caleb bore witness before the congregation, and his reward was a share in the land. [57] David was a man of loyalty, and he was granted the throne of an everlasting kingdom. [58] Elijah never flagged in his zeal for the law, and he was taken up to heaven. [59] Hananiah, Azariah, and Mishael had

faith, and they were saved from the flames. [60] Daniel was a man of integrity, and he was rescued from the lions' jaws. [61] So bear in mind how in the history of the generations no one who trusts in Heaven ever lacks strength. [62] Do not fear a wicked man's threats; his success will turn to filth and worms. [63] Today he may be high in honour, but tomorrow not a trace of him will be found; he will have returned to the dust, and his schemes will have come to naught. [64] But you, my sons, draw your courage and strength from the law, for through it glory will be yours.

[65] 'Now here is Symeon your brother, whom I know to be wise in counsel; listen always to him, for he will be a father to you. [66] Judas Maccabaeus has been strong and brave from boyhood; he is to be your commander in the field, and wage war against the peoples. [67] Assemble to your side all who observe the law, and avenge your people's wrongs. [68] Repay the Gentiles in their own coin, and give heed to what the law decrees.'

[69] Mattathias blessed them, and was gathered to his fathers. [70] He died in the year 146, and was buried by his sons in the family tomb at Modin; and there was great lamentation for him throughout Israel.

The war under Judas Maccabaeus

3 JUDAS Maccabaeus came forward to take his father's place. [2] He had the support of all his brothers and his father's followers, and they carried on Israel's campaign with zest.

[3] He enhanced his people's glory.
Like a giant he put on his breastplate
and girt himself with weapons of
war.
He waged many a campaign
from a camp well guarded with the
sword.
[4] He was like a lion in his exploits,
like a young lion roaring for prey.
[5] He tracked down and pursued the
renegades;
he consumed with fire the troublers
of his people.
[6] The renegades cowered in fear of
him,

and all such wrongdoers were utterly
confounded,
while the cause of freedom prospered
in his hands.
⁷ He roused many kings to anger,
but to Jacob his deeds brought joy.
He is remembered for ever in blessing.
⁸ He passed through the towns of
Judaea,
wiping out the apostates there;
he turned wrath away from Israel.
⁹ His renown spread to the ends of the
earth,
and he rallied a people near to
destruction.

¹⁰ Apollonius raised an army, consisting
of Gentiles and a large contingent from
Samaria, to wage war against Israel.
¹¹ Informed of this, Judas marched out
and in the encounter defeated and killed
him. Many of the enemy fell; the survivors took flight. ¹² From the arms which
were captured, Judas obtained the sword
of Apollonius, and for the rest of his life he
used it in his campaigns.

¹³ When Seron, the commander of the
army in Syria, heard that Judas had
mustered a considerable force, all his
loyal followers of military age, ¹⁴ he said,
'I shall make a name for myself and win
renown throughout the empire by taking
up arms against Judas and his followers,
who set at naught the king's command.'
¹⁵ Seron was reinforced by a strong contingent of apostate Jews, who marched up
with him to help wreak vengeance on
Israel. ¹⁶ As he reached the pass of Beth-
horon, Judas advanced to meet him with
a handful of men, ¹⁷ who at the sight of
the host coming against them said to
Judas, 'How can so few of us fight against
so many? Besides, we have had nothing
to eat all day and are faint with hunger.'
¹⁸ Judas replied: 'Many can easily be
overpowered by a few; Heaven can save
just as well by few as by many. ¹⁹ Victory
does not depend on numbers; strength
is from Heaven alone. ²⁰ Our enemies,
inflated with insolence and lawlessness,
are coming against us; they mean to kill
us and our wives and children for the sake
of the plunder they will get. ²¹ But we are
fighting for our lives and for our laws and
customs, ²² and Heaven will crush them

before our eyes; you have no need to be
afraid of them.'
²³ As soon as he finished speaking, he
launched a surprise attack, which overwhelmed Seron and his army. ²⁴ They
were pursued down the pass of Beth-horon
as far as the plain; some eight hundred of
them fell; the rest fled to Philistia.
²⁵ Judas and his brothers came to be
regarded with fear, and alarm spread
among the Gentiles round about. ²⁶ His
fame reached the ears of the king, and the
story of his battles was told in every
nation. ²⁷ Incensed by those reports, King
Antiochus issued orders for the mobiliza-
tion of all the forces of his empire, an
immensely powerful army. ²⁸ He opened
his treasury and gave a year's pay to his
troops, with a command to be prepared to
serve as required. ²⁹ But he found that his
resources were running low; his income
from tribute had dwindled as a result of
the disaffection and violence he had
brought on his empire by abolishing
traditional laws and customs. ³⁰ He was
worried that, as had happened once or
twice before, he might be short of money,
both for his normal expenses and for the
gifts he had been accustomed to distribute
with an even more lavish hand than any
of his predecessors on the throne.
³¹ Greatly disconcerted, he resolved to
go to Persia and collect the tribute due
from the provinces, and so raise a large
sum of ready money. ³² He left Lysias, a
distinguished member of the royal family,
as viceroy of the territories between the
Euphrates and the Egyptian frontier,
³³ and he also appointed him guardian of
his son Antiochus until his return. ³⁴ He
transferred to him half the armed forces,
together with the elephants, and gave
him detailed instructions about what he
wanted done, especially in regard to the
inhabitants of Judaea and Jerusalem.
³⁵ Lysias was to dispatch a force against
them so as to crush and destroy the power
of Israel and those left in Jerusalem, and to
blot out all memory of them from the
place. ³⁶ Foreigners were to be settled
throughout the territory and the land was
to be parcelled out among them. ³⁷ The
remaining half of his forces the king
retained and, setting out with them from
Antioch, his capital, in the year 147, he

3:37 147: *that is* 165 B.C.

crossed the Euphrates and marched through the upper provinces.

[38] Lysias chose Ptolemaeus son of Dorymenes, with Nicanor and Gorgias, all three powerful members of the order of king's Friends, [39] and sent forty thousand infantry and seven thousand cavalry under their command to invade and devastate Judaea in accordance with the king's orders. [40] They set out with their entire force and occupied a position near Emmaus in the lowlands. [41] The traders of the region, impressed by what they heard of the army, came to the camp to buy the Israelites for slaves, bringing with them a very large quantity of silver and gold as well as a stock of fetters. The army was also reinforced by troops from Syria and Philistia.

[42] When Judas and his brothers saw how much graver their plight had become with the enemy encamped inside their frontiers, and, further, when they learnt of the orders the king had given for the complete destruction of the nation, [43] they said among themselves, 'Let us restore the shattered fortunes of our people; let us fight for our nation and for the holy place.' [44] They gathered in full assembly both to prepare for battle and to pray and seek divine mercy and compassion.

[45] Jerusalem lay deserted like a
   wilderness,
   with none of her children going in or
       out.
   The holy place was trodden
       underfoot;
   aliens and heathen lodged in her
       citadel.
   Joy had been banished from Jacob,
   and flute and harp were silent.

[46] They assembled at Mizpah, which is opposite Jerusalem, for there in former times Israel had had a place of worship. [47] They fasted that day, put on sackcloth, sprinkled ashes on their heads, and tore their garments. [48] They unrolled the scroll of the law, seeking there the guidance which Gentiles seek from the images of their gods. [49] They brought the priestly vestments, together with the firstfruits and the tithes, and presented Nazirites who had completed their vows, [50] and they cried aloud to Heaven: 'What shall we do about these? Where shall we take

them? [51] Your holy place is trodden underfoot and profaned, and for your priests there is only mourning and humiliation. [52] And now, the Gentiles have gathered against us to destroy us. You know the fate they plan for us; [53] how can we withstand them unless you come to our aid?' [54] The trumpets were sounded, and a great shout was raised.

[55] Judas then appointed leaders of the people, officers over thousands, hundreds, fifties, and tens. [56] In accordance with the law, he ordered back to their homes those who were building their houses or were betrothed or were planting vineyards or were faint-hearted. [57] The army moved off and took up position to the south of Emmaus. [58] There Judas addressed them: 'Prepare for action and show yourselves men. Be ready at dawn to fight these Gentiles massed against us to destroy us and our holy place. [59] Better we should die fighting than look on while calamity overwhelms our people and the holy place. [60] But it will be as Heaven wills.'

4 Gorgias, with a detachment of five thousand men and a thousand picked cavalry, set out by night [2] to launch a surprise attack on the Jewish position; his guides were men from the citadel. [3] But Judas had word of it, and he and his soldiers moved out to strike at the king's army in Emmaus [4] while the troops under Gorgias's command were still away from their base. [5] Gorgias reached Judas's camp during the night, but, finding no one there, began to search the hills for them. 'These Jews', he said, 'are running away from us.'

[6] Daybreak saw Judas in the plain with three thousand men, though they had not all the armour or swords they needed. [7] They found the gentile camp to be strongly fortified with breastworks, while mounted guards, seasoned troops, patrolled round it.

[8] Judas said to his men: 'Do not be afraid of their numbers or panic at their onslaught. [9] Remember how our forefathers were saved at the Red Sea, when pursued by Pharaoh and his army. [10] Now let us call on Heaven to favour our cause and, remembering the covenant made with our forefathers, to crush this army which today opposes us. [11] Then all the

Gentiles will know there is One who liberates and saves Israel.'

¹² When the foreigners saw them advancing to the attack, ¹³ they moved out from their camp to give battle. Sounding their trumpets, Judas and his men ¹⁴ closed with them, and the Gentiles broke and fled into the plain; ¹⁵ all who fell behind were put to the sword. The pursuit was pressed as far as Gazara and the lowlands of Idumaea, to Azotus and Jamnia; some three thousand of the enemy were killed.

¹⁶ Judas and his force then broke off the pursuit and withdrew. ¹⁷ He said to the people: 'Curb your desire for spoil; there is more fighting ahead of us; ¹⁸ Gorgias and his force are in the hills near by. Stand firm now against our enemies and fight; after that, plunder as much as you please.'

¹⁹ Before Judas had finished speaking, an enemy patrol appeared, reconnoitring from the hills. ²⁰ They saw that their army had been routed and their camp was being set on fire, for the smoke that met their gaze showed what had happened. ²¹ They were panic-stricken as they took in the scene, and when, further, they saw the army of Judas in the plain, ready for action, ²² they fled one and all to Philistia.

²³ Judas turned back to plunder the camp, and large quantities of gold and silver, violet and purple stuffs, and great riches were seized. ²⁴ At their homecoming there were songs of thanksgiving and praise to Heaven, 'for it is right, because his mercy endures for ever'. ²⁵ That day saw a great deliverance for Israel.

²⁶ Those of the Gentiles who escaped with their lives went to Lysias and reported all that had happened. ²⁷ He was stunned at the news, bitterly disappointed that matters with Israel had not gone as he intended; they had turned out very differently from the king's instructions to him.

²⁸ The following year Lysias mustered sixty thousand picked infantry and five thousand cavalry to bring the war with the Jews to an end. ²⁹ Marching into Idumaea, they encamped at Bethsura, where Judas opposed them with ten thousand men. ³⁰ When he saw the strength of the enemy's army, he prayed:

'All praise to you, Saviour of Israel, who by the hand of your servant David broke the giant's onslaught and who delivered the Philistine army into the hands of Jonathan, Saul's son, and of his armour-bearer. ³¹ Now let this army be hemmed in by the power of your people Israel, and let the enemy's pride in their troops and mounted men be humbled; ³² fill them with cowardice, make their insolent strength melt away, let them reel under a crushing defeat; ³³ may they fall by the sword of those who love you. And let all who know your name praise you with songs of thanksgiving.'

³⁴ Battle was joined, and in the hand-to-hand fighting Lysias lost about five thousand men. ³⁵ When he saw his own army routed and Judas's army in fighting spirit, ready to live or to die nobly, he withdrew to Antioch, where he recruited a force of mercenaries, intending to return to Judaea with a much larger army.

³⁶ Judas and his brothers said: 'Now that our enemies have been crushed, let us go up to cleanse and rededicate the temple.' ³⁷ When the whole army had assembled, they went up to Mount Zion, ³⁸ where they found the temple laid waste, the altar desecrated, the gates burnt down, the courts overgrown like a thicket or wooded hillside, and the priests' rooms in ruin. ³⁹ They tore their garments, lamented loudly, put ashes on their heads, ⁴⁰ and threw themselves face downwards on the ground. They cried aloud to Heaven, and the ceremonial trumpets were sounded.

⁴¹ Then Judas detailed men to engage the citadel garrison while the temple was being cleansed. ⁴² He selected priests without blemish and faithful to the law, ⁴³ and they purified the temple, removing to an unclean place the stones which defiled it. ⁴⁴ They discussed what to do about the desecrated altar of whole-offerings, ⁴⁵ and rightly decided to demolish it, for fear it might become a lasting reproach to them because it had been defiled by the Gentiles. They therefore pulled down the altar, ⁴⁶ and stored away the stones in a suitable place on the temple hill, until there should arise a prophet to give a decision about them. ⁴⁷ They took

---

4:35 **intending … army:** *prob. mng; Gk obscure.*

unhewn stones, as the law directs, and built a new altar on the model of the previous one. [48] They also repaired the temple and restored its interior, and they consecrated the temple courts. [49] New sacred vessels were made; the lampstand, the altar of incense, and the table were brought into the temple. [50] They burnt incense on the altar, and they lit the lamps on the lampstand to shine within the temple. [51] When they had set the Bread of the Presence on the table and spread out the curtains, their work was completed.

[52] Early on the twenty-fifth day of the ninth month, the month of Kislev, in the year 148, [53] sacrifice was offered, as laid down by the law, on the newly constructed altar of whole-offerings. [54] On the anniversary of the day of its desecration by the Gentiles, on that very day it was dedicated with hymns of thanksgiving, to the music of harps and lutes and cymbals. [55] All the people prostrated themselves in worship and gave praise to Heaven for prospering their cause.

[56] They celebrated the dedication of the altar for eight days; there was rejoicing as they brought whole-offerings and sacrificed shared-offerings and thank-offerings. [57] They decorated the front of the temple with gold garlands and ornamental shields. They renovated the gates and restored the priests' rooms, fitting them with doors. [58] At the lifting of the disgrace brought on them by the Gentiles there was very great rejoicing among the people.

[59] Judas, his brothers, and the whole congregation of Israel decreed that, at the same season each year, the dedication of the altar should be observed with joy and gladness for eight days, beginning on the twenty-fifth of Kislev.

[60] At that time they encircled Mount Zion with high walls and strong towers to prevent the Gentiles from coming in and overrunning it as they had done before. [61] Judas set a garrison there, and he also fortified Bethsura, so that the people should have a fortress facing Idumaea.

5 The Gentiles round about were greatly incensed when they heard of the building of the altar and rededication of the temple. [2] Determined to wipe out all of Jacob's race living among them, they set about the work of massacre and extermination.

[3] Judas made war on the descendants of Esau in Idumaea and attacked Acrabattene, because they had encircled Israel. He inflicted a heavy and humiliating defeat on them and stripped their corpses of armour and weapons. [4] He remembered also the wrong done by the Baeanites, who with traps and road-blocks were continually ambushing the Israelites. [5] He shut them up in their forts and positioned his troops against them; then, calling down a solemn curse on them, he set ablaze the forts with all their occupants. [6] He crossed over to attack the Ammonites and was confronted by a strong force and a large crowd of people, all under the leadership of Timotheus. [7] In the course of many engagements, they broke before Judas's attack and were crushed. [8] After Judas had taken Jazer and its dependent villages, he returned to Judaea.

[9] The Gentiles in Gilead gathered against the Israelites within their territory, intent on destroying them; but the Israelites took refuge in the fortress of Dathema, [10] from where they sent this letter to Judas and his brothers:

The Gentiles in this region have gathered to wipe us out. [11] With Timotheus in command of their army, they are preparing to come and seize the fortress where we have taken refuge. [12] Therefore come now at once and rescue us from their clutches, for many of our number have already fallen. [13] All our fellow-Jews in the region of Tubias have been massacred, their wives and children seized, and their property carried off, and about a thousand men have lost their lives.

[14] While the letter was being read, other messengers with their garments torn arrived from Galilee. [15] 'Ptolemais, Tyre and Sidon,' they reported, 'and all heathen Galilee have mobilized armies for our destruction.'

[16] When Judas and the people heard this, a full assembly was called to decide what should be done for their fellow-countrymen under persecution and enemy attack. [17] Judas said to his brother Simon, 'You go to the rescue of your

4:52 **148**: *that is* 164 B.C.

countrymen in Galilee with such troops as you need, while I and our brother Jonathan go to Gilead.' [18] The remainder of the forces he left with Josephus son of Zacharias, and Azarias, a leading citizen, for the defence of Judaea. [19] Their orders were: 'Take charge of the people, but on no account engage the Gentiles in battle while we are away.' [20] Simon was allotted three thousand men for the march on Galilee, and Judas eight thousand for the march on Gilead.

[21] Simon invaded Galilee and, after many battles, broke the resistance of the Gentiles. [22] Pursuing them as far as the gate of Ptolemais, he killed nearly three thousand of them, and stripped their corpses. [23] He brought back with him the Jews from Galilee and Arbatta, together with their wives and children and all they possessed, and amid great jubilation conducted them to Judaea.

[24] Meanwhile Judas Maccabaeus and his brother Jonathan crossed the Jordan and made a three days' march through the desert. [25] They came upon some Nabataeans, who met them peaceably, and gave them a full account of what had happened to the Jews in Gilead: [26] many of them were held prisoner in the large fortified towns of Bozrah and Bezer, in Alema, Casphor, Maked, and Carnaim; [27] some were enclosed in the other towns of Gilead. 'Your enemies', they reported, 'are marshalling their forces to storm your strongholds tomorrow so as to capture them and destroy all the Jews in them in a single day.'

[28] Judas and his army abruptly turned aside to Bozrah by way of the desert, and captured the town. He put the entire male population to the sword, plundered all their property, and set the place on fire. [29] Making a night march from Bozrah he came within reach of the fortress of Dathema. [30] When dawn broke, there in front of them were troops past counting; they were bringing up scaling-ladders and siege-engines to breach the fortress and begin the attack. [31] When Judas saw that battle was joined, and heard a cry go up to heaven from the town, with the sound of trumpets and loud shouting, [32] he said to his men: 'Fight this day for our brothers!'

[33] They advanced in three columns to take the enemy in the rear; they sounded the trumpets and cried aloud in prayer. [34] When the army of Timotheus realized it was Maccabaeus, they fled. In the heavy defeat inflicted on them, there fell that day nearly eight thousand of the enemy. [35] Judas then turned aside to Alema, which he attacked and captured; he killed all the males, plundered the town, and set it on fire. [36] Moving from there, he occupied Casphor, Maked, Bezer, and the other towns of Gilead.

[37] After these events Timotheus gathered another army and took up position opposite Raphon, on the far side of the wadi. [38] Judas sent spies to their camp, and they reported that all the Gentiles in the neighbourhood had rallied in very great strength to Timotheus, [39] who had also hired the help of Arab mercenaries. The enemy were encamped on the far side of the wadi, ready to give battle. So Judas marched to meet them.

[40] As Judas and his army were approaching the wadi, Timotheus said to his officers: 'If he crosses over to our side first, we shall not be able to stand up to him; he will certainly get the better of us. [41] If, however, his courage fails him and he takes up a position on the other side of the river, then we will cross over and get the better of him.' [42] When Judas reached the wadi, he stationed the officers of the muster on its bank with instructions that the whole army should advance to the battle; no one was to be allowed to take up a fixed position. [43] Thus Judas forestalled the enemy by crossing to attack them at the head of all his people. The gentile army broke before him; one and all they threw away their weapons and sought refuge in the temple at Carnaim. [44] Judas captured the town and burnt the temple and everyone in it. With the overthrow of Carnaim, all resistance came to an end.

[45] Judas assembled the Israelites who were in Gilead to escort them all back to Judaea. There was a great host of them, men high and low, women and children, together with their possessions. [46] They arrived at Ephron, a large and strongly fortified town on the road. It was impossible to bypass it on either side; the only

5:35 **Alema:** *some witnesses read* Maapha.

route lay through the town. ⁴⁷ The inhabitants, however, barricaded their gates with boulders and denied them passage. ⁴⁸ Judas made peaceful overtures to them: 'We have to go through your territory to reach our own. No one will do you any harm: we will simply pass through on foot.' But they refused to open their gates to him. ⁴⁹ Judas issued orders to those under his command: everyone was to halt where he was. ⁵⁰ The fighting men took up battle positions and attacked the town all that day and all the night, until it fell into their hands. ⁵¹ They put every male to the sword, razed the town to the ground and plundered it, and then marched through it over the bodies of the slain. ⁵² They crossed the Jordan to the broad plain opposite Bethshan, ⁵³ while Judas kept the stragglers together and encouraged the people all along the way till he arrived in Judaea. ⁵⁴ With gladness and jubilation they went up to Mount Zion and offered whole-offerings, because they had returned in safety and without loss.

⁵⁵ While Judas and Jonathan were in Gilead, and Simon their brother was besieging Ptolemais in Galilee, ⁵⁶ their heroic military achievements were reported to the two commanders, Azarias and Josephus son of Zacharias, ⁵⁷ and they said: 'We too must make a name for ourselves; let us undertake a campaign against the Gentiles in our neighbourhood.' ⁵⁸ They gave orders to the forces in their command to advance on Jamnia. ⁵⁹ When Gorgias and his men marched from the town to give battle, ⁶⁰ Josephus and Azarias were put to rout and pursued to the frontier of Judaea, with the loss that day of some two thousand Israelites. ⁶¹ The people suffered this heavy defeat because those in command of them, thinking to play the hero themselves, had not obeyed Judas and his brothers. ⁶² Those men were not, however, of that family whose prerogative it was to bring deliverance to Israel.

⁶³ The valiant Judas and his brothers won a great reputation throughout Israel and among all the Gentiles, wherever their fame spread, ⁶⁴ and crowds flocked to acclaim them.

⁶⁵ After this, Judas marched out with his brothers and made war on the descendants of Esau in the country to the south.

He struck at Hebron and its villages, demolished its fortifications, and everywhere burnt down its forts. ⁶⁶ He then set out to invade Philistia and marched through Marisa. ⁶⁷ Several priests who, from a desire to distinguish themselves, had ill-advisedly gone into action, fell in the battle that day. ⁶⁸ Judas turned aside to Azotus in the territory of the Philistines; he pulled down their altars and burnt the images of their gods; he carried off spoil from the towns, and then went back to Judaea.

6 As King Antiochus made his way through the upper provinces he heard that in Persia there was a city, Elymais, famous for its wealth in silver and gold. ² Its temple was very rich, full of gold shields, coats of mail, and weapons left there by Philip's son Alexander, king of Macedon and the first to be king over the Greeks. ³ Antiochus came to the city, but in his attempt to take and plunder it he was unsuccessful because his plan had become known to the citizens. ⁴ They gave battle and drove him off; in bitter disappointment he withdrew towards Babylon.

⁵ In Persia a messenger brought him the news that the armies which had invaded Judaea had suffered defeat, ⁶ and that Lysias, who had marched up with an exceptionally strong force, had been flung back in open battle. Further, the strength of the Jews had increased through the capture of weapons, equipment, and spoil in plenty from the armies they destroyed; ⁷ they had pulled down the abomination built by him on the altar in Jerusalem and surrounded their temple with high walls as before; they had even fortified Bethsura, his city.

⁸ The king was dismayed and so sorely shaken by this report that he took to his bed, ill with grief at the miscarriage of his plans. ⁹ There he lay for many days, overcome again and again by bitter grief, and he realized that he was dying. ¹⁰ He summoned all his Friends and said: 'Sleep has deserted me; the weight of care has broken my heart. ¹¹ At first I asked myself: Why am I engulfed in this sea of troubles, I who was kind and well loved in the day of my power? ¹² But now I recall the wrong I did in Jerusalem: I carried off all the vessels of silver and gold that were there, and with no justification sent

armies to wipe out the inhabitants of Judaea. [13] I know that is why these misfortunes have come upon me; and here I am, dying of bitter grief in a foreign land.'

[14] He summoned Philip, one of his Friends, and appointed him regent over his whole empire, [15] giving him the crown, his royal robe, and the signet ring, with authority to bring up his son Antiochus and train him for the throne. [16] King Antiochus died in Persia in the year 149.

[17] When Lysias learnt that the king was dead, he placed on the throne in succession to his father the young Antiochus, whom he had trained from boyhood, and he gave him the name Eupator.

[18] MEANWHILE the garrison of the citadel was confining the Israelites to the neighbourhood of the temple, and, by harassing tactics, giving continual support to the Gentiles. [19] Judas determined to make an end of them; he gathered all the people together to lay siege to the citadel [20] in the year 150, erecting emplacements and siege-engines against the enemy.

[21] But some of the beleaguered garrison escaped and were joined by a number of apostate Israelites. [22] They went to the king and complained: 'How long must we wait for you to support our cause and avenge our comrades? [23] We were happy to serve your father, to follow his instructions and obey his decrees. [24] And what was the result? Our own countrymen turned against us; indeed they put to death as many of us as they could lay hold of, and they robbed us of our property. [25] Nor are we the only ones to suffer at their hands; they have attacked all the neighbouring lands as well. [26] At this very moment the citadel in Jerusalem is closely invested, and they are intent on its capture. They have also fortified both the temple and Bethsura. [27] Unless your majesty quickly takes the initiative against them they will go to yet greater lengths. There will be no stopping them!'

[28] The king became furious as he listened. He assembled all his Friends, his generals, and cavalry commanders, [29] and he was joined by mercenary troops from other kingdoms and from overseas. [30] His forces numbered one hundred thousand infantry, twenty thousand cavalry, and thirty-two war elephants. [31] They advanced through Idumaea and laid siege to Bethsura, keeping up the attack for many days. They erected siege-engines, but the defenders, fighting back manfully, made a sortie and set them on fire.

[32] Judas now withdrew from the citadel and took up his position at Bethzacharia facing towards the royal encampment. [33] Early next morning the king broke camp and after a forced march along the Bethzacharia road he drew up his army in battle order and the trumpets were sounded. [34] The elephants were roused for combat with the blood of grapes and of mulberries. [35] The great beasts were distributed among the phalanxes; by each were stationed a thousand men, equipped with coats of chain-mail and bronze helmets. Five hundred picked horsemen were also assigned to each animal; [36] they were stationed beforehand where the beast was, and wherever it went, they went also, never leaving its side. [37] Each animal had, by way of protection, a strong wooden turret fastened on its back with a special harness, and carried four fighting men as well as an Indian driver. [38] The rest of his cavalry Lysias stationed on either flank of the army, to harass the enemy while themselves protected by the phalanxes. [39] When the sun shone on the gold and bronze shields, the hills gleamed and flashed like blazing torches.

[40] Part of the king's army was deployed over the heights, and part over the low ground. They advanced steadily and in good order, [41] and trembling seized all who heard the din and clash of arms of this multitude on the march, for it was indeed a very great and powerful force.

[42] Judas drew near with his army and gave battle, and six hundred of the king's men were killed. [43] Eleazar Avaran saw that one of the elephants wore royal armour and stood out above all the rest, and, thinking that the king must be on it, [44] he gave his life to save his people and win for himself everlasting renown. [45] He ran boldly towards it, into the middle of the phalanx, dealing death right and left, so that the enemy fell back on either side before him. [46] He got in underneath the

6:16 149: *that is* 163 B.C.　　　6:20 150: *that is* 162 B.C.　　　6:37 four: *prob. rdg; Gk* thirty-two.

elephant, thrust at it from below, and killed it. It sank to the ground on top of him, crushing him to death. ⁴⁷ When the Jews saw the strength and impetus of the royal forces, they gave ground before them.

⁴⁸ A part of the royal army marched up to Jerusalem to renew the engagement, and the king encamped against Judaea and Mount Zion. ⁴⁹ He came to terms with the people of Bethsura, who abandoned the town, not having the food to withstand a siege, as it was a sabbatical year when the land was left fallow. ⁵⁰ So Bethsura was occupied by the king, who detailed a garrison to hold it.

⁵¹ He then subjected the temple to a lengthy siege; he set up emplacements and siege-engines, with flamethrowers, catapults for discharging stones and barbed missiles, and slings. ⁵² The defenders for their part constructed engines to counter his engines, and put up a prolonged resistance. ⁵³ But there was no food in the storerooms because it was the sabbatical year; those who from time to time had arrived in Judaea as refugees from the Gentiles had consumed all that remained of the provisions. ⁵⁴ The shortage had been so severe that men had dispersed to their homes, leaving only a few in the temple.

⁵⁵ Lysias heard that Philip, whom King Antiochus, before he died, had appointed to bring up his son Antiochus and train him for the throne, ⁵⁶ had now returned from Persia and Media with the late king's expeditionary force and was seeking to take over the government. ⁵⁷ Hastily he gave orders for departure, saying to the king and to the army officers and men: 'Every day we grow weaker, our provisions are running low, the place we are besieging is strong, and the affairs of the empire are pressing. ⁵⁸ Let us now offer these men terms, and make peace with them and with their whole nation. ⁵⁹ Let us guarantee them the right to follow their laws and customs as they used to do, for it was our abolition of these laws and customs that roused their resentment and led to all the troubles.'

⁶⁰ The proposal having met with approval from both king and commanders, an offer of peace was sent and accepted.

⁶¹ The king and his commanders bound themselves by oath, and on the terms agreed the defenders emerged from their stronghold. ⁶² But when the king entered Mount Zion and saw how strongly the place was fortified, he went back on his oath, and ordered the demolition of the surrounding wall. ⁶³ Then with all speed he departed for Antioch, where he found Philip in possession. In the ensuing battle Antiochus took the city by storm.

7 IN the year 151, Demetrius son of Seleucus left Rome, and, landing with a handful of men at a town on the coast, there made himself king. ² While he was on his way to the palace of his ancestors, the army placed Antiochus and Lysias under arrest, with a view to handing them over to him. ³ But when he was informed of their action, he said, 'Do not let me set eyes on them.' ⁴ The soldiers accordingly put them to death, and Demetrius ascended the throne of his kingdom.

⁵ All the apostates and renegades from Israel, led by Alcimus, who aspired to the high-priesthood, came to the king ⁶ with charges against their people. 'Judas and his brothers have wiped out everybody who supported you and have driven us from our country,' they said. ⁷ 'Be pleased now to send a man you trust, to go and see what devastation they have brought on us and on the king's territory, and to punish them along with all who aid and abet them.' ⁸ The king chose one of the royal Friends, Bacchides, who was governor of the province of Beyond-Euphrates, a man of high standing in the empire and loyal to the king; ⁹ he and Alcimus the apostate, on whom the king had conferred the high-priesthood, were sent with orders to wreak vengeance on Israel. ¹⁰ They set out and marched on Judaea with a large force. There Bacchides sent envoys with false offers of friendship, ¹¹ but when Judas and his brothers saw how large an army had come they disregarded those offers.

¹² A deputation of doctors of the law appeared before Alcimus and Bacchides, to ask for a just settlement. ¹³ The Hasidaeans were the first group in Israel to make overtures, ¹⁴ for they said, 'A priest of the

6:53 **in the storerooms:** *some witnesses read* in the temple.   7:1 **151:** *that is* 161 B.C.

family of Aaron is come with their forces, and he will not treat us unjustly.' [15] The language of Alcimus was conciliatory; he assured them on oath that no harm was intended to them or to their friends. [16] But once he had gained their confidence, he arrested sixty of them and put them to death all on one day. As scripture says:

[17] The bodies of your saints were
　　scattered;
　all round Jerusalem their blood was
　　shed,
　and there was none to give them
　　burial.

[18] Fear and dread fell on the whole people. 'There is neither truth nor justice among them,' they said to one another; 'they have broken their agreement and the oath they swore.'

[19] Bacchides then left Jerusalem and encamped in Bethzaith, where he issued orders for the arrest of many of those who had deserted to him, together with some of the people, and had them slaughtered and thrown into a great cistern. [20] He assigned the whole district to Alcimus and detailed troops to assist him, while he himself went back to the king.

[21] Alcimus put up a strong fight for his high-priesthood, [22] and all the trouble-makers rallied to him. They gained control over Judaea and inflicted great damage on Israel. [23] When Judas saw the extent of the havoc which Alcimus and his followers had wrought among the Israelites, far worse than anything done by the Gentiles, [24] he went throughout the territory of Judaea and its environs, punishing deserters and debarring them from access to the country districts. [25] Judging that Judas and his supporters had grown too powerful for him to withstand, Alcimus returned to the king and accused them of atrocities.

[26] Then the king dispatched Nicanor, one of his most distinguished commanders and a bitter enemy of Israel, with orders to wipe out that people. [27] Nicanor arrived at Jerusalem with a large force and sent envoys to Judas and his brothers with false offers of friendship: [28] 'Let there be no quarrel between us,' he said; 'I propose to come with only a small escort to meet you as a friend.'

[29] When he came, they greeted one another in friendly fashion, yet the enemy were preparing to kidnap Judas. [30] That Nicanor's visit involved duplicity became known to Judas, and taking alarm he refused to meet him again. [31] Realizing that his plot had been detected, Nicanor marched out to engage Judas near Capharsalama. [32] About five hundred of Nicanor's men were killed; the rest made good their escape to the City of David.

[33] After those events, Nicanor went up to Mount Zion, where some of the priests and members of the senate came out from the holy place to extend a friendly welcome to him, and to show him the whole-offering which was being sacrificed for the king. [34] But he mocked and jeered at them and polluted them with his spittle, talking arrogantly [35] and vowing in anger: 'Unless Judas and his army are turned over to me at once, I shall burn down this house when I return victorious.' And he departed in a rage. [36] The priests went in again and stood in tears, facing the altar and the temple, and said, [37] 'Lord, you chose this house to bear your name, to be a house of prayer and supplication for your people; [38] take vengeance on this man and his army, and let them perish by the sword. Let their blasphemy not be forgotten; grant them no reprieve.'

[39] Nicanor moved from Jerusalem and set up his camp at Beth-horon, where he was joined by an army from Syria. [40] Meanwhile Judas, encamping at Adasa with three thousand men, uttered this prayer: [41] 'When the followers of a certain king were guilty of blasphemy, your angel came forth and struck down one hundred and eighty-five thousand of them. [42] In the same way crush this army before us today. Let generations to come know that Nicanor has reviled your holy place; judge him as his wickedness deserves.'

[43] Battle was joined on the thirteenth of the month of Adar, and Nicanor's forces suffered a crushing defeat, he himself being the first to fall in the fighting. [44] Seeing Nicanor fall, his men threw away their arms and fled. [45] The Jews, with their trumpets sounding a signal behind the fleeing enemy, pursued them as far as Gazara, a day's journey from Adasa. [46] From every Judaean village round about, the inhabitants came out and, attacking the fugitives on the flanks, forced them back upon their pursuers, so that they all fell by the sword; not one of

them survived. [47] The Jews gathered up the weapons of the slain and other spoils of war; they cut off Nicanor's head and that right hand he had stretched out so arrogantly, and brought them to be displayed at Jerusalem. [48] There was great public rejoicing, and that day was kept as a special day of jubilation. [49] It was ordained that the day, the thirteenth of Adar, should be celebrated annually. [50] Judaea then entered on a short period of peace.

8 JUDAS had had reports about the Romans: that they were renowned for their military power and for the favour they showed to those who became their allies, and that any who joined them could be sure of their friendship [2] and strong military support. He was told of the campaigns they had fought, and the valour they had shown in their conquest of the Gauls, whom they had laid under tribute. [3] He heard of their successes in Spain, where they had seized the silver and gold mines, [4] maintaining by perseverance and good judgement their hold on the entire country, distant though it was from their own land. There were kings from the ends of the earth who had marched against them, only to be beaten off, heavily defeated; others there were who paid them annual tribute.

[5] Philip, and Perseus king of Kittim, and all who had set themselves in opposition to the Romans had been crushed in battle and conquered. [6] Antiochus the Great, king of Asia, had advanced against them with one hundred and twenty elephants, with cavalry and chariots and an immense force, only to be totally defeated. [7] They had captured the king alive, and had required that he and his successors should pay a large annual tribute, give hostages, [8] and cede the territories of India, Media, and Lydia, together with some of their finest provinces; these they had taken from him and handed over to King Eumenes. [9] The Greeks planned to attack and destroy them, [10] but the Romans got to know of it and sent just one general against them. When battle was joined many of the Greeks fell, and their women and children were made captive. The Romans plundered and annexed their territory, demolishing their strongholds and making the inhabitants slaves,

as they remain to this day. [11] The other kingdoms and the islands, any who ever opposed them, they destroyed or reduced to slavery. [12] With their friends, however, and with all who relied on them for protection, they maintained firm friendship.

Thus they overcame rulers near and far, and all who heard of their reputation went in dread of them. [13] Those whom they wished to help and appoint as kings, became kings; those whom they wished to depose, they deposed. By such means they attained to great heights of power. [14] Yet for all this, not one of them ever gave himself the airs of a prince, assuming a crown or putting on the purple. [15] They had established a senate where each day three hundred and twenty senators met for deliberation, giving constant thought to the proper ordering of public affairs. [16] Every year they entrusted their government and the rule of all their dominions to one of their number, all obeying this one man without jealousy or envy.

[17] So Judas chose Eupolemus son of John, son of Accos, and Jason son of Eleazar, and sent them to Rome to make a treaty of friendship and alliance, [18] in order that the Romans might rid them of foreign oppression, for it was clear that the Greek empire was reducing Israel to abject slavery. [19] The envoys made the journey to Rome, a very long journey, and when they came into the senate house they spoke as follows: [20] 'Judas Maccabaeus, his brothers, and the Jewish people have sent us to conclude with you a treaty of alliance, so that we may be enrolled as your allies and friends.' [21] The Romans gave their approval to the proposal, [22] and the following is a copy of the reply which they inscribed on bronze tablets and sent to Jerusalem, so that the Jews might have a record there of the treaty:

[23] Success attend the Romans and the Jewish nation by sea and land for ever! May sword and foe be far from them! [24] But if an unprovoked attack is made on Rome or on any of her allies throughout her dominion, [25] then the Jewish nation shall afford them whole-hearted support as occasion may require. [26] In accordance with Rome's decision Jews shall neither give nor

supply provisions, arms, money, or ships to the enemies of Rome. They are to observe their commitments without compensation.

27 In like manner, if an unprovoked attack is made on the Jewish nation, then the Romans shall afford them wholehearted support as occasion may require. 28 In accordance with Rome's decision there shall be given neither provisions, arms, money, nor ships to the enemies of the Jewish nation. These commitments are to be kept without breach of faith.

29 Those are the terms of the treaty which the Romans have made with the Jewish people. 30 But if, hereafter, both parties agree to add or to rescind anything, what they decide shall be done; any such addition or rescindment shall be valid.

31 To this the Romans added: 'As for the wrongs which King Demetrius is perpetrating against the Jews, we have written to him as follows: "Why have you so harshly oppressed our friends and allies the Jews? 32 If they bring any further complaint against you, we shall open hostilities against you by sea and by land in support of their cause."'

9 When Demetrius heard that Nicanor and his men had fallen in battle, he sent Bacchides and Alcimus a second time into Judaea, and with them the right wing of his army. 2 They marched along the Gilgal road, laid siege to Messaloth in Arbela, and captured it, inflicting heavy loss of life.

3 In the first month of the year 152, they moved camp to Jerusalem, 4 and from there they marched to Berea with twenty thousand infantry and two thousand cavalry. 5 Judas had established his camp at Alasa. He had with him three thousand picked troops, 6 but, when his men saw the size of the enemy forces, their courage failed and many deserted, until a mere eight hundred remained.

7 Aware that his army had melted away and the campaign was going against him, Judas was greatly disheartened, for there was not time to reassemble his forces. Though himself despondent, 8 he said to those who were left, 'Let us take the offensive and see if we can defeat the enemy.' 9 His men tried to dissuade him: 'Impossible!' they said. 'No, we are too few. Let us save our lives now, and come back later to fight them when we have our comrades with us.' 10 But Judas replied: 'Heaven forbid that I should do such a thing as run away! If our time has come, let us die bravely for our fellow-countrymen, and leave no stain on our honour.'

11 The Syrian army moved from its camp and took up its battle position against Judas's men. The cavalry was divided into two squadrons; the slingers and the archers went ahead of the main force, and the crack troops were in the front line. 12 Bacchides was on the right wing. The phalanx advanced with trumpets sounding and flanked by the two cavalry squadrons; 13 Judas's men also sounded their trumpets. The earth shook as the armies met, and the fighting went on from morning till night.

14 When he saw that Bacchides and the main strength of his army were on the right flank, Judas with all his most valiant troops rallying to him 15 broke the Syrian right and pursued them as far as Mount Azotus. 16 The Syrians on the left, seeing their right wing broken, wheeled about and, following closely after Judas and his men, attacked them from the rear. 17 The fighting became very heavy, and many fell on both sides. 18 Judas was among the fallen; the rest of the Jews fled. 19 Jonathan and Simon carried Judas their brother away and laid him in the family tomb at Modin, 20 and there they wept over him. There was great grief throughout Israel, and the people mourned him for many days, saying,

21 How is our champion fallen,
　　the saviour of Israel!

22 The rest of the history of Judas, his wars, exploits, and achievements—these were so numerous that they have not been recorded.

Jonathan: leader and high priest

23 AFTER the death of Judas, the renegades in every part of Israel emerged from hiding, and all the evildoers reappeared, 24 and the country, afflicted at that time by a terrible famine, went over to their

9:3 152: *that is* 160 B.C.

side. ²⁵ Bacchides chose apostates to be in control of the land. ²⁶ They searched out and hunted down the friends of Judas to bring them before Bacchides, who wreaked his vengeance on them and loaded them with indignities. ²⁷ It was a time of harsh oppression for Israel, worse than any since the days when prophets ceased to appear among them. ²⁸ So the friends of Judas all assembled and said to Jonathan, ²⁹ 'Since the death of your brother Judas there has not been a man like him to take the lead against our enemies, Bacchides and those of our own nation who are hostile to us. ³⁰ Today, therefore, we have chosen you to succeed him as our ruler and our leader to fight our battles.' ³¹ From then Jonathan took over the leadership in the place of his brother Judas.

³² When this became known to Bacchides, he sought to kill Jonathan; ³³ but Jonathan, his brother Simon, and all who were with them got to know of it and took refuge in the wilderness of Tekoa, where they encamped by the pool of Asphar. ³⁴ Bacchides discovered this on the sabbath, and he crossed the Jordan with his whole army. ³⁵ Jonathan sent his brother John away in charge of the camp followers and appealed to his friends the Nabataeans to look after the baggage train, which was of some size. ³⁶ But the Jambrites, in a sortie from Medaba, kidnapped John and made off with the baggage. ³⁷ Some time afterwards, news was brought to Jonathan and his brother Simon that the Jambrites were celebrating an important wedding and bringing the bride, the daughter of one of the great nobles of Canaan, from Nadabath with a large retinue. ³⁸ The fate of their brother John still fresh in their minds, Jonathan and his men went up and hid themselves under cover of a hill. ³⁹ As they watched, there, coming to meet the bridal party in the middle of a bustling crowd and a train of baggage, was the bridegroom, escorted, to the sound of drums and musical instruments, by his friends and kinsmen all fully armed. ⁴⁰ Jonathan's men leapt from their ambush and cut them down; many fell, while the survivors made off into the hills, and the Jews took all their goods as spoil. ⁴¹ So the wedding was turned into mourn-ing, and the sound of music to lamentation. ⁴² The blood of their brother fully avenged, Jonathan and Simon returned to the marshes by Jordan.

⁴³ Hearing of this, Bacchides came on the sabbath right to the banks of Jordan with a large force. ⁴⁴ Jonathan said to his men, 'Up, fight for our lives! Today we are in worse plight than ever: ⁴⁵ a battle in front, the waters of Jordan behind, to right and left marsh and thicket—there is no escape! ⁴⁶ Cry to Heaven to save you from the enemy.' ⁴⁷ Battle was joined, and Jonathan had raised his hand to strike down Bacchides, when the Syrian leader eluded him and got away. ⁴⁸ Then Jonathan and his men leapt into the Jordan and swam over to the other side; but the enemy did not pursue them across the river. ⁴⁹ That day the army of Bacchides lost about a thousand men.

⁵⁰ Bacchides returned to Jerusalem, and he fortified with high walls and barred gates a number of places in Judaea: Jericho's fortress, Emmaus and Beth-horon, Bethel, Timnath-pharathon, and Tephon, ⁵¹ in all of which he stationed garrisons to harass Israel. ⁵² He strengthened the towns of Bethsura and Gazara and the citadel, placing troops and stores of provisions in them. ⁵³ He took as hostages the sons of the leading men of the country and put them under guard in the citadel at Jerusalem.

⁵⁴ In the second month of the year 153, Alcimus gave orders for the wall of the inner court of the temple to be demolished, thereby destroying the work of the prophets. ⁵⁵ But he had only begun the work of demolition, when he suffered a stroke which put a stop to his activities. Paralysed and with his speech impaired, he could not utter a word or give final instructions about his property, ⁵⁶ and subsequently he died in great agony. ⁵⁷ On learning that Alcimus was dead, Bacchides returned to the king, and for two years Judaea had peace.

⁵⁸ The renegades all took counsel together: 'Here are Jonathan and his people living in peace and security,' they said; 'if we bring back Bacchides now, he will lay hold of every one of them in a single night.' ⁵⁹ They went and conferred with Bacchides, ⁶⁰ who set off with a large

9:54 153: *that is* 159 B.C.

force. At the same time he sent letters secretly to all his supporters in Judaea, with instructions to seize Jonathan and his men. But because the plan leaked out they were unable to do so, [61] and some fifty of the ringleaders of this villainy in Judaea were taken and put to death. [62] Jonathan and Simon withdrew with their men to Bethbasi in the desert, rebuilt its ruined fortifications, and strengthened it. [63] Informed of this, Bacchides mustered his whole army, summoned his allies in Judaea, [64] and marched against Bethbasi. He took up his position against it, erected siege-engines, and pressed the attack for many days. [65] Jonathan left his brother Simon in the town and, slipping out into the country with a few men, [66] attacked Odomera and his people and the Phasirites in their encampment. [67] Gradually he gained the upper hand and began to advance towards Bethbasi with his forces.

Simon and his men made a sortie from the town, set fire to the siege-engines, [68] and inflicted a shattering attack on Bacchides. They kept up such heavy pressure on him that his plans for an assault were frustrated. [69] Incensed with the renegades at whose instance he had invaded the land, he had many of them put to death. He then decided to return to his own country.

[70] When Jonathan learnt of this, he sent envoys to Bacchides to secure peace terms and the return of prisoners. [71] Bacchides agreed and accepted Jonathan's proposals, swearing to him that as long as he lived he would harm him no more. [72] He handed over the prisoners he had taken earlier from Judaea, and then returned to his own country, never again to set foot on Jewish soil. [73] So the war in Israel came to an end. Taking up residence in Michmash, Jonathan began to govern the people and root the apostates out of Israel.

10 IN the year 160, Alexander Epiphanes son of Antiochus arrived by ship and took possession of Ptolemais, where he was welcomed and proclaimed king. [2] On hearing of this King Demetrius raised a very large army and marched out to give battle. [3] At the same time he sent Jonathan a letter in friendly and flattering terms. [4] He said to himself,

'Let us forestall Alexander by making peace with the Jews before Jonathan comes to terms with him against us, [5] for Jonathan will not have forgotten all the harm we did him by our treatment of his brothers and of his nation.' [6] So he granted him authority to raise and equip an army, conferred on him the title of ally, and gave orders for the hostages in the citadel to be handed over to him. [7] Jonathan came to Jerusalem and read out the letter to all the people and also to the men of the garrison in the citadel, [8] who were filled with apprehension on hearing that the king had given Jonathan authority to raise an army. [9] They surrendered the hostages, who were then restored to their parents.

[10] Jonathan took up his quarters in Jerusalem and began to rebuild and renovate the city. [11] He instructed those engaged on the work to build the walls and surround Mount Zion with a fortification of squared stones, and this was done. [12] The foreigners who occupied the strongholds built by Bacchides made good their escape, [13] every man of them deserting his post and making off to his own country; [14] only in Bethsura were there still left some of those who had abandoned the law and ordinances and found refuge there.

[15] When King Alexander heard of the promises made to Jonathan by Demetrius, and was given an account of the battles and heroic deeds of Jonathan and his brothers, and of the hardships they had endured, he exclaimed, [16] 'Where shall we ever find another man like this? Let us make him our Friend and ally at once.' [17] He therefore wrote Jonathan the following letter:

[18] From King Alexander to his brother Jonathan.
   Greeting.
   [19] Reports have reached us of your valour and of how worthy you are to be our Friend. [20] Now this day we appoint you to be high priest of your nation with the title of king's Friend, to support our cause and to maintain friendship with us.

He also sent him a purple robe and a gold crown.

10:1 *160: that is* 152 B.C.

21 Jonathan assumed the sacred vestments in the seventh month of the year 160 at the feast of Tabernacles; he gathered an army and got ready a large supply of weapons.

22 Demetrius was mortified at the news. 23 'How did we come to let Alexander forestall us in gaining the friendship and support of the Jews?' he demanded. 24 'I too shall write to them in cordial terms and offer honours and gifts to keep them on my side.' 25 So he sent the Jews the following message:

From King Demetrius to the Jewish nation.
Greeting.
26 We have heard with much pleasure that you have honoured your agreements and remained in friendship with us and have not gone over to our enemies. 27 Continue now to keep faith with us, and we shall reward you well for what you do in our cause, 28 both by granting you numerous exemptions and by making you gifts.

29 I hereby release and exempt you and all Jews whatsoever from tribute, from the tax on salt, and from the crown-levy. 30 From today and hereafter I exempt you from the one-third of the grain harvest and the half of the fruit harvest due to me; from today and for all time, I shall no longer exact them from Judaea or from the three administrative districts, formerly part of Samaria and Galilee, which I now attach to Judaea. 31 Jerusalem and its environs, with its tithes and tolls, shall be sacred and free of taxes. 32 I surrender also authority over the citadel in Jerusalem and grant the high priest the right to garrison it with men of his own choice. 33 All Jewish prisoners of war taken from Judaea into any part of my realm I now set at liberty without ransom. No one shall exact any levy whatsoever on the livestock of the Jews. 34 All their festivals, sabbaths, new moons, and appointed days, with three days preceding and following each festival, shall be days of exemption and release for all Jews in my kingdom; 35 no one shall have authority to impose on a Jew any exaction or burden whatsoever.

36 Jews shall be enlisted in the forces of the crown to the number of thirty thousand men; they shall receive the standard rate of army pay. 37 Some of them shall be stationed in the important royal strongholds, others placed in positions of trust in the kingdom. Their commanders and officers shall be of their own race, and they may follow their own customs, just as the king has ordered for Judaea.

38 The three districts annexed to Judaea from the territory of Samaria shall be so annexed as to be deemed under a single control and subject to no authority other than that of the high priest.

39 Ptolemais and the adjoining land I make over to the temple in Jerusalem, to meet the expenses proper to it. 40 I myself shall make an annual grant of fifteen thousand silver shekels, charged on my own royal accounts, to be drawn from such places as may prove convenient. 41 And the arrears of the subsidy, in so far as it has not been paid by the revenue officials, as it formerly was, shall henceforth be paid in for the needs of the temple. 42 Further, the five thousand silver shekels which used to be taken from the annual income of the temple are also remitted, because they belong to the ministering priests. 43 Whoever takes sanctuary in the temple at Jerusalem or in any part of its precincts, because of a debt to the crown or any other debt, shall be free from distraint on his person or on his property within my kingdom. 44 The cost of the rebuilding and renovation of the temple shall be borne by the royal revenue; 45 in addition, the repair of the walls of Jerusalem and its surrounding fortification, as well as of the fortresses in Judaea, shall become a charge on the royal revenue.

46 Jonathan and the people put no faith in those proposals when they heard them, and declined to accept them, for they recalled the great harm the king had done Israel and his harsh oppression of them. 47 They favoured Alexander, because he had been the first to make overtures of peace, and they remained his allies to the end.

48 King Alexander mustered large

10:21 160: *that is* 152 B.C.

forces and took up position over against Demetrius. ⁴⁹ When the two kings joined battle, Alexander's army was put to flight. Demetrius pursued with vigour, ⁵⁰ pressing home the attack till sunset; but Demetrius fell that day.

⁵¹ Alexander sent envoys to Ptolemy, the king of Egypt, with this message: ⁵² 'I have returned to my kingdom and now sit on the throne of my ancestors. I have assumed the government, defeated Demetrius, and made myself master of our country; ⁵³ when I gave battle, he and his army were routed, and I occupy the throne of his kingdom. ⁵⁴ Now let us form an alliance; make me your son-in-law by giving me your daughter in marriage, and both to you and to her I shall make gifts worthy of your royal state.'

⁵⁵ King Ptolemy replied: 'It was a happy day when you returned to the land of your ancestors and ascended the throne of their realm. ⁵⁶ I now accede to your request; but come to Ptolemais so that we may meet, and I shall become your father-in-law as you propose.'

⁵⁷ In the year 162, Ptolemy set out from Egypt with his daughter Cleopatra, and arrived at Ptolemais, ⁵⁸ where King Alexander met him. Ptolemy gave him his daughter in marriage, and the wedding was celebrated there in royal style with great pomp.

⁵⁹ King Alexander wrote to Jonathan to come and meet him. ⁶⁰ Jonathan went in state to Ptolemais, where he met the two kings; he presented them with silver and gold, and also made many gifts to their Friends; and so he won their favour.

⁶¹ There were some pestilent Jewish renegades who conspired to lodge complaints against Jonathan. The king, however, paid no heed to them, ⁶² but gave orders for Jonathan to be divested of the garment he wore and to be robed in purple, and this was done. ⁶³ The king then seated him at his side, and bade his officers escort Jonathan into the centre of the city and proclaim that no one should bring any complaint against him or make trouble for him for any reason whatsoever. ⁶⁴ When this proclamation was made and the men who had planned to lodge complaints saw Jonathan's splendour and the purple robe he wore, one

and all decamped. ⁶⁵ So, honoured by the king, enrolled in the first class of the order of king's Friends, and appointed a general and a provincial governor, ⁶⁶ Jonathan returned to Jerusalem well pleased with his success.

⁶⁷ In the year 165, Demetrius, the son of King Demetrius, arrived in the land of his fathers from Crete, ⁶⁸ which greatly perturbed King Alexander when he heard of it, and made him return to Antioch. ⁶⁹ Demetrius appointed as his commander Apollonius the governor of Coele-Syria, who raised a powerful force and encamped at Jamnia. From there he sent this message to Jonathan the high priest: ⁷⁰ 'You are alone in offering resistance to us, and your opposition is bringing me ridicule and disgrace. Why do you defy us up there in the hills? ⁷¹ Now if you have confidence in your forces, come down and meet us on the plain, and let us try conclusions with each other there, for I have the power of the cities behind me. ⁷² Make enquiries; find out who I am, and who are our allies. You will be told that you cannot stand your ground against us: your predecessors were routed twice in their own territory, ⁷³ and now you will not be able to resist my cavalry and such a force as mine on the plain, where there is not so much as a stone or a pebble, or any place to which you can escape.'

⁷⁴ Provoked by this message from Apollonius, Jonathan marched out from Jerusalem with ten thousand picked men and was joined by his brother Simon with reinforcements. ⁷⁵ He laid siege to Joppa, where the citizens had closed the gates against him because Apollonius had a garrison there. ⁷⁶ But when the fighting started, the citizens were frightened and opened the gates; so Jonathan became master of Joppa. ⁷⁷ Hearing of this, Apollonius with three thousand cavalry and a large body of infantry marched to Azotus as if to pass through it, but at the same time, relying on his numerous cavalry, he advanced into the plain. ⁷⁸ Jonathan pursued him as far as Azotus, where battle was joined. ⁷⁹ Apollonius had left behind a thousand cavalry in concealment, ⁸⁰ and Jonathan now discovered this ambush at his rear. Though surrounded by

10:57 **162**: *that is* 150 B.C.   10:67 **165**: *that is* 147 B.C.

the enemy raining arrows on them from dawn till dusk, [81] his army stood firm as Jonathan had ordered, and the enemy's horses grew weary. [82] At that point, with the cavalry now exhausted, Simon led out his troops and engaged the enemy phalanx, which, routed by him, took to flight. [83] The horsemen scattered across the plain and the infantry fled to Azotus, where they sought refuge in the temple of Dagon their idol. [84] But Jonathan set fire to Azotus and its surrounding villages, and plundered them; the temple of Dagon, with those who had fled there, he burnt to the ground. [85] The numbers of those who fell by the sword, together with those who lost their lives in the fire, reached eight thousand. [86] Jonathan marched from Azotus, and encamped at Ascalon, where with great pomp the citizens came out to meet him. [87] He and his men returned to Jerusalem loaded with spoil.

[88] When these events were reported to King Alexander, he conferred still greater honour on Jonathan, [89] sending him the gold clasp which it is the custom to present to the king's Kinsmen; he also granted him Accaron and all its environs as a personal gift.

11 The king of Egypt gathered a huge army, countless as the sand on the seashore, and with it a great fleet of ships; his intention was to make himself master of Alexander's kingdom by a subterfuge and to add it to his own. [2] He set out for Syria with protestations of peace, and the people of the towns proceeded to open their gates to him and went to meet him; this they had been ordered to do by King Alexander, because Ptolemy was his father-in-law.

[3] As he continued his progress from town to town, Ptolemy left in each of them a detachment of troops as a garrison. [4] When he reached Azotus, he was shown the burnt-out temple of Dagon, the city itself and its ruined suburbs strewn with corpses, and, piled up along his way, the bodies of those burnt in the course of the fighting. [5] The people told the king that it was all Jonathan's doing, for they hoped he would find fault with him; but the king said nothing. [6] When Jonathan met him in state at Joppa, they exchanged

greetings and passed the night there, and [7] Jonathan accompanied the king to the river Eleutherus before returning to Jerusalem. [8] King Ptolemy made himself master of the coastal towns as far as Seleucia-by-the-sea, all the time hatching designs hostile to Alexander.

[9] He sent envoys to King Demetrius with this message: 'I propose that you and I should make a compact: I will give you my daughter, now Alexander's wife, and you shall reign over the kingdom of your father. [10] I regret having given my daughter to Alexander, for he has tried to kill me.' [11] He maligned him in this way because he coveted his kingdom, [12] and he took back his daughter and gave her to Demetrius. The estrangement between Ptolemy and Alexander turned to open enmity.

[13] Ptolemy now entered Antioch, where he assumed the crown of Asia, in addition to the crown of Egypt which he already wore.

[14] All this time King Alexander was in Cilicia, because the inhabitants of that region were in revolt, [15] but when he heard what had been taking place he marched against Ptolemy, who met him with a strong force. Alexander was defeated [16] and fled to Arabia for protection; King Ptolemy was triumphant. [17] Zabdiel, an Arab chieftain, cut off Alexander's head and sent it to Ptolemy. [18] On the third day after that, however, King Ptolemy died, and his garrisons in the fortresses were wiped out by the local inhabitants. [19] So in the year 167 Demetrius became king.

[20] At this time Jonathan mustered the Judaeans for an attack on the citadel in Jerusalem, and they constructed a large number of siege-engines for the purpose. [21] Some renegades, enemies of their own people, went to the king and reported that Jonathan was laying siege to the citadel, [22] news which excited the king's anger. At once he moved his quarters to Ptolemais, and, in a letter to Jonathan, ordered him to raise the siege and with all speed meet him for conference at Ptolemais.

[23] When Jonathan received this summons, he gave orders for the siege to be continued, and then, selecting elders of Israel and priests to accompany him, he

11:19 167: *that is* 145 B.C.

set out on his dangerous mission. ²⁴ He took with him silver and gold, and robes, and many other gifts, with which he won the favour of Demetrius when they met at Ptolemais.

²⁵ Although certain renegade Jews tried to lodge complaints against Jonathan, ²⁶ the king treated him just as his predecessors had done and honoured him in the presence of all his Friends. ²⁷ He confirmed him in the high-priesthood and in all his former dignities, and bestowed on him the rank of head of the first class of king's Friends.

²⁸ Jonathan requested the king to exempt Judaea and the three Samaritan districts from tribute, promising in return three hundred talents. ²⁹ The king gave his consent, and on all these matters wrote as follows:

³⁰ From King Demetrius to his brother Jonathan, and to the Jewish nation. Greeting.

³¹ This is what we have written in a letter to our Kinsman Lasthenes about you; we have had a copy made for your information:

³² 'From King Demetrius to his respected cousin Lasthenes.

'Greeting.

³³ 'Since the Jewish people are well disposed towards us and observe their obligations to us, we are resolved to recognize their loyalty by becoming their benefactor. ³⁴ We have, therefore, confirmed them in the possession of the lands of Judaea and the three districts Apherema, Lydda, and Ramathaim, which are now transferred from Samaria to Judaea, together with all the lands adjacent thereto, for the benefit of all who sacrifice at Jerusalem; this is a transfer of the annual payments which the king formerly received from these territories, from the produce of the soil and of the orchards. ³⁵ Other of our revenues, the tithes and tolls now pertaining to us, the salt-pans, and the crown-levy, all these we shall cede to them.

³⁶ 'These concessions are from now irrevocable for all future time. ³⁷ See to it then that you make a copy of them to be given to Jonathan for display in a prominent position on the holy mountain.'

³⁸ When King Demetrius saw that the country was quiet under his rule and resistance at an end, he disbanded his forces, dismissing them all to their homes, with the exception of the foreign mercenaries he had recruited from the islands of the Gentiles. As a result the troops who had served under his predecessors all turned against him. ³⁹ A certain Trypho, formerly of the party of Alexander, aware of the widespread disaffection towards Demetrius among the soldiers, went to Imalcue, the Arab chieftain, who had charge of the child Antiochus, Alexander's son, ⁴⁰ and kept pressing him to hand the boy over to him to be made king in place of his father. He informed Imalcue of all the measures Demetrius was taking and of his unpopularity with his troops; and he remained there for some time.

⁴¹ Meanwhile Jonathan sent a request to King Demetrius that the garrisons which were constantly harassing Israel should be withdrawn from the citadel in Jerusalem and from the fortresses. ⁴² To this Demetrius replied: 'I will not only meet your request, but when opportunity arises I will do you and your people the highest honour. ⁴³ Therefore be so good now as to send men to support me, for my own troops have all defected.'

⁴⁴ Jonathan dispatched three thousand seasoned fighting men to Antioch, and the king was delighted at their coming. ⁴⁵ The citizens, a hundred and twenty thousand strong, poured into the centre of the city bent on killing Demetrius, ⁴⁶ and while they seized control of the streets and fighting broke out, the king took refuge in the palace. ⁴⁷ He summoned the Jews to his aid, and at once they all rallied to him; they deployed throughout the city and slaughtered as many as a hundred thousand that day, ⁴⁸ setting the city on fire and taking much booty. And thus the king's life was saved. ⁴⁹ When the citizens saw that the Jews had the city completely at their mercy, their courage failed and they clamoured to the king ⁵⁰ to accept their surrender and to stop the Jews making war on them

---

11:28 **three ... districts:** *prob. rdg; Gk* three districts and Samaria.

and the city. 51 They threw down their weapons and made peace; and the Jews, now in high repute with the king and his subjects throughout the kingdom, returned to Jerusalem laden with booty. 52 But when King Demetrius was secure on his throne, with the country quiet under him, 53 he went back on all his promises and became estranged from Jonathan; instead of repaying the benefits he had received, he treated him with great harshness.

54 After this Trypho returned, and with him Antiochus, a mere lad, who was now crowned king. 55 The soldiers, so contemptuously discharged by Demetrius, all rallied to Antiochus and fought against Demetrius until he was defeated and fled. 56 Trypho, who had captured the elephants, made himself master of Antioch.

57 The young Antiochus in a letter to Jonathan confirmed him in the high-priesthood, with authority over the four districts, and appointed him one of the king's Friends. 58 He also sent him a service of gold plate, and conferred on him the right to drink from a gold cup, to be robed in purple, and to wear the gold clasp. 59 To Jonathan's brother Simon he assigned command of the area from the Ladder of Tyre to the Egyptian frontier.

60 Jonathan made a tour through the country on the far side of the river, including the towns there, and the whole Syrian army gathered to his support. He went to Ascalon, where he was received with great honour by the citizens. 61 From there he went on to Gaza, but the inhabitants closed the gates against him; so he blockaded it, set fire to its suburbs, and plundered them. 62 The inhabitants of Gaza then sued for peace, and he granted them terms, taking the sons of their magistrates as hostages and sending them off to Jerusalem; he himself continued his progress through the country as far as Damascus. 63 Jonathan heard that Demetrius's officers had arrived at Kedesh-in-Galilee with a large force to divert him from his objective. 64 He went to meet them, leaving his brother Simon in Judaea. 65 Simon took up position against Bethsura, which he succeeded in blockading after a prolonged attack. 66 Finally the inhabitants sued for terms, which Simon granted; he

expelled them from the town, occupied it, and installed a garrison.

67 Jonathan, who had encamped with his army by the lake of Gennesaret, marched out early in the morning into the plain of Hazor. 68 There in the plain were the gentile forces advancing to meet him; they had set an ambush for him in the hills, while they themselves made a frontal attack. 69 When the troops started up from the ambush and joined in the fighting, Jonathan's men took to their heels; 70 except for the two commanders, Mattathias son of Absalom and Judas son of Chalphi, not a man of them stood his ground. 71 Jonathan tore his clothes, threw dust on his head, and prayed. 72 Then he returned to the attack and utterly routed the enemy. 73 Seeing this, the fugitives of Jonathan's army rallied to him and joined in the pursuit as far as the enemy base at Kedesh; there they set up camp. 74 That day about three thousand of the Gentiles fell. Jonathan then returned to Jerusalem.

12 JONATHAN considered that the time was now opportune to select representatives and dispatch them on a mission to Rome to confirm and renew the treaty of friendship with that city. 2 He also sent letters to the same effect to Sparta and elsewhere. 3 The envoys, having reached Rome, entered the senate house, where they said: 'Jonathan the high priest and the Jewish people have sent us to renew their former pact of friendship and alliance.' 4 The Romans provided them with letters requiring the authorities in each place to accord them safe conduct to Judaea.

5 This is a transcript of Jonathan's letter to the Spartans:

6 From Jonathan the High Priest, the Senate of the Jews, the priests, and the rest of the Jewish people, to our brothers of Sparta.

Greeting.

7 On a former occasion a letter from Arius your king to Onias the high priest acknowledged our kinship; a copy is given below. 8 Onias welcomed your envoy with full honours and accepted the letter in which the terms of alliance and friendship were set forth. 9 We do not regard ourselves as being in need of

such alliances, since the sacred books we possess afford us encouragement. [10] Nevertheless, we now venture to make contact with you to renew our pact of brotherhood and friendship so that we may not become estranged, for many years have passed since your previous approach to us. [11] We never neglect any opportunity, on festal and other appropriate days, of making mention of you at our sacrifices and in our prayers, as it is right and proper to remember kinsmen; [12] and we rejoice at your fame.

[13] We ourselves have been under the constant pressure of hostile attacks on every side, as the surrounding kings have made war upon us. [14] During the course of these wars we had no wish to trouble you or our other allies and friends. [15] Having had the support of aid from Heaven, we have been saved from our enemies, and they have been humbled. [16] Accordingly, we have chosen Numenius son of Antiochus and Antipater son of Jason and have sent them to the Romans to renew our former friendship and alliance with them. [17] We have instructed them to bear our greetings to you also, and to deliver this letter regarding the renewal of our pact of brotherhood. [18] Now we ask you to favour us with a reply.

[19] This is the copy of the letter sent by the Spartans to Onias:

[20] From Arius, King of Sparta, to Onias the High Priest.

Greeting.

[21] A document has come to light which shows that Spartans and Jews are kinsmen, both being descended from Abraham. [22] Now that we have learnt of this, we beg you to write and tell us how your affairs prosper. [23] Our own response is this: 'What is yours, your livestock and every kind of property, is ours, and what is ours is yours.' We are instructing our envoys, therefore, to report to you in these terms.

[24] When Jonathan heard that Demetrius's generals had come with an even larger force to renew the attack, [25] he marched out from Jerusalem and met them in the region of Hamath, to give them no chance

of setting foot on his territory. [26] Spies sent to the enemy camp reported on their return that dispositions were being made for a night assault. [27] At sunset Jonathan issued orders to his men that throughout the night they were to stay awake and stand to arms ready for battle; he also stationed outposts all round the camp. [28] The enemy were alarmed when they learnt that Jonathan and his men were prepared for their attack; their courage failed them and they withdrew, first lighting watch-fires in their camp. [29] Jonathan and his men saw the fires burning and did not realize what had happened until morning. [30] Though he took up the pursuit, he did not overtake them, for they had crossed the river Eleutherus. [31] Turning aside he attacked and plundered the Arabs called Zabadaeans. [32] He moved on to Damascus, marching through the whole country.

[33-34] Meanwhile Simon set out, and, after advancing as far as Ascalon and the neighbouring fortresses, he turned towards Joppa. He had heard that the inhabitants intended to hand over the fort to the supporters of Demetrius, but, before they could do so, he occupied it and placed a garrison there for its defence.

[35] On his return Jonathan convened the senate and with its agreement decided to build fortresses in Judaea, [36] to increase the height of the walls of Jerusalem, and to erect a high barrier which would cut off the citadel from the city and so isolate it that the garrison could neither buy nor sell. [37] The people assembled to rebuild the city, for the wall along the ravine to the east had partly collapsed; he also repaired the section called Chaphenatha. [38] Simon rebuilt Adida in the Shephelah, and strengthened it with barred gates.

[39] Trypho now aspired to the sovereignty of Asia; he planned to assume the crown and launch an offensive against King Antiochus. [40] But fearing that Jonathan would resort to war to prevent this, he cast about for some means of capturing and killing him. He set off and reached Bethshan. [41] Jonathan went out to confront him with forty thousand picked warriors, and he too reached Bethshan. [42] When Trypho saw the size of the force with Jonathan, he hesitated to take the offensive. [43] Instead he received Jonathan with full honours: he commended him to

all his Friends, loaded him with gifts, and ordered his Friends and his troops to obey him as they would himself. [44] He said to him: 'Why have you put all these men to so much trouble? We are not at war! [45] Send them home now and choose a few to accompany you, and come with me to Ptolemais. I shall hand it over to you together with the other fortresses, a large number of troops, and all the officials, and then I shall take my leave. This is the sole purpose of my coming.' [46] Jonathan believed him and did as he said: he dismissed his forces, and they returned to Judaea. [47] He kept back three thousand men, of whom he left two thousand in Galilee, while a thousand accompanied him. [48] But as soon as Jonathan entered Ptolemais, the people closed the gates and seized him, and put to the sword everyone who had come with him.

[49] Trypho sent a force of infantry and cavalry into Galilee to the great plain, to wipe out Jonathan's men, [50] who only now learnt that Jonathan had been seized and was lost, along with his escort; however, they put heart into one another and marched off in close formation, ready for battle. [51] When their pursuers saw that they would fight for their lives they turned back. [52] Though all came safely home to Judaea, they were greatly afraid and mourned for Jonathan and those who were with him; the whole of Israel was plunged into grief. [53] The Gentiles round about were all bent on destroying them root and branch. 'The Jews have no leader or champion,' they said; 'so now is the time for us to attack, and we shall blot out all memory of them from among men.'

The leadership of Simon

13 WHEN a report reached Simon that Trypho had got together a large force for the invasion and destruction of Judaea, [2] the people were reduced to a state of panic. Seeing this, Simon went up to Jerusalem, where he called an assembly [3] and to afford them encouragement said: 'I do not need to remind you how much my brothers and I and my father's house have done for the laws and the holy place, what battles we have fought, what hardships we have endured. [4] All my brothers have fallen in this cause, fighting for Israel; only I am left. [5] Now Heaven forbid that I should grudge my life

when danger threatens, for I am in no way a better man than my brothers. [6] Rather, since the Gentiles in their hatred have all gathered to destroy us, I shall take up the cause of my nation and of the holy place, of your wives and children.' [7] With these words he rekindled the spirit of the people, [8] and they responded by calling out: 'You shall be our leader in place of Judas and your brother Jonathan. [9] Fight our wars, and we shall do whatever you say.' [10] Simon assembled all the fighting men and hurried on the completion of the walls until Jerusalem was fortified on every side. [11] Jonathan son of Absalom was sent with a considerable force to Joppa, where he drove out the inhabitants and remained in occupation of the town.

[12] Trypho marched from Ptolemais at the head of a large force to invade Judaea, taking Jonathan with him under guard; [13] Simon meanwhile established his camp at Adida on the edge of the plain. [14] When Trypho learnt that Simon had come forward to take the place of his brother Jonathan and was about to offer battle, he sent envoys to him with this message: [15] 'We are detaining your brother Jonathan because of certain moneys owed by him to the royal treasury in connection with the offices he held. [16] To ensure that once released he will not again revolt, send now one hundred talents of silver and two of his sons as hostages, and we shall let him go.' [17] Although he was sure the proposal was a trick, Simon had the money and the children brought to him, fearing that otherwise he might arouse widespread animosity among the people, [18] who would say, 'It was because you did not send the money and the children that Jonathan lost his life.' [19] So he sent the children and the hundred talents; but Trypho broke his word and did not release Jonathan.

[20] After this, Trypho set out to invade and ravage the country. He made a detour by way of Adora, and Simon with his army marched parallel with him everywhere he went. [21] Meanwhile the garrison of the citadel kept sending emissaries to Trypho, urging him to come by the desert route and to send supplies. [22] Trypho prepared to dispatch the whole of his cavalry, but that night there was a severe storm, and they failed to get through

because of the snow; so he withdrew into Gilead. ²³ When he was near Bascama, he had Jonathan put to death and buried there. ²⁴ Trypho then turned and went off to his own country.

²⁵ Simon had the body of his brother brought for burial to Modin, the town of his forefathers. ²⁶ There was great grief for Jonathan throughout Israel and the mourning lasted for many days. ²⁷ Over the tomb of his father and brothers Simon raised a lofty monument, visible at a great distance and faced, back and front, with polished stone. ²⁸ He erected seven pyramids, arranged in pairs, for his father and mother and four brothers. ²⁹ He contrived an elaborate setting for the pyramids: he surrounded them with tall columns surmounted with trophies of armour as a perpetual memorial, and with carved ships alongside the trophies, plainly visible to those at sea. ³⁰ This mausoleum which he made at Modin stands to the present day.

³¹ Trypho now conspired against Antiochus the young king and put him to death. ³² He usurped the throne and assumed the crown of Asia, and he inflicted great damage on the country.

³³ Simon rebuilt the fortresses of Judaea, furnishing them with high towers and with massive walls and barred gates; he also stocked the fortresses with provisions. ³⁴ He selected delegates and sent them to King Demetrius to negotiate a remission of taxes for the country, on the ground that all Trypho's exactions had been exorbitant. ³⁵ In reply to this request Demetrius sent a letter in the following terms:

³⁶ From King Demetrius to Simon the High Priest and Friend of kings, and to the elders and nation of the Jews. Greeting.
³⁷ We have received the gold crown and the palm branch which you sent, and we are prepared to make a lasting peace with you and to instruct the revenue officers to grant you remissions of tax. ³⁸ All our agreements with you stand confirmed, and the strongholds which you built shall remain yours. ³⁹ For any errors of omission or commission we grant a free pardon, to take effect from the date of

this letter. We remit the crown-levy which you owed us, and every other tax formerly exacted in Jerusalem is henceforth cancelled. ⁴⁰ Any of you who are suitable for enrolment in our retinue shall be so enrolled.

Let there be peace between us.

⁴¹ In the year 170, Israel was released from the gentile yoke; ⁴² the people began to write on their contracts and agreements: 'In the first year of Simon, the great high priest, general, and leader of the Jews'.

⁴³ At that time Simon surrounded and closely invested Gazara with his troops. He constructed a siege-engine, and bringing it up to the town he made a breach in one of the towers and captured it. ⁴⁴ The men on the siege-engine leapt from it into the town, and there was great commotion. ⁴⁵ The defenders along with their wives and children climbed on to the city wall with their garments torn, clamouring loudly to Simon to grant them terms. ⁴⁶ 'Do not treat us as our wickedness deserves,' they cried, 'but as your mercy prompts you.' ⁴⁷ Simon agreed terms and called off the attack. But he expelled them from the town, and after purifying the houses in which there were idols, he made his entry with songs of thanksgiving and praise. ⁴⁸ Everything which was polluted he threw out, and he settled there men who would keep the law. He strengthened the fortifications, and he built himself a residence in the town.

⁴⁹ The occupants of the citadel at Jerusalem were prevented from going in and out to buy and sell in the countryside; famine ensued, and many died of starvation. ⁵⁰ The survivors cried out to Simon to accept their surrender; this he granted; then expelling them from the citadel he cleansed it from its defilement. ⁵¹ It was on the twenty-third day of the second month in the year 171 that the Jews entered the city amid a chorus of praise and the waving of palm branches, with lutes, cymbals, and zithers, with hymns and songs, to celebrate Israel's final riddance of a formidable enemy. ⁵² Simon decreed that this day should be observed as an annual festival. He strengthened the fortifications of the temple hill opposite the citadel, and he and his men made it their

13:41 **170**: *that is* 142 B.C.   13:43 **Gazara**: *prob. rdg: Gk* Gaza.   13:51 **171**: *that is* 141 B.C.

base. [53] In recognition of the fact that his son John had now reached manhood, he appointed him commander of all the forces, with Gazara as his headquarters.

14 In the year 172, King Demetrius mustered his army and moved into Media to obtain support for his war against Trypho. [2] When Arsakes king of Persia and Media heard that Demetrius had entered his territory, he dispatched one of his generals to take him alive. [3] The general marched out, defeated and captured Demetrius, and brought him to Arsakes, who kept him under guard.

[4] As long as Simon ruled, Judaea was undisturbed. He sought his nation's good, and they lived happily all through the glorious days of his reign. [5] Notable among his achievements was his capture of the port of Joppa to secure his communications overseas. [6] He extended his nation's borders and made himself master of the land. [7] Many prisoners of war were repatriated. He gained control over Gazara and Bethsura and over the citadel, from which he removed all pollution. None could withstand him.

[8] The people farmed the land in peace; it produced its crops, and the trees in the plains their fruit. [9] Old men sat in the streets, talking together of their blessings; and the young men arrayed themselves in splendid military style. [10] Simon supplied the towns with food in plenty and equipped them with weapons for defence, so that his renown spread to the ends of the earth. [11] Peace was restored to the land, and throughout Israel there was great rejoicing. [12] Everyone sat under his own vine and fig tree, and there was none to cause alarm. [13] Those were days when no enemy was seen in the land and every hostile king was crushed. [14] Simon gave his protection to the poor among the people; he fulfilled the demands of the law, and rid the country of renegades and evil men. [15] He enhanced the splendour of the temple and furnished it with a wealth of sacred vessels.

[16] THE report of Jonathan's death reached Rome and even Sparta, and caused widespread grief. [17] When they heard, however, that his brother Simon had succeeded him as high priest and was firmly in control of both country and towns, [18] they sent him a renewal of the treaty of friendship and alliance they had established with his brothers Judas and Jonathan; this was inscribed on bronze tablets [19] which were read before the assembly in Jerusalem. [20] The following is a copy of the letter which the Spartans sent:

From the magistrates and city of Sparta to the High Priest Simon, to the Senate, the priests, and the rest of the Jewish people, our brothers.
Greeting.
[21] The envoys sent to our people have informed us of your honour and fame, and their visit has given us much pleasure. [22] We have entered a record of the message they brought in the minutes of the public assembly; it reads: 'Numenius son of Antiochus and Antipater son of Jason came as envoys of the Jews to renew the treaty of friendship. [23] It was resolved by the public assembly to receive these men with honour and to place a copy of their address in the public archives, so that the people of Sparta might have it on permanent record. A copy of this document has been made for Simon the high priest.'

[24] After this, Simon sent Numenius to Rome bearing a large gold shield, worth a thousand minas, to confirm the alliance with the Romans.

[25] When the people heard an account of these events they asked themselves how they could show their gratitude to Simon and his sons, [26] for he, with his brothers and his father's family, had proved resolute in repulsing the enemies of Israel and ensuring the nation's freedom. [27] So the people had an inscription engraved on bronze tablets and placed on a monument on Mount Zion; this is a copy of the inscription:

On the eighteenth day of the month of Elul, in the year 172, the third year of Simon's high-priesthood, [28] at Asaramel, before a large assembly of priests, people, rulers of the nation, and elders of the land, the following resolution was passed: [29] 'Whereas our land had been subject to frequent wars, Simon son of Mattathias, a priest of the Joarib

14:1 **172**: *that is* 140 B.C.   14:27 **172**: *that is* 140 B.C.

family, and his brothers put their lives in jeopardy by their resistance to the enemies of the people, in order to safeguard the temple and the law, and they brought great glory to their nation. ³⁰ Jonathan rallied the nation and became high priest, and then was gathered to his forefathers. ³¹ When enemies resolved to invade and destroy the land and to make an assault on the temple, ³² Simon came forward and fought for his nation. He expended large sums of his own money to arm the soldiers of his nation and to provide their pay. ³³ He fortified the towns of Judaea, including Bethsura, a frontier town formerly used by the enemy as an arsenal, and he stationed in it a garrison of Jewish soldiers. ³⁴ The coastal town of Joppa was also fortified, as was Gazara near Azotus, formerly occupied by the enemy. He settled Jews there, and provided these towns with everything requisite for their restoration.

³⁵ 'Simon's patriotism and his resolution to win renown for his nation were such that the people made him their leader and high priest, in recognition of his achievements, his just conduct, his loyalty towards the nation, and constant efforts to enhance its power. ³⁶ In his time and under his leadership the Gentiles were successfully evicted from the land; so too were those who had occupied the City of David in Jerusalem and made for themselves a citadel from which they used to sally forth and bring defilement on the whole precinct of the temple and do violence to its purity. ³⁷ He installed Jewish soldiers in it and fortified it for the greater security of the land and city; he also heightened the walls of Jerusalem. ³⁸ In consideration of all this King Demetrius confirmed him in the office of high priest, ³⁹ appointed him one of his Friends, and granted him the highest honours; ⁴⁰ for he had heard that the Romans were addressing the Jews as friends, allies, and brothers and had received Simon's envoys with much honour.

⁴¹ 'The Jews and their priests confirmed Simon as their leader and high priest in perpetuity until a true prophet should appear. ⁴² He was to be their general, and to have full charge of the temple and of the work of reconstruction; in addition the supervision of the country and of the arms and fortifications was to be entrusted to him. ⁴³ He was to be obeyed by the whole people; all official documents throughout the land were to be drawn up in his name. He was to be entitled to wear the purple robe and gold clasp.

⁴⁴ 'None of the people or the priests is to have authority to abrogate any of these decrees, to oppose commands issued by Simon, or to convene any assembly in the land without his permission; none of them is to be robed in purple or to wear the gold clasp. ⁴⁵ Whoever contravenes these provisions or neglects any of them is to be liable to punishment.

⁴⁶ 'It was the unanimous decision of the people that Simon should officiate in the ways here laid down. ⁴⁷ Simon accepted, and consented to be high priest, general, and ethnarch of the Jews and the priests, and to be the protector of them all.'

⁴⁸ This inscription, it was declared, should be engraved on bronze tablets and set up in a prominent position within the precincts of the temple, ⁴⁹ and copies were to be placed in the treasury in the keeping of Simon and his sons.

15 Antiochus son of King Demetrius sent a letter from overseas to Simon, priest and ethnarch of the Jews, and to the whole nation. ² It read:

From King Antiochus to Simon, High Priest and Ethnarch, and to the Jewish nation.

Greeting.

³ Whereas certain rebels have seized control of my ancestral kingdom, now I have decided to assert my claim to it, so that I may restore it to its former state. For this I have recruited a large body of mercenaries and fitted out ships of war. ⁴ It is my intention to land in my country and to seek out and punish those who have ravaged my kingdom and laid waste many of its cities. ⁵ Therefore I now confirm all the remissions which my royal predecessors granted you, whether of tribute or of other contributions. ⁶ I authorize you to mint your own coinage as currency for your country. ⁷ Jerusalem and the temple is to be free. All the arms you

have prepared and the fortresses you have built and now occupy may remain in your hands. ⁸All debts now owing to the royal treasury and all future liabilities thereto are cancelled from this time forward for ever. ⁹When we have re-established our kingdom, we shall confer the highest honours on you and on your nation and temple, to make your country's fame apparent to the whole world.

¹⁰In the year 174, Antiochus entered the land of his forefathers, and all the armed forces came over to him, leaving Trypho only a few supporters. ¹¹With Antiochus in pursuit of him, Trypho fled along the coastal road to Dor, ¹²for he well knew how desperate was his position now that his troops had deserted. ¹³Antiochus, with a hundred and twenty thousand trained soldiers and eight thousand horsemen under his command, laid siege to Dor. ¹⁴He drew a cordon round the town, his ships joining in the blockade from the sea, and thus, both by land and sea, he exerted heavy pressure on it and prevented anyone from leaving or entering.

¹⁵NUMENIUS and his party arrived from Rome with letters to the various kings and nations. That to Ptolemy read as follows:

¹⁶From Lucius, Consul of the Romans, to King Ptolemy.
   Greeting.
   ¹⁷Envoys have come to us from our friends and allies the Jews. They were sent by Simon the high priest and the Jewish people, to renew their original treaty of friendship and alliance, ¹⁸and they brought with them a gold shield valued at a thousand minas. ¹⁹We have resolved, therefore, to write to kings and nations, that they do nothing to the detriment of the Jews; they must not make war on them or on their cities or their country, nor are they to ally themselves with those who so make war. ²⁰We have decided to accept the shield from them. ²¹If, therefore, any rebels have escaped from their country to you, they are to be handed over to Simon the high priest to be punished by him according to Jewish law.

²²The same message was sent to King Demetrius, to Attalus, Ariarathes, Arsakes, ²³Sampsakes, and the Spartans, and also to the following places: Delos, Myndos, Sicyon, Caria, Samos, Pamphylia, Lycia, Halicarnassus, Rhodes, Phaselis, Cos, Sideh, Aradus, Gortyna, Cnidus, Cyprus, and Cyrene. ²⁴A copy was written out for Simon the high priest.

²⁵KING Antiochus laid siege to Dor for the second time, and launched repeated attacks against it; he had siege-engines constructed and blockaded Trypho, preventing all movement in or out of the town.

²⁶Simon sent two thousand picked men to assist him, as well as silver and gold and much equipment. ²⁷But Antiochus refused the offer; instead, he repudiated all his previous agreements with Simon and broke off relations. ²⁸He sent Athenobius, one of the Friends, to convey this message: 'You are occupying Joppa and Gazara and the citadel in Jerusalem, cities that belong to my kingdom. ²⁹You have laid waste their territories and done great damage to the country, and you have made yourselves masters of many places in my kingdom. ³⁰Therefore I now demand the return of the cities you have seized and the surrender of the tribute exacted from places beyond the frontiers of Judaea over which you have assumed control. ³¹Otherwise, you must pay five hundred talents of silver on their account, and another five hundred as compensation for the destruction you have caused and for the loss of tribute from the cities. Failing this, we shall resort to war.'

³²Athenobius, the king's Friend, came to Jerusalem, and when he saw the magnificence of Simon's establishment, and the gold and silver vessels on his sideboard, and his display of wealth, he was amazed. He delivered the king's message, ³³to which Simon replied: 'We have neither occupied other people's land nor taken possession of other people's property; we have taken only our ancestral heritage, unjustly seized for a time by our enemies. ³⁴We have grasped the opportunity to reclaim our patrimony. ³⁵But with regard to Joppa and Gazara, which you demand, these towns were doing great damage among our people and in our land; for these we offer one hundred talents.'

15:10 174: *that is* 138 B.C.   15:25 **for the second time:** *some witnesses read* on the second day.

Without a word, [36] Athenobius went off in anger to the king, who was furious when Athenobius told him what Simon had said, and described Simon's splendour and all else he had seen.

[37] Meanwhile Trypho boarded a ship and made his escape to Orthosia. [38] The king appointed Kendebaeus as commander-in-chief of the coastal zone, and gave him infantry and cavalry, [39] with instructions to blockade Judaea, to rebuild Kedron and strengthen its gates, and to make war on our people; he himself would continue the pursuit of Trypho. [40] Kendebaeus arrived in Jamnia, and by invading Judaea began to harass our people, capturing and killing them. [41] He rebuilt Kedron and stationed cavalry and foot-soldiers there to sally forth and patrol the roads of Judaea, as instructed by the king.

16 John went up from Gazara and reported to Simon, his father, the results of Kendebaeus's campaign. [2] Simon summoned his two eldest sons Judas and John, and said to them: 'My brothers and I and my father's family have fought Israel's battles from our youth until this day, and many a time have we been successful in rescuing Israel. [3] Now I am old, but mercifully you are in the prime of life. Take my brother's place and mine, and go out and fight for our nation. And may help from Heaven be with you!'

[4] John levied twenty thousand warriors, foot-soldiers and cavalry, from the country and marched against Kendebaeus. After a night at Modin [5] they advanced early next morning into the plain, where a large force of infantry and cavalry stood ready to meet them on the far side of a wadi. [6] John and his troops were in position facing the enemy, when he realized that his men were afraid to cross the gully. So he himself led the way, and seeing this his men followed him across. [7] John drew up his army with the cavalry in the centre of the infantry, for the opposing cavalry were very numerous. [8] The trumpets sounded for the attack, and Kendebaeus and his army were routed; many fell, and the remainder took refuge in the fortress. [9] John's brother Judas was wounded in the fighting, but John kept up the pursuit until Kendebaeus reached Kedron, which he had rebuilt. [10] The fugitives fled to the forts in the open country round Azotus, whereupon John set fire to Azotus, and some two thousand of the enemy perished. He then returned to Judaea in safety.

[11] Ptolemaeus son of Abubus had been appointed commander for the plain of Jericho. He had great wealth in silver and gold, [12] for he was the high priest's son-in-law, [13] but he became over-ambitious and, proposing to make himself master of the country, plotted to put Simon and his sons out of the way. [14] When, in the course of a tour to inspect the towns in that region and to attend to their needs, Simon went down to Jericho with his sons Mattathias and Judas in the year 177, in the eleventh month, the month of Shebat, [15] the son of Abubus, with treachery in his heart, received them at the small fort called Dok which he had built, and entertained them lavishly. But he had men in concealment there, [16] and when Simon and his sons were drunk, Ptolemaeus and his accomplices started up and seized their weapons; bursting into the banqueting hall, they attacked Simon and killed him, along with his two sons and some of his servants. [17] It was an act of base treachery in which evil was returned for good.

[18] Ptolemaeus forwarded an account of his action to the king, with a request for troops to be sent to his assistance and for him to be given authority over the country and its towns. [19] He ordered some of his men to Gazara to make away with John, and he wrote to the senior officers of the army urging them to come over to him and be given silver and gold and gifts. [20] Other troops he detailed to seize control of Jerusalem and the temple hill. [21] But someone ran ahead and reported to John at Gazara that his father and brothers had been murdered, and that Ptolemaeus had sent men to kill him as well. [22] The news came as a great shock to John, and, learning of the plot against his life, he arrested and put to death the men who came to kill him.

[23] The rest of the story of John, his wars and the deeds of valour he performed, the walls he built, and his achievements, [24] are recorded in the annals of his high-priesthood from the time when he succeeded his father.

16:14 177: *that is* 134 B.C.

THE SECOND BOOK OF THE
MACCABEES

1 From the Jews in Jerusalem and in the country of Judaea to their Jewish kinsmen in Egypt.

Greeting and peace.

² May God prosper you, and may he keep in mind the covenant he made with Abraham, Isaac, and Jacob, his faithful servants. ³ May he give to you all hearts to worship him and to fulfil his purposes with high courage and willing spirit. ⁴ May he make your minds open to his law and ordinances. May he bring you peace, ⁵ and grant you an answer to your prayers; may he be reconciled to you and never forsake you in an evil hour. ⁶ Here and now we are praying for you.

⁷ In the reign of Demetrius, in the year 169, we wrote to you during the persecution and crisis that we Jews experienced after Jason and his followers defected from the holy land and the kingdom, ⁸ setting the temple porch on fire and spilling innocent blood. We prayed to the Lord and were answered; we brought a sacrifice and an offering of fine flour, we lit the lamps, and laid out the Bread of the Presence. ⁹ Now we instruct you to observe the celebration of a feast of Tabernacles in the month of Kislev.

¹⁰ Written in the year 188.

From the people of Jerusalem and Judaea, from the Senate, and from Judas: to Aristobulus, tutor of King Ptolemy and a member of the family of anointed priests, and to the Jews in Egypt.

Greeting and health.

¹¹ We have been rescued by God from great dangers, for which we give him profound thanks as our champion against the king; ¹² God it was who drove out the enemy stationed in the Holy City.

¹³ When King Antiochus went into Persia with a force that seemed invincible, they were cut to pieces in the temple of the goddess Nanaea through a stratagem employed by her priests. ¹⁴ On the pretext of a ritual marriage with the goddess, Antiochus, escorted by his Friends, had come to the temple to secure the considerable treasure by way of dowry. ¹⁵ After this was laid out by the priests, he entered the temple precinct with a small bodyguard. As soon as he was inside, the priests shut the sanctuary; ¹⁶ then, opening a secret trapdoor in the panelled ceiling, they hurled stones at them, and the king fell as if struck by a thunderbolt. They hacked off limbs and heads and threw them to those outside. ¹⁷ Blessed in all things be our God, who handed over the godless to death!

¹⁸ We think it right and proper to inform you that we are about to celebrate the purification of the temple on the twenty-fifth of Kislev, so that you also may celebrate a feast of Tabernacles; this is in honour of the fire which appeared when Nehemiah offered sacrifices, after he had rebuilt the temple and the altar. ¹⁹ When our forefathers were being carried off to Persia, the devout priests of those days secretly took fire from the altar and concealed it inside a dry well. This proved a safe hiding-place and remained undiscovered. ²⁰ After many years had passed, in God's good time Nehemiah was sent back by the king of Persia. He dispatched in search of the fire the descendants of the priests who had hidden it, and they reported to our people that they found, not fire, but a thick liquid. ²¹ Nehemiah told them to draw some out and bring it to him. When the materials of the sacrifice had been presented, he ordered the priests to sprinkle this liquid over the wood and the sacrifice. ²² This was done, and after some time the sun, till then hidden by clouds, began to shine and to every-

1:7 **169**: *that is* 143 B.C.   1:10 **188**: *that is* 124 B.C.

one's astonishment there was a great blaze of fire on the altar. ²³While the sacrifice was burning, the priests offered prayer, they and all those present: Jonathan began and the rest responded, led by Nehemiah.

²⁴The prayer was in this style: 'Lord God, the Creator of all things, the terrible and mighty, the just and merciful, the only King, you alone are gracious; ²⁵you are the only Giver, the only just and omnipotent and eternal One, the Deliverer of Israel from every evil, who chose the patriarchs and set them apart. ²⁶Accept, we pray, this sacrifice on behalf of your whole people Israel; watch over them and sanctify them, for they are your own possession. ²⁷Bring together those of our people who are dispersed, set free those who are enslaved among the heathen, look favourably on those who are despised and detested; so let the heathen know that you are our God. ²⁸Punish with torments our arrogant and insolent oppressors, ²⁹and, as promised by Moses, plant your people in your holy land.' ³⁰The priests then chanted the hymns.

³¹After the sacrifice had been consumed, Nehemiah ordered that what remained of the liquid be poured over some great stones. ³²At this a flame shot up, but it burnt itself out as soon as the fire on the altar outshone it.

³³These events became widely known. The king of Persia was told that, in the place where the exiled priests had hidden the fire, a liquid had appeared, which Nehemiah and his companions had used to burn up the materials of the sacrifice. ³⁴After he had verified this, the king had the site enclosed and declared it sacred. ³⁵The custodians he appointed received a share of the very substantial revenue the king derived from it. ³⁶Nehemiah and his companions called the liquid nephthar, which means 'purification'; but most people call it naphtha.

2 The records show that it was Jeremiah the prophet who ordered the exiles to hide the fire, in the way just described. ²After giving them the law,

the prophet charged them not to neglect the ordinances of the Lord, or let their minds be led astray by the sight of gold and silver images in all their finery. ³In similar terms he appealed to them never to let the law be far from their hearts.

⁴It is recorded also that, in obedience to a divine command, the prophet gave orders for the Tent of Meeting and the Ark to accompany him, and he went off to the mountain from the top of which Moses had seen God's promised land. ⁵Arriving at the mountain, Jeremiah found a cave-dwelling into which he carried the Tent, the Ark, and the altar of incense; he then blocked up the entrance. ⁶Some of his companions went to mark out the way, but were unable to find it. ⁷Jeremiah learnt of this and took them to task. 'The place is to remain unknown', he said, 'until God finally gathers his people together and shows them his favour. ⁸The Lord will then bring these things to light once more, and his glory will appear together with the cloud, as it was revealed in the time of Moses and also when Solomon prayed that the shrine might be worthily consecrated.'

⁹Further, it is related that Solomon, who had the gift of wisdom, offered a dedication sacrifice at the completion of the temple; ¹⁰and that, just as Moses had prayed to the Lord and fire had come down from heaven and burnt up the sacrificial offerings, so in answer to Solomon's prayer the fire came down and consumed the whole-offerings. ¹¹(Moses said, 'The sin-offering was burnt in the same way because it was not eaten.') ¹²The feast celebrated by Solomon went on for eight days.

¹³These same facts are set out in the official records and in the memoirs of Nehemiah. Just as Nehemiah collected the chronicles of the kings, the writings of prophets, the works of David, and royal letters about sacred offerings, to found his library, ¹⁴in the same way Judas has collected for us all the documents that had been dispersed as a result of the recent conflict. These are in our possession, ¹⁵and if ever you

---

1:31 **that what remained … stones:** *so some witnesses; others read* that great stones should enclose what remained of the liquid.   1:32 **but … outshone it:** *or* but hardly had the light been reflected from the altar, when it burnt itself out.   2:11 **sin-offering:** *or* purification-offering.

need any of them, send messengers for them.

¹⁶ Since we are about to celebrate the purification of the temple, we are writing to impress upon you the duty of holding this festival. ¹⁷ God has rescued his whole people and granted to all of us the holy land, the kingship, the priesthood, and the consecration, ¹⁸ as he promised by the law. We have confidence that God will soon show us compassion and gather us from everywhere under heaven to the holy place, for he has delivered us from great evils and purified that place.

¹⁹ J ASON of Cyrene has set out in five books the story of Judas Maccabaeus and his brothers, of the purification of the great temple, and of the dedication of the altar. ²⁰ He has also given an account of the wars with Antiochus Epiphanes and with his son Eupator, ²¹ and he has described the apparitions from heaven which appeared to those who, in the cause of the Jewish religion, vied with one another in heroism. Few though they were, they ranged through the whole country, taking booty and routing the foreign hordes; ²² they recovered the world-renowned temple, liberated the city of Jerusalem, and reaffirmed the laws, which were in danger of being abolished. All this they achieved because the Lord showed them clemency and favour.

²³ These five books of Jason I shall attempt to summarize in a single work; ²⁴ for I was struck by the mass of statistics and the difficulty which the sheer bulk of the material occasions to those wishing to master the narratives of this history. ²⁵ I have tried to provide entertainment for those who peruse for pleasure, an aid for students who must commit the facts to memory, and in general a service to readers. ²⁶ The task which I have taken on myself in making this summary is no easy one; it means hard work and late nights, ²⁷ just as the man who prepares a banquet and aims to satisfy his guests has no light task. Yet I shall gladly undergo this labour to earn general gratitude ²⁸ and, while concentrating on the main points of my outline, I shall leave to the original author the minute discussion of every particular. ²⁹ While the architect of a new house

must concern himself with the whole of the structure, the man who paints in encaustic on the walls needs to discover only what is necessary for the ornamentation; I reckon it is much the same with me. ³⁰ It is the province of the original author of a history to take possession of the field, to spread himself in discussion, and to busy himself with matters of detail; ³¹ on the other hand, whoever makes an abridgement must be allowed to aim at conciseness of expression and to renounce an exhaustive treatment of the subject matter.

³² Here then, without further comment, I begin my narrative, for it would be absurd to give a lengthy introduction to the history and cut short the history itself.

Syrian oppression of the Jews

3 DURING the rule of the high priest Onias, the Holy City enjoyed unbroken peace and prosperity, and there was exemplary observance of the laws, because he was pious and hated wickedness. ² The kings themselves held the sanctuary in honour and embellished the temple with the most magnificent gifts; ³ King Seleucus of Asia even met the whole cost of the sacrificial worship from his own revenues.

⁴ But a certain Simon, of the clan Bilgah, who had been appointed administrator of the temple, quarrelled with the high priest about the regulation of the city market. ⁵ Unable to get the better of Onias, he went to Apollonius son of Thrasaeus, then governor of Coele-Syria and Phoenicia, ⁶ and alleged that the treasury at Jerusalem was so packed with untold riches that the total of the accumulated balances was beyond all reckoning; it bore no relation to the account for the sacrifices, and he suggested that these balances might be brought under the control of the king. ⁷ In the course of a meeting with the king, Apollonius reported what he had been told about the riches, whereupon the king chose Heliodorus, his chief minister, to be sent with orders to effect the removal of these treasures.

⁸ Heliodorus set off at once, ostensibly to make a tour of inspection of the cities of Coele-Syria and Phoenicia, but in fact to

3:4 **Bilgah:** *so some witnesses; others read* Benjamin.

carry out the king's design. ⁹ When he arrived at Jerusalem and had been cordially received by the high priest and the citizens, he disclosed the purpose of his visit: he told them about the allegations and asked if they were true. ¹⁰ The high priest explained that the deposits were held in trust for widows and orphans, ¹¹ apart from what belonged to Hyrcanus son of Tobias, a man of very high standing. The matter was being misrepresented by the godless Simon; the total sum was four hundred talents of silver and two hundred of gold. ¹² It was unthinkable, he said, that injury should be done to those who had relied on the sanctity of the place, on the dignity and inviolability of a temple held in reverence the whole world over. ¹³ But, in virtue of the king's orders, Heliodorus insisted that these deposits must without question be confiscated for the royal treasury.

¹⁴ On the day appointed, when he entered the temple to draw up an inventory, there was great distress throughout the city. ¹⁵ The priests, prostrating themselves in their vestments before the altar, prayed to Heaven, whose law had made deposits sacred, to keep them intact for their rightful owners. ¹⁶ The high priest's looks pierced every beholder to the heart, for his face and changing colour betrayed the anguish of his spirit. ¹⁷ Alarm and shuddering gripped him, and the pain he felt was clearly apparent to the onlookers. ¹⁸ The people flocked from their houses and rushed to join in universal supplication because of the dishonour which threatened the holy place. ¹⁹ Women in sackcloth, their breasts bare, thronged the streets; unmarried girls who were kept in seclusion ran to the gates or the walls, while others leaned out from windows; ²⁰ with outstretched hands all made solemn entreaty to Heaven. ²¹ It was pitiful to see the crowd lying prostrate in utter disarray and the high priest in an agony of apprehension.

²² While the people were imploring the Lord Almighty to keep the deposits intact and safe for those who had lodged them, ²³ Heliodorus proceeded to put into effect what had been decided. ²⁴ But just as he was arriving with his escort at the treasury, the Ruler of spirits and of all power sent a mighty apparition, so that everyone who had dared to accompany Helio-

dorus collapsed in terror, stricken with panic before the might of God. ²⁵ There appeared to them a horse, splendidly caparisoned, with a rider of terrifying aspect who was clad all in golden armour; it rushed fiercely at Heliodorus and, rearing up, attacked him with its hooves. ²⁶ There also appeared to Heliodorus two young men of surpassing strength and glorious beauty, magnificently attired. Taking their stand on either side of him, they flogged him, raining on him blow after blow. ²⁷ Suddenly, overwhelmed by a great darkness, he fell to the ground, and his men quickly took him up and placed him on a stretcher. ²⁸ This man, who so recently had entered the treasury accompanied by his whole bodyguard and an attendant crowd, was now borne off utterly helpless, publicly compelled to acknowledge the sovereignty of God.

²⁹ While Heliodorus lay speechless, deprived by this divine act of all hope of recovery, ³⁰ the Jews were praising the Lord for the miracle he had performed in his holy place; the temple, which only a short time before was the scene of alarm and confusion, now overflowed with joy and gladness at the manifestation of the Lord Almighty.

³¹ Some of Heliodorus's companions lost no time in begging Onias to pray to the Most High that the life of their master, now lying at his very last gasp, might be spared. ³² Fearing that the king might suspect that Heliodorus had met with foul play at the hands of the Jews, the high priest offered a sacrifice for the man's recovery. ³³ As the expiation was being made, the same young men, dressed as before, again appeared to Heliodorus, and standing over him said: 'You should be very grateful to Onias the high priest; it is for his sake the Lord has spared your life. ³⁴ You have been scourged by God; now proclaim his mighty power to all men.' With these words they vanished.

³⁵ Heliodorus offered a sacrifice and made lavish freewill-offerings to the Lord who had spared his life; then, taking leave of Onias, he returned with his troops to the king. ³⁶ To everyone he bore witness of the miracles of the supreme God which he had seen with his own eyes.

³⁷ When the king asked him what sort of man would be suitable to send to

Jerusalem another time, Heliodorus replied: [38] 'If you have an enemy or someone plotting against your government, that is the place to send him; you will receive him back soundly flogged, if he survives at all, for beyond doubt there is a divine power surrounding the place. [39] He whose habitation is in heaven watches over it himself and gives it his aid; those who approach the place with evil intent he strikes down and destroys.'
[40] So runs the story of Heliodorus and the preservation of the treasury.

4 BUT Simon, the man mentioned above, who in the matter of the money had laid information against his country, went on to slander Onias by alleging that it was he who had incited Heliodorus and so been the author of these troubles. [2] He had the effrontery to accuse of conspiracy against the government one who was a benefactor of the city, a protector of his fellow-Jews, and a staunch upholder of the law. [3] The feud reached such a pitch that one of Simon's trusted adherents even resorted to murder. [4] Realizing how dangerous this rivalry had become and that Apollonius son of Menestheus, governor of Coele-Syria and Phoenicia, was encouraging Simon in his evil ways, [5] Onias had recourse to the king. He did not appear as an accuser of his fellow-citizens but rather as one concerned for the interests of all the Jews, both as a nation and as individuals. [6] He saw that unless the king intervened there could be no peace in public affairs, nor would Simon be stopped in his mad course.
[7] When, on the death of Seleucus, Antiochus known as Epiphanes succeeded to the throne, Jason, Onias's brother, procured for himself the office of high priest by underhand means. [8] In a petition to the king he promised him three hundred and sixty talents in silver coin immediately, and eighty talents from future revenue; [9] further, he undertook to pay an additional hundred and fifty talents if authority were given him to set up a gymnasium for the physical education of young men, and to enrol in Jerusalem a group to be known as 'Antiochenes'. [10] The king gave his as-

sent; and Jason, as soon as he had secured the high-priesthood, made his fellow-Jews conform to the Greek way of life.
[11] He set aside the royal privileges accorded the Jews through the agency of John, the father of that Eupolemus who at a later date negotiated a treaty of friendship and alliance with the Romans. He abolished the institutions founded on the law and introduced practices which ran counter to it. [12] He lost no time in establishing a gymnasium at the foot of the citadel itself, and he made the most outstanding of the young men adopt the hat worn by Greek athletes. [13] So with the introduction of foreign customs Hellenism reached a high point through the inordinate wickedness of Jason, an apostate and no true high priest. [14] As a result, the priests no longer showed any enthusiasm for their duties at the altar; they treated the temple with disdain, they neglected the sacrifices, and whenever the opening gong called them they hurried to join in the sports at the wrestling school in defiance of the law. [15] They placed no value on dignities prized by their forefathers, but cared above everything for Hellenic honours. [16] This brought misfortune upon them from every side, and the very people whose way of life they admired and tried so hard to emulate turned out to be vindictive enemies. [17] To act profanely against God's laws is no light matter, as will in due course become clear.
[18] When the quinquennial games were being held at Tyre in the presence of the king, [19] the villainous Jason sent, as envoys to represent Jerusalem, Antiochenes bearing three hundred drachmas in silver for the sacrifice to Hercules. Even the bearers considered it improper that this money should be used for a sacrifice, and thought it should be spent differently. [20] Thanks to them, the money intended by its sender for the sacrifice to Hercules went in fact to fit out triremes.
[21] From Apollonius son of Menestheus, who was sent to Egypt for the coronation of King Philomotor, Antiochus learnt that Philometor was now hostile to his interests. Anxious for his own security, he removed to Joppa, and then to Jerusalem, [22] where he was lavishly welcomed by Jason and the city, and received with

4:9 enrol ... 'Antiochenes': *or* enrol the inhabitants of Jerusalem as citizens of Antioch.

torchlight processions and ovations. Afterwards he quartered his army in Phoenicia.

²³ Three years later, Jason sent Menelaus, brother of the Simon mentioned above, to convey money to the king and to carry out agreed decisions on some urgent business. ²⁴ But Menelaus, once in the king's presence, flattered him with an air of authority, and diverted the high-priesthood to himself, outbidding Jason by three hundred talents in silver. ²⁵ He arrived back with the royal mandate, but with nothing else to make him worthy of the high-priesthood; he had the passions of a cruel tyrant and the temper of a savage beast. ²⁶ Jason, who had supplanted his own brother, was now supplanted in his turn and forced to seek refuge in Ammonite territory. ²⁷ Menelaus continued to hold the high-priesthood but without ever paying any of the money he had promised the king, however often it was demanded by Sostratus, the commander of the citadel, ²⁸ who was responsible for collecting the revenues. In consequence both were summoned to appear before the king. ²⁹ Menelaus left as his deputy in the high-priesthood his brother Lysimachus, while Sostratus left Crates, the commander of the Cypriot mercenaries, to act for him.

³⁰ While those events were taking place the inhabitants of Tarsus and Mallus rose in revolt, because their cities had been handed over as a gift to Antiochis, the king's concubine. ³¹ The king went off hurriedly to restore order, leaving Andronicus, one of his ministers, as regent. ³² Thinking to seize a favourable opportunity, Menelaus made a present to Andronicus of some of the gold plate which he had appropriated from the temple. Some he had already sold to Tyre and neighbouring cities. ³³ When Onias learnt of it on good authority, he withdrew to sanctuary at Daphne near Antioch and denounced him. ³⁴ For this, Menelaus approached Andronicus privately and urged him to have Onias put to death. The regent came to Onias and, though bent on treachery, greeted him and with assurances on oath persuaded him to leave the sanctuary in spite of his suspicions. Then at once, with no respect for justice, he made away with him.

³⁵ This wicked murder caused indignation and resentment not only among Jews but among many from other nations as well. ³⁶ When the king returned from Cilicia, the Jews of Antioch sent him a petition about the indefensible killing of Onias, a crime detested equally by the Gentiles. ³⁷ Antiochus, deeply grieved, was moved to pity and tears as he thought of the high character and disciplined conduct of the dead man. ³⁸ His anger flared up and without more ado he stripped Andronicus of the purple and tore off his clothes; then leading him right round the city to that very place where he had committed the sacrilegious crime against Onias, he dispatched the murderer, who was thus repaid by the Lord with richly deserved punishment.

³⁹ Lysimachus, with the connivance of Menelaus, entered on a career of sacrilege and plunder in Jerusalem. When this became widely known and the people heard that much of the gold plate had been disposed of, they combined against Lysimachus. ⁴⁰ As the crowds, now aroused and furious, were getting out of hand, Lysimachus armed some three thousand men and launched a vicious attack, led by a certain Auranus, a man advanced in years and no less in folly. ⁴¹ Recognizing that Lysimachus was behind the attack, some of the crowd seized stones, others blocks of wood, others again handfuls of burning embers that were lying about, and they hurled them indiscriminately at Lysimachus and his men. ⁴² The result was that many were wounded, some were killed, and the rout was complete; the temple robber himself they put to death near the treasury.

⁴³ A charge was laid against Menelaus in connection with this incident ⁴⁴ and, on the king's arrival at Tyre, three men sent by the Jewish senate stated their case before him. ⁴⁵ Menelaus's cause being as good as lost, he promised Ptolemaeus son of Dorymenes a substantial sum of money if he would win over the king. ⁴⁶ Ptolemaeus led the king aside into a colonnade, as though to take the air, and persuaded him to change his mind. ⁴⁷ Menelaus, the author of all the mischief, was acquitted and the charges brought against him were dismissed, but the king condemned to death the unfortunate accusers, men who would have been let go as entirely

innocent had they appeared even before Scythians. [48]At once those who had pleaded for their city, their people, and their sacred vessels, suffered this undeserved penalty. [49]It caused even some of the Tyrians to show their detestation of the crime by providing a splendid funeral for the victims. [50]Yet thanks to the cupidity of those in power, Menelaus, this arch-plotter against his fellow-citizens, continued in office and went from bad to worse.

5 About that time Antiochus undertook his second expedition against Egypt. [2]For nearly forty days apparitions were seen in the sky all over Jerusalem: galloping horsemen in golden armour, companies of spearmen standing to arms, [3]swordsmen at the ready, and squadrons of cavalry in battle order. Charges and countercharges were made in this direction and that; shields were brandished, spears massed, javelins hurled; breast-plates and golden ornaments of every kind blazed with light. [4]That the phenomenon might portend good was the prayer of everyone.

[5]On a false report of Antiochus's death, Jason at the head of no less than a thousand men launched a surprise attack on Jerusalem. The defenders on the wall were driven back and, with the city on the point of being taken, Menelaus sought refuge in the citadel. [6]Jason embarked upon an unsparing massacre of his fellow-citizens, for he did not grasp that success against one's own kin is the greatest of failures; he imagined that the trophies he raised marked the defeat of enemies, not of fellow-countrymen. [7]However, he failed to secure control of the government; all he achieved as the result of his scheming was dishonour, and once again he sought asylum in Ammonite territory. [8]His career came to a miserable end, for after being imprisoned by Aretas the ruler of the Arabs he fled from city to city, hunted by all, hated as a renegade against the laws, detested as the butcher of his country and his fellow-citizens, until he landed up in Egypt. [9]Then, having crossed by sea to Sparta, where he hoped to obtain shelter because of the Spartans' kinship with the Jews, he, who had driven so many into exile, himself died an exile. [10]He who had cast out so many to lie unburied was himself unmourned; he

had no obsequies of any kind, no resting-place in the ancestral grave.

[11]It was clear to the king, when news of those happenings reached him, that Judaea was in a state of insurrection, and he set out from Egypt in savage mood. He took Jerusalem by storm, [12]ordering his troops to cut down unsparingly everyone they met, and to slaughter those who took refuge in the houses. [13]Young and old were murdered, women and children massacred, girls and infants butchered. [14]At the end of three days the victims numbered eighty thousand: forty thousand killed in the fighting, and as many again sold into slavery.

[15]Not satisfied with this, and guided by Menelaus, who had turned traitor to both religion and country, the king had the audacity to enter the most holy temple on earth. [16]The villain laid his polluted hands on the sacred vessels, and profanely swept up the votive offerings which other kings had made to enhance the splendour and fame of the shrine.

[17]The pride of Antiochus passed all bounds. He did not understand that the sins of the people of Jerusalem had for a short time angered the Lord, and that this was the reason why the temple was left to its fate. [18]Had they not been guilty of many sinful acts, Antiochus would have fared no better than Heliodorus, who was sent by King Seleucus to inspect the treasury; like him, he would have been flogged and his presumption foiled at once. [19]But the Lord did not choose the nation for the sake of the sanctuary; he chose the sanctuary for the sake of the nation. [20]That was why the sanctuary itself had its part in the misfortunes that befell the nation, and afterwards shared its good fortune; it was abandoned when the Almighty was roused to anger, but restored again in all its splendour when the great Master was reconciled with his people.

[21]So Antiochus hastened back to Antioch, taking with him eighteen hundred talents from the temple. Carried away by arrogance he thought that he could make ships sail on dry land and men walk over the sea! [22]He left behind commissioners to oppress the people: in Jerusalem he left Philip, by race a Phrygian, by disposition more barbarous than the man who appointed him, [23]and in Mount

Gerizim, Andronicus; and in addition to these there was Menelaus, who was more brutally overbearing to the citizens than the others. Further, such was the king's hostility towards the Jewish population [24] that he sent Apollonius, commander of the Mysian mercenaries, with an army of twenty-two thousand men; his orders were to slaughter all the adult males and to sell the women and children into slavery. [25] When Apollonius arrived at Jerusalem, he pretended he had come in peace; waiting until the holy sabbath day and finding the Jews abstaining from work, he paraded his troops under arms. [26] All who came out to witness the spectacle he put to the sword; then, charging into the city with his soldiers, he cut down an even greater number of the people.

[27] BUT Judas, also called Maccabaeus, escaped with about nine others into the desert, where he and his companions lived in the mountains, fending for themselves like the wild animals, and all the while feeding on what vegetation they found there, so as to have no share in the pollution.

6 Not long afterwards King Antiochus sent an elderly Athenian to compel the Jews to give up their ancestral customs and to cease regulating their lives by the laws of God. [2] He was commissioned also to pollute the temple at Jerusalem and dedicate it to Olympian Zeus; the sanctuary on Mount Gerizim he was to dedicate to Zeus God of Hospitality, as requested by the local inhabitants.

[3] This evil onslaught bore hard on the people and tried them grievously, [4] for the Gentiles filled the temple with licentious revelry: they took their pleasure with prostitutes and had intercourse with women in the sacred precincts. Moreover, they introduced things which the law forbade, [5] and heaped the altar with offerings prohibited as impure. [6] No one was allowed to observe the sabbath or to keep the traditional festivals or even to admit to being a Jew at all. [7] Each month during the celebration of the king's birthday, the Jews were forcibly compelled to eat the entrails of sacrificial victims, and on the feast of Dionysus to wear ivy-wreaths and join the procession in his honour. [8] At the

instigation of the inhabitants of Ptolemais a royal decree was published in the neighbouring Greek cities to the effect that they should adopt the same policy of compelling the Jews to eat the entrails, [9] and that they should put to death everyone who refused to conform to Greek ways.

The miserable fate of the Jews was there for all to see. [10] For instance, two women who had had their children circumcised were brought to trial; then, with their babies hanging at their breasts, they were paraded through the city and hurled headlong from the ramparts. [11] Other Jews, who had assembled secretly in nearby caves to observe the sabbath, were denounced to Philip and, since out of regard for the sanctity of the day they had scruples about defending themselves, they were burnt alive.

[12] Now I beg my readers not to be disheartened by those tragic events, but to reflect that such penalties were inflicted for the discipline, not the destruction, of our race. [13] It is a sign of great benevolence that acts of impiety should not be overlooked for long but rather should meet their due recompense at once. [14] The Lord has not seen fit to deal with us as he does with other nations: with them he patiently holds his hand until they have reached the full extent of their sins, [15] but on us he inflicts retribution before our sins reach their limit. [16] So he never withdraws his mercy from us; although he may discipline his people by disaster, he does not desert them. [17] So much by way of reminder; I must now continue with my summary of events.

[18] Eleazar, one of the leading teachers of the law, a man of great age and distinguished bearing, was being forced to open his mouth and eat pork; [19] but preferring death with honour to life with impiety, he spat it out and voluntarily submitted to the torture. [20] So should men act who have the courage to reject food which despite a natural desire to save their lives it is not lawful to eat. [21] Because of their long acquaintance with him, the officials in charge of this sacrilegious meal had a word with Eleazar in private; they urged him to bring meat which he was permitted to eat and had himself prepared; he need only pretend to comply with the

---

6:8 At ... Ptolemais: *some witnesses read* At the instigation of Ptolemaeus.

king's order to eat the sacrificial meat. [22] In that way he would escape death by taking advantage of the clemency which their long-standing friendship merited. [23] But Eleazar made an honourable decision, one worthy of his years and the authority of old age, worthy of the grey hairs he had attained to and wore with such distinction, worthy of his faultless conduct from childhood, but above all worthy of the holy and God-given law; he replied at once: 'Send me to my grave! [24] If I went through with this pretence at my time of life, many of the young might believe that at the age of ninety Eleazar had turned apostate. [25] If I practised deceit for the sake of a brief moment of life, I should lead them astray and stain my old age with dishonour. [26] I might for the present avoid man's punishment, but alive or dead I should never escape the hand of the Almighty. [27] If I now die bravely, I shall show that I have deserved my long life [28] and leave to the young a noble example; I shall be teaching them how to die a good death, gladly and nobly, for our revered and holy laws.'

With these words he went straight to the torture, [29] while those who a short time before had shown him friendship now turned hostile because, to them, what he had said was madness. [30] When Eleazar was on the point of death from the blows he had received, he groaned aloud and said: 'To the Lord belongs all holy knowledge; he knows what terrible agony I endure in my body from this flogging, though I could have escaped death; yet he knows also that in my soul I suffer gladly, because I stand in awe of him.'

[31] So he died; and by his death he left a noble example and a memorial of virtue, not only to the young but also to the great mass of his countrymen.

7 Another incident concerned the arrest of seven brothers along with their mother. They were being tortured by the king with whips and thongs to force them to eat pork, contrary to the law. [2] But one of them, speaking for all, said: 'What do you expect to learn by interrogating us? Rather than break our ancestral laws we are prepared to die.' [3] In fury the king ordered great pans and cauldrons to be heated. [4] This was attended to without delay; meanwhile he gave orders that the spokesman's tongue should be cut out

and that he should be scalped and mutilated before the eyes of his mother and six brothers. [5] A wreck of a man, but still breathing, he was taken at the king's direction to the fire and roasted in one of the pans. As the smoke from it streamed out, the mother and her sons encouraged each other to die nobly. [6] 'The Lord God is looking on,' they said, 'and we may be sure he has compassion on us. Did not Moses say to Israel in the song plainly denouncing apostasy, "He will have compassion on his servants"?'

[7] After the first brother had died in this way, the second was subjected to the same indignities. The skin and hair of his head were torn off, and he was asked: 'Will you eat, or must we tear you limb from limb?' [8] 'Eat? Never!' he replied in his native language, and so he in turn underwent torture like the first. [9] With his final breath he said: 'Fiend though you are, you are setting us free from this present life, and the King of the universe will raise us up to a life everlastingly made new, since it is for his laws that we are dying.'

[10] After him the third was tortured. When the question was put to him, he at once showed his tongue, courageously held out his hands, [11] and spoke nobly: 'The God of heaven gave these to me, but his laws mean far more to me than they do, and it is from him that I trust to receive them again.' [12] Both the king himself and those with him were astounded at the young man's spirit and his utter disregard for suffering.

[13] When he too was dead, they tortured the fourth in the same cruel manner. [14] At the point of death, he uttered these words: 'Better to be killed by men and to cherish God's promise to raise us again! But for you there will be no resurrection.'

[15] Next the fifth was dragged forward for torture. [16] Looking at the king, he said: 'Mortal as you are, you have authority among human beings and can do as you please. But do not imagine that God has abandoned our nation. [17] Wait, and you will see how his mighty power will torment you and your descendants!'

[18] After him the sixth was brought and he, with his dying breath, said: 'Do not delude yourself: it is through our own fault that we suffer these things; we have sinned against our God and brought these

appalling events on ourselves. ¹⁹ But do not suppose you yourself will escape the consequences of trying to contend with God.'

²⁰ The mother was the most remarkable of all, and she deserves to be remembered with special honour. She watched her seven sons perish within the space of a single day, yet she bore it bravely, for she trusted in the Lord. ²¹ She encouraged each in turn in her native language; filled with noble resolution, her woman's thoughts fired by a manly spirit, she said to them: ²² 'You appeared in my womb, I know not how; it was not I who gave you life and breath, not I who set in order the elements of your being. ²³ The Creator of the universe, who designed the beginning of mankind and devised the origin of all, will in his mercy give you back again breath and life, since now you put his laws above every thought of self.'

²⁴ Antiochus felt that he was being treated with contempt and suspected an insult in her words. As the youngest brother was still left, the king, not content with appealing to him, even assured him on oath that once he abandoned his ancestral customs he would make him rich and enviable by enrolling him as a king's Friend and entrusting him with high office. ²⁵ Since the youth paid no regard whatsoever, the king summoned the mother and urged her to advise her boy to save his life. ²⁶ After much urging from the king, she agreed to persuade her son. ²⁷ She leant towards him and, flouting the cruel tyrant, said in their native language: 'Son, take pity on me, who carried you nine months in the womb, nursed you for three years, reared you and brought you up to your present age. ²⁸ I implore you, my child, to look at the heavens and the earth; consider all that is in them, and realize that God did not create them from what already existed and that a human being comes into existence in the same way. ²⁹ Do not be afraid of this butcher; accept death willingly and prove yourself worthy of your brothers, so that by God's mercy I may receive back both you and them together.'

³⁰ She had barely finished when the young man spoke out: 'What are you all waiting for? I will not submit to the king's command; I obey the command of the law given through Moses to our forefathers. ³¹ And you, King Antiochus, who have devised all manner of atrocities for the Hebrews, you will not escape God's hand. ³² It is for our own sins that we are suffering, ³³ and, though to correct and discipline us our living Lord is angry for a brief time, yet he will be reconciled with his servants. ³⁴ But you, impious creature, most villainous of the human race, do not let vain hopes buoy you up or empty delusions carry you away when you lay hands on Heaven's servants. ³⁵ You are not yet safe from the judgement of the omnipotent, all-seeing God. ³⁶ My brothers, after a short period of pain, have under God's covenant drunk of the waters of everlasting life; but you by God's verdict will pay the just penalty of your brutal insolence. ³⁷ I, like my brothers, surrender my body and my life for our ancestral laws. I appeal to God to show favour speedily to his people and by whips and scourges to bring you to admit that he alone is God. ³⁸ May the Almighty's anger, which has justly fallen on all our race, end with me and my brothers!'

³⁹ Roused by this defiance, the king in his fury used him worse than the others, ⁴⁰ and the young man, putting his whole trust in the Lord, died without having incurred defilement.

⁴¹ Last of all, after her sons, the mother died.

⁴² This then must conclude our account of the eating of the entrails and the monstrous tortures.

Judas Maccabaeus revolts

8 MEANWHILE Judas, who was called Maccabaeus, and his companions were making their way into the villages unobserved, summoning their kinsmen to their side and recruiting others who had remained faithful to the Jewish religion, until they had collected up to six thousand men. ² They appealed to the Lord to look with compassion on his people whom all were trampling underfoot, to take pity on the temple now profaned by apostates, ³ and to have mercy on Jerusalem, which was being destroyed and would soon be levelled to the ground. They prayed him also to give

7:36 **drunk**: *prob. rdg*; *Gk* fallen.

ear to the blood that cried to him for vengeance, [4] to keep in mind the infamous massacre of innocent children and the blasphemous deeds against his name, and to show his hatred of wickedness.

[5] Once his band of partisans was organized, the Gentiles found Maccabaeus invincible, now that the Lord's anger had changed to mercy. [6] Maccabaeus came on towns and villages without warning and burnt them down; he recaptured strategic positions, and inflicted many reverses on the enemy, [7] choosing the night-time as being especially favourable for these attacks. Everywhere there was talk of his heroism.

[8] When Philip realized that the gains made by Judas, though small, were occurring with increasing frequency, he wrote to Ptolemaeus, the governor of Coele-Syria and Phoenicia, asking for help in protecting the royal interests. [9] Ptolemaeus at once appointed Nicanor son of Patroclus, a member of the highest order of king's Friends, and sent him at the head of no fewer than twenty thousand troops of various nationalities to exterminate the whole population of Judaea; with him Ptolemaeus associated Gorgias, a general of wide military experience. [10] Nicanor purposed, by the sale of the Jews he would take prisoner, to pay off the two thousand talents due from the king as tribute to the Romans; [11] and he immediately made an offer of Jewish slaves to the coastal towns, undertaking to deliver them at the rate of ninety to the talent. But he had not reckoned with the punishment soon to overtake him from the Almighty.

[12] When word of Nicanor's advance reached Judas, and his men were informed that the enemy was at hand, [13] the faint-hearted who doubted God's justice deserted and fled. [14] But the rest, disposing of their remaining possessions, joined in prayer to the Lord for deliverance from the godless Nicanor, who had put them up for sale even before any fighting took place; [15] and, if they could not ask this for their own merits, they did so on the ground of the covenants God had made with their forefathers, and because they bore his holy and majestic name.

[16] Maccabaeus assembled his followers, six thousand in number, and urged them

not to give way to panic in the face of the enemy nor to be afraid of the great horde of Gentiles coming against them without just cause. They should fight nobly, [17] keeping before their eyes the outrages committed by the Gentiles against the holy temple, the callous indignities inflicted on Jerusalem, and, moreover, the suppression of the traditional Jewish institutions. [18] 'They rely on weapons and deeds of daring,' he said, 'but we put our trust in Almighty God, who is able with a nod to overthrow our present assailants and, if need be, the whole world.' [19] He went on to recount to them the occasions when God had come to the help of their ancestors: how, in Sennacherib's time, one hundred and eighty-five thousand of the enemy were destroyed, [20] and how, on the occasion of the battle in Babylonia against the Galatians, all the Jews engaged in the combat had numbered no more than eight thousand, with four thousand Macedonians, yet, when the Macedonians were hard pressed, the eight thousand through Heaven's aid had destroyed one hundred and twenty thousand and taken much spoil.

[21] His words put heart into his men and made them ready to die for their laws and their country. He divided the army into four, [22] putting each of his brothers, Simon, Josephus, and Jonathan, in command of a division of fifteen hundred men. [23] Besides this, Judas appointed Eleazar to read aloud from the holy book; then, giving the signal for battle with the cry 'God is our help' and taking command of the leading detachment, he joined battle with Nicanor. [24] With the Almighty fighting on their side they slaughtered over nine thousand of the enemy, wounded and disabled the greater part of Nicanor's forces, and routed them completely. [25] They also seized the money of those who had come to buy them as slaves. After chasing the enemy a considerable way, they were forced to break off because of the lateness of the hour; [26] it was the day before the sabbath, and for that reason they did not continue the pursuit. [27] They collected the enemy's weapons and stripped the dead, then turned to keep the sabbath, offering thanks and praises loud and long to the Lord who had kept

8:23 **Besides ... book:** *prob. rdg; Gk obscure.*   8:27 **kept ... day:** *so some witnesses; others read* brought them safely to that day and had appointed it as the beginning of mercy for them.

the first drops of his mercy to shed on them that day. ²⁸ When the sabbath was over, they distributed some of the spoils among the victims of persecution and among the widows and orphans; the remainder they divided among themselves and their children. ²⁹ This done, all together made supplication to the merciful Lord, praying him to be fully reconciled with his servants.

³⁰ The Jews now engaged the forces of Timotheus and Bacchides, killed over twenty thousand of them, and gained firm control of some of the high strongholds. They divided the immense booty, allocating to the victims of persecution, to the orphans and widows, as well as to the old, shares equal to their own. ³¹ All the enemy's weapons were carefully collected and stored at strategic points; the remainder of the spoils they brought into Jerusalem. ³² The officer commanding the bodyguard of Timotheus was put to death; he was an utterly godless man who had caused the Jews great suffering. ³³ During the victory celebrations in their ancestral capital, they burnt alive the men who had set fire to the sacred gates, including Callisthenes, who had taken refuge in some small house; so he received the due reward of his impiety.

³⁴ Thus Nicanor, that double-dyed villain who had brought along the thousand traders to buy the Jewish captives, ³⁵ was with the Lord's help humiliated by the very people whom he had dismissed as of no consequence. He threw off his magnificent garment, and all alone made his escape across country like a runaway slave; he was, indeed, exceedingly fortunate to reach Antioch after the destruction of his army. ³⁶ He who had undertaken to secure tribute for the Romans by taking prisoner the inhabitants of Jerusalem now proclaimed to the world that the Jews had a champion and were invulnerable, because they kept the laws this champion had given them.

9 It so happened that about this time Antiochus had returned in disorder from Persia. ² He had entered the city called Persepolis and attempted to plunder its temples and gain control of the place. But the populace rose and resorted to arms, with the result that Antiochus was defeated by the inhabitants and forced into a humiliating withdrawal.

³ When he was near Ecbatana, a report reached him of what had befallen Nicanor and the forces of Timotheus, ⁴ and this so roused his anger that he proposed to make the Jews suffer for the injury inflicted by those who had routed him; to this end he ordered his charioteer not to stop until he reached his destination.

But riding with him was the divine judgement! In his arrogance he said: 'Once I reach Jerusalem, I will make it one big Jewish graveyard.' ⁵ But the all-seeing Lord, the God of Israel, dealt him a fatal, invisible blow. No sooner had he uttered the words than he was seized with incurable pains in his bowels and acute internal suffering—⁶ a punishment entirely fitting for one who had inflicted many unheard-of torments on the bowels of others. ⁷ Still he did not in the least abate his insolence; more arrogant than ever and breathing fiery threats against the Jews, he gave orders for more speed on his journey. But as the chariot hurtled along he fell from it, and so violent was his fall that he suffered agony in every limb. ⁸ He, who in his pretension to be superhuman had been thinking that he could command the waves of the sea and weigh high mountains on the scales, was brought to the ground and had to be carried on a stretcher. The power of God was thus made manifest to all. ⁹ Worms swarmed from the body of this godless man and, while he was still alive and in agony, his flesh rotted off, and the whole army was overwhelmed by the stench of decay. ¹⁰ It was so unbearably offensive that no one was able to convey the man who only a short time before had seemed to reach to the stars in the heavens.

¹¹ In this broken state, Antiochus began to moderate his monstrous arrogance; scourged by God and racked with incessant pain, he was coming to see things in their true light. ¹² He was unable to endure his own stench and cried, 'It is right for mortals to submit to God and not claim equality with him.' ¹³ Though the Lord would spare him no longer, the villain made him a solemn promise: he vowed ¹⁴ that the Holy City, which he had been hurrying to level to the ground and transform into a graveyard, he would publicly declare to be free; ¹⁵ to all the Jews, a people he had considered not worthy of burial but fit only to be thrown

out with their children as carrion for birds and beasts, he would now give privileges equal to those enjoyed by the citizens of Athens; [16] the holy temple, which he had earlier plundered, he would adorn with the most magnificent gifts, and would replace all the sacred vessels on a much more lavish scale, and he would meet the cost of the sacrifices from his own revenues. [17] In addition, he would even turn Jew and visit every inhabited place to proclaim God's might.

[18] When his pain in no way abated, because the just judgement of God had befallen him, he was in despair and wrote to the Jews the following letter, as a kind of olive branch:

[19] From Antiochus, King and Chief Magistrate, to my worthy citizens, the Jews.

Warm greetings and good wishes for your health and prosperity.

[20] May you and your children flourish and your affairs progress as you wish. As I have my hope in Heaven, [21] I keep an affectionate remembrance of your respect and goodwill.

On my way back from Persia, I suffered a troublesome illness, and so I have judged it necessary to provide for the general security of all. [22] Not that I despair of my condition—on the contrary I have good hopes of recovery—[23] but I observed that my father, whenever he undertook a campaign east of the Euphrates, nominated a successor, [24] so that, if anything unforeseen should happen or if some untoward report should spread, his subjects would not be disturbed, since they would know to whom the government had been entrusted. [25] Further, I am well aware that the neighbouring princes, those on the frontiers of my kingdom, are waiting on events and watching for their opportunity. I have therefore designated as king my son Antiochus, whom I frequently placed in your care and commended to most of you during my regular visits to the satrapies beyond the Euphrates. I have written to him and enclose a copy. [26] Wherefore most earnestly I urge each one of you to maintain your existing goodwill towards me and my son, remembering the services I have rendered to you, both as a community and as individuals. [27] I am confident my son will follow my policy of moderation and benevolence and will accommodate himself to your wishes.

[28] So this murderer and blasphemer, suffering the greatest agony, such as he had made others suffer, met a pitiable end in the mountains of a foreign land. [29] His close friend Philip brought the body back, but being afraid of Antiochus's son went over to Ptolemy Philometor in Egypt.

The temple rededicated

10 UNDER the Lord's guidance, Maccabaeus and his followers recovered the temple and city of Jerusalem, [2] and demolished the altars erected by the heathen in the public square, together with their sacred precincts. [3] When they had purified the sanctuary, they made another altar, and striking fire with flints they offered sacrifice for the first time in two whole years; they restored the incense, the lamps, and the Bread of the Presence. [4] This done, they prostrated themselves and prayed to the Lord that he would never again allow them to fall into such disasters but, were they ever to sin, would discipline them himself with clemency rather than hand them over to blasphemous and barbarous Gentiles. [5] The sanctuary was purified on the twenty-fifth of Kislev, the same day of the same month as that on which foreigners had profaned it. [6] The joyful celebration lasted for eight days, like the feast of Tabernacles, and they recalled how, only a short time before, they had kept that feast while living like wild animals in the mountains and caves. [7] So carrying garlanded wands and flowering branches, as well as palm-fronds, they chanted hymns to the One who had so triumphantly achieved the purification of his own temple. [8] A decree was passed by the public assembly that every year the entire Jewish nation should keep these days holy.

[9] WE have already given an account of the end of Antiochus called Epiphanes. [10] Now we shall describe what transpired under that godless man's son, Antiochus Eupator, in a brief summary of the evils brought about by his wars. [11] At his

accession, Eupator appointed as vicegerent a man called Lysias who had succeeded Ptolemaeus Macron as governor-
general of Coele-Syria and Phoenicia.
[12] Because of the injustice formerly done
to the Jews, Ptolemaeus had taken the
lead in treating them with justice and
endeavoured to maintain amicable relations with them. [13] For this he was denounced to Eupator by the king's Friends;
on every side he heard himself called
traitor, because he had previously abandoned Cyprus, which had been entrusted
to him by Philometor, and had gone over
to Antiochus Epiphanes. He still enjoyed
power, but no longer respect, and he
ended his life by taking poison.

[14] When Gorgias became governor of
the region, he hired mercenaries and
seized every opportunity of attacking the
Jews. [15] At the same time the Idumaeans,
who controlled strategic strongholds,
were also harassing them; they harboured fugitives from Jerusalem and
made every effort to foment hostilities.
[16] But Maccabaeus and his men, after
public prayers entreating God to fight on
their side, launched an assault on the
Idumaean strongholds. [17] They pressed
the attack vigorously and captured them,
driving off those who manned the walls
and cutting down everyone they encountered. No less than twenty thousand of the
enemy were killed.

[18] But nine thousand or more took
refuge in two exceedingly strong forts,
which were fully equipped to withstand
a siege. [19] Maccabaeus left Simon and
Josephus behind with Zacchaeus and his
troops in sufficient strength to besiege
them, while he himself set out for areas
which were being hard pressed. [20] But
Simon's men were avaricious, and when
they were offered seventy thousand
drachmas by some of those in the forts,
they accepted the bribe and let them slip
through their lines. [21] On being informed
of this, Maccabaeus denounced the men
before the assembled leaders of the army
for having sold their brothers for money
by letting their enemies escape to fight
again, [22] and he had them executed as
traitors. He promptly reduced the two
forts, [23] and his military operations were
crowned with complete success. In the
two strongholds he destroyed over twenty
thousand of the enemy.

[24] Timotheus, who had earlier suffered
defeat at the hands of the Jews, now
mustered a huge army of mercenaries and
no small force of Asian cavalry, and
marched on Judaea to take it by storm.
[25] At his approach, Maccabaeus and his
men made their prayer to God; they
sprinkled dust on their heads and put
sackcloth round their waists, [26] prostrated
themselves on the altar-step and entreated God to show them favour—in the
words of the law: 'to be an enemy of their
enemies and an opponent of their opponents'.

[27] After this prayer, they took up their
weapons and, advancing a considerable
distance from Jerusalem, halted near the
enemy. [28] At first light the two armies
came to grips. For the Jews success and
victory were assured, not only because of
their courage but still more because they
had recourse to the Lord, whereas the
other side had only their own fury to lead
them into battle. [29] As the fighting grew
fierce, there appeared to the enemy five
magnificent figures in the sky, each riding
a horse with a golden bridle. Placing
themselves at the head of the Jews, [30] they
formed a circle round Maccabaeus and
kept him unharmed under the protection
of their armour, while they launched
arrows and thunderbolts at the enemy,
who, confused and blinded, broke in
complete disarray. [31] Twenty thousand
five hundred of the infantry as well as six
hundred cavalry were slain.

[32] Timotheus himself fled to Gazara, a
stoutly garrisoned stronghold under the
command of Chaereas. [33] This outcome
suited Maccabaeus and his men, and for
four days they laid siege to the place.
[34] The defenders, confident in the strength
of their position, hurled horrible and
wicked blasphemies at them [35] until, at
dawn on the fifth day, twenty young men
from the Maccabaean force, burning with
rage at the blasphemy, bravely stormed
the wall and in savage fury cut down all
they encountered. [36] Under cover of this
distraction others got up the same way
and attacked the defenders, setting alight
the towers and kindling fires on which
they burnt the blasphemers alive. Others
broke down the gates and let in the rest of
the army, and thus the city was occupied.
[37] Timotheus, who had hidden in a cistern, was killed along with his brother

Chaereas and Apollophanes. [38] In celebration of their achievement, the Jews praised with hymns and thanksgivings the Lord who showers benefits on Israel and gives them the victory.

11 Very shortly afterwards, in anger at what had happened, the vicegerent Lysias, the king's guardian and Kinsman, [2] mustered about eighty thousand foot-soldiers, in addition to all his cavalry, and marched against the Jews. He planned to make Jerusalem a settlement for Gentiles, [3] with the temple subject to taxation like all gentile shrines and the high-priesthood up for auction each year. [4] Reckoning not at all with the might of God, he was carried away by the thought of his tens of thousands of infantry, his thousands of cavalry, his eighty elephants. [5] He invaded Judaea, and advancing on Bethsura, a fortified place about twenty miles distant from Jerusalem, he closely invested it.

[6] When Maccabaeus and his men were informed that Lysias was besieging their strongholds, they and all the people, wailing and weeping, prayed the Lord to send a good angel to deliver Israel. [7] Maccabaeus himself was the first to take up arms, and he urged the others to share the danger with him and go to the rescue of their fellow-Jews. Readily they all set out together. [8] While they were still in the neighbourhood of Jerusalem, there appeared at their head a horseman arrayed in white and brandishing golden weapons. [9] With one voice they praised their merciful God and felt so strong in spirit that they could have attacked not only men but also the most savage animals, or even walls of iron. [10] Under the Lord's mercy and with their heavenly ally they came on in battle array. [11] Like lions they hurled themselves on the enemy, laid low eleven thousand foot-soldiers, as well as sixteen hundred cavalry, and put the remainder to flight. [12] Most of those who escaped had lost their weapons and were wounded, and Lysias himself saved his life, if not his honour, by ignominiously taking to his heels.

[13] Yet Lysias was no fool, and as he took stock of the defeat he had suffered he realized that the Hebrews were invincible, because God in his power fought on their side. So he sent emissaries [14] to persuade the Jews to make a settlement on terms that were entirely acceptable, promising also to make the king well disposed towards them. [15] Out of regard for the general welfare, Maccabaeus agreed to all the proposals of Lysias, for the king had accepted whatever written terms Maccabaeus had forwarded to Lysias from the Jewish side.

[16] Lysias's letter to the Jews ran as follows:

From Lysias to the Jewish community. Greeting.

[17] Your representatives John and Absalom have laid before me the document a copy of which is attached, and have asked me to give my views on its contents. [18] Whatever required to be brought to the king's attention I have communicated to him, and what was within my own competence I have granted. [19] Provided, therefore, you maintain your goodwill towards the government, I for my part shall endeavour to promote your wellbeing for the future. [20] I have charged your representatives and mine to confer with you about the details. [21] Farewell.

The twenty-fourth day of Dioscorus in the year 148.

[22] The king's letter was as follows:

From King Antiochus to his brother Lysias.

Greeting.

[23] Now that our royal father has joined the company of the gods, we desire that our subjects shall be left undisturbed in the conduct of their own affairs. [24] It has been brought to our notice that the Jews are not prepared to accept our father's policy and adopt Greek ways; they prefer their own mode of life and request that they be allowed to observe their own laws. [25] It is our pleasure, therefore, that this nation like others shall continue undisturbed. We hereby decree that their temple be restored to them and that they be allowed to regulate their lives in accordance with their ancestral customs. [26] Have the goodness, therefore, to inform them of this and to ratify it, so

11:21 **148**: *that is* 164 B.C.

that, apprised of our policy, they may be reassured and manage their affairs to their own satisfaction.

27 The king's letter to the people ran thus:

From King Antiochus to the Senate of the Jews and to the Jewish people. Greeting. 28 We trust that all is well with you; we ourselves prosper. 29 Menelaus has made plain to us that it is your wish to return to your homes. 30 We therefore declare an amnesty for all who return before the thirtieth day of Xanthicus. 31 The Jews may follow their own food-laws as heretofore, and none of them will be in any way victimized for any previous offence committed in ignorance. 32 I am sending Menelaus to reassure you. 33 Farewell.

The fifteenth day of Xanthicus in the year 148.

34 The Romans also sent the Jews a letter. It read as follows:

From Quintus Memmius, Titus Manilius, and Manius Sergius, envoys of the Romans, to the Jewish people. Greeting. 35 We give our assent to all the concessions that Lysias, the king's Kinsman, has granted you. 36 Be pleased to examine carefully the questions which he reserved for reference to the king; and then send someone without delay, so that we may make suitable proposals on your behalf, for we are proceeding to Antioch. 37 Send messengers immediately, therefore, so that we also may know what is your opinion. 38 Farewell.

The fifteenth day of Xanthicus in the year 148.

12 After the conclusion of these agreements, Lysias left and went to the king. The Jews busied themselves on their farms, 2 but they were prevented from leading stable and tranquil lives by some of the governors in the region, Timotheus and Apollonius son of Gennaeus, as well as Hieronymus and Demophon, and also by Nicanor, chief of the Cypriot mercenaries.

3 A DASTARDLY atrocity was perpetrated by the inhabitants of Joppa: they invited the Jews living among them to embark with their wives and children in boats they had provided, giving no indication of any animosity towards them. 4 As it was a public decision by the whole town and because they wished to live in peace and suspected nothing, the Jews accepted; but once out at sea the people of Joppa sank the boats, drowning no fewer than two hundred of the Jews. 5 As soon as Judas learnt of this brutal treatment of his fellow-countrymen he issued orders to his troops, 6 and, invoking God the just judge, he fell upon the murderers. Under cover of night he set the harbour of Joppa on fire, burnt the shipping, and put to the sword those who had taken refuge there. 7 But finding that the town was closed against him he withdrew, with the intention nevertheless of returning to wipe out the entire community. 8 When he learnt that the people of Jamnia planned to deal in the same way with the Jews living there, 9 he made a night attack on the town and set both harbour and fleet alight, so that the glow of the flames was visible at Jerusalem, thirty miles away.

10 When, in their advance against Timotheus, Judas and his men had marched more than a mile from Jamnia, they were set upon by not less than five thousand Arabs on foot, supported by five hundred horsemen. 11 Through God's help, the Jews were the victors in a hard-fought battle. The defeated nomads begged Judas to make an alliance with them, promising to supply cattle and to furnish the Jews with all other assistance. 12 Accepting that they could indeed be useful in many ways, Judas agreed to make peace, and with assurances from him the Arabs went back to their tents.

13 Judas also attacked Caspin, a walled and strongly fortified town inhabited by a mixed population of Gentiles. 14 Confident in the strength of their walls and in their stock of provisions, the defenders treated Judas and his men with insolence, abusing them and uttering the most wicked blasphemies. 15 But Judas's men invoked the great Ruler of the universe, who in the days of Joshua threw down the walls of

11:33 148: *that is* 164 B.C.   11:34 Titus ... Sergius: *so some MSS; others* Titus Manius.   11:38 148: *that is* 164 B.C.

Jericho without the aid of battering-ram or siege-engine; then in a fierce onslaught they rushed the wall [16] and, by the will of God, captured the town. The carnage was indescribable; the nearby lake, a quarter of a mile wide, appeared to be overflowing with blood.

[17] From there they advanced about ninety-five miles until they reached Charax, which is inhabited by the Tubian Jews, as they are called. [18] They did not catch Timotheus, for having had no success he had by that time withdrawn from the district, though in one place he left behind an exceedingly strong garrison. [19] Dositheus and Sosipater, Maccabaeus's generals, set out for the stronghold and destroyed the garrison stationed there by Timotheus; it consisted of over ten thousand men. [20] Maccabaeus for his part grouped his forces in a number of detachments, appointed commanders for them, and hurried in pursuit of Timotheus, who had with him a hundred and twenty thousand infantry and two thousand five hundred cavalry. [21] When Timotheus learnt of Judas's approach, he sent on the women and children with the rest of the baggage train to a town called Carnaim, this being an inaccessible place, hard to storm because all the approaches to it were so narrow. [22] As soon as Judas's first detachment came into sight, panic seized the enemy, who were terrified at a hostile manifestation of the all-seeing One. In headlong flight they rushed in all directions, so that frequently they were injured by their own comrades and run through by the points of their swords. [23] Judas pressed the pursuit vigorously and cut down these wicked men, destroying up to thirty thousand of them. [24] Timotheus himself was taken prisoner by the troops of Dositheus and Sosipater, but with great cunning he begged them to let him go unmolested, pointing out that he held in his power the brothers of some of them and the parents of most of them, and it might well be that scant regard would be paid them. [25] On his repeated pledge to restore those hostages unharmed, they let him go in order to save their relatives.

[26] Judas moved on Carnaim and the sanctuary of Atargatis, where he slaughtered twenty-five thousand people.

[27] From this defeat and massacre of his enemies he marched on Ephron, a fortified town with a mixture of nationalities. Stalwart young men positioned themselves before the walls, where they put up a stout fight, while inside there was a great supply of engines of war and missiles. [28] But the Jews, invoking the Ruler whose might shatters the enemy's strength, made themselves masters of the town and laid low as many as twenty-five thousand of the defenders. [29] Leaving it behind, they pushed on to Scythopolis, some seventy-five miles from Jerusalem. [30] When the Jewish settlers there testified to the goodwill shown them by the people and the kindness with which they had been treated in times of misfortune, [31] Judas and his men thanked them, charging them to be no less friendly to the Jews in the future. Then, as the feast of Weeks was near, they proceeded to Jerusalem.

[32] Immediately after celebrating Pentecost, as the feast is called, they marched against Gorgias, the general in charge of Idumaea, [33] who came out with three thousand infantry and four hundred cavalry. [34] Battle was joined and a small number of Jews fell. [35] But one of the Tubian Jews, Dositheus by name, a cavalryman of great strength, caught hold of Gorgias by his cloak and was dragging the villain off by main force, with the object of taking him alive, when a Thracian horseman bore down on Dositheus and chopped off his arm, and Gorgias escaped to Marisa.

[36] As the troop under Esdrias were exhausted by the prolonged fighting, Judas appealed to the Lord to show himself their ally and leader in battle; [37] then, raising the battle cry with hymns in his native language, he launched a surprise attack and put Gorgias's army to flight. [38] Regrouping his forces, Judas led them to the town of Adullam, and since the seventh day was at hand they purified themselves according to custom and kept the sabbath there. [39] Next day they went to collect the bodies of the fallen, as by now had become necessary, in order to take them for burial with their kinsfolk in their family graves. [40] On each one of the dead they found under the tunic amulets sacred to the idols of Jamnia, objects forbidden to Jews

12:27 **nationalities:** *some witnesses add* where Lysias had his headquarters.

by the law. It was evident to all that here was the reason these men had fallen. [41] So everyone praised the acts of the Lord, the just Judge and Revealer of secrets, [42] and turning to prayer they begged that every trace of this offence might be blotted out. The noble Judas exhorted the people to keep themselves free from wrongdoing, for they had seen with their own eyes what had happened because of the sin of those who had fallen. [43] He levied a contribution from each man, and sent to Jerusalem the total of two thousand silver drachmas to provide a sin-offering—a fit and proper act in which he took due account of the resurrection. [44] Had he not been expecting the fallen to rise again, it would have been superfluous and senseless to pray for the dead; [45] but since he had in view the splendid reward reserved for those who die a godly death, his purpose was holy and devout. That was why he offered the atoning sacrifice, to free the dead from their sin.

13 In the year 149, information reached Judas and those with him that Antiochus Eupator was advancing on Judaea with a large army; [2] he was accompanied by Lysias, his guardian and vicegerent, bringing in addition a Greek force consisting of one hundred and ten thousand infantry, five thousand three hundred cavalry, twenty-two elephants, and three hundred chariots fitted with scythes. [3] Menelaus, who had also joined them, kept egging Antiochus on. This he did most disingenuously, not for his country's good, but because he believed he would be established in office. [4] The King of kings, however, stirred up the anger of Antiochus against this wicked man, and when Lysias produced evidence that Menelaus was responsible for all the troubles, the king ordered him to be taken to Beroea and there executed in the manner customary at that place. [5] In Beroea there is a tower some seventy-five feet high, filled with ashes; it has a circular device sloping down sheer on all sides into the ashes. [6] This is where the citizens take anyone guilty of sacrilege or any other heinous crime, and thrust him to his doom; [7] and such was the fate of the renegade Menelaus, who, in accordance with his just deserts, was not even given burial in the earth. [8] Many a time he had desecrated the sacred ashes of the altar-fire, and by ashes he met his death.

[9] In savage arrogance the king came on, aiming to inflict sufferings on the Jews far worse than they had endured under his father. [10] When Judas learnt of this, he ordered the people to invoke the Lord day and night, and pray that now more than ever he would come to their aid, since law, country, and holy temple were all at risk; [11] and that he would not allow them, just when they had begun to revive, to fall into the hands of blaspheming Gentiles. [12] They all complied: for three days without respite they prayed to their merciful Lord, they wailed, they fasted, they prostrated themselves. Then, with many an exhortation, Judas called upon them to stand by him.

[13] After a council of war with the elders, he decided not to wait for the king's army to invade Judaea and take Jerusalem, but to march out and with God's help put matters to the test. [14] He committed the outcome to the Lord of the universe, and exhorted his troops to fight nobly to the death for law, temple, and city, for their country and their way of life. He pitched camp near Modin, [15] and giving his men the watchword 'Victory with God!' he launched a night attack towards the royal tent with a picked force of his bravest young warriors. As many as two thousand in the enemy camp were killed, and Judas's men stabbed to death the leading elephant and its driver. [16] In the end they reduced the whole camp to panic and confusion, and then made a successful withdrawal. [17] Through the help and protection which Judas had received from the Lord it was all over by daybreak.

[18] Now that he had had a taste of Jewish daring, the king resorted to stratagem in probing their positions. [19] He advanced on Bethsura, one of their strong forts, and was repulsed; he attacked again, and was defeated. [20] Judas meanwhile sent in supplies to the garrison. [21] A soldier in the Jewish ranks, Rhodocus by name, passed secret information to the enemy; but he was tracked down, caught, and put away.

12:43 sin-offering: *or* purification-offering.   13:1 149: *that is 163* B.C.   13:5 some ... feet: *Gk* fifty cubits.   13:15 stabbed to death: *prob. rdg, based on one version.*

[22] A second time the king parleyed with the inhabitants of Bethsura; after giving and receiving guarantees he took his departure; he attacked Judas and his men, but had the worst of it. [23] He now received a report that Philip, who had been left in charge of affairs of state in Antioch, had made a mad bid for power. In consternation the king summoned the Jews, agreed to their terms, and took an oath to respect all their rights. After reaching this settlement he offered a sacrifice, paid honour to the sanctuary and its precincts, [24] and received Maccabaeus in a friendly manner. He left Hegemonides as governor of the region from Ptolemais to Gerra, [25] while he himself went to Ptolemais, where the inhabitants resented the treaty he had made, and in their anger wanted to repudiate the terms. [26] Lysias mounted the rostrum and put forward the best defence he could. He won the people over, calmed them down, and, having thus gained their support, departed from Antioch.

Such was the course of the king's offensive and retreat.

14 AFTER three years had passed, information reached Judas and his followers that Demetrius son of Seleucus had sailed into the harbour at Tripolis with a powerful army and fleet, [2] and, having disposed of Antiochus and his guardian Lysias, had taken control of the country.

[3] A certain Alcimus, who had formerly been high priest, had willingly submitted to defilement at the time of the revolt. Realizing now that there was no guarantee whatsoever of his safety, nor any possibility of access to the holy altar, [4] he went to King Demetrius about the year 151 and presented him with a gold crown and a palm, together with some of the customary olive branches from the temple. On that occasion he kept silent. [5] But when Demetrius summoned him to his council and questioned him about the attitude and aims of the Jews, he seized the opportunity to forward his own misguided scheme, and replied: [6] 'Those Jews called Hasidaeans who are led by Judas Maccabaeus are keeping the war alive

and fomenting sedition; they refuse to let the kingdom have peace. [7] Thus, although I have been deprived of my hereditary dignity, by which I mean the high-priesthood, I have two motives in coming here today: [8] first, a genuine concern for the king's interests; and secondly, a regard for my fellow-citizens, since our whole race is suffering considerable hardship as a result of the senseless conduct of those people I have mentioned. [9] My advice to your majesty is to get to know the details of these matters and then, as befits your universal kindness and goodwill, make provision for our country and our beleaguered nation. [10] For as long as Judas remains alive there can be no peace for the state.'

[11] No sooner had he spoken in this vein than the other Friends, who were hostile to Judas, added fresh fuel to Demetrius's anger. [12] There and then the king selected Nicanor, commander of the elephant corps, made him military governor of Judaea, and sent him [13] with a commission to make away with Judas and disperse his army, and to install Alcimus as high priest of the great temple. [14] The gentile population of Judaea, refugees from the attacks of Judas, now flocked to join Nicanor, supposing that defeat and misfortune for the Jews would spell prosperity for them.

[15] When the Jews heard of Nicanor's offensive and the onset of the Gentiles, they sprinkled dust over themselves and prayed to him who has established his people for ever, who never fails to manifest himself and afford help when his chosen are in need. [16] At their leader's command, they moved forward immediately and made contact with the enemy at the village of Adasa. [17] Simon, the brother of Judas, had fought an engagement with Nicanor, but because the enemy came up unexpectedly he had suffered a slight reverse. [18] In spite of this, when Nicanor learnt how brave Judas and his troops were and how courageously they fought for their country, he shrank from deciding the issue by the sword; [19] so he sent Posidonius, Theodotus, and Mattathias to negotiate a settlement.

[20] After a full consideration of the pro-

14:4 *151: that is* 161 B.C.   14:16 **Adasa**: *prob. rdg*; *cp. 1 Macc. 7:40.*   14:17 **came up**: *prob. rdg, based on one version.*

posals Judas put them to his men, all of whom were in favour of accepting the terms. ²¹ On the day fixed for a private meeting of the leaders, a chariot advanced from each of the two lines, and seats were placed in position; ²² Judas posted armed men at strategic points ready to deal with any sudden treachery on the enemy's part. The discussion between the two leaders was harmonious. ²³ Nicanor stayed some time in Jerusalem and behaved correctly. Dismissing the crowds that had flocked from round about, ²⁴ he kept Judas close to himself at all times, for he had developed a real affection for him. ²⁵ He urged him to marry and have children; so Judas married and settled down to the quiet life of an ordinary citizen.

²⁶ Alcimus, observing their friendliness, got hold of a copy of the agreement they had concluded, and went to Demetrius and claimed that Nicanor was pursuing a policy detrimental to the interests of the state by appointing Judas, a man guilty of conspiracy, as king's Friend designate. ²⁷ Incensed by these villainous slanders, the king wrote angrily to Nicanor expressing his dissatisfaction with the terms agreed upon; he ordered him to arrest Maccabaeus and send him to Antioch at once. ²⁸ The instructions dismayed Nicanor, and he took it hard that he should have to go back on his agreement when the man had committed no offence; ²⁹ but since there was no gainsaying the king, he watched for an opportunity of carrying out the order by some stratagem. ³⁰ Maccabaeus, on his part, noticed that Nicanor had become less friendly towards him and no longer showed him the same civility. He realized that this coolness boded ill for him, and collecting a good number of his followers he went into hiding.

³¹ Recognizing that he had been outmanoeuvred by the resolute action of Judas, Nicanor appeared before the great and holy temple at the time when the priests were offering the regular sacrifices, and ordered them to surrender Judas. ³² Though the priests declared on oath that they did not know the whereabouts of the wanted man, ³³ Nicanor stretched out his right hand towards the shrine and swore this oath: 'Unless you surrender Judas to me in chains, I shall level this sanctuary of God to the ground and destroy the altar; on this spot I shall build

a temple to Dionysus for all the world to see'; ³⁴ and with those words he left. Then the priests, their hands uplifted to Heaven, prayed to the constant champion of our nation: ³⁵ 'Lord, you have no need of anything in the world, yet it was your pleasure that among us there should be a shrine for your dwelling-place; ³⁶ now, holy Lord from whom all holiness comes, keep this house, so recently purified, free from defilement for ever.'

³⁷ A MAN called Razis, a member of the Jerusalem senate, was denounced to Nicanor. He was a patriot and very highly spoken of, one who for his loyalty was known as Father of the Jews. ³⁸ In the early days of the revolt he had stood trial for practising the Jewish religion, and with no hesitation had risked life and limb for that cause. ³⁹ Nicanor, wishing to demonstrate his hostility towards the Jews, sent more than five hundred soldiers to arrest Razis; ⁴⁰ he reckoned that this would be a severe blow to the Jews. ⁴¹ The tower of his house was on the point of being captured by this mob of soldiers, the outer gate was being forced, and there were calls for fire to burn down the inner doors, when Razis, beset on every side, turned his sword on himself; ⁴² he preferred to die nobly rather than fall into the hands of evil men and be subjected to gross humiliation. ⁴³ With everything happening so quickly, he misjudged the stroke and, now that troops were pouring through the doorways, he ran up without hesitation on to the wall and heroically threw himself down into the crowd. ⁴⁴ They hurriedly gave way and he fell to the ground in the space they left. ⁴⁵ He was still breathing and still ablaze with courage; streaming with blood and severely wounded as he was, he picked himself up and dashed through the crowd. Finally, standing on a sheer rock, ⁴⁶ and now completely drained of blood, he tore out his entrails and with both hands flung them at the crowd. And thus, invoking him who disposes of life and breath to give them back to him again, he died.

15 NICANOR, advised that Judas and his men were in the neighbourhood of Samaria, planned to attack them on their day of rest, when it could be done

without risk. ² Those Jews who were forced to accompany his army begged him not to carry out so savage and barbarous a massacre. 'Have regard for the day singled out and made holy by the all-seeing One,' they said. ³ The double-dyed villain retorted, 'Is there some ruler in the sky who has ordered the sabbath-day observance?' ⁴ The Jews declared, 'The living Lord himself is ruler in the sky, and he commanded the seventh day to be kept holy.' ⁵ 'And I am a ruler on earth,' countered Nicanor; 'I order you to take up arms and do your duty to the king.' However, he did not succeed in carrying out this outrage he had planned.

⁶ In his pretentious and extravagant conceit, Nicanor had resolved to erect a public trophy from the spoils taken from Judas's army. ⁷ But Maccabaeus's confidence never wavered, and he had not the least doubt that he would obtain help from the Lord. ⁸ He urged his men to have no fear of the gentile attack, but to bear in mind the aid they had received from Heaven in the past and look with confidence to the Almighty for the victory he would send them on this occasion also. ⁹ He drew encouragement for them from the law and the prophets and, by reminding them of the struggles they had already come through, filled them with a fresh ardour. ¹⁰ When he had roused their courage, he issued his orders, reminding them at the same time of the Gentiles' broken faith and perjury. ¹¹ He armed each one of them, not so much with shield and spear for protection, as with brave and reassuring words; and he cheered them all by recounting a dream he had had, a waking vision worthy of belief.

¹² What he had seen was this: there had appeared to him the former high priest Onias, a good and noble man of modest bearing and mild disposition, a ready and apt speaker, an exemplar from childhood of every virtue; with uplifted hands Onias was praying for the whole Jewish community. ¹³ Next there appeared in the same attitude a figure of great age and dignity, whose wonderful air of authority marked him as a man of the utmost distinction. ¹⁴ Onias then spoke: 'This is God's prophet Jeremiah,' he said, 'one who loves his fellow-Jews and constantly offers prayers for the people and for the Holy City.' ¹⁵ Extending his right hand Jeremiah pre-sented a golden sword to Judas, saying as he did so, ¹⁶ 'Take this holy sword, a gift from God, and with it shatter the enemy.'

The Jews triumph

¹⁷ THE heroic words of Judas had the effect of evoking the bravery of everyone and of giving boys the courage of men. The Jews resolved not to undertake a long campaign, but nobly to go over to the offensive and decide the issue by fighting in close combat with all their courage. This they did because Jerusalem, their religion, and the temple were in peril. ¹⁸ Their fear was not chiefly for their wives and children, or for brothers and relatives, but first and foremost for the sacred shrine. ¹⁹ The distress of those shut up in Jerusalem was no less, for they were anxious about the outcome of a battle on open ground.

²⁰ All were awaiting the decisive struggle which lay ahead. The enemy had already concentrated his forces: his army drawn up in battle order, the elephants strategically positioned, and the cavalry ranged on the flanks. ²¹ Maccabaeus observed the deployment of the troops, the variety of their weapons, and the ferocity of the elephants, and raising his hands towards heaven he invoked the Lord, the worker of miracles; he knew that God grants victory to those who deserve it, not because of their military strength but as he himself decides. ²² This was his prayer: 'Lord, in the days of King Hezekiah of Judah you sent your angel and he destroyed as many as a hundred and eighty-five thousand men in Sennacherib's camp. ²³ Now, Ruler of heaven, send a good angel once again to go before us spreading fear and panic. ²⁴ May these blasphemers who are coming to attack your holy people be struck down by your strong arm!' Such was his prayer.

²⁵ Nicanor and his forces advanced to the sound of trumpets and war-songs, ²⁶ but Judas and his men engaged the enemy with invocations and prayers on their lips. ²⁷ Praying to God in their hearts and greatly cheered by his care, they killed no fewer than thirty-five thousand in hand-to-hand fighting.

²⁸ The action over, they were joyfully disbanding, when they discovered Nicanor lying dead in full armour, ²⁹ and with tumultuous shouts they praised the

heavenly Ruler in their native language. [30] Judas their leader, who had always fought body and soul on behalf of his fellow-countrymen, without ever losing his youthful patriotism, ordered that Nicanor's head and whole arm should be cut off and taken to Jerusalem. [31] On arrival there he called together the people, stationed the priests before the altar, sent for the men in the citadel, [32] and put on display the head of that villainous Nicanor and the hand which the bragging blasphemer had stretched out against the Almighty's holy temple. [33] He cut out the godless Nicanor's tongue and swore he would feed it to the birds bit by bit; and he gave orders that the evidence of what Nicanor's folly had brought upon him should be hung up opposite the shrine. [34] All made the sky ring with the praises of the Lord who had shown his power: 'Praise to him who has preserved his own sanctuary from defilement!' [35] Judas hung Nicanor's head from the citadel, as a clear proof of the Lord's help for everyone to see. [36] It was unanimously decreed that this day should never pass unnoticed, but that the thirteenth of the twelfth month, called Adar in Aramaic, should be duly celebrated; it is the eve of Mordecai's Day. [37] Such, then, was the fate of Nicanor, and from that time Jerusalem has remained in the possession of the Hebrews.

At this point I shall bring my work to an end. [38] If it is found to be well written and aptly composed, that is what I myself aimed at; if superficial and mediocre, it was the best I could do. [39] For, just as it is disagreeable to drink wine by itself or water by itself, whereas the mixing of the two produces a pleasant and delightful taste, so too variety of style in a literary work charms the ear of the reader. Let this, then, be my final word.

THE NEW TESTAMENT

THE GOSPEL ACCORDING TO

MATTHEW

The ancestry of the Messiah

1 THE genealogy of Jesus Christ, son of David, son of Abraham.

2 Abraham was the father of Isaac, Isaac of Jacob, Jacob of Judah and his brothers, 3 Judah of Perez and Zarah (their mother was Tamar), Perez of Hezron, Hezron of Ram, 4 Ram of Amminadab, Amminadab of Nahshon, Nahshon of Salmon, 5 Salmon of Boaz (his mother was Rahab), Boaz of Obed (his mother was Ruth), Obed of Jesse; 6 and Jesse was the father of King David.

David was the father of Solomon (his mother had been the wife of Uriah), 7 Solomon of Rehoboam, Rehoboam of Abijah, Abijah of Asa, 8 Asa of Jehoshaphat, Jehoshaphat of Joram, Joram of Uzziah, 9 Uzziah of Jotham, Jotham of Ahaz, Ahaz of Hezekiah, 10 Hezekiah of Manasseh, Manasseh of Amon, Amon of Josiah; 11 and Josiah was the father of Jeconiah and his brothers at the time of the deportation to Babylon.

12 After the deportation Jeconiah was the father of Shealtiel, Shealtiel of Zerubbabel, 13 Zerubbabel of Abiud, Abiud of Eliakim, Eliakim of Azor, 14 Azor of Zadok, Zadok of Achim, Achim of Eliud, 15 Eliud of Eleazar, Eleazar of Matthan, Matthan of Jacob, 16 Jacob of Joseph, the husband of Mary, who gave birth to Jesus called Messiah.

17 There were thus fourteen generations in all from Abraham to David, fourteen from David until the deportation to Babylon, and fourteen from the deportation until the Messiah.

The birth and infancy of Jesus

18 THIS is how the birth of Jesus Christ came about. His mother Mary was betrothed to Joseph; before their marriage she found she was going to have a child through the Holy Spirit. 19 Being a man of principle, and at the same time wanting to save her from exposure, Joseph made up his mind to have the marriage contract quietly set aside. 20 He had resolved on this, when an angel of the Lord appeared to him in a dream and said, 'Joseph, son of David, do not be afraid to take Mary home with you to be your wife. It is through the Holy Spirit that she has conceived. 21 She will bear a son; and you shall give him the name Jesus, for he will save his people from their sins.' 22 All this happened in order to fulfil what the Lord declared through the prophet: 23 'A virgin will conceive and bear a son, and he shall be called Emmanuel,' a name which means 'God is with us'. 24 When he woke Joseph did as the angel of the Lord had directed him; he took Mary home to be his wife, 25 but had no intercourse with her until her son was born. And he named the child Jesus.

2 JESUS was born at Bethlehem in Judaea during the reign of Herod. After his birth astrologers from the east arrived in Jerusalem, 2 asking, 'Where is the newborn king of the Jews? We observed the rising of his star, and we have come to pay him homage.' 3 King Herod was greatly perturbed when he heard this, and so was the whole of Jerusalem. 4 He called together the chief priests and scribes of the Jews, and asked them where the Messiah was to be born. 5 'At Bethlehem in Judaea,' they replied, 'for this is what the prophet wrote: 6 "Bethlehem in the land of Judah, you are by no means least among the rulers of Judah; for out of you shall come a ruler to be the shepherd of my people Israel."'

7 Then Herod summoned the astrologers to meet him secretly, and ascertained from them the exact time when the star had appeared. 8 He sent them to Bethlehem, and said, 'Go and make a careful search for the child, and when you have found him, bring me word, so that I may go myself and pay him homage.'

9-10 After hearing what the king had to say they set out; there before them was the star they had seen rising, and it went ahead of them until it stopped above the

1:21 Jesus: *that is* Saviour.

1

place where the child lay. They were overjoyed at the sight of it [11] and, entering the house, they saw the child with Mary his mother and bowed low in homage to him; they opened their treasure chests and presented gifts to him: gold, frankincense, and myrrh. [12] Then they returned to their own country by another route, for they had been warned in a dream not to go back to Herod.

[13] After they had gone, an angel of the Lord appeared to Joseph in a dream, and said, 'Get up, take the child and his mother and escape with them to Egypt, and stay there until I tell you; for Herod is going to search for the child to kill him.' [14] So Joseph got up, took mother and child by night, and sought refuge with them in Egypt, [15] where he stayed till Herod's death. This was to fulfil what the Lord had declared through the prophet: 'Out of Egypt I have called my son.'

[16] When Herod realized that the astrologers had tricked him he flew into a rage, and gave orders for the massacre of all the boys aged two years or under, in Bethlehem and throughout the whole district, in accordance with the time he had ascertained from the astrologers. [17] So the words spoken through Jeremiah the prophet were fulfilled: [18] 'A voice was heard in Rama, sobbing in bitter grief; it was Rachel weeping for her children, and refusing to be comforted, because they were no more.'

[19] After Herod's death an angel of the Lord appeared in a dream to Joseph in Egypt [20] and said to him, 'Get up, take the child and his mother, and go to the land of Israel, for those who threatened the child's life are dead.' [21] So he got up, took mother and child with him, and came to the land of Israel. [22] But when he heard that Archelaus had succeeded his father Herod as king of Judaea, he was afraid to go there. Directed by a dream, he withdrew to the region of Galilee, [23] where he settled in a town called Nazareth. This was to fulfil the words spoken through the prophets: 'He shall be called a Nazarene.'

John the Baptist and Jesus

3 IN the course of time John the Baptist appeared in the Judaean wilderness, proclaiming this message: [2] 'Repent, for the kingdom of Heaven is upon you!' [3] It was of him that the prophet Isaiah spoke when he said,

A voice cries in the wilderness,
'Prepare the way for the Lord;
clear a straight path for him.'

[4] John's clothing was a rough coat of camel's hair, with a leather belt round his waist, and his food was locusts and wild honey. [5] Everyone flocked to him from Jerusalem, Judaea, and the Jordan valley, [6] and they were baptized by him in the river Jordan, confessing their sins.

[7] When he saw many of the Pharisees and Sadducees coming for baptism he said to them: 'Vipers' brood! Who warned you to escape from the wrath that is to come? [8] Prove your repentance by the fruit you bear; [9] and do not imagine you can say, "We have Abraham for our father." I tell you that God can make children for Abraham out of these stones. [10] The axe lies ready at the roots of the trees; every tree that fails to produce good fruit is cut down and thrown on the fire. [11] I baptize you with water, for repentance; but the one who comes after me is mightier than I am, whose sandals I am not worthy to remove. He will baptize you with the Holy Spirit and with fire. [12] His winnowing-shovel is ready in his hand and he will clear his threshing-floor; he will gather the wheat into his granary, but the chaff he will burn on a fire that can never be put out.'

[13] Then Jesus arrived at the Jordan from Galilee, and came to John to be baptized by him. [14] John tried to dissuade him. 'Do you come to me?' he said. 'It is I who need to be baptized by you.' [15] Jesus replied, 'Let it be so for the present; it is right for us to do all that God requires.' Then John allowed him to come. [16] No sooner had Jesus been baptized and come up out of the water than the heavens were opened and he saw the Spirit of God descending like a dove to alight on him. [17] And there came a voice from heaven saying, 'This is my beloved Son, in whom I take delight.'

The temptation of Jesus

4 JESUS was then led by the Spirit into the wilderness, to be tempted by the devil.

[2] For forty days and nights he fasted, and at the end of them he was famished.

3:17 **This ... Son:** *or* This is my only Son.   4:1 **tempted:** *or* tested.

³ The tempter approached him and said, 'If you are the Son of God, tell these stones to become bread.' ⁴ Jesus answered, 'Scripture says, "Man is not to live on bread alone, but on every word that comes from the mouth of God."'

⁵ The devil then took him to the Holy City and set him on the parapet of the temple. ⁶ 'If you are the Son of God,' he said, 'throw yourself down; for scripture says, "He will put his angels in charge of you, and they will support you in their arms, for fear you should strike your foot against a stone."' ⁷ Jesus answered him, 'Scripture also says, "You are not to put the Lord your God to the test."'

⁸ The devil took him next to a very high mountain, and showed him all the kingdoms of the world in their glory. ⁹ 'All these', he said, 'I will give you, if you will only fall down and do me homage.' ¹⁰ But Jesus said, 'Out of my sight, Satan! Scripture says, "You shall do homage to the Lord your God and worship him alone."'

¹¹ Then the devil left him; and angels came and attended to his needs.

The first disciples

¹² WHEN he heard that John had been arrested, Jesus withdrew to Galilee; ¹³ and leaving Nazareth he went and settled at Capernaum on the sea of Galilee, in the district of Zebulun and Naphtali. ¹⁴ This was to fulfil the words of the prophet Isaiah about ¹⁵ 'the land of Zebulun, the land of Naphtali, the road to the sea, the land beyond Jordan, Galilee of the Gentiles':

¹⁶ The people that lived in darkness
  have seen a great light;
  light has dawned on those
  who lived in the land of death's dark
    shadow.

¹⁷ From that day Jesus began to proclaim the message: 'Repent, for the kingdom of Heaven is upon you.'

¹⁸ JESUS was walking by the sea of Galilee when he saw two brothers, Simon called Peter and his brother Andrew, casting a net into the lake; for they were fishermen. ¹⁹ Jesus said to them, 'Come with me, and I will make you fishers of men.' ²⁰ At once they left their nets and followed him.

²¹ Going on farther, he saw another pair of brothers, James son of Zebedee and his brother John; they were in a boat with their father Zebedee, mending their nets. He called them, ²² and at once they left the boat and their father, and followed him.

²³ He travelled throughout Galilee, teaching in the synagogues, proclaiming the good news of the kingdom, and healing every kind of illness and infirmity among the people. ²⁴ His fame spread throughout Syria; and they brought to him sufferers from various diseases, those racked with pain or possessed by demons, those who were epileptic or paralysed, and he healed them all. ²⁵ Large crowds followed him, from Galilee and the Decapolis, from Jerusalem and Judaea, and from Transjordan.

The Sermon on the Mount

5 WHEN he saw the crowds he went up a mountain. There he sat down, and when his disciples had gathered round him ² he began to address them. And this is the teaching he gave:

³ 'Blessed are the poor in spirit;
  the kingdom of Heaven is theirs.
⁴ Blessed are the sorrowful;
  they shall find consolation.
⁵ Blessed are the gentle;
  they shall have the earth for their
    possession.
⁶ Blessed are those who hunger and
    thirst to see right prevail;
  they shall be satisfied.
⁷ Blessed are those who show mercy;
  mercy shall be shown to them.
⁸ Blessed are those whose hearts are
    pure;
  they shall see God.
⁹ Blessed are the peacemakers;
  they shall be called God's children.
¹⁰ Blessed are those who are persecuted
    in the cause of right;
  the kingdom of Heaven is theirs.

¹¹ 'Blessed are you, when you suffer insults and persecution and calumnies of every kind for my sake. ¹² Exult and be glad, for you have a rich reward in heaven; in the same way they persecuted the prophets before you.

¹³ 'You are salt to the world. And if salt becomes tasteless, how is its saltness to be

5:6 to ... **prevail**: *or* to do what is right.

3

restored? It is good for nothing but to be thrown away and trodden underfoot.

¹⁴ 'You are light for all the world. A town that stands on a hill cannot be hidden. ¹⁵ When a lamp is lit, it is not put under the meal-tub, but on the lampstand, where it gives light to everyone in the house. ¹⁶ Like the lamp, you must shed light among your fellows, so that, when they see the good you do, they may give praise to your Father in heaven.

¹⁷ 'Do NOT suppose that I have come to abolish the law and the prophets; I did not come to abolish, but to complete. ¹⁸ Truly I tell you: so long as heaven and earth endure, not a letter, not a dot, will disappear from the law until all that must happen has happened. ¹⁹ Anyone therefore who sets aside even the least of the law's demands, and teaches others to do the same, will have the lowest place in the kingdom of Heaven, whereas anyone who keeps the law, and teaches others to do so, will rank high in the kingdom of Heaven. ²⁰ I tell you, unless you show yourselves far better than the scribes and Pharisees, you can never enter the kingdom of Heaven.

²¹ 'You have heard that our forefathers were told, "Do not commit murder; anyone who commits murder must be brought to justice." ²² But what I tell you is this: Anyone who nurses anger against his brother must be brought to justice. Whoever calls his brother "good for nothing" deserves the sentence of the court; whoever calls him "fool" deserves hellfire. ²³ So if you are presenting your gift at the altar and suddenly remember that your brother has a grievance against you, ²⁴ leave your gift where it is before the altar. First go and make your peace with your brother; then come back and offer your gift. ²⁵ If someone sues you, come to terms with him promptly while you are both on your way to court; otherwise he may hand you over to the judge, and the judge to the officer, and you will be thrown into jail. ²⁶ Truly I tell you: once you are there you will not be let out until you have paid the last penny.

²⁷ 'You have heard that they were told, "Do not commit adultery." ²⁸ But what I tell you is this: If a man looks at a woman with a lustful eye, he has already committed adultery with her in his heart. ²⁹ If your right eye causes your downfall, tear it out and fling it away; it is better for you to lose one part of your body than for the whole of it to be thrown into hell. ³⁰ If your right hand causes your downfall, cut it off and fling it away; it is better for you to lose one part of your body than for the whole of it to go to hell.

³¹ 'They were told, "A man who divorces his wife must give her a certificate of dismissal." ³² But what I tell you is this: If a man divorces his wife for any cause other than unchastity he involves her in adultery; and whoever marries her commits adultery.

³³ 'Again, you have heard that our forefathers were told, "Do not break your oath," and "Oaths sworn to the Lord must be kept." ³⁴ But what I tell you is this: You are not to swear at all—not by heaven, for it is God's throne, ³⁵ nor by the earth, for it is his footstool, nor by Jerusalem, for it is the city of the great King, ³⁶ nor by your own head, because you cannot turn one hair of it white or black. ³⁷ Plain "Yes" or "No" is all you need to say; anything beyond that comes from the evil one.

³⁸ 'You have heard that they were told, "An eye for an eye, a tooth for a tooth." ³⁹ But what I tell you is this: Do not resist those who wrong you. If anyone slaps you on the right cheek, turn and offer him the other also. ⁴⁰ If anyone wants to sue you and takes your shirt, let him have your cloak as well. ⁴¹ If someone in authority presses you into service for one mile, go with him two. ⁴² Give to anyone who asks; and do not turn your back on anyone who wants to borrow.

⁴³ 'You have heard that they were told, "Love your neighbour and hate your enemy." ⁴⁴ But what I tell you is this: Love your enemies and pray for your persecutors; ⁴⁵ only so can you be children of your heavenly Father, who causes the sun to rise on good and bad alike, and sends the rain on the innocent and the wicked. ⁴⁶ If you love only those who love you, what reward can you expect? Even the tax-collectors do as much as that. ⁴⁷ If you greet only your brothers, what is there extraordinary about that? Even the

5:18 **until ... happened:** *or* before all that it stands for is achieved.

4

heathen do as much. [48] There must be no limit to your goodness, as your heavenly Father's goodness knows no bounds.

6 'BE careful not to parade your religion before others; if you do, no reward awaits you with your Father in heaven.

[2] 'So, when you give alms, do not announce it with a flourish of trumpets, as the hypocrites do in synagogues and in the streets to win the praise of others. Truly I tell you: they have their reward already. [3] But when you give alms, do not let your left hand know what your right is doing; [4] your good deed must be secret, and your Father who sees what is done in secret will reward you.

[5] 'Again, when you pray, do not be like the hypocrites; they love to say their prayers standing up in synagogues and at street corners for everyone to see them. Truly I tell you: they have their reward already. [6] But when you pray, go into a room by yourself, shut the door, and pray to your Father who is in secret; and your Father who sees what is done in secret will reward you.

[7] 'In your prayers do not go babbling on like the heathen, who imagine that the more they say the more likely they are to be heard. [8] Do not imitate them, for your Father knows what your needs are before you ask him.

[9] 'This is how you should pray:

Our Father in heaven,
　may your name be hallowed;
[10] your kingdom come,
　your will be done,
　on earth as in heaven.
[11] Give us today our daily bread.
[12] Forgive us the wrong we have done,
　as we have forgiven those who have
　　wronged us.
[13] And do not put us to the test,
　but save us from the evil one.

[14] 'For if you forgive others the wrongs they have done, your heavenly Father will also forgive you; [15] but if you do not forgive others, then your Father will not forgive the wrongs that you have done.

[16] 'So too when you fast, do not look gloomy like the hypocrites: they make their faces unsightly so that everybody may see that they are fasting. Truly I tell you: they have their reward already. [17] But when you fast, anoint your head and wash your face, [18] so that no one sees that you are fasting, but only your Father who is in secret; and your Father who sees what is done in secret will give you your reward.

[19] 'DO NOT store up for yourselves treasure on earth, where moth and rust destroy, and thieves break in and steal; [20] but store up treasure in heaven, where neither moth nor rust will destroy, nor thieves break in and steal. [21] For where your treasure is, there will your heart be also.

[22] 'The lamp of the body is the eye. If your eyes are sound, you will have light for your whole body; [23] if your eyes are bad, your whole body will be in darkness. If then the only light you have is darkness, how great a darkness that will be.

[24] 'No one can serve two masters; for either he will hate the first and love the second, or he will be devoted to the first and despise the second. You cannot serve God and Money.

[25] 'This is why I tell you not to be anxious about food and drink to keep you alive and about clothes to cover your body. Surely life is more than food, the body more than clothes. [26] Look at the birds in the sky; they do not sow and reap and store in barns, yet your heavenly Father feeds them. Are you not worth more than the birds? [27] Can anxious thought add a single day to your life? [28] And why be anxious about clothes? Consider how the lilies grow in the fields; they do not work, they do not spin; [29] yet I tell you, even Solomon in all his splendour was not attired like one of them. [30] If that is how God clothes the grass in the fields, which is there today and tomorrow is thrown on the stove, will he not all the more clothe you? How little faith you have! [31] Do not ask anxiously, "What are we to eat? What are we to drink? What shall we wear?" [32] These are the things that occupy the minds of the heathen, but

---

6:11 **our ... bread**: *or* our bread for the morrow.　　6:13 **from the evil one**: *or* from evil. *Some witnesses add* For yours is the kingdom and the power and the glory, for ever. Amen.　　6:27 **add ... life**: *or* add one foot to your height.　　6:28 **Consider ... spin**: *one witness reads* Consider the lilies: they neither card, nor spin, nor work.

your heavenly Father knows that you need them all. ³³ Set your mind on God's kingdom and his justice before everything else, and all the rest will come to you as well. ³⁴ So do not be anxious about tomorrow; tomorrow will look after itself. Each day has troubles enough of its own.

7 'Do NOT judge, and you will not be judged. ² For as you judge others, so you will yourselves be judged, and whatever measure you deal out to others will be dealt to you. ³ Why do you look at the speck of sawdust in your brother's eye, with never a thought for the plank in your own? ⁴ How can you say to your brother, "Let me take the speck out of your eye," when all the time there is a plank in your own? ⁵ You hypocrite! First take the plank out of your own eye, and then you will see clearly to take the speck out of your brother's.

⁶ 'Do not give dogs what is holy; do not throw your pearls to the pigs: they will only trample on them, and turn and tear you to pieces.

⁷ 'Ask, and you will receive; seek, and you will find; knock, and the door will be opened to you. ⁸ For everyone who asks receives, those who seek find, and to those who knock, the door will be opened.

⁹ 'Would any of you offer his son a stone when he asks for bread, ¹⁰ or a snake when he asks for a fish? ¹¹ If you, bad as you are, know how to give good things to your children, how much more will your heavenly Father give good things to those who ask him!

¹² 'Always treat others as you would like them to treat you: that is the law and the prophets.

¹³ 'Enter by the narrow gate. Wide is the gate and broad the road that leads to destruction, and many enter that way; ¹⁴ narrow is the gate and constricted the road that leads to life, and those who find them are few.

¹⁵ 'Beware of false prophets, who come to you dressed up as sheep while underneath they are savage wolves. ¹⁶ You will recognize them by their fruit. Can grapes be picked from briars, or figs from thistles? ¹⁷ A good tree always yields sound fruit, and a poor tree bad fruit. ¹⁸ A good tree cannot bear bad fruit, or a poor tree sound fruit. ¹⁹ A tree that does not yield sound fruit is cut down and thrown on the fire.

²⁰ That is why I say you will recognize them by their fruit.

²¹ 'Not everyone who says to me, "Lord, Lord" will enter the kingdom of Heaven, but only those who do the will of my heavenly Father. ²² When the day comes, many will say to me, "Lord, Lord, did we not prophesy in your name, drive out demons in your name, and in your name perform many miracles?" ²³ Then I will tell them plainly, "I never knew you. Out of my sight; your deeds are evil!"

²⁴ 'So whoever hears these words of mine and acts on them is like a man who had the sense to build his house on rock. ²⁵ The rain came down, the floods rose, the winds blew and beat upon that house; but it did not fall, because its foundations were on rock. ²⁶ And whoever hears these words of mine and does not act on them is like a man who was foolish enough to build his house on sand. ²⁷ The rain came down, the floods rose, the winds blew and battered against that house; and it fell with a great crash.'

²⁸ When Jesus had finished this discourse the people were amazed at his teaching; ²⁹ unlike their scribes he taught with a note of authority.

Miracles and teaching

8 WHEN he came down from the mountain great crowds followed him. ² And now a leper approached him, bowed before him, and said, 'Sir, if only you will, you can make me clean.' ³ Jesus stretched out his hand and touched him, saying, 'I will; be clean.' And his leprosy was cured immediately. ⁴ Then Jesus said to him, 'See that you tell nobody; but go and show yourself to the priest, and make the offering laid down by Moses to certify the cure.'

⁵ As Jesus entered Capernaum a centurion came up to ask his help. ⁶ 'Sir,' he said, 'my servant is lying at home paralysed and racked with pain.' ⁷ Jesus said, 'I will come and cure him.' ⁸ But the centurion replied, 'Sir, I am not worthy to have you under my roof. You need only say the word and my servant will be cured. ⁹ I know, for I am myself under orders, with soldiers under me. I say to one, "Go," and he goes; to another, "Come here," and he comes; and to my servant, "Do this," and he does it.' ¹⁰ Jesus heard him with astonishment, and said to the people who were

following him, 'Truly I tell you: nowhere in Israel have I found such faith. [11] Many, I tell you, will come from east and west to sit with Abraham, Isaac, and Jacob at the banquet in the kingdom of Heaven. [12] But those who were born to the kingdom will be thrown out into the dark, where there will be wailing and grinding of teeth.' [13] Then Jesus said to the centurion, 'Go home; as you have believed, so let it be.' At that very moment the boy recovered.

[14] Jesus then went to Peter's house and found Peter's mother-in-law in bed with fever. [15] So he took her by the hand; the fever left her, and she got up and attended to his needs.

[16] That evening they brought to him many who were possessed by demons; and he drove the spirits out with a word and healed all who were sick, [17] to fulfil the prophecy of Isaiah: 'He took our illnesses from us and carried away our diseases.'

[18] AT the sight of the crowd surrounding him Jesus gave word to cross to the other side of the lake. [19] A scribe came up and said to him, 'Teacher, I will follow you wherever you go.' [20] Jesus replied, 'Foxes have their holes and birds their roosts; but the Son of Man has nowhere to lay his head.' [21] Another man, one of his disciples, said to him, 'Lord, let me go and bury my father first.' [22] Jesus replied, 'Follow me, and leave the dead to bury their dead.'

[23] Jesus then got into the boat, and his disciples followed. [24] All at once a great storm arose on the lake, till the waves were breaking right over the boat; but he went on sleeping. [25] So they came and woke him, saying: 'Save us, Lord; we are sinking!' [26] 'Why are you such cowards?' he said. 'How little faith you have!' With that he got up and rebuked the wind and the sea, and there was a dead calm. [27] The men were astonished at what had happened, and exclaimed, 'What sort of man is this? Even the wind and the sea obey him.'

[28] When he reached the country of the Gadarenes on the other side, two men came to meet him from among the tombs; they were possessed by demons, and so violent that no one dared pass that way. [29] 'Son of God,' they shouted, 'what do you want with us? Have you come here to torment us before our time?' [30] In the distance a large herd of pigs was feeding; [31] and the demons begged him: 'If you drive us out, send us into that herd of pigs.' [32] 'Go!' he said. Then they came out and went into the pigs, and the whole herd rushed over the edge into the lake, and perished in the water. [33] The men in charge of them took to their heels, and made for the town, where they told the whole story, and what had happened to the madmen. [34] Then the whole town came out to meet Jesus; and when they saw him they begged him to leave the district. [1] So he got into the boat and crossed over, and came to his own town.

9

[2] Some men appeared, bringing to Jesus a paralysed man on a bed. When he saw their faith Jesus said to the man, 'Take heart, my son; your sins are forgiven.' [3] At this some of the scribes said to themselves, 'This man is blaspheming!' [4] Jesus realized what they were thinking, and said, 'Why do you harbour evil thoughts? [5] Is it easier to say, "Your sins are forgiven," or to say, "Stand up and walk"? [6] But to convince you that the Son of Man has authority on earth to forgive sins'— he turned to the paralysed man—'stand up, take your bed, and go home.' [7] And he got up and went off home. [8] The people were filled with awe at the sight, and praised God for granting such authority to men.

[9] AS HE went on from there Jesus saw a man named Matthew at his seat in the custom-house, and said to him, 'Follow me'; and Matthew rose and followed him. [10] When Jesus was having a meal in the house, many tax-collectors and sinners were seated with him and his disciples. [11] Noticing this, the Pharisees said to his disciples, 'Why is it that your teacher eats with tax-collectors and sinners?' [12] Hearing this he said, 'It is not the healthy who need a doctor, but the sick. [13] Go and learn what this text means, "I require mercy, not sacrifice." I did not come to call the virtuous, but sinners.'

[14] Then John's disciples came to him with the question: 'Why is it that we and the Pharisees fast but your disciples do not?' [15] Jesus replied, 'Can you expect the bridegroom's friends to be sad while the bridegroom is with them? The time will

come when the bridegroom will be taken away from them; then they will fast.

¹⁶ 'No one puts a patch of unshrunk cloth on an old garment; for then the patch tears away from the garment, and leaves a bigger hole. ¹⁷ Nor do people put new wine into old wineskins; if they do, the skins burst, and then the wine runs out and the skins are ruined. No, they put new wine into fresh skins; then both are preserved.'

¹⁸ EVEN as he spoke, an official came up, who bowed before him and said, 'My daughter has just died; but come and lay your hand on her, and she will live.' ¹⁹ Jesus rose and went with him, and so did his disciples.

²⁰ Just then a woman who had suffered from haemorrhages for twelve years came up from behind, and touched the edge of his cloak; ²¹ for she said to herself, 'If I can only touch his cloak, I shall be healed.' ²² But Jesus turned and saw her, and said, 'Take heart, my daughter; your faith has healed you.' And from that moment she recovered.

²³ When Jesus arrived at the official's house and saw the flute-players and the general commotion, ²⁴ he said, 'Go away! The girl is not dead: she is asleep'; and they laughed at him. ²⁵ After turning them all out, he went into the room and took the girl by the hand, and she got up. ²⁶ The story became the talk of the whole district.

²⁷ As he went on from there Jesus was followed by two blind men, shouting, 'Have pity on us, Son of David!' ²⁸ When he had gone indoors they came to him, and Jesus asked, 'Do you believe that I have the power to do what you want?' 'We do,' they said. ²⁹ Then he touched their eyes, and said, 'As you have believed, so let it be'; ³⁰ and their sight was restored. Jesus said to them sternly, 'See that no one hears about this.' ³¹ But as soon as they had gone out they talked about him all over the region.

³² They were on their way out when a man was brought to him, who was dumb and possessed by a demon; ³³ the demon was driven out and the dumb man spoke. The crowd was astonished and said,

'Nothing like this has ever been seen in Israel.'

³⁵ So JESUS went round all the towns and villages teaching in their synagogues, proclaiming the good news of the kingdom, and curing every kind of illness and infirmity. ³⁶ The sight of the crowds moved him to pity: they were like sheep without a shepherd, harassed and helpless. ³⁷ Then he said to his disciples, 'The crop is heavy, but the labourers too few; ³⁸ you must ask the owner to send labourers to bring in the harvest.'

The Twelve are commissioned

10 THEN he called his twelve disciples to him and gave them authority to drive out unclean spirits and to cure every kind of illness and infirmity.

² These are the names of the twelve apostles: first Simon, also called Peter, and his brother Andrew; James son of Zebedee, and his brother John; ³ Philip and Bartholomew, Thomas and Matthew the tax-collector, James son of Alphaeus, Thaddaeus, ⁴ Simon the Zealot, and Judas Iscariot, the man who betrayed him.

⁵ These twelve Jesus sent out with the following instructions: 'Do not take the road to gentile lands, and do not enter any Samaritan town; ⁶ but go rather to the lost sheep of the house of Israel. ⁷ And as you go proclaim the message: "The kingdom of Heaven is upon you." ⁸ Heal the sick, raise the dead, cleanse lepers, drive out demons. You received without cost; give without charge.

⁹ 'Take no gold, silver, or copper in your belts, ¹⁰ no pack for the road, no second coat, no sandals, no stick; the worker deserves his keep.

¹¹ 'Whatever town or village you enter, look for some suitable person in it, and stay with him until you leave. ¹² Wish the house peace as you enter it; ¹³ if it is welcoming, let your peace descend on it, and if it is not, let your peace come back to you. ¹⁴ If anyone will not receive you or listen to what you say, then as you leave that house or that town shake the dust of it off your feet. ¹⁵ Truly I tell you: on the day of judgement it will be more bearable for the land of Sodom and Gomorrah than for that town.

9:20 **edge:** *or* tassel.   9:33 **in Israel:** *some witnesses add* ³⁴ But the Pharisees said, 'He drives out devils by the prince of devils.'   10:3 **Thaddaeus:** *some witnesses read* Lebbaeus.

[16] 'I send you out like sheep among wolves; be wary as serpents, innocent as doves.

[17] 'Be on your guard, for you will be handed over to the courts, they will flog you in their synagogues, [18] and you will be brought before governors and kings on my account, to testify before them and the Gentiles. [19] But when you are arrested, do not worry about what you are to say, for when the time comes, the words you need will be given you; [20] it will not be you speaking, but the Spirit of your Father speaking in you.

[21] 'Brother will hand over brother to death, and a father his child; children will turn against their parents and send them to their death. [22] Everyone will hate you for your allegiance to me, but whoever endures to the end will be saved. [23] When you are persecuted in one town, take refuge in another; truly I tell you: before you have gone through all the towns of Israel the Son of Man will have come.

[24] 'No pupil ranks above his teacher, no servant above his master. [25] The pupil should be content to share his teacher's lot, the servant to share his master's. If the master has been called Beelzebul, how much more his household!

[26] 'So do not be afraid of them. There is nothing covered up that will not be uncovered, nothing hidden that will not be made known. [27] What I say to you in the dark you must repeat in broad daylight; what you hear whispered you must shout from the housetops. [28] Do not fear those who kill the body, but cannot kill the soul. Fear him rather who is able to destroy both soul and body in hell.

[29] 'Are not two sparrows sold for a penny? Yet without your Father's knowledge not one of them can fall to the ground. [30] As for you, even the hairs of your head have all been counted. [31] So do not be afraid; you are worth more than any number of sparrows.

[32] 'Whoever will acknowledge me before others, I will acknowledge before my Father in heaven; [33] and whoever disowns me before others, I will disown before my Father in heaven.

[34] 'You must not think that I have come to bring peace to the earth; I have not come to bring peace, but a sword. [35] I have come to set a man against his father, a daughter against her mother, a daughter-in-law against her mother-in-law; [36] and a man will find his enemies under his own roof.

[37] 'No one is worthy of me who cares more for father or mother than for me; no one is worthy of me who cares more for son or daughter; [38] no one is worthy of me who does not take up his cross and follow me. [39] Whoever gains his life will lose it; whoever loses his life for my sake will gain it.

[40] 'To receive you is to receive me, and to receive me is to receive the One who sent me. [41] Whoever receives a prophet because he is a prophet will be given a prophet's reward, and whoever receives a good man because he is a good man will be given a good man's reward. [42] Truly I tell you: anyone who gives so much as a cup of cold water to one of these little ones because he is a disciple of mine, will certainly not go unrewarded.'

11 When Jesus had finished giving instructions to his twelve disciples, he went from there to teach and preach in the neighbouring towns.

Recognizing the Messiah

[2] JOHN, who was in prison, heard what Christ was doing, and sent his own disciples [3] to put this question to him: 'Are you the one who is to come, or are we to expect someone else?' [4] Jesus answered, 'Go and report to John what you hear and see: [5] the blind recover their sight, the lame walk, lepers are made clean, the deaf hear, the dead are raised to life, the poor are brought good news—[6] and blessed are those who do not find me an obstacle to faith.'

[7] When the messengers were on their way back, Jesus began to speak to the crowds about John: 'What was the spectacle that drew you to the wilderness? A reed swaying in the wind? [8] No? Then what did you go out to see? A man dressed in finery? Fine clothes are to be found in palaces. [9] But why did you go out? To see a prophet? Yes indeed, and far more than a prophet. [10] He is the man of whom scripture says,

Here is my herald, whom I send
　　ahead of you,
and he will prepare your way before
　　you.

11 'Truly I tell you: among all who have ever been born, no one has been greater than John the Baptist, and yet the least in the kingdom of Heaven is greater than he.
12 'Since the time of John the Baptist the kingdom of Heaven has been subjected to violence and violent men are taking it by force. 13 For until John, all the prophets and the law foretold things to come; 14 and John is the destined Elijah, if you will but accept it. 15 If you have ears, then hear.

16 'How can I describe this generation? They are like children sitting in the market-place and calling to each other,

17 We piped for you and you would not dance.
We lamented, and you would not mourn.

18 'For John came, neither eating nor drinking, and people say, "He is possessed"; 19 the Son of Man came, eating and drinking, and they say, "Look at him! A glutton and a drinker, a friend of tax-collectors and sinners!" Yet God's wisdom is proved right by its results.'

20 THEN he spoke of the towns in which most of his miracles had been performed, and denounced them for their impenitence. 21 'Alas for you, Chorazin!' he said. 'Alas for you, Bethsaida! If the miracles performed in you had taken place in Tyre and Sidon, they would have repented long ago in sackcloth and ashes. 22 But it will be more bearable, I tell you, for Tyre and Sidon on the day of judgement than for you. 23 As for you, Capernaum, will you be exalted to heaven? No, you will be brought down to Hades! For if the miracles performed in you had taken place in Sodom, Sodom would be standing to this day. 24 But it will be more bearable, I tell you, for the land of Sodom on the day of judgement than for you.'

25 At that time Jesus spoke these words: 'I thank you, Father, Lord of heaven and earth, for hiding these things from the learned and wise, and revealing them to the simple. 26 Yes, Father, such was your choice. 27 Everything is entrusted to me by my Father; and no one knows the Son but the Father, and no one knows the Father but the Son and those to whom the Son chooses to reveal him.

28 'Come to me, all who are weary and whose load is heavy; I will give you rest. 29 Take my yoke upon you, and learn from me, for I am gentle and humble-hearted; and you will find rest for your souls. 30 For my yoke is easy to wear, my load is light.'

Opposition to Jesus

12 ABOUT that time Jesus was going through the cornfields on the sabbath; and his disciples, feeling hungry, began to pluck some ears of corn and eat them. 2 When the Pharisees saw this, they said to him, 'Look, your disciples are doing what is forbidden on the sabbath.' 3 He answered, 'Have you not read what David did when he and his men were hungry? 4 He went into the house of God and ate the sacred bread, though neither he nor his men had a right to eat it, but only the priests. 5 Or have you not read in the law that on the sabbath the priests in the temple break the sabbath and they are not held to be guilty? 6 But I tell you, there is something greater than the temple here. 7 If you had known what this text means, "It is mercy I require, not sacrifice," you would not have condemned the innocent. 8 For the Son of Man is lord of the sabbath.'

9 He went on to another place, and entered their synagogue. 10 A man was there with a withered arm, and they asked Jesus, 'Is it permitted to heal on the sabbath?' (They wanted to bring a charge against him.) 11 But he said to them, 'Suppose you had one sheep, and it fell into a ditch on the sabbath; is there a single one of you who would not catch hold of it and lift it out? 12 Surely a man is worth far more than a sheep! It is therefore permitted to do good on the sabbath.' 13 Then he said to the man, 'Stretch out your arm.' He stretched it out, and it was made sound again like the other. 14 But the Pharisees, on leaving the synagogue, plotted to bring about Jesus's death.

15 Jesus was aware of it and withdrew, and many followed him. He healed all who were ill, 16 and gave strict instructions that they were not to make him known. 17 This was to fulfil Isaiah's prophecy:

11:12 has been ... force: *or* has been forcing its way forward, and men of force are seizing it.   11:26 Yes ... such: *or* Yes, I thank you, Father, that such.

[18] Here is my servant, whom I have
chosen,
my beloved, in whom I take delight;
I will put my Spirit upon him,
and he will proclaim justice among
the nations.
[19] He will not strive, he will not shout,
nor will his voice be heard in the
streets.
[20] He will not snap off a broken reed,
nor snuff out a smouldering wick,
until he leads justice on to victory.
[21] In him the nations shall put their
hope.

[22] THEN they brought him a man who was
possessed by a demon; he was blind and
dumb, and Jesus cured him, restoring
both speech and sight. [23] The bystanders
were all amazed, and the word went
round: 'Can this be the Son of David?'
[24] But when the Pharisees heard it they
said, 'It is only by Beelzebul prince of
devils that this man drives the devils out.'
[25] Knowing what was in their minds,
he said to them, 'Every kingdom divided
against itself is laid waste; and no town or
household that is divided against itself can
stand. [26] And if it is Satan who drives out
Satan, he is divided against himself; how
then can his kingdom stand? [27] If it is by
Beelzebul that I drive out devils, by whom
do your own people drive them out? If this
is your argument, they themselves will
refute you. [28] But if it is by the Spirit of God
that I drive out the devils, then be sure the
kingdom of God has already come upon
you.
[29] 'Or again, how can anyone break
into a strong man's house and make off
with his goods, unless he has first tied up
the strong man? Then he can ransack the
house.
[30] 'He who is not with me is against me,
and he who does not gather with me
scatters.
[31] 'So I tell you this: every sin and every
slander can be forgiven, except slander
spoken against the Spirit; that will not be
forgiven. [32] Anyone who speaks a word
against the Son of Man will be forgiven;
but if anyone speaks against the Holy
Spirit, for him there will be no forgiveness,
either in this age or in the age to come.
[33] 'Get a good tree and its fruit will be

good; get a bad tree and its fruit will be
bad. You can tell a tree by its fruit.
[34] Vipers' brood! How can your words be
good when you yourselves are evil? It is
from the fullness of the heart that the
mouth speaks. [35] Good people from their
store of good produce good; and evil
people from their store of evil produce evil.
[36] 'I tell you this: every thoughtless
word you speak you will have to account
for on the day of judgement. [37] For out of
your own mouth you will be acquitted;
out of your own mouth you will be
condemned.'
[38] At this some of the scribes and the
Pharisees said, 'Teacher, we would like
you to show us a sign.' [39] He answered: 'It
is a wicked, godless generation that asks
for a sign, and the only sign that will be
given it is the sign of the prophet Jonah.
[40] Just as Jonah was in the sea monster's
belly for three days and three nights, so
the Son of Man will be three days and
three nights in the bowels of the earth.
[41] The men of Nineveh will appear in
court when this generation is on trial, and
ensure its condemnation, for they repented at the preaching of Jonah; and
what is here is greater than Jonah. [42] The
queen of the south will appear in court
when this generation is on trial, and
ensure its condemnation; for she came
from the ends of the earth to listen to the
wisdom of Solomon, and what is here is
greater than Solomon.
[43] 'When an unclean spirit comes out of
someone it wanders over the desert sands
seeking a resting-place, and finds none.
[44] Then it says, "I will go back to the home
I left." So it returns and finds the house
unoccupied, swept clean, and tidy. [45] It
goes off and collects seven other spirits
more wicked than itself, and they all come
in and settle there; and in the end that
person's plight is worse than before. That is
how it will be with this wicked generation.'
[46] He was still speaking to the crowd
when his mother and brothers appeared;
they stood outside, wanting to speak to
him. [47] Someone said, 'Your mother and
your brothers are standing outside; they
want to speak to you.' [48] Jesus turned to
the man who brought the message, and
said, 'Who is my mother? Who are my
brothers?' [49] and pointing to his disciples,

12:41 **will appear ... trial:** *or* will rise again with this generation at the judgement.   12:42 **The queen ...**
trial: *or* The queen of the south will be raised to life with this generation at the judgement.

he said, 'Here are my mother and my brothers. ⁵⁰ Whoever does the will of my heavenly Father is my brother and sister and mother.'

Parables

13 THAT same day Jesus went out and sat by the lakeside, ² where so many people gathered round him that he had to get into a boat. He sat there, and all the people stood on the shore. ³ He told them many things in parables.

He said: 'A sower went out to sow. ⁴ And as he sowed, some of the seed fell along the footpath; and the birds came and ate it up. ⁵ Some fell on rocky ground, where it had little soil, and it sprouted quickly because it had no depth of earth; ⁶ but when the sun rose it was scorched, and as it had no root it withered away. ⁷ Some fell among thistles; and the thistles grew up and choked it. ⁸ And some of the seed fell on good soil, where it produced a crop, some a hundredfold, some sixtyfold, and some thirtyfold. ⁹ If you have ears, then hear.'

¹⁰ The disciples came to him and asked, 'Why do you speak to them in parables?' ¹¹ He replied, 'To you it has been granted to know the secrets of the kingdom of Heaven, but not to them. ¹² For those who have will be given more, till they have enough and to spare; and those who have not will forfeit even what they have. ¹³ That is why I speak to them in parables; for they look without seeing, and listen without hearing or understanding. ¹⁴ The prophecy of Isaiah is being fulfilled in them: "You may listen and listen, but you will never understand; you may look and look, but you will never see. ¹⁵ For this people's mind has become dull; they have stopped their ears and shut their eyes. Otherwise, their eyes might see, their ears hear, and their mind understand, and then they might turn to me, and I would heal them."

¹⁶ 'But happy are your eyes because they see, and your ears because they hear! ¹⁷ Truly I tell you: many prophets and saints longed to see what you now see, yet never saw it; to hear what you hear, yet never heard it.

¹⁸ 'Hear then the parable of the sower. ¹⁹ When anyone hears the word that tells of the Kingdom, but fails to understand it, the evil one comes and carries off what has been sown in his heart; that is the seed sown along the footpath. ²⁰ The seed sown on rocky ground stands for the person who hears the word and accepts it at once with joy; ²¹ it strikes no root in him and he has no staying-power; when there is trouble or persecution on account of the word he quickly loses faith. ²² The seed sown among thistles represents the person who hears the word, but worldly cares and the false glamour of wealth choke it, and it proves barren. ²³ But the seed sown on good soil is the person who hears the word and understands it; he does bear fruit and yields a hundredfold, or sixtyfold, or thirtyfold.'

²⁴ Here is another parable he gave them: 'The kingdom of Heaven is like this. A man sowed his field with good seed; ²⁵ but while everyone was asleep his enemy came, sowed darnel among the wheat, and made off. ²⁶ When the corn sprouted and began to fill out, the darnel could be seen among it. ²⁷ The farmer's men went to their master and said, "Sir, was it not good seed that you sowed in your field? So where has the darnel come from?" ²⁸ "This is an enemy's doing," he replied. "Well then," they said, "shall we go and gather the darnel?" ²⁹ "No," he answered; "in gathering it you might pull up the wheat at the same time. ³⁰ Let them both grow together till harvest; and at harvest time I will tell the reapers, 'Gather the darnel first, and tie it in bundles for burning; then collect the wheat into my barn.'"'

³¹ This is another parable he gave them: 'The kingdom of Heaven is like a mustard seed, which a man took and sowed in his field. ³² Mustard is smaller than any other seed, but when it has grown it is taller than other plants; it becomes a tree, big enough for the birds to come and roost among its branches.'

³³ He told them also this parable: 'The kingdom of Heaven is like yeast, which a woman took and mixed with three measures of flour till it was all leavened.'

³⁴ In all this teaching to the crowds Jesus spoke in parables; indeed he never spoke to them except in parables. ³⁵ This was to fulfil the saying of the prophet:

13: 35 **prophet:** *some witnesses add* Isaiah.

I will open my mouth in parables;
I will utter things kept secret since
the world was made.

³⁶ Then he sent the people away, and went into the house, where his disciples came to him and said, 'Explain to us the parable of the darnel in the field.' ³⁷ He replied, 'The sower of the good seed is the Son of Man. ³⁸ The field is the world; the good seed stands for the children of the Kingdom, the darnel for the children of the evil one, ³⁹ and the enemy who sowed the darnel is the devil. The harvest is the end of time, and the reapers are angels. ⁴⁰ As the darnel is gathered up and burnt, so at the end of time ⁴¹ the Son of Man will send his angels, who will gather out of his kingdom every cause of sin, and all whose deeds are evil; ⁴² these will be thrown into the blazing furnace, where there will be wailing and grinding of teeth. ⁴³ Then the righteous will shine like the sun in the kingdom of their Father. If you have ears, then hear.

⁴⁴ 'The kingdom of Heaven is like treasure which a man found buried in a field. He buried it again, and in joy went and sold everything he had, and bought the field.

⁴⁵ 'Again, the kingdom of Heaven is like this. A merchant looking out for fine pearls ⁴⁶ found one of very special value; so he went and sold everything he had and bought it.

⁴⁷ 'Again the kingdom of Heaven is like a net cast into the sea, where it caught fish of every kind. ⁴⁸ When it was full, it was hauled ashore. Then the men sat down and collected the good fish into baskets and threw the worthless away. ⁴⁹ That is how it will be at the end of time. The angels will go out, and they will separate the wicked from the good, ⁵⁰ and throw them into the blazing furnace, where there will be wailing and grinding of teeth.

⁵¹ 'Have you understood all this?' he asked; and they answered, 'Yes.' ⁵² So he said to them, 'When, therefore, a teacher of the law has become a learner in the kingdom of Heaven, he is like a house-holder who can produce from his store things new and old.'

⁵³ WHEN Jesus had finished these parables he left that place, ⁵⁴ and came to his home town, where he taught the people in their synagogue. In amazement they asked, 'Where does he get this wisdom from, and these miraculous powers? ⁵⁵ Is he not the carpenter's son? Is not his mother called Mary, his brothers James, Joseph, Simon, and Judas? ⁵⁶ And are not all his sisters here with us? Where does he get all this from?' ⁵⁷ So they turned against him. Jesus said to them, 'A prophet never lacks honour, except in his home town and in his own family.' ⁵⁸ And he did not do many miracles there, such was their want of faith.

Death of John the Baptist

14 IT was at that time that reports about Jesus reached Herod the tetrarch. ² 'This is John the Baptist,' he said to his attendants; 'he has been raised from the dead, and that is why these miraculous powers are at work in him.'

³ Now Herod had arrested John, put him in chains, and thrown him into prison, on account of Herodias, his brother Philip's wife; ⁴ for John had told him: 'You have no right to her.' ⁵ Herod would have liked to put him to death, but he was afraid of the people, in whose eyes John was a prophet. ⁶ But at his birthday celebrations the daughter of Herodias danced before the guests, and Herod was so delighted ⁷ that he promised on oath to give her anything she asked for. ⁸ Prompted by her mother, she said, 'Give me here on a dish the head of John the Baptist.' ⁹ At this the king was distressed, but because of his oath and his guests, he ordered the request to be granted, ¹⁰ and had John beheaded in prison. ¹¹ The head was brought on a dish and given to the girl; and she carried it to her mother. ¹² Then John's disciples came and took away the body, and buried it; and they went and told Jesus.

More miracles and teaching

¹³ WHEN he heard what had happened Jesus withdrew privately by boat to a remote place; but large numbers of people heard of it, and came after him on foot from the towns. ¹⁴ When he came ashore and saw a large crowd, his heart went out to them, and he healed those who were sick. ¹⁵ As evening drew on, the disciples came up to him and said, 'This is a remote place and the day has gone; send the

people off to the villages to buy themselves food.' ¹⁶ Jesus answered, 'There is no need for them to go; give them something to eat yourselves.' ¹⁷ 'All we have here', they said, 'is five loaves and two fish.' ¹⁸ 'Bring them to me,' he replied. ¹⁹ So he told the people to sit down on the grass; then, taking the five loaves and the two fish, he looked up to heaven, said the blessing, broke the loaves, and gave them to the disciples; and the disciples gave them to the people. ²⁰ They all ate and were satisfied; and twelve baskets were filled with what was left over. ²¹ Some five thousand men shared in this meal, not counting women and children.

²² As soon as they had finished, he made the disciples embark and cross to the other side ahead of him, while he dismissed the crowd; ²³ then he went up the hill by himself to pray. It had grown late, and he was there alone. ²⁴ The boat was already some distance from the shore, battling with a head wind and a rough sea. ²⁵ Between three and six in the morning he came towards them, walking across the lake. ²⁶ When the disciples saw him walking on the lake they were so shaken that they cried out in terror: 'It is a ghost!' ²⁷ But at once Jesus spoke to them: 'Take heart! It is I; do not be afraid.'

²⁸ Peter called to him: 'Lord, if it is you, tell me to come to you over the water.' ²⁹ 'Come,' said Jesus. Peter got down out of the boat, and walked over the water towards Jesus. ³⁰ But when he saw the strength of the gale he was afraid; and beginning to sink, he cried, 'Save me, Lord!' ³¹ Jesus at once reached out and caught hold of him. 'Why did you hesitate?' he said. 'How little faith you have!' ³² Then they climbed into the boat; and the wind dropped. ³³ And the men in the boat fell at his feet, exclaiming, 'You must be the Son of God.'

³⁴ So they completed the crossing and landed at Gennesaret. ³⁵ The people there recognized Jesus and sent word to all the country round. They brought to him all who were ill ³⁶ and begged him to let them simply touch the edge of his cloak; and all who touched it were completely cured.

15 THEN Jesus was approached by a group of Pharisees and scribes from Jerusalem, with the question:

² 'Why do your disciples break the ancient tradition? They do not wash their hands before eating.' ³ He answered them: 'And what about you? Why do you break God's commandment in the interest of your tradition? ⁴ For God said, "Honour your father and mother," and "Whoever curses his father or mother shall be put to death." ⁵ But you say, "Whoever says to his father or mother, 'Anything I have which might have been used for your benefit is set apart for God,' ⁶ must not honour his father or his mother." You have made God's law null and void out of regard for your tradition. ⁷ What hypocrites! How right Isaiah was when he prophesied about you: ⁸ "This people pays me lip-service, but their heart is far from me; ⁹ they worship me in vain, for they teach as doctrines the commandments of men."'

¹⁰ He called the crowd and said to them, 'Listen and understand! ¹¹ No one is defiled by what goes into his mouth; only by what comes out of it.'

¹² Then the disciples came to him and said, 'Do you know that the Pharisees have taken great offence at what you have been saying?' ¹³ He answered: 'Any plant that is not of my heavenly Father's planting will be rooted up. ¹⁴ Leave them alone; they are blind guides, and if one blind man guides another they will both fall into the ditch.'

¹⁵ Then Peter said, 'Tell us what that parable means.' ¹⁶ Jesus said, 'Are you still as dull as the rest? ¹⁷ Do you not see that whatever goes in by the mouth passes into the stomach and so is discharged into the drain? ¹⁸ But what comes out of the mouth has its origins in the heart; and that is what defiles a person. ¹⁹ Wicked thoughts, murder, adultery, fornication, theft, perjury, slander—these all proceed from the heart; ²⁰ and these are the things that defile a person; but to eat without first washing his hands, that cannot defile him.'

²¹ JESUS then withdrew to the region of Tyre and Sidon. ²² And a Canaanite woman from those parts came to meet him crying, 'Son of David! Have pity on me; my daughter is tormented by a devil.' ²³ But he said not a word in reply. His

14:36 **edge:** *or* tassel.   15:14 **blind guides:** *some witnesses add* of blind men.

14

disciples came and urged him: 'Send her away! See how she comes shouting after us.' ²⁴ Jesus replied, 'I was sent to the lost sheep of the house of Israel, and to them alone.' ²⁵ But the woman came and fell at his feet and cried, 'Help me, sir.' ²⁶ Jesus replied, 'It is not right to take the children's bread and throw it to the dogs.' ²⁷ 'True, sir,' she answered, 'and yet the dogs eat the scraps that fall from their master's table.' ²⁸ Hearing this Jesus replied, 'What faith you have! Let it be as you wish!' And from that moment her daughter was restored to health.

²⁹ After leaving that region Jesus took the road by the sea of Galilee, where he climbed a hill and sat down. ³⁰ Crowds flocked to him, bringing with them the lame, blind, dumb, and crippled, and many other sufferers; they put them down at his feet, and he healed them. ³¹ Great was the amazement of the people when they saw the dumb speaking, the crippled made strong, the lame walking, and the blind with their sight restored; and they gave praise to the God of Israel.

³² Jesus called his disciples and said to them, 'My heart goes out to these people; they have been with me now for three days and have nothing to eat. I do not want to send them away hungry; they might faint on the way.' ³³ The disciples replied, 'Where in this remote place can we find bread enough to feed such a crowd?' ³⁴ 'How many loaves have you?' Jesus asked. 'Seven,' they replied, 'and a few small fish.' ³⁵ So he ordered the people to sit down on the ground; ³⁶ then he took the seven loaves and the fish, and after giving thanks to God he broke them and gave them to the disciples, and the disciples gave them to the people. ³⁷ They all ate and were satisfied; and seven baskets were filled with what was left over. ³⁸ Those who were fed numbered four thousand men, not counting women and children. ³⁹ After dismissing the crowd, he got into a boat and went to the neighbourhood of Magadan.

16 The Pharisees and Sadducees came, and to test him they asked him to show them a sign from heaven.

² He answered: ⁴ 'It is a wicked, godless generation that asks for a sign; and the only sign that will be given it is the sign of Jonah.' With that he left them and went away.

⁵ In crossing to the other side the disciples had forgotten to take any bread. ⁶ So when Jesus said to them, 'Take care; be on your guard against the leaven of the Pharisees and Sadducees,' ⁷ they began to say to one another, 'We have brought no bread!' ⁸ Knowing what they were discussing, Jesus said, 'Why are you talking about having no bread? Where is your faith? ⁹ Do you still not understand? Have you forgotten the five loaves for the five thousand, and how many basketfuls you picked up? ¹⁰ Or the seven loaves for the four thousand, and how many basketfuls you picked up? ¹¹ How can you fail to see that I was not talking about bread? Be on your guard, I said, against the leaven of the Pharisees and Sadducees.' ¹² Then they understood: they were to be on their guard, not against baker's leaven, but against the teaching of the Pharisees and Sadducees.

Jesus the Son of God

¹³ WHEN he came to the territory of Caesarea Philippi, Jesus asked his disciples, 'Who do people say that the Son of Man is?' ¹⁴ They answered, 'Some say John the Baptist, others Elijah, others Jeremiah, or one of the prophets.' ¹⁵ 'And you,' he asked, 'who do you say I am?' ¹⁶ Simon Peter answered: 'You are the Messiah, the Son of the living God.' ¹⁷ Then Jesus said: 'Simon son of Jonah, you are favoured indeed! You did not learn that from any human being; it was revealed to you by my heavenly Father. ¹⁸ And I say to you: you are Peter, the Rock; and on this rock I will build my church, and the powers of death shall never conquer it. ¹⁹ I will give you the keys of the kingdom of Heaven; what you forbid on earth shall be forbidden in heaven, and what you allow on earth shall be allowed in heaven.' ²⁰ He then gave his disciples strict orders not to tell anyone that he was the Messiah.

²¹ From that time Jesus began to make it

16:2 **He answered**: *some witnesses here insert* 'In the evening you say, "It will be fine weather, for the sky is red"; ³ and in the morning you say, "It will be stormy today; the sky is red and lowering." You know how to interpret the appearance of the sky; can you not interpret the signs of the times?'   16:18 **powers of death**: *lit.* gates of Hades.

clear to his disciples that he had to go to Jerusalem, and endure great suffering at the hands of the elders, chief priests, and scribes; to be put to death, and to be raised again on the third day. [22] At this Peter took hold of him and began to rebuke him: 'Heaven forbid!' he said. 'No, Lord, this shall never happen to you.' [23] Then Jesus turned and said to Peter, 'Out of my sight, Satan; you are a stumbling block to me. You think as men think, not as God thinks.'

[24] Jesus then said to his disciples, 'Anyone who wishes to be a follower of mine must renounce self; he must take up his cross and follow me. [25-26] Whoever wants to save his life will lose it, but whoever loses his life for my sake will find it. What will anyone gain by winning the whole world at the cost of his life? Or what can he give to buy his life back? [27] For the Son of Man is to come in the glory of his Father with his angels, and then he will give everyone his due reward. [28] Truly I tell you: there are some of those standing here who will not taste death before they have seen the Son of Man coming in his kingdom.'

17 Six days later Jesus took Peter, James, and John the brother of James, and led them up a high mountain by themselves. [2] And in their presence he was transfigured; his face shone like the sun, and his clothes became a brilliant white. [3] And they saw Moses and Elijah appear, talking with him. [4] Then Peter spoke: 'Lord,' he said, 'it is good that we are here. Would you like me to make three shelters here, one for you, one for Moses, and one for Elijah?' [5] While he was still speaking, a bright cloud suddenly cast its shadow over them, and a voice called from the cloud: 'This is my beloved Son, in whom I take delight; listen to him.' [6] At the sound of the voice the disciples fell on their faces in terror. [7] Then Jesus came up to them, touched them, and said, 'Stand up; do not be afraid.' [8] And when they raised their eyes there was no one but Jesus to be seen.

[9] On their way down the mountain, Jesus commanded them not to tell anyone of the vision until the Son of Man had been raised from the dead. [10] The disciples put a question to him: 'Why then do the scribes say that Elijah must come first?' [11] He replied, 'Elijah is to come and set everything right. [12] But I tell you that Elijah has already come, and they failed to recognize him, and did to him as they wanted; in the same way the Son of Man is to suffer at their hands.' [13] Then the disciples understood that he meant John the Baptist.

[14] When they returned to the crowd, a man came up to Jesus, fell on his knees before him, and said, [15] 'Have pity, sir, on my son: he is epileptic and has bad fits; he keeps falling into the fire or into the water. [16] I brought him to your disciples, but they could not cure him.' [17] Jesus answered, 'What an unbelieving and perverse generation! How long shall I be with you? How long must I endure you? Bring him here to me.' [18] Then Jesus spoke sternly to him; the demon left the boy, and from that moment he was cured.

[19] Afterwards the disciples came to Jesus and asked him privately, 'Why could we not drive it out?' [20] He answered, 'Your faith is too small. Truly I tell you: if you have faith no bigger than a mustard seed, you will say to this mountain, "Move from here to there!" and it will move; nothing will be impossible for you.'

[22] They were going about together in Galilee when Jesus said to them, 'The Son of Man is to be handed over into the power of men, [23] and they will kill him; then on the third day he will be raised again.' And they were filled with grief.

[24] On their arrival at Capernaum the collectors of the temple tax came up to Peter and asked, 'Does your master not pay temple tax?' [25] 'He does,' said Peter. When he went indoors Jesus forestalled him by asking, 'Tell me, Simon, from whom do earthly monarchs collect tribute money? From their own people, or from aliens?' [26] 'From aliens,' said Peter. 'Yes,' said Jesus, 'and their own people are exempt. [27] But as we do not want to cause offence, go and cast a line in the lake; take the first fish you catch, open its mouth, and you will find a silver coin; take that and pay the tax for us both.'

17:5 This ... Son: *or* This is my only Son.   17:20 impossible for you: *some witnesses add* [21] But there is no means of driving out this sort but prayer and fasting.

Teaching about the kingdom

18 AT that time the disciples came to Jesus and asked, 'Who is the greatest in the kingdom of Heaven?' [2] He called a child, set him in front of them, [3] and said, 'Truly I tell you: unless you turn round and become like children, you will never enter the kingdom of Heaven. [4] Whoever humbles himself and becomes like this child will be the greatest in the kingdom of Heaven, [5] and whoever receives one such child in my name receives me. [6] But if anyone causes the downfall of one of these little ones who believe in me, it would be better for him to have a millstone hung round his neck and be drowned in the depths of the sea. [7] Alas for the world that any of them should be made to fall! Such things must happen, but alas for the one through whom they happen!

[8] 'If your hand or your foot causes your downfall, cut it off and fling it away; it is better for you to enter into life maimed or lame, than to keep two hands or two feet and be thrown into the eternal fire. [9] And if your eye causes your downfall, tear it out and fling it away; it is better to enter into life with one eye than to keep both eyes and be thrown into the fires of hell.

[10] 'See that you do not despise one of these little ones; I tell you, they have their angels in heaven, who look continually on the face of my heavenly Father.

[12] 'What do you think? Suppose someone has a hundred sheep, and one of them strays, does he not leave the other ninety-nine on the hillside and go in search of the one that strayed? [13] Truly I tell you: if he should find it, he is more delighted over that sheep than over the ninety-nine that did not stray. [14] In the same way, it is not your heavenly Father's will that one of these little ones should be lost.

[15] 'If your brother does wrong, go and take the matter up with him, strictly between yourselves. If he listens to you, you have won your brother over. [16] But if he will not listen, take one or two others with you, so that every case may be settled on the evidence of two or three witnesses. [17] If he refuses to listen to them, report the matter to the congregation; and if he will not listen even to the congregation, then treat him as you would a pagan or a tax-collector.

[18] 'Truly I tell you: whatever you forbid on earth shall be forbidden in heaven, and whatever you allow on earth shall be allowed in heaven.

[19] 'And again I tell you: if two of you agree on earth about any request you have to make, that request will be granted by my heavenly Father. [20] For where two or three meet together in my name, I am there among them.'

[21] Then Peter came to him and asked, 'Lord, how often am I to forgive my brother if he goes on wronging me? As many as seven times?' [22] Jesus replied, 'I do not say seven times but seventy times seven.

[23] 'The kingdom of Heaven, therefore, should be thought of in this way: There was once a king who decided to settle accounts with the men who served him. [24] At the outset there appeared before him a man who owed ten thousand talents. [25] Since he had no means of paying, his master ordered him to be sold, with his wife, his children, and everything he had, to meet the debt. [26] The man fell at his master's feet. "Be patient with me," he implored, "and I will pay you in full"; [27] and the master was so moved with pity that he let the man go and cancelled the debt. [28] But no sooner had the man gone out than he met a fellow-servant who owed him a hundred denarii; he took hold of him, seizing him by the throat, and said, "Pay me what you owe." [29] The man fell at his fellow-servant's feet, and begged him, "Be patient with me, and I will pay you"; [30] but he refused, and had him thrown into jail until he should pay the debt. [31] The other servants were deeply distressed when they saw what had happened, and they went to their master and told him the whole story. [32] Then he sent for the man and said, "You scoundrel! I cancelled the whole of your debt when you appealed to me; [33] ought you not to have shown mercy to your fellow-servant just as I showed mercy to you?" [34] And so angry was the master that he condemned the man to be tortured until he should pay the debt in full. [35] That is how my heavenly Father

18:10 **Father**: *some witnesses add* [11] For the Son of Man came to save the lost.   18:15 **wrong**: *some witnesses add* to you.   18:22 **seventy times seven**: *or* seventy-seven times.   18:24 **talents**: *see p. xi*   18:28 **denarii**: *see p. xi.*

will deal with you, unless you each forgive your brother from your hearts.'

On the road to Jerusalem

19 WHEN Jesus had finished this discourse he left Galilee and came into the region of Judaea on the other side of the Jordan. ² Great crowds followed him, and he healed them there.

³ Some Pharisees came and tested him by asking, 'Is it lawful for a man to divorce his wife for any cause he pleases?' ⁴ He responded by asking, 'Have you never read that in the beginning the Creator made them male and female?' ⁵ and he added, 'That is why a man leaves his father and mother, and is united to his wife, and the two become one flesh. ⁶ It follows that they are no longer two individuals: they are one flesh. Therefore what God has joined together, man must not separate.' ⁷ 'Then why', they objected, 'did Moses lay it down that a man might divorce his wife by a certificate of dismissal?' ⁸ He answered, 'It was because of your stubbornness that Moses gave you permission to divorce your wives; but it was not like that at the beginning. ⁹ I tell you, if a man divorces his wife for any cause other than unchastity, and marries another, he commits adultery.'

¹⁰ The disciples said to him, 'If that is how things stand for a man with a wife, it is better not to marry.' ¹¹ To this he replied, 'That is a course not everyone can accept, but only those for whom God has appointed it. ¹² For while some are incapable of marriage because they were born so, or were made so by men, there are others who have renounced marriage for the sake of the kingdom of Heaven. Let those accept who can.'

¹³ They brought children for him to lay his hands on them with prayer. The disciples rebuked them, ¹⁴ but Jesus said, 'Let the children come to me; do not try to stop them; for the kingdom of Heaven belongs to such as these.' ¹⁵ And he laid his hands on the children, and went on his way.

¹⁶ A man came up and asked him, 'Teacher, what good must I do to gain eternal life?' ¹⁷ 'Good?' said Jesus. 'Why do you ask me about that? One alone is good. But if you wish to enter into life, keep the commandments.' ¹⁸ 'Which commandments?' he asked. Jesus answered, 'Do not murder; do not commit adultery; do not steal; do not give false evidence; ¹⁹ honour your father and mother; and love your neighbour as yourself.' ²⁰ The young man answered, 'I have kept all these. What do I still lack?' ²¹ Jesus said to him, 'If you wish to be perfect, go, sell your possessions, and give to the poor, and you will have treasure in heaven; then come and follow me.' ²² When the young man heard this, he went away with a heavy heart; for he was a man of great wealth.

²³ Jesus said to his disciples, 'Truly I tell you: a rich man will find it hard to enter the kingdom of Heaven. ²⁴ I repeat, it is easier for a camel to pass through the eye of a needle than for a rich man to enter the kingdom of God.' ²⁵ The disciples were astonished when they heard this, and exclaimed, 'Then who can be saved?' ²⁶ Jesus looked at them and said, 'For men this is impossible; but everything is possible for God.'

²⁷ Then Peter said, 'What about us? We have left everything to follow you. How shall we fare?' ²⁸ Jesus replied, 'Truly I tell you: in the world that is to be, when the Son of Man is seated on his glorious throne, you also will sit on twelve thrones, judging the twelve tribes of Israel. ²⁹ And anyone who has left houses, or brothers or sisters, or father or mother, or children, or land for the sake of my name will be repaid many times over, and gain eternal life. ³⁰ But many who are first will be last, and the last first.

20 'The kingdom of Heaven is like this. There was once a landowner who went out early one morning to hire labourers for his vineyard; ² and after agreeing to pay them the usual day's wage he sent them off to work. ³ Three hours later he went out again and saw some more men standing idle in the market-place. ⁴ "Go and join the others in the vineyard," he said, "and I will pay you a fair wage"; so off they went. ⁵ At midday he went out again, and at three in the afternoon, and made the same

19:9 **adultery**: *some witnesses add* And the man who marries a woman so divorced commits adultery.
20:2 **the ... wage**: *lit.* one denarius for the day.

18

arrangement as before. ⁶An hour before sunset he went out and found another group standing there; so he said to them, "Why are you standing here all day doing nothing?" ⁷"Because no one has hired us," they replied; so he told them, "Go and join the others in the vineyard." ⁸When evening fell, the owner of the vineyard said to the overseer, "Call the labourers and give them their pay, beginning with those who came last and ending with the first." ⁹Those who had started work an hour before sunset came forward, and were paid the full day's wage. ¹⁰When it was the turn of the men who had come first, they expected something extra, but were paid the same as the others. ¹¹As they took it, they grumbled at their employer: ¹²"These latecomers did only one hour's work, yet you have treated them on a level with us, who have sweated the whole day long in the blazing sun!" ¹³The owner turned to one of them and said, "My friend, I am not being unfair to you. You agreed on the usual wage for the day, did you not? ¹⁴Take your pay and go home. I choose to give the last man the same as you. ¹⁵Surely I am free to do what I like with my own money? Why be jealous because I am generous?" ¹⁶So the last will be first, and the first last.'

¹⁷JESUS was journeying towards Jerusalem, and on the way he took the Twelve aside and said to them, ¹⁸'We are now going up to Jerusalem, and the Son of Man will be handed over to the chief priests and the scribes; they will condemn him to death ¹⁹and hand him over to the Gentiles, to be mocked and flogged and crucified; and on the third day he will be raised to life again.'

²⁰The mother of Zebedee's sons then approached him with her sons. She bowed before him and begged a favour. ²¹'What is it you want?' asked Jesus. She replied, 'Give orders that in your kingdom these two sons of mine may sit next to you, one at your right hand and the other at your left.' ²²Jesus turned to the brothers and said, 'You do not understand what you are asking. Can you drink the cup that I am to drink?' 'We can,' they

replied. ²³'You shall indeed drink my cup,' he said; 'but to sit on my right or on my left is not for me to grant; that honour is for those to whom it has already been assigned by my Father.'

²⁴When the other ten heard this, they were indignant with the two brothers. ²⁵So Jesus called them to him and said, 'You know that, among the Gentiles, rulers lord it over their subjects, and the great make their authority felt. ²⁶It shall not be so with you; among you, whoever wants to be great must be your servant, ²⁷and whoever wants to be first must be the slave of all—²⁸just as the Son of Man did not come to be served but to serve, and to give his life as a ransom for many.'

²⁹As they were leaving Jericho he was followed by a huge crowd. ³⁰At the roadside sat two blind men. When they heard that Jesus was passing by they shouted, 'Have pity on us, Son of David.' ³¹People told them to be quiet, but they shouted all the more, 'Sir, have pity on us; have pity on us, Son of David.' ³²Jesus stopped and called the men. 'What do you want me to do for you?' ³³he asked. 'Sir,' they answered, 'open our eyes.' ³⁴Jesus was deeply moved, and touched their eyes. At once they recovered their sight and followed him.

Jesus in the temple

21 THEY were approaching Jerusalem, and when they reached Bethphage at the mount of Olives Jesus sent off two disciples, ²and told them: 'Go into the village opposite, where you will at once find a donkey tethered with her foal beside her. Untie them, and bring them to me. ³If anyone says anything to you, answer, "The Master needs them"; and he will let you have them at once.' ⁴This was to fulfil the prophecy which says, ⁵'Tell the daughter of Zion, "Here is your king, who comes to you in gentleness, riding on a donkey, on the foal of a beast of burden."'

⁶The disciples went and did as Jesus had directed, ⁷and brought the donkey and her foal; they laid their cloaks on them and Jesus mounted. ⁸Crowds of people carpeted the road with their cloaks, and some cut branches from the

20:9 the … wage: *lit.* one denarius each.   20:13 You … day: *lit.* You agreed on a denarius.   21:3 The Master … once: *or* "The Master needs them and will send them back without delay."

trees to spread in his path. [9] Then the crowds in front and behind raised the shout: 'Hosanna to the Son of David! Blessed is he who comes in the name of the Lord! Hosanna in the heavens!'

[10] When he entered Jerusalem the whole city went wild with excitement. 'Who is this?' people asked, [11] and the crowds replied, 'This is the prophet Jesus, from Nazareth in Galilee.'

[12] Jesus went into the temple and drove out all who were buying and selling in the temple precincts; he upset the tables of the money-changers and the seats of the dealers in pigeons, [13] and said to them, 'Scripture says, "My house shall be called a house of prayer"; but you are making it a bandits' cave.'

[14] In the temple the blind and the crippled came to him, and he healed them. [15] When the chief priests and scribes saw the wonderful things he did, and heard the boys in the temple shouting, 'Hosanna to the Son of David!' they were indignant [16] and asked him, 'Do you hear what they are saying?' Jesus answered, 'I do. Have you never read the text, "You have made children and babes at the breast sound your praise aloud"?' [17] Then he left them and went out of the city to Bethany, where he spent the night.

[18] Next morning on his way to the city he felt hungry; [19] and seeing a fig tree at the roadside he went up to it, but found nothing on it but leaves. He said to the tree, 'May you never bear fruit again!' and at once the tree withered away. [20] The disciples were amazed at the sight. 'How is it', they asked, 'that the tree has withered so suddenly?' [21] Jesus answered them, 'Truly I tell you: if only you have faith and have no doubts, you will do what has been done to the fig tree. And more than that: you need only say to this mountain, "Be lifted from your place and hurled into the sea," and what you say will be done. [22] Whatever you pray for in faith you will receive.'

[23] He entered the temple, and, as he was teaching, the chief priests and elders of the nation came up to him and asked: 'By what authority are you acting like this? Who gave you this authority?' [24] Jesus replied, 'I also have a question for you. If you answer it, I will tell you by what authority I act. [25] The baptism of John: was it from God, or from men?' This set them arguing among themselves: 'If we say, "From God," he will say, "Then why did you not believe him?" [26] But if we say, "From men," we are afraid of the people's reaction, for they all take John for a prophet.' [27] So they answered, 'We do not know.' And Jesus said: 'Then I will not tell you either by what authority I act.

[28] 'But what do you think about this? There was a man who had two sons. He went to the first, and said, "My son, go and work today in the vineyard." [29] "I will, sir," the boy replied; but he did not go. [30] The father came to the second and said the same. "I will not," he replied; but afterwards he changed his mind and went. [31] Which of the two did what his father wanted?' 'The second,' they replied. Then Jesus said, 'Truly I tell you: tax-collectors and prostitutes are entering the kingdom of God ahead of you. [32] For when John came to show you the right way to live, you did not believe him, but the tax-collectors and prostitutes did; and even when you had seen that, you did not change your minds and believe him.

[33] 'Listen to another parable. There was a landowner who planted a vineyard: he put a wall round it, hewed out a wine-press, and built a watch-tower; then he let it out to vine-growers and went abroad. [34] When the harvest season approached, he sent his servants to the tenants to collect the produce due to him. [35] But they seized his servants, thrashed one, killed another, and stoned a third. [36] Again, he sent other servants, this time a larger number; and they treated them in the same way. [37] Finally he sent his son. "They will respect my son," he said. [38] But when they saw the son the tenants said to one another, "This is the heir; come on, let us kill him, and get his inheritance." [39] So they seized him, flung him out of the vineyard, and killed him. [40] When the owner of the vineyard comes, how do you think he will deal with those tenants?' [41] 'He will bring those bad men to a bad end,' they answered, 'and hand the vineyard over to other tenants, who will give him his share of the crop when the season comes.' [42] Jesus said to them, 'Have you never read in the scriptures: "The stone which the builders rejected has become the main corner-stone. This is the Lord's doing, and it is wonderful in

our eyes"? ⁴³ Therefore, I tell you, the kingdom of God will be taken away from you, and given to a nation that yields the proper fruit.'

⁴⁵ When the chief priests and Pharisees heard his parables, they saw that he was referring to them. ⁴⁶ They wanted to arrest him, but were afraid of the crowds, who looked on Jesus as a prophet.

22 JESUS spoke to them again in parables: ² 'The kingdom of Heaven is like this. There was a king who arranged a banquet for his son's wedding; ³ but when he sent his servants to summon the guests he had invited, they refused to come. ⁴ Then he sent other servants, telling them to say to the guests, "Look! I have prepared this banquet for you. My bullocks and fatted beasts have been slaughtered, and everything is ready. Come to the wedding." ⁵ But they took no notice; one went off to his farm, another to his business, ⁶ and the others seized the servants, attacked them brutally, and killed them. ⁷ The king was furious; he sent troops to put those murderers to death and set their town on fire. ⁸ Then he said to his servants, "The wedding banquet is ready; but the guests I invited did not deserve the honour. ⁹ Go out therefore to the main thoroughfares, and invite everyone you can find to the wedding." ¹⁰ The servants went out into the streets, and collected everyone they could find, good and bad alike. So the hall was packed with guests.

¹¹ 'When the king came in to watch them feasting, he observed a man who was not dressed for a wedding. ¹² "My friend," said the king, "how do you come to be here without wedding clothes?" But he had nothing to say. ¹³ The king then said to his attendants, "Bind him hand and foot; fling him out into the dark, the place of wailing and grinding of teeth." ¹⁴ For many are invited, but few are chosen.'

¹⁵ THEN the Pharisees went away and agreed on a plan to trap him in argument. ¹⁶ They sent some of their followers to him, together with members of Herod's party. 'Teacher,' they said, 'we know you are a sincere man; you teach in all sincerity the way of life that God requires, courting no man's favour, whoever he may be. ¹⁷ Give us your ruling on this: are we or are we not permitted to pay taxes to the Roman emperor?' ¹⁸ Jesus was aware of their malicious intention and said, 'You hypocrites! Why are you trying to catch me out? ¹⁹ Show me the coin used for the tax.' They handed him a silver piece. ²⁰ Jesus asked, 'Whose head is this, and whose inscription?' ²¹ 'Caesar's,' they replied. He said to them, 'Then pay to Caesar what belongs to Caesar, and to God what belongs to God.' ²² Taken aback by this reply, they went away and left him alone.

²³ The same day Sadducees, who maintain that there is no resurrection, came to him and asked: ²⁴ 'Teacher, Moses said that if a man dies childless, his brother shall marry the widow and provide an heir for his brother. ²⁵ We know a case involving seven brothers. The first married and died, and as he was without issue his wife was left to his brother. ²⁶ The same thing happened with the second, and the third, and so on with all seven. ²⁷ Last of all the woman died. ²⁸ At the resurrection, then, whose wife will she be, since they had all married her?' ²⁹ Jesus answered: 'How far you are from the truth! You know neither the scriptures nor the power of God. ³⁰ In the resurrection men and women do not marry; they are like angels in heaven.

³¹ 'As for the resurrection of the dead, have you never read what God himself said to you: ³² "I am the God of Abraham, the God of Isaac, the God of Jacob"? God is not God of the dead but of the living.' ³³ When the crowds heard this, they were amazed at his teaching.

³⁴ Hearing that he had silenced the Sadducees, the Pharisees came together in a body, ³⁵ and one of them tried to catch him out with this question: ³⁶ 'Teacher, which is the greatest commandment in the law?' ³⁷ He answered, '"Love the Lord your God with all your heart, with all your soul, and with all your mind." ³⁸ That is the greatest, the first commandment. ³⁹ The second is like it: "Love your neighbour as yourself." ⁴⁰ Everything in the law and the prophets hangs on these two commandments.'

21:43 **proper fruit:** *some witnesses add* ⁴⁴ Any man who falls on this stone will be dashed to pieces; and if it falls on a man he will be crushed by it.   22:35 **one of them:** *some witnesses add* an expert in the law.

41 Turning to the assembled Pharisees Jesus asked them, 42 'What is your opinion about the Messiah? Whose son is he?' 'The son of David,' they replied. 43 'Then how is it', he asked, 'that David by inspiration calls him "Lord"? For he says, 44 "The Lord said to my Lord, 'Sit at my right hand until I put your enemies under your feet.'" 45 If then David calls him "Lord", how can he be David's son?' 46 Nobody was able to give him an answer; and from that day no one dared to put any more questions to him.

23 JESUS then addressed the crowds and his disciples 2 in these words: 'The scribes and the Pharisees occupy Moses' seat; 3 so be careful to do whatever they tell you. But do not follow their practice; for they say one thing and do another. 4 They make up heavy loads and pile them on the shoulders of others, but will not themselves lift a finger to ease the burden. 5 Whatever they do is done for show. They go about wearing broad phylacteries and with large tassels on their robes; 6 they love to have the place of honour at feasts and the chief seats in synagogues, 7 to be greeted respectfully in the street, and to be addressed as "rabbi".

8 'But you must not be called "rabbi", for you have one Rabbi, and you are all brothers. 9 Do not call any man on earth "father", for you have one Father, and he is in heaven. 10 Nor must you be called "teacher"; you have one Teacher, the Messiah. 11 The greatest among you must be your servant. 12 Whoever exalts himself will be humbled; and whoever humbles himself will be exalted.

13 'Alas for you, scribes and Pharisees, hypocrites! You shut the door of the kingdom of Heaven in people's faces; you do not enter yourselves, and when others try to enter, you stop them.

15 'Alas for you, scribes and Pharisees, hypocrites! You travel over sea and land to win one convert; and when you have succeeded you make him twice as fit for hell as you are yourselves.

16 'Alas for you, blind guides! You say, "If someone swears by the sanctuary, that is nothing; but if he swears by the gold in the sanctuary, he is bound by his oath." 17 Blind fools! Which is the more important, the gold, or the sanctuary which sanctifies the gold? 18 Or you say, "If someone swears by the altar, that is nothing; but if he swears by the offering that lies on the altar, he is bound by his oath." 19 What blindness! Which is the more important, the offering, or the altar which sanctifies it? 20 To swear by the altar, then, is to swear both by the altar and by whatever lies on it; 21 to swear by the sanctuary is to swear both by the sanctuary and by him who dwells there; 22 and to swear by Heaven is to swear both by the throne of God and by him who sits upon it.

23 'Alas for you, scribes and Pharisees, hypocrites! You pay tithes of mint and dill and cummin; but you have overlooked the weightier demands of the law—justice, mercy, and good faith. It is these you should have practised, without neglecting the others. 24 Blind guides! You strain off a midge, yet gulp down a camel!

25 'Alas for you, scribes and Pharisees, hypocrites! You clean the outside of a cup or a dish, and leave the inside full of greed and self-indulgence! 26 Blind Pharisee! Clean the inside of the cup first; then the outside will be clean also.

27 'Alas for you, scribes and Pharisees, hypocrites! You are like tombs covered with whitewash; they look fine on the outside, but inside they are full of dead men's bones and of corruption. 28 So it is with you: outwardly you look like honest men, but inside you are full of hypocrisy and lawlessness.

29 'Alas for you, scribes and Pharisees, hypocrites! You build up the tombs of the prophets and embellish the monuments of the saints, 30 and you say, "If we had been living in the time of our forefathers, we should never have taken part with them in the murder of the prophets." 31 So you acknowledge that you are the sons of those who killed the prophets. 32 Go on then, finish off what your fathers began! 33 Snakes! Vipers' brood! How can you escape being condemned to hell?

34 'I am sending you therefore prophets and wise men and teachers of the law; some of them you will kill and crucify, others you will flog in your synagogues

23:13 you stop them: *some witnesses add* 14 Alas for you, scribes and Pharisees, hypocrites! You eat up the property of widows, while for appearance' sake you say long prayers. You will receive the severest sentence. 23:32 Go on ... began: *or* You too must come up to your fathers' standards.

and hound from city to city. [35] So on you will fall the guilt of all the innocent blood spilt on the ground, from the blood of innocent Abel to the blood of Zechariah son of Berachiah, whom you murdered between the sanctuary and the altar. [36] Truly I tell you: this generation will bear the guilt of it all.

[37] 'O Jerusalem, Jerusalem, city that murders the prophets and stones the messengers sent to her! How often have I longed to gather your children, as a hen gathers her brood under her wings; but you would not let me. [38] Look! There is your temple, forsaken by God and laid waste. [39] I tell you, you will not see me until the time when you say, "Blessed is he who comes in the name of the Lord!"'

Warnings about the end

24 JESUS left the temple and was walking away when his disciples came and pointed to the temple buildings. [2] He answered, 'Yes, look at it all. Truly I tell you: not one stone will be left upon another; they will all be thrown down.'

[3] As he sat on the mount of Olives the disciples came to speak to him privately. 'Tell us,' they said, 'when will this happen? And what will be the sign of your coming and the end of the age?'

[4] Jesus replied: 'Take care that no one misleads you. [5] For many will come claiming my name and saying, "I am the Messiah," and many will be misled by them. [6] The time is coming when you will hear of wars and rumours of wars. See that you are not alarmed. Such things are bound to happen; but the end is still to come. [7] For nation will go to war against nation, kingdom against kingdom; there will be famines and earthquakes in many places. [8] All these things are the first birth-pangs of the new age.

[9] 'You will then be handed over for punishment and execution; all nations will hate you for your allegiance to me. [10] At that time many will fall from their faith; they will betray one another and hate one another. [11] Many false prophets will arise, and will mislead many; [12] and as lawlessness spreads, the love of many will grow cold. [13] But whoever endures to the end will be saved. [14] And this gospel of the kingdom will be proclaimed through-out the earth as a testimony to all nations; and then the end will come.

[15] 'So when you see "the abomination of desolation", of which the prophet Daniel spoke, standing in the holy place (let the reader understand), [16] then those who are in Judaea must take to the hills. [17] If anyone is on the roof, he must not go down to fetch his goods from the house; [18] if anyone is in the field, he must not turn back for his coat. [19] Alas for women with child in those days, and for those who have children at the breast! [20] Pray that it may not be winter or a sabbath when you have to make your escape. [21] It will be a time of great distress, such as there has never been before since the beginning of the world, and will never be again. [22] If that time of troubles were not cut short, no living thing could survive; but for the sake of God's chosen it will be cut short.

[23] 'If anyone says to you then, "Look, here is the Messiah," or "There he is," do not believe it. [24] Impostors will come claiming to be messiahs or prophets, and they will produce great signs and wonders to mislead, if possible, even God's chosen. [25] See, I have forewarned you. [26] If therefore they tell you, "He is there in the wilderness," do not go out; or if they say, "He is there in the inner room," do not believe it. [27] Like a lightning-flash, that lights the sky from east to west, will be the coming of the Son of Man.

[28] 'Wherever the carcass is, there will the vultures gather.

[29] 'As soon as that time of distress has passed,

the sun will be darkened,
the moon will not give her light;
the stars will fall from the sky,
the celestial powers will be shaken.

[30] 'Then will appear in heaven the sign that heralds the Son of Man. All the peoples of the world will make lamentation, and they will see the Son of Man coming on the clouds of heaven with power and great glory. [31] With a trumpet-blast he will send out his angels, and they will gather his chosen from the four winds, from the farthest bounds of heaven on every side.

[32] 'Learn a lesson from the fig tree.

23:38 *Some witnesses omit* and laid waste.

23

When its tender shoots appear and are breaking into leaf, you know that summer is near. [33] In the same way, when you see all these things, you may know that the end is near, at the very door. [34] Truly I tell you: the present generation will live to see it all. [35] Heaven and earth will pass away, but my words will never pass away.

[36] 'Yet about that day and hour no one knows, not even the angels in heaven, not even the Son; no one but the Father alone.

[37] 'As it was in the days of Noah, so will it be when the Son of Man comes. [38] In the days before the flood they ate and drank and married, until the day that Noah went into the ark, [39] and they knew nothing until the flood came and swept them all away. That is how it will be when the Son of Man comes. [40] Then there will be two men in the field: one will be taken, the other left; [41] two women grinding at the mill: one will be taken, the other left.

[42] 'Keep awake, then, for you do not know on what day your Lord will come. [43] Remember, if the householder had known at what time of night the burglar was coming, he would have stayed awake and not let his house be broken into. [44] Hold yourselves ready, therefore, because the Son of Man will come at the time you least expect him.

[45] 'Who is the faithful and wise servant, charged by his master to manage his household and supply them with food at the proper time? [46] Happy that servant if his master comes home and finds him at work! [47] Truly I tell you: he will be put in charge of all his master's property. [48] But if he is a bad servant and says to himself, "The master is a long time coming," [49] and begins to bully the other servants and to eat and drink with his drunken friends, [50] then the master will arrive on a day when the servant does not expect him, at a time he has not been told. [51] He will cut him in pieces and assign him a place among the hypocrites, where there is wailing and grinding of teeth.

25 'When the day comes, the kingdom of Heaven will be like this. There were ten girls, who took their lamps and went out to meet the bridegroom. [2] Five of them were foolish, and five prudent; [3] when the foolish ones took their lamps, they took no oil with them, [4] but the others took flasks of oil with their lamps. [5] As the bridegroom was a long time in coming, they all dozed off to sleep. [6] But at midnight there came a shout: "Here is the bridegroom! Come out to meet him." [7] Then the girls all got up and trimmed their lamps. [8] The foolish said to the prudent, "Our lamps are going out; give us some of your oil." [9] "No," they answered; "there will never be enough for all of us. You had better go to the dealers and buy some for yourselves." [10] While they were away the bridegroom arrived; those who were ready went in with him to the wedding banquet; and the door was shut. [11] Later the others came back. "Sir, sir, open the door for us," they cried. [12] But he answered, "Truly I tell you: I do not know you." [13] Keep awake then, for you know neither the day nor the hour.

[14] 'It is like a man going abroad, who called his servants and entrusted his capital to them; [15] to one he gave five bags of gold, to another two, to another one, each according to his ability. Then he left the country. [16] The man who had the five bags went at once and employed them in business, and made a profit of five bags, [17] and the man who had the two bags made two. [18] But the man who had been given one bag of gold went off and dug a hole in the ground, and hid his master's money. [19] A long time afterwards their master returned, and proceeded to settle accounts with them. [20] The man who had been given the five bags of gold came and produced the five he had made: "Master," he said, "you left five bags with me; look, I have made five more." [21] "Well done, good and faithful servant!" said the master. "You have proved trustworthy in a small matter; I will now put you in charge of something big. Come and share your master's joy." [22] The man with the two bags then came and said, "Master, you left two bags with me; look, I have made two more." [23] "Well done, good and faithful servant!" said the master. "You have proved trustworthy in a small matter; I will now put you in charge of something big. Come and share your master's joy." [24] Then the man who

24:33 **that ... near**: *or* that he is near.

had been given one bag came and said, "Master, I knew you to be a hard man: you reap where you have not sown, you gather where you have not scattered; 25 so I was afraid, and I went and hid your gold in the ground. Here it is—you have what belongs to you." 26 "You worthless, lazy servant!" said the master. "You knew, did you, that I reap where I have not sown, and gather where I have not scattered? 27 Then you ought to have put my money on deposit, and on my return I should have got it back with interest. 28 Take the bag of gold from him, and give it to the one with the ten bags. 29 For everyone who has will be given more, till he has enough and to spare; and everyone who has nothing will forfeit even what he has. 30 As for the useless servant, throw him out into the dark, where there will be wailing and grinding of teeth!"

31 'When the Son of Man comes in his glory and all the angels with him, he will sit on his glorious throne, 32 with all the nations gathered before him. He will separate people into two groups, as a shepherd separates the sheep from the goats; 33 he will place the sheep on his right hand and the goats on his left. 34 Then the king will say to those on his right, "You have my Father's blessing; come, take possession of the kingdom that has been ready for you since the world was made. 35 For when I was hungry, you gave me food; when thirsty, you gave me drink; when I was a stranger, you took me into your home; 36 when naked, you clothed me; when I was ill, you came to my help; when in prison, you visited me." 37 Then the righteous will reply, "Lord, when was it that we saw you hungry and fed you, or thirsty and gave you drink, 38 a stranger and took you home, or naked and clothed you? 39 When did we see you ill or in prison, and come to visit you?" 40 And the king will answer, "Truly I tell you: anything you did for one of my brothers here, however insignificant, you did for me." 41 Then he will say to those on his left, "A curse is on you; go from my sight to the eternal fire that is ready for the devil and his angels. 42 For when I was hungry, you gave me nothing to eat; when thirsty, nothing to drink; 43 when I was a stranger, you did not welcome me; when I was naked, you did not clothe me; when I was ill and in prison, you did not come to my help." 44 And they in their turn will reply, "Lord, when was it that we saw you hungry or thirsty or a stranger or naked or ill or in prison, and did nothing for you?" 45 And he will answer, "Truly I tell you: anything you failed to do for one of these, however insignificant, you failed to do for me." 46 And they will go away to eternal punishment, but the righteous will enter eternal life.'

The trial and crucifixion of Jesus

26 WHEN Jesus had finished all these discourses he said to his disciples, 2 'You know that in two days' time it will be Passover, when the Son of Man will be handed over to be crucified.'

3 Meanwhile the chief priests and the elders of the people met in the house of the high priest, Caiaphas, 4 and discussed a scheme to seize Jesus and put him to death. 5 'It must not be during the festival,' they said, 'or there may be rioting among the people.'

6 JESUS was at Bethany in the house of Simon the leper, 7 when a woman approached him with a bottle of very costly perfume; and she began to pour it over his head as he sat at table. 8 The disciples were indignant when they saw it. 'Why this waste?' they said. 9 'It could have been sold for a large sum and the money given to the poor.' 10 Jesus noticed, and said to them, 'Why make trouble for the woman? It is a fine thing she has done for me. 11 You have the poor among you always, but you will not always have me. 12 When she poured this perfume on my body it was her way of preparing me for burial. 13 Truly I tell you: wherever this gospel is proclaimed throughout the world, what she has done will be told as her memorial.'

14 THEN one of the Twelve, the man called Judas Iscariot, went to the chief priests 15 and said, 'What will you give me to betray him to you?' They weighed him out thirty silver pieces. 16 From that moment he began to look for an opportunity to betray him.

17 On the first day of Unleavened Bread the disciples came and asked Jesus, 'Where would you like us to prepare the Passover for you?' 18 He told them to go to

a certain man in the city with this message: 'The Teacher says, "My appointed time is near; I shall keep the Passover with my disciples at your house."' [19] The disciples did as Jesus directed them and prepared the Passover.

[20] In the evening he sat down with the twelve disciples; [21] and during supper he said, 'Truly I tell you: one of you will betray me.' [22] Greatly distressed at this, they asked him one by one, 'Surely you do not mean me, Lord?' [23] He answered, 'One who has dipped his hand into the bowl with me will betray me. [24] The Son of Man is going the way appointed for him in the scriptures; but alas for that man by whom the Son of Man is betrayed! It would be better for that man if he had never been born.' [25] Then Judas spoke, the one who was to betray him: 'Rabbi, surely you do not mean me?' Jesus replied, 'You have said it.'

[26] During supper Jesus took bread, and having said the blessing he broke it and gave it to the disciples with the words: 'Take this and eat; this is my body.' [27] Then he took a cup, and having offered thanks to God he gave it to them with the words: 'Drink from it, all of you. [28] For this is my blood, the blood of the covenant, shed for many for the forgiveness of sins. [29] I tell you, never again shall I drink from this fruit of the vine until that day when I drink it new with you in the kingdom of my Father.'

[30] After singing the Passover hymn, they went out to the mount of Olives. [31] Then Jesus said to them, 'Tonight you will all lose faith because of me; for it is written: "I will strike the shepherd and the sheep of his flock will be scattered." [32] But after I am raised, I shall go ahead of you into Galilee.' [33] Peter replied, 'Everyone else may lose faith because of you, but I never will.' [34] Jesus said to him, 'Truly I tell you: tonight before the cock crows you will disown me three times.' [35] Peter said, 'Even if I have to die with you, I will never disown you.' And all the disciples said the same.

[36] JESUS then came with his disciples to a place called Gethsemane, and he said to them, 'Sit here while I go over there to pray.' [37] He took with him Peter and the two sons of Zebedee. Distress and anguish overwhelmed him, [38] and he said to them,

'My heart is ready to break with grief. Stop here, and stay awake with me.' [39] Then he went on a little farther, threw himself down, and prayed, 'My Father, if it is possible, let this cup pass me by. Yet not my will but yours.'

[40] He came back to the disciples and found them asleep; and he said to Peter, 'What! Could none of you stay awake with me for one hour? [41] Stay awake, and pray that you may be spared the test. The spirit is willing, but the flesh is weak.'

[42] He went away a second time and prayed: 'My Father, if it is not possible for this cup to pass me by without my drinking it, your will be done.' [43] He came again and found them asleep, for their eyes were heavy. [44] So he left them and went away again and prayed a third time, using the same words as before.

[45] Then he came to the disciples and said to them, 'Still asleep? Still resting? The hour has come! The Son of Man is betrayed into the hands of sinners. [46] Up, let us go! The traitor is upon us.'

[47] He was still speaking when Judas, one of the Twelve, appeared, and with him a great crowd armed with swords and cudgels, sent by the chief priests and the elders of the nation. [48] The traitor had given them this sign: 'The one I kiss is your man; seize him.' [49] Going straight up to Jesus, he said, 'Hail, Rabbi!' and kissed him. [50] Jesus replied, 'Friend, do what you are here to do.' Then they came forward, seized Jesus, and held him fast.

[51] At that moment one of those with Jesus reached for his sword and drew it, and struck the high priest's servant, cutting off his ear. [52] But Jesus said to him, 'Put up your sword. All who take the sword die by the sword. [53] Do you suppose that I cannot appeal for help to my Father, and at once be sent more than twelve legions of angels? [54] But how then would the scriptures be fulfilled, which say that this must happen?'

[55] Then Jesus spoke to the crowd: 'Do you take me for a bandit, that you have come out with swords and cudgels to arrest me? Day after day I sat teaching in the temple, and you did not lay hands on me. [56] But this has all happened to fulfil what the prophets wrote.'

Then the disciples all deserted him and ran away.

[57] JESUS was led away under arrest to the house of Caiaphas the high priest, where the scribes and elders were assembled. [58] Peter followed him at a distance till he came to the high priest's courtyard; he went in and sat down among the attendants, to see how it would all end. [59] The chief priests and the whole Council tried to find some allegation against Jesus that would warrant a death sentence; [60] but they failed to find one, though many came forward with false evidence. Finally two men [61] alleged that he had said, 'I can pull down the temple of God, and rebuild it in three days.' [62] At this the high priest rose and said to him, 'Have you no answer to the accusations that these witnesses bring against you?' [63] But Jesus remained silent. The high priest then said, 'By the living God I charge you to tell us: are you the Messiah, the Son of God?' [64] Jesus replied, 'The words are yours. But I tell you this: from now on you will see the Son of Man seated at the right hand of the Almighty and coming on the clouds of heaven.' [65] At these words the high priest tore his robes and exclaimed, 'This is blasphemy! Do we need further witnesses? You have just heard the blasphemy. [66] What is your verdict?' 'He is guilty,' they answered; 'he should die.' [67] Then they spat in his face and struck him with their fists; some said, as they beat him, [68] 'Now, Messiah, if you are a prophet, tell us who hit you.'

[69] Meanwhile Peter was sitting outside in the courtyard when a servant-girl accosted him; 'You were with Jesus the Galilean,' she said. [70] Peter denied it in front of them all. 'I do not know what you are talking about,' he said. [71] He then went out to the gateway, where another girl, seeing him, said to the people there, 'He was with Jesus of Nazareth.' [72] Once again he denied it, saying with an oath, 'I do not know the man.' [73] Shortly afterwards the bystanders came up and said to Peter, 'You must be one of them; your accent gives you away!' [74] At this he started to curse and declared with an oath: 'I do not know the man.' At that moment a cock crowed; [75] and Peter remembered how Jesus had said, 'Before the cock crows you will disown me three times.' And he went outside, and wept bitterly.

27 WHEN morning came, the chief priests and the elders of the nation all met together to plan the death of Jesus. [2] They bound him and led him away, to hand him over to Pilate, the Roman governor.

[3] When Judas the traitor saw that Jesus had been condemned, he was seized with remorse, and returned the thirty silver pieces to the chief priests and elders. [4] 'I have sinned,' he said; 'I have brought an innocent man to his death.' But they said, 'What is that to us? It is your concern.' [5] So he threw the money down in the temple and left; he went away and hanged himself.

[6] The chief priests took up the money, but they said, 'This cannot be put into the temple fund; it is blood-money.' [7] So after conferring they used it to buy the Potter's Field, as a burial-place for foreigners. [8] This explains the name Blood Acre, by which that field has been known ever since; [9] and in this way fulfilment was given to the saying of the prophet Jeremiah: 'They took the thirty silver pieces, the price set on a man's head (for that was his price among the Israelites), [10] and gave the money for the potter's field, as the Lord directed me.'

[11] Jesus was now brought before the governor; 'Are you the king of the Jews?' the governor asked him. 'The words are yours,' said Jesus; [12] and when the chief priests and elders brought charges against him he made no reply. [13] Then Pilate said to him, 'Do you not hear all this evidence they are bringing against you?' [14] but to the governor's great astonishment he refused to answer a single word.

[15] At the festival season it was customary for the governor to release one prisoner chosen by the people. [16] There was then in custody a man of some notoriety, called Jesus Barabbas. [17] When the people assembled Pilate said to them, 'Which would you like me to release to you—Jesus Barabbas, or Jesus called Messiah?' [18] For he knew it was out of malice that Jesus had been handed over to him. [19] While Pilate was sitting in court a

26:64 **The words are yours:** *or* It is as you say.   27:9 **They took:** *or* I took.   27:11 **The words are yours:** *or* It is as you say.   27:16, 17 **Jesus Barabbas:** *many witnesses omit* Jesus *in both verses.*

message came to him from his wife: 'Have nothing to do with that innocent man; I was much troubled on his account in my dreams last night.'

20 Meanwhile the chief priests and elders had persuaded the crowd to ask for the release of Barabbas and to have Jesus put to death. 21 So when the governor asked, 'Which of the two would you like me to release to you?' they said, 'Barabbas.' 22 'Then what am I to do with Jesus called Messiah?' asked Pilate; and with one voice they answered, 'Crucify him!' 23 'Why, what harm has he done?' asked Pilate; but they shouted all the louder, 'Crucify him!'

24 When Pilate saw that he was getting nowhere, and that there was danger of a riot, he took water and washed his hands in full view of the crowd. 'My hands are clean of this man's blood,' he declared. 'See to that yourselves.' 25 With one voice the people cried, 'His blood be on us and on our children.' 26 He then released Barabbas to them; but he had Jesus flogged, and then handed him over to be crucified.

27 THEN the soldiers of the governor took Jesus into his residence, the Praetorium, where they collected the whole company round him. 28 They stripped him and dressed him in a scarlet cloak; 29 and plaiting a crown of thorns they placed it on his head, and a stick in his right hand. Falling on their knees before him they jeered at him: 'Hail, king of the Jews!' 30 They spat on him, and used the stick to beat him about the head. 31 When they had finished mocking him, they stripped off the cloak and dressed him in his own clothes.

Then they led him away to be crucified. 32 On their way out they met a man from Cyrene, Simon by name, and pressed him into service to carry his cross.

33 Coming to a place called Golgotha (which means 'Place of a Skull'), 34 they offered him a drink of wine mixed with gall; but after tasting it he would not drink.

35 When they had crucified him they shared out his clothes by casting lots, 36 and then sat down there to keep watch. 37 Above his head was placed the inscription giving the charge against him: 'This is Jesus, the king of the Jews.' 38 Two bandits were crucified with him, one on his right and the other on his left.

39 The passers-by wagged their heads and jeered at him, 40 crying, 'So you are the man who was to pull down the temple and rebuild it in three days! If you really are the Son of God, save yourself and come down from the cross.' 41 The chief priests with the scribes and elders joined in the mockery: 42 'He saved others,' they said, 'but he cannot save himself. King of Israel, indeed! Let him come down now from the cross, and then we shall believe him. 43 He trusted in God, did he? Let God rescue him, if he wants him—for he said he was God's Son.' 44 Even the bandits who were crucified with him taunted him in the same way.

45 From midday a darkness fell over the whole land, which lasted until three in the afternoon; 46 and about three Jesus cried aloud, 'Eli, Eli, lema sabachthani?' which means, 'My God, my God, why have you forsaken me?' 47 Hearing this, some of the bystanders said, 'He is calling Elijah.' 48 One of them ran at once and fetched a sponge, which he soaked in sour wine and held to his lips on the end of a stick. 49 But the others said, 'Let us see if Elijah will come to save him.'

50 Jesus again cried aloud and breathed his last. 51 At that moment the curtain of the temple was torn in two from top to bottom. The earth shook, rocks split, 52 and graves opened; many of God's saints were raised from sleep, 53 and coming out of their graves after his resurrection entered the Holy City, where many saw them. 54 And when the centurion and his men who were keeping watch over Jesus saw the earthquake and all that was happening, they were filled with awe and said, 'This must have been a son of God.'

55 A NUMBER of women were also present, watching from a distance; they had followed Jesus from Galilee and looked after him. 56 Among them were Mary of Magdala, Mary the mother of James and Joseph, and the mother of the sons of Zebedee.

57 When evening fell, a wealthy man from Arimathaea, Joseph by name, who had himself become a disciple of Jesus,

27: 54 **a son of God**: *or* the Son of God.

[58] approached Pilate and asked for the body of Jesus; and Pilate gave orders that he should have it. [59] Joseph took the body, wrapped it in a clean linen sheet, [60] and laid it in his own unused tomb, which he had cut out of the rock. He then rolled a large stone against the entrance, and went away. [61] Mary of Magdala was there, and the other Mary, sitting opposite the grave.

[62] Next day, the morning after the day of preparation, the chief priests and the Pharisees came in a body to Pilate. [63] 'Your excellency,' they said, 'we recall how that impostor said while he was still alive, "I am to be raised again after three days." [64] We request you to give orders for the grave to be made secure until the third day. Otherwise his disciples may come and steal the body, and then tell the people that he has been raised from the dead; and the final deception will be worse than the first.' [65] 'You may have a guard,' said Pilate; 'go and make the grave as secure as you can.' [66] So they went and made it secure by sealing the stone and setting a guard.

The resurrection

28 ABOUT daybreak on the first day of the week, when the sabbath was over, Mary of Magdala and the other Mary came to look at the grave. [2] Suddenly there was a violent earthquake; an angel of the Lord descended from heaven and came and rolled away the stone, and sat down on it. [3] His face shone like lightning; his garments were white as snow. [4] At the sight of him the guards shook with fear and fell to the ground as though dead.

[5] The angel spoke to the women: 'You', he said, 'have nothing to fear. I know you are looking for Jesus who was crucified.

[6] He is not here; he has been raised, as he said he would be. Come and see the place where he was laid, [7] and then go quickly and tell his disciples: "He has been raised from the dead and is going ahead of you into Galilee; there you will see him." That is what I came to tell you.'

[8] They hurried away from the tomb in awe and great joy, and ran to bring the news to the disciples. [9] Suddenly Jesus was there in their path, greeting them. They came up and clasped his feet, kneeling before him. [10] 'Do not be afraid,' Jesus said to them. 'Go and take word to my brothers that they are to leave for Galilee. They will see me there.'

[11] While the women were on their way, some of the guard went into the city and reported to the chief priests everything that had happened. [12] After meeting and conferring with the elders, the chief priests offered the soldiers a substantial bribe [13] and told them to say, 'His disciples came during the night and stole the body while we were asleep.' [14] They added, 'If this should reach the governor's ears, we will put matters right with him and see you do not suffer.' [15] So they took the money and did as they were told. Their story became widely known, and is current in Jewish circles to this day.

[16] The eleven disciples made their way to Galilee, to the mountain where Jesus had told them to meet him. [17] When they saw him, they knelt in worship, though some were doubtful. [18] Jesus came near and said to them: 'Full authority in heaven and on earth has been committed to me. [19] Go therefore to all nations and make them my disciples; baptize them in the name of the Father and the Son and the Holy Spirit, [20] and teach them to observe all that I have commanded you. I will be with you always, to the end of time.'

THE GOSPEL ACCORDING TO
MARK

John the Baptist and Jesus

1 THE beginning of the gospel of Jesus Christ the Son of God.

² IN the prophet Isaiah it stands written:

I am sending my herald ahead of you;
    he will prepare your way.
³ A voice cries in the wilderness,
    'Prepare the way for the Lord;
    clear a straight path for him.'

⁴ John the Baptist appeared in the wilderness proclaiming a baptism in token of repentance, for the forgiveness of sins; ⁵ and everyone flocked to him from the countryside of Judaea and the city of Jerusalem, and they were baptized by him in the river Jordan, confessing their sins. ⁶ John was dressed in a rough coat of camel's hair, with a leather belt round his waist, and he fed on locusts and wild honey. ⁷ He proclaimed: 'After me comes one mightier than I am, whose sandals I am not worthy to stoop down and unfasten. ⁸ I have baptized you with water; he will baptize you with the Holy Spirit.'

⁹ It was at this time that Jesus came from Nazareth in Galilee and was baptized in the Jordan by John. ¹⁰ As he was coming up out of the water, he saw the heavens break open and the Spirit descend on him, like a dove. ¹¹ And a voice came from heaven: 'You are my beloved Son; in you I take delight.'

¹² At once the Spirit drove him out into the wilderness, ¹³ and there he remained for forty days tempted by Satan. He was among the wild beasts; and angels attended to his needs.

Proclaiming the kingdom

¹⁴ AFTER John had been arrested, Jesus came into Galilee proclaiming the gospel of God: ¹⁵ 'The time has arrived; the kingdom of God is upon you. Repent, and believe the gospel.'

¹⁶ Jesus was walking by the sea of Galilee when he saw Simon and his brother Andrew at work with casting-nets in the lake; for they were fishermen. ¹⁷ Jesus said to them, 'Come, follow me, and I will make you fishers of men.' ¹⁸ At once they left their nets and followed him.

¹⁹ Going a little farther, he saw James son of Zebedee and his brother John in a boat mending their nets. ²⁰ At once he called them; and they left their father Zebedee in the boat with the hired men and followed him.

²¹ They came to Capernaum, and on the sabbath he went to the synagogue and began to teach. ²² The people were amazed at his teaching, for, unlike the scribes, he taught with a note of authority. ²³ Now there was a man in their synagogue possessed by an unclean spirit. He shrieked at him: ²⁴ 'What do you want with us, Jesus of Nazareth? Have you come to destroy us? I know who you are—the Holy One of God.' ²⁵ Jesus rebuked him: 'Be silent', he said, 'and come out of him.' ²⁶ The unclean spirit threw the man into convulsions and with a loud cry left him. ²⁷ They were all amazed and began to ask one another, 'What is this? A new kind of teaching! He speaks with authority. When he gives orders, even the unclean spirits obey.' ²⁸ His fame soon spread far and wide throughout Galilee.

²⁹ On leaving the synagogue, they went straight to the house of Simon and Andrew; and James and John went with them. ³⁰ Simon's mother-in-law was in bed with a fever. As soon as they told him about her, ³¹ Jesus went and took hold of her hand, and raised her to her feet. The fever left her, and she attended to their needs.

³² That evening after sunset they brought to him all who were ill or possessed by demons; ³³ and the whole town was there, gathered at the door. ³⁴ He healed many who suffered from various diseases, and drove out many

1:1 *Some witnesses omit* the Son of God.   1:11 **You are ... Son:** *or* You are my only Son.   1:24 **Have you:** *or* You have.

demons. He would not let the demons speak, because they knew who he was. [35] Very early next morning he got up and went out. He went away to a remote spot and remained there in prayer. [36] But Simon and his companions went in search of him, [37] and when they found him, they said, 'Everybody is looking for you.' [38] He answered, 'Let us move on to the neighbouring towns, so that I can proclaim my message there as well, for that is what I came out to do.' [39] So he went through the whole of Galilee, preaching in their synagogues and driving out demons.

[40] On one occasion he was approached by a leper, who knelt before him and begged for help. 'If only you will,' said the man, 'you can make me clean.' [41] Jesus was moved to anger; he stretched out his hand, touched him, and said, 'I will; be clean.' [42] The leprosy left him immediately, and he was clean. [43] Then he dismissed him with this stern warning: [44] 'See that you tell nobody, but go and show yourself to the priest, and make the offering laid down by Moses for your cleansing; that will certify the cure.' [45] But the man went away and made the whole story public, spreading it far and wide, until Jesus could no longer show himself in any town. He stayed outside in remote places; yet people kept coming to him from all quarters.

2 After some days he returned to Capernaum, and news went round that he was at home; [2] and such a crowd collected that there was no room for them even in the space outside the door. While he was proclaiming the message to them, [3] a man was brought who was paralysed. Four men were carrying him, [4] but because of the crowd they could not get him near. So they made an opening in the roof over the place where Jesus was, and when they had broken through they lowered the bed on which the paralysed man was lying. [5] When he saw their faith, Jesus said to the man, 'My son, your sins are forgiven.'

[6] Now there were some scribes sitting there, thinking to themselves, [7] 'How can the fellow talk like that? It is blasphemy! Who but God can forgive sins?' [8] Jesus knew at once what they were thinking,

and said to them, 'Why do you harbour such thoughts? [9] Is it easier to say to this paralysed man, "Your sins are forgiven," or to say, "Stand up, take your bed, and walk"? [10] But to convince you that the Son of Man has authority on earth to forgive sins'—he turned to the paralysed man— [11] 'I say to you, stand up, take your bed, and go home.' [12] And he got up, and at once took his bed and went out in full view of them all, so that they were astounded and praised God. 'Never before', they said, 'have we seen anything like this.'

[13] Once more he went out to the lakeside. All the crowd came to him there, and he taught them. [14] As he went along, he saw Levi son of Alphaeus at his seat in the custom-house, and said to him, 'Follow me'; and he rose and followed him.

[15] When Jesus was having a meal in his house, many tax-collectors and sinners were seated with him and his disciples, for there were many of them among his followers. [16] Some scribes who were Pharisees, observing the company in which he was eating, said to his disciples, 'Why does he eat with tax-collectors and sinners?' [17] Hearing this, Jesus said to them, 'It is not the healthy who need a doctor, but the sick; I did not come to call the virtuous, but sinners.'

[18] Once, when John's disciples and the Pharisees were keeping a fast, some people came and asked him, 'Why is it that John's disciples and the disciples of the Pharisees are fasting, but yours are not?' [19] Jesus replied, 'Can you expect the bridegroom's friends to fast while the bridegroom is with them? As long as he is with them, there can be no fasting. [20] But the time will come when the bridegroom will be taken away from them; that will be the time for them to fast.

[21] 'No one sews a patch of unshrunk cloth on to an old garment; if he does, the patch tears away from it, the new from the old, and leaves a bigger hole. [22] No one puts new wine into old wineskins; if he does, the wine will burst the skins, and then wine and skins are both lost. New wine goes into fresh skins.'

[23] One sabbath he was going through the cornfields; and as they went along his disciples began to pluck ears of corn.

1:41 **to anger:** *many witnesses read* with pity.

24 The Pharisees said to him, 'Why are they doing what is forbidden on the sabbath?' 25 He answered, 'Have you never read what David did when he and his men were hungry and had nothing to eat? 26 He went into the house of God, in the time of Abiathar the high priest, and ate the sacred bread, though no one but a priest is allowed to eat it, and even gave it to his men.'

27 He also said to them, 'The sabbath was made for man, not man for the sabbath: 28 so the Son of Man is lord even of the sabbath.'

3 On another occasion when he went to synagogue, there was a man in the congregation who had a withered arm; 2 and they were watching to see whether Jesus would heal him on the sabbath, so that they could bring a charge against him. 3 He said to the man with the withered arm, 'Come and stand out here.' 4 Then he turned to them: 'Is it permitted to do good or to do evil on the sabbath, to save life or to kill?' They had nothing to say; 5 and, looking round at them with anger and sorrow at their obstinate stupidity, he said to the man, 'Stretch out your arm.' He stretched it out and his arm was restored. 6 Then the Pharisees, on leaving the synagogue, at once began plotting with the men of Herod's party to bring about Jesus's death.

7 JESUS went away to the lakeside with his disciples. Great numbers from Galilee, Judaea 8 and Jerusalem, Idumaea and Transjordan, and the neighbourhood of Tyre and Sidon, heard what he was doing and came to him. 9 So he told his disciples to have a boat ready for him, to save him from being crushed by the crowd. 10 For he healed so many that the sick all came crowding round to touch him. 11 The unclean spirits too, when they saw him, would fall at his feet and cry aloud, 'You are the Son of God'; 12 but he insisted that they should not make him known. 13 Then he went up into the hill-country and summoned the men he wanted; and they came and joined him. 14 He appointed twelve to be his companions, and to be sent out to proclaim the gospel, 15 with authority to drive out demons. 16 The Twelve he appointed were: Simon, whom he named Peter; 17 the sons of Zebedee, James and his brother John,

whom he named Boanerges, Sons of Thunder; 18 Andrew, Philip, Bartholomew, Matthew, Thomas, James son of Alphaeus, Thaddaeus, Simon the Zealot, 19 and Judas Iscariot, the man who betrayed him.

He entered a house, 20 and once more such a crowd collected round them that they had no chance even to eat. 21 When his family heard about it they set out to take charge of him. 'He is out of his mind,' they said.

22 The scribes, too, who had come down from Jerusalem, said, 'He is possessed by Beelzebul,' and, 'He drives out demons by the prince of demons.' 23 So he summoned them, and spoke to them in parables: 'How can Satan drive out Satan? 24 If a kingdom is divided against itself, that kingdom cannot stand; 25 if a household is divided against itself, that house cannot stand; 26 and if Satan is divided and rebels against himself, he cannot stand, and that is the end of him.

27 'On the other hand, no one can break into a strong man's house and make off with his goods unless he has first tied up the strong man; then he can ransack the house.

28 'Truly I tell you: every sin and every slander can be forgiven; 29 but whoever slanders the Holy Spirit can never be forgiven; he is guilty of an eternal sin.' 30 He said this because they had declared that he was possessed by an unclean spirit.

31 Then his mother and his brothers arrived; they stayed outside and sent in a message asking him to come out to them. 32 A crowd was sitting round him when word was brought that his mother and brothers were outside asking for him. 33 'Who are my mother and my brothers?' he replied. 34 And looking round at those who were sitting in the circle about him he said, 'Here are my mother and my brothers. 35 Whoever does the will of God is my brother and sister and mother.'

Parables

4 ON another occasion he began to teach by the lakeside. The crowd that gathered round him was so large that he had to get into a boat on the lake and sit there, with the whole crowd on the beach right down to the water's edge. 2 And he taught them many things by parables.

As he taught he said:

3 'Listen! A sower went out to sow. 4 And it happened that as he sowed, some of the seed fell along the footpath; and the birds came and ate it up. 5 Some fell on rocky ground, where it had little soil, and it sprouted quickly because it had no depth of earth; 6 but when the sun rose it was scorched, and as it had no root it withered away. 7 Some fell among thistles; and the thistles grew up and choked the corn, and it produced no crop. 8 And some of the seed fell into good soil, where it came up and grew, and produced a crop; and the yield was thirtyfold, sixtyfold, even a hundredfold.' 9 He added, 'If you have ears to hear, then hear.'

10 When Jesus was alone with the Twelve and his other companions they questioned him about the parables. 11 He answered, 'To you the secret of the kingdom of God has been given; but to those who are outside, everything comes by way of parables, 12 so that (as scripture says) they may look and look, but see nothing; they may listen and listen, but understand nothing; otherwise they might turn to God and be forgiven.'

13 He went on: 'Do you not understand this parable? How then are you to understand any parable? 14 The sower sows the word. 15 With some the seed falls along the footpath; no sooner have they heard it than Satan comes and carries off the word which has been sown in them. 16 With others the seed falls on rocky ground; as soon as they hear the word, they accept it with joy, 17 but it strikes no root in them; they have no staying-power, and when there is trouble or persecution on account of the word, they quickly lose faith. 18 With others again the seed falls among thistles; they hear the word, 19 but worldly cares and the false glamour of wealth and evil desires of all kinds come in and choke the word, and it proves barren. 20 But there are some with whom the seed is sown on good soil; they accept the word when they hear it, and they bear fruit thirtyfold, sixtyfold, or a hundredfold.'

21 He said to them, 'Is a lamp brought in to be put under the measuring bowl or under the bed? No, it is put on the lampstand. 22 Nothing is hidden except to be disclosed, and nothing concealed except to be brought into the open. 23 If you have ears to hear, then hear.'

24 He also said to them, 'Take note of what you hear; the measure you give is the measure you will receive, with something more besides. 25 For those who have will be given more, and those who have not will forfeit even what they have.'

26 He said, 'The kingdom of God is like this. A man scatters seed on the ground; 27 he goes to bed at night and gets up in the morning, and meanwhile the seed sprouts and grows—how, he does not know. 28 The ground produces a crop by itself, first the blade, then the ear, then full grain in the ear; 29 but as soon as the crop is ripe, he starts reaping, because harvest time has come.'

30 He said, 'How shall we picture the kingdom of God, or what parable shall we use to describe it? 31 It is like a mustard seed; when sown in the ground it is smaller than any other seed, 32 but once sown, it springs up and grows taller than any other plant, and forms branches so large that birds can roost in its shade.'

33 With many such parables he used to give them his message, so far as they were able to receive it. 34 He never spoke to them except in parables; but privately to his disciples he explained everything.

Miracles

35 THAT day, in the evening, he said to them, 'Let us cross over to the other side of the lake.' 36 So they left the crowd and took him with them in the boat in which he had been sitting; and some other boats went with him. 37 A fierce squall blew up and the waves broke over the boat until it was all but swamped. 38 Now he was in the stern asleep on a cushion; they roused him and said, 'Teacher, we are sinking! Do you not care?' 39 He awoke and rebuked the wind, and said to the sea, 'Silence! Be still!' The wind dropped and there was a dead calm. 40 He said to them, 'Why are you such cowards? Have you no faith even now?' 41 They were awestruck and said to one another, 'Who can this be? Even the wind and the sea obey him.'

5 So they came to the country of the Gerasenes on the other side of the lake. 2 As he stepped ashore, a man possessed by an unclean spirit came up to him from among the tombs 3 where he had made his home. Nobody could control him any longer; even chains were useless, 4 for he had often been fettered

and chained up, but had snapped his chains and broken the fetters. No one was strong enough to master him. ⁵ Unceasingly, night and day, he would cry aloud among the tombs and on the hillsides and gash himself with stones. ⁶ When he saw Jesus in the distance, he ran up and flung himself down before him, ⁷ shouting at the top of his voice, 'What do you want with me, Jesus, son of the Most High God? In God's name do not torment me.' ⁸ For Jesus was already saying to him, 'Out, unclean spirit, come out of the man!' ⁹ Jesus asked him, 'What is your name?' 'My name is Legion,' he said, 'there are so many of us.' ¹⁰ And he implored Jesus not to send them out of the district. ¹¹ There was a large herd of pigs nearby, feeding on the hillside, ¹² and the spirits begged him, 'Send us among the pigs; let us go into them.' ¹³ He gave them leave; and the unclean spirits came out and went into the pigs; and the herd, of about two thousand, rushed over the edge into the lake and were drowned.

¹⁴ The men in charge of them took to their heels and carried the news to the town and countryside; and the people came out to see what had happened. ¹⁵ When they came to Jesus and saw the madman who had been possessed by the legion of demons, sitting there clothed and in his right mind, they were afraid. ¹⁶ When eyewitnesses told them what had happened to the madman and what had become of the pigs, ¹⁷ they begged Jesus to leave the district. ¹⁸ As he was getting into the boat, the man who had been possessed begged to go with him. ¹⁹ But Jesus would not let him. 'Go home to your own people,' he said, 'and tell them what the Lord in his mercy has done for you.' ²⁰ The man went off and made known throughout the Decapolis what Jesus had done for him; and everyone was amazed.

²¹ As soon as Jesus had returned by boat to the other shore, a large crowd gathered round him. While he was by the lakeside, ²² there came a synagogue president named Jairus; and when he saw him, he threw himself down at his feet ²³ and pleaded with him. 'My little daughter is at death's door,' he said. 'I beg you to come and lay your hands on her so that her life may be saved.' ²⁴ So Jesus went with him, accompanied by a great crowd which pressed round him.

²⁵ Among them was a woman who had suffered from haemorrhages for twelve years; ²⁶ and in spite of long treatment by many doctors, on which she had spent all she had, she had become worse rather than better. ²⁷ She had heard about Jesus, and came up behind him in the crowd and touched his cloak; ²⁸ for she said, 'If I touch even his clothes, I shall be healed.' ²⁹ And there and then the flow of blood dried up and she knew in herself that she was cured of her affliction. ³⁰ Aware at once that power had gone out of him, Jesus turned round in the crowd and asked, 'Who touched my clothes?' ³¹ His disciples said to him, 'You see the crowd pressing round you and yet you ask, "Who touched me?"' ³² But he kept looking around to see who had done it. ³³ Then the woman, trembling with fear because she knew what had happened to her, came and fell at his feet and told him the whole truth. ³⁴ He said to her, 'Daughter, your faith has healed you. Go in peace, free from your affliction.'

³⁵ While he was still speaking, a message came from the president's house, 'Your daughter has died; why trouble the teacher any more?' ³⁶ But Jesus, overhearing the message as it was delivered, said to the president of the synagogue, 'Do not be afraid; simply have faith.' ³⁷ Then he allowed no one to accompany him except Peter and James and James's brother John. ³⁸ They came to the president's house, where he found a great commotion, with loud crying and wailing. ³⁹ So he went in and said to them, 'Why this crying and commotion? The child is not dead: she is asleep'; ⁴⁰ and they laughed at him. After turning everyone out, he took the child's father and mother and his own companions into the room where the child was. ⁴¹ Taking hold of her hand, he said to her, 'Talitha cum,' which means, 'Get up, my child.' ⁴² Immediately the girl got up and walked about—she was twelve years old. They were overcome with amazement; ⁴³ but he gave them strict instructions not to let anyone know about it, and told them to give her something to eat.

6 From there he went to his home town accompanied by his disciples. ² When the sabbath came he began to teach in the synagogue; and the large congregation who heard him asked in amazement,

'Where does he get it from? What is this wisdom he has been given? How does he perform such miracles? ³ Is he not the carpenter, the son of Mary, the brother of James and Joses and Judas and Simon? Are not his sisters here with us?' So they turned against him. ⁴ Jesus said to them, 'A prophet never lacks honour except in his home town, among his relations and his own family.' ⁵ And he was unable to do any miracle there, except that he put his hands on a few sick people and healed them; ⁶ and he was astonished at their want of faith.

Death of John the Baptist

AS HE went round the villages teaching,⁷ he summoned the Twelve and sent them out two by two with authority over unclean spirits. ⁸ He instructed them to take nothing for the journey except a stick—no bread, no pack, no money in their belts. ⁹ They might wear sandals, but not a second coat. ¹⁰ 'When you enter a house,' he told them, 'stay there until you leave that district. ¹¹ At any place where they will not receive you or listen to you, shake the dust off your feet as you leave, as a solemn warning.' ¹² So they set out and proclaimed the need for repentance; ¹³ they drove out many demons, and anointed many sick people with oil and cured them.

¹⁴ Now King Herod heard of Jesus, for his fame had spread, and people were saying, 'John the Baptist has been raised from the dead, and that is why these miraculous powers are at work in him.' ¹⁵ Others said, 'It is Elijah.' Others again, 'He is a prophet like one of the prophets of old.' ¹⁶ But when Herod heard of it, he said, 'This is John, whom I beheaded, raised from the dead.'

¹⁷ It was this Herod who had sent men to arrest John and put him in prison at the instance of his brother Philip's wife, Herodias, whom he had married. ¹⁸ John had told him, 'You have no right to take your brother's wife.' ¹⁹ Herodias nursed a grudge against John and would willingly have killed him, but she could not, ²⁰ for Herod went in awe of him, knowing him to be a good and holy man; so he gave him his protection. He liked to listen to

him, although what he heard left him greatly disturbed.

²¹ Herodias found her opportunity when Herod on his birthday gave a banquet to his chief officials and commanders and the leading men of Galilee. ²² Her daughter came in and danced, and so delighted Herod and his guests that the king said to the girl, 'Ask me for anything you like and I will give it to you.' ²³ He even said on oath: 'Whatever you ask I will give you, up to half my kingdom.' ²⁴ She went out and said to her mother, 'What shall I ask for?' She replied, 'The head of John the Baptist.' ²⁵ The girl hurried straight back to the king with her request: 'I want you to give me, here and now, on a dish, the head of John the Baptist.' ²⁶ The king was greatly distressed, yet because of his oath and his guests he could not bring himself to refuse her. ²⁷ He sent a soldier of the guard with orders to bring John's head; and the soldier went to the prison and beheaded him; ²⁸ then he brought the head on a dish, and gave it to the girl; and she gave it to her mother.

²⁹ When John's disciples heard the news, they came and took his body away and laid it in a tomb.

Miracles of feeding and their significance

³⁰ THE apostles rejoined Jesus and reported to him all that they had done and taught. ³¹ He said to them, 'Come with me, by yourselves, to some remote place and rest a little.' With many coming and going they had no time even to eat. ³² So they set off by boat privately for a remote place. ³³ But many saw them leave and recognized them, and people from all the towns hurried round on foot and arrived there first. ³⁴ When he came ashore and saw a large crowd, his heart went out to them, because they were like sheep without a shepherd; and he began to teach them many things. ³⁵ It was already getting late, and his disciples came to him and said, 'This is a remote place and it is already very late; ³⁶ send the people off to the farms and villages round about, to buy themselves something to eat.' ³⁷ 'Give them something to eat yourselves,' he answered. They replied, 'Are we to go and

6:3 the carpenter ... Mary: *some witnesses read* the son of the carpenter and Mary.   6:14 and ... saying: *some witnesses read* and he said.

spend two hundred denarii to provide them with food?' [38] 'How many loaves have you?' he asked. 'Go and see.' They found out and told him, 'Five, and two fish.' [39] He ordered them to make the people sit down in groups on the green grass, [40] and they sat down in rows, in companies of fifty and a hundred. [41] Then, taking the five loaves and the two fish, he looked up to heaven, said the blessing, broke the loaves, and gave them to the disciples to distribute. He also divided the two fish among them. [42] They all ate and were satisfied; [43] and twelve baskets were filled with what was left of the bread and the fish. [44] Those who ate the loaves numbered five thousand men.

[45] As soon as they had finished, he made his disciples embark and cross to Bethsaida ahead of him, while he himself dismissed the crowd. [46] After taking leave of them, he went up the hill to pray. [47] It was now late and the boat was already well out on the water, while he was alone on the land. [48] Somewhere between three and six in the morning, seeing them labouring at the oars against a head wind, he came towards them, walking on the lake. He was going to pass by them; [49] but when they saw him walking on the lake, they thought it was a ghost and cried out; [50] for they all saw him and were terrified. But at once he spoke to them: 'Take heart! It is I; do not be afraid.' [51] Then he climbed into the boat with them, and the wind dropped. At this they were utterly astounded, [52] for they had not understood the incident of the loaves; their minds were closed.

[53] So they completed the crossing and landed at Gennesaret, where they made fast. [54] When they came ashore, he was recognized at once; [55] and the people scoured the whole countryside and brought the sick on their beds to any place where he was reported to be. [56] Wherever he went, to village or town or farm, they laid the sick in the market-place and begged him to let them simply touch the edge of his cloak; and all who touched him were healed.

7 A GROUP of Pharisees, with some scribes who had come from Jerusalem, met him [2] and noticed that some of his disciples were eating their food with defiled hands—in other words, without washing them. [3] (For Pharisees and Jews in general never eat without washing their hands, in obedience to ancient tradition; [4] and on coming from the market-place they never eat without first washing. And there are many other points on which they maintain traditional rules, for example in the washing of cups and jugs and copper bowls.) [5] These Pharisees and scribes questioned Jesus: 'Why do your disciples not conform to the ancient tradition, but eat their food with defiled hands?' [6] He answered, 'How right Isaiah was when he prophesied about you hypocrites in these words: "This people pays me lip-service, but their heart is far from me: [7] they worship me in vain, for they teach as doctrines the commandments of men." [8] You neglect the commandment of God, in order to maintain the tradition of men.'

[9] He said to them, 'How clever you are at setting aside the commandment of God in order to maintain your tradition! [10] Moses said, "Honour your father and your mother," and again, "Whoever curses his father or mother shall be put to death." [11] But you hold that if someone says to his father or mother, "Anything I have which might have been used for your benefit is Corban,"' (that is, set apart for God) [12] 'he is no longer allowed to do anything for his father or mother. [13] In this way by your tradition, handed down among you, you make God's word null and void. And you do many other things just like that.'

[14] On another occasion he called the people and said to them, 'Listen to me, all of you, and understand this: [15] nothing that goes into a person from outside can defile him; no, it is the things that come out of a person that defile him.'

[17] When he had left the people and gone indoors, his disciples questioned him about the parable. [18] He said to them, 'Are you as dull as the rest? Do you not see that nothing that goes into a person from outside can defile him, [19] because it does not go into the heart but into the stomach, and so goes out into the drain?' By saying this he declared all foods clean.

6:37 denarii: *see p. xi.*   6:56 edge: *or tassel.*   7:3 washing their hands: *some witnesses add* with the fist; *others add* frequently; *or* thoroughly.   7:9 maintain: *some witnesses read* establish.   7:15 that defile him: *some witnesses here add* [16] If you have ears to hear, then hear.

20 He went on, 'It is what comes out of a person that defiles him. 21 From inside, from the human heart, come evil thoughts, acts of fornication, theft, murder, 22 adultery, greed, and malice; fraud, indecency, envy, slander, arrogance, and folly; 23 all these evil things come from within, and they are what defile a person.'

24 He moved on from there into the territory of Tyre. He found a house to stay in, and would have liked to remain unrecognized, but that was impossible. 25 Almost at once a woman whose small daughter was possessed by an unclean spirit heard of him and came and fell at his feet. 26 (The woman was a Gentile, a Phoenician of Syria by nationality.) She begged him to drive the demon out of her daughter. 27 He said to her, 'Let the children be satisfied first; it is not right to take the children's bread and throw it to the dogs.' 28 'Sir,' she replied, 'even the dogs under the table eat the children's scraps.' 29 He said to her, 'For saying that, go, and you will find the demon has left your daughter.' 30 And when she returned home, she found the child lying in bed; the demon had left her.

31 On his journey back from Tyrian territory he went by way of Sidon to the sea of Galilee, well within the territory of the Decapolis. 32 They brought to him a man who was deaf and had an impediment in his speech, and begged Jesus to lay his hand on him. 33 He took him aside, away from the crowd; then he put his fingers in the man's ears, and touched his tongue with spittle. 34 Looking up to heaven, he sighed, and said to him, 'Ephphatha,' which means 'Be opened.' 35 With that his hearing was restored, and at the same time the impediment was removed and he spoke clearly. 36 Jesus forbade them to tell anyone; but the more he forbade them, the more they spread it abroad. 37 Their astonishment knew no bounds: 'All that he does, he does well,' they said; 'he even makes the deaf hear and the dumb speak.'

8 THERE was another occasion about this time when a huge crowd had collected, and, as they had no food, Jesus called his disciples and said to them, 2 'My heart goes out to these people; they have been with me now for three days and have nothing to eat. 3 If I send them home hungry, they will faint on the way, and some of them have a long way to go.' 4 His disciples answered, 'How can anyone provide these people with bread in this remote place?' 5 'How many loaves have you?' he asked; and they answered, 'Seven.' 6 So he ordered the people to sit down on the ground; then he took the seven loaves, and after giving thanks to God he broke the bread and gave it to his disciples to distribute; and they distributed it to the people. 7 They had also a few small fish, which he blessed and ordered them to distribute. 8 They ate and were satisfied, and seven baskets were filled with what was left over. 9 The people numbered about four thousand. Then he dismissed them, 10 and at once got into the boat with his disciples and went to the district of Dalmanutha.

11 Then the Pharisees came out and began to argue with him. To test him they asked him for a sign from heaven. 12 He sighed deeply and said, 'Why does this generation ask for a sign? Truly I tell you: no sign shall be given to this generation.' 13 With that he left them, re-embarked, and made for the other shore.

14 Now they had forgotten to take bread with them, and had only one loaf in the boat. 15 He began to warn them: 'Beware,' he said, 'be on your guard against the leaven of the Pharisees and the leaven of Herod.' 16 So they began to talk among themselves about having no bread. 17 Knowing this, he said to them, 'Why are you talking about having no bread? Have you no inkling yet? Do you still not understand? Are your minds closed? 18 You have eyes: can you not see? You have ears: can you not hear? Have you forgotten? 19 When I broke the five loaves among five thousand, how many basketfuls of pieces did you pick up?' 'Twelve,' they said. 20 'And how many when I broke the seven loaves among four thousand?' 'Seven,' they answered. 21 He said to them, 'Do you still not understand?'

22 They arrived at Bethsaida. There the people brought a blind man to Jesus and begged him to touch him. 23 He took the blind man by the hand and led him out of

8:10 **Dalmanutha**: *some witnesses read* Magedan; *others read* Magdala.

the village. Then he spat on his eyes, laid his hands upon him, and asked whether he could see anything. [24] The man's sight began to come back, and he said, 'I see people—they look like trees, but they are walking about.' [25] Jesus laid his hands on his eyes again; he looked hard, and now he was cured and could see everything clearly. [26] Then Jesus sent him home, saying, 'Do not even go into the village.'

The cross foreshadowed

[27] JESUS and his disciples set out for the villages of Caesarea Philippi, and on the way he asked his disciples, 'Who do people say I am?' [28] They answered, 'Some say John the Baptist, others Elijah, others one of the prophets.' [29] 'And you,' he asked, 'who do you say I am?' Peter replied: 'You are the Messiah.' [30] Then he gave them strict orders not to tell anyone about him; [31] and he began to teach them that the Son of Man had to endure great suffering, and to be rejected by the elders, chief priests, and scribes; to be put to death, and to rise again three days afterwards. [32] He spoke about it plainly. At this Peter took hold of him and began to rebuke him. [33] But Jesus, turning and looking at his disciples, rebuked Peter. 'Out of my sight, Satan!' he said. 'You think as men think, not as God thinks.'

[34] Then he called the people to him, as well as his disciples, and said to them, 'Anyone who wants to be a follower of mine must renounce self; he must take up his cross and follow me. [35] Whoever wants to save his life will lose it, but whoever loses his life for my sake and for the gospel's will save it. [36] What does anyone gain by winning the whole world at the cost of his life? [37] What can he give to buy his life back? [38] If anyone is ashamed of me and my words in this wicked and godless age, the Son of Man will be ashamed of him, when he comes in the glory of his Father with the holy angels.'

9 He said to them, 'Truly I tell you: there are some of those standing here who will not taste death before they have seen the kingdom of God come with power.'

[2] Six days later Jesus took Peter, James,

and John with him and led them up a high mountain by themselves. And in their presence he was transfigured; [3] his clothes became dazzling white, with a whiteness no bleacher on earth could equal. [4] They saw Elijah appear and Moses with him, talking with Jesus. [5] Then Peter spoke: 'Rabbi,' he said, 'it is good that we are here! Shall we make three shelters, one for you, one for Moses, and one for Elijah?' [6] For he did not know what to say; they were so terrified. [7] Then a cloud appeared, casting its shadow over them, and out of the cloud came a voice: 'This is my beloved Son; listen to him.' [8] And suddenly, when they looked around, only Jesus was with them; there was no longer anyone else to be seen.

[9] On their way down the mountain, he instructed them not to tell anyone what they had seen until the Son of Man had risen from the dead. [10] They seized upon those words, and discussed among themselves what this 'rising from the dead' could mean. [11] And they put a question to him: 'Why do the scribes say that Elijah must come first?' [12] He replied, 'Elijah does come first to set everything right. How is it, then, that the scriptures say of the Son of Man that he is to endure great suffering and be treated with contempt? [13] However, I tell you, Elijah has already come and they have done to him what they wanted, as the scriptures say of him.'

[14] When they came back to the disciples they saw a large crowd surrounding them and scribes arguing with them. [15] As soon as they saw Jesus the whole crowd were overcome with awe and ran forward to welcome him. [16] He asked them, 'What is this argument about?' [17] A man in the crowd spoke up: 'Teacher, I brought my son for you to cure. He is possessed by a spirit that makes him dumb. [18] Whenever it attacks him, it flings him to the ground, and he foams at the mouth, grinds his teeth, and goes rigid. I asked your disciples to drive it out, but they could not.' [19] Jesus answered: 'What an unbelieving generation! How long shall I be with you? How long must I endure you? Bring him to me.' [20] So they brought the boy to him; and as soon as the spirit saw him it threw the boy into convulsions, and he fell on

8:26 Do ... village: *some witnesses read* Do not tell anyone in the village. 8:38 me and my words: *some witnesses read* me and mine. Father ... angels: *some witnesses read* Father and of the holy angels. 9:7 This ... Son: *or* This is my only Son.

the ground and rolled about foaming at the mouth. [21] Jesus asked his father, 'How long has he been like this?' 'From childhood,' he replied; [22] 'it has often tried to destroy him by throwing him into the fire or into water. But if it is at all possible for you, take pity on us and help us.' [23] 'If it is possible!' said Jesus. 'Everything is possible to one who believes.' [24] At once the boy's father cried: 'I believe; help my unbelief.' [25] When Jesus saw that the crowd was closing in on them, he spoke sternly to the unclean spirit. 'Deaf and dumb spirit,' he said, 'I command you, come out of him and never go back!' [26] It shrieked aloud and threw the boy into repeated convulsions, and then came out, leaving him looking like a corpse; in fact, many said, 'He is dead.' [27] But Jesus took hold of his hand and raised him to his feet, and he stood up.

[28] Then Jesus went indoors, and his disciples asked him privately, 'Why could we not drive it out?' [29] He said, 'This kind cannot be driven out except by prayer.'

Learning what discipleship means

[30] THEY left that district and made their way through Galilee. Jesus did not want anyone to know, [31] because he was teaching his disciples, and telling them, 'The Son of Man is now to be handed over into the power of men, and they will kill him; and three days after being killed he will rise again.' [32] But they did not understand what he said, and were afraid to ask.

[33] So they came to Capernaum; and when he had gone indoors, he asked them, 'What were you arguing about on the way?' [34] They were silent, because on the way they had been discussing which of them was the greatest. [35] So he sat down, called the Twelve, and said to them, 'If anyone wants to be first, he must make himself last of all and servant of all.' [36] Then he took a child, set him in front of them, and put his arm round him. [37] 'Whoever receives a child like this in my name,' he said, 'receives me; and whoever receives me, receives not me but the One who sent me.'

[38] John said to him, 'Teacher, we saw someone driving out demons in your name, and as he was not one of us, we tried to stop him.' [39] Jesus said, 'Do not stop him, for no one who performs a miracle in my name will be able the next moment to speak evil of me. [40] He who is not against us is on our side. [41] Truly I tell you: whoever gives you a cup of water to drink because you are followers of the Messiah will certainly not go unrewarded.

[42] 'If anyone causes the downfall of one of these little ones who believe, it would be better for him to be thrown into the sea with a millstone round his neck. [43] If your hand causes your downfall, cut it off; it is better for you to enter into life maimed than to keep both hands and go to hell, to the unquenchable fire. [45] If your foot causes your downfall, cut it off; it is better to enter into life crippled than to keep both your feet and be thrown into hell. [47] And if your eye causes your downfall, tear it out; it is better to enter into the kingdom of God with one eye than to keep both eyes and be thrown into hell, [48] where the devouring worm never dies and the fire is never quenched.

[49] 'Everyone will be salted with fire.

[50] 'Salt is good; but if the salt loses its saltness, how will you season it?

'You must have salt within yourselves, and be at peace with one another.'

10

ON leaving there he came into the regions of Judaea and Transjordan. Once again crowds gathered round him, and he taught them as was his practice. [2] He was asked: 'Is it lawful for a man to divorce his wife?' This question was put to test him. [3] He responded by asking, 'What did Moses command you?' [4] They answered, 'Moses permitted a man to divorce his wife by a certificate of dismissal.' [5] Jesus said to them, 'It was because of your stubbornness that he made this rule for you. [6] But in the beginning, at the creation, "God made them male and female." [7] "That is why a man leaves his father and mother, and is united to his wife, [8] and the two become one flesh." It follows that they are no longer two individuals: they are one flesh.

9:29 **by prayer:** *some witnesses add* and fasting.   9:43 **unquenchable fire:** *some witnesses add* [44] where the devouring worm never dies and the fire is never quenched.   9:45 **into hell:** *some witnesses add* [46] where the devouring worm never dies and the fire is never quenched.   10:2 **He was asked:** *some witnesses read* Pharisees approached and asked him.

⁹ Therefore what God has joined together, man must not separate.'

¹⁰ When they were indoors again, the disciples questioned him about this. ¹¹ He said to them, 'Whoever divorces his wife and remarries commits adultery against her; ¹² so too, if she divorces her husband and remarries, she commits adultery.'

¹³ They brought children for him to touch. The disciples rebuked them, ¹⁴ but when Jesus saw it he was indignant, and said to them, 'Let the children come to me; do not try to stop them; for the kingdom of God belongs to such as these. ¹⁵ Truly I tell you: whoever does not accept the kingdom of God like a child will never enter it.' ¹⁶ And he put his arms round them, laid his hands on them, and blessed them.

¹⁷ As he was starting out on a journey, a stranger ran up, and, kneeling before him, asked, 'Good Teacher, what must I do to win eternal life?' ¹⁸ Jesus said to him, 'Why do you call me good? No one is good except God alone. ¹⁹ You know the commandments: "Do not murder; do not commit adultery; do not steal; do not give false evidence; do not defraud; honour your father and mother."' ²⁰ 'But Teacher,' he replied, 'I have kept all these since I was a boy.' ²¹ As Jesus looked at him, his heart warmed to him. 'One thing you lack,' he said. 'Go, sell everything you have, and give to the poor, and you will have treasure in heaven; then come and follow me.' ²² At these words his face fell and he went away with a heavy heart; for he was a man of great wealth.

²³ Jesus looked round at his disciples and said to them, 'How hard it will be for the wealthy to enter the kingdom of God!' ²⁴ They were amazed that he should say this, but Jesus insisted, 'Children, how hard it is to enter the kingdom of God! ²⁵ It is easier for a camel to pass through the eye of a needle than for a rich man to enter the kingdom of God.' ²⁶ They were more astonished than ever, and said to one another, 'Then who can be saved?' ²⁷ Jesus looked at them and said, 'For men it is impossible, but not for God; everything is possible for God.'

²⁸ 'What about us?' said Peter. 'We have left everything to follow you.' ²⁹ Jesus said, 'Truly I tell you: there is no one who has given up home, brothers or sisters, mother, father or children, or land, for my sake and for the gospel, ³⁰ who will not receive in this age a hundred times as much—houses, brothers and sisters, mothers and children, and land—and persecutions besides; and in the age to come eternal life. ³¹ But many who are first will be last, and the last first.'

³² THEY were on the road going up to Jerusalem, and Jesus was leading the way; and the disciples were filled with awe, while those who followed behind were afraid. Once again he took the Twelve aside and began to tell them what was to happen to him. ³³ 'We are now going up to Jerusalem,' he said, 'and the Son of Man will be handed over to the chief priests and the scribes; they will condemn him to death and hand him over to the Gentiles. ³⁴ He will be mocked and spat upon, and flogged and killed; and three days afterwards, he will rise again.'

³⁵ James and John, the sons of Zebedee, approached him and said, 'Teacher, we should like you to do us a favour.' ³⁶ 'What is it you want me to do for you?' he asked. ³⁷ They answered, 'Allow us to sit with you in your glory, one at your right hand and the other at your left.' ³⁸ Jesus said to them, 'You do not understand what you are asking. Can you drink the cup that I drink, or be baptized with the baptism I am baptized with?' ³⁹ 'We can,' they answered. Jesus said, 'The cup that I drink you shall drink, and the baptism I am baptized with shall be your baptism; ⁴⁰ but to sit on my right or on my left is not for me to grant; that honour is for those to whom it has already been assigned.'

⁴¹ When the other ten heard this, they were indignant with James and John. ⁴² Jesus called them to him and said, 'You know that among the Gentiles the recognized rulers lord it over their subjects, and the great make their authority felt. ⁴³ It shall not be so with you; among you, whoever wants to be great must be your servant, ⁴⁴ and whoever wants to be first must be the slave of all. ⁴⁵ For the Son of Man did not come to be served but to serve, and to give his life as a ransom for many.'

10:24 **how hard it is:** *some witnesses add* for those who trust in riches.

40

⁴⁶ They came to Jericho; and as he was leaving the town, with his disciples and a large crowd, Bartimaeus (that is, son of Timaeus), a blind beggar, was seated at the roadside. ⁴⁷ Hearing that it was Jesus of Nazareth, he began to shout, 'Son of David, Jesus, have pity on me!' ⁴⁸ Many of the people told him to hold his tongue; but he shouted all the more, 'Son of David, have pity on me.' ⁴⁹ Jesus stopped and said, 'Call him'; so they called the blind man: 'Take heart,' they said. 'Get up; he is calling you.' ⁵⁰ At that he threw off his cloak, jumped to his feet, and came to Jesus. ⁵¹ Jesus said to him, 'What do you want me to do for you?' 'Rabbi,' the blind man answered, 'I want my sight back.' ⁵² Jesus said to him, 'Go; your faith has healed you.' And at once he recovered his sight and followed him on the road.

The challenge to Jerusalem

11 THEY were now approaching Jerusalem, and when they reached Bethphage and Bethany, close by the mount of Olives, he sent off two of his disciples. ² 'Go into the village opposite,' he told them, 'and just as you enter you will find tethered there a colt which no one has yet ridden. Untie it and bring it here. ³ If anyone asks why you are doing this, say, "The Master needs it, and will send it back here without delay."' ⁴ So they went off, and found the colt outside in the street, tethered beside a door. As they were untying it, ⁵ some of the by-standers asked, 'What are you doing, untying that colt?' ⁶ They answered as Jesus had told them, and were then allowed to take it. ⁷ So they brought the colt to Jesus, and when they had spread their cloaks on it he mounted it. ⁸ Many people carpeted the road with their cloaks, while others spread greenery which they had cut in the fields; ⁹ and those in front and those behind shouted, 'Hosanna! Blessed is he who comes in the name of the Lord! ¹⁰ Blessed is the kingdom of our father David which is coming! Hosanna in the heavens!'
¹¹ He entered Jerusalem and went into the temple. He looked round at everything; then, as it was already late, he went out to Bethany with the Twelve.

¹² On the following day, as they left Bethany, he felt hungry, ¹³ and, noticing in the distance a fig tree in leaf, he went to see if he could find anything on it. But when he reached it he found nothing but leaves; for it was not the season for figs. ¹⁴ He said to the tree, 'May no one ever again eat fruit from you!' And his disciples were listening.
¹⁵ So they came to Jerusalem, and he went into the temple and began to drive out those who bought and sold there. He upset the tables of the money-changers and the seats of the dealers in pigeons; ¹⁶ and he would not allow anyone to carry goods through the temple court. ¹⁷ Then he began to teach them, and said, 'Does not scripture say, "My house shall be called a house of prayer for all nations"? But you have made it a robbers' cave.'
¹⁸ The chief priests and the scribes heard of this and looked for a way to bring about his death; for they were afraid of him, because the whole crowd was spellbound by his teaching. ¹⁹ And when evening came they went out of the city.
²⁰ Early next morning, as they passed by, they saw that the fig tree had withered from the roots up; ²¹ and Peter, recalling what had happened, said to him, 'Rabbi, look, the fig tree which you cursed has withered.' ²² Jesus answered them, 'Have faith in God. ²³ Truly I tell you: if anyone says to this mountain, "Be lifted from your place and hurled into the sea," and has no inward doubts, but believes that what he says will happen, it will be done for him. ²⁴ I tell you, then, whatever you ask for in prayer, believe that you have received it and it will be yours.
²⁵ 'And when you stand praying, if you have a grievance against anyone, forgive him, so that your Father in heaven may forgive you the wrongs you have done.'

²⁷ THEY came once more to Jerusalem. And as he was walking in the temple court the chief priests, scribes, and elders came to him ²⁸ and said, 'By what authority are you acting like this? Who gave you authority to act in this way?' ²⁹ Jesus said to them, 'I also have a question for you, and if you give me an answer, I will tell you by what authority I act. ³⁰ The

---

11:3 **The Master:** *or* Its owner.   11:25 **wrongs you have done:** *some witnesses add* ²⁶ But if you do not forgive others, then the wrongs you have done will not be forgiven by your Father in heaven.

baptism of John: was it from God, or from men? Answer me.' [31] This set them arguing among themselves: 'What shall we say? If we say, "From God," he will say, "Then why did you not believe him?" [32] Shall we say, "From men"?'— but they were afraid of the people, for all held that John was in fact a prophet. [33] So they answered, 'We do not know.' And Jesus said to them, 'Then I will not tell you either by what authority I act.'

12 He went on to speak to them in parables: 'A man planted a vineyard and put a wall round it, hewed out a winepress, and built a watch-tower; then he let it out to vine-growers and went abroad. [2] When the season came, he sent a servant to the tenants to collect from them his share of the produce. [3] But they seized him, thrashed him, and sent him away empty-handed. [4] Again, he sent them another servant, whom they beat about the head and treated outrageously, [5] and then another, whom they killed. He sent many others and they thrashed some and killed the rest. [6] He had now no one left to send except his beloved son, and in the end he sent him. "They will respect my son," he said; [7] but the tenants said to one another, "This is the heir; come on, let us kill him, and the inheritance will be ours." [8] So they seized him and killed him, and flung his body out of the vineyard. [9] What will the owner of the vineyard do? He will come and put the tenants to death and give the vineyard to others. [10] 'Have you never read this text: "The stone which the builders rejected has become the main corner-stone. [11] This is the Lord's doing, and it is wonderful in our eyes"?'

[12] They saw that the parable was aimed at them and wanted to arrest him; but they were afraid of the people, so they left him alone and went away.

[13] A NUMBER of Pharisees and men of Herod's party were sent to trap him with a question. [14] They came and said, 'Teacher, we know you are a sincere man and court no one's favour, whoever he may be; you teach in all sincerity the way of life that God requires. Are we or are we not permitted to pay taxes to the Roman emperor? [15] Shall we pay or not?' He saw through their duplicity, and said, 'Why are you trying to catch me out? Fetch me a silver piece, and let me look at it.' [16] They brought one, and he asked them, 'Whose head is this, and whose inscription?' 'Caesar's,' they replied. [17] Then Jesus said, 'Pay Caesar what belongs to Caesar, and God what belongs to God.' His reply left them completely taken aback.

[18] Next Sadducees, who maintain that there is no resurrection, came to him and asked: [19] 'Teacher, Moses laid it down for us that if there are brothers, and one dies leaving a wife but no child, then the next should marry the widow and provide an heir for his brother. [20] Now there were seven brothers. The first took a wife and died without issue. [21] Then the second married her, and he too died without issue; so did the third; [22] none of the seven left any issue. Finally the woman died. [23] At the resurrection, when they rise from the dead, whose wife will she be, since all seven had married her?' [24] Jesus said to them, 'How far you are from the truth! You know neither the scriptures nor the power of God. [25] When they rise from the dead, men and women do not marry; they are like angels in heaven.

[26] 'As for the resurrection of the dead, have you not read in the book of Moses, in the story of the burning bush, how God spoke to him and said, "I am the God of Abraham, the God of Isaac, the God of Jacob"? [27] He is not God of the dead but of the living. You are very far from the truth.'

[28] Then one of the scribes, who had been listening to these discussions and had observed how well Jesus answered, came forward and asked him, 'Which is the first of all the commandments?' [29] He answered, 'The first is, "Hear, O Israel: the Lord our God is the one Lord, [30] and you must love the Lord your God with all your heart, with all your soul, with all your mind, and with all your strength." [31] The second is this: "You must love your neighbour as yourself." No other commandment is greater than these.' [32] The scribe said to him, 'Well said, Teacher. You are right in saying that God is one and beside him there is no other. [33] And to love him with all your heart, all your

---

12:6 **his beloved son**: *or* his only son.

understanding, and all your strength, and to love your neighbour as yourself—that means far more than any whole-offerings and sacrifices.' [34] When Jesus saw how thoughtfully he answered, he said to him, 'You are not far from the kingdom of God.' After that nobody dared put any more questions to him.

[35] As he taught in the temple, Jesus went on to say, 'How can the scribes maintain that the Messiah is a son of David? [36] It was David himself who said, when inspired by the Holy Spirit, "The Lord said to my Lord, 'Sit at my right hand until I put your enemies under your feet.'" [37] David himself calls him "Lord"; how can he be David's son?'

There was a large crowd listening eagerly. [38] As he taught them, he said, 'Beware of the scribes, who love to walk up and down in long robes and be greeted respectfully in the street, [39] to have the chief seats in synagogues and places of honour at feasts. [40] Those who eat up the property of widows, while for appearance' sake they say long prayers, will receive a sentence all the more severe.'

[41] As he was sitting opposite the temple treasury, he watched the people dropping their money into the chest. Many rich people were putting in large amounts. [42] Presently there came a poor widow who dropped in two tiny coins, together worth a penny. [43] He called his disciples to him and said, 'Truly I tell you: this poor widow has given more than all those giving to the treasury; [44] for the others who have given had more than enough, but she, with less than enough, has given all that she had to live on.'

Warnings about the end

13 As HE was leaving the temple, one of his disciples exclaimed, 'Look, Teacher, what huge stones! What fine buildings!' [2] Jesus said to him, 'You see these great buildings? Not one stone will be left upon another; they will all be thrown down.'

[3] As he sat on the mount of Olives opposite the temple he was questioned privately by Peter, James, John, and Andrew. [4] 'Tell us,' they said, 'when will this happen? What will be the sign that all these things are about to be fulfilled?'

[5] Jesus began: 'Be on your guard; let no one mislead you. [6] Many will come claim-

ing my name, and saying, "I am he"; and many will be misled by them. [7] When you hear of wars and rumours of wars, do not be alarmed. Such things are bound to happen; but the end is still to come. [8] For nation will go to war against nation, kingdom against kingdom; there will be earthquakes in many places; there will be famines. These are the first birth-pangs of the new age.

[9] 'As for you, be on your guard. You will be handed over to the courts; you will be beaten in synagogues; you will be summoned to appear before governors and kings on my account to testify in their presence. [10] Before the end the gospel must be proclaimed to all nations. [11] So when you are arrested and put on trial do not worry beforehand about what you will say, but when the time comes say whatever is given you to say, for it is not you who will be speaking, but the Holy Spirit. [12] Brother will hand over brother to death, and a father his child; children will turn against their parents and send them to their death. [13] Everyone will hate you for your allegiance to me, but whoever endures to the end will be saved.

[14] 'But when you see "the abomination of desolation" usurping a place which is not his (let the reader understand), then those who are in Judaea must take to the hills. [15] If anyone is on the roof, he must not go down into the house to fetch anything out; [16] if anyone is in the field, he must not turn back for his coat. [17] Alas for women with child in those days, and for those who have children at the breast! [18] Pray that it may not come in winter. [19] For those days will bring distress such as there has never been before since the beginning of the world which God created, and will never be again. [20] If the Lord had not cut short that time of troubles, no living thing could survive. However, for the sake of his own, whom he has chosen, he has cut short the time.

[21] 'If anyone says to you then, "Look, here is the Messiah," or, "Look, there he is," do not believe it. [22] Impostors will come claiming to be messiahs or prophets, and they will produce signs and wonders to mislead, if possible, God's chosen. [23] Be on your guard; I have forewarned you of it all.

²⁴ 'But in those days, after that distress,

the sun will be darkened,
the moon will not give her light;
²⁵ the stars will come falling from the
sky,
the celestial powers will be shaken.

²⁶ 'Then they will see the Son of Man coming in the clouds with great power and glory, ²⁷ and he will send out the angels and gather his chosen from the four winds, from the farthest bounds of earth to the farthest bounds of heaven. ²⁸ 'Learn a lesson from the fig tree. When its tender shoots appear and are breaking into leaf, you know that summer is near. ²⁹ In the same way, when you see all this happening, you may know that the end is near, at the very door. ³⁰ Truly I tell you: the present generation will live to see it all. ³¹ Heaven and earth will pass away, but my words will never pass away.

³² 'Yet about that day or hour no one knows, not even the angels in heaven, not even the Son; no one but the Father. ³³ 'Be on your guard, keep watch. You do not know when the moment is coming. ³⁴ It is like a man away from home: he has left his house and put his servants in charge, each with his own work to do, and he has ordered the door-keeper to stay awake. ³⁵ Keep awake, then, for you do not know when the master of the house will come. Evening or midnight, cock-crow or early dawn — ³⁶ if he comes suddenly, do not let him find you asleep. ³⁷ And what I say to you, I say to everyone: Keep awake.'

The trial and crucifixion of Jesus

14 It was two days before the festival of Passover and Unleavened Bread, and the chief priests and the scribes were trying to devise some scheme to seize him and put him to death. ² 'It must not be during the festival,' they said, 'or we should have rioting among the people.' ³ Jesus was at Bethany, in the house of Simon the leper. As he sat at table, a woman came in carrying a bottle of very costly perfume, pure oil of nard. She broke it open and poured the oil over his head.

⁴ Some of those present said indignantly to one another, 'Why this waste? ⁵ The perfume might have been sold for more than three hundred denarii and the money given to the poor'; and they began to scold her. ⁶ But Jesus said, 'Leave her alone. Why make trouble for her? It is a fine thing she has done for me. ⁷ You have the poor among you always, and you can help them whenever you like; but you will not always have me. ⁸ She has done what lay in her power; she has anointed my body in anticipation of my burial. ⁹ Truly I tell you: wherever the gospel is proclaimed throughout the world, what she has done will be told as her memorial.'

¹⁰ Then Judas Iscariot, one of the Twelve, went to the chief priests to betray him to them. ¹¹ When they heard what he had come for, they were glad and promised him money; and he began to look for an opportunity to betray him.

¹² Now ON the first day of Unleavened Bread, when the Passover lambs were being slaughtered, his disciples said to him, 'Where would you like us to go and prepare the Passover for you?' ¹³ So he sent off two of his disciples with these instructions: 'Go into the city, and a man will meet you carrying a jar of water. Follow him, ¹⁴ and when he enters a house give this message to the householder: "The Teacher says, 'Where is the room in which I am to eat the Passover with my disciples?'" ¹⁵ He will show you a large upstairs room, set out in readiness. Make the preparations for us there.' ¹⁶ Then the disciples went off, and when they came into the city they found everything just as he had told them. So they prepared the Passover.

¹⁷ In the evening he came to the house with the Twelve. ¹⁸ As they sat at supper Jesus said, 'Truly I tell you: one of you will betray me—one who is eating with me.' ¹⁹ At this they were distressed; and one by one they said to him, 'Surely you do not mean me?' ²⁰ 'It is one of the Twelve', he said, 'who is dipping into the bowl with me. ²¹ The Son of Man is going the way appointed for him in the scriptures; but alas for that man by whom the Son of Man is betrayed! It would be better for that man if he had never been born.'

13:29 **the end is near:** *or* he is near.   13:33 **keep watch:** *some witnesses add* and pray.
14:5 **denarii:** *see p. xi.*

²² During supper he took bread, and having said the blessing he broke it and gave it to them, with the words: 'Take this; this is my body.' ²³ Then he took a cup, and having offered thanks to God he gave it to them; and they all drank from it. ²⁴ And he said to them, 'This is my blood, the blood of the covenant, shed for many. ²⁵ Truly I tell you: never again shall I drink from the fruit of the vine until that day when I drink it new in the kingdom of God.'

²⁶ After singing the Passover hymn, they went out to the mount of Olives. ²⁷ And Jesus said to them, 'You will all lose faith; for it is written: "I will strike the shepherd and the sheep will be scattered." ²⁸ Nevertheless, after I am raised I shall go ahead of you into Galilee.' ²⁹ Peter answered, 'Everyone else may lose faith, but I will not.' ³⁰ Jesus said to him, 'Truly I tell you: today, this very night, before the cock crows twice, you yourself will disown me three times.' ³¹ But Peter insisted: 'Even if I have to die with you, I will never disown you.' And they all said the same.

³² WHEN they reached a place called Gethsemane, he said to his disciples, 'Sit here while I pray.' ³³ And he took Peter and James and John with him. Horror and anguish overwhelmed him, ³⁴ and he said to them, 'My heart is ready to break with grief; stop here, and stay awake.' ³⁵ Then he went on a little farther, threw himself on the ground, and prayed that if it were possible this hour might pass him by. ³⁶ 'Abba, Father,' he said, 'all things are possible to you; take this cup from me. Yet not my will but yours.'

³⁷ He came back and found them asleep; and he said to Peter, 'Asleep, Simon? Could you not stay awake for one hour? ³⁸ Stay awake, all of you; and pray that you may be spared the test. The spirit is willing, but the flesh is weak.' ³⁹ Once more he went away and prayed. ⁴⁰ On his return he found them asleep again, for their eyes were heavy; and they did not know how to answer him.

⁴¹ He came a third time and said to them, 'Still asleep? Still resting? Enough! The hour has come. The Son of Man is betrayed into the hands of sinners. ⁴² Up, let us go! The traitor is upon us.'

⁴³ He was still speaking when Judas, one of the Twelve, appeared, and with him a crowd armed with swords and cudgels, sent by the chief priests, scribes, and elders. ⁴⁴ Now the traitor had agreed with them on a signal: 'The one I kiss is your man; seize him and get him safely away.' ⁴⁵ When he reached the spot, he went straight up to him and said, 'Rabbi,' and kissed him. ⁴⁶ Then they seized him and held him fast.

⁴⁷ One of the bystanders drew his sword, and struck the high priest's servant, cutting off his ear. ⁴⁸ Then Jesus spoke: 'Do you take me for a robber, that you have come out with swords and cudgels to arrest me? ⁴⁹ Day after day I have been among you teaching in the temple, and you did not lay hands on me. But let the scriptures be fulfilled.' ⁵⁰ Then the disciples all deserted him and ran away.

⁵¹ Among those who had followed Jesus was a young man with nothing on but a linen cloth. They tried to seize him; ⁵² but he slipped out of the linen cloth and ran away naked.

⁵³ THEN they led Jesus away to the high priest's house, where the chief priests, elders, and scribes were all assembling. ⁵⁴ Peter followed him at a distance right into the high priest's courtyard; and there he remained, sitting among the attendants and warming himself at the fire.

⁵⁵ The chief priests and the whole Council tried to find evidence against Jesus that would warrant a death sentence, but failed to find any. ⁵⁶ Many gave false evidence against him, but their statements did not tally. ⁵⁷ Some stood up and gave false evidence against him to this effect: ⁵⁸ 'We heard him say, "I will pull down this temple, made with human hands, and in three days I will build another, not made with hands."' ⁵⁹ But even on this point their evidence did not agree.

⁶⁰ Then the high priest rose to his feet and questioned Jesus: 'Have you no answer to the accusations that these

14:39 **prayed**: *some witnesses add* using the same words. 14:41 **Enough**: *the meaning of the Greek cannot be confidently decided.*

witnesses bring against you?' [61] But he remained silent and made no reply.

Again the high priest questioned him: 'Are you the Messiah, the Son of the Blessed One?' [62] 'I am,' said Jesus; 'and you will see the Son of Man seated at the right hand of the Almighty and coming with the clouds of heaven.' [63] Then the high priest tore his robes and said, 'Do we need further witnesses? [64] You have heard the blasphemy. What is your decision?' Their judgement was unanimous: that he was guilty and should be put to death.

[65] Some began to spit at him; they blindfolded him and struck him with their fists, crying out, 'Prophesy!' And the attendants slapped him in the face.

[66] Meanwhile Peter was still below in the courtyard. One of the high priest's servant-girls came by [67] and saw him there warming himself. She looked closely at him and said, 'You were with this man from Nazareth, this Jesus.' [68] But he denied it: 'I know nothing,' he said; 'I have no idea what you are talking about,' and he went out into the forecourt. [69] The servant-girl saw him there and began to say again to the bystanders, 'He is one of them'; [70] and again he denied it.

Again, a little later, the bystanders said to Peter, 'You must be one of them; you are a Galilean.' [71] At this he started to curse, and declared with an oath, 'I do not know this man you are talking about.' [72] At that moment the cock crowed for the second time; and Peter remembered how Jesus had said to him, 'Before the cock crows twice, you will disown me three times.' And he burst into tears.

15 As soon as morning came, the whole Council, chief priests, elders, and scribes, made their plans. They bound Jesus and led him away to hand him over to Pilate. [2] 'Are you the king of the Jews?' Pilate asked him. 'The words are yours,' he replied. [3] And the chief priests brought many charges against him. [4] Pilate questioned him again: 'Have you nothing to say in your defence? You see how many charges they are bringing against you.' [5] But, to Pilate's astonishment, Jesus made no further reply.

[6] At the festival season the governor used to release one prisoner requested by the people. [7] As it happened, a man known as Barabbas was then in custody with the rebels who had committed murder in the rising. [8] When the crowd appeared and began asking for the usual favour, [9] Pilate replied, 'Would you like me to release the king of the Jews?' [10] For he knew it was out of malice that Jesus had been handed over to him. [11] But the chief priests incited the crowd to ask instead for the release of Barabbas. [12] Pilate spoke to them again: 'Then what shall I do with the man you call king of the Jews?' [13] They shouted back, 'Crucify him!' [14] 'Why, what wrong has he done?' Pilate asked; but they shouted all the louder, 'Crucify him!' [15] So Pilate, in his desire to satisfy the mob, released Barabbas to them; and he had Jesus flogged, and then handed him over to be crucified.

[16] The soldiers took him inside the governor's residence, the Praetorium, and called the whole company together. [17] They dressed him in purple and, plaiting a crown of thorns, placed it on his head. [18] Then they began to salute him: 'Hail, king of the Jews!' [19] They beat him about the head with a stick and spat at him, and then knelt and paid homage to him. [20] When they had finished their mockery, they stripped off the purple robe and dressed him in his own clothes.

THEN they led him out to crucify him. [21] A man called Simon, from Cyrene, the father of Alexander and Rufus, was passing by on his way in from the country, and they pressed him into service to carry his cross. [22] They brought Jesus to the place called Golgotha, which means 'Place of a Skull', [23] and they offered him drugged wine, but he did not take it. [24] Then they fastened him to the cross. They shared out his clothes, casting lots to decide what each should have.

[25] It was nine in the morning when they crucified him; [26] and the inscription giving the charge against him read, 'The King of the Jews'. [27] Two robbers were crucified with him, one on his right and the other on his left.

14:65 **Prophesy**: *some witnesses add* Who hit you? *as in Matthew and Luke.*   14:68 **into the forecourt**: *some witnesses add* and a cock crowed.   15:2 **The words are yours**: *or* It is as you say.   15:8 **appeared**: *some witnesses read* shouted.   15:27 **on his left**: *some witnesses add* [28] So was fulfilled the text of scripture which says, 'He was reckoned among criminals.'

[29] The passers-by wagged their heads and jeered at him: 'Bravo!' they cried, 'So you are the man who was to pull down the temple, and rebuild it in three days! [30] Save yourself and come down from the cross.' [31] The chief priests and scribes joined in, jesting with one another: 'He saved others,' they said, 'but he cannot save himself. [32] Let the Messiah, the king of Israel, come down now from the cross. If we see that, we shall believe.' Even those who were crucified with him taunted him.

[33] At midday a darkness fell over the whole land, which lasted till three in the afternoon; [34] and at three Jesus cried aloud, 'Eloï, Eloï, lema sabachthani?' which means, 'My God, my God, why have you forsaken me?' [35] Hearing this, some of the bystanders said, 'Listen! He is calling Elijah.' [36] Someone ran and soaked a sponge in sour wine and held it to his lips on the end of a stick. 'Let us see', he said, 'if Elijah will come to take him down.' [37] Then Jesus gave a loud cry and died; [38] and the curtain of the temple was torn in two from top to bottom. [39] When the centurion who was standing opposite him saw how he died, he said, 'This man must have been a son of God.'

[40] A NUMBER of women were also present, watching from a distance. Among them were Mary of Magdala, Mary the mother of James the younger and of Joses, and Salome, [41] who had all followed him and looked after him when he was in Galilee, and there were many others who had come up to Jerusalem with him.

[42] By this time evening had come; and as it was the day of preparation (that is, the day before the sabbath), [43] Joseph of Arimathaea, a respected member of the Council, a man who looked forward to the kingdom of God, bravely went in to Pilate and asked for the body of Jesus. [44] Pilate was surprised to hear that he had died so soon, and sent for the centurion to make sure that he was already dead. [45] And when he heard the centurion's report, he gave Joseph leave to take the body. [46] So Joseph bought a linen sheet, took him down from the cross, and wrapped him in the sheet. Then he laid him in a tomb cut out of the rock, and rolled a stone against the entrance. [47] And Mary of Magdala and Mary the mother of Joses were watching and saw where he was laid.

The resurrection of Jesus

16 WHEN the sabbath was over, Mary of Magdala, Mary the mother of James, and Salome bought aromatic oils, intending to go and anoint him; [2] and very early on the first day of the week, just after sunrise, they came to the tomb. [3] They were wondering among themselves who would roll away the stone for them from the entrance to the tomb, [4] when they looked up and saw that the stone, huge as it was, had been rolled back already. [5] They went into the tomb, where they saw a young man sitting on the right-hand side, wearing a white robe; and they were dumbfounded. [6] But he said to them, 'Do not be alarmed; you are looking for Jesus of Nazareth, who was crucified. He has been raised; he is not here. Look, there is the place where they laid him. [7] But go and say to his disciples and to Peter: "He is going ahead of you into Galilee: there you will see him, as he told you."' [8] Then they went out and ran away from the tomb, trembling with amazement. They said nothing to anyone, for they were afraid.

And they delivered all these instructions briefly to Peter and his companions. Afterwards Jesus himself sent out by them, from east to west, the sacred and imperishable message of eternal salvation.

[9] WHEN he had risen from the dead, early on the first day of the week, he appeared first to Mary of Magdala, from whom he had driven out seven demons. [10] She went and carried the news to his mourning and sorrowful followers, [11] but when they were told that he was alive and that she had seen him they did not believe it.

[12] Later he appeared in a different form

15:39 **a son of God**: *or* the Son of God.   16:1 **When ... Salome**: *some witnesses omit, reading* And they went and bought ...   16:8 **afraid**: *at this point some of the most ancient witnesses bring the book to a close.* **And they delivered ... salvation**: *some witnesses add this passage, which in one of them is the conclusion of the book.* 16:9–20 *Some witnesses give these verses either instead of, or in addition to, the passage* And they delivered ... salvation *(here printed before verse 9), and so bring the book to a close. Others insert further additional matter.*

to two of them while they were on their way into the country. [13] These also went and took the news to the others, but again no one believed them.

[14] Still later he appeared to the eleven while they were at table, and reproached them for their incredulity and dullness, because they had not believed those who had seen him after he was raised from the dead. [15] Then he said to them: 'Go to every part of the world, and proclaim the gospel to the whole creation. [16] Those who believe it and receive baptism will be saved; those who do not believe will be condemned. [17] Faith will bring with it these miracles: believers will drive out demons in my name and speak in strange tongues; [18] if they handle snakes or drink any deadly poison, they will come to no harm; and the sick on whom they lay their hands will recover.'

[19] So after talking with them the Lord Jesus was taken up into heaven and took his seat at the right hand of God; [20] but they went out to proclaim their message far and wide, and the Lord worked with them and confirmed their words by the miracles that followed.

THE GOSPEL ACCORDING TO

LUKE

[1] To Theophilus: Many writers have undertaken to draw up an account of the events that have taken place among us, [2] following the traditions handed down to us by the original eyewitnesses and servants of the gospel. [3] So I in my turn, as one who has investigated the whole course of these events in detail, have decided to write an orderly narrative for you, your excellency, [4] so as to give you authentic knowledge about the matters of which you have been informed.

The coming of Christ

[5] In the reign of Herod king of Judaea there was a priest named Zechariah, of the division of the priesthood called after Abijah. His wife, whose name was Elizabeth, was also of priestly descent. [6] Both of them were upright and devout, blamelessly observing all the commandments and ordinances of the Lord. [7] But they had no children, for Elizabeth was barren, and both were well on in years.

[8] Once, when it was the turn of his division and he was there to take part in the temple service, [9] he was chosen by lot, by priestly custom, to enter the sanctuary of the Lord and offer the incense; [10] and at the hour of the offering the people were all assembled at prayer outside. [11] There appeared to him an angel of the Lord, standing on the right of the altar of incense. [12] At this sight, Zechariah was startled and overcome by fear. [13] But the angel said to him, 'Do not be afraid, Zechariah; your prayer has been heard: your wife Elizabeth will bear you a son, and you are to name him John. [14] His birth will fill you with joy and delight, and will bring gladness to many; [15] for he will be great in the eyes of the Lord. He is never to touch wine or strong drink. From his very birth he will be filled with the Holy Spirit; [16] and he will bring back many Israelites to the Lord their God. [17] He will go before him as forerunner, possessed by the spirit and power of Elijah, to reconcile father and child, to convert the rebellious to the ways of the righteous, to prepare a people that shall be fit for the Lord.'

[18] Zechariah said to the angel, 'How can I be sure of this? I am an old man and my wife is well on in years.'

[19] The angel replied, 'I am Gabriel; I stand in attendance on God, and I have been sent to speak to you and bring you this good news. [20] But now, because you have not believed me, you will lose all power of speech and remain silent until the day when these things take place; at their proper time my words will be proved true.'

[21] Meanwhile the people were waiting for Zechariah, surprised that he was staying so long inside the sanctuary. [22] When

he did come out he could not speak to them, and they realized that he had had a vision. He stood there making signs to them, and remained dumb.

23 When his period of duty was completed Zechariah returned home. 24 His wife Elizabeth conceived, and for five months she lived in seclusion, thinking, 25 'This is the Lord's doing; now at last he has shown me favour and taken away from me the disgrace of childlessness.'

26 In the sixth month the angel Gabriel was sent by God to Nazareth, a town in Galilee, 27 with a message for a girl betrothed to a man named Joseph, a descendant of David; the girl's name was Mary. 28 The angel went in and said to her, 'Greetings, most favoured one! The Lord is with you.' 29 But she was deeply troubled by what he said and wondered what this greeting could mean. 30 Then the angel said to her, 'Do not be afraid, Mary, for God has been gracious to you; 31 you will conceive and give birth to a son, and you are to give him the name Jesus. 32 He will be great, and will be called Son of the Most High. The Lord God will give him the throne of his ancestor David, 33 and he will be king over Israel for ever; his reign shall never end.' 34 'How can this be?' said Mary. 'I am still a virgin.' 35 The angel answered, 'The Holy Spirit will come upon you, and the power of the Most High will overshadow you; for that reason the holy child to be born will be called Son of God. 36 Moreover your kinswoman Elizabeth has herself conceived a son in her old age; and she who is reputed barren is now in her sixth month, 37 for God's promises can never fail.' 38 'I am the Lord's servant,' said Mary; 'may it be as you have said.' Then the angel left her.

39 Soon afterwards Mary set out and hurried away to a town in the uplands of Judah. 40 She went into Zechariah's house and greeted Elizabeth. 41 And when Elizabeth heard Mary's greeting, the baby stirred in her womb. Then Elizabeth was filled with the Holy Spirit 42 and exclaimed in a loud voice, 'God's blessing is on you above all women, and his blessing is on the fruit of your womb. 43 Who am I, that the mother of my Lord should visit me? 44 I tell you, when your greeting sounded

in my ears, the baby in my womb leapt for joy. 45 Happy is she who has had faith that the Lord's promise to her would be fulfilled!'

46 And Mary said:

'My soul tells out the greatness of the Lord,
47 my spirit has rejoiced in God my Saviour;
48 for he has looked with favour on his servant,
lowly as she is.
From this day forward
all generations will count me blessed,
49 for the Mighty God has done great things for me.
His name is holy,
50 his mercy sure from generation to generation
toward those who fear him.
51 He has shown the might of his arm,
he has routed the proud and all their schemes;
52 he has brought down monarchs from their thrones,
and raised on high the lowly.
53 He has filled the hungry with good things,
and sent the rich away empty.
54-55 He has come to the help of Israel his servant,
as he promised to our forefathers;
he has not forgotten to show mercy
to Abraham and his children's children for ever.'

56 Mary stayed with Elizabeth about three months and then returned home.

57 WHEN the time came for Elizabeth's child to be born, she gave birth to a son. 58 Her neighbours and relatives heard what great kindness the Lord had shown her, and they shared her delight. 59 On the eighth day they came to circumcise the child; and they were going to name him Zechariah after his father, 60 but his mother spoke up: 'No!' she said. 'He is to be called John.' 61 'But', they said, 'there is nobody in your family who has that name.' 62 They enquired of his father by signs what he would like him to be called. 63 He asked for a writing tablet and to everybody's astonishment wrote, 'His

---

1:33 **Israel:** *lit.* the house of Jacob.   1:35 **the holy child . . . God:** *or* the child to be born will be called holy, Son of God.   1:37 **for God's . . . fail:** *some witnesses read* for with God nothing will prove impossible. 1:46 **Mary:** *a few witnesses read* Elizabeth.

name is John.' [64] Immediately his lips and tongue were freed and he began to speak, praising God. [65] All the neighbours were overcome with awe, and throughout the uplands of Judaea the whole story became common talk. [66] All who heard it were deeply impressed and said, 'What will this child become?' For indeed the hand of the Lord was upon him.

[67] And Zechariah his father was filled with the Holy Spirit and uttered this prophecy:

[68] 'Praise to the Lord, the God of Israel!
  For he has turned to his people and
    set them free.
[69] He has raised for us a strong
    deliverer
  from the house of his servant David.

[70] 'So he promised: age after age he
    proclaimed
  by the lips of his holy prophets,
[71] that he would deliver us from our
    enemies,
  out of the hands of all who hate us;
[72] that, calling to mind his solemn
    covenant,
  he would deal mercifully with our
    fathers.

[73] 'This was the oath he swore to our
    father Abraham,
[74] to rescue us from enemy hands and
    set us free from fear,
  so that we might worship [75] in his
    presence
  in holiness and righteousness our
    whole life long.

[76] 'And you, my child, will be called
    Prophet of the Most High,
  for you will be the Lord's forerunner,
    to prepare his way
[77] and lead his people to a knowledge of
    salvation
  through the forgiveness of their sins:
[78] for in the tender compassion of our
    God
  the dawn from heaven will break
    upon us,
[79] to shine on those who live in
    darkness, under the shadow of
    death,
  and to guide our feet into the way of
    peace.'

[80] As the child grew up he became strong in spirit; he lived out in the wilderness until the day when he appeared publicly before Israel.

2 In those days a decree was issued by the emperor Augustus for a census to be taken throughout the Roman world. [2] This was the first registration of its kind; it took place when Quirinius was governor of Syria. [3] Everyone made his way to his own town to be registered. [4-5] Joseph went up to Judaea from the town of Nazareth in Galilee, to register in the city of David called Bethlehem, because he was of the house of David by descent; and with him went Mary, his betrothed, who was expecting her child. [6] While they were there the time came for her to have her baby, [7] and she gave birth to a son, her firstborn. She wrapped him in swaddling clothes, and laid him in a manger, because there was no room for them at the inn.

[8] Now in this same district there were shepherds out in the fields, keeping watch through the night over their flock. [9] Suddenly an angel of the Lord appeared to them, and the glory of the Lord shone round them. They were terrified, [10] but the angel said, 'Do not be afraid; I bring you good news, news of great joy for the whole nation. [11] Today there has been born to you in the city of David a deliverer—the Messiah, the Lord. [12] This will be the sign for you: you will find a baby wrapped in swaddling clothes, and lying in a manger.' [13] All at once there was with the angel a great company of the heavenly host, singing praise to God:

[14] 'Glory to God in highest heaven,
  and on earth peace to all in whom
    he delights.'

[15] After the angels had left them and returned to heaven the shepherds said to one another, 'Come, let us go straight to Bethlehem and see this thing that has happened, which the Lord has made known to us.' [16] They hurried off and found Mary and Joseph, and the baby lying in the manger. [17] When they saw the child, they related what they had been told about him; [18] and all who heard were astonished at what the shepherds said.

2:2 **registration ... Quirinius:** *or* registration carried out while Quirinius.   2:7 **no ... inn:** *or* no other space in their lodging.   2:11 **the Messiah, the Lord:** *some witnesses read* the Lord's Messiah.

[19] But Mary treasured up all these things and pondered over them. [20] The shepherds returned glorifying and praising God for what they had heard and seen; it had all happened as they had been told.

[21] Eight days later the time came to circumcise him, and he was given the name Jesus, the name given by the angel before he was conceived.

[22] Then, after the purification had been completed in accordance with the law of Moses, they brought him up to Jerusalem to present him to the Lord [23] (as prescribed in the law of the Lord: 'Every firstborn male shall be deemed to belong to the Lord'), [24] and also to make the offering as stated in the law: 'a pair of turtle-doves or two young pigeons'.

[25] There was at that time in Jerusalem a man called Simeon. This man was upright and devout, one who watched and waited for the restoration of Israel, and the Holy Spirit was upon him. [26] It had been revealed to him by the Holy Spirit that he would not see death until he had seen the Lord's Messiah. [27] Guided by the Spirit he came into the temple; and when the parents brought in the child Jesus to do for him what the law required, [28] he took him in his arms, praised God, and said:

[29] 'Now, Lord, you are releasing your
    servant in peace,
    according to your promise.
[30] For I have seen with my own eyes
    the deliverance [31] you have made
    ready in full view of all nations:
[32] a light that will bring revelation to
    the Gentiles
    and glory to your people Israel.'

[33] The child's father and mother were full of wonder at what was being said about him. [34-35] Simeon blessed them and said to Mary his mother, 'This child is destined to be a sign that will be rejected; and you too will be pierced to the heart. Many in Israel will stand or fall because of him; and so the secret thoughts of many will be laid bare.'

[36] There was also a prophetess, Anna the daughter of Phanuel, of the tribe of Asher. She was a very old woman, who had lived seven years with her husband after she was first married, [37] and then alone as a widow to the age of eighty-four. She never left the temple, but worshipped night and day with fasting and prayer. [38] Coming up at that very moment, she gave thanks to God; and she talked about the child to all who were looking for the liberation of Jerusalem.

[39] When they had done everything prescribed in the law of the Lord, they returned to Galilee to their own town of Nazareth. [40] The child grew big and strong and full of wisdom; and God's favour was upon him.

[41] Now it was the practice of his parents to go to Jerusalem every year for the Passover festival; [42] and when he was twelve, they made the pilgrimage as usual. [43] When the festive season was over and they set off for home, the boy Jesus stayed behind in Jerusalem. His parents did not know of this; [44] but supposing that he was with the party they travelled for a whole day, and only then did they begin looking for him among their friends and relations. [45] When they could not find him they returned to Jerusalem to look for him; [46] and after three days they found him sitting in the temple surrounded by the teachers, listening to them and putting questions; [47] and all who heard him were amazed at his intelligence and the answers he gave. [48] His parents were astonished to see him there, and his mother said to him, 'My son, why have you treated us like this? Your father and I have been anxiously searching for you.' [49] 'Why did you search for me?' he said. 'Did you not know that I was bound to be in my Father's house?' [50] But they did not understand what he meant. [51] Then he went back with them to Nazareth, and continued to be under their authority; his mother treasured up all these things in her heart. [52] As Jesus grew he advanced in wisdom and in favour with God and men.

John the Baptist and Jesus

3 IN the fifteenth year of the emperor Tiberius, when Pontius Pilate was governor of Judaea, when Herod was tetrarch of Galilee, his brother Philip prince of Ituraea and Trachonitis, and Lysanias prince of Abilene, [2] during the high-priesthood of Annas and Caiaphas,

2:49 **in ... house:** *or* about my Father's business.

the word of God came to John son of Zechariah in the wilderness. ³And he went all over the Jordan valley proclaiming a baptism in token of repentance for the forgiveness of sins, ⁴ as it is written in the book of the prophecies of Isaiah:

> A voice cries in the wilderness,
> 'Prepare the way for the Lord;
> clear a straight path for him.
> ⁵ Every ravine shall be filled in,
>   and every mountain and hill levelled;
> winding paths shall be straightened,
>   and rough ways made smooth;
> ⁶ and all mankind shall see God's
>   deliverance.'

⁷ Crowds of people came out to be baptized by him, and he said to them: 'Vipers' brood! Who warned you to escape from the wrath that is to come? ⁸ Prove your repentance by the fruit you bear; and do not begin saying to yourselves, "We have Abraham for our father." I tell you that God can make children for Abraham out of these stones. ⁹ Already the axe is laid to the roots of the trees; and every tree that fails to produce good fruit is cut down and thrown on the fire.'

¹⁰ The people asked him, 'Then what are we to do?' ¹¹ He replied, 'Whoever has two shirts must share with him who has none, and whoever has food must do the same.' ¹² Among those who came to be baptized were tax-collectors, and they said to him, 'Teacher, what are we to do?' ¹³ He told them, 'Exact no more than the assessment.' ¹⁴ Some soldiers also asked him, 'And what of us?' To them he said, 'No bullying; no blackmail; make do with your pay!'

¹⁵ The people were all agog, wondering about John, whether perhaps he was the Messiah, ¹⁶ but he spoke out and said to them all: 'I baptize you with water; but there is one coming who is mightier than I am. I am not worthy to unfasten the straps of his sandals. He will baptize you with the Holy Spirit and with fire. ¹⁷ His winnowing-shovel is ready in his hand, to clear his threshing-floor and gather the wheat into his granary; but the chaff he will burn on a fire that can never be put out.'

¹⁸ In this and many other ways he made his appeal to the people and announced the good news. ¹⁹ But Herod the tetrarch, when he was rebuked by him over the affair of his brother's wife Herodias and all his other misdeeds, ²⁰ crowned them all by shutting John up in prison.

The ancestry of the Messiah

²¹ DURING a general baptism of the people, when Jesus too had been baptized and was praying, heaven opened ²² and the Holy Spirit descended on him in bodily form like a dove, and there came a voice from heaven, 'You are my beloved Son; in you I delight.'

²³ When Jesus began his work he was about thirty years old, the son, as people thought, of Joseph son of Heli, ²⁴ son of Matthat, son of Levi, son of Melchi, son of Jannai, son of Joseph, ²⁵ son of Mattathias, son of Amos, son of Nahum, son of Esli, son of Naggai, ²⁶ son of Maath, son of Mattathias, son of Semein, son of Josech, son of Joda, ²⁷ son of Johanan, son of Rhesa, son of Zerubbabel, son of Shealtiel, son of Neri, ²⁸ son of Melchi, son of Addi, son of Cosam, son of Elmadam, son of Er, ²⁹ son of Joshua, son of Eliezer, son of Jorim, son of Matthat, son of Levi, ³⁰ son of Symeon, son of Judah, son of Joseph, son of Jonam, son of Eliakim, ³¹ son of Melea, son of Menna, son of Mattatha, son of Nathan, son of David, ³² son of Jesse, son of Obed, son of Boaz, son of Salma, son of Nahshon, ³³ son of Amminadab, son of Arni, son of Hezron, son of Perez, son of Judah, ³⁴ son of Jacob, son of Isaac, son of Abraham, son of Terah, son of Nahor, ³⁵ son of Serug, son of Reu, son of Peleg, son of Eber, son of Shelah, ³⁶ son of Cainan, son of Arphaxad, son of Shem, son of Noah, son of Lamech, ³⁷ son of Methuselah, son of Enoch, son of Jared, son of Mahalaleel, son of Cainan, ³⁸ son of Enosh, son of Seth, son of Adam, son of God.

The temptation of Jesus

4 ¹⁻² FULL of the Holy Spirit, Jesus returned from the Jordan, and for forty days he wandered in the wilderness, led by the Spirit and tempted by the devil. During that time he ate nothing, and at the end of it he was famished. ³ The devil

---

3:22 **You are ... Son:** *or* You are my only Son. **You are ... delight:** *some witnesses read* You are my Son; this day I have begotten you.   3:33 **Amminadab:** *some witnesses add* son of Admin.

said to him, 'If you are the Son of God, tell this stone to become bread.' ⁴ Jesus answered, 'Scripture says, "Man is not to live on bread alone."'

⁵ Next the devil led him to a height and showed him in a flash all the kingdoms of the world. ⁶ 'All this dominion will I give to you,' he said, 'and the glory that goes with it; for it has been put in my hands and I can give it to anyone I choose. ⁷ You have only to do homage to me and it will all be yours.' ⁸ Jesus answered him, 'Scripture says, "You shall do homage to the Lord your God and worship him alone."'

⁹ The devil took him to Jerusalem and set him on the parapet of the temple. 'If you are the Son of God,' he said, 'throw yourself down from here; ¹⁰ for scripture says, "He will put his angels in charge of you," ¹¹ and again, "They will support you in their arms for fear you should strike your foot against a stone."' ¹² Jesus answered him, 'It has been said, "You are not to put the Lord your God to the test."'

¹³ So, having come to the end of all these temptations, the devil departed, biding his time.

Jesus in Galilee

¹⁴ THEN Jesus, armed with the power of the Spirit, returned to Galilee; and reports about him spread through the whole countryside. ¹⁵ He taught in their synagogues and everyone sang his praises.

¹⁶ He came to Nazareth, where he had been brought up, and went to the synagogue on the sabbath day as he regularly did. He stood up to read the lesson ¹⁷ and was handed the scroll of the prophet Isaiah. He opened the scroll and found the passage which says,

¹⁸ 'The spirit of the Lord is upon me
   because he has anointed me;
he has sent me to announce good
   news to the poor,
to proclaim release for prisoners
and recovery of sight for the blind;
to let the broken victims go free,
¹⁹ to proclaim the year of the Lord's
   favour.'

²⁰ He rolled up the scroll, gave it back to the attendant, and sat down; and all eyes in the synagogue were fixed on him.

²¹ He began to address them: 'Today', he said, 'in your hearing this text has come true.' ²² There was general approval; they were astonished that words of such grace should fall from his lips. 'Is not this Joseph's son?' they asked. ²³ Then Jesus said, 'No doubt you will quote to me the proverb, "Physician, heal yourself!" and say, "We have heard of all your doings at Capernaum; do the same here in your own home town." ²⁴ Truly I tell you,' he went on: 'no prophet is recognized in his own country. ²⁵ There were indeed many widows in Israel in Elijah's time, when for three and a half years the skies never opened, and famine lay hard over the whole country; ²⁶ yet it was to none of these that Elijah was sent, but to a widow at Sarepta in the territory of Sidon. ²⁷ Again, in the time of the prophet Elisha there were many lepers in Israel, and not one of them was healed, but only Naaman, the Syrian.' ²⁸ These words roused the whole congregation to fury; ²⁹ they leapt up, drove him out of the town, and took him to the brow of the hill on which it was built, meaning to hurl him over the edge. ³⁰ But he walked straight through the whole crowd, and went away.

³¹ Coming down to Capernaum, a town in Galilee, he taught the people on the sabbath, ³² and they were amazed at his teaching, for what he said had the note of authority. ³³ Now there was a man in the synagogue possessed by a demon, an unclean spirit. He shrieked at the top of his voice, ³⁴ 'What do you want with us, Jesus of Nazareth? Have you come to destroy us? I know who you are—the Holy One of God.' ³⁵ Jesus rebuked him: 'Be silent', he said, 'and come out of him.' Then the demon, after throwing the man down in front of the people, left him without doing him any injury. ³⁶ Amazement fell on them all and they said to one another: 'What is there in this man's words? He gives orders to the unclean spirits with authority and power, and they go.' ³⁷ So the news spread, and he was the talk of the whole district.

³⁸ On leaving the synagogue he went to Simon's house. Simon's mother-in-law was in the grip of a high fever; and they asked him to help her. ³⁹ He stood over her

4:34 **Have you:** *or* You have.

and rebuked the fever. It left her, and she got up at once and attended to their needs. ⁴⁰ At sunset all who had friends ill with diseases of one kind or another brought them to him; and he laid his hands on them one by one and healed them. ⁴¹ Demons also came out of many of them, shouting, 'You are the Son of God.' But he rebuked them and forbade them to speak, because they knew he was the Messiah.

⁴² When day broke he went out and made his way to a remote spot. But the crowds went in search of him, and when they came to where he was they pressed him not to leave them. ⁴³ But he said, 'I must give the good news of the kingdom of God to the other towns also, for that is what I was sent to do.' ⁴⁴ So he proclaimed the gospel in the synagogues of Judaea.

5 One day as he stood by the lake of Gennesaret, with people crowding in on him to listen to the word of God, ² he noticed two boats lying at the water's edge; the fishermen had come ashore and were washing their nets. ³ He got into one of the boats, which belonged to Simon, and asked him to put out a little way from the shore; then he went on teaching the crowds as he sat in the boat. ⁴ When he had finished speaking, he said to Simon, 'Put out into deep water and let down your nets for a catch.' ⁵ Simon answered, 'Master, we were hard at work all night and caught nothing; but if you say so, I will let down the nets.' ⁶ They did so and made such a huge catch of fish that their nets began to split. ⁷ So they signalled to their partners in the other boat to come and help them. They came, and loaded both boats to the point of sinking. ⁸ When Simon saw what had happened he fell at Jesus's knees and said, 'Go, Lord, leave me, sinner that I am!' ⁹ For he and all his companions were amazed at the catch they had made; ¹⁰ so too were his partners James and John, Zebedee's sons. 'Do not be afraid,' said Jesus to Simon; 'from now on you will be catching people.' ¹¹ As soon as they had brought the boats to land, they left everything and followed him.

¹² He was once in a certain town where there was a man covered with leprosy; when he saw Jesus, he threw himself to the ground and begged his help. 'Sir,' he said, 'if only you will, you can make me clean.' ¹³ Jesus stretched out his hand and touched him, saying, 'I will; be clean.' The leprosy left him immediately. ¹⁴ Jesus then instructed him not to tell anybody. 'But go,' he said, 'show yourself to the priest, and make the offering laid down by Moses for your cleansing; that will certify the cure.' ¹⁵ But the talk about him spread ever wider, so that great crowds kept gathering to hear him and to be cured of their ailments. ¹⁶ And from time to time he would withdraw to remote places for prayer.

¹⁷ One day as he was teaching, Pharisees and teachers of the law were sitting round him. People had come from every village in Galilee and from Judaea and Jerusalem, and the power of the Lord was with him to heal the sick. ¹⁸ Some men appeared carrying a paralysed man on a bed, and tried to bring him in and set him down in front of Jesus. ¹⁹ Finding no way to do so because of the crowd, they went up onto the roof and let him down through the tiling, bed and all, into the middle of the company in front of Jesus. ²⁰ When Jesus saw their faith, he said to the man, 'Your sins are forgiven you.'

²¹ The scribes and Pharisees began asking among themselves, 'Who is this fellow with his blasphemous talk? Who but God alone can forgive sins?' ²² But Jesus knew what they were thinking and answered them: 'Why do you harbour these thoughts? ²³ Is it easier to say, "Your sins are forgiven you," or to say, "Stand up and walk"? ²⁴ But to convince you that the Son of Man has the right on earth to forgive sins'—he turned to the paralysed man—'I say to you, stand up, take your bed, and go home.' ²⁵ At once the man rose to his feet before their eyes, took up the bed he had been lying on, and went home praising God. ²⁶ They were all lost in amazement and praised God; filled with awe they said, 'The things we have seen today are beyond belief!'

²⁷ Later, when he went out, he saw a tax-collector, Levi by name, at his seat in the custom-house, and said to him, 'Follow me.' ²⁸ Leaving everything, he got up and followed him.

²⁹ Afterwards Levi held a big reception

5:17 **Pharisees … Jerusalem**: *some witnesses read* Pharisees and teachers of the law, who had come from every village in Galilee and from Judaea and Jerusalem, were sitting round him.

in his house for Jesus; among the guests was a large party of tax-collectors and others. ³⁰ The Pharisees, some of whom were scribes, complained to his disciples: 'Why', they said, 'do you eat and drink with tax-collectors and sinners?' ³¹ Jesus answered them: 'It is not the healthy that need a doctor, but the sick; ³² I have not come to call the virtuous but sinners to repentance.'

³³ Then they said to him, 'John's disciples are much given to fasting and the practice of prayer, and so are the disciples of the Pharisees; but yours eat and drink.' ³⁴ Jesus replied, 'Can you make the bridegroom's friends fast while the bridegroom is with them? ³⁵ But the time will come when the bridegroom will be taken away from them; that will be the time for them to fast.'

³⁶ He told them this parable also: 'No one tears a piece from a new garment to patch an old one; if he does, he will have made a hole in the new garment, and the patch taken from the new will not match the old. ³⁷ No one puts new wine into old wineskins; if he does, the new wine will burst the skins, the wine will spill out, and the skins be ruined. ³⁸ New wine goes into fresh skins! ³⁹ And no one after drinking old wine wants new; for he says, "The old wine is good."'

6 One sabbath he was going through the cornfields, and his disciples were plucking the ears of corn, rubbing them in their hands, and eating them. ² Some Pharisees said, 'Why are you doing what is forbidden on the sabbath?' ³ Jesus answered, 'Have you not read what David did when he and his men were hungry? ⁴ He went into the house of God and took the sacred bread to eat and gave it to his men, though only the priests are allowed to eat it.' ⁵ He also said to them, 'The Son of Man is master of the sabbath.'

⁶ On another sabbath he had gone to synagogue and was teaching. There was a man in the congregation whose right arm was withered; ⁷ and the scribes and Pharisees were on the watch to see whether Jesus would heal him on the sabbath, so that they could find a charge to bring against him. ⁸ But he knew what was in their minds and said to the man with the withered arm, 'Stand up and come out here.' So he stood up and came out. ⁹ Then Jesus said to them, 'I put this question to you: is it permitted to do good or to do evil on the sabbath, to save life or to destroy it?' ¹⁰ He looked round at them all, and then he said to the man, 'Stretch out your arm.' He did so, and his arm was restored. ¹¹ But they totally failed to understand, and began to discuss with one another what they could do to Jesus.

¹² During this time he went out one day into the hill-country to pray, and spent the night in prayer to God. ¹³ When day broke he called his disciples to him, and from among them he chose twelve and named them apostles: ¹⁴ Simon, to whom he gave the name Peter, and Andrew his brother, James and John, Philip and Bartholomew, ¹⁵ Matthew and Thomas, James son of Alphaeus, and Simon who was called the Zealot, ¹⁶ Judas son of James, and Judas Iscariot who turned traitor.

¹⁷ He came down the hill with them and stopped on some level ground where a large crowd of his disciples had gathered, and with them great numbers of people from Jerusalem and all Judaea and from the coastal region of Tyre and Sidon, who had come to listen to him, and to be cured of their diseases. ¹⁸ Those who were troubled with unclean spirits were healed; ¹⁹ and everyone in the crowd was trying to touch him, because power went out from him and cured them all.

Jesus's sermon to the disciples

²⁰ TURNING to his disciples he began to speak:

'Blessed are you who are in need;
the kingdom of God is yours.
²¹ Blessed are you who now go hungry;
you will be satisfied.
Blessed are you who weep now;
you will laugh.

²² 'Blessed are you when people hate you and ostracize you, when they insult you and slander your very name, because of the Son of Man. ²³ On that day exult and dance for joy, for you have a rich reward in heaven; that is how their fathers treated the prophets.

²⁴ 'But alas for you who are rich;
you have had your time of happiness.
²⁵ Alas for you who are well fed now;
you will go hungry.
Alas for you who laugh now;
you will mourn and weep.

26 Alas for you when all speak well of
    you;
    that is how their fathers treated the
    false prophets.

27 'But to you who are listening I say:
Love your enemies; do good to those who
hate you; 28 bless those who curse you;
pray for those who treat you spitefully.
29 If anyone hits you on the cheek, offer
the other also; if anyone takes your coat,
let him have your shirt as well. 30 Give to
everyone who asks you; if anyone takes
what is yours, do not demand it back.
31 'Treat others as you would like them
to treat you. 32 If you love only those who
love you, what credit is that to you? Even
sinners love those who love them.
33 Again, if you do good only to those who
do good to you, what credit is there in
that? Even sinners do as much. 34 And if
you lend only where you expect to be
repaid, what credit is there in that? Even
sinners lend to each other to be repaid in
full. 35 But you must love your enemies
and do good, and lend without expecting
any return; and you will have a rich
reward: you will be sons of the Most High,
because he himself is kind to the ungrateful and the wicked. 36 Be compassionate,
as your Father is compassionate.
37 'Do not judge, and you will not be
judged; do not condemn, and you will not
be condemned; pardon, and you will be
pardoned; 38 give, and gifts will be given
you. Good measure, pressed and shaken
down and running over, will be poured
into your lap; for whatever measure you
deal out to others will be dealt to you in
turn.'
39 He also spoke to them in a parable:
'Can one blind man guide another? Will
not both fall into the ditch? 40 No pupil
ranks above his teacher; fully trained he
can but reach his teacher's level.
41 'Why do you look at the speck in your
brother's eye, with never a thought for
the plank in your own? 42 How can you
say to your brother, "Brother, let me take
the speck out of your eye," when you are
blind to the plank in your own? You
hypocrite! First take the plank out of your
own eye, and then you will see clearly to
take the speck out of your brother's.
43 'There is no such thing as a good tree
producing bad fruit, nor yet a bad tree
producing good fruit. 44 Each tree is

known by its own fruit: you do not gather
figs from brambles or pick grapes from
thistles. 45 Good people produce good from
the store of good within themselves; and
evil people produce evil from the evil
within them. For the words that the
mouth utters come from the overflowing
of the heart.
46 'Why do you call me "Lord, Lord" —
and never do what I tell you? 47 Everyone
who comes to me and hears my words
and acts on them—I will show you what
he is like. 48 He is like a man building a
house, who dug deep and laid the foundations on rock. When the river was in
flood, it burst upon that house, but could
not shift it, because it had been soundly
built. 49 But he who hears and does not act
is like a man who built his house on the
soil without foundations. As soon as the
river burst upon it, the house collapsed,
and fell with a great crash.'

Miracles and parables

7 WHEN he had finished addressing the
   people, he entered Capernaum. 2 A
centurion there had a servant whom he
valued highly, but the servant was ill and
near to death. 3 Hearing about Jesus, he
sent some Jewish elders to ask him to
come and save his servant's life. 4 They
approached Jesus and made an urgent
appeal to him: 'He deserves this favour
from you,' they said, 5 'for he is a friend of
our nation and it is he who built us our
synagogue.' 6 Jesus went with them; but
when he was not far from the house, the
centurion sent friends with this message:
'Do not trouble further, sir; I am not
worthy to have you come under my roof,
7 and that is why I did not presume to
approach you in person. But say the word
and my servant will be cured. 8 I know, for
I am myself under orders, with soldiers
under me. I say to one, "Go," and he
goes; to another, "Come here," and he
comes; and to my servant, "Do this," and
he does it.' 9 When Jesus heard this, he
was astonished, and, turning to the
crowd that was following him, he said, 'I
tell you, not even in Israel have I found
such faith.' 10 When the messengers
returned to the house, they found the
servant in good health.
11 Afterwards Jesus went to a town
called Nain, accompanied by his disciples
and a large crowd. 12 As he approached

the gate of the town he met a funeral. The dead man was the only son of his widowed mother; and many of the townspeople were there with her. [13] When the Lord saw her his heart went out to her, and he said, 'Do not weep.' [14] He stepped forward and laid his hand on the bier; and the bearers halted. Then he spoke: 'Young man, I tell you to get up.' [15] The dead man sat up and began to speak; and Jesus restored him to his mother. [16] Everyone was filled with awe and praised God. 'A great prophet has arisen among us,' they said; 'God has shown his care for his people.' [17] The story of what he had done spread through the whole of Judaea and all the region around.

[18] When John was informed of all this by his disciples, [19] he summoned two of them and sent them to the Lord with this question: 'Are you the one who is to come, or are we to expect someone else?' [20] The men made their way to Jesus and said, 'John the Baptist has sent us to ask you, "Are you the one who is to come, or are we to expect someone else?"' [21] There and then he healed many sufferers from diseases, plagues, and evil spirits; and on many blind people he bestowed sight. [22] Then he gave them this answer: 'Go and tell John what you have seen and heard: the blind regain their sight, the lame walk, lepers are made clean, the deaf hear, the dead are raised to life, the poor are brought good news—[23] and happy is he who does not find me an obstacle to faith.'

[24] After John's messengers had left, Jesus began to speak about him to the crowds: 'What did you go out into the wilderness to see? A reed swaying in the wind? [25] No? Then what did you go out to see? A man dressed in finery? Grand clothes and luxury are to be found in palaces. [26] But what did you go out to see? A prophet? Yes indeed, and far more than a prophet. [27] He is the man of whom scripture says,

Here is my herald, whom I send
 ahead of you,
and he will prepare your way before
 you.

[28] 'I tell you, among all who have been born, no one has been greater than John; yet the least in the kingdom of God is greater than he is.'

[29] When they heard him, all the people, including the tax-collectors, acknowledged the goodness of God, for they had accepted John's baptism; [30] but the Pharisees and lawyers, who had refused his baptism, rejected God's purpose for themselves.

[31] 'How can I describe the people of this generation? What are they like? [32] They are like children sitting in the marketplace and calling to each other,

We piped for you and you would not
 dance.
We lamented, and you would not
 mourn.

[33] 'For John the Baptist came, neither eating bread nor drinking wine, and you say, "He is possessed." [34] The Son of Man came, eating and drinking, and you say, "Look at him! A glutton and a drinker, a friend of tax-collectors and sinners!" [35] And yet God's wisdom is proved right by all who are her children.'

[36] One of the Pharisees invited Jesus to a meal; he went to the Pharisee's house and took his place at table. [37] A woman who was living an immoral life in the town had learned that Jesus was a guest in the Pharisee's house and had brought oil of myrrh in a small flask. [38] She took her place behind him, by his feet, weeping. His feet were wet with her tears and she wiped them with her hair, kissing them and anointing them with the myrrh. [39] When his host the Pharisee saw this he said to himself, 'If this man were a real prophet, he would know who this woman is who is touching him, and what a bad character she is.' [40] Jesus took him up: 'Simon,' he said, 'I have something to say to you.' 'What is it, Teacher?' he asked. [41] 'Two men were in debt to a moneylender: one owed him five hundred silver pieces, the other fifty. [42] As they did not have the means to pay he cancelled both debts. Now, which will love him more?' [43] Simon replied, 'I should think the one that was let off more.' 'You are right,' said Jesus. [44] Then turning to the woman, he said to Simon, 'You see this woman? I came to your house: you provided no water for my feet; but this woman has made my feet wet with her tears and wiped them with her hair. [45] You gave me no kiss; but she has been kissing my feet ever since I came in. [46] You

did not anoint my head with oil; but she has anointed my feet with myrrh. [47] So, I tell you, her great love proves that her many sins have been forgiven; where little has been forgiven, little love is shown.' [48] Then he said to her, 'Your sins are forgiven.' [49] The other guests began to ask themselves, 'Who is this, that he can forgive sins?' [50] But he said to the woman, 'Your faith has saved you; go in peace.'

8 AFTER this he went journeying from town to town and village to village, proclaiming the good news of the kingdom of God. With him were the Twelve [2] and a number of women who had been set free from evil spirits and infirmities: Mary, known as Mary of Magdala, from whom seven demons had come out, [3] Joanna, the wife of Chuza a steward of Herod's, Susanna, and many others. These women provided for them out of their own resources.

[4] People were now gathering in large numbers, and as they made their way to him from one town after another, he said in a parable: [5] 'A sower went out to sow his seed. And as he sowed, some of the seed fell along the footpath, where it was trampled on, and the birds ate it up. [6] Some fell on rock and, after coming up, it withered for lack of moisture. [7] Some fell among thistles, and the thistles grew up with it and choked it. [8] And some of the seed fell into good soil, and grew, and yielded a hundredfold.' As he said this he called out, 'If you have ears to hear, then hear.'

[9] His disciples asked him what this parable meant, [10] and he replied, 'It has been granted to you to know the secrets of the kingdom of God; but the others have only parables, so that they may look but see nothing, hear but understand nothing.

[11] 'This is what the parable means. The seed is the word of God. [12] The seed along the footpath stands for those who hear it, and then the devil comes and carries off the word from their hearts for fear they should believe and be saved. [13] The seed sown on rock stands for those who receive the word with joy when they hear it, but have no root; they are believers for a

while, but in the time of testing they give up. [14] That which fell among thistles represents those who hear, but their growth is choked by cares and wealth and the pleasures of life, and they bring nothing to maturity. [15] But the seed in good soil represents those who bring a good and honest heart to the hearing of the word, hold it fast, and by their perseverance yield a harvest.

[16] 'Nobody lights a lamp and then covers it with a basin or puts it under the bed. You put it on a lampstand so that those who come in may see the light. [17] For there is nothing hidden that will not be disclosed, nothing concealed that will not be made known and brought into the open.

[18] 'Take care, then, how you listen; for those who have will be given more, and those who have not will forfeit even what they think they have.'

[19] His mother and his brothers arrived but could not get to him for the crowd. [20] He was told, 'Your mother and brothers are standing outside, and want to see you.' [21] He replied, 'My mother and my brothers are those who hear the word of God and act upon it.'

[22] One day he got into a boat with his disciples and said to them, 'Let us cross over to the other side of the lake.' So they put out; [23] and as they sailed along he fell asleep. Then a heavy squall struck the lake; they began to ship water and were in grave danger. [24] They came and roused him: 'Master, Master, we are sinking!' they cried. He awoke, and rebuked the wind and the turbulent waters. The storm subsided and there was calm. [25] 'Where is your faith?' he asked. In fear and astonishment they said to one another, 'Who can this be? He gives his orders to the wind and the waves, and they obey him.'

[26] So they landed in the country of the Gerasenes, which is opposite Galilee. [27] As he stepped ashore he was met by a man from the town who was possessed by demons. For a long time he had neither worn clothes nor lived in a house, but stayed among the tombs. [28] When he saw Jesus he cried out, and fell at his feet. 'What do you want with me, Jesus, Son of the Most High God?' he shouted. 'I

7:47 **her great ... have been forgiven**: *or* her sins, which are many, have been forgiven because she has loved much.   8:26 **Gerasenes**: *some witnesses read* Gergesenes; *others read* Gadarenes.

implore you, do not torment me.' ²⁹ For Jesus was already ordering the unclean spirit to come out of the man. Many a time it had seized him, and then, for safety's sake, they would secure him with chains and fetters; but each time he broke loose and was driven by the demon out into the wilds.

³⁰ Jesus asked him, 'What is your name?' 'Legion,' he replied. This was because so many demons had taken possession of him. ³¹ And they begged him not to banish them to the abyss.

³² There was a large herd of pigs nearby, feeding on the hillside; and the demons begged him to let them go into these pigs. He gave them leave; ³³ the demons came out of the man and went into the pigs, and the herd rushed over the edge into the lake and were drowned.

³⁴ When the men in charge of them saw what had happened, they took to their heels and carried the news to the town and countryside; ³⁵ and the people came out to see what had happened. When they came to Jesus, and found the man from whom the demons had gone out sitting at his feet clothed and in his right mind, they were afraid. ³⁶ Eyewitnesses told them how the madman had been cured. ³⁷ Then the whole population of the Gerasene district was overcome by fear and asked Jesus to go away. So he got into the boat and went away. ³⁸ The man from whom the demons had gone out begged to go with him; but Jesus sent him away: ³⁹ 'Go back home,' he said, 'and tell them what God has done for you.' The man went all over the town proclaiming what Jesus had done for him.

⁴⁰ When Jesus returned, the people welcomed him, for they were all expecting him. ⁴¹ Then a man appeared—Jairus was his name and he was president of the synagogue. Throwing himself down at Jesus's feet he begged him to come to his house, ⁴² because his only daughter, who was about twelve years old, was dying.

While Jesus was on his way he could hardly breathe for the crowds. ⁴³ Among them was a woman who had suffered from haemorrhages for twelve years; and nobody had been able to cure her. ⁴⁴ She came up from behind and touched the edge of his cloak, and at once her haemorrhage stopped. ⁴⁵ Jesus said, 'Who was it who touched me?' All disclaimed it, and Peter said, 'Master, the crowds are hemming you in and pressing upon you!' ⁴⁶ But Jesus said, 'Someone did touch me, for I felt that power had gone out from me.' ⁴⁷ Then the woman, seeing that she was detected, came trembling and fell at his feet. Before all the people she explained why she had touched him and how she had been cured instantly. ⁴⁸ He said to her, 'Daughter, your faith has healed you. Go in peace.'

⁴⁹ While he was still speaking, a man came from the president's house with the message, 'Your daughter is dead; do not trouble the teacher any more.' ⁵⁰ But Jesus heard, and said, 'Do not be afraid; simply have faith and she will be well again.' ⁵¹ When he arrived at the house he allowed no one to go in with him except Peter, John, and James, and the child's father and mother. ⁵² Everyone was weeping and lamenting for her. He said, 'Stop your weeping; she is not dead: she is asleep'; ⁵³ and they laughed at him, well knowing that she was dead. ⁵⁴ But Jesus took hold of her hand and called to her: 'Get up, my child.' ⁵⁵ Her spirit returned, she stood up immediately, and he told them to give her something to eat. ⁵⁶ Her parents were astounded; but he forbade them to tell anyone what had happened.

Jesus and the Twelve

9 CALLING the Twelve together he gave them power and authority to overcome all demons and to cure diseases, ² and sent them out to proclaim the kingdom of God and to heal the sick. ³ 'Take nothing for the journey,' he told them, 'neither stick nor pack, neither bread nor money; nor are you to have a second coat. ⁴ When you enter a house, stay there until you leave that place. ⁵ As for those who will not receive you, when you leave their town shake the dust off your feet as a warning to them.' ⁶ So they set out and travelled from village to village, and everywhere they announced the good news and healed the sick.

⁷ Now Herod the tetrarch heard of all that was happening, and did not know

8:37 **Gerasene:** *some witnesses read* Gergesene; *others read* Gadarene.   8:43 **years; and:** *some witnesses add* though she had spent all she had on doctors.   8:44 **edge:** *or* tassel.

what to make of it; for some were saying that John had been raised from the dead, [8] others that Elijah had appeared, others again that one of the prophets of old had come back to life. [9] Herod said, 'As for John, I beheaded him; but who is this I hear so much about?' And he was anxious to see him.

[10] On their return the apostles gave Jesus an account of all they had done. Then he took them with him and withdrew privately to a town called Bethsaida, [11] but the crowds found out and followed. He welcomed them, and spoke to them about the kingdom of God, and cured those who were in need of healing. [12] When evening was drawing on, the Twelve came to him and said, 'Send the people off, so that they can go into the villages and farms round about to find food and lodging, for this is a remote place we are in.' [13] 'Give them something to eat yourselves,' he replied. But they said, 'All we have is five loaves and two fish, nothing more—or do you intend us to go and buy food for all these people?' [14] For there were about five thousand men. Then he said to his disciples, 'Make them sit down in groups of about fifty.' [15] They did so and got them all seated. [16] Then, taking the five loaves and the two fish, he looked up to heaven, said the blessing over them, broke them, and gave them to the disciples to distribute to the people. [17] They all ate and were satisfied; and the scraps they left were picked up and filled twelve baskets.

[18] One day, when he had been praying by himself in the company of his disciples, he asked them, 'Who do the people say I am?' [19] They answered, 'Some say John the Baptist, others Elijah, others that one of the prophets of old has come back to life.' [20] 'And you,' he said, 'who do you say I am?' Peter answered, 'God's Messiah.' [21] Then he gave them strict orders not to tell this to anyone. [22] And he said, 'The Son of Man has to endure great sufferings, and to be rejected by the elders, chief priests, and scribes, to be put to death, and to be raised again on the third day.'

[23] To everybody he said, 'Anyone who wants to be a follower of mine must renounce self; day after day he must take up his cross, and follow me. [24] Whoever wants to save his life will lose it, but whoever loses his life for my sake will save it. [25] What does anyone gain by winning the whole world at the cost of destroying himself? [26] If anyone is ashamed of me and my words, the Son of Man will be ashamed of him, when he comes in his glory and the glory of the Father and the holy angels. [27] In truth I tell you: there are some of those standing here who will not taste death before they have seen the kingdom of God.'

[28] About a week after this he took Peter, John, and James and went up a mountain to pray. [29] And while he was praying the appearance of his face changed and his clothes became dazzling white. [30] Suddenly there were two men talking with him—Moses and Elijah—[31] who appeared in glory and spoke of his departure, the destiny he was to fulfil in Jerusalem. [32] Peter and his companions had been overcome by sleep; but when they awoke, they saw his glory and the two men who stood beside him. [33] As these two were moving away from Jesus, Peter said to him, 'Master, it is good that we are here. Shall we make three shelters, one for you, one for Moses, and one for Elijah?' but he spoke without knowing what he was saying. [34] As he spoke there came a cloud which cast its shadow over them; they were afraid as they entered the cloud, [35] and from it a voice spoke: 'This is my Son, my Chosen; listen to him.' [36] After the voice had spoken, Jesus was seen to be alone. The disciples kept silence and did not at that time say a word to anyone of what they had seen.

[37] Next day when they came down from the mountain a large crowd came to meet him. [38] A man in the crowd called out: 'Teacher, I implore you to look at my son, my only child. [39] From time to time a spirit seizes him and with a sudden scream throws him into convulsions so that he foams at the mouth; it keeps on tormenting him and can hardly be made to let him go. [40] I begged your disciples to drive it out, but they could not.' [41] Jesus answered, 'What an unbelieving and perverse generation! How long shall I be with you and endure you? Bring your son here.' [42] But before the boy could reach

9:26 **me and my words:** *some witnesses read* me and mine.   9:31 **departure:** *lit.* exodus.

him the demon dashed him to the ground and threw him into convulsions. Jesus spoke sternly to the unclean spirit, cured the boy, and gave him back to his father. ⁴³And they were all struck with awe at the greatness of God.

Amid the general astonishment at all he was doing, Jesus said to his disciples, ⁴⁴'Listen to what I have to tell you. The Son of Man is to be given up into the power of men.' ⁴⁵But they did not understand what he said; its meaning had been hidden from them, so that they could not grasp it, and they were afraid to ask him about it.

⁴⁶An argument started among them as to which of them was the greatest. ⁴⁷Jesus, who knew what was going on in their minds, took a child, stood him by his side, ⁴⁸and said, 'Whoever receives this child in my name receives me; and whoever receives me receives the one who sent me. For the least among you all is the greatest.'

⁴⁹'Master,' said John, 'we saw someone driving out demons in your name, but as he is not one of us we tried to stop him.' ⁵⁰Jesus said to him, 'Do not stop him, for he who is not against you is on your side.'

The journey to Jerusalem

⁵¹As the time approached when he was to be taken up to heaven, he set his face resolutely towards Jerusalem, ⁵²and sent messengers ahead. They set out and went into a Samaritan village to make arrangements for him; ⁵³but the villagers would not receive him because he was on his way to Jerusalem. ⁵⁴When the disciples James and John saw this they said, 'Lord, do you want us to call down fire from heaven to consume them?' ⁵⁵But he turned and rebuked them, ⁵⁶and they went on to another village.

⁵⁷As they were going along the road a man said to him, 'I will follow you wherever you go.' ⁵⁸Jesus answered, 'Foxes have their holes and birds their roosts; but the Son of Man has nowhere to lay his head.' ⁵⁹To another he said, 'Follow me,' but the man replied, 'Let me first go and bury my father.' ⁶⁰Jesus said, 'Leave the dead to bury their dead; you must go and announce the kingdom of God.' ⁶¹Yet another said, 'I will follow you, sir; but let me first say goodbye to my people at home.' ⁶²To him Jesus said, 'No one who sets his hand to the plough and then looks back is fit for the kingdom of God.'

10 After this the Lord appointed a further seventy-two and sent them on ahead in pairs to every town and place he himself intended to visit. ²He said to them: 'The crop is heavy, but the labourers are few. Ask the owner therefore to send labourers to bring in the harvest. ³Be on your way; I am sending you like lambs among wolves. ⁴Carry no purse or pack, and travel barefoot. Exchange no greetings on the road. ⁵When you go into a house, let your first words be, "Peace to this house." ⁶If there is a man of peace there, your peace will rest on him; if not, it will return to you. ⁷Stay in that house, sharing their food and drink; for the worker deserves his pay. Do not move around from house to house. ⁸When you enter a town and you are made welcome, eat the food provided for you; ⁹heal the sick there, and say, "The kingdom of God has come upon you." ¹⁰But when you enter a town and you are not made welcome, go out into its streets and say, ¹¹"The very dust of your town that clings to our feet we wipe off to your shame. Only take note of this: the kingdom of God has come." ¹²I tell you, on the day of judgement the fate of Sodom will be more bearable than the fate of that town.

¹³'Alas for you, Chorazin! Alas for you, Bethsaida! If the miracles performed in you had taken place in Tyre and Sidon, they would have repented long ago, sitting in sackcloth and ashes. ¹⁴But it will be more bearable for Tyre and Sidon at the judgement than for you. ¹⁵As for you, Capernaum, will you be exalted to heaven? No, you will be brought down to Hades!

¹⁶'Whoever listens to you listens to me; whoever rejects you rejects me. And whoever rejects me rejects the One who sent me.'

¹⁷The seventy-two came back jubilant. 'In your name, Lord,' they said, 'even the

9:54 **consume them:** *some witnesses add* as Elijah did.   9:55 **rebuked them:** *some witnesses add* 'You do not know', he said, 'to what spirit you belong; ⁽⁵⁶⁾for the Son of Man did not come to destroy men's lives but to save them.'   10:1 **seventy-two:** *some witnesses read* seventy.   10:9 **come upon you:** *or* come close to you. 10:11 **has come:** *or* has come close.   10:17 **seventy-two:** *some witnesses read* seventy.

demons submit to us.' ¹⁸ He replied, 'I saw Satan fall, like lightning, from heaven. ¹⁹ And I have given you the power to tread underfoot snakes and scorpions and all the forces of the enemy. Nothing will ever harm you. ²⁰ Nevertheless, do not rejoice that the spirits submit to you, but that your names are enrolled in heaven.'

²¹ At that moment Jesus exulted in the Holy Spirit and said, 'I thank you, Father, Lord of heaven and earth, for hiding these things from the learned and wise, and revealing them to the simple. Yes, Father, such was your choice. ²² Everything is entrusted to me by my Father; no one knows who the Son is but the Father, or who the Father is but the Son, and those to whom the Son chooses to reveal him.'

²³ When he was alone with his disciples he turned to them and said, 'Happy the eyes that see what you are seeing! ²⁴ I tell you, many prophets and kings wished to see what you now see, yet never saw it; to hear what you hear, yet never heard it.'

²⁵ A LAWYER once came forward to test him by asking: 'Teacher, what must I do to inherit eternal life?' ²⁶ Jesus said, 'What is written in the law? What is your reading of it?' ²⁷ He replied, 'Love the Lord your God with all your heart, and with all your soul, with all your strength, and with all your mind; and your neighbour as yourself.' ²⁸ 'That is the right answer,' said Jesus; 'do that and you will have life.'

²⁹ Wanting to justify his question, he asked, 'But who is my neighbour?' ³⁰ Jesus replied, 'A man was on his way from Jerusalem down to Jericho when he was set upon by robbers, who stripped and beat him, and went off leaving him half dead. ³¹ It so happened that a priest was going down by the same road, and when he saw him, he went past on the other side. ³² So too a Levite came to the place, and when he saw him went past on the other side. ³³ But a Samaritan who was going that way came upon him, and when he saw him he was moved to pity. ³⁴ He went up and bandaged his wounds, bathing them with oil and wine. Then he lifted him on to his own beast, brought him to an inn, and looked after him. ³⁵ Next day he produced two silver pieces and gave them to the innkeeper, and said, "Look after him; and if you spend more, I will repay you on my way back." ³⁶ Which of these three do you think was neighbour to the man who fell into the hands of the robbers?' ³⁷ He answered, 'The one who showed him kindness.' Jesus said to him, 'Go and do as he did.'

³⁸ While they were on their way Jesus came to a village where a woman named Martha made him welcome. ³⁹ She had a sister, Mary, who seated herself at the Lord's feet and stayed there listening to his words. ⁴⁰ Now Martha was distracted by her many tasks, so she came to him and said, 'Lord, do you not care that my sister has left me to get on with the work by myself? Tell her to come and give me a hand.' ⁴¹ But the Lord answered, 'Martha, Martha, you are fretting and fussing about so many things; ⁴² only one thing is necessary. Mary has chosen what is best; it shall not be taken away from her.'

11 At one place after Jesus had been praying, one of his disciples said, 'Lord, teach us to pray, as John taught his disciples.' ² He answered, 'When you pray, say,

Father, may your name be hallowed;
   your kingdom come.
³ Give us each day our daily bread.
⁴ And forgive us our sins,
   for we too forgive all who have done
      us wrong.
And do not put us to the test.'

⁵ Then he said to them, 'Suppose one of you has a friend who comes to him in the middle of the night and says, "My friend, lend me three loaves, ⁶ for a friend of mine on a journey has turned up at my house, and I have nothing to offer him"; ⁷ and he replies from inside, "Do not bother me. The door is shut for the night; my children and I have gone to bed; and I cannot get up and give you what you want." ⁸ I tell you that even if he will not get up and provide for him out of friendship, his very

---

10:21 **Holy Spirit:** *some witnesses omit* Holy. **Yes ... such:** *or* Yes, I thank you, Father, that such.
10:42 **only ... necessary:** *some witnesses read* only few things are necessary, or rather, one alone.
11:2 **Father:** *some witnesses read* Our Father in heaven. **your kingdom come:** *one witness reads* your kingdom come upon us; *some others have* your Holy Spirit come upon us and cleanse us; *some add* your will be done, on earth as in heaven.   11:3 **daily bread:** *or* bread for the morrow.   11:4 **to the test:** *some witnesses add* but save us from the evil one (*or* from evil).

persistence will make the man get up and give him all he needs. ⁹ So I say to you, ask, and you will receive; seek, and you will find; knock, and the door will be opened to you. ¹⁰ For everyone who asks receives, those who seek find, and to those who knock, the door will be opened.

¹¹ 'Would any father among you offer his son a snake when he asks for a fish, ¹² or a scorpion when he asks for an egg? ¹³ If you, bad as you are, know how to give good things to your children, how much more will the heavenly Father give the Holy Spirit to those who ask him!'

Opposition and questioning

¹⁴ HE was driving out a demon which was dumb; and when the demon had come out, the dumb man began to speak. The people were astonished, ¹⁵ but some of them said, 'It is by Beelzebul prince of demons that he drives the demons out.' ¹⁶ Others, by way of a test, demanded of him a sign from heaven. ¹⁷ But he knew what was in their minds, and said, 'Every kingdom divided against itself is laid waste, and a divided household falls. ¹⁸ And if Satan is divided against himself, how can his kingdom stand—since, as you claim, I drive out the demons by Beelzebul? ¹⁹ If it is by Beelzebul that I drive out demons, by whom do your own people drive them out? If this is your argument, they themselves will refute you. ²⁰ But if it is by the finger of God that I drive out the demons, then be sure the kingdom of God has already come upon you.

²¹ 'When a strong man fully armed is on guard over his palace, his possessions are safe. ²² But when someone stronger attacks and overpowers him, he carries off the arms and armour on which the man had relied and distributes the spoil.

²³ 'He who is not with me is against me, and he who does not gather with me scatters.

²⁴ 'When an unclean spirit comes out of someone it wanders over the desert sands seeking a resting-place; and if it finds none, it says, "I will go back to the home I left." ²⁵ So it returns and finds the house swept clean and tidy. ²⁶ It goes off and collects seven other spirits more wicked than itself, and they all come in and settle there; and in the end that person's plight is worse than before.'

²⁷ While he was speaking thus, a woman in the crowd called out, 'Happy the womb that carried you and the breasts that suckled you!' ²⁸ He rejoined, 'No, happy are those who hear the word of God and keep it.'

²⁹ With the crowds swarming round him he went on to say: 'This is a wicked generation. It demands a sign, and the only sign that will be given it is the sign of Jonah. ³⁰ For just as Jonah was a sign to the Ninevites, so will the Son of Man be to this generation. ³¹ The queen of the south will appear in court when the men of this generation are on trial, and ensure their condemnation; for she came from the ends of the earth to listen to the wisdom of Solomon, and what is here is greater than Solomon. ³² The men of Nineveh will appear in court when this generation is on trial, and ensure its condemnation; for they repented at the preaching of Jonah; and what is here is greater than Jonah.

³³ 'No one lights a lamp and puts it in a cellar, but on the lampstand so that those who come in may see the light. ³⁴ The lamp of your body is the eye. When your eyes are sound, you have light for your whole body; but when they are bad, your body is in darkness. ³⁵ See to it then that the light you have is not darkness. ³⁶ If you have light for your whole body with no trace of darkness, it will all be full of light, as when the light of a lamp shines on you.'

³⁷ WHEN he had finished speaking, a Pharisee invited him to a meal, and he came in and sat down. ³⁸ The Pharisee noticed with surprise that he had not begun by washing before the meal. ³⁹ But the Lord said to him, 'You Pharisees clean the outside of cup and plate; but inside you are full of greed and wickedness. ⁴⁰ You fools! Did not he who made the outside make the inside too? ⁴¹ But let what is inside be given in charity, and all is clean.

⁴² 'Alas for you Pharisees! You pay

11:11 **offer his son**: *some witnesses add* a stone when he asks for bread, or.   11:31 **will appear ... trial**: *or* will be raised to life at the judgement together with the men of this generation.   11:32 **The men ... ensure**: *or* At the judgement the men of Nineveh will rise again together with this generation and will ensure. 11:33 **in a cellar**: *some witnesses add* or under the measuring bowl.

63

tithes of mint and rue and every garden herb, but neglect justice and the love of God. It is these you should have practised, without overlooking the others.

⁴³ 'Alas for you Pharisees! You love to have the chief seats in synagogues, and to be greeted respectfully in the street.

⁴⁴ 'Alas, alas, you are like unmarked graves which people walk over unawares.'

⁴⁵ At this one of the lawyers said, 'Teacher, when you say things like this you are insulting us too.' ⁴⁶ Jesus rejoined: 'Alas for you lawyers also! You load men with intolerable burdens, and will not lift a finger to lighten the load.

⁴⁷ 'Alas, you build monuments to the prophets whom your fathers murdered, ⁴⁸ and so testify that you approve of the deeds your fathers did; they committed the murders and you provide the monuments.

⁴⁹ 'This is why the Wisdom of God said, "I will send them prophets and messengers; and some of these they will persecute and kill"; ⁵⁰ so that this generation will have to answer for the blood of all the prophets shed since the foundation of the world; ⁵¹ from the blood of Abel to the blood of Zechariah who met his death between the altar and the sanctuary. I tell you, this generation will have to answer for it all.

⁵² 'Alas for you lawyers! You have taken away the key of knowledge. You did not go in yourselves, and those who were trying to go in, you prevented.'

⁵³ After he had left the house, the scribes and Pharisees began to assail him fiercely and to ply him with a host of questions, ⁵⁴ laying snares to catch him with his own words.

12 MEANWHILE, when a crowd of many thousands had gathered, packed so close that they were trampling on one another, he began to speak first to his disciples: 'Be on your guard against the leaven of the Pharisees—I mean their hypocrisy. ² There is nothing covered up that will not be uncovered, nothing hidden that will not be made known. ³ Therefore everything you have said in the dark will be heard in broad daylight, and what you have whispered behind closed doors will be shouted from the housetops.

⁴ 'To you who are my friends I say: do not fear those who kill the body and after that have nothing more they can do. ⁵ I will show you whom to fear: fear him who, after he has killed, has authority to cast into hell. Believe me, he is the one to fear.

⁶ 'Are not five sparrows sold for twopence? Yet not one of them is overlooked by God. ⁷ More than that, even the hairs of your head have all been counted. Do not be afraid; you are worth more than any number of sparrows.

⁸ 'I tell you this: whoever acknowledges me before others, the Son of Man will acknowledge before the angels of God; ⁹ but whoever disowns me before others will be disowned before the angels of God.

¹⁰ 'Anyone who speaks a word against the Son of Man will be forgiven; but for him who slanders the Holy Spirit there will be no forgiveness.

¹¹ 'When you are brought before synagogues and state authorities, do not worry about how you will conduct your defence or what you will say. ¹² When the time comes the Holy Spirit will instruct you what to say.'

¹³ Someone in the crowd said to him, 'Teacher, tell my brother to divide the family property with me.' ¹⁴ He said to the man, 'Who set me over you to judge or arbitrate?' ¹⁵ Then to the people he said, 'Beware! Be on your guard against greed of every kind, for even when someone has more than enough, his possessions do not give him life.' ¹⁶ And he told them this parable: 'There was a rich man whose land yielded a good harvest. ¹⁷ He debated with himself: "What am I to do? I have not the space to store my produce. ¹⁸ This is what I will do," said he: "I will pull down my barns and build them bigger. I will collect in them all my grain and other goods, ¹⁹ and I will say to myself, 'You have plenty of good things laid by, enough for many years to come: take life easy, eat, drink, and enjoy yourself.'" ²⁰ But God said to him, "You fool, this very night you must surrender your life; and the money you have made, who will get it now?" ²¹ That is how it is with the man who piles up treasure for himself and remains a pauper in the sight of God.'

²² To his disciples he said, 'This is why I tell you not to worry about food to keep you alive or clothes to cover your body.

23 Life is more than food, the body more than clothes. 24 Think of the ravens: they neither sow nor reap; they have no storehouse or barn; yet God feeds them. You are worth far more than the birds! 25 Can anxious thought add a day to your life? 26 If, then, you cannot do even a very little thing, why worry about the rest?

27 'Think of the lilies: they neither spin nor weave; yet I tell you, even Solomon in all his splendour was not attired like one of them. 28 If that is how God clothes the grass, which is growing in the field today, and tomorrow is thrown on the stove, how much more will he clothe you! How little faith you have! 29 Do not set your minds on what you are to eat or drink; do not be anxious. 30 These are all things that occupy the minds of the Gentiles, but your Father knows that you need them. 31 No, set your minds on his kingdom, and the rest will come to you as well.

32 'Have no fear, little flock; for your Father has chosen to give you the kingdom. 33 Sell your possessions and give to charity. Provide for yourselves purses that do not wear out, and never-failing treasure in heaven, where no thief can get near it, no moth destroy it. 34 For where your treasure is, there will your heart be also.

35 'Be ready for action, with your robes hitched up and your lamps alight. 36 Be like people who wait for their master's return from a wedding party, ready to let him in the moment he arrives and knocks. 37 Happy are those servants whom the master finds awake when he comes. Truly I tell you: he will hitch up his robe, seat them at table, and come and wait on them. 38 If it is the middle of the night or before dawn when he comes and he still finds them awake, then are they happy indeed. 39 Remember, if the householder had known at what time the burglar was coming he would not have let his house be broken into. 40 So hold yourselves in readiness, because the Son of Man will come at the time you least expect him.'

41 Peter said, 'Lord, do you intend this parable specially for us or is it for everyone?' 42 The Lord said, 'Who is the trusty and sensible man whom his master will appoint as his steward, to manage his servants and issue their rations at the proper time? 43 Happy that servant if his master comes home and finds him at work! 44 I tell you this: he will be put in charge of all his master's property. 45 But if that servant says to himself, "The master is a long time coming," and begins to bully the menservants and maids, and to eat and drink and get drunk, 46 then the master will arrive on a day when the servant does not expect him, at a time he has not been told. He will cut him in pieces and assign him a place among the faithless.

47 'The servant who knew his master's wishes, yet made no attempt to carry them out, will be flogged severely. 48 But one who did not know them and earned a beating will be flogged less severely. Where someone has been given much, much will be expected of him; and the more he has had entrusted to him the more will be demanded of him.

49 'I have come to set fire to the earth, and how I wish it were already kindled! 50 I have a baptism to undergo, and what constraint I am under until it is over! 51 Do you suppose I came to establish peace on the earth? No indeed, I have come to bring dissension. 52 From now on, a family of five will be divided, three against two and two against three; 53 father against son and son against father, mother against daughter and daughter against mother, mother-in-law against daughter-in-law and daughter-in-law against mother-in-law.'

54 He also said to the people, 'When you see clouds gathering in the west, you say at once, "It is going to rain," and rain it does. 55 And when the wind is from the south, you say, "It will be hot," and it is. 56 What hypocrites you are! You know how to interpret the appearance of earth and sky, but cannot interpret this fateful hour.

57 'Why can you not judge for yourselves what is right? 58 When you are going with your opponent to court, make an effort to reach a settlement with him while you are still on the way; otherwise he may drag you before the judge, and the judge hand you over to the officer, and the officer throw you into jail. 59 I tell you, you will not be let out until you have paid the very last penny.'

12:25 **a day ... life**: *or* a foot to your height.

13 At that time some people came and told him about the Galileans whose blood Pilate had mixed with their sacrifices. ²He answered them: 'Do you suppose that, because these Galileans suffered this fate, they must have been greater sinners than anyone else in Galilee? ³No, I tell you; but unless you repent, you will all of you come to the same end. ⁴Or the eighteen people who were killed when the tower fell on them at Siloam—do you imagine they must have been more guilty than all the other people living in Jerusalem? ⁵No, I tell you; but unless you repent, you will all come to an end like theirs.'

⁶He told them this parable: 'A man had a fig tree growing in his vineyard; and he came looking for fruit on it, but found none. ⁷So he said to the vine-dresser, "For the last three years I have come looking for fruit on this fig tree without finding any. Cut it down. Why should it go on taking goodness from the soil?" ⁸But he replied, "Leave it, sir, for this one year, while I dig round it and manure it. ⁹And if it bears next season, well and good; if not, you shall have it down."'

¹⁰He was teaching in one of the synagogues on the sabbath, ¹¹and there was a woman there possessed by a spirit that had crippled her for eighteen years. She was bent double and quite unable to stand up straight. ¹²When Jesus saw her he called her and said, 'You are rid of your trouble,' ¹³and he laid his hands on her. Immediately she straightened up and began to praise God. ¹⁴But the president of the synagogue, indignant with Jesus for healing on the sabbath, intervened and said to the congregation, 'There are six working days: come and be cured on one of them, and not on the sabbath.' ¹⁵The Lord gave him this answer: 'What hypocrites you are!' he said. 'Is there a single one of you who does not loose his ox or his donkey from its stall and take it out to water on the sabbath? ¹⁶And here is this woman, a daughter of Abraham, who has been bound by Satan for eighteen long years: was it not right for her to be loosed from her bonds on the sabbath?' ¹⁷At these words all his opponents were covered with confusion, while the mass of the people were delighted at all the wonderful things he was doing.

¹⁸'What is the kingdom of God like?' he continued. 'To what shall I compare it? ¹⁹It is like a mustard seed which a man took and sowed in his garden; and it grew to be a tree and the birds came to roost among its branches.'

²⁰Again he said, 'To what shall I compare the kingdom of God? ²¹It is like yeast which a woman took and mixed with three measures of flour till it was all leavened.'

²²He continued his journey through towns and villages, teaching as he made his way towards Jerusalem. ²³Someone asked him, 'Sir, are only a few to be saved?' His answer was: ²⁴'Make every effort to enter through the narrow door; for I tell you that many will try to enter but will not succeed.

²⁵'When once the master of the house has got up and locked the door, you may stand outside and knock, and say, "Sir, let us in!" but he will only answer, "I do not know where you come from." ²⁶Then you will protest, "We used to eat and drink with you, and you taught in our streets." ²⁷But he will repeat, "I tell you, I do not know where you come from. Out of my sight, all of you, you and your wicked ways!" ²⁸There will be wailing and grinding of teeth there, when you see Abraham, Isaac, Jacob, and all the prophets, in the kingdom of God, and you yourselves are driven away. ²⁹From east and west, from north and south, people will come and take their places at the banquet in the kingdom of God. ³⁰Yes, and some who are now last will be first, and some who are first will be last.'

³¹At that time a number of Pharisees came and warned him, 'Leave this place and be on your way; Herod wants to kill you.' ³²He replied, 'Go and tell that fox, "Listen: today and tomorrow I shall be driving out demons and working cures; on the third day I reach my goal." ³³However, I must go on my way today and tomorrow and the next day, because it is unthinkable for a prophet to meet his death anywhere but in Jerusalem.

³⁴'O Jerusalem, Jerusalem, city that murders the prophets and stones the messengers sent to her! How often have I longed to gather your children, as a hen gathers her brood under her wings; but you would not let me. ³⁵Look! There is

your temple, forsaken by God. I tell you, you will not see me until the time comes when you say, "Blessings on him who comes in the name of the Lord!"'

14 ONE sabbath he went to have a meal in the house of one of the leading Pharisees; and they were watching him closely. ² There, in front of him, was a man suffering from dropsy, ³ and Jesus asked the lawyers and the Pharisees: 'Is it permitted to heal people on the sabbath or not?' ⁴ They said nothing. So he took the man, cured him, and sent him away. ⁵ Then he turned to them and said, 'If one of you has a son or an ox that falls into a well, will he hesitate to pull him out on the sabbath day?' ⁶ To this they could find no reply.

⁷ When he noticed how the guests were trying to secure the places of honour, he spoke to them in a parable: ⁸ 'When somebody asks you to a wedding feast, do not sit down in the place of honour. It may be that some person more distinguished than yourself has been invited; ⁹ and the host will come to say to you, "Give this man your seat." Then you will look foolish as you go to take the lowest place. ¹⁰ No, when you receive an invitation, go and sit down in the lowest place, so that when your host comes he will say, "Come up higher, my friend." Then all your fellow-guests will see the respect in which you are held. ¹¹ For everyone who exalts himself will be humbled; and whoever humbles himself will be exalted.'

¹² Then he said to his host, 'When you are having guests for lunch or supper, do not invite your friends, your brothers or other relations, or your rich neighbours; they will only ask you back again and so you will be repaid. ¹³ But when you give a party, ask the poor, the crippled, the lame, and the blind. ¹⁴ That is the way to find happiness, because they have no means of repaying you. You will be repaid on the day when the righteous rise from the dead.'

¹⁵ Hearing this one of the company said to him, 'Happy are those who will sit at the feast in the kingdom of God!' ¹⁶ Jesus answered, 'A man was giving a big dinner party and had sent out many invitations. ¹⁷ At dinner-time he sent his servant to tell his guests, "Come please, everything is now ready." ¹⁸ One after another they all sent excuses. The first said, "I have bought a piece of land, and I must go and inspect it; please accept my apologies." ¹⁹ The second said, "I have bought five yoke of oxen, and I am on my way to try them out; please accept my apologies." ²⁰ The next said, "I cannot come; I have just got married." ²¹ When the servant came back he reported this to his master. The master of the house was furious and said to him, "Go out quickly into the streets and alleys of the town, and bring in the poor, the crippled, the blind, and the lame." ²² When the servant informed him that his orders had been carried out and there was still room, ²³ his master replied, "Go out on the highways and along the hedgerows and compel them to come in; I want my house full. ²⁴ I tell you, not one of those who were invited shall taste my banquet."'

²⁵ Once when great crowds were accompanying him, he turned to them and said: ²⁶ 'If anyone comes to me and does not hate his father and mother, wife and children, brothers and sisters, even his own life, he cannot be a disciple of mine. ²⁷ No one who does not carry his cross and come with me can be a disciple of mine. ²⁸ Would any of you think of building a tower without first sitting down and calculating the cost, to see whether he could afford to finish it? ²⁹ Otherwise, if he has laid its foundation and then is unable to complete it, everyone who sees it will laugh at him. ³⁰ "There goes the man", they will say, "who started to build and could not finish." ³¹ Or what king will march to battle against another king, without first sitting down to consider whether with ten thousand men he can face an enemy coming to meet him with twenty thousand? ³² If he cannot, then, long before the enemy approaches, he sends envoys and asks for terms. ³³ So also, if you are not prepared to leave all your possessions behind, you cannot be my disciples.

³⁴ 'Salt is good; but if salt itself becomes tasteless, how will it be seasoned? ³⁵ It is useless either on the land or on the dungheap; it can only be thrown away. If you have ears to hear, then hear.'

14:5 **son:** *some witnesses read* donkey.

Finding the lost

15 ANOTHER time, the tax-collectors and sinners were all crowding in to listen to him; [2] and the Pharisees and scribes began murmuring their disapproval: 'This fellow', they said, 'welcomes sinners and eats with them.' [3] He answered them with this parable: [4] 'If one of you has a hundred sheep and loses one of them, does he not leave the ninety-nine in the wilderness and go after the one that is missing until he finds it? [5] And when he does, he lifts it joyfully on to his shoulders, [6] and goes home to call his friends and neighbours together. "Rejoice with me!" he cries. "I have found my lost sheep." [7] In the same way, I tell you, there will be greater joy in heaven over one sinner who repents than over ninety-nine righteous people who do not need to repent.

[8] 'Or again, if a woman has ten silver coins and loses one of them, does she not light the lamp, sweep out the house, and look in every corner till she finds it? [9] And when she does, she calls her friends and neighbours together, and says, "Rejoice with me! I have found the coin that I lost." [10] In the same way, I tell you, there is joy among the angels of God over one sinner who repents.'

[11] Again he said: 'There was once a man who had two sons; [12] and the younger said to his father, "Father, give me my share of the property." So he divided his estate between them. [13] A few days later the younger son turned the whole of his share into cash and left home for a distant country, where he squandered it in dissolute living. [14] He had spent it all, when a severe famine fell upon that country and he began to be in need. [15] So he went and attached himself to one of the local landowners, who sent him on to his farm to mind the pigs. [16] He would have been glad to fill his belly with the pods that the pigs were eating, but no one gave him anything. [17] Then he came to his senses: "How many of my father's hired servants have more food than they can eat," he said, "and here am I, starving to death! [18] I will go at once to my father, and say to him, 'Father, I have sinned against God and against you; [19] I am no longer fit to be called your son; treat me as one of your hired servants.'" [20] So he set out for his father's house. But while he was still a long way off his father saw him, and his heart went out to him; he ran to meet him, flung his arms round him, and kissed him. [21] The son said, "Father, I have sinned against God and against you; I am no longer fit to be called your son." [22] But the father said to his servants, "Quick! Fetch a robe, the best we have, and put it on him; put a ring on his finger and sandals on his feet. [23] Bring the fatted calf and kill it, and let us celebrate with a feast. [24] For this son of mine was dead and has come back to life; he was lost and is found." And the festivities began.

[25] 'Now the elder son had been out on the farm; and on his way back, as he approached the house, he heard music and dancing. [26] He called one of the servants and asked what it meant. [27] The servant told him, "Your brother has come home, and your father has killed the fatted calf because he has him back safe and sound." [28] But he was angry and refused to go in. His father came out and pleaded with him; [29] but he retorted, "You know how I have slaved for you all these years; I never once disobeyed your orders; yet you never gave me so much as a kid, to celebrate with my friends. [30] But now that this son of yours turns up, after running through your money with his women, you kill the fatted calf for him." [31] "My boy," said the father, "you are always with me, and everything I have is yours. [32] How could we fail to celebrate this happy day? Your brother here was dead and has come back to life; he was lost and has been found."'

Instructing the disciples

16 HE said to his disciples, 'There was a rich man who had a steward, and he received complaints that this man was squandering the property. [2] So he sent for him, and said, "What is this that I hear about you? Produce your accounts, for you cannot be steward any longer." [3] The steward said to himself, "What am I to do now that my master is going to dismiss me from my post? I am not strong enough to dig, and I am too proud to beg. [4] I know what I must do, to make sure that, when I am dismissed, there will be people who will take me into their homes." [5] He summoned his master's debtors one by one. To the first he said, "How much do you owe my master?" [6] He replied, "A hundred jars of olive oil." He said, "Here is your account. Sit down and make it fifty, and be quick about it." ⁷Then he said to another, "And you, how much do you owe?" He said, "A hundred measures of wheat," and was told, "Here is your account; make it eighty." ⁸And the master applauded the dishonest steward for acting so astutely. For in dealing with their own kind the children of this world are more astute than the children of light.

⁹'So I say to you, use your worldly wealth to win friends for yourselves, so that when money is a thing of the past you may be received into an eternal home.

¹⁰'Anyone who can be trusted in small matters can be trusted also in great; and anyone who is dishonest in small matters is dishonest also in great. ¹¹If, then, you have not proved trustworthy with the wealth of this world, who will trust you with the wealth that is real? ¹²And if you have proved untrustworthy with what belongs to another, who will give you anything of your own?

¹³'No slave can serve two masters; for either he will hate the first and love the second, or he will be devoted to the first and despise the second. You cannot serve God and Money.'

¹⁴The Pharisees, who loved money, heard all this and scoffed at him. ¹⁵He said to them, 'You are the people who impress others with your righteousness; but God sees through you; for what is considered admirable in human eyes is detestable in the sight of God.

¹⁶'The law and the prophets were until John: since then, the good news of the kingdom of God is proclaimed, and everyone forces a way in.

¹⁷'It is easier for heaven and earth to come to an end than for one letter of the law to lose its force.

¹⁸'A man who divorces his wife and marries another commits adultery; and anyone who marries a woman divorced from her husband commits adultery.

¹⁹'There was once a rich man, who used to dress in purple and the finest linen, and feasted sumptuously every day. ²⁰At his gate lay a poor man named Lazarus, who was covered with sores. ²¹He would have been glad to satisfy his hunger with the scraps from the rich man's table. Dogs used to come and lick his sores. ²²One day the poor man died

and was carried away by the angels to be with Abraham. The rich man also died and was buried. ²³In Hades, where he was in torment, he looked up and there, far away, was Abraham with Lazarus close beside him. ²⁴"Abraham, my father," he called out, "take pity on me! Send Lazarus to dip the tip of his finger in water, to cool my tongue, for I am in agony in this fire." ²⁵But Abraham said, "My child, remember that the good things fell to you in your lifetime, and the bad to Lazarus. Now he has his consolation here and it is you who are in agony. ²⁶But that is not all: there is a great gulf fixed between us; no one can cross it from our side to reach you, and none may pass from your side to us." ²⁷"Then, father," he replied, "will you send him to my father's house, ²⁸where I have five brothers, to warn them, so that they may not come to this place of torment?" ²⁹But Abraham said, "They have Moses and the prophets; let them listen to them." ³⁰"No, father Abraham," he replied, "but if someone from the dead visits them, they will repent." ³¹Abraham answered, "If they do not listen to Moses and the prophets they will pay no heed even if someone should rise from the dead."'

17 HE said to his disciples, 'There are bound to be causes of stumbling; but woe betide the person through whom they come. ²It would be better for him to be thrown into the sea with a millstone round his neck than to cause the downfall of one of these little ones. ³So be on your guard.

'If your brother does wrong, reprove him; and if he repents, forgive him. ⁴Even if he wrongs you seven times in a day and comes back to you seven times saying, "I am sorry," you are to forgive him.'

⁵The apostles said to the Lord, 'Increase our faith'; ⁶and the Lord replied, 'If you had faith no bigger than a mustard seed, you could say to this mulberry tree, "Be rooted up and planted in the sea"; and it would obey you.

⁷'Suppose one of you has a servant ploughing or minding sheep. When he comes in from the fields, will the master say, "Come and sit down straight away"? ⁸Will he not rather say, "Prepare my supper; hitch up your robe, and wait on me while I have my meal. You can have

yours afterwards"? [9] Is he grateful to the servant for carrying out his orders? [10] So with you: when you have carried out all you have been ordered to do, you should say, "We are servants and deserve no credit; we have only done our duty."'

[11] In the course of his journey to Jerusalem he was travelling through the borderlands of Samaria and Galilee. [12] As he was entering a village he was met by ten men with leprosy. They stood some way off [13] and called out to him, 'Jesus, Master, take pity on us.' [14] When he saw them he said, 'Go and show yourselves to the priests'; and while they were on their way, they were made clean. [15] One of them, finding himself cured, turned back with shouts of praise to God. [16] He threw himself down at Jesus's feet and thanked him. And he was a Samaritan. [17] At this Jesus said: 'Were not all ten made clean? The other nine, where are they? [18] Was no one found returning to give praise to God except this foreigner?' [19] And he said to the man, 'Stand up and go on your way; your faith has cured you.'

[20] THE Pharisees asked him, 'When will the kingdom of God come?' He answered, 'You cannot tell by observation when the kingdom of God comes. [21] You cannot say, "Look, here it is," or "There it is!" For the kingdom of God is among you!'

[22] He said to the disciples, 'The time will come when you will long to see one of the days of the Son of Man and will not see it. [23] They will say to you, "Look! There!" and "Look! Here!" Do not go running off in pursuit. [24] For like a lightning-flash, that lights up the earth from end to end, will the Son of Man be in his day. [25] But first he must endure much suffering and be rejected by this generation.

[26] 'As it was in the days of Noah, so will it be in the days of the Son of Man. [27] They ate and drank and married, until the day that Noah went into the ark and the flood came and made an end of them all. [28] So too in the days of Lot, they ate and drank, they bought and sold, they planted and built; [29] but on the day that Lot left Sodom, fire and sulphur rained from the sky and made an end of them all. [30] It will

be like that on the day when the Son of Man is revealed.

[31] 'On that day if anyone is on the roof while his belongings are in the house, he must not go down to fetch them; and if anyone is in the field, he must not turn back. [32] Remember Lot's wife. [33] Whoever seeks to preserve his life will lose it; and whoever loses his life will gain it.

[34] 'I tell you, on that night there will be two people in one bed: one will be taken, the other left. [35] There will be two women together grinding corn: one will be taken, the other left.' [37] When they heard this they asked, 'Where, Lord?' He said, 'Where the carcass is, there will the vultures gather.'

18 HE told them a parable to show that they should keep on praying and never lose heart: [2] 'In a certain city there was a judge who had no fear of God or respect for man, [3] and in the same city there was a widow who kept coming before him to demand justice against her opponent. [4] For a time he refused; but in the end he said to himself, "Although I have no fear of God or respect for man, [5] yet this widow is so great a nuisance that I will give her justice before she wears me out with her persistence."' [6] The Lord said, 'You hear what the unjust judge says. [7] Then will not God give justice to his chosen, to whom he listens patiently while they cry out to him day and night? [8] I tell you, he will give them justice soon enough. But when the Son of Man comes, will he find faith on earth?'

[9] Here is another parable that he told; it was aimed at those who were sure of their own goodness and looked down on everyone else. [10] 'Two men went up to the temple to pray, one a Pharisee and the other a tax-collector. [11] The Pharisee stood up and prayed this prayer: "I thank you, God, that I am not like the rest of mankind—greedy, dishonest, adulterous —or, for that matter, like this tax-collector. [12] I fast twice a week; I pay tithes on all that I get." [13] But the other kept his distance and would not even raise his eyes to heaven, but beat upon his breast, saying, "God, have mercy on me,

---

17:21 **For ... among you!**: *or* For the kingdom of God is within you! *or* For the kingdom of God is within your grasp! *or* For suddenly the kingdom of God will be among you.   17:35 **the other left**: *some witnesses add* [36] 'There will be two men in the fields: one will be taken, the other left.'

sinner that I am." ¹⁴ It was this man, I tell you, and not the other, who went home acquitted of his sins. For everyone who exalts himself will be humbled; and whoever humbles himself will be exalted.'

¹⁵ They brought babies for him to touch, and when the disciples saw them they rebuked them. ¹⁶ But Jesus called for the children and said, 'Let the children come to me; do not try to stop them; for the kingdom of God belongs to such as these. ¹⁷ Truly I tell you: whoever does not accept the kingdom of God like a child will never enter it.'

¹⁸ One of the rulers put this question to him: 'Good Teacher, what must I do to win eternal life?' ¹⁹ Jesus said to him, 'Why do you call me good? No one is good except God alone. ²⁰ You know the commandments: "Do not commit adultery; do not murder; do not steal; do not give false evidence; honour your father and mother."' ²¹ The man answered, 'I have kept all these since I was a boy.' ²² On hearing this Jesus said, 'There is still one thing you lack: sell everything you have and give to the poor, and you will have treasure in heaven; then come and follow me.' ²³ When he heard this his heart sank, for he was a very rich man. ²⁴ When Jesus saw it he said, 'How hard it is for the wealthy to enter the kingdom of God! ²⁵ It is easier for a camel to go through the eye of a needle than for a rich man to enter the kingdom of God.' ²⁶ Those who heard asked, 'Then who can be saved?' ²⁷ He answered, 'What is impossible for men is possible for God.'

²⁸ Peter said, 'What about us? We left all we had to follow you.' ²⁹ Jesus said to them, 'Truly I tell you: there is no one who has given up home, or wife, brothers, parents, or children, for the sake of the kingdom of God, ³⁰ who will not be repaid many times over in this age, and in the age to come have eternal life.'

Jesus's challenge to Jerusalem

³¹ HE took the Twelve aside and said, 'We are now going up to Jerusalem; and everything that was written by the prophets will find its fulfilment in the Son of Man. ³² He will be handed over to the Gentiles. He will be mocked, maltreated, and spat upon; ³³ they will flog him and kill him; and on the third day he will rise again.' ³⁴ But they did not understand this

at all or grasp what he was talking about; its meaning was concealed from them.

³⁵ As he approached Jericho a blind man sat at the roadside begging. ³⁶ Hearing a crowd going past, he asked what was happening, ³⁷ and was told that Jesus of Nazareth was passing by. ³⁸ Then he called out, 'Jesus, Son of David, have pity on me.' ³⁹ The people in front told him to hold his tongue; but he shouted all the more, 'Son of David, have pity on me.' ⁴⁰ Jesus stopped and ordered the man to be brought to him. When he came up Jesus asked him, ⁴¹ 'What do you want me to do for you?' 'Sir, I want my sight back,' he answered. ⁴² Jesus said to him, 'Have back your sight; your faith has healed you.' ⁴³ He recovered his sight instantly and followed Jesus, praising God. And all the people gave praise to God for what they had seen.

19 Entering Jericho he made his way through the city. ² There was a man there named Zacchaeus; he was superintendent of taxes and very rich. ³ He was eager to see what Jesus looked like; but, being a little man, he could not see him for the crowd. ⁴ So he ran on ahead and climbed a sycomore tree in order to see him, for he was to pass that way. ⁵ When Jesus came to the place, he looked up and said, 'Zacchaeus, be quick and come down, for I must stay at your house today.' ⁶ He climbed down as quickly as he could and welcomed him gladly. ⁷ At this there was a general murmur of disapproval. 'He has gone in to be the guest of a sinner,' they said. ⁸ But Zacchaeus stood there and said to the Lord, 'Here and now, sir, I give half my possessions to charity; and if I have defrauded anyone, I will repay him four times over.' ⁹ Jesus said to him, 'Today salvation has come to this house—for this man too is a son of Abraham. ¹⁰ The Son of Man has come to seek and to save what is lost.'

¹¹ While they were listening to this, he went on to tell them a parable, because he was now close to Jerusalem and they thought the kingdom of God might dawn at any moment. ¹² He said, 'A man of noble birth went on a long journey abroad, to have himself appointed king and then return. ¹³ But first he called ten of his servants and gave them each a sum of money, saying, "Trade with this while I

am away." [14] His fellow-citizens hated him and sent a delegation after him to say, "We do not want this man as our king." [15] He returned however as king, and sent for the servants to whom he had given the money, to find out what profit each had made. [16] The first came and said, "Your money, sir, has increased tenfold." [17] "Well done," he replied; "you are a good servant. Because you have shown yourself trustworthy in a very small matter, you shall have charge of ten cities." [18] The second came and said, "Your money, sir, has increased fivefold"; [19] and he was told, "You shall be in charge of five cities." [20] The third came and said, "Here is your money, sir; I kept it wrapped up in a handkerchief. [21] I was afraid of you, because you are a hard man: you draw out what you did not put in and reap what you did not sow." [22] "You scoundrel!" he replied. "I will condemn you out of your own mouth. You knew me to be a hard man, did you, drawing out what I never put in, and reaping what I did not sow? [23] Then why did you not put my money on deposit, and I could have claimed it with interest when I came back?" [24] Turning to his attendants he said, "Take the money from him and give it to the man with the most." [25] "But, sir," they replied, "he has ten times as much already." [26] "I tell you," he said, "everyone who has will be given more; but whoever has nothing will forfeit even what he has. [27] But as for those enemies of mine who did not want me for their king, bring them here and slaughter them in my presence.'"

[28] WITH that Jesus set out on the ascent to Jerusalem. [29] As he approached Bethphage and Bethany at the hill called Olivet, he sent off two of the disciples, [30] telling them: 'Go into the village opposite; as you enter it you will find tethered there a colt which no one has yet ridden. Untie it and bring it here. [31] If anyone asks why you are untying it, say, "The Master needs it."' [32] The two went on their errand and found everything just as he had told them. [33] As they were untying the colt, its owners asked, 'Why are you untying that colt?' [34] They answered, 'The Master needs it.'

[35] So they brought the colt to Jesus, and threw their cloaks on it for Jesus to mount. [36] As he went along people laid their cloaks on the road. [37] And when he reached the descent from the mount of Olives, the whole company of his disciples in their joy began to sing aloud the praises of God for all the great things they had seen:

[38] 'Blessed is he who comes as king in the name of the Lord!
Peace in heaven, glory in highest heaven!'

[39] Some Pharisees in the crowd said to him, 'Teacher, restrain your disciples.' [40] He answered, 'I tell you, if my disciples are silent the stones will shout aloud.'

[41] When he came in sight of the city, he wept over it [42] and said, 'If only you had known this day the way that leads to peace! But no; it is hidden from your sight. [43] For a time will come upon you, when your enemies will set up siegeworks against you; they will encircle you and hem you in at every point; [44] they will bring you to the ground, you and your children within your walls, and not leave you one stone standing on another, because you did not recognize the time of God's visitation.'

[45] Then he went into the temple and began driving out the traders, [46] with these words: 'Scripture says, "My house shall be a house of prayer"; but you have made it a bandits' cave.'

[47] Day by day he taught in the temple. The chief priests and scribes, with the support of the leading citizens, wanted to bring about his death, [48] but found they were helpless, because the people all hung on his words.

20 ONE day, as he was teaching the people in the temple and telling them the good news, the chief priests and scribes, accompanied by the elders, confronted him. [2] 'Tell us', they said, 'by what authority you are acting like this; who gave you this authority?' [3] He answered them, 'I also have a question for you: tell me, [4] was the baptism of John from God or from man?' [5] This set them arguing among themselves: 'If we say, "From God," he will say, "Why did you not believe him?" [6] And if we say, "From man," the people will all stone us, for they are convinced that John was a prophet.' [7] So they answered that they could not tell. [8] And Jesus said to them, 'Then neither will I tell you by what authority I act.'

[9] He went on to tell the people this parable: 'A man planted a vineyard, let it out to vine-growers, and went abroad for a long time. [10] When the season came, he sent a servant to the tenants to collect from them his share of the produce; but the tenants thrashed him and sent him away empty-handed. [11] He tried again and sent a second servant; but they thrashed him too, treated him outrageously, and sent him away empty-handed. [12] He tried once more and sent a third; him too they wounded and flung out. [13] Then the owner of the vineyard said, "What am I to do? I will send my beloved son; perhaps they will respect him." [14] But when the tenants saw him they discussed what they should do. "This is the heir," they said; "let us kill him so that the inheritance may come to us." [15] So they flung him out of the vineyard and killed him. What, therefore, will the owner of the vineyard do to them? [16] He will come and put those tenants to death and give the vineyard to others.'

When they heard this, they said, 'God forbid!' [17] But he looked straight at them and said, 'Then what does this text of scripture mean: "The stone which the builders rejected has become the main corner-stone"? [18] Everyone who falls on that stone will be dashed to pieces; anyone on whom it falls will be crushed.'

[19] The scribes and chief priests wanted to seize him there and then, for they saw that this parable was aimed at them; but they were afraid of the people. [20] So they watched their opportunity and sent agents in the guise of honest men, to seize on some word of his that they could use as a pretext for handing him over to the authority and jurisdiction of the governor. [21] They put a question to him: 'Teacher,' they said, 'we know that what you speak and teach is sound; you pay deference to no one, but teach in all sincerity the way of life that God requires. [22] Are we or are we not permitted to pay taxes to the Roman emperor?' [23] He saw through their trick and said, [24] 'Show me a silver piece. Whose head does it bear, and whose inscription?' 'Caesar's,' they

replied. [25] 'Very well then,' he said, 'pay to Caesar what belongs to Caesar, and to God what belongs to God.' [26] Thus their attempt to catch him out in public failed, and, taken aback by his reply, they fell silent.

[27] Then some Sadducees, who deny that there is a resurrection, came forward and asked: [28] 'Teacher, Moses laid it down for us that if there are brothers, and one dies leaving a wife but no child, then the next should marry the widow and provide an heir for his brother. [29] Now, there were seven brothers: the first took a wife and died childless; [30] then the second married her, [31] then the third. In this way the seven of them died leaving no children. [32] Last of all the woman also died. [33] At the resurrection, therefore, whose wife is she to be, since all seven had married her?' [34] Jesus said to them, 'The men and women of this world marry; [35] but those who have been judged worthy of a place in the other world, and of the resurrection from the dead, do not marry, [36] for they are no longer subject to death. They are like angels; they are children of God, because they share in the resurrection. [37] That the dead are raised to life again is shown by Moses himself in the story of the burning bush, when he calls the Lord "the God of Abraham, the God of Isaac, the God of Jacob". [38] God is not God of the dead but of the living; in his sight all are alive.'

[39] At this some of the scribes said, 'Well spoken, Teacher.' [40] And nobody dared put any further question to him.

[41] He said to them, 'How can they say that the Messiah is David's son? [42] For David himself says in the book of Psalms: "The Lord said to my Lord, 'Sit at my right hand [43] until I make your enemies your footstool.'"' [44] Thus David calls him "Lord"; how then can he be David's son?'

[45] In the hearing of all the people Jesus said to his disciples: [46] 'Beware of the scribes, who like to walk up and down in long robes, and love to be greeted respectfully in the street, to have the chief seats in synagogues and places of honour at feasts. [47] These are the men who eat up the property of widows, while for appearance' sake they say long prayers; the

---

20:13 **my beloved son**: *or* my only son.

sentence they receive will be all the more severe.'

Warnings about the end

21 As JESUS looked up and saw rich people dropping their gifts into the chest of the temple treasury, [2] he noticed a poor widow putting in two tiny coins. [3] 'I tell you this,' he said: 'this poor widow has given more than any of them; [4] for those others who have given had more than enough, but she, with less than enough, has given all she had to live on.'

[5] SOME people were talking about the temple and the beauty of its fine stones and ornaments. He said, [6] 'These things you are gazing at—the time will come when not one stone will be left upon another; they will all be thrown down.' [7] 'Teacher,' they asked, 'when will that be? What will be the sign that these things are about to happen?'

[8] He said, 'Take care that you are not misled. For many will come claiming my name and saying, "I am he," and, "The time has come." Do not follow them. [9] And when you hear of wars and insurrections, do not panic. These things are bound to happen first; but the end does not follow at once.' [10] Then he added, 'Nation will go to war against nation, kingdom against kingdom; [11] there will be severe earthquakes, famines and plagues in many places, and in the sky terrors and great portents.

[12] 'But before all this happens they will seize you and persecute you. You will be handed over to synagogues and put in prison; you will be haled before kings and governors for your allegiance to me. [13] This will be your opportunity to testify. [14] So resolve not to prepare your defence beforehand, [15] because I myself will give you such words and wisdom as no opponent can resist or refute. [16] Even your parents and brothers, your relations and friends, will betray you. Some of you will be put to death; [17] and everyone will hate you for your allegiance to me. [18] But not a hair of your head will be lost. [19] By standing firm you will win yourselves life.

[20] 'But when you see Jerusalem encircled by armies, then you may be sure that her devastation is near. [21] Then those who are in Judaea must take to the hills; those who are in the city itself must leave it, and those who are out in the country must not return; [22] because this is the time of retribution, when all that stands written is to be fulfilled. [23] Alas for women with child in those days, and for those who have children at the breast! There will be great distress in the land and a terrible judgement on this people. [24] They will fall by the sword; they will be carried captive into all countries; and Jerusalem will be trampled underfoot by Gentiles until the day of the Gentiles has run its course.

[25] 'Portents will appear in sun and moon and stars. On earth nations will stand helpless, not knowing which way to turn from the roar and surge of the sea. [26] People will faint with terror at the thought of all that is coming upon the world; for the celestial powers will be shaken. [27] Then they will see the Son of Man coming in a cloud with power and great glory. [28] When all this begins to happen, stand upright and hold your heads high, because your liberation is near.'

[29] He told them a parable: 'Look at the fig tree, or at any other tree. [30] As soon as it buds, you can see for yourselves that summer is near. [31] In the same way, when you see all this happening, you may know that the kingdom of God is near.

[32] 'Truly I tell you: the present generation will live to see it all. [33] Heaven and earth will pass away, but my words will never pass away.

[34] 'Be on your guard; do not let your minds be dulled by dissipation and drunkenness and worldly cares so that the great day catches you suddenly [35] like a trap; for that day will come on everyone, the whole world over. [36] Be on the alert, praying at all times for strength to pass safely through all that is coming and to stand in the presence of the Son of Man.'

[37] His days were given to teaching in the temple; every evening he would leave the city and spend the night on the hill called Olivet. [38] And in the early morning the people flocked to listen to him in the temple.

The last supper

22 THE festival of Unleavened Bread, known as Passover, was approaching, [2] and the chief priests and the

---

21: 38 **in the temple:** *some witnesses here insert the passage printed on p. 102.*

scribes were trying to devise some means of doing away with him; for they were afraid of the people.

[3] Then Satan entered into Judas, who was called Iscariot, one of the Twelve; [4] and he went to the chief priests and temple guards to discuss ways of betraying Jesus to them. [5] They were glad and undertook to pay him a sum of money. [6] He agreed, and began to look for an opportunity to betray him to them without collecting a crowd.

[7] Then came the day of Unleavened Bread, on which the Passover lambs had to be slaughtered, [8] and Jesus sent off Peter and John, saying, 'Go and prepare the Passover supper for us.' [9] 'Where would you like us to make the preparations?' they asked. [10] He replied, 'As soon as you set foot in the city a man will meet you carrying a jar of water. Follow him into the house that he enters [11] and give this message to the householder: "The Teacher says, 'Where is the room in which I am to eat the Passover with my disciples?'" [12] He will show you a large room upstairs all set out: make the preparations there.' [13] They went and found everything as he had said. So they prepared for Passover.

[14] When the hour came he took his place at table, and the apostles with him; [15] and he said to them, 'How I have longed to eat this Passover with you before my death! [16] For I tell you, never again shall I eat it until the time when it finds its fulfilment in the kingdom of God.'

[17] Then he took a cup, and after giving thanks he said, 'Take this and share it among yourselves; [18] for I tell you, from this moment I shall not drink the fruit of the vine until the time when the kingdom of God comes.' [19] Then he took bread, and after giving thanks he broke it, and gave it to them with the words: 'This is my body.'

[21] 'Even now my betrayer is here, his hand with mine on the table. [22] For the Son of Man is going his appointed way; but alas for that man by whom he is betrayed!' [23] At that they began to ask among themselves which of them it could possibly be who was to do this.

[24] Then a dispute began as to which of them should be considered the greatest. [25] But he said, 'Among the Gentiles, kings lord it over their subjects; and those in authority are given the title Benefactor. [26] Not so with you: on the contrary, the greatest among you must bear himself like the youngest, the one who rules like one who serves. [27] For who is greater— the one who sits at table or the servant who waits on him? Surely the one who sits at table. Yet I am among you like a servant.

[28] 'You have stood firmly by me in my times of trial; [29] and I now entrust to you the kingdom which my Father entrusted to me; [30] in my kingdom you shall eat and drink at my table and sit on thrones as judges of the twelve tribes of Israel.

[31] 'Simon, Simon, take heed: Satan has been given leave to sift all of you like wheat; [32] but I have prayed for you, Simon, that your faith may not fail; and when you are restored, give strength to your brothers.' [33] 'Lord,' he replied, 'I am ready to go with you to prison and to death.' [34] Jesus said, 'I tell you, Peter, the cock will not crow tonight until you have denied three times over that you know me.'

[35] He said to them, 'When I sent you out barefoot without purse or pack, were you ever short of anything?' 'No,' they answered. [36] 'It is different now,' he said; 'whoever has a purse had better take it with him, and his pack too; and if he has no sword, let him sell his cloak to buy one. [37] For scripture says, "And he was reckoned among transgressors," and this, I tell you, must be fulfilled in me; indeed, all that is written of me is reaching its fulfilment.' [38] 'Lord,' they said, 'we have two swords here.' 'Enough!' he replied.

[39] Then he went out and made his way as usual to the mount of Olives, accompanied by the disciples. [40] When he reached the place he said to them, 'Pray that you may be spared the test.' [41] He himself withdrew from them about a stone's throw, knelt down, and began to pray: [42] 'Father, if it be your will, take this cup

---

22:16 **For ... shall I:** *some witnesses read* But I tell you, I shall not.   22:19 **my body:** *some witnesses add, in whole or in part, and with various arrangements, the following:* 'which is given for you; do this as a memorial of me.' [20] In the same way he took the cup after supper, and said, 'This cup, poured out for you, is the new covenant sealed by my blood.'   22:29-30 **and I now ... and sit:** *or* and as my Father gave me the right to reign, so I give you the right to eat and to drink at my table in my kingdom and to sit.

from me. Yet not my will but yours be done.'

[43] And now there appeared to him an angel from heaven bringing him strength, [44] and in anguish of spirit he prayed the more urgently; and his sweat was like drops of blood falling to the ground. [45] When he rose from prayer and came to the disciples he found them asleep, worn out by grief. [46] 'Why are you sleeping?' he said. 'Rise and pray that you may be spared the test.'

The trial and crucifixion of Jesus

[47] WHILE he was still speaking a crowd appeared with the man called Judas, one of the Twelve, at their head. He came up to Jesus to kiss him; [48] but Jesus said, 'Judas, would you betray the Son of Man with a kiss?'

[49] When his followers saw what was coming, they said, 'Lord, shall we use our swords?' [50] And one of them struck at the high priest's servant, cutting off his right ear. [51] But Jesus answered, 'Stop! No more of that!' Then he touched the man's ear and healed him.

[52] Turning to the chief priests, the temple guards, and the elders, who had come to seize him, he said, 'Do you take me for a robber, that you have come out with swords and cudgels? [53] Day after day, I have been with you in the temple, and you did not raise a hand against me. But this is your hour—when darkness reigns.'

[54] Then they arrested him and led him away. They brought him to the high priest's house, and Peter followed at a distance. [55] They lit a fire in the middle of the courtyard and sat round it, and Peter sat among them. [56] A serving-maid who saw him sitting in the firelight stared at him and said, 'This man was with him too.' [57] But he denied it: 'I do not know him,' he said. [58] A little later a man noticed him and said, 'You also are one of them.' But Peter said to him, 'No, I am not.' [59] About an hour passed and someone else spoke more strongly still: 'Of course he was with him. He must have been; he is a Galilean.' [60] But Peter said, 'I do not know what you are talking about.' At that moment, while he was still speaking, a cock crowed; [61] and the Lord turned and looked at Peter. Peter remembered the Lord's words, 'Tonight before the cock crows you will disown me three times.' [62] And he went outside, and wept bitterly.

[63] The men who were guarding Jesus mocked him. They beat him, [64] they blindfolded him, and kept asking him, 'If you are a prophet, tell us who hit you.' [65] And so they went on heaping insults upon him.

[66] As SOON as it was day, the elders of the people, chief priests, and scribes assembled, and he was brought before their Council. [67] 'Tell us,' they said, 'are you the Messiah?' 'If I tell you,' he replied, 'you will not believe me; [68] and if I ask questions, you will not answer. [69] But from now on, the Son of Man will be seated at the right hand of Almighty God.' [70] 'You are the Son of God, then?' they all said, and he replied, 'It is you who say I am.' [71] At that they said, 'What further evidence do we need? We have heard this ourselves from his own lips.'

23 With that the whole assembly rose and brought him before Pilate. [2] They opened the case against him by saying, 'We found this man subverting our nation, opposing the payment of taxes to Caesar, and claiming to be Messiah, a king.' [3] Pilate asked him, 'Are you the king of the Jews?' He replied, 'The words are yours.' [4] Pilate then said to the chief priests and the crowd, 'I find no case for this man to answer.' [5] But they insisted: 'His teaching is causing unrest among the people all over Judaea. It started from Galilee and now has spread here.'

[6] When Pilate heard this, he asked if the man was a Galilean, [7] and on learning that he belonged to Herod's jurisdiction he remitted the case to him, for Herod was also in Jerusalem at that time. [8] When Herod saw Jesus he was greatly pleased; he had heard about him and had long been wanting to see him in the hope of witnessing some miracle performed by him. [9] He questioned him at some length without getting any reply; [10] but the chief priests and scribes appeared and pressed the case against him vigorously. [11] Then Herod and his troops treated him with

22:43–44 *Some witnesses omit* And now … ground. way.   22:69 **of Almighty God:** *lit.* of the Power of God. 23:3 **The words are yours:** *or* It is as you say.   22:51 **Stop! No more of that:** *or* Let them have their 22:70 **It is … I am:** *or* You are right, for I am.

contempt and ridicule, and sent him back to Pilate dressed in a gorgeous robe. [12] That same day Herod and Pilate became friends; till then there had been a feud between them.

[13] Pilate now summoned the chief priests, councillors, and people, [14] and said to them, 'You brought this man before me on a charge of subversion. But, as you see, I have myself examined him in your presence and found nothing in him to support your charges. [15] No more did Herod, for he has referred him back to us. Clearly he has done nothing to deserve death. [16] I therefore propose to flog him and let him go.' [18] But there was a general outcry. 'Away with him! Set Barabbas free!' [19] (Now Barabbas had been put in prison for his part in a rising in the city and for murder.) [20] Pilate addressed them again, in his desire to release Jesus, [21] but they shouted back, 'Crucify him, crucify him!' [22] For the third time he spoke to them: 'Why, what wrong has he done? I have not found him guilty of any capital offence. I will therefore flog him and let him go.' [23] But they persisted with their demand, shouting that Jesus should be crucified. Their shouts prevailed, [24] and Pilate decided that they should have their way. [25] He released the man they asked for, the man who had been put in prison for insurrection and murder, and gave Jesus over to their will.

[26] As THEY led him away to execution they took hold of a man called Simon, from Cyrene, on his way in from the country; putting the cross on his back they made him carry it behind Jesus.

[27] Great numbers of people followed, among them many women who mourned and lamented over him. [28] Jesus turned to them and said, 'Daughters of Jerusalem, do not weep for me; weep for yourselves and your children. [29] For the days are surely coming when people will say, "Happy are the barren, the wombs that never bore a child, the breasts that never fed one." [30] Then they will begin to say to the mountains, "Fall on us," and to the hills, "Cover us." [31] For if these things are done when the wood is green, what will happen when it is dry?'

[32] There were two others with him, criminals who were being led out to execution; [33] and when they reached the place called The Skull, they crucified him there, and the criminals with him, one on his right and the other on his left. [34] Jesus said, 'Father, forgive them; they do not know what they are doing.'

They shared out his clothes by casting lots. [35] The people stood looking on, and their rulers jeered at him: 'He saved others: now let him save himself, if this is God's Messiah, his Chosen.' [36] The soldiers joined in the mockery and came forward offering him sour wine. [37] 'If you are the king of the Jews,' they said, 'save yourself.' [38] There was an inscription above his head which ran: 'This is the king of the Jews.'

[39] One of the criminals hanging there taunted him: 'Are not you the Messiah? Save yourself, and us.' [40] But the other rebuked him: 'Have you no fear of God? You are under the same sentence as he is. [41] In our case it is plain justice; we are paying the price for our misdeeds. But this man has done nothing wrong.' [42] And he said, 'Jesus, remember me when you come to your throne.' [43] Jesus answered, 'Truly I tell you: today you will be with me in Paradise.'

[44] By now it was about midday and a darkness fell over the whole land, which lasted until three in the afternoon: [45] the sun's light failed. And the curtain of the temple was torn in two. [46] Then Jesus uttered a loud cry and said, 'Father, into your hands I commit my spirit'; and with these words he died. [47] When the centurion saw what had happened, he gave praise to God. 'Beyond all doubt', he said, 'this man was innocent.'

[48] The crowd who had assembled for the spectacle, when they saw what had happened, went home beating their breasts.

[49] His friends had all been standing at a distance; the women who had accompanied him from Galilee stood with them and watched it all.

[50] Now there was a man called Joseph, a member of the Council, a good and upright man, [51] who had dissented from

23:18 **But there was:** *some witnesses read* [17] At festival time he was obliged to release one person for them; [18] and now there was. 23:34 *Some witnesses omit* Jesus said, 'Father ... doing.'

their policy and the action they had taken. He came from the Judaean town of Arimathaea, and he was one who looked forward to the kingdom of God. [52] This man now approached Pilate and asked for the body of Jesus. [53] Taking it down from the cross, he wrapped it in a linen sheet, and laid it in a tomb cut out of the rock, in which no one had been laid before. [54] It was the day of preparation, and the sabbath was about to begin.

[55] The women who had accompanied Jesus from Galilee followed; they took note of the tomb and saw his body laid in it. [56] Then they went home and prepared spices and perfumes; and on the sabbath they rested in obedience to the commandment.

The resurrection

24 BUT very early on the first day of the week they came to the tomb bringing the spices they had prepared. [2] They found that the stone had been rolled away from the tomb, [3] but when they went inside, they did not find the body of the Lord Jesus. [4] While they stood utterly at a loss, suddenly two men in dazzling garments were at their side. [5] They were terrified, and stood with eyes cast down, but the men said, 'Why search among the dead for one who is alive? [6] Remember how he told you, while he was still in Galilee, [7] that the Son of Man must be given into the power of sinful men and be crucified, and must rise again on the third day.' [8] Then they recalled his words [9] and, returning from the tomb, they reported everything to the eleven and all the others.

[10] The women were Mary of Magdala, Joanna, and Mary the mother of James, and they, with the other women, told these things to the apostles. [11] But the story appeared to them to be nonsense, and they would not believe them.

[13] THAT same day two of them were on their way to a village called Emmaus, about seven miles from Jerusalem, [14] talking together about all that had happened. [15] As they talked and argued, Jesus himself came up and walked with them; [16] but something prevented them from recogniz-

ing him. [17] He asked them, 'What is it you are debating as you walk?' They stood still, their faces full of sadness, [18] and one, called Cleopas, answered, 'Are you the only person staying in Jerusalem not to have heard the news of what has happened there in the last few days?' [19] 'What news?' he said. 'About Jesus of Nazareth,' they replied, 'who, by deeds and words of power, proved himself a prophet in the sight of God and the whole people; [20] and how our chief priests and rulers handed him over to be sentenced to death, and crucified him. [21] But we had been hoping that he was to be the liberator of Israel. What is more, this is the third day since it happened, [22] and now some women of our company have astounded us: they went early to the tomb, [23] but failed to find his body, and returned with a story that they had seen a vision of angels who told them he was alive. [24] Then some of our people went to the tomb and found things just as the women had said; but him they did not see.'

[25] 'How dull you are!' he answered. 'How slow to believe all that the prophets said! [26] Was not the Messiah bound to suffer in this way before entering upon his glory?' [27] Then, starting from Moses and all the prophets, he explained to them in the whole of scripture the things that referred to himself.

[28] By this time they had reached the village to which they were going, and he made as if to continue his journey. [29] But they pressed him: 'Stay with us, for evening approaches, and the day is almost over.' So he went in to stay with them. [30] And when he had sat down with them at table, he took bread and said the blessing; he broke the bread, and offered it to them. [31] Then their eyes were opened, and they recognized him; but he vanished from their sight. [32] They said to one another, 'Were not our hearts on fire as he talked with us on the road and explained the scriptures to us?'

[33] Without a moment's delay they set out and returned to Jerusalem. There they found that the eleven and the rest of the company had assembled, [34] and were saying, 'It is true: the Lord has risen; he has appeared to Simon.' [35] Then they

24:5 **who is alive:** *some witnesses add* He is not here: he has been raised.   24:11 **believe them:** *some witnesses add* [12] Peter, however, got up and ran to the tomb, and, peering in, saw the wrappings and nothing more; and he went home amazed at what had happened.

described what had happened on their journey and told how he had made himself known to them in the breaking of the bread.

[36] As they were talking about all this, there he was, standing among them. [37] Startled and terrified, they thought they were seeing a ghost. [38] But he said, 'Why are you so perturbed? Why do doubts arise in your minds? [39] Look at my hands and feet. It is I myself. Touch me and see; no ghost has flesh and bones as you can see that I have.' [41] They were still incredulous, still astounded, for it seemed too good to be true. So he asked them, 'Have you anything here to eat?' [42] They offered him a piece of fish they had cooked, [43] which he took and ate before their eyes.

[44] And he said to them, 'This is what I meant by saying, while I was still with you, that everything written about me in the law of Moses and in the prophets and psalms was bound to be fulfilled.' [45] Then he opened their minds to understand the scriptures. [46] 'So you see', he said, 'that scripture foretells the sufferings of the Messiah and his rising from the dead on the third day, [47] and declares that in his name repentance bringing the forgiveness of sins is to be proclaimed to all nations beginning from Jerusalem. [48] You are to be witnesses to it all. [49] I am sending on you the gift promised by my Father; wait here in this city until you are armed with power from above.'

[50] Then he led them out as far as Bethany, and blessed them with uplifted hands; [51] and in the act of blessing he parted from them. [52] And they returned to Jerusalem full of joy, [53] and spent all their time in the temple praising God.

24:36 **among them:** *some witnesses add* And he said to them, 'Peace be with you!' 24:39 **I have:** *some witnesses add* [40] After saying this he showed them his hands and feet. 24:51 **parted from them:** *some witnesses add* and was carried up into heaven. 24:52 **And they:** *some witnesses add* worshipped him and.

THE GOSPEL ACCORDING TO

JOHN

The coming of Christ

1 IN the beginning the Word already was. The Word was in God's presence, and what God was, the Word was. [2] He was with God at the beginning, [3] and through him all things came to be; without him no created thing came into being. [4] In him was life, and that life was the light of mankind. [5] The light shines in the darkness, and the darkness has never mastered it.

[6] There appeared a man named John. He was sent from God, [7] and came as a witness to testify to the light, so that through him all might become believers. [8] He was not himself the light; he came to bear witness to the light. [9] The true light which gives light to everyone was even then coming into the world.

[10] He was in the world; but the world, though it owed its being to him, did not recognize him. [11] He came to his own, and his own people would not accept him. [12] But to all who did accept him, to those who put their trust in him, he gave the right to become children of God, [13] born not of human stock, by the physical desire of a human father, but of God. [14] So the Word became flesh; he made his home among us, and we saw his glory, such glory as befits the Father's only Son, full of grace and truth.

[15] John bore witness to him and proclaimed: 'This is the man of whom I said, "He comes after me, but ranks ahead of me"; before I was born, he already was.'

[16] From his full store we have all received grace upon grace; [17] for the law

1:3–4 **through him ... was life:** *or* without him no single thing was created. All that came to be was alive with his life. 1:9 **The true ... world:** *or* The true light was in being, which gives light to everyone entering the world.

was given through Moses, but grace and truth came through Jesus Christ. ¹⁸ No one has ever seen God; God's only Son, he who is nearest to the Father's heart, has made him known.

Testimony of the Baptist and the first disciples

¹⁹ THIS is the testimony John gave when the Jews of Jerusalem sent a deputation of priests and Levites to ask him who he was. ²⁰ He readily acknowledged, 'I am not the Messiah.' ²¹ 'What then? Are you Elijah?' 'I am not,' he replied. 'Are you the Prophet?' 'No,' he said. ²² 'Then who are you?' they asked. 'We must give an answer to those who sent us. What account do you give of yourself?' ²³ He answered in the words of the prophet Isaiah: 'I am a voice crying in the wilderness, "Make straight the way for the Lord."'

²⁴ Some Pharisees who were in the deputation ²⁵ asked him, 'If you are not the Messiah, nor Elijah, nor the Prophet, then why are you baptizing?' ²⁶ 'I baptize in water,' John replied, 'but among you, though you do not know him, stands the one ²⁷ who is to come after me. I am not worthy to unfasten the strap of his sandal.' ²⁸ This took place at Bethany beyond Jordan, where John was baptizing.

²⁹ The next day he saw Jesus coming towards him. 'There is the Lamb of God,' he said, 'who takes away the sin of the world. ³⁰ He it is of whom I said, "After me there comes a man who ranks ahead of me"; before I was born, he already was. ³¹ I did not know who he was; but the reason why I came, baptizing in water, was that he might be revealed to Israel.'

³² John testified again: 'I saw the Spirit come down from heaven like a dove and come to rest on him. ³³ I did not know him; but he who sent me to baptize in water had told me, "The man on whom you see the Spirit come down and rest is the one who is to baptize in Holy Spirit." ³⁴ I have seen it and have borne witness: this is God's Chosen One.'

³⁵ The next day again, John was standing with two of his disciples ³⁶ when Jesus passed by. John looked towards him and said, 'There is the Lamb of God!' ³⁷ When the two disciples heard what he said, they followed Jesus. ³⁸ He turned and saw them following; 'What are you looking for?' he asked. They said, 'Rabbi,' (which means 'Teacher') 'where are you staying?' ³⁹ 'Come and see,' he replied. So they went and saw where he was staying, and spent the rest of the day with him. It was about four in the afternoon.

⁴⁰ One of the two who followed Jesus after hearing what John said was Andrew, Simon Peter's brother. ⁴¹ The first thing he did was to find his brother Simon and say to him, 'We have found the Messiah' (which is the Hebrew for Christ). ⁴² He brought Simon to Jesus, who looked at him and said, 'You are Simon son of John; you shall be called Cephas' (that is, Peter, 'the Rock').

⁴³⁻⁴⁴ The next day Jesus decided to leave for Galilee. He met Philip, who, like Andrew and Peter, came from Bethsaida, and said to him, 'Follow me.' ⁴⁵ Philip went to find Nathanael and told him, 'We have found the man of whom Moses wrote in the law, the man foretold by the prophets: it is Jesus son of Joseph, from Nazareth.' ⁴⁶ 'Nazareth!' Nathanael exclaimed. 'Can anything good come from Nazareth?' Philip said, 'Come and see.' ⁴⁷ When Jesus saw Nathanael coming towards him, he said, 'Here is an Israelite worthy of the name; there is nothing false in him.' ⁴⁸ Nathanael asked him, 'How is it you know me?' Jesus replied, 'I saw you under the fig tree before Philip spoke to you.' ⁴⁹ 'Rabbi,' said Nathanael, 'you are the Son of God; you are king of Israel.' ⁵⁰ Jesus answered, 'Do you believe this because I told you I saw you under the fig tree? You will see greater things than that.' ⁵¹ Then he added, 'In very truth I tell you all: you will see heaven wide open and God's angels ascending and descending upon the Son of Man.'

Signs and discourses

2 TWO DAYS later there was a wedding at Cana-in-Galilee. The mother of Jesus was there, ² and Jesus and his disciples were also among the guests. ³ The wine gave out, so Jesus's mother said to him, 'They have no wine left.' ⁴ He answered, 'That is no concern of mine.

1:18 *God's only Son*: *some witnesses read* the only begotten God.   1:34 *this ... One*: *some witnesses read* this is the Son of God.

My hour has not yet come.' ⁵ His mother said to the servants, 'Do whatever he tells you.' ⁶ There were six stone water-jars standing near, of the kind used for Jewish rites of purification; each held from twenty to thirty gallons. ⁷ Jesus said to the servants, 'Fill the jars with water,' and they filled them to the brim. ⁸ 'Now draw some off,' he ordered, 'and take it to the master of the feast'; and they did so. ⁹ The master tasted the water now turned into wine, not knowing its source, though the servants who had drawn the water knew. He hailed the bridegroom ¹⁰ and said, 'Everyone else serves the best wine first, and the poorer only when the guests have drunk freely; but you have kept the best wine till now.'

¹¹ So Jesus performed at Cana-in-Galilee the first of the signs which revealed his glory and led his disciples to believe in him.

¹² AFTER this he went down to Capernaum with his mother, his brothers, and his disciples, and they stayed there a few days. ¹³ As it was near the time of the Jewish Passover, Jesus went up to Jerusalem. ¹⁴ In the temple precincts he found the dealers in cattle, sheep, and pigeons, and the money-changers seated at their tables. ¹⁵ He made a whip of cords and drove them out of the temple, sheep, cattle, and all. He upset the tables of the money-changers, scattering their coins. ¹⁶ Then he turned on the dealers in pigeons: 'Take them out of here,' he said; 'do not turn my Father's house into a market.' ¹⁷ His disciples recalled the words of scripture: 'Zeal for your house will consume me.' ¹⁸ The Jews challenged Jesus: 'What sign can you show to justify your action?' ¹⁹ 'Destroy this temple,' Jesus replied, 'and in three days I will raise it up again.' ²⁰ The Jews said, 'It has taken forty-six years to build this temple. Are you going to raise it up again in three days?' ²¹ But the temple he was speaking of was his body. ²² After his resurrection his disciples recalled what he had said, and they believed the scripture and the words that Jesus had spoken.

²³ WHILE he was in Jerusalem for Passover many put their trust in him when they saw the signs that he performed. ²⁴ But Jesus for his part would not trust himself to them. He knew them all, ²⁵ and had no need of evidence from others about anyone, for he himself could tell what was in people.

3 ONE of the Pharisees, called Nicodemus, a member of the Jewish Council, ² came to Jesus by night. 'Rabbi,' he said, 'we know that you are a teacher sent by God; no one could perform these signs of yours unless God were with him.' ³ Jesus answered, 'In very truth I tell you, no one can see the kingdom of God unless he has been born again.' ⁴ 'But how can someone be born when he is old?' asked Nicodemus. 'Can he enter his mother's womb a second time and be born?' ⁵ Jesus answered, 'In very truth I tell you, no one can enter the kingdom of God without being born from water and spirit. ⁶ Flesh can give birth only to flesh; it is spirit that gives birth to spirit. ⁷ You ought not to be astonished when I say, "You must all be born again." ⁸ The wind blows where it wills; you hear the sound of it, but you do not know where it comes from or where it is going. So it is with everyone who is born from the Spirit.'

⁹ 'How is this possible?' asked Nicodemus. ¹⁰ 'You a teacher of Israel and ignorant of such things!' said Jesus. ¹¹ 'In very truth I tell you, we speak of what we know, and testify to what we have seen, and yet you all reject our testimony. ¹² If you do not believe me when I talk to you about earthly things, how are you to believe if I should talk about the things of heaven?

¹³ 'No one has gone up into heaven except the one who came down from heaven, the Son of Man who is in heaven. ¹⁴ Just as Moses lifted up the serpent in the wilderness, so the Son of Man must be lifted up, ¹⁵ in order that everyone who has faith may in him have eternal life.

¹⁶ 'God so loved the world that he gave his only Son, that everyone who has faith in him may not perish but have eternal life. ¹⁷ It was not to judge the world that God sent his Son into the world, but that through him the world might be saved. ¹⁸ 'No one who puts his faith in him comes under judgement; but the

---

3:8 **wind** *and* **spirit** *are translations of the same Greek word, which has both meanings.*   3:13 *Some witnesses* omit *who is in heaven.*

unbeliever has already been judged because he has not put his trust in God's only Son. ¹⁹ This is the judgement: the light has come into the world, but people preferred darkness to light because their deeds were evil. ²⁰ Wrongdoers hate the light and avoid it, for fear their misdeeds should be exposed. ²¹ Those who live by the truth come to the light so that it may be clearly seen that God is in all they do.'

²² AFTER this Jesus went with his disciples into Judaea; he remained there with them and baptized. ²³ John too was baptizing at Aenon, near Salim, because water was plentiful in that region; and all the time people were coming for baptism. ²⁴ This was before John's imprisonment.

²⁵ John's disciples were engaged in a debate with some Jews about purification; ²⁶ so they came to John and said, 'Rabbi, there was a man with you on the other side of the Jordan, to whom you bore your witness. Now he is baptizing, and everyone is flocking to him.' ²⁷ John replied: 'One can have only what is given one from Heaven. ²⁸ You yourselves can testify that I said, "I am not the Messiah; I have been sent as his forerunner." ²⁹ It is the bridegroom who marries the bride. The bridegroom's friend, who stands by and listens to him, is overjoyed at hearing the bridegroom's voice. This is my joy and now it is complete. ³⁰ He must grow greater; I must become less.'

³¹ He who comes from above is above all others; he who is from the earth belongs to the earth and uses earthly speech. He who comes from heaven ³² bears witness to what he has seen and heard, even though no one accepts his witness. ³³ To accept his witness is to affirm that God speaks the truth; ³⁴ for he whom God sent utters the words of God, so measureless is God's gift of the Spirit. ³⁵ The Father loves the Son and has entrusted him with complete authority. ³⁶ Whoever puts his faith in the Son has eternal life. Whoever disobeys the Son will not see that life; God's wrath rests upon him.

4 ¹⁻² NEWS now reached the Pharisees that Jesus was winning and baptizing more disciples than John; although, in fact, it was his disciples who were baptizing, not Jesus himself. When Jesus heard this, ³ he left Judaea and set out once more for Galilee. ⁴ He had to pass through Samaria, ⁵ and on his way came to a Samaritan town called Sychar, near the plot of ground which Jacob gave to his son Joseph; ⁶ Jacob's well was there. It was about noon, and Jesus, tired after his journey, was sitting by the well.

⁸ His disciples had gone into the town to buy food. ⁷ Meanwhile a Samaritan woman came to draw water, and Jesus said to her, 'Give me a drink.' ⁹ The woman said, 'What! You, a Jew, ask for a drink from a Samaritan woman?' (Jews do not share drinking vessels with Samaritans.) ¹⁰ Jesus replied, 'If only you knew what God gives, and who it is that is asking you for a drink, you would have asked him and he would have given you living water.' ¹¹ 'Sir,' the woman said, 'you have no bucket and the well is deep, so where can you get "living water"? ¹² Are you greater than Jacob our ancestor who gave us the well and drank from it himself, he and his sons and his cattle too?' ¹³ Jesus answered, 'Everyone who drinks this water will be thirsty again; ¹⁴ but whoever drinks the water I shall give will never again be thirsty. The water that I shall give will be a spring of water within him, welling up and bringing eternal life.' ¹⁵ 'Sir,' said the woman, 'give me this water, and then I shall not be thirsty, nor have to come all this way to draw water.'

¹⁶ 'Go and call your husband,' said Jesus, 'and come back here.' ¹⁷ She answered, 'I have no husband.' Jesus said, 'You are right in saying that you have no husband, ¹⁸ for though you have had five husbands, the man you are living with now is not your husband. You have spoken the truth!' ¹⁹ 'Sir,' replied the woman, 'I can see you are a prophet. ²⁰ Our fathers worshipped on this mountain, but you Jews say that the place where God must be worshipped is in Jerusalem.' ²¹ 'Believe me,' said Jesus, 'the time is coming when you will worship the Father neither on this mountain nor in Jerusalem. ²² You Samaritans worship you know not what; we worship what we

---

3:25 some Jews: *some witnesses read* a Jew.   3:31 from heaven: *some witnesses add* is above all and.
4:9 Jews ... Samaritans: *some witnesses omit these words.*

know. It is from the Jews that salvation comes. ²³ But the time is coming, indeed it is already here, when true worshippers will worship the Father in spirit and in truth. These are the worshippers the Father wants. ²⁴ God is spirit, and those who worship him must worship in spirit and in truth.' ²⁵ The woman answered, 'I know that Messiah' (that is, Christ) 'is coming. When he comes he will make everything clear to us.' ²⁶ Jesus said to her, 'I am he, I who am speaking to you.'

²⁷ At that moment his disciples returned, and were astonished to find him talking with a woman; but none of them said, 'What do you want?' or, 'Why are you talking with her?' ²⁸ The woman left her water-jar and went off to the town, where she said to the people, ²⁹ 'Come and see a man who has told me everything I ever did. Could this be the Messiah?' ³⁰ They left the town and made their way towards him.

³¹ MEANWHILE the disciples were urging him, 'Rabbi, have something to eat.' ³² But he said, 'I have food to eat of which you know nothing.' ³³ At this the disciples said to one another, 'Can someone have brought him food?' ³⁴ But Jesus said, 'For me it is meat and drink to do the will of him who sent me until I have finished his work. ³⁵ 'Do you not say, "Four months more and then comes harvest"? But look, I tell you, look around at the fields: they are already white, ripe for harvesting. ³⁶ The reaper is drawing his pay and harvesting a crop for eternal life, so that sower and reaper may rejoice together. ³⁷ That is how the saying comes true: "One sows, another reaps." ³⁸ I sent you to reap a crop for which you have not laboured. Others laboured and you have come in for the harvest of their labour.'

³⁹ Many Samaritans of that town came to believe in him because of the woman's testimony: 'He told me everything I ever did.' ⁴⁰ So when these Samaritans came to him they pressed him to stay with them; and he stayed there two days. ⁴¹ Many more became believers because of what they heard from his own lips. ⁴² They told the woman, 'It is no longer because of

what you said that we believe, for we have heard him ourselves; and we are convinced that he is the Saviour of the world.'

Jesus the giver of life

⁴³ WHEN the two days were over Jesus left for Galilee; ⁴⁴ for he himself had declared that a prophet is without honour in his own country. ⁴⁵ On his arrival the Galileans made him welcome, because they had seen all he did at the festival in Jerusalem; they had been at the festival themselves.

⁴⁶ Once again he visited Cana-in-Galilee, where he had turned the water into wine. An officer in the royal service was there, whose son was lying ill at Capernaum. ⁴⁷ When he heard that Jesus had come from Judaea into Galilee, he went to him and begged him to go down and cure his son, who was at the point of death. ⁴⁸ Jesus said to him, 'Will none of you ever believe without seeing signs and portents?' ⁴⁹ The officer pleaded with him, 'Sir, come down before my boy dies.' ⁵⁰ 'Return home,' said Jesus; 'your son will live.' The man believed what Jesus said and started for home. ⁵¹ While he was on his way down his servants met him with the news that his child was going to live. ⁵² So he asked them at what time he had begun to recover, and they told him, 'It was at one o'clock yesterday afternoon that the fever left him.' ⁵³ The father realized that this was the time at which Jesus had said to him, 'Your son will live,' and he and all his household became believers.

⁵⁴ This was the second sign which Jesus performed after coming from Judaea into Galilee.

5 SOME time later, Jesus went up to Jerusalem for one of the Jewish festivals. ² Now at the Sheep Gate in Jerusalem there is a pool whose Hebrew name is Bethesda. It has five colonnades ³ and in them lay a great number of sick people, blind, lame, and paralysed. ⁵ Among them was a man who had been crippled for thirty-eight years. ⁶ Jesus saw him lying there, and knowing that he had been ill a long time he asked him, 'Do you want to

---

5: 3 **paralysed**: *some witnesses add* waiting for the disturbance of the water; *some also add* ⁴ for from time to time an angel came down into the pool and stirred up the water. The first to plunge in after this disturbance recovered from whatever disease had afflicted him.

get well?' 7 'Sir,' he replied, 'I have no one to put me in the pool when the water is disturbed; while I am getting there, someone else steps into the pool before me.' 8 Jesus answered, 'Stand up, take your bed and walk.' 9 The man recovered instantly; he took up his bed, and began to walk.

That day was a sabbath. 10 So the Jews said to the man who had been cured, 'It is the sabbath. It is against the law for you to carry your bed.' 11 He answered, 'The man who cured me, he told me, "Take up your bed and walk."' 12 They asked him, 'Who is this man who told you to take it up and walk?' 13 But the man who had been cured did not know who it was; for the place was crowded and Jesus had slipped away. 14 A little later Jesus found him in the temple and said to him, 'Now that you are well, give up your sinful ways, or something worse may happen to you.' 15 The man went off and told the Jews that it was Jesus who had cured him.

16 It was for doing such things on the sabbath that the Jews began to take action against Jesus. 17 He defended himself by saying, 'My Father continues to work, and I must work too.' 18 This made the Jews all the more determined to kill him, because not only was he breaking the sabbath but, by calling God his own Father, he was claiming equality with God.

19 To this charge Jesus replied, 'In very truth I tell you, the Son can do nothing by himself; he does only what he sees the Father doing: whatever the Father does, the Son does. 20 For the Father loves the Son and shows him all that he himself is doing, and will show him even greater deeds, to fill you with wonder. 21 As the Father raises the dead and gives them life, so the Son gives life as he chooses. 22 Again, the Father does not judge anyone, but has given full jurisdiction to the Son; 23 it is his will that all should pay the same honour to the Son as to the Father. To deny honour to the Son is to deny it to the Father who sent him.

24 'In very truth I tell you, whoever heeds what I say and puts his trust in him who sent me has eternal life; he does not come to judgement, but has already passed from death to life. 25 In very truth I tell you, the time is coming, indeed it is already here, when the dead shall hear

the voice of the Son of God, and those who hear shall come to life. 26 For as the Father has life in himself, so by his gift the Son also has life in himself.

27 'As Son of Man he has also been given authority to pass judgement. 28 Do not be surprised at this, because the time is coming when all who are in the grave shall hear his voice 29 and come out: those who have done right will rise to life; those who have done wrong will rise to judgement. 30 I cannot act by myself; I judge as I am bidden, and my sentence is just, because I seek to do not my own will, but the will of him who sent me.

31 'If I testify on my own behalf, that testimony is not valid. 32 There is another who bears witness for me, and I know that his testimony about me is valid. 33 You sent messengers to John and he has testified to the truth. 34 Not that I rely on human testimony, but I remind you of it for your own salvation. 35 John was a brightly burning lamp, and for a time you were ready to exult in his light. 36 But I rely on a testimony higher than John's: the work my Father has given me to do and to finish, the very work I have in hand, testifies that the Father has sent me. 37 And the Father who has sent me has borne witness on my behalf. His voice you have never heard, his form you have never seen; 38 his word has found no home in you, because you do not believe the one whom he sent. 39 You study the scriptures diligently, supposing that in having them you have eternal life; their testimony points to me, 40 yet you refuse to come to me to receive that life.

41 'I do not look to men for honour. 42 But I know that with you it is different, for you have no love of God in you. 43 I have come accredited by my Father, and you have no welcome for me; but let someone self-accredited come, and you will give him a welcome. 44 How can you believe when you accept honour from one another, and care nothing for the honour that comes from him who alone is God? 45 Do not imagine that I shall be your accuser at the Father's tribunal. Your accuser is Moses, the very Moses on whom you have set your hope. 46 If you believed him you would believe me, for it was of me that he wrote. 47 But if you do not believe what he wrote, how are you to believe what I say?'

Bread from heaven

6 SOME time later Jesus withdrew to the farther shore of the sea of Galilee (or Tiberias), [2] and a large crowd of people followed him because they had seen the signs he performed in healing the sick. [3] Jesus went up the hillside and sat down with his disciples. [4] It was near the time of Passover, the great Jewish festival. [5] Looking up and seeing a large crowd coming towards him, Jesus said to Philip, 'Where are we to buy bread to feed these people?' [6] He said this to test him; Jesus himself knew what he meant to do. [7] Philip replied, 'We would need two hundred denarii to buy enough bread for each of them to have a little.' [8] One of his disciples, Andrew, the brother of Simon Peter, said to him, [9] 'There is a boy here who has five barley loaves and two fish; but what is that among so many?' [10] Jesus said, 'Make the people sit down.' There was plenty of grass there, so the men sat down, about five thousand of them. [11] Then Jesus took the loaves, gave thanks, and distributed them to the people as they sat there. He did the same with the fish, and they had as much as they wanted. [12] When everyone had had enough, he said to his disciples, 'Gather up the pieces left over, so that nothing is wasted.' [13] They gathered them up, and filled twelve baskets with the pieces of the five barley loaves that were left uneaten.

[14] When the people saw the sign Jesus had performed, the word went round, 'Surely this must be the Prophet who was to come into the world.' [15] Jesus, realizing that they meant to come and seize him to proclaim him king, withdrew again to the hills by himself.

[16] At nightfall his disciples went down to the sea, [17] and set off by boat to cross to Capernaum. Though darkness had fallen, Jesus had not yet joined them; [18] a strong wind was blowing and the sea grew rough. [19] When they had rowed about three or four miles they saw Jesus walking on the sea and approaching the boat. They were terrified, [20] but he called out, 'It is I; do not be afraid.' [21] With that they were ready to take him on board, and immediately the boat reached the land they were making for.

[22] NEXT morning the crowd was still on the opposite shore. They had seen only one boat there, and Jesus, they knew, had not embarked with his disciples, who had set off by themselves. [23] Boats from Tiberias, however, had come ashore near the place where the people had eaten the bread over which the Lord gave thanks. [24] When the crowd saw that Jesus had gone as well as his disciples, they went on board these boats and made for Capernaum in search of him. [25] They found him on the other side. 'Rabbi,' they asked, 'when did you come here?' [26] Jesus replied, 'In very truth I tell you, it is not because you saw signs that you came looking for me, but because you ate the bread and your hunger was satisfied. [27] You should work, not for this perishable food, but for the food that lasts, the food of eternal life.

'This food the Son of Man will give you, for on him God the Father has set the seal of his authority.' [28] 'Then what must we do', they asked him, 'if our work is to be the work of God?' [29] Jesus replied, 'This is the work that God requires: to believe in the one whom he has sent.'

[30] They asked, 'What sign can you give us, so that we may see it and believe you? What is the work you are doing? [31] Our ancestors had manna to eat in the desert; as scripture says, "He gave them bread from heaven to eat."' [32] Jesus answered, 'In very truth I tell you, it was not Moses who gave you the bread from heaven; it is my Father who gives you the true bread from heaven. [33] The bread that God gives comes down from heaven and brings life to the world.' [34] 'Sir,' they said to him, 'give us this bread now and always.' [35] Jesus said to them, 'I am the bread of life. Whoever comes to me will never be hungry, and whoever believes in me will never be thirsty. [36] But you, as I said, have seen and yet you do not believe. [37] All that the Father gives me will come to me, and anyone who comes to me I will never turn away. [38] I have come down from heaven, to do not my own will, but the will of him who sent me. [39] It is his will that I should not lose even one of those he has given me, but should raise them all up on the last day. [40] For it is my Father's will that

---

6:7 *denarii: see p. xi.*   6:23 *Some witnesses omit* over which the Lord gave thanks.   6:36 you ... **have seen**: *some witnesses add* me.

everyone who sees the Son and has faith in him should have eternal life; and I will raise them up on the last day.'

⁴¹At this the Jews began to grumble because he said, 'I am the bread which came down from heaven.' ⁴²They said, 'Surely this is Jesus, Joseph's son! We know his father and mother. How can he say, "I have come down from heaven"?' ⁴³'Stop complaining among yourselves,' Jesus told them. ⁴⁴'No one can come to me unless he is drawn by the Father who sent me; and I will raise him up on the last day. ⁴⁵It is written in the prophets: "They will all be taught by God." Everyone who has listened to the Father and learned from him comes to me.

⁴⁶'I do not mean that anyone has seen the Father; he who has come from God has seen the Father, and he alone. ⁴⁷In very truth I tell you, whoever believes has eternal life. ⁴⁸I am the bread of life. ⁴⁹Your ancestors ate manna in the wilderness, yet they are dead. ⁵⁰I am speaking of the bread that comes down from heaven; whoever eats it will never die. ⁵¹I am the living bread that has come down from heaven; if anyone eats this bread, he will live for ever. The bread which I shall give is my own flesh, given for the life of the world.'

⁵²This led to a fierce dispute among the Jews. 'How can this man give us his flesh to eat?' they protested. ⁵³Jesus answered them, 'In very truth I tell you, unless you eat the flesh of the Son of Man and drink his blood you can have no life in you. ⁵⁴Whoever eats my flesh and drinks my blood has eternal life, and I will raise him up on the last day. ⁵⁵My flesh is real food; my blood is real drink. ⁵⁶Whoever eats my flesh and drinks my blood dwells in me and I in him. ⁵⁷As the living Father sent me, and I live because of the Father, so whoever eats me will live because of me. ⁵⁸This is the bread which came down from heaven; it is not like the bread which our fathers ate; they are dead, but whoever eats this bread will live for ever.'

⁵⁹JESUS said these things in the synagogue as he taught in Capernaum. ⁶⁰On hearing them, many of his disciples exclaimed, 'This is more than we can stand! How can anyone listen to such talk?'

⁶¹Jesus was aware that his disciples were grumbling about it and asked them, 'Does this shock you? ⁶²Then what if you see the Son of Man ascending to where he was before? ⁶³It is the spirit that gives life; the flesh can achieve nothing; the words I have spoken to you are both spirit and life. ⁶⁴Yet there are some of you who have no faith.' For Jesus knew from the outset who were without faith and who was to betray him. ⁶⁵So he said, 'This is why I told you that no one can come to me unless it has been granted to him by the Father.'

⁶⁶From that moment many of his disciples drew back and no longer went about with him. ⁶⁷So Jesus asked the Twelve, 'Do you also want to leave?' ⁶⁸Simon Peter answered him, 'Lord, to whom shall we go? Your words are words of eternal life. ⁶⁹We believe and know that you are God's Holy One.' ⁷⁰Jesus answered, 'Have I not chosen the twelve of you? Yet one of you is a devil.' ⁷¹He meant Judas son of Simon Iscariot. It was he who would betray him, and he was one of the Twelve.

The great controversy

7 AFTER that Jesus travelled around within Galilee; he decided to avoid Judaea because the Jews were looking for a chance to kill him. ²But when the Jewish feast of Tabernacles was close at hand, ³his brothers said to him, 'You should leave here and go into Judaea, so that your disciples may see the great things you are doing. ⁴No one can hope for recognition if he works in obscurity. If you can really do such things as these, show yourself to the world.' ⁵For even his brothers had no faith in him. ⁶Jesus answered: 'The right time for me has not yet come, but any time is right for you. ⁷The world cannot hate you; but it hates me for exposing the wickedness of its ways. ⁸Go up to the festival yourselves. I am not going to this festival, because the right time for me has not yet come.' ⁹So saying he stayed behind in Galilee.

¹⁰Later, when his brothers had gone to the festival, he went up too, not openly, but in secret. ¹¹At the festival the Jews were looking for him and asking where he was, ¹²and there was much murmuring about him in the crowds. 'He is a good

7:8 **not going:** *some witnesses read* not yet going.

man,' said some. 'No,' said others, 'he is leading the people astray.' 13 No one talked freely about him, however, for fear of the Jews.

14 WHEN the festival was already half over, Jesus went up to the temple and began to teach. 15 The Jews were astonished: 'How is it', they said, 'that this untrained man has such learning?' 16 Jesus replied, 'My teaching is not my own but his who sent me. 17 Whoever chooses to do the will of God will know whether my teaching comes from him or is merely my own. 18 Anyone whose teaching is merely his own seeks his own glory; but if anyone seeks the glory of him who sent him, he is sincere and there is nothing false in him.

19 'Did not Moses give you the law? Yet not one of you keeps it. Why are you trying to kill me?' 20 The crowd answered, 'You are possessed! Who wants to kill you?' 21 Jesus replied, 'I did one good deed, and you are all taken aback. 22 But consider: Moses gave you the law of circumcision (not that it originated with Moses, but with the patriarchs) and you circumcise even on the sabbath. 23 Well then, if someone can be circumcised on the sabbath to avoid breaking the law of Moses, why are you indignant with me for making someone's whole body well on the sabbath? 24 Stop judging by appearances; be just in your judgements.'

25 This prompted some of the people of Jerusalem to say, 'Is not this the man they want to put to death? 26 Yet here he is, speaking in public, and they say not one word to him. Can it be that our rulers have decided that this is the Messiah? 27 Yet we know where this man comes from; when the Messiah appears no one is to know where he comes from.' 28 Jesus responded to this as he taught in the temple: 'Certainly you know me,' he declared, 'and you know where I come from. Yet I have not come of my own accord; I was sent by one who is true, and him you do not know. 29 I know him because I come from him, and he it is who sent me.' 30 At this they tried to seize him, but no one could lay hands on him because his appointed hour had not yet

come. 31 Among the people many believed in him. 'When the Messiah comes,' they said, 'is it likely that he will perform more signs than this man?'

32 The Pharisees overheard these mutterings about him among the people, so the chief priests and the Pharisees sent temple police to arrest him. 33 Then Jesus said, 'For a little longer I shall be with you; then I am going away to him who sent me. 34 You will look for me, but you will not find me; and where I am, you cannot come.' 35 So the Jews said to one another, 'Where does he intend to go, that we should not be able to find him? Will he go to the Dispersion among the Gentiles, and teach Gentiles? 36 What does he mean by saying, "You will look for me, but you will not find me; and where I am, you cannot come"?'

37 ON the last and greatest day of the festival Jesus stood and declared, 'If anyone is thirsty, let him come to me and drink. 38 Whoever believes in me, as scripture says, "Streams of living water shall flow from within him."' 39 He was speaking of the Spirit which believers in him would later receive; for the Spirit had not yet been given, because Jesus had not yet been glorified.

40 On hearing his words some of the crowd said, 'This must certainly be the Prophet.' 41 Others said, 'This is the Messiah.' But others argued, 'Surely the Messiah is not to come from Galilee? 42 Does not scripture say that the Messiah is to be of the family of David, from David's village of Bethlehem?' 43 Thus he was the cause of a division among the people. 44 Some were for arresting him, but no one laid hands on him.

45 The temple police went back to the chief priests and Pharisees, who asked them, 'Why have you not brought him?' 46 'No one ever spoke as this man speaks,' they replied. 47 The Pharisees retorted, 'Have you too been misled? 48 Has a single one of our rulers believed in him, or any of the Pharisees? 49 As for this rabble, which cares nothing for the law, a curse is on them.' 50 Then one of their number, Nicodemus (the man who once visited Jesus), intervened. 51 'Does our law', he asked

7:28 **Certainly … come from:** *or* Do you know me? And do you know where I come from?   7:37–38 **If anyone … within him:** *or* If anyone is thirsty, let him come to me; whoever believes in me, let him drink. As scripture says, "Streams of living water shall flow from within him."

them, 'permit us to pass judgement on someone without first giving him a hearing and learning the facts?' [52] 'Are you a Galilean too?' they retorted. 'Study the scriptures and you will find that the Prophet does not come from Galilee.'

8 [12] ONCE again Jesus addressed the people: 'I am the light of the world. No follower of mine shall walk in darkness; he shall have the light of life.' [13] The Pharisees said to him, 'You are witness in your own cause; your testimony is not valid.' [14] Jesus replied, 'My testimony is valid, even though I do testify on my own behalf; because I know where I come from, and where I am going. But you know neither where I come from nor where I am going. [15] You judge by worldly standards; I pass judgement on no one. [16] If I do judge, my judgement is valid because it is not I alone who judge, but I and he who sent me. [17] In your own law it is written that the testimony of two witnesses is valid. [18] I am a witness in my own cause, and my other witness is the Father who sent me.' [19] 'Where is your father?' they asked him. Jesus replied, 'You do not know me or my Father; if you knew me you would know my Father too.'

[20] Jesus was teaching near the treasury in the temple when he said this; but no one arrested him, because his hour had not yet come.

[21] Again he said to them, 'I am going away. You will look for me, but you will die in your sin; where I am going, you cannot come.' [22] At this the Jews said, 'Perhaps he will kill himself: is that what he means when he says, "Where I am going, you cannot come"?' [23] Jesus continued, 'You belong to this world below, I to the world above. Your home is in this world, mine is not. [24] That is why I told you that you would die in your sins; and you will die in your sins unless you believe that I am what I am.' [25] 'And who are you?' they asked him. Jesus answered, 'What I have told you all along. [26] I have much to say about you—and in judgement. But he who sent me speaks the truth, and what I heard from him I report to the world.'

[27] They did not understand that he was speaking to them about the Father. [28] So Jesus said to them, 'When you have lifted up the Son of Man you will know that I am what I am. I do nothing on my own authority, but in all I say, I have been taught by my Father. [29] He who sent me is present with me, and has not left me on my own; for I always do what is pleasing to him.' [30] As he said this, many put their faith in him.

[31] Turning to the Jews who had believed him, Jesus said, 'If you stand by my teaching, you are truly my disciples; [32] you will know the truth, and the truth will set you free.' [33] 'We are Abraham's descendants,' they replied; 'we have never been in slavery to anyone. What do you mean by saying, "You will become free"?' [34] 'In very truth I tell you', said Jesus, 'that everyone who commits sin is a slave. [35] The slave has no permanent standing in the household, but the son belongs to it for ever. [36] If then the Son sets you free, you will indeed be free.

[37] 'I know that you are descended from Abraham, yet you are bent on killing me because my teaching makes no headway with you. [38] I tell what I have seen in my Father's presence; you do what you have learned from your father.' [39] They retorted, 'Abraham is our father.' 'If you were Abraham's children', Jesus replied, 'you would do as Abraham did. [40] As it is, you are bent on killing me, because I have told you the truth, which I heard from God. That is not how Abraham acted. [41] You are doing your own father's work.'

They said, 'We are not illegitimate; God is our father, and God alone.' [42] Jesus said to them, 'If God were your father, you would love me, for God is the source of my being, and from him I come. I have not come of my own accord; he sent me. [43] Why do you not understand what I am saying? It is because my teaching is beyond your grasp. [44] Your father is the devil and you choose to carry out your father's desires. He was a murderer from the beginning, and is not rooted in the truth; there is no truth in him. When he tells a lie he is speaking his own language, for he is a liar and the father of lies. [45] But because I speak the truth, you do not believe me. [46] Which of you can convict

7:52 **the Prophet does not:** *most witnesses read* the prophets do not. **Galilee:** *some witnesses here insert the passage 7:53—8:11, which is printed on p. 102.*   8:25 **What ... along:** *or* Why should I speak to you at all?

me of sin? If what I say is true, why do you not believe me? [47] He who has God for his father listens to the words of God. You are not God's children, and that is why you do not listen.'

[48] The Jews answered, 'Are we not right in saying that you are a Samaritan, and that you are possessed?' [49] 'I am not possessed,' said Jesus; 'I am honouring my Father, but you dishonour me. [50] I do not care about my own glory; there is one who does care, and he is judge. [51] In very truth I tell you, if anyone obeys my teaching he will never see death.'

[52] The Jews said, 'Now we are certain that you are possessed. Abraham is dead and so are the prophets; yet you say, "If anyone obeys my teaching he will never taste death." [53] Are you greater than our father Abraham? He is dead and the prophets too are dead. Who do you claim to be?'

[54] Jesus replied, 'If I glorify myself, that glory of mine is worthless. It is the Father who glorifies me, he of whom you say, "He is our God," [55] though you do not know him. But I know him; if I were to say that I did not know him I should be a liar like you. I do know him and I obey his word. [56] Your father Abraham was overjoyed to see my day; he saw it and was glad.' [57] The Jews protested, 'You are not yet fifty years old. How can you have seen Abraham?' [58] Jesus said, 'In very truth I tell you, before Abraham was born, I am.' [59] They took up stones to throw at him, but he was not to be seen; and he left the temple.

Seeing and believing

9 As HE went on his way Jesus saw a man who had been blind from birth. [2] His disciples asked him, 'Rabbi, why was this man born blind? Who sinned, this man or his parents?' [3] 'It is not that he or his parents sinned,' Jesus answered; 'he was born blind so that God's power might be displayed in curing him. [4] While daylight lasts we must carry on the work of him who sent me; night is coming, when no one can work. [5] While I am in the world I am the light of the world.'

[6] With these words he spat on the ground and made a paste with the spittle; he spread it on the man's eyes, [7] and said

to him, 'Go and wash in the pool of Siloam.' (The name means 'Sent'.) The man went off and washed, and came back able to see.

[8] His neighbours and those who were accustomed to see him begging said, 'Is not this the man who used to sit and beg?' [9] Some said, 'Yes, it is.' Others said, 'No, but it is someone like him.' He himself said, 'I am the man.' [10] They asked him, 'How were your eyes opened?' [11] He replied, 'The man called Jesus made a paste and smeared my eyes with it, and told me to go to Siloam and wash. So I went and washed, and found I could see.' [12] 'Where is he?' they asked. 'I do not know,' he said.

[13] The man who had been blind was brought before the Pharisees. [14] As it was a sabbath day when Jesus made the paste and opened his eyes, [15] the Pharisees too asked him how he had gained his sight. The man told them, 'He spread a paste on my eyes; then I washed, and now I can see.' [16] Some of the Pharisees said, 'This man cannot be from God; he does not keep the sabbath.' Others said, 'How could such signs come from a sinful man?' So they took different sides. [17] Then they continued to question him: 'What have you to say about him? It was your eyes he opened.' He answered, 'He is a prophet.'

[18] The Jews would not believe that the man had been blind and had gained his sight, until they had summoned his parents [19] and questioned them: 'Is this your son? Do you say that he was born blind? How is it that he can see now?' [20] The parents replied, 'We know that he is our son, and that he was born blind. [21] But how it is that he can now see, or who opened his eyes, we do not know. Ask him; he is of age; let him speak for himself.' [22] His parents gave this answer because they were afraid of the Jews; for the Jewish authorities had already agreed that anyone who acknowledged Jesus as Messiah should be banned from the synagogue. [23] That is why the parents said, 'He is of age; ask him.'

[24] So for the second time they summoned the man who had been blind, and said, 'Speak the truth before God. We know that this man is a sinner.'

9:4 **we:** *some witnesses read* I.

²⁵ 'Whether or not he is a sinner, I do not know,' the man replied. 'All I know is this: I was blind and now I can see.' ²⁶ 'What did he do to you?' they asked. 'How did he open your eyes?' ²⁷ 'I have told you already,' he retorted, 'but you took no notice. Why do you want to hear it again? Do you also want to become his disciples?' ²⁸ Then they became abusive. 'You are that man's disciple,' they said, 'but we are disciples of Moses. ²⁹ We know that God spoke to Moses, but as for this man, we do not know where he comes from.'

³⁰ The man replied, 'How extraordinary! Here is a man who has opened my eyes, yet you do not know where he comes from! ³¹ We know that God does not listen to sinners; he listens to anyone who is devout and obeys his will. ³² To open the eyes of a man born blind—that is unheard of since time began. ³³ If this man was not from God he could do nothing.' ³⁴ 'Who are you to lecture us?' they retorted. 'You were born and bred in sin.' Then they turned him out.

³⁵ Hearing that they had turned him out, Jesus found him and asked, 'Have you faith in the Son of Man?' ³⁶ The man answered, 'Tell me who he is, sir, that I may put my faith in him.' ³⁷ 'You have seen him,' said Jesus; 'indeed, it is he who is speaking to you.' ³⁸ 'Lord, I believe,' he said, and fell on his knees before him.

³⁹ Jesus said, 'It is for judgement that I have come into this world—to give sight to the sightless and to make blind those who see.' ⁴⁰ Some Pharisees who were present asked, 'Do you mean that we are blind?' ⁴¹ 'If you were blind,' said Jesus, 'you would not be guilty, but because you claim to see, your guilt remains.

Victory over death

10 'IN very truth I tell you, the man who does not enter the sheepfold by the door, but climbs in some other way, is nothing but a thief and a robber. ² He who enters by the door is the shepherd in charge of the sheep. ³ The doorkeeper admits him, and the sheep hear his voice; he calls his own sheep by name, and leads them out. ⁴ When he has brought them all out, he goes ahead of them and the sheep follow, because they

know his voice. ⁵ They will not follow a stranger; they will run away from him, because they do not recognize the voice of strangers.'

⁶ This was a parable that Jesus told them, but they did not understand what he meant by it.

⁷ So Jesus spoke again: 'In very truth I tell you, I am the door of the sheepfold. ⁸ The sheep paid no heed to any who came before me, for they were all thieves and robbers. ⁹ I am the door; anyone who comes into the fold through me will be safe. He will go in and out and find pasture.

¹⁰ 'A thief comes only to steal, kill, and destroy; I have come that they may have life, and may have it in all its fullness. ¹¹ I am the good shepherd; the good shepherd lays down his life for the sheep. ¹² The hired man, when he sees the wolf coming, abandons the sheep and runs away, because he is not the shepherd and the sheep are not his. Then the wolf harries the flock and scatters the sheep. ¹³ The man runs away because he is a hired man and cares nothing for the sheep.

¹⁴ 'I am the good shepherd; I know my own and my own know me, ¹⁵ as the Father knows me and I know the Father; and I lay down my life for the sheep. ¹⁶ But there are other sheep of mine, not belonging to this fold; I must lead them as well, and they too will listen to my voice. There will then be one flock, one shepherd. ¹⁷ The Father loves me because I lay down my life, to receive it back again. ¹⁸ No one takes it away from me; I am laying it down of my own free will. I have the right to lay it down, and I have the right to receive it back again; this charge I have received from my Father.'

¹⁹ These words once again caused a division among the Jews. ²⁰ Many of them said, 'He is possessed, he is out of his mind. Why listen to him?' ²¹ Others said, 'No one possessed by a demon could speak like this. Could a demon open the eyes of the blind?'

²² IT was winter, and the festival of the Dedication was being held in Jerusalem. ²³ As Jesus was walking in the temple precincts, in Solomon's Portico, ²⁴ the Jews gathered round him and asked:

9:35 **Son of Man**: *some witnesses read* Son of God.

'How long are you going to keep us in suspense? Tell us plainly: are you the Messiah?' [25] 'I have told you,' said Jesus, 'and you do not believe. My deeds done in my Father's name are my credentials, [26] but because you are not sheep of my flock you do not believe. [27] My own sheep listen to my voice; I know them and they follow me. [28] I give them eternal life and they will never perish; no one will snatch them from my care. [29] My Father who has given them to me is greater than all, and no one can snatch them out of the Father's care. [30] The Father and I are one.'

[31] Once again the Jews picked up stones to stone him. [32] At this Jesus said to them, 'By the Father's power I have done many good deeds before your eyes; for which of these are you stoning me?' [33] 'We are not stoning you for any good deed,' the Jews replied, 'but for blasphemy: you, a man, are claiming to be God.' [34] Jesus answered, 'Is it not written in your law, "I said: You are gods"? [35] It is those to whom God's word came who are called gods—and scripture cannot be set aside. [36] Then why do you charge me with blasphemy for saying, "I am God's son," I whom the Father consecrated and sent into the world?

[37] 'If my deeds are not the deeds of my Father, do not believe me. [38] But if they are, then even if you do not believe me, believe the deeds, so that you may recognize and know that the Father is in me, and I in the Father.'

[39] This provoked them to make another attempt to seize him, but he escaped from their clutches.

[40] JESUS withdrew again across the Jordan, to the place where John had been baptizing earlier, and stayed there [41] while crowds came to him. 'John gave us no miraculous sign,' they said, 'but all that he told us about this man was true.' [42] And many came to believe in him there.

11 There was a man named Lazarus who had fallen ill. His home was at Bethany, the village of Mary and her sister Martha. [2] This Mary, whose brother Lazarus had fallen ill, was the woman who anointed the Lord with ointment and wiped his feet with her hair. [3] The sisters sent a message to him: 'Sir, you should know that your friend lies ill.' [4] When Jesus heard this he said, 'This illness is not to end in death; through it God's glory is to be revealed and the Son of God glorified.' [5] Therefore, though he loved Martha and her sister and Lazarus, [6] he stayed where he was for two days after hearing of Lazarus's illness.

[7] He then said to his disciples, 'Let us go back to Judaea.' [8] 'Rabbi,' his disciples said, 'it is not long since the Jews there were wanting to stone you. Are you going there again?' [9] Jesus replied, 'Are there not twelve hours of daylight? Anyone can walk in the daytime without stumbling, because he has this world's light to see by. [10] But if he walks after nightfall he stumbles, because the light fails him.'

[11] After saying this he added, 'Our friend Lazarus has fallen asleep, but I shall go and wake him.' [12] The disciples said, 'Master, if he is sleeping he will recover.' [13] Jesus had been speaking of Lazarus's death, but they thought that he meant natural sleep. [14] Then Jesus told them plainly: 'Lazarus is dead. [15] I am glad for your sake that I was not there; for it will lead you to believe. But let us go to him.' [16] Thomas, called 'the Twin', said to his fellow-disciples, 'Let us also go and die with him.'

[17] ON his arrival Jesus found that Lazarus had already been four days in the tomb. [18] Bethany was just under two miles from Jerusalem, [19] and many of the Jews had come from the city to visit Martha and Mary and condole with them about their brother. [20] As soon as Martha heard that Jesus was on his way, she went to meet him, and left Mary sitting at home. [21] Martha said to Jesus, 'Lord, if you had been here my brother would not have died. [22] Even now I know that God will grant you whatever you ask of him.' [23] Jesus said, 'Your brother will rise again.' [24] 'I know that he will rise again', said Martha, 'at the resurrection on the last day.' [25] Jesus said, 'I am the resurrection and the life. Whoever has faith in me shall live, even though he dies; [26] and no one who lives and has faith in me shall ever die. Do you believe this?' [27] 'I do,

10:29 **My Father ... snatch them:** *some witnesses read* That which my Father has given me is greater than all, and no one can snatch it.   10:33 **claiming ... God:** *or* claiming to be a god.   11:25 *Some witnesses omit* and the life.

Lord,' she answered; 'I believe that you are the Messiah, the Son of God who was to come into the world.'

[28] So saying she went to call her sister Mary, and, taking her aside, she said, 'The Master is here and is asking for you.' [29] As soon as Mary heard this she rose and went to him. [30] Jesus had not yet entered the village, but was still at the place where Martha had met him. [31] When the Jews who were in the house condoling with Mary saw her hurry out, they went after her, assuming that she was going to the tomb to weep there.

[32] Mary came to the place where Jesus was, and as soon as she saw him she fell at his feet and said, 'Lord, if you had been here my brother would not have died.' [33] When Jesus saw her weeping and the Jews who had come with her weeping, he was moved with indignation and deeply distressed. [34] 'Where have you laid him?' he asked. They replied, 'Come and see.' [35] Jesus wept. [36] The Jews said, 'How dearly he must have loved him!' [37] But some of them said, 'Could not this man, who opened the blind man's eyes, have done something to keep Lazarus from dying?'

[38] Jesus, again deeply moved, went to the tomb. It was a cave, with a stone placed against it. [39] Jesus said, 'Take away the stone.' Martha, the dead man's sister, said to him, 'Sir, by now there will be a stench; he has been there four days.' [40] Jesus said, 'Did I not tell you that if you have faith you will see the glory of God?' [41] Then they removed the stone.

Jesus looked upwards and said, 'Father, I thank you for hearing me. [42] I know that you always hear me, but I have spoken for the sake of the people standing round, that they may believe it was you who sent me.'

[43] Then he raised his voice in a great cry: 'Lazarus, come out.' [44] The dead man came out, his hands and feet bound with linen bandages, his face wrapped in a cloth. Jesus said, 'Loose him; let him go.'

[45] MANY of the Jews who had come to visit Mary, and had seen what Jesus did, put their faith in him. [46] But some of them went off to the Pharisees and reported what he had done.

[47] Thereupon the chief priests and the Pharisees convened a meeting of the Council. 'This man is performing many signs,' they said, 'and what action are we taking? [48] If we let him go on like this the whole populace will believe in him, and then the Romans will come and sweep away our temple and our nation.' [49] But one of them, Caiaphas, who was high priest that year, said, 'You have no grasp of the situation at all; [50] you do not realize that it is more to your interest that one man should die for the people, than that the whole nation should be destroyed.' [51] He did not say this of his own accord, but as the high priest that year he was prophesying that Jesus would die for the nation, [52] and not for the nation alone but to gather together the scattered children of God. [53] So from that day on they plotted his death.

[54] Accordingly Jesus no longer went about openly among the Jews, but withdrew to a town called Ephraim, in the country bordering on the desert, and stayed there with his disciples.

The Passover in Jerusalem

[55] THE Jewish Passover was now at hand, and many people went up from the country to Jerusalem to purify themselves before the festival. [56] They looked out for Jesus, and as they stood in the temple they asked one another, 'What do you think? Perhaps he is not coming to the festival.' [57] Now the chief priests and the Pharisees had given orders that anyone who knew where he was must report it, so that they might arrest him.

12 SIX days before the Passover festival Jesus came to Bethany, the home of Lazarus whom he had raised from the dead. [2] They gave a supper in his honour, at which Martha served, and Lazarus was among the guests with Jesus. [3] Then Mary brought a pound of very costly perfume, pure oil of nard, and anointed Jesus's feet and wiped them with her hair, till the house was filled with the fragrance. [4] At this, Judas Iscariot, one of his disciples—the one who was to betray him—protested, [5] 'Could not this perfume have been sold for three hundred denarii and the money given to the poor?' [6] He

12:5 denarii: *see p. xi.*

92

said this, not out of any concern for the poor, but because he was a thief; he had charge of the common purse and used to pilfer the money kept in it. ⁷'Leave her alone,' said Jesus. 'Let her keep it for the day of my burial. ⁸The poor you have always among you, but you will not always have me.'

⁹Learning he was there the Jews came in large numbers, not only because of Jesus but also to see Lazarus whom he had raised from the dead. ¹⁰The chief priests then resolved to do away with Lazarus as well, ¹¹since on his account many Jews were going over to Jesus and putting their faith in him.

¹²THE next day the great crowd of pilgrims who had come for the festival, hearing that Jesus was on the way to Jerusalem, ¹³went out to meet him with palm branches in their hands, shouting, 'Hosanna! Blessed is he who comes in the name of the Lord! Blessed is the king of Israel!' ¹⁴Jesus found a donkey and mounted it, in accordance with the words of scripture: ¹⁵'Fear no more, daughter of Zion; see, your king is coming, mounted on a donkey's colt.' ¹⁶At the time his disciples did not understand this, but after Jesus had been glorified they remembered that this had been written about him, and that it had happened to him.

¹⁷The people who were present when he called Lazarus out of the tomb and raised him from the dead kept telling what they had seen and heard. ¹⁸That is why the crowd went to meet him: they had heard of this sign that he had performed. ¹⁹The Pharisees said to one another, 'You can see we are getting nowhere; all the world has gone after him!'

²⁰AMONG those who went up to worship at the festival were some Gentiles. ²¹They approached Philip, who was from Bethsaida in Galilee, and said to him, 'Sir, we should like to see Jesus.' ²²Philip went and told Andrew, and the two of them went to tell Jesus. ²³Jesus replied: 'The hour has come for the Son of Man to be glorified. ²⁴In very truth I tell you, unless a grain of wheat falls into the ground and dies, it remains that and nothing more; but if it dies, it bears a rich harvest.

²⁵Whoever loves himself is lost, but he who hates himself in this world will be kept safe for eternal life. ²⁶If anyone is to serve me, he must follow me; where I am, there will my servant be. Whoever serves me will be honoured by the Father.

²⁷'Now my soul is in turmoil, and what am I to say? "Father, save me from this hour"? No, it was for this that I came to this hour. ²⁸Father, glorify your name.' A voice came from heaven: 'I have glorified it, and I will glorify it again.' ²⁹The crowd standing by said it was thunder they heard, while others said, 'An angel has spoken to him.' ³⁰Jesus replied, 'This voice spoke for your sake, not mine. ³¹Now is the hour of judgement for this world; now shall the prince of this world be driven out. ³²And when I am lifted up from the earth I shall draw everyone to myself.' ³³This he said to indicate the kind of death he was to die.

³⁴The people answered, 'Our law teaches us that the Messiah remains for ever. What do you mean by saying that the Son of Man must be lifted up? What Son of Man is this?' ³⁵Jesus answered them: 'The light is among you still, but not for long. Go on your way while you have the light, so that darkness may not overtake you. He who journeys in the dark does not know where he is going. ³⁶Trust to the light while you have it, so that you may become children of light.' After these words Jesus went away from them into hiding.

³⁷IN spite of the many signs which Jesus had performed in their presence they would not believe in him, ³⁸for the prophet Isaiah's words had to be fulfilled: 'Lord, who has believed what we reported, and to whom has the power of the Lord been revealed?' ³⁹And there is another saying of Isaiah which explains why they could not believe: ⁴⁰'He has blinded their eyes and dulled their minds, lest they should see with their eyes, and perceive with their minds, and turn to me to heal them.' ⁴¹Isaiah said this because he saw his glory and spoke about him.

⁴²For all that, even among those in authority many believed in him, but would not acknowledge him on account of the Pharisees, for fear of being banned

12:8 *Some witnesses omit* The poor ... have me.

from the synagogue. ⁴³ For they valued human reputation rather than the honour which comes from God.

⁴⁴ JESUS proclaimed: 'To believe in me, is not to believe in me but in him who sent me; ⁴⁵ to see me, is to see him who sent me. ⁴⁶ I have come into the world as light, so that no one who has faith in me should remain in darkness. ⁴⁷ But if anyone hears my words and disregards them, I am not his judge; I have not come to judge the world, but to save the world. ⁴⁸ There is a judge for anyone who rejects me and does not accept my words; the word I have spoken will be his judge on the last day. ⁴⁹ I do not speak on my own authority, but the Father who sent me has himself commanded me what to say and how to speak. ⁵⁰ I know that his commands are eternal life. What the Father has said to me, therefore—that is what I speak.'

Farewell discourses

13 IT was before the Passover festival, and Jesus knew that his hour had come and that he must leave this world and go to the Father. He had always loved his own who were in the world, and he loved them to the end.

² The devil had already put it into the mind of Judas son of Simon Iscariot to betray him. During supper, ³ Jesus, well aware that the Father had entrusted everything to him, and that he had come from God and was going back to God, ⁴ rose from the supper table, took off his outer garment and, taking a towel, tied it round him. ⁵ Then he poured water into a basin, and began to wash his disciples' feet and to wipe them with the towel.

⁶ When he came to Simon Peter, Peter said to him, 'You, Lord, washing my feet?' ⁷ Jesus replied, 'You do not understand now what I am doing, but one day you will.' ⁸ Peter said, 'I will never let you wash my feet.' 'If I do not wash you,' Jesus replied, 'you have no part with me.' ⁹ 'Then, Lord,' said Simon Peter, 'not my feet only; wash my hands and head as well!' ¹⁰ Jesus said to him, 'Anyone who has bathed needs no further washing; he is clean all over; and you are clean, though not every one of you.' ¹¹ He added the

words 'not every one of you' because he knew who was going to betray him.

¹² After washing their feet he put on his garment and sat down again. 'Do you understand what I have done for you?' he asked. ¹³ 'You call me Teacher and Lord, and rightly so, for that is what I am. ¹⁴ Then if I, your Lord and Teacher, have washed your feet, you also ought to wash one another's feet. ¹⁵ I have set you an example: you are to do as I have done for you. ¹⁶ In very truth I tell you, a servant is not greater than his master, nor a messenger than the one who sent him. ¹⁷ If you know this, happy are you if you act upon it.

¹⁸ 'I am not speaking about all of you; I know whom I have chosen. But there is a text of scripture to be fulfilled: "He who eats bread with me has turned against me." ¹⁹ I tell you this now, before the event, so that when it happens you may believe that I am what I am. ²⁰ In very truth I tell you, whoever receives any messenger of mine receives me; and receiving me, he receives the One who sent me.'

²¹ After saying this, Jesus exclaimed in deep distress, 'In very truth I tell you, one of you is going to betray me.' ²² The disciples looked at one another in bewilderment: which of them could he mean? ²³ One of them, the disciple he loved, was reclining close beside Jesus. ²⁴ Simon Peter signalled to him to find out which one he meant. ²⁵ That disciple leaned back close to Jesus and asked, 'Lord, who is it?' ²⁶ Jesus replied, 'It is the one to whom I give this piece of bread when I have dipped it in the dish.' Then he took it, dipped it in the dish, and gave it to Judas son of Simon Iscariot. ²⁷ As soon as Judas had received it Satan entered him. Jesus said to him, 'Do quickly what you have to do.' ²⁸ No one at the table understood what he meant by this. ²⁹ Some supposed that, as Judas was in charge of the common purse, Jesus was telling him to buy what was needed for the festival, or to make some gift to the poor. ³⁰ As soon as Judas had received the bread he went out. It was night.

³¹ WHEN he had gone out, Jesus said, 'Now the Son of Man is glorified, and in

13:10 **needs … washing:** *some witnesses read* needs only to wash his feet.

him God is glorified. [32] If God is glorified in him, God will also glorify him in himself; and he will glorify him now. [33] My children, I am to be with you for a little longer; then you will look for me, and, as I told the Jews, I tell you now: where I am going you cannot come. [34] I give you a new commandment: love one another; as I have loved you, so you are to love one another. [35] If there is this love among you, then everyone will know that you are my disciples.'

[36] Simon Peter said to him, 'Lord, where are you going?' Jesus replied, 'I am going where you cannot follow me now, but one day you will.' [37] Peter said, 'Lord, why cannot I follow you now? I will lay down my life for you.' [38] Jesus answered, 'Will you really lay down your life for me? In very truth I tell you, before the cock crows you will have denied me three times.

14 'Set your troubled hearts at rest. Trust in God always; trust also in me. [2] There are many dwelling-places in my Father's house; if it were not so I should have told you; for I am going to prepare a place for you. [3] And if I go and prepare a place for you, I shall come again and take you to myself, so that where I am you may be also; [4] and you know the way I am taking.' [5] Thomas said, 'Lord, we do not know where you are going, so how can we know the way?' [6] Jesus replied, 'I am the way, the truth, and the life; no one comes to the Father except by me.

[7] 'If you knew me you would know my Father too. From now on you do know him; you have seen him.' [8] Philip said to him, 'Lord, show us the Father; we ask no more.' [9] Jesus answered, 'Have I been all this time with you, Philip, and still you do not know me? Anyone who has seen me has seen the Father. Then how can you say, "Show us the Father"? [10] Do you not believe that I am in the Father, and the Father in me? I am not myself the source of the words I speak to you: it is the Father who dwells in me doing his own work. [11] Believe me when I say that I am in the Father and the Father in me; or else accept the evidence of the deeds themselves. [12] In very truth I tell you, whoever has faith in me will do what I am doing;

indeed he will do greater things still because I am going to the Father. [13] Anything you ask in my name I will do, so that the Father may be glorified in the Son. [14] If you ask anything in my name I will do it.

[15] 'If you love me you will obey my commands; [16] and I will ask the Father, and he will give you another to be your advocate, who will be with you for ever— [17] the Spirit of truth. The world cannot accept him, because the world neither sees nor knows him; but you know him, because he dwells with you and will be in you. [18] I will not leave you bereft; I am coming back to you. [19] In a little while the world will see me no longer, but you will see me; because I live, you too will live. [20] When that day comes you will know that I am in my Father, and you in me and I in you. [21] Anyone who has received my commands and obeys them—he it is who loves me; and he who loves me will be loved by my Father; and I will love him and disclose myself to him.'

[22] Judas said—the other Judas, not Iscariot—'Lord, how has it come about that you mean to disclose yourself to us and not to the world?' [23] Jesus replied, 'Anyone who loves me will heed what I say; then my Father will love him, and we will come to him and make our dwelling with him; [24] but whoever does not love me does not heed what I say. And the word you hear is not my own: it is the word of the Father who sent me. [25] I have told you these things while I am still with you; [26] but the advocate, the Holy Spirit whom the Father will send in my name, will teach you everything and remind you of all that I have told you.

[27] 'Peace is my parting gift to you, my own peace, such as the world cannot give. Set your troubled hearts at rest, and banish your fears. [28] You heard me say, "I am going away, and I am coming back to you." If you loved me you would be glad that I am going to the Father; for the Father is greater than I am. [29] I have told you now, before it happens, so that when it does happen you may have faith.

[30] 'I shall not talk much longer with you, for the prince of this world approaches. He has no rights over me; [31] but the world must be shown that I love the

13:32 *Some witnesses omit* If God ... in him.   14:3 **also:** *some witnesses add* you know where I am going.
14:7 **If you ... too:** *some witnesses read* If you know me you will know my Father too.   14:14 **If you ask:** *some witnesses add* me.   14:17 **will be:** *some witnesses read* is.

Father and am doing what he commands; come, let us go!

15 'I AM the true vine, and my Father is the gardener. ²Any branch of mine that is barren he cuts away; and any fruiting branch he prunes clean, to make it more fruitful still. ³You are already clean because of the word I have spoken to you. ⁴Dwell in me, as I in you. No branch can bear fruit by itself, but only if it remains united with the vine; no more can you bear fruit, unless you remain united with me.

⁵'I am the vine; you are the branches. Anyone who dwells in me, as I dwell in him, bears much fruit; apart from me you can do nothing. ⁶Anyone who does not dwell in me is thrown away like a withered branch. The withered branches are gathered up, thrown on the fire, and burnt.

⁷'If you dwell in me, and my words dwell in you, ask whatever you want, and you shall have it. ⁸This is how my Father is glorified: you are to bear fruit in plenty and so be my disciples. ⁹As the Father has loved me, so I have loved you. Dwell in my love. ¹⁰If you heed my commands, you will dwell in my love, as I have heeded my Father's commands and dwell in his love.

¹¹'I have spoken thus to you, so that my joy may be in you, and your joy complete. ¹²This is my commandment: love one another, as I have loved you. ¹³There is no greater love than this, that someone should lay down his life for his friends. ¹⁴You are my friends, if you do what I command you. ¹⁵No longer do I call you servants, for a servant does not know what his master is about. I have called you friends, because I have disclosed to you everything that I heard from my Father. ¹⁶You did not choose me: I chose you. I appointed you to go on and bear fruit, fruit that will last; so that the Father may give you whatever you ask in my name. ¹⁷This is my commandment to you: love one another.

¹⁸'If the world hates you, it hated me first, as you know well. ¹⁹If you belonged to the world, the world would love its own; but you do not belong to the world, now that I have chosen you out of the world, and for that reason the world hates

you. ²⁰Remember what I said: "A servant is not greater than his master." If they persecuted me, they will also persecute you; if they have followed my teaching, they will follow yours. ²¹All this will they do to you on my account, because they do not know the One who sent me.

²²'If I had not come and spoken to them, they would not be guilty of sin; but now they have no excuse for their sin: ²³whoever hates me, hates my Father also. ²⁴If I had not done such deeds among them as no one else has ever done, they would not be guilty of sin; but now they have seen and hated both me and my Father. ²⁵This text in their law had to come true: "They hated me without reason."

²⁶'When the advocate has come, whom I shall send you from the Father— the Spirit of truth that issues from the Father—he will bear witness to me. ²⁷And you also are my witnesses, because you have been with me from the first.

16 'I have told you all this to guard you against the breakdown of your faith. ²They will ban you from the synagogue; indeed, the time is coming when anyone who kills you will suppose that he is serving God. ³They will do these things because they did not know either the Father or me. ⁴I have told you all this so that when the time comes for it to happen you may remember my warning. I did not tell you this at first, because then I was with you; ⁵but now I am going away to him who sent me. None of you asks me, "Where are you going?" ⁶Yet you are plunged into grief at what I have told you. ⁷Nevertheless I assure you that it is in your interest that I am leaving you. If I do not go, the advocate will not come, whereas if I go, I will send him to you. ⁸When he comes, he will prove the world wrong about sin, justice, and judgement: ⁹about sin, because they refuse to believe in me; ¹⁰about justice, because I go to the Father when I pass from your sight; ¹¹about judgement, because the prince of this world stands condemned.

¹²'There is much more that I could say to you, but the burden would be too great for you now. ¹³However, when the Spirit of truth comes, he will guide you into all the truth; for he will not speak on his own

---

15:18 **it hated … well:** *or* bear in mind that it hated me first.

authority, but will speak only what he hears; and he will make known to you what is to come. ¹⁴ He will glorify me, for he will take what is mine and make it known to you. ¹⁵ All that the Father has is mine, and that is why I said, "He will take what is mine and make it known to you."

¹⁶ 'A LITTLE while, and you see me no more; again a little while, and you will see me.' ¹⁷ Some of his disciples said to one another, 'What does he mean by this: "A little while, and you will not see me, and again a little while, and you will see me," and by this: "Because I am going to the Father"?' ¹⁸ So they asked, 'What is this "little while" that he is talking about? We do not know what he means.'

¹⁹ Jesus knew that they were wanting to question him, and said, 'Are you discussing that saying of mine: "A little while, and you will not see me, and again a little while, and you will see me"? ²⁰ In very truth I tell you, you will weep and mourn, but the world will be glad. But though you will be plunged in grief, your grief will be turned to joy. ²¹ A woman in labour is in pain because her time has come; but when her baby is born she forgets the anguish in her joy that a child has been born into the world. ²² So it is with you: for the moment you are sad; but I shall see you again, and then you will be joyful, and no one shall rob you of your joy. ²³ When that day comes you will ask me nothing more. In very truth I tell you, if you ask the Father for anything in my name, he will give it you. ²⁴ So far you have asked nothing in my name. Ask and you will receive, that your joy may be complete.

²⁵ 'Till now I have been using figures of speech; a time is coming when I shall no longer use figures, but tell you of the Father in plain words. ²⁶ When that day comes you will make your request in my name, and I do not say that I shall pray to the Father for you, ²⁷ for the Father loves you himself, because you have loved me and believed that I came from God. ²⁸ I came from the Father and have come into the world; and now I am leaving the world again and going to the Father.'

²⁹ His disciples said, 'Now you are speaking plainly, not in figures of speech! ³⁰ We are certain now that you know everything, and do not need to be asked; because of this we believe that you have come from God.'

³¹ Jesus answered, 'Do you now believe? ³² I warn you, the hour is coming, has indeed already come, when you are to be scattered, each to his own home, leaving me alone. Yet I am not alone, for the Father is with me. ³³ I have told you all this so that in me you may find peace. In the world you will have suffering. But take heart! I have conquered the world.'

17 THEN Jesus looked up to heaven and said:

'Father, the hour has come. Glorify your Son, that the Son may glorify you. ² For you have made him sovereign over all mankind, to give eternal life to all whom you have given him. ³ This is eternal life: to know you the only true God, and Jesus Christ whom you have sent.

⁴ 'I have glorified you on earth by finishing the work which you gave me to do; ⁵ and now, Father, glorify me in your own presence with the glory which I had with you before the world began.

⁶ 'I have made your name known to the men whom you gave me out of the world. They were yours and you gave them to me, and they have obeyed your command. ⁷ Now they know that all you gave me has come from you; ⁸ for I have taught them what I learned from you, and they have received it: they know with certainty that I came from you, and they have believed that you sent me.

⁹ 'I pray for them; I am not praying for the world but for those whom you have given me, because they belong to you. ¹⁰ All that is mine is yours, and what is yours is mine; and through them is my glory revealed.

¹¹ 'I am no longer in the world; they are still in the world, but I am coming to you. Holy Father, protect them by the power of your name, the name you have given me, that they may be one, as we are one. ¹² While I was with them, I protected them by the power of your name which

---

16:23 **if you ask ... you:** *some witnesses read* if you ask the Father for anything, he will give it you in my name. 17:11 **protect ... given me:** *some witnesses read* protect by the power of your name those whom you have given me. 17:12 **protected ... gave me:** *some witnesses read* protected by the power of your name those whom you have given me.

you gave me, and kept them safe. Not one of them is lost except the man doomed to be lost, for scripture has to be fulfilled.

[13] 'Now I am coming to you; but while I am still in the world I speak these words, so that they may have my joy within them in full measure. [14] I have delivered your word to them, and the world hates them because they are strangers in the world, as I am. [15] I do not pray you to take them out of the world, but to keep them from the evil one. [16] They are strangers in the world, as I am. [17] Consecrate them by the truth; your word is truth. [18] As you sent me into the world, I have sent them into the world, [19] and for their sake I consecrate myself, that they too may be consecrated by the truth.

[20] 'It is not for these alone that I pray, but for those also who through their words put their faith in me. [21] May they all be one; as you, Father, are in me, and I in you, so also may they be in us, that the world may believe that you sent me. [22] The glory which you gave me I have given to them, that they may be one, as we are one; [23] I in them and you in me, may they be perfectly one. Then the world will know that you sent me, and that you loved them as you loved me.

[24] 'Father, they are your gift to me; and my desire is that they may be with me where I am, so that they may look upon my glory, which you have given me because you loved me before the world began. [25] Righteous Father, although the world does not know you, I know you, and they know that you sent me. [26] I made your name known to them, and will make it known, so that the love you had for me may be in them, and I in them.'

The trial and crucifixion of Jesus

18 AFTER this prayer, Jesus went out with his disciples across the Kedron ravine. There was a garden there, and he and his disciples went into it. [2] The place was known to Judas, his betrayer, because Jesus had often met there with his disciples. [3] So Judas made his way there with a detachment of soldiers, and with temple police provided by the chief priests and the Pharisees; they were equipped with lanterns, torches, and weapons. [4] Jesus, knowing everything that was to happen to him, stepped forward and asked them, 'Who is it you want?' [5] 'Jesus

of Nazareth,' they answered. Jesus said, 'I am he.' And Judas the traitor was standing there with them. [6] When Jesus said, 'I am he,' they drew back and fell to the ground. [7] Again he asked, 'Who is it you want?' 'Jesus of Nazareth,' they repeated. [8] 'I have told you that I am he,' Jesus answered. 'If I am the man you want, let these others go.' [9] (This was to make good his words, 'I have not lost one of those you gave me.') [10] Thereupon Simon Peter drew the sword he was wearing and struck at the high priest's servant, cutting off his right ear. The servant's name was Malchus. [11] Jesus said to Peter, 'Put away your sword. This is the cup the Father has given me; shall I not drink it?'

[12] THE troops with their commander, and the Jewish police, now arrested Jesus and secured him. [13] They took him first to Annas, father-in-law of Caiaphas, the high priest for that year—[14] the same Caiaphas who had advised the Jews that it would be to their interest if one man died for the people. [15] Jesus was followed by Simon Peter and another disciple. This disciple, who was known to the high priest, went with Jesus into the high priest's courtyard, [16] but Peter stayed outside at the door. So the other disciple, the high priest's acquaintance, went back and spoke to the girl on duty at the door, and brought Peter in. [17] The girl said to Peter, 'Are you another of this man's disciples?' 'I am not,' he said. [18] As it was cold, the servants and the police had made a charcoal fire, and were standing round it warming themselves. Peter too was standing with them, sharing the warmth.

[19] The high priest questioned Jesus about his disciples and about his teaching. [20] Jesus replied, 'I have spoken openly for all the world to hear; I have always taught in synagogues or in the temple, where all Jews congregate; I have said nothing in secret. [21] Why are you questioning me? Question those who heard me; they know what I said.' [22] When he said this, one of the police standing near him struck him on the face. 'Is that the way to answer the high priest?' he demanded. [23] Jesus replied, 'If I was wrong to speak what I did, produce evidence to prove it; if I was right, why strike me?'

[24] So Annas sent him bound to Caiaphas the high priest.

25 Meanwhile, as Simon Peter stood warming himself, he was asked, 'Are you another of his disciples?' But he denied it: 'I am not,' he said. 26 One of the high priest's servants, a relation of the man whose ear Peter had cut off, insisted, 'Did I not see you with him in the garden?' 27 Once again Peter denied it; and at that moment a cock crowed.

28 FROM Caiaphas Jesus was led into the governor's headquarters. It was now early morning, and the Jews themselves stayed outside the headquarters to avoid defilement, so that they could eat the Passover meal. 29 So Pilate came out to them and asked, 'What charge do you bring against this man?' 30 'If he were not a criminal', they replied, 'we would not have brought him before you.' 31 Pilate said, 'Take him yourselves and try him by your own law.' The Jews answered, 'We are not allowed to put anyone to death.' 32 Thus they ensured the fulfilment of the words by which Jesus had indicated the kind of death he was to die.

33 Pilate then went back into his headquarters and summoned Jesus. 'So you are the king of the Jews?' he said. 34 Jesus replied, 'Is that your own question, or have others suggested it to you?' 35 'Am I a Jew?' said Pilate. 'Your own nation and their chief priests have brought you before me. What have you done?' 36 Jesus replied, 'My kingdom does not belong to this world. If it did, my followers would be fighting to save me from the clutches of the Jews. My kingdom belongs elsewhere.' 37 'You are a king, then?' said Pilate. Jesus answered, '"King" is your word. My task is to bear witness to the truth. For this I was born; for this I came into the world, and all who are not deaf to truth listen to my voice.' 38 Pilate said, 'What is truth?' With those words he went out again to the Jews and said, 'For my part I find no case against him. 39 But you have a custom that I release one prisoner for you at Passover. Would you like me to release the king of the Jews?' 40 At this they shouted back: 'Not him; we want Barabbas!' Barabbas was a bandit.

19 Pilate now took Jesus and had him flogged; 2 and the soldiers plaited a crown of thorns and placed it on his head, and robed him in a purple cloak. 3 Then one after another they came up to him, crying, 'Hail, king of the Jews!' and struck him on the face.

4 Once more Pilate came out and said to the Jews, 'Here he is; I am bringing him out to let you know that I find no case against him'; 5 and Jesus came out, wearing the crown of thorns and the purple cloak. 'Here is the man,' said Pilate. 6 At the sight of him the chief priests and the temple police shouted, 'Crucify! Crucify!' 'Take him yourselves and crucify him,' said Pilate; 'for my part I find no case against him.' 7 The Jews answered, 'We have a law; and according to that law he ought to die, because he has claimed to be God's Son.'

8 When Pilate heard that, he was more afraid than ever, 9 and going back into his headquarters he asked Jesus, 'Where have you come from?' But Jesus gave him no answer. 10 'Do you refuse to speak to me?' said Pilate. 'Surely you know that I have authority to release you, and authority to crucify you?' 11 'You would have no authority at all over me', Jesus replied, 'if it had not been granted you from above; and therefore the deeper guilt lies with the one who handed me over to you.'

12 From that moment Pilate tried hard to release him; but the Jews kept shouting, 'If you let this man go, you are no friend to Caesar; anyone who claims to be a king is opposing Caesar.' 13 When Pilate heard what they were saying, he brought Jesus out and took his seat on the tribunal at the place known as The Pavement (in Hebrew, 'Gabbatha'). 14 It was the day of preparation for the Passover, about noon. Pilate said to the Jews, 'Here is your king.' 15 They shouted, 'Away with him! Away with him! Crucify him!' 'Am I to crucify your king?' said Pilate. 'We have no king but Caesar,' replied the chief priests. 16 Then at last, to satisfy them, he handed Jesus over to be crucified.

JESUS was taken away, 17 and went out, carrying the cross himself, to the place called The Skull (in Hebrew, 'Golgotha'); 18 there they crucified him, and with him two others, one on either side, with Jesus in between.

19:14 **It was ... Passover:** *or* It was Friday in Passover.

¹⁹ Pilate had an inscription written and fastened to the cross; it read, 'Jesus of Nazareth, King of the Jews'. ²⁰ This inscription, in Hebrew, Latin, and Greek, was read by many Jews, since the place where Jesus was crucified was not far from the city. ²¹ So the Jewish chief priests said to Pilate, 'You should not write "King of the Jews", but rather "He claimed to be king of the Jews".' ²² Pilate replied, 'What I have written, I have written.'

²³ When the soldiers had crucified Jesus they took his clothes and, leaving aside the tunic, divided them into four parts, one for each soldier. The tunic was seamless, woven in one piece throughout; ²⁴ so they said to one another, 'We must not tear this; let us toss for it.' Thus the text of scripture came true: 'They shared my garments among them, and cast lots for my clothing.'

That is what the soldiers did. ²⁵ Meanwhile near the cross on which Jesus hung, his mother was standing with her sister, Mary wife of Clopas, and Mary of Magdala. ²⁶ Seeing his mother, with the disciple whom he loved standing beside her, Jesus said to her, 'Mother, there is your son'; ²⁷ and to the disciple, 'There is your mother'; and from that moment the disciple took her into his home.

²⁸ After this, Jesus, aware that all had now come to its appointed end, said in fulfilment of scripture, 'I am thirsty.' ²⁹ A jar stood there full of sour wine; so they soaked a sponge with the wine, fixed it on hyssop, and held it up to his lips. ³⁰ Having received the wine, he said, 'It is accomplished!' Then he bowed his head and gave up his spirit.

³¹ Because it was the eve of the sabbath, the Jews were anxious that the bodies should not remain on the crosses, since that sabbath was a day of great solemnity; so they requested Pilate to have the legs broken and the bodies taken down. ³² The soldiers accordingly came to the men crucified with Jesus and broke the legs of each in turn, ³³ but when they came to Jesus and found he was already dead, they did not break his legs. ³⁴ But one of the soldiers thrust a lance into his side, and at once there was a flow of blood and water. ³⁵ This is vouched for by an eyewitness, whose evidence is to be trusted. He knows that he speaks the truth, so that you too may believe; ³⁶ for this happened in fulfilment of the text of scripture: 'No bone of his shall be broken.' ³⁷ And another text says, 'They shall look on him whom they pierced.'

³⁸ AFTER that, Joseph of Arimathaea, a disciple of Jesus, but a secret disciple for fear of the Jews, asked Pilate for permission to remove the body of Jesus. He consented; so Joseph came and removed the body. ³⁹ He was joined by Nicodemus (the man who had visited Jesus by night), who brought with him a mixture of myrrh and aloes, more than half a hundredweight. ⁴⁰ They took the body of Jesus and following Jewish burial customs they wrapped it, with the spices, in strips of linen cloth. ⁴¹ Near the place where he had been crucified there was a garden, and in the garden a new tomb, not yet used for burial; ⁴² and there, since it was the eve of the Jewish sabbath and the tomb was near at hand, they laid Jesus.

The resurrection

20 EARLY on the first day of the week, while it was still dark, Mary of Magdala came to the tomb. She saw that the stone had been moved away from the entrance, ² and ran to Simon Peter and the other disciple, the one whom Jesus loved. 'They have taken the Lord out of the tomb,' she said, 'and we do not know where they have laid him.' ³ So Peter and the other disciple set out and made their way to the tomb. ⁴ They ran together, but the other disciple ran faster than Peter and reached the tomb first. ⁵ He peered in and saw the linen wrappings lying there, but he did not enter. ⁶ Then Simon Peter caught up with him and went into the tomb. He saw the linen wrappings lying there, ⁷ and the napkin which had been round his head, not with the wrappings but rolled up in a place by itself. ⁸ Then the disciple who had reached the tomb first also went in, and he saw and believed; ⁹ until then they had not understood the scriptures, which showed that he must rise from the dead.

¹⁰ So the disciples went home again; ¹¹ but Mary stood outside the tomb weep-

---

19:29 **hyssop**: *one witness reads* a javelin.

ing. And as she wept, she peered into the tomb, [12] and saw two angels in white sitting there, one at the head, and one at the feet, where the body of Jesus had lain. [13] They asked her, 'Why are you weeping?' She answered, 'They have taken my Lord away, and I do not know where they have laid him.' [14] With these words she turned round and saw Jesus standing there, but she did not recognize him. [15] Jesus asked her, 'Why are you weeping? Who are you looking for?' Thinking it was the gardener, she said, 'If it is you, sir, who removed him, tell me where you have laid him, and I will take him away.' [16] Jesus said, 'Mary!' She turned and said to him, 'Rabbuni!' (which is Hebrew for 'Teacher'). [17] 'Do not cling to me,' said Jesus, 'for I have not yet ascended to the Father. But go to my brothers, and tell them that I am ascending to my Father and your Father, to my God and your God.' [18] Mary of Magdala went to tell the disciples. 'I have seen the Lord!' she said, and gave them his message.

[19] Late that same day, the first day of the week, when the disciples were together behind locked doors for fear of the Jews, Jesus came and stood among them. 'Peace be with you!' he said; [20] then he showed them his hands and his side. On seeing the Lord the disciples were overjoyed. [21] Jesus said again, 'Peace be with you! As the Father sent me, so I send you.' [22] Then he breathed on them, saying, 'Receive the Holy Spirit! [23] If you forgive anyone's sins, they are forgiven; if you pronounce them unforgiven, unforgiven they remain.'

[24] One of the Twelve, Thomas the Twin, was not with the rest when Jesus came. [25] So the others kept telling him, 'We have seen the Lord.' But he said, 'Unless I see the mark of the nails on his hands, unless I put my finger into the place where the nails were, and my hand into his side, I will never believe it.'

[26] A week later his disciples were once again in the room, and Thomas was with them. Although the doors were locked, Jesus came and stood among them, saying, 'Peace be with you!' [27] Then he said to Thomas, 'Reach your finger here; look at my hands. Reach your hand here and put it into my side. Be unbelieving no longer, but believe.' [28] Thomas said, 'My Lord and my God!' [29] Jesus said to him, 'Because you have seen me you have found faith. Happy are they who find faith without seeing me.'

[30] There were indeed many other signs that Jesus performed in the presence of his disciples, which are not recorded in this book. [31] Those written here have been recorded in order that you may believe that Jesus is the Christ, the Son of God, and that through this faith you may have life by his name.

21 SOME time later, Jesus showed himself to his disciples once again, by the sea of Tiberias. This is how it happened. [2] Simon Peter was with Thomas the Twin, Nathanael from Cana-in-Galilee, the sons of Zebedee, and two other disciples. [3] 'I am going out fishing,' said Simon Peter. 'We will go with you,' said the others. So they set off and got into the boat; but that night they caught nothing.

[4] Morning came, and Jesus was standing on the beach, but the disciples did not know that it was Jesus. [5] He called out to them, 'Friends, have you caught anything?' 'No,' they answered. [6] He said, 'Throw out the net to starboard, and you will make a catch.' They did so, and found they could not haul the net on board, there were so many fish in it. [7] Then the disciple whom Jesus loved said to Peter, 'It is the Lord!' As soon as Simon Peter heard him say, 'It is the Lord,' he fastened his coat about him (for he had stripped) and plunged into the sea. [8] The rest of them came on in the boat, towing the net full of fish. They were only about a hundred yards from land.

[9] When they came ashore, they saw a charcoal fire there with fish laid on it, and some bread. [10] Jesus said, 'Bring some of the fish you have caught.' [11] Simon Peter went on board and hauled the net to land; it was full of big fish, a hundred and fifty-three in all; and yet, many as they were, the net was not torn. [12] Jesus said, 'Come and have breakfast.' None of the disciples dared to ask 'Who are you?' They knew it was the Lord. [13] Jesus came, took the bread and gave it to them, and the fish in the same way. [14] This makes

20: 31 **believe**: *witnesses read different tenses, some implying* continue to believe, *others* come to believe.

the third time that Jesus appeared to his disciples after his resurrection from the dead.

[15] After breakfast Jesus said to Simon Peter, 'Simon son of John, do you love me more than these others?' 'Yes, Lord,' he answered, 'you know that I love you.' 'Then feed my lambs,' he said. [16] A second time he asked, 'Simon son of John, do you love me?' 'Yes, Lord, you know I love you.' 'Then tend my sheep.' [17] A third time he said, 'Simon son of John, do you love me?' Peter was hurt that he asked him a third time, 'Do you love me?' 'Lord,' he said, 'you know everything; you know I love you.' Jesus said, 'Then feed my sheep.

[18] 'In very truth I tell you: when you were young you fastened your belt about you and walked where you chose; but when you are old you will stretch out your arms, and a stranger will bind you fast, and carry you where you have no wish to go.' [19] He said this to indicate the manner of death by which Peter was to glorify God. Then he added, 'Follow me.'

[20] Peter looked round, and saw the disciple whom Jesus loved following—the one who at supper had leaned back close to him to ask the question, 'Lord, who is it that will betray you?' [21] When he saw him, Peter asked, 'Lord, what about him?' [22] Jesus said, 'If it should be my will that he stay until I come, what is it to you? Follow me.'

[23] That saying of Jesus became current among his followers, and was taken to mean that that disciple would not die. But in fact Jesus did not say he would not die; he only said, 'If it should be my will that he stay until I come, what is it to you?'

[24] It is this same disciple who vouches for what has been written here. He it is who wrote it, and we know that his testimony is true.

[25] There is much else that Jesus did. If it were all to be recorded in detail, I suppose the world could not hold the books that would be written.

21:24 **is true:** *some witnesses here insert the passage printed below.*

An incident in the temple*

8 [53] AND they all went home, [1] while Jesus went to the mount of Olives. [2] At daybreak he appeared again in the temple, and all the people gathered round him. He had taken his seat and was engaged in teaching them [3] when the scribes and the Pharisees brought in a woman caught committing adultery. Making her stand in the middle [4] they said to him, 'Teacher, this woman was caught in the very act of adultery. [5] In the law Moses has laid down that such women are to be stoned. What do you say about it?' [6] They put the question as a test, hoping to frame a charge against him.

Jesus bent down and wrote with his finger on the ground. [7] When they continued to press their question he sat up straight and said, 'Let whichever of you is free from sin throw the first stone at her.' [8] Then once again he bent down and wrote on the ground. [9] When they heard what he said, one by one they went away, the eldest first; and Jesus was left alone, with the woman still standing there. [10] Jesus again sat up and said to the woman, 'Where are they? Has no one condemned you?' [11] She answered, 'No one, sir.' 'Neither do I condemn you,' Jesus said. 'Go; do not sin again.'

*This passage, which in most editions of the New Testament is printed in the text of John, 7:53—8:11, has no fixed place in our witnesses. Some of them do not contain it at all. Some place it after Luke 21:38, others after John 7:36, or 7:52, or 21:24.   8:9 **they went away:** *some witnesses add* convicted by their conscience.

ACTS OF THE APOSTLES

1 In the first part of my work, Theophilus, I gave an account of all that Jesus did and taught from the beginning ² until the day when he was taken up to heaven, after giving instructions through the Holy Spirit to the apostles whom he had chosen. ³ To these men he showed himself after his death and gave ample proof that he was alive: he was seen by them over a period of forty days and spoke to them about the kingdom of God. ⁴ While he was in their company he directed them not to leave Jerusalem. 'You must wait', he said, 'for the gift promised by the Father, of which I told you; ⁵ John, as you know, baptized with water, but within the next few days you will be baptized with the Holy Spirit.'

⁶ When they were all together, they asked him, 'Lord, is this the time at which you are to restore sovereignty to Israel?' ⁷ He answered, 'It is not for you to know about dates or times which the Father has set within his own control. ⁸ But you will receive power when the Holy Spirit comes upon you; and you will bear witness for me in Jerusalem, and throughout all Judaea and Samaria, and even in the farthest corners of the earth.'

⁹ After he had said this, he was lifted up before their very eyes, and a cloud took him from their sight. ¹⁰ They were gazing intently into the sky as he went, and all at once there stood beside them two men robed in white, ¹¹ who said, 'Men of Galilee, why stand there looking up into the sky? This Jesus who has been taken from you up to heaven will come in the same way as you have seen him go.'

The church in Jerusalem

¹² They then returned to Jerusalem from the hill called Olivet, which is near the city, no farther than a sabbath day's journey. ¹³ On their arrival they went to the upstairs room where they were lodging: Peter and John and James and Andrew, Philip and Thomas, Bartholomew and Matthew, James son of Alphaeus, Simon the Zealot, and Judas son of James. ¹⁴ All these with one accord were constantly at prayer, together with a group of women, and Mary the mother of Jesus, and his brothers.

¹⁵ It was during this time that Peter stood up before the assembled brotherhood, about one hundred and twenty in all, and said: ¹⁶ 'My friends, the prophecy in scripture, which the Holy Spirit uttered concerning Judas through the mouth of David, was bound to come true; Judas acted as guide to those who arrested Jesus—¹⁷ he was one of our number and had his place in this ministry.' ¹⁸ (After buying a plot of land with the price of his villainy, this man fell headlong and burst open so that all his entrails spilled out; ¹⁹ everyone in Jerusalem came to hear of this, and in their own language they named the plot Akeldama, which means 'Blood Acre'.) ²⁰ 'The words I have in mind', Peter continued, 'are in the book of Psalms: "Let his homestead fall desolate; let there be none to inhabit it." And again, "Let his charge be given to another." ²¹ Therefore one of those who bore us company all the while the Lord Jesus was going about among us, ²² from his baptism by John until the day when he was taken up from us—one of those must now join us as a witness to his resurrection.'

²³ Two names were put forward: Joseph, who was known as Barsabbas and bore the added name of Justus, and Matthias. ²⁴ Then they prayed and said, 'You know the hearts of everyone, Lord; declare which of these two you have chosen ²⁵ to receive this office of ministry and apostleship which Judas abandoned to go where he belonged.' ²⁶ They drew lots, and the lot fell to Matthias; so he was elected to be an apostle with the other eleven.

2 The day of Pentecost had come, and they were all together in one place. ² Suddenly there came from the sky what sounded like a strong, driving wind, a noise which filled the whole house where they were sitting. ³ And there appeared to them flames like tongues of fire distributed among them and coming to rest on each one. ⁴ They were all filled with the Holy

Spirit and began to talk in other tongues, as the Spirit gave them power of utterance.

⁵ Now there were staying in Jerusalem devout Jews drawn from every nation under heaven. ⁶ At this sound a crowd of them gathered, and were bewildered because each one heard his own language spoken; ⁷ they were amazed and in astonishment exclaimed, 'Surely these people who are speaking are all Galileans! ⁸ How is it that each of us can hear them in his own native language? ⁹ Parthians, Medes, Elamites; inhabitants of Mesopotamia, of Judaea and Cappadocia, of Pontus and Asia, ¹⁰ of Phrygia and Pamphylia, of Egypt and the districts of Libya around Cyrene; visitors from Rome, both Jews and proselytes; ¹¹ Cretans and Arabs—all of us hear them telling in our own tongues the great things God has done.' ¹² They were all amazed and perplexed, saying to one another, 'What can this mean?' ¹³ Others said contemptuously, 'They have been drinking!'

¹⁴ But Peter stood up with the eleven, and in a loud voice addressed the crowd: 'Fellow-Jews, and all who live in Jerusalem, listen and take note of what I say. ¹⁵ These people are not drunk, as you suppose; it is only nine in the morning! ¹⁶ No, this is what the prophet Joel spoke of: ¹⁷ "In the last days, says God, I will pour out my Spirit on all mankind; and your sons and daughters shall prophesy; your young men shall see visions, and your old men shall dream dreams. ¹⁸ Yes, on my servants and my handmaids I will pour out my Spirit in those days, and they shall prophesy. ¹⁹ I will show portents in the sky above, and signs on the earth below—blood and fire and a pall of smoke. ²⁰ The sun shall be turned to darkness, and the moon to blood, before that great, resplendent day, the day of the Lord, shall come. ²¹ Everyone who calls on the name of the Lord on that day shall be saved."

²² 'Men of Israel, hear me: I am speaking of Jesus of Nazareth, singled out by God and made known to you through miracles, portents, and signs, which God worked among you through him, as you well know. ²³ By the deliberate will and plan of God he was given into your power,

and you killed him, using heathen men to crucify him. ²⁴ But God raised him to life again, setting him free from the pangs of death, because it could not be that death should keep him in its grip.

²⁵ 'For David says of him:

I foresaw that the Lord would be
    with me for ever,
with him at my right hand I cannot
    be shaken;
²⁶ therefore my heart is glad
and my tongue rejoices;
moreover, my flesh shall dwell in
    hope,
²⁷ for you will not abandon me to
    death,
nor let your faithful servant suffer
    corruption.
²⁸ You have shown me the paths of life;
    your presence will fill me with joy.

²⁹ 'My friends, nobody can deny that the patriarch David died and was buried; we have his tomb here to this very day. ³⁰ It is clear therefore that he spoke as a prophet who knew that God had sworn to him that one of his own direct descendants should sit on his throne; ³¹ and when he said he was not abandoned to death, and his flesh never saw corruption, he spoke with foreknowledge of the resurrection of the Messiah. ³² Now Jesus has been raised by God, and of this we are all witnesses. ³³ Exalted at God's right hand he received from the Father the promised Holy Spirit, and all that you now see and hear flows from him. ³⁴ For it was not David who went up to heaven; his own words are: "The Lord said to my Lord, 'Sit at my right hand ³⁵ until I make your enemies your footstool.'" ³⁶ Let all Israel then accept as certain that God has made this same Jesus, whom you crucified, both Lord and Messiah.'

³⁷ When they heard this they were cut to the heart, and said to Peter and the other apostles, 'Friends, what are we to do?' ³⁸ 'Repent', said Peter, 'and be baptized, every one of you, in the name of Jesus the Messiah; then your sins will be forgiven and you will receive the gift of the Holy Spirit. ³⁹ The promise is to you and to your children and to all who are far away, to everyone whom the Lord our God may call.'

2:33 **at:** *or* by.

⁴⁰ He pressed his case with many other arguments and pleaded with them: 'Save yourselves from this crooked age.' ⁴¹ Those who accepted what he said were baptized, and some three thousand were added to the number of believers that day. ⁴² They met constantly to hear the apostles teach and to share the common life, to break bread, and to pray.

⁴³ A sense of awe was felt by everyone, and many portents and signs were brought about through the apostles. ⁴⁴ All the believers agreed to hold everything in common: ⁴⁵ they began to sell their property and possessions and distribute to everyone according to his need. ⁴⁶ One and all they kept up their daily attendance at the temple, and, breaking bread in their homes, they shared their meals with unaffected joy, ⁴⁷ as they praised God and enjoyed the favour of the whole people. And day by day the Lord added new converts to their number.

3 ONE day at three in the afternoon, the hour of prayer, Peter and John were on their way up to the temple. ² Now a man who had been a cripple from birth used to be carried there and laid every day by the temple gate called Beautiful to beg from people as they went in. ³ When he saw Peter and John on their way into the temple, he asked for alms. ⁴ They both fixed their eyes on him, and Peter said, 'Look at us.' ⁵ Expecting a gift from them, the man was all attention. ⁶ Peter said, 'I have no silver or gold; but what I have I give you: in the name of Jesus Christ of Nazareth, get up and walk.' ⁷ Then, grasping him by the right hand he helped him up; and at once his feet and ankles grew strong; ⁸ he sprang to his feet, and started to walk. He entered the temple with them, leaping and praising God as he went. ⁹ Everyone saw him walking and praising God, ¹⁰ and when they recognized him as the man who used to sit begging at Beautiful Gate they were filled with wonder and amazement at what had happened to him.

¹¹ While he still clung to Peter and John all the people came running in astonishment towards them in Solomon's Portico, as it is called. ¹² Peter saw them coming and met them with these words: 'Men of

Israel, why be surprised at this? Why stare at us as if we had made this man walk by some power or godliness of our own? ¹³⁻¹⁴ The God of Abraham, Isaac, and Jacob, the God of our fathers, has given the highest honour to his servant Jesus, whom you handed over for trial and disowned in Pilate's court—disowned the holy and righteous one when Pilate had decided to release him. You asked for the reprieve of a murderer, ¹⁵ and killed the Prince of life. But God raised him from the dead; of that we are witnesses. ¹⁶ The name of Jesus, by awakening faith, has given strength to this man whom you see and know, and this faith has made him completely well as you can all see.

¹⁷ 'Now, my friends, I know quite well that you acted in ignorance, as did your rulers; ¹⁸ but this is how God fulfilled what he had foretold through all the prophets: that his Messiah would suffer. ¹⁹ Repent, therefore, and turn to God, so that your sins may be wiped out. Then the Lord may grant you a time of recovery ²⁰ and send the Messiah appointed for you, that is, Jesus. ²¹ He must be received into heaven until the time comes for the universal restoration of which God has spoken through his holy prophets from the beginning. ²² Moses said, "The Lord God will raise up for you a prophet like me from among yourselves. Listen to everything he says to you, ²³ for anyone who refuses to listen to that prophet must be cut off from the people." ²⁴ From Samuel onwards, every prophet who spoke predicted this present time.

²⁵ 'You are the heirs of the prophets, and of that covenant which God made with your fathers when he said to Abraham, "And in your offspring all the families on earth shall find blessing." ²⁶ When God raised up his servant, he sent him to you first, to bring you blessing by turning every one of you from your wicked ways.'

4 They were still addressing the people when the chief priests, together with the controller of the temple and the Sadducees, broke in on them, ² annoyed because they were proclaiming the resurrection from the dead by teaching the people about Jesus. ³ They were arrested

3:22 **a prophet like me:** *or* a prophet as he raised up me.   4:1 **the chief priests:** *some witnesses omit* chief.

105

and, as it was already evening, put in prison for the night. ⁴ But many of those who had heard the message became believers, bringing the number of men to about five thousand.

⁵ Next day the Jewish rulers, elders, and scribes met in Jerusalem. ⁶ There were present Annas the high priest, Caiaphas, John, Alexander, and all who were of the high-priestly family. ⁷ They brought the apostles before the court and began to interrogate them. 'By what power', they asked, 'or by what name have such men as you done this?' ⁸ Then Peter, filled with the Holy Spirit, answered, 'Rulers of the people and elders, ⁹ if it is about help given to a sick man that we are being questioned today, and the means by which he was cured, ¹⁰ this is our answer to all of you and to all the people of Israel: it was by the name of Jesus Christ of Nazareth, whom you crucified, and whom God raised from the dead; through him this man stands here before you fit and well. ¹¹ This Jesus is the stone, rejected by you the builders, which has become the corner-stone. ¹² There is no salvation through anyone else; in all the world no other name has been granted to mankind by which we can be saved.'

¹³ Observing that Peter and John were uneducated laymen, they were astonished at their boldness and took note that they had been companions of Jesus; ¹⁴ but with the man who had been cured standing in full view beside them, they had nothing to say in reply. ¹⁵ So they ordered them to leave the court, and then conferred among themselves. ¹⁶ 'What are we to do with these men?' they said. 'It is common knowledge in Jerusalem that a notable miracle has come about through them; and we cannot deny it. ¹⁷ But to stop this from spreading farther among the people, we had better caution them never again to speak to anyone in this name.' ¹⁸ They then called them in and ordered them to refrain from all public speaking and teaching in the name of Jesus.

¹⁹ But Peter and John replied: 'Is it right in the eyes of God for us to obey you rather than him? Judge for yourselves. ²⁰ We cannot possibly give up speaking about what we have seen and heard.'

²¹ With a repeated caution the court discharged them. They could not see how they were to punish them, because the people were all giving glory to God for what had happened. ²² The man upon whom this miracle of healing had been performed was over forty years old.

²³ As soon as they were discharged the apostles went back to their friends and told them everything that the chief priests and elders had said. ²⁴ When they heard it, they raised their voices with one accord and called upon God.

'Sovereign Lord, Maker of heaven and earth and sea and of everything in them, ²⁵ you said by the Holy Spirit, through the mouth of David your servant,

Why did the Gentiles rage
and the peoples hatch their futile
   plots?
²⁶ The kings of the earth took their
   stand
and the rulers made common cause
against the Lord and against his
   Messiah.

²⁷ 'They did indeed make common cause in this very city against your holy servant Jesus whom you anointed as Messiah. Herod and Pontius Pilate conspired with the Gentiles and with the peoples of Israel ²⁸ to do all the things which, under your hand and by your decree, were foreordained. ²⁹ And now, O Lord, mark their threats, and enable those who serve you to speak your word with all boldness. ³⁰ Stretch out your hand to heal and cause signs and portents to be done through the name of your holy servant Jesus.'

³¹ When they had ended their prayer, the building where they were assembled rocked, and all were filled with the Holy Spirit and spoke God's word with boldness.

³² THE whole company of believers was united in heart and soul. Not one of them claimed any of his possessions as his own; everything was held in common. ³³ With great power the apostles bore witness to the resurrection of the Lord Jesus, and all were held in high esteem. ³⁴ There was never a needy person among them, because those who had property in land or houses would sell it, bring the proceeds of

4:6 **John:** *some witnesses read* Jonathan.   4:33 **all ... esteem:** *or* grace was strongly at work in them all.

the sale, [35] and lay them at the feet of the apostles, to be distributed to any who were in need. [36] For instance Joseph, surnamed by the apostles Barnabas (which means 'Son of Encouragement'), a Levite and by birth a Cypriot, [37] sold an estate which he owned; he brought the money and laid it at the apostles' feet.

5 But a man called Ananias sold a property, [2] and with the connivance of his wife Sapphira kept back some of the proceeds, and brought part only to lay at the apostles' feet. [3] Peter said, 'Ananias, how was it that Satan so possessed your mind that you lied to the Holy Spirit by keeping back part of the price of the land? [4] While it remained unsold, did it not remain yours? Even after it was turned into money, was it not still at your own disposal? What made you think of doing this? You have lied not to men but to God.' [5] When Ananias heard these words he dropped dead; and all who heard were awestruck. [6] The younger men rose and covered his body, then carried him out and buried him.

[7] About three hours passed, and his wife came in, unaware of what had happened. [8] Peter asked her, 'Tell me, were you paid such and such a price for the land?' 'Yes,' she replied, 'that was the price.' [9] Peter said, 'Why did the two of you conspire to put the Spirit of the Lord to the test? Those who buried your husband are there at the door, and they will carry you away.' [10] At once she dropped dead at his feet. When the young men came in, they found her dead; and they carried her out and buried her beside her husband.

[11] Great awe fell on the whole church and on all who heard of this. [12] Many signs and wonders were done among the people by the apostles. All the believers used to meet by common consent in Solomon's Portico; [13] no one from outside their number ventured to join them, yet people in general spoke highly of them. [14] An ever-increasing number of men and women who believed in the Lord were added to their ranks. [15] As a result the sick were carried out into the streets and laid there on beds and stretchers, so that at least Peter's shadow might fall on one or another as he passed by; [16] and the people from the towns round Jerusalem flocked in, bringing those who were ill or harassed by unclean spirits, and all were cured.

[17] Then the high priest and his colleagues, the Sadducean party, were goaded by jealousy [18] to arrest the apostles and put them in official custody. [19] But during the night, an angel of the Lord opened the prison doors, led them out, and said, [20] 'Go, stand in the temple and tell the people all about this new life.' [21] Accordingly they entered the temple at daybreak and went on with their teaching.

When the high priest arrived with his colleagues they summoned the Sanhedrin, the full Council of the Israelite nation, and sent to the jail for the prisoners. [22] The officers who went to the prison failed to find them there, so they returned and reported, [23] 'We found the jail securely locked at every point, with the warders at their posts by the doors, but on opening them we found no one inside.' [24] When they heard this, the controller of the temple and the chief priests were at a loss to know what could have become of them, [25] until someone came and reported: 'The men you put in prison are standing in the temple teaching the people.' [26] Then the controller went off with the officers and fetched them, but without use of force, for fear of being stoned by the people.

[27] When they had been brought in and made to stand before the Council, the high priest began his examination. [28] 'We gave you explicit orders', he said, 'to stop teaching in that name; and what has happened? You have filled Jerusalem with your teaching, and you are trying to hold us responsible for that man's death.' [29] Peter replied for the apostles: 'We must obey God rather than men. [30] The God of our fathers raised up Jesus; after you had put him to death by hanging him on a gibbet, [31] God exalted him at his right hand as leader and saviour, to grant Israel repentance and forgiveness of sins. [32] And we are witnesses to all this, as is the Holy Spirit who is given by God to those obedient to him.'

[33] This touched them on the raw, and they wanted to put them to death. [34] But a member of the Council rose to his feet, a Pharisee called Gamaliel, a teacher of the

5:31 **at his right hand:** *or* with his right hand.

law held in high regard by all the people. He had the men put outside for a while, [35] and then said, 'Men of Israel, be very careful in deciding what to do with these men. [36] Some time ago Theudas came forward, making claims for himself, and a number of our people, about four hundred, joined him. But he was killed and his whole movement was destroyed and came to nothing. [37] After him came Judas the Galilean at the time of the census; he induced some people to revolt under his leadership, but he too perished and his whole movement was broken up. [38] Now, my advice to you is this: keep clear of these men; let them alone. For if what is being planned and done is human in origin, it will collapse; [39] but if it is from God, you will never be able to stamp it out, and you risk finding yourselves at war with God.'

[40] Convinced by this, they sent for the apostles and had them flogged; then they ordered them to give up speaking in the name of Jesus, and discharged them. [41] The apostles went out from the Council rejoicing that they had been found worthy to suffer humiliation for the sake of the name. [42] And every day they went steadily on with their teaching in the temple and in private houses, telling the good news of Jesus the Messiah.

The church moves outwards

6 DURING this period, when disciples were growing in number, a grievance arose on the part of those who spoke Greek, against those who spoke the language of the Jews; they complained that their widows were being overlooked in the daily distribution. [2] The Twelve called the whole company of disciples together and said, 'It would not be fitting for us to neglect the word of God in order to assist in the distribution. [3] Therefore, friends, pick seven men of good repute from your number, men full of the Spirit and of wisdom, and we will appoint them for this duty; [4] then we can devote ourselves to prayer and to the ministry of the word.' [5] This proposal proved acceptable to the whole company. They elected Stephen, a man full of faith and of the Holy Spirit, along with Philip, Prochorus, Nicanor, Timon, Parmenas, and Nicolas

of Antioch, who had been a convert to Judaism, [6] and presented them to the apostles, who prayed and laid their hands on them.

[7] The word of God spread more and more widely; the number of disciples in Jerusalem was increasing rapidly, and very many of the priests adhered to the faith.

[8] Stephen, full of grace and power, began to do great wonders and signs among the people. [9] Some members of the synagogue called the Synagogue of Freedmen, comprising Cyrenians and Alexandrians and people from Cilicia and Asia, came forward and argued with Stephen, [10] but could not hold their own against the inspired wisdom with which he spoke. [11] They then put up men to allege that they had heard him make blasphemous statements against Moses and against God. [12] They stirred up the people and the elders and scribes, set upon him and seized him, and brought him before the Council. [13] They produced false witnesses who said, 'This fellow is for ever saying things against this holy place and against the law. [14] For we have heard him say this Jesus of Nazareth will destroy this place and alter the customs handed down to us by Moses.' [15] All who were sitting in the Council fixed their eyes on him, and his face seemed to them like the face of an angel.

7 Then the high priest asked him, 'Is this true?' [2] He replied, 'My brothers, fathers of this nation, listen to me. The God of glory appeared to Abraham our ancestor while he was in Mesopotamia, before he had settled in Harran, [3] and said: "Leave your country and your kinsfolk, and come away to a land that I will show you." [4] Thereupon he left the land of the Chaldaeans and settled in Harran. From there, after his father's death, God led him to migrate to this land where you now live. [5] He gave him no foothold in it, nothing to call his own, but promised to give it as a possession for ever to him and to his descendants after him, though he was then childless. [6] This is what God said: "Abraham's descendants shall live as aliens in a foreign land, held in slavery and oppression for four hundred years. [7] And I will pass judgement", he said, "on

6:1 **those who spoke Greek:** *lit.* the Hellenists.   **those who spoke the language of the Jews:** *lit.* the Hebrews.

the nation whose slaves they are; and after that they shall escape and worship me in this place." ⁸ God gave Abraham the covenant of circumcision, and so, when his son Isaac was born, he circumcised him on the eighth day; and Isaac was the father of Jacob, and Jacob of the twelve patriarchs.

⁹ 'The patriarchs out of jealousy sold Joseph into slavery in Egypt, but God was with him ¹⁰ and rescued him from all his troubles. He gave him wisdom which so commended him to Pharaoh king of Egypt that he appointed him governor of Egypt and of the whole royal household.

¹¹ 'When famine struck all Egypt and Canaan, causing great distress, and our ancestors could find nothing to eat, ¹² Jacob heard that there was food in Egypt and sent our fathers there. This was their first visit. ¹³ On the second visit Joseph made himself known to his brothers, and his ancestry was disclosed to Pharaoh. ¹⁴ Joseph sent for his father Jacob and the whole family, seventy-five persons in all; ¹⁵ and Jacob went down into Egypt. There he and our fathers ended their days. ¹⁶ Their remains were later removed to Shechem and buried in the tomb for which Abraham paid a sum of money to the sons of Hamor at Shechem.

¹⁷ 'Now as the time approached for God to fulfil the promise he had made to Abraham, our people in Egypt grew and increased in numbers. ¹⁸ At length another king, who knew nothing of Joseph, ascended the throne of Egypt. ¹⁹ He employed cunning to harm our race, and forced our ancestors to expose their children so that they should not survive. ²⁰ It was at this time that Moses was born. He was a fine child, and pleasing to God. For three months he was nursed in his father's house; ²¹ then when he was exposed, Pharaoh's daughter adopted him and brought him up as her own son. ²² So Moses was trained in all the wisdom of the Egyptians, a powerful speaker and a man of action.

²³ 'He was approaching the age of forty, when it occurred to him to visit his fellow-countrymen the Israelites. ²⁴ Seeing one of them being ill-treated, he went to his aid, and avenged the victim by striking down the Egyptian. ²⁵ He thought his countrymen would understand that God was offering them deliverance through him, but they did not understand. ²⁶ The next day he came upon two of them fighting, and tried to persuade them to make up their quarrel. "Men, you are brothers!" he said. "Why are you ill-treating one another?" ²⁷ But the man who was at fault pushed him away. "Who made you ruler and judge over us?" he said. ²⁸ "Are you going to kill me as you killed the Egyptian yesterday?" ²⁹ At this Moses fled the country and settled in Midianite territory. There two sons were born to him.

³⁰ 'After forty years had passed, an angel appeared to him in the flame of a burning bush in the desert near Mount Sinai. ³¹ Moses was amazed at the sight, and as he approached to look more closely, the voice of the Lord came to him: ³² "I am the God of your fathers, the God of Abraham, Isaac, and Jacob." Moses was terrified and did not dare to look. ³³ Then the Lord said to him, "Take off your sandals; the place where you are standing is holy ground. ³⁴ I have indeed seen how my people are oppressed in Egypt and have heard their groans; and I have come down to rescue them. Come now, I will send you to Egypt."

³⁵ 'This Moses, whom they had rejected with the words, "Who made you ruler and judge?"—this very man was commissioned as ruler and liberator by God himself, speaking through the angel who appeared to him in the bush. ³⁶ It was Moses who led them out, doing signs and wonders in Egypt, at the Red Sea, and for forty years in the desert. ³⁷ It was he who said to the Israelites, "God will raise up for you from among yourselves a prophet like me." ³⁸ It was he again who, in the assembly in the desert, kept company with the angel, who spoke to him on Mount Sinai, and with our forefathers, and received the living utterances of God to pass on to us.

³⁹ 'Our forefathers would not accept his leadership but thrust him aside. They wished themselves back in Egypt, ⁴⁰ and said to Aaron, "Make us gods to go before us. As for this fellow Moses, who brought us out of Egypt, we do not know what has become of him." ⁴¹ That was when they

7:37 **like me:** *or* as he raised up me.

made the bull-calf and offered sacrifice to the idol, and held festivities in honour of what their hands had made. ⁴²So God turned away from them and gave them over to the worship of the host of heaven, as it stands written in the book of the prophets: "Did you bring me victims and offerings those forty years in the desert, you people of Israel? ⁴³No, you carried aloft the shrine of Moloch and the star of the god Rephan, the images which you had made for your adoration. I will banish you beyond Babylon."

⁴⁴'Our forefathers had the Tent of the Testimony in the desert, as God commanded when he told Moses to make it after the pattern which he had seen. ⁴⁵In the next generation, our fathers under Joshua brought it with them when they dispossessed the nations whom God drove out before them, and so it was until the time of David. ⁴⁶David found favour with God and begged leave to provide a dwelling-place for the God of Jacob; ⁴⁷but it was Solomon who built him a house. ⁴⁸However, the Most High does not live in houses made by men; as the prophet says: ⁴⁹"Heaven is my throne and earth my footstool. What kind of house will you build for me, says the Lord; where shall my resting-place be? ⁵⁰Are not all these things of my own making?"

⁵¹'How stubborn you are, heathen still at heart and deaf to the truth! You always resist the Holy Spirit. You are just like your fathers! ⁵²Was there ever a prophet your fathers did not persecute? They killed those who foretold the coming of the righteous one, and now you have betrayed him and murdered him. ⁵³You received the law given by God's angels and yet you have not kept it.'

⁵⁴This touched them on the raw, and they ground their teeth with fury. ⁵⁵But Stephen, filled with the Holy Spirit, and gazing intently up to heaven, saw the glory of God, and Jesus standing at God's right hand. ⁵⁶'Look!' he said. 'I see the heavens opened and the Son of Man standing at the right hand of God.' ⁵⁷At this they gave a great shout, and stopped their ears; they made a concerted rush at him, ⁵⁸threw him out of the city, and set about stoning him. The witnesses laid their coats at the feet of a young man named Saul. ⁵⁹As they stoned him Stephen called out, 'Lord Jesus, receive my spirit.' ⁶⁰He fell on his knees and cried aloud, 'Lord, do not hold this sin against them,' and with that he died. ¹Saul was among those who approved of his execution.

The church in Judaea and Samaria

THAT day was the beginning of a time of violent persecution for the church in Jerusalem; and all except the apostles were scattered over the country districts of Judaea and Samaria. ²Stephen was given burial by devout men, who made a great lamentation for him. ³Saul, meanwhile, was harrying the church; he entered house after house, seizing men and women and sending them to prison.

⁴As for those who had been scattered, they went through the country preaching the word. ⁵Philip came down to a city in Samaria and began proclaiming the Messiah there. ⁶As the crowds heard Philip and saw the signs he performed, everyone paid close attention to what he had to say. ⁷In many cases of possession the unclean spirits came out with a loud cry, and many paralysed and crippled folk were cured; ⁸and there was great rejoicing in that city.

⁹A man named Simon had been in the city for some time and had captivated the Samaritans with his magical arts, making large claims for himself. ¹⁰Everybody, high and low, listened intently to him. 'This man', they said, 'is that power of God which is called "The Great Power".' ¹¹They listened because they had for so long been captivated by his magic. ¹²But when they came to believe Philip, with his good news about the kingdom of God and the name of Jesus Christ, men and women alike were baptized. ¹³Even Simon himself believed, and after his baptism was constantly in Philip's company. He was captivated when he saw the powerful signs and miracles that were taking place.

¹⁴When the apostles in Jerusalem heard that Samaria had accepted the word of God, they sent off Peter and John, ¹⁵who went down there and prayed for the converts, asking that they might receive the Holy Spirit. ¹⁶Until then the Spirit had not come upon any of them;

7:46 **for ... Jacob**: *some witnesses read* for the house of Jacob.

they had been baptized into the name of the Lord Jesus, that and nothing more. [17] So Peter and John laid their hands on them, and they received the Holy Spirit. [18] When Simon observed that the Spirit was bestowed through the laying on of the apostles' hands, he offered them money [19] and said, 'Give me too the same power, so that anyone I lay my hands on will receive the Holy Spirit.' [20] Peter replied, 'You thought God's gift was for sale? Your money can go with you to damnation! [21] You have neither part nor share in this, for you are corrupt in the eyes of God. [22] Repent of this wickedness of yours and pray the Lord to forgive you for harbouring such a thought. [23] I see that bitter gall and the chains of sin will be your fate.' [24] Simon said to them, 'Pray to the Lord for me, and ask that none of the things you have spoken of may befall me.'

[25] After giving their testimony and speaking the word of the Lord, they took the road back to Jerusalem, bringing the good news to many Samaritan villages on the way.

[26] Then the angel of the Lord said to Philip, 'Start out and go south to the road that leads down from Jerusalem to Gaza.' (This is the desert road.) [27] He set out and was on his way when he caught sight of an Ethiopian. This man was a eunuch, a high official of the Kandake, or queen, of Ethiopia, in charge of all her treasure; he had been to Jerusalem on a pilgrimage [28] and was now returning home, sitting in his carriage and reading aloud from the prophet Isaiah. [29] The Spirit said to Philip, 'Go and meet the carriage.' [30] When Philip ran up he heard him reading from the prophet Isaiah and asked, 'Do you understand what you are reading?' [31] He said, 'How can I without someone to guide me?' and invited Philip to get in and sit beside him. [32] The passage he was reading was this: 'He was led like a sheep to the slaughter; like a lamb that is dumb before the shearer, he does not open his mouth. [33] He has been humiliated and has no redress. Who will be able to speak of his posterity? For he is cut off from the world of the living.' [34] 'Please tell me', said the eunuch to

Philip, 'who it is that the prophet is speaking about here: himself or someone else?' [35] Then Philip began and, starting from this passage, he told him the good news of Jesus. [36] As they were going along the road, they came to some water. 'Look,' said the eunuch, 'here is water: what is to prevent my being baptized?' [38] and he ordered the carriage to stop. Then they both went down into the water, Philip and the eunuch, and he baptized him. [39] When they came up from the water the Spirit snatched Philip away; the eunuch did not see him again, but went on his way rejoicing. [40] Philip appeared at Azotus, and toured the country, preaching in all the towns till he reached Caesarea.

9 SAUL, still breathing murderous threats against the Lord's disciples, went to the high priest [2] and applied for letters to the synagogues at Damascus authorizing him to arrest any followers of the new way whom he found, men or women, and bring them to Jerusalem. [3] While he was still on the road and nearing Damascus, suddenly a light from the sky flashed all around him. [4] He fell to the ground and heard a voice saying, 'Saul, Saul, why are you persecuting me?' [5] 'Tell me, Lord,' he said, 'who you are.' The voice answered, 'I am Jesus, whom you are persecuting. [6] But now get up and go into the city, and you will be told what you have to do.' [7] Meanwhile the men who were travelling with him stood speechless; they heard the voice but could see no one. [8] Saul got up from the ground, but when he opened his eyes he could not see; they led him by the hand and brought him into Damascus. [9] He was blind for three days, and took no food or drink.

[10] There was in Damascus a disciple named Ananias. He had a vision in which he heard the Lord say: 'Ananias!' 'Here I am, Lord,' he answered. [11] The Lord said to him, 'Go to Straight Street, to the house of Judas, and ask for a man from Tarsus named Saul. You will find him at prayer; [12] he has had a vision of a man named Ananias coming in and laying hands on him to restore his sight.' [13] Ananias

---

8:36 **baptized**: *some witnesses add* [37] Philip said, 'If you wholeheartedly believe, it is permitted.' He replied, 'I believe that Jesus Christ is the Son of God.'

answered, 'Lord, I have often heard about this man and all the harm he has done your people in Jerusalem. ¹⁴ Now he is here with authority from the chief priests to arrest all who invoke your name.' ¹⁵ But the Lord replied, 'You must go, for this man is my chosen instrument to bring my name before the nations and their kings, and before the people of Israel. ¹⁶ I myself will show him all that he must go through for my name's sake.'

¹⁷ So Ananias went and, on entering the house, laid his hands on him and said, 'Saul, my brother, the Lord Jesus, who appeared to you on your way here, has sent me to you so that you may recover your sight and be filled with the Holy Spirit.' ¹⁸ Immediately it was as if scales had fallen from his eyes, and he regained his sight. He got up and was baptized, ¹⁹ and when he had eaten his strength returned.

He stayed some time with the disciples in Damascus. ²⁰ Without delay he proclaimed Jesus publicly in the synagogues, declaring him to be the Son of God. ²¹ All who heard were astounded. 'Is not this the man', they said, 'who was in Jerusalem hunting down those who invoke this name? Did he not come here for the sole purpose of arresting them and taking them before the chief priests?' ²² But Saul went from strength to strength, and confounded the Jews of Damascus with his cogent proofs that Jesus was the Messiah. ²³ When some time had passed, the Jews hatched a plot against his life; ²⁴ but their plans became known to Saul. They kept watch on the city gates day and night so that they might murder him; ²⁵ but one night some disciples took him and, lowering him in a basket, let him down over the wall.

²⁶ On reaching Jerusalem he tried to join the disciples, but they were all afraid of him, because they did not believe that he really was a disciple. ²⁷ Barnabas, however, took him and introduced him to the apostles; he described to them how on his journey Saul had seen the Lord and heard his voice, and how at Damascus he had spoken out boldly in the name of Jesus. ²⁸ Saul now stayed with them, moving about freely in Jerusalem. ²⁹ He spoke out boldly and openly in the name

of the Lord, talking and debating with the Greek-speaking Jews. But they planned to murder him, ³⁰ and when the brethren discovered this they escorted him down to Caesarea and sent him away to Tarsus.

³¹ MEANWHILE the church, throughout Judaea, Galilee, and Samaria, was left in peace to build up its strength, and to live in the fear of the Lord. Encouraged by the Holy Spirit, it grew in numbers.

³² In the course of a tour Peter was making throughout the region he went down to visit God's people at Lydda. ³³ There he found a man named Aeneas who had been bedridden with paralysis for eight years. ³⁴ Peter said to him, 'Aeneas, Jesus Christ cures you; get up and make your bed!' and immediately he stood up. ³⁵ All who lived in Lydda and Sharon saw him; and they turned to the Lord.

³⁶ In Joppa there was a disciple named Tabitha (in Greek, Dorcas, meaning 'Gazelle'), who filled her days with acts of kindness and charity. ³⁷ At that time she fell ill and died; and they washed her body and laid it in a room upstairs. ³⁸ As Lydda was near Joppa, the disciples, who had heard that Peter was there, sent two men to him with the urgent request, 'Please come over to us without delay.' ³⁹ At once Peter went off with them. When he arrived he was taken up to the room, and all the widows came and stood round him in tears, showing him the shirts and coats that Dorcas used to make while she was with them. ⁴⁰ Peter sent them all outside, and knelt down and prayed; then, turning towards the body, he said, 'Tabitha, get up.' She opened her eyes, saw Peter, and sat up. ⁴¹ He gave her his hand and helped her to her feet. Then he called together the members of the church and the widows and showed her to them alive. ⁴² News of it spread all over Joppa, and many came to believe in the Lord. ⁴³ Peter stayed on in Joppa for some time at the house of a tanner named Simon.

10 At Caesarea there was a man named Cornelius, a centurion in the Italian Cohort, as it was called. ² He was a devout man, and he and his whole family joined in the worship of God; he gave generously to help the Jewish

9:29 **Greek-speaking Jews:** *lit.* Hellenists.

people, and was regular in his prayers to God. [3] One day about three in the afternoon he had a vision in which he clearly saw an angel of God come into his room and say, 'Cornelius!' [4] Cornelius stared at him in terror. 'What is it, my lord?' he asked. The angel said, 'Your prayers and acts of charity have gone up to heaven to speak for you before God. [5] Now send to Joppa for a man named Simon, also called Peter: [6] he is lodging with another Simon, a tanner, whose house is by the sea.' [7] When the angel who spoke to him had gone, he summoned two of his servants and a military orderly who was a religious man, [8] told them the whole story, and ordered them to Joppa.

[9] Next day about noon, while they were still on their way and approaching the city, Peter went up on the roof to pray. [10] He grew hungry and wanted something to eat, but while they were getting it ready, he fell into a trance. [11] He saw heaven opened, and something coming down that looked like a great sheet of sailcloth; it was slung by the four corners and was being lowered to the earth, [12] and in it he saw creatures of every kind, four-footed beasts, reptiles, and birds. [13] There came a voice which said to him, 'Get up, Peter, kill and eat.' [14] But Peter answered, 'No, Lord! I have never eaten anything profane or unclean.' [15] The voice came again, a second time: 'It is not for you to call profane what God counts clean.' [16] This happened three times, and then the thing was taken up into heaven.

[17] While Peter was still puzzling over the meaning of the vision he had seen, the messengers from Cornelius had been asking the way to Simon's house, and now arrived at the entrance. [18] They called out and asked if Simon Peter was lodging there. [19] Peter was thinking over the vision, when the Spirit said to him, 'Some men are here looking for you; [20] get up and go downstairs. You may go with them without any misgiving, for it was I who sent them.' [21] Peter came down to the men and said, 'You are looking for me? Here I am. What brings you here?' [22] 'We are from the centurion Cornelius,' they replied, 'a good and religious man, acknowledged as such by the whole Jewish nation. He was directed by a holy angel to send for you to his house and hear what you have to say.' [23] So Peter

asked them in and gave them a night's lodging.

Next day he set out with them, accompanied by some members of the congregation at Joppa, [24] and on the following day arrived at Caesarea. Cornelius was expecting them and had called together his relatives and close friends. [25] When Peter arrived, Cornelius came to meet him, and bowed to the ground in deep reverence. [26] But Peter raised him to his feet and said, 'Stand up; I am only a man like you.' [27] Still talking with him he went in and found a large gathering. [28] He said to them, 'I need not tell you that a Jew is forbidden by his religion to visit or associate with anyone of another race. Yet God has shown me clearly that I must not call anyone profane or unclean; [29] that is why I came here without demur when you sent for me. May I ask what was your reason for doing so?'

[30] Cornelius said, 'Three days ago, just about this time, I was in the house here saying the afternoon prayers, when suddenly a man in shining robes stood before me. [31] He said: "Cornelius, your prayer has been heard and your acts of charity have spoken for you before God. [32] Send to Simon Peter at Joppa, and ask him to come; he is lodging in the house of Simon the tanner, by the sea." [33] I sent to you there and then, and you have been good enough to come. So now we are all met here before God, to listen to everything that the Lord has instructed you to say.'

[34] Peter began: 'I now understand how true it is that God has no favourites, [35] but that in every nation those who are god-fearing and do what is right are acceptable to him. [36] He sent his word to the Israelites and gave the good news of peace through Jesus Christ, who is Lord of all. [37] I need not tell you what has happened lately all over the land of the Jews, starting from Galilee after the baptism proclaimed by John. [38] You know how God anointed Jesus of Nazareth with the Holy Spirit and with power. Because God was with him he went about doing good and healing all who were oppressed by the devil. [39] And we can bear witness to all that he did in the Jewish countryside and in Jerusalem. They put him to death, hanging him on a gibbet; [40] but God raised him to life on the third day, and allowed him to be clearly seen, [41] not by

the whole people, but by witnesses whom God had chosen in advance—by us, who ate and drank with him after he rose from the dead. ⁴²He commanded us to proclaim him to the people, and affirm that he is the one designated by God as judge of the living and the dead. ⁴³It is to him that all the prophets testify, declaring that everyone who trusts in him receives forgiveness of sins through his name.'

⁴⁴Peter was still speaking when the Holy Spirit came upon all who were listening to the message. ⁴⁵The believers who had come with Peter, men of Jewish birth, were amazed that the gift of the Holy Spirit should have been poured out even on Gentiles, ⁴⁶for they could hear them speaking in tongues of ecstasy and acclaiming the greatness of God. Then Peter spoke: ⁴⁷'Is anyone prepared to withhold the water of baptism from these persons, who have received the Holy Spirit just as we did?' ⁴⁸Then he ordered them to be baptized in the name of Jesus Christ. After that they asked him to stay on with them for a time.

11 News came to the apostles and the members of the church in Judaea that Gentiles too had accepted the word of God; ²and when Peter came up to Jerusalem those who were of Jewish birth took issue with him. ³'You have been visiting men who are uncircumcised,' they said, 'and sitting at table with them!' ⁴Peter began by laying before them the facts as they had happened.

⁵'I was at prayer in the city of Joppa,' he said, 'and while in a trance I had a vision: I saw something coming down that looked like a great sheet of sailcloth, slung by the four corners and lowered from heaven till it reached me. ⁶I looked intently to make out what was in it and I saw four-footed beasts, wild animals, reptiles, and birds. ⁷Then I heard a voice saying to me, "Get up, Peter, kill and eat." ⁸But I said, "No, Lord! Nothing profane or unclean has ever entered my mouth." ⁹A voice from heaven came a second time: "It is not for you to call profane what God counts clean." ¹⁰This happened three times, and then they were all drawn up again into heaven. ¹¹At that very moment three men who had been

sent to me from Caesarea arrived at the house where I was staying; ¹²and the Spirit told me to go with them. My six companions here came with me and we went into the man's house. ¹³He told us how he had seen an angel standing in his house who said, "Send to Joppa for Simon Peter. ¹⁴He will speak words that will bring salvation to you and all your household." ¹⁵Hardly had I begun speaking, when the Holy Spirit came upon them, just as upon us at the beginning, ¹⁶and I recalled what the Lord had said: "John baptized with water, but you will be baptized with the Holy Spirit." ¹⁷God gave them no less a gift than he gave us when we came to believe in the Lord Jesus Christ. How could I stand in God's way?'

¹⁸When they heard this their doubts were silenced, and they gave praise to God. 'This means', they said, 'that God has granted life-giving repentance to the Gentiles also.'

¹⁹MEANWHILE those who had been scattered after the persecution that arose over Stephen made their way to Phoenicia, Cyprus, and Antioch, bringing the message to Jews only and to no others. ²⁰But there were some natives of Cyprus and Cyrene among them, and these, when they arrived at Antioch, began to speak to Gentiles as well, telling them the good news of the Lord Jesus. ²¹The power of the Lord was with them, and a great many became believers and turned to the Lord.

²²The news reached the ears of the church in Jerusalem; and they sent Barnabas to Antioch. ²³When he arrived and saw the divine grace at work, he rejoiced and encouraged them all to hold fast to the Lord with resolute hearts, ²⁴for he was a good man, full of the Holy Spirit and of faith. And large numbers were won over to the Lord.

²⁵He then went off to Tarsus to look for Saul; ²⁶and when he had found him, he brought him to Antioch. For a whole year the two of them lived in fellowship with the church there, and gave instruction to large numbers. It was in Antioch that the disciples first got the name of Christians.

²⁷During this period some prophets came down from Jerusalem to Antioch,

---

11:11 **I was:** *some witnesses read* we were.   11:12 **with them:** *some witnesses add* making no distinctions; *others add* without any misgiving, *as in 10:20.*

[28] and one of them, Agabus by name, was inspired to stand up and predict a severe and world-wide famine, which in fact occurred in the reign of Claudius. [29] So the disciples agreed to make a contribution, each according to his means, for the relief of their fellow-Christians in Judaea. [30] This they did, and sent it off to the elders, entrusting it to Barnabas and Saul.

12 It was about this time that King Herod launched an attack on certain members of the church. [2] He beheaded James, the brother of John, [3] and, when he saw that the Jews approved, proceeded to arrest Peter also. This happened during the festival of Unleavened Bread. [4] Having secured him, he put him in prison under a military guard, four squads of four men each, meaning to produce him in public after Passover. [5] So, while Peter was held in prison, the church kept praying fervently to God for him.

[6] On the very night before Herod had planned to produce him, Peter was asleep between two soldiers, secured by two chains, while outside the doors sentries kept guard over the prison. [7] All at once an angel of the Lord stood there, and the cell was ablaze with light. He tapped Peter on the shoulder to wake him. 'Quick! Get up!' he said, and the chains fell away from Peter's wrists. [8] The angel said, 'Do up your belt and put on your sandals.' He did so. 'Now wrap your cloak round you and follow me.' [9] Peter followed him out, with no idea that the angel's intervention was real: he thought it was just a vision. [10] They passed the first guard-post, then the second, and reached the iron gate leading out into the city. This opened for them of its own accord; they came out and had walked the length of one street when suddenly the angel left him. [11] Then Peter came to himself. 'Now I know it is true,' he said: 'the Lord has sent his angel and rescued me from Herod's clutches and from all that the Jewish people were expecting.' [12] Once he had realized this, he made for the house of Mary, the mother of John Mark, where a large company was at prayer. [13] He knocked at the outer door and a maidservant called Rhoda came to answer it. [14] She recognized Peter's voice and was so overjoyed that instead of opening the door she ran in and announced that Peter was standing outside. [15] 'You are crazy,' they told her; but she insisted that it was so. Then they said, 'It must be his angel.'

[16] Peter went on knocking, and when they opened the door and saw him, they were astounded. [17] He motioned to them with his hand to keep quiet, and described to them how the Lord had brought him out of prison. 'Tell James and the members of the church,' he said. Then he left the house and went off elsewhere.

[18] When morning came, there was consternation among the soldiers: what could have become of Peter? [19] Herod made careful search, but failed to find him, so he interrogated the guards and ordered their execution.

Afterwards Herod left Judaea to reside for a while at Caesarea. [20] He had for some time been very angry with the people of Tyre and Sidon, who now by common agreement presented themselves at his court. There they won over Blastus the royal chamberlain, and sued for peace, because their country drew its supplies from the king's territory. [21] On an appointed day Herod, attired in his royal robes and seated on the rostrum, addressed the populace; [22] they responded, 'It is a god speaking, not a man!' [23] Instantly an angel of the Lord struck him down, because he had usurped the honour due to God; he was eaten up with worms and so died.

[24] Meanwhile the word of God continued to grow and spread; [25] and Barnabas and Saul, their task fulfilled, returned from Jerusalem, taking John Mark with them.

Paul's work among the Gentiles

13 THERE were in the church at Antioch certain prophets and teachers: Barnabas, Simeon called Niger, Lucius of Cyrene, Manaen, a close friend of Prince Herod, and Saul. [2] While they were offering worship to the Lord and fasting, the Holy Spirit said, 'Set Barnabas and Saul apart for me, to do the work to which I have called them.' [3] Then, after further fasting and prayer, they laid their hands on them and sent them on their way.

12:25 **from Jerusalem**: *some witnesses read* to Jerusalem.

4 These two, sent out on their mission by the Holy Spirit, came down to Seleucia, and from there sailed to Cyprus. 5 Arriving at Salamis, they declared the word of God in the Jewish synagogues; they had John with them as their assistant. 6 They went through the whole island as far as Paphos, and there they came upon a sorcerer, a Jew who posed as a prophet, Barjesus by name. 7 He was in the retinue of the governor, Sergius Paulus, a learned man, who had sent for Barnabas and Saul and wanted to hear the word of God. 8 This Elymas the sorcerer (so his name may be translated) opposed them, trying to turn the governor away from the faith. 9 But Saul, also known as Paul, filled with the Holy Spirit, fixed his eyes on him 10 and said, 'You are a swindler, an out-and-out fraud! You son of the devil and enemy of all goodness, will you never stop perverting the straight ways of the Lord? 11 Look now, the hand of the Lord strikes: you shall be blind, and for a time you shall not see the light of the sun.' At once mist and darkness came over his eyes, and he groped about for someone to lead him by the hand. 12 When the governor saw what had happened he became a believer, deeply impressed by what he learnt about the Lord.

13 Sailing from Paphos, Paul and his companions went to Perga in Pamphylia; John, however, left them and returned to Jerusalem. 14 From Perga they continued their journey as far as Pisidian Antioch. On the sabbath they went to synagogue and took their seats; 15 and after the readings from the law and the prophets, the officials of the synagogue sent this message to them: 'Friends, if you have anything to say to the people by way of exhortation, let us hear it.' 16 Paul stood up, raised his hand for silence, and began.

'Listen, men of Israel and you others who worship God! 17 The God of this people, Israel, chose our forefathers. When they were still living as aliens in Egypt, he made them into a great people and, with arm outstretched, brought them out of that country. 18 For some forty years he bore with their conduct in the desert. 19 Then in the Canaanite country, after overthrowing seven nations, whose lands he gave them to be their heritage 20 for some four hundred and fifty years, he appointed judges for them until the time of the prophet Samuel.

21 'It was then that they asked for a king, and God gave them Saul son of Kish, a man of the tribe of Benjamin. He reigned for forty years 22 before God removed him and appointed David as their king, with this commendation: "I have found David the son of Jesse to be a man after my own heart; he will carry out all my purposes." 23 This is the man from whose descendants God, as he promised, has brought Israel a saviour, Jesus. 24 John had made ready for his coming by proclaiming a baptism in token of repentance to the whole people of Israel; 25 and, nearing the end of his earthly course, John said, "I am not the one you think I am. No, after me comes one whose sandals I am not worthy to unfasten."

26 'My brothers, who come of Abraham's stock, and others among you who worship God, we are the people to whom this message of salvation has been sent. 27 The people of Jerusalem and their rulers did not recognize Jesus, or understand the words of the prophets which are read sabbath by sabbath; indeed, they fulfilled them by condemning him. 28 Though they failed to find grounds for the sentence of death, they asked Pilate to have him executed. 29 When they had carried out all that the scriptures said about him, they took him down from the gibbet and laid him in a tomb. 30 But God raised him from the dead; 31 and over a period of many days he appeared to those who had come up with him from Galilee to Jerusalem, and they are now his witnesses before our people.

32 'We are here to give you the good news that God, who made the promise to the fathers, 33 has fulfilled it for the children by raising Jesus from the dead, as indeed it stands written in the second Psalm: "You are my son; this day I have begotten you." 34 Again, that he raised him from the dead, never to be subjected to corruption, he declares in these words: "I will give you the blessings promised to David, holy and sure." 35 This is borne out by another passage: "You will not let

---

13:18 **he … conduct:** *some witnesses read* he sustained them.   13:33 **for the children:** *some witnesses read* for our children; *others read* for us their children.

your faithful servant suffer corruption." [36] As for David, when he had served the purpose of God in his own generation, he died and was gathered to his fathers, and suffered corruption; [37] but the one whom God raised up did not suffer corruption. [38] You must understand, my brothers, it is through him that forgiveness of sins is now being proclaimed to you. [39] It is through him that everyone who has faith is acquitted of everything for which there was no acquittal under the law of Moses. [40] Beware, then, lest you bring down upon yourselves the doom proclaimed by the prophets: [41] "See this, you scoffers, marvel, and begone; for I am doing a deed in your days, a deed which you will never believe when you are told of it."'

[42] As they were leaving the synagogue they were asked to come again and speak on these subjects next sabbath; [43] and after the congregation had dispersed, many Jews and gentile worshippers went with Paul and Barnabas, who spoke to them and urged them to hold fast to the grace of God.

[44] On the following sabbath almost the whole city gathered to hear the word of God. [45] When the Jews saw the crowds, they were filled with jealous resentment, and contradicted what Paul had said with violent abuse. [46] But Paul and Barnabas were outspoken in their reply. 'It was necessary', they said, 'that the word of God should be declared to you first. But since you reject it and judge yourselves unworthy of eternal life, we now turn to the Gentiles. [47] For these are our instructions from the Lord: "I have appointed you to be a light for the Gentiles, and a means of salvation to earth's farthest bounds."' [48] When the Gentiles heard this, they were overjoyed and thankfully acclaimed the word of the Lord, and those who were marked out for eternal life became believers. [49] Thus the word of the Lord spread throughout the region. [50] But the Jews stirred up feeling among those worshippers who were women of standing, and among the leading men of the city; a campaign of persecution was started against Paul and Barnabas, and they were expelled from the district. [51] They shook the dust off their feet in protest against them and went to Iconium. [52] And the disciples were filled with joy and with the Holy Spirit.

14 At Iconium they went together into the Jewish synagogue and spoke to such purpose that Jews and Greeks in large numbers became believers. [2] But the unconverted Jews stirred up the Gentiles and poisoned their minds against the Christians. [3] So Paul and Barnabas stayed on for some time, and spoke boldly and openly in reliance on the Lord, who confirmed the message of his grace by enabling them to work signs and miracles. [4] The populace was divided, some siding with the Jews, others with the apostles. [5] A move was made by Gentiles and Jews together, with the connivance of the city authorities, to maltreat them and stone them, [6] and when they became aware of this, they made their escape to the Lycaonian cities of Lystra and Derbe and the surrounding country. [7] There they continued to spread the good news.

[8] At Lystra a cripple, lame from birth, who had never walked in his life, [9] sat listening to Paul as he spoke. Paul fixed his eyes on him and, seeing that he had the faith to be cured, [10] said in a loud voice, 'Stand up straight on your feet'; and he sprang up and began to walk. [11] When the crowds saw what Paul had done, they shouted, in their native Lycaonian, 'The gods have come down to us in human form!' [12] They called Barnabas Zeus, and Paul they called Hermes, because he was the spokesman. [13] The priest of Zeus, whose temple was just outside the city, brought oxen and garlands to the gates, and he and the people were about to offer sacrifice.

[14] But when the apostles Barnabas and Paul heard of it, they tore their clothes and rushed into the crowd shouting, [15] 'Men, why are you doing this? We are human beings, just like you. The good news we bring tells you to turn from these follies to the living God, who made heaven and earth and sea and everything in them. [16] In past ages he has allowed all nations to go their own way; [17] and yet he has not left you without some clue to his nature, in the benefits he bestows: he sends you rain from heaven and the crops in their seasons, and gives you food in plenty and keeps you in good heart.' [18] Even with these words they barely managed to prevent the crowd from offering sacrifice to them.

[19] Then Jews from Antioch and Iconium

came on the scene and won over the crowds. They stoned Paul, and dragged him out of the city, thinking him dead. [20] The disciples formed a ring round him, and he got to his feet and went into the city. Next day he left with Barnabas for Derbe.

[21] After bringing the good news to that town and gaining many converts, they returned to Lystra, then to Iconium, and then to Antioch, [22] strengthening the disciples and encouraging them to be true to the faith. They warned them that to enter the kingdom of God we must undergo many hardships. [23] They also appointed for them elders in each congregation, and with prayer and fasting committed them to the Lord in whom they had put their trust.

[24] They passed through Pisidia and came into Pamphylia. [25] When they had delivered the message at Perga, they went down to Attalia, [26] and from there sailed to Antioch, where they had originally been commended to the grace of God for the task which they had now completed. [27] On arrival there, they called the congregation together and reported all that God had accomplished through them, and how he had thrown open the gates of faith to the Gentiles. [28] And they stayed for some time with the disciples there.

15 SOME people who had come down from Judaea began to teach the brotherhood that those who were not circumcised in accordance with Mosaic practice could not be saved. [2] That brought them into fierce dissension and controversy with Paul and Barnabas, and it was arranged that these two and some others from Antioch should go up to Jerusalem to see the apostles and elders about this question.

[3] They were sent on their way by the church, and travelled through Phoenicia and Samaria, telling the full story of the conversion of the Gentiles, and causing great rejoicing among all the Christians. [4] When they reached Jerusalem they were welcomed by the church and the apostles and elders, and they reported all that God had accomplished through them. [5] But some of the Pharisaic party

who had become believers came forward and declared, 'Those Gentiles must be circumcised and told to keep the law of Moses.'

[6] The apostles and elders met to look into this matter, [7] and, after a long debate, Peter rose to address them. 'My friends,' he said, 'in the early days, as you yourselves know, God made his choice among you: from my lips the Gentiles were to hear and believe the message of the gospel. [8] And God, who can read human hearts, showed his approval by giving the Holy Spirit to them as he did to us. [9] He made no difference between them and us; for he purified their hearts by faith. [10] Then why do you now try God's patience by laying on the shoulders of these converts a yoke which neither we nor our forefathers were able to bear? [11] For our belief is that we are saved in the same way as they are: by the grace of the Lord Jesus.'

[12] At that the whole company fell silent and listened to Barnabas and Paul as they described all the signs and portents that God had worked among the Gentiles through them.

[13] When they had finished speaking, James summed up: 'My friends,' he said, 'listen to me. [14] Simon has described how it first happened that God, in his providence, chose from among the Gentiles a people to bear his name. [15] This agrees with the words of the prophets: as scripture has it,

[16] Thereafter I will return and
　　rebuild the fallen house of David;
　I will rebuild its ruins and set it up
　　again,
[17] that the rest of mankind may seek
　　the Lord,
　all the Gentiles whom I have claimed
　　for my own.
　Thus says the Lord, who is doing this
[18] as he made known long ago.

[19] 'In my judgement, therefore, we should impose no irksome restrictions on those of the Gentiles who are turning to God; [20] instead we should instruct them by letter to abstain from things polluted by contact with idols, from fornication, from anything that has been strangled,

15:14 **Simon:** *Gk* Simeon.　15:20 **from fornication ... blood:** *some witnesses omit* from fornication; *others omit* from anything that has been strangled; *some add* (*after* blood) and to refrain from doing to others what they would not like done to themselves.

and from blood. [21] Moses, after all, has never lacked spokesmen in every town for generations past; he is read in the synagogues sabbath by sabbath.'

[22] Then, with the agreement of the whole church, the apostles and elders resolved to choose representatives and send them to Antioch with Paul and Barnabas. They chose two leading men in the community, Judas Barsabbas and Silas, [23] and gave them this letter to deliver:

From the apostles and elders to our brothers of gentile origin in Antioch, Syria, and Cilicia. Greetings!

[24] We have heard that some of our number, without any instructions from us, have disturbed you with their talk and unsettled your minds. [25] In consequence, we have resolved unanimously to send to you our chosen representatives with our well-beloved Barnabas and Paul, [26] who have given up their lives to the cause of our Lord Jesus Christ; [27] so we are sending Judas and Silas, who will, by word of mouth, confirm what is written in this letter. [28] It is the decision of the Holy Spirit, and our decision, to lay no further burden upon you beyond these essentials: [29] you are to abstain from meat that has been offered to idols, from blood, from anything that has been strangled, and from fornication. If you keep yourselves free from these things you will be doing well. Farewell.

[30] So they took their leave and travelled down to Antioch, where they called the congregation together and delivered the letter. [31] When it was read, all rejoiced at the encouragement it brought, [32] and Judas and Silas, who were themselves prophets, said much to encourage and strengthen the members. [33] After spending some time there, they took their leave with the good wishes of the brethren, to return to those who had sent them. [35] But Paul and Barnabas stayed on at Antioch, where, along with many others, they taught and preached the word of the Lord.

[36] AFTER a while Paul said to Barnabas, 'Let us go back and see how our brothers are getting on in the various towns where we proclaimed the word of the Lord.' [37] Barnabas wanted to take John Mark with them; [38] but Paul insisted that the man who had deserted them in Pamphylia and had not gone on to share in their work was not the man to take with them now. [39] The dispute was so sharp that they parted company. Barnabas took Mark with him and sailed for Cyprus. [40] Paul chose Silas and started on his journey, commended by the brothers to the grace of the Lord. [41] He travelled through Syria and Cilicia bringing new strength to the churches.

16 He went on to Derbe and then to Lystra, where he found a disciple named Timothy, the son of a Jewish Christian mother and a gentile father, [2] well spoken of by the Christians at Lystra and Iconium. [3] Paul wanted to take him with him when he left, so he had him circumcised out of consideration for the Jews who lived in those parts, for they all knew that his father was a Gentile. [4] As they made their way from town to town they handed on the decisions taken by the apostles and elders in Jerusalem and enjoined their observance. [5] So, day by day, the churches grew stronger in faith and increased in numbers.

[6] They travelled through the Phrygian and Galatian region, prevented by the Holy Spirit from delivering the message in the province of Asia. [7] When they approached the Mysian border they tried to enter Bithynia, but, as the Spirit of Jesus would not allow them, [8] they passed through Mysia and reached the coast at Troas. [9] During the night a vision came to Paul: a Macedonian stood there appealing to him, 'Cross over to Macedonia and help us.' [10] As soon as he had seen this vision, we set about getting a passage to Macedonia, convinced that God had called us to take the good news there.

[11] We sailed from Troas and made a straight run to Samothrace, the next day to Neapolis, [12] and from there to Philippi, a leading city in that district of Macedonia and a Roman colony. Here we stayed for

---

15:29 **from anything ... fornication:** *some witnesses omit* from anything that has been strangled; *some omit* and from fornication; *and some witnesses add* and refrain from doing to others what you would not like done to yourselves.   15:33 **sent them:** *some witnesses add* [34] But Silas decided to remain there.   16:6 **through ... region:** *or* through Phrygia and the Galatian region.

some days, ¹³ and on the sabbath we went outside the city gate by the riverside, where we thought there would be a place of prayer; we sat down and talked to the women who had gathered there. ¹⁴ One of those listening was called Lydia, a dealer in purple fabric, who came from the city of Thyatira; she was a worshipper of God, and the Lord opened her heart to respond to what Paul said. ¹⁵ She was baptized, and her household with her, and then she urged us, 'Now that you have accepted me as a believer in the Lord, come and stay at my house.' And she insisted on our going.

¹⁶ Once, on our way to the place of prayer, we met a slave-girl who was possessed by a spirit of divination and brought large profits to her owners by telling fortunes. ¹⁷ She followed Paul and the rest of us, shouting, 'These men are servants of the Most High God, and are declaring to you a way of salvation.' ¹⁸ She did this day after day, until, in exasperation, Paul rounded on the spirit. 'I command you in the name of Jesus Christ to come out of her,' he said, and it came out instantly.

¹⁹ When the girl's owners saw that their hope of profit had gone, they seized Paul and Silas and dragged them to the city authorities in the main square; ²⁰ bringing them before the magistrates, they alleged, 'These men are causing a disturbance in our city; they are Jews, ²¹ and they are advocating practices which it is illegal for us Romans to adopt and follow.' ²² The mob joined in the attack; and the magistrates had the prisoners stripped and gave orders for them to be flogged. ²³ After a severe beating they were flung into prison and the jailer was ordered to keep them under close guard. ²⁴ In view of these orders, he put them into the inner prison and secured their feet in the stocks.

²⁵ About midnight Paul and Silas, at their prayers, were singing praises to God, and the other prisoners were listening, ²⁶ when suddenly there was such a violent earthquake that the foundations of the jail were shaken; the doors burst open and all the prisoners found their fetters unfastened. ²⁷ The jailer woke up to see the prison doors wide open and, assuming

that the prisoners had escaped, drew his sword intending to kill himself. ²⁸ But Paul shouted, 'Do yourself no harm; we are all here.' ²⁹ The jailer called for lights, rushed in, and threw himself down before Paul and Silas, trembling with fear. ³⁰ He then escorted them out and said, 'Sirs, what must I do to be saved?' ³¹ They answered, 'Put your trust in the Lord Jesus, and you will be saved, you and your household,' ³² and they imparted the word of the Lord to him and to everyone in his house. ³³ At that late hour of the night the jailer took them and washed their wounds, and there and then he and his whole family were baptized. ³⁴ He brought them up into his house, set out a meal, and rejoiced with his whole household in his new-found faith in God.

³⁵ When daylight came, the magistrates sent their officers with the order, 'Release those men.' ³⁶ The jailer reported these instructions to Paul: 'The magistrates have sent an order for your release. Now you are free to go in peace.' ³⁷ But Paul said to the officers: 'We are Roman citizens! They gave us a public flogging and threw us into prison without trial. Are they now going to smuggle us out by stealth? No indeed! Let them come in person and escort us out.' ³⁸ The officers reported his words to the magistrates. Alarmed to hear that they were Roman citizens, ³⁹ they came and apologized to them, and then escorted them out and requested them to go away from the city. ⁴⁰ On leaving the prison, they went to Lydia's house, where they met their fellow-Christians and spoke words of encouragement to them, and then they took their departure.

17 THEY now travelled by way of Amphipolis and Apollonia and came to Thessalonica, where there was a Jewish synagogue. ² Following his usual practice Paul went to their meetings; and for the next three sabbaths he argued with them, quoting texts of scripture ³ which he expounded and applied to show that the Messiah had to suffer and rise from the dead. 'And this Jesus', he said, 'whom I am proclaiming to you is the Messiah.' ⁴ Some of them were convinced and joined Paul and Silas, as did a

16:13 where ... prayer: *some witnesses read* where there was a recognized place of prayer.

great number of godfearing Gentiles and a good many influential women.

[5] The Jews in their jealousy recruited some ruffians from the dregs of society to gather a mob. They put the city in an uproar, and made for Jason's house with the intention of bringing Paul and Silas before the town assembly. [6] Failing to find them, they dragged Jason himself and some members of the congregation before the magistrates, shouting, 'The men who have made trouble the whole world over have now come here, [7] and Jason has harboured them. All of them flout the emperor's laws, and assert there is a rival king, Jesus.' [8] These words alarmed the mob and the magistrates also, [9] who took security from Jason and the others before letting them go.

[10] As soon as darkness fell, the members of the congregation sent Paul and Silas off to Beroea; and, on arrival, they made their way to the synagogue. [11] The Jews here were more fair-minded than those at Thessalonica: they received the message with great eagerness, studying the scriptures every day to see whether it was true. [12] Many of them therefore became believers, and so did a fair number of Gentiles, women of standing as well as men. [13] But when the Thessalonian Jews learnt that the word of God had now been proclaimed by Paul in Beroea, they followed him there to stir up trouble and rouse the rabble. [14] At once the members of the congregation sent Paul down to the coast, while Silas and Timothy both stayed behind. [15] Paul's escort brought him as far as Athens, and came away with instructions for Silas and Timothy to rejoin him with all speed.

[16] While Paul was waiting for them at Athens, he was outraged to see the city so full of idols. [17] He argued in the synagogue with the Jews and gentile worshippers, and also in the city square every day with casual passers-by. [18] Moreover, some of the Epicurean and Stoic philosophers joined issue with him. Some said, 'What can this charlatan be trying to say?' and others, 'He would appear to be a propagandist for foreign deities'—this because he was preaching about Jesus and the Resurrection. [19] They brought him to the Council of the Areopagus and asked, 'May we know what this new doctrine is that you propound? [20] You are introducing ideas that sound strange to us, and we should like to know what they mean.' [21] Now, all the Athenians and the resident foreigners had time for nothing except talking or hearing about the latest novelty.

[22] Paul stood up before the Council of the Areopagus and began: 'Men of Athens, I see that in everything that concerns religion you are uncommonly scrupulous. [23] As I was going round looking at the objects of your worship, I noticed among other things an altar bearing the inscription "To an Unknown God". What you worship but do not know—this is what I now proclaim.

[24] 'The God who created the world and everything in it, and who is Lord of heaven and earth, does not live in shrines made by human hands. [25] It is not because he lacks anything that he accepts service at our hands, for he is himself the universal giver of life and breath—indeed of everything. [26] He created from one stock every nation of men to inhabit the whole earth's surface. He determined their eras in history and the limits of their territory. [27] They were to seek God in the hope that, groping after him, they might find him; though indeed he is not far from each one of us, [28] for in him we live and move, in him we exist; as some of your own poets have said, "We are also his offspring." [29] Being God's offspring, then, we ought not to suppose that the deity is like an image in gold or silver or stone, shaped by human craftsmanship and design. [30] God has overlooked the age of ignorance; but now he commands men and women everywhere to repent, [31] because he has fixed the day on which he will have the world judged, and justly judged, by a man whom he has designated; of this he has given assurance to all by raising him from the dead.'

[32] When they heard about the raising of the dead, some scoffed; others said, 'We will hear you on this subject some other time.' [33] So Paul left the assembly. [34] Some men joined him and became believers, including Dionysius, a member of the

---

17:19 **to ... Areopagus:** *or* to Mars' Hill.   17:22 **before ... Areopagus:** *or* in the middle of Mars' Hill.
17:26 **determined ... history:** *or* fixed the ordered seasons.

Council of the Areopagus; and also a woman named Damaris, with others besides.

18 After this he left Athens and went to Corinth. ² There he met a Jew named Aquila, a native of Pontus, and his wife Priscilla; they had recently arrived from Italy because Claudius had issued an edict that all Jews should leave Rome. Paul approached them ³ and, because he was of the same trade, he made his home with them; they were tentmakers and Paul worked with them. ⁴ He also held discussions in the synagogue sabbath by sabbath, trying to convince both Jews and Gentiles.

⁵ Then Silas and Timothy came down from Macedonia, and Paul devoted himself entirely to preaching, maintaining before the Jews that the Messiah is Jesus. ⁶ When, however, they opposed him and resorted to abuse, he shook out the folds of his cloak and declared, 'Your blood be on your own heads! My conscience is clear! From now on I shall go to the Gentiles.' ⁷ With that he left, and went to the house of a worshipper of God named Titius Justus, who lived next door to the synagogue. ⁸ Crispus, the president of the synagogue, became a believer in the Lord, as did all his household; and a number of Corinthians who heard him believed and were baptized. ⁹ One night in a vision the Lord said to Paul, 'Have no fear: go on with your preaching and do not be silenced. ¹⁰ I am with you, and no attack shall harm you, for I have many in this city who are my people.' ¹¹ So he settled there for eighteen months, teaching the word of God among them.

¹² But when Gallio was proconsul of Achaia, the Jews made a concerted attack on Paul and brought him before the court. ¹³ 'This man', they said, 'is inducing people to worship God in ways that are against the law.' ¹⁴ Paul was just about to speak when Gallio declared, 'If it had been a question of crime or grave misdemeanour, I should, of course, have given you Jews a patient hearing, ¹⁵ but if it is some bickering about words and names and your Jewish law, you may settle it yourselves. I do not intend to be a judge of these matters.' ¹⁶ And he dismissed them from the court. ¹⁷ Then they all attacked Sosthenes, the president of the synagogue, and beat him up in full view of the tribunal. But all this left Gallio quite unconcerned.

¹⁸ Paul stayed on at Corinth for some time, and then took leave of the congregation. Accompanied by Priscilla and Aquila, he sailed for Syria, having had his hair cut off at Cenchreae in fulfilment of a vow. ¹⁹ They put in at Ephesus, where he parted from his companions; he himself went into the synagogue and held a discussion with the Jews. ²⁰ He was asked to stay longer, but he declined ²¹ and set sail from Ephesus, promising, as he took leave of them, 'I shall come back to you if it is God's will.' ²² On landing at Caesarea, he went up and greeted the church; and then went down to Antioch. ²³ After some time there he set out again on a journey through the Galatian country and then through Phrygia, bringing new strength to all the disciples.

²⁴ THERE arrived at Ephesus a Jew named Apollos, an Alexandrian by birth, an eloquent man, powerful in his use of the scriptures. ²⁵ He had been instructed in the way of the Lord and was full of spiritual fervour; and in his discourses he taught accurately the facts about Jesus, though the only baptism he knew was John's. ²⁶ He now began to speak boldly in the synagogue, where Priscilla and Aquila heard him; they took him in hand and expounded the way to him in greater detail. ²⁷ Finding that he wanted to go across to Achaia, the congregation gave him their support, and wrote to the disciples there to make him welcome. From the time of his arrival, he was very helpful to those who had by God's grace become believers, ²⁸ for he strenuously confuted the Jews, demonstrating publicly from the scriptures that the Messiah is Jesus.

19 While Apollos was at Corinth, Paul travelled through the inland regions till he came to Ephesus, where he found a number of disciples. ² When he asked them, 'Did you receive the Holy Spirit when you became believers?' they replied, 'No, we were not even told that there is a Holy Spirit.' ³ He asked, 'Then what baptism were you given?' 'John's

---

18:24 **an eloquent man:** *or* a learned man.   18:26 **the way:** *some witnesses read* the way of God.

baptism,' they answered. ⁴ Paul said, 'The baptism that John gave was a baptism in token of repentance, and he told the people to put their trust in one who was to come after him, that is, in Jesus.' ⁵ On hearing this they were baptized into the name of the Lord Jesus; ⁶ and when Paul had laid his hands on them, the Holy Spirit came upon them and they spoke in tongues of ecstasy and prophesied. ⁷ There were about a dozen men in all.

⁸ During the next three months he attended the synagogue and with persuasive argument spoke boldly about the kingdom of God. ⁹ When some proved obdurate and would not believe, speaking evil of the new way before the congregation, he withdrew from them, taking the disciples with him, and continued to hold discussions daily in the lecture hall of Tyrannus. ¹⁰ This went on for two years, with the result that the whole population of the province of Asia, both Jews and Gentiles, heard the word of the Lord. ¹¹ God worked extraordinary miracles through Paul: ¹² when handkerchiefs and scarves which had been in contact with his skin were carried to the sick, they were cured of their diseases, and the evil spirits came out of them.

¹³ Some itinerant Jewish exorcists tried their hand at using the name of the Lord Jesus on those possessed by evil spirits; they would say, 'I adjure you by Jesus whom Paul proclaims.' ¹⁴ There were seven sons of Sceva, a Jewish chief priest, who were doing this, ¹⁵ when the evil spirit responded, 'Jesus I recognize, Paul I know, but who are you?' ¹⁶ The man with the evil spirit flew at them, overpowered them all, and handled them with such violence that they ran out of the house battered and naked. ¹⁷ Everybody in Ephesus, Jew and Gentile alike, got to know of it, and all were awestruck, while the name of the Lord Jesus gained in honour. ¹⁸ Moreover many of those who had become believers came and openly confessed that they had been using magical spells. ¹⁹ A good many of those who formerly practised magic collected their books and burnt them publicly, and when the total value was reckoned up it came to fifty thousand pieces of silver. ²⁰ In such ways the word of the Lord showed its power, spreading more and more widely and effectively.

²¹ When matters had reached this stage, Paul made up his mind to visit Macedonia and Achaia and then go on to Jerusalem. 'After I have been there,' he said, 'I must see Rome also.' ²² He sent two of his assistants, Timothy and Erastus, to Macedonia, while he himself stayed some time longer in the province of Asia.

²³ It was about this time that the Christian movement gave rise to a serious disturbance. ²⁴ There was a man named Demetrius, a silversmith who made silver shrines of Artemis, and provided considerable employment for the craftsmen. ²⁵ He called a meeting of them and of the workers in allied trades, and addressed them: 'As you men know, our prosperity depends on this industry. ²⁶ But this fellow Paul, as you can see and hear for yourselves, has perverted crowds of people with his propaganda, not only at Ephesus but also in practically the whole of the province of Asia; he tells them that gods made by human hands are not gods at all. ²⁷ There is danger for us here; it is not only that our line of business will be discredited, but also that the sanctuary of the great goddess Artemis will cease to command respect; and then it will not be long before she who is worshipped by all Asia and the civilized world is brought down from her divine pre-eminence.'

²⁸ On hearing this, they were enraged, and began to shout, 'Great is Artemis of the Ephesians!' ²⁹ The whole city was in an uproar; they made a concerted rush into the theatre, hustling along with them Paul's travelling companions, the Macedonians Gaius and Aristarchus. ³⁰ Paul wanted to appear before the assembly but the other Christians would not let him. ³¹ Even some of the dignitaries of the province, who were friendly towards him, sent a message urging him not to venture into the theatre. ³² Meanwhile some were shouting one thing, some another, for the assembly was in an uproar and most of them did not know what they had all come for. ³³ Some of the crowd explained the trouble to Alexander, whom the Jews had pushed to the front, and he, motioning for silence, attempted to make a defence before the assembly. ³⁴ But when they recognized that he was a Jew, one shout arose from them all: 'Great is Artemis of the Ephesians!' and they kept it up for about two hours.

³⁵ The town clerk, however, quietened the crowd. 'Citizens of Ephesus,' he said, 'all the world knows that our city of Ephesus is temple warden of the great Artemis and of that image of her which fell from heaven. ³⁶ Since these facts are beyond dispute, your proper course is to keep calm and do nothing rash. ³⁷ These men whom you have brought here as offenders have committed no sacrilege and uttered no blasphemy against our goddess. ³⁸ If, therefore, Demetrius and his craftsmen have a case against anyone, there are assizes and there are proconsuls; let the parties bring their charges and countercharges. ³⁹ But if it is a larger question you are raising, it will be dealt with in the statutory assembly. ⁴⁰ We certainly run the risk of being charged with riot for this day's work. There is no justification for it, and it would be impossible for us to give any explanation of this turmoil.' ⁴¹ With that he dismissed the assembly.

20 WHEN the disturbance was over, Paul sent for the disciples and, after encouraging them, said goodbye and set out on his journey to Macedonia. ² He travelled through that region, constantly giving encouragement to the Christians, and finally reached Greece. ³ When he had spent three months there and was on the point of embarking for Syria, a plot was laid against him by the Jews, so he decided to return by way of Macedonia. ⁴ He was accompanied by Sopater son of Pyrrhus from Beroea, Aristarchus and Secundus from Thessalonica, Gaius of Derbe, and Timothy, and from Asia Tychicus and Trophimus. ⁵ These went ahead and waited for us at Troas; ⁶ we ourselves sailed from Philippi after the Passover season, and five days later rejoined them at Troas, where we spent a week.

⁷ On the Saturday night, when we gathered for the breaking of bread, Paul, who was to leave next day, addressed the congregation and went on speaking until midnight. ⁸ Now there were many lamps in the upstairs room where we were assembled, ⁹ and a young man named Eutychus, who was sitting on the window-ledge, grew more and more

drowsy as Paul went on talking, until, completely overcome by sleep, he fell from the third storey to the ground, and was picked up dead. ¹⁰ Paul went down, threw himself upon him, and clasped him in his arms. 'Do not distress yourselves,' he said to them; 'he is alive.' ¹¹ He then went upstairs, broke bread and ate, and after much conversation, which lasted until dawn, he departed. ¹² And they took the boy home, greatly relieved that he was alive.

¹³ We went on ahead to the ship and embarked for Assos, where we were to take Paul aboard; this was the arrangement he had made, since he was going to travel by road. ¹⁴ When he met us at Assos, we took him aboard and proceeded to Mitylene. ¹⁵ We sailed from there and next day arrived off Chios. On the second day we made Samos, and the following day we reached Miletus. ¹⁶ Paul had decided to bypass Ephesus and so avoid having to spend time in the province of Asia; he was eager to be in Jerusalem on the day of Pentecost, if that were possible. ¹⁷ He did, however, send from Miletus to Ephesus and summon the elders of the church. ¹⁸ When they joined him, he spoke to them as follows.

'You know how, from the day that I first set foot in the province of Asia, I spent my whole time with you, ¹⁹ serving the Lord in all humility amid the sorrows and trials that came upon me through the intrigues of the Jews. ²⁰ You know that I kept back nothing that was for your good: I delivered the message to you, and taught you, in public and in your homes; ²¹ with Jews and Gentiles alike I insisted on repentance before God and faith in our Lord Jesus. ²² Now, as you see, I am constrained by the Spirit to go to Jerusalem. I do not know what will befall me there, ²³ except that in city after city the Holy Spirit assures me that imprisonment and hardships await me. ²⁴ For myself, I set no store by life; all I want is to finish the race, and complete the task which the Lord Jesus assigned to me, that of bearing my testimony to the gospel of God's grace.

²⁵ 'One thing more: I have gone about among you proclaiming the kingdom, but now I know that none of you will ever see my face again. ²⁶ That being so, I here and

20:6 **after ... season**: *lit.* after the days of Unleavened Bread.

now declare that no one's fate can be laid at my door; I have kept back nothing; [27] I have disclosed to you the whole purpose of God. [28] Keep guard over yourselves and over all the flock of which the Holy Spirit has given you charge, as shepherds of the church of the Lord, which he won for himself by his own blood. [29] I know that when I am gone, savage wolves will come in among you and will not spare the flock. [30] Even from your own number men will arise who will distort the truth in order to get the disciples to break away and follow them. [31] So be on the alert; remember how with tears I never ceased to warn each one of you night and day for three years.

[32] 'And now I commend you to God and to the word of his grace, which has power to build you up and give you your heritage among all those whom God has made his own. [33] I have not wanted anyone's money or clothes for myself; [34] you all know that these hands of mine earned enough for the needs of myself and my companions. [35] All along I showed you that it is our duty to help the weak in this way, by hard work, and that we should keep in mind the words of the Lord Jesus, who himself said, "Happiness lies more in giving than in receiving."'

[36] As he finished speaking, he knelt down with them all and prayed. [37] There were loud cries of sorrow from them all, as they folded Paul in their arms and kissed him; [38] what distressed them most was his saying that they would never see his face again. Then they escorted him to the ship.

21 We tore ourselves away from them and, putting to sea, made a straight run and came to Cos; next day to Rhodes, and thence to Patara. [2] There we found a ship bound for Phoenicia, so we went aboard and sailed in her. [3] We came in sight of Cyprus and, leaving it to port, we continued our voyage to Syria and put in at Tyre, where the ship was to unload her cargo. [4] We sought out the disciples and stayed there a week. Warned by the Spirit, they urged Paul to abandon his visit to Jerusalem. [5] But when our time ashore was ended, we left and continued our journey; and they and their wives and children all escorted us out of the city.

We knelt down on the beach and prayed, [6] and then bade each other goodbye; we went on board, and they returned home.

[7] We made the passage from Tyre and reached Ptolemais, where we greeted the brotherhood and spent a day with them. [8] Next day we left and came to Caesarea, where we went to the home of Philip the evangelist, who was one of the Seven, and stayed with him. [9] He had four unmarried daughters, who possessed the gift of prophecy. [10] When we had been there several days, a prophet named Agabus arrived from Judaea. [11] He came to us, took Paul's belt, bound his own feet and hands with it, and said, 'These are the words of the Holy Spirit: Thus will the Jews in Jerusalem bind the man to whom this belt belongs, and hand him over to the Gentiles.' [12] When we heard this, we and the local people begged and implored Paul to abandon his visit to Jerusalem. [13] Then Paul gave his answer: 'Why all these tears? Why are you trying to weaken my resolution? I am ready, not merely to be bound, but even to die at Jerusalem for the name of the Lord Jesus.' [14] So, as he would not be dissuaded, we gave up and said, 'The Lord's will be done.'

[15] At the end of our stay we packed our baggage and took the road up to Jerusalem. [16] Some of the disciples from Caesarea came along with us, to direct us to a Cypriot named Mnason, a Christian from the early days, with whom we were to spend the night. [17] On our arrival at Jerusalem, the congregation welcomed us gladly.

[18] Next day Paul paid a visit to James; we accompanied him, and all the elders were present. [19] After greeting them, he described in detail all that God had done among the Gentiles by means of his ministry. [20] When they heard this, they gave praise to God. Then they said to Paul: 'You observe, brother, how many thousands of converts we have among the Jews, all of them staunch upholders of the law. [21] Now they have been given certain information about you: it is said that you teach all the Jews in the gentile world to turn their backs on Moses, and tell them not to circumcise their children or follow our way of life. [22] What is to be done,

---

20:28 **of the Lord ... blood:** *some witnesses read* of God, which he won for himself by the blood of his Own.

then? They are sure to hear that you have arrived. ²³ Our proposal is this: we have four men here who are under a vow; ²⁴ take them with you and go through the ritual of purification together, and pay their expenses, so that they may have their heads shaved; then everyone will know that there is nothing in the reports they have heard about you, but that you are yourself a practising Jew and observe the law. ²⁵ As for the gentile converts, we sent them our decision that they should abstain from meat that has been offered to idols, from blood, from anything that has been strangled, and from fornication.' ²⁶ So Paul took the men, and next day, after going through the ritual of purification with them, he went into the temple to give notice of the date when the period of purification would end and the offering be made for each of them.

Paul's work in Jerusalem

²⁷ But just before the seven days were up, the Jews from the province of Asia saw him in the temple. They stirred up all the crowd and seized him, ²⁸ shouting, 'Help us, men of Israel! This is the fellow who attacks our people, our law, and this sanctuary, and spreads his teaching the whole world over. What is more, he has brought Gentiles into the temple and profaned this holy place.' ²⁹ They had previously seen Trophimus the Ephesian with him in the city, and assumed that Paul had brought him into the temple.

³⁰ The whole city was in a turmoil, and people came running from all directions. They seized Paul and dragged him out of the temple, and at once the doors were shut. ³¹ They were bent on killing him, but word came to the officer commanding the cohort that all Jerusalem was in an uproar. ³² He immediately took a force of soldiers with their centurions and came down at the double to deal with the riot. When the crowd saw the commandant and his troops, they stopped beating Paul. ³³ As soon as the commandant could reach Paul, he arrested him and ordered him to be shackled with two chains; he enquired who he was and what he had been doing. ³⁴ Some in the crowd shouted one thing, some another, and as the commandant could not get at the truth

because of the hubbub, he ordered him to be taken to the barracks. ³⁵ When Paul reached the steps, he found himself carried up by the soldiers because of the violence of the mob; ³⁶ for the whole crowd was at their heels yelling, 'Kill him!'

³⁷ Just before he was taken into the barracks Paul said to the commandant, 'May I have a word with you?' The commandant said, 'So you speak Greek? ³⁸ Then you are not the Egyptian who started a revolt some time ago and led a force of four thousand terrorists out into the desert?' ³⁹ Paul replied, 'I am a Jew from Tarsus in Cilicia, a citizen of no mean city. May I have your permission to speak to the people?' ⁴⁰ When this was given, Paul stood on the steps and raised his hand to call for the attention of the people. As soon as quiet was restored, he addressed them in the Jewish language:

22 'Brothers and fathers, give me a hearing while I put my case to you.' ² When they heard him speaking to them in their own language, they listened more quietly. ³ 'I am a true-born Jew,' he began, 'a native of Tarsus in Cilicia. I was brought up in this city, and as a pupil of Gamaliel I was thoroughly trained in every point of our ancestral law. I have always been ardent in God's service, as you all are today. ⁴ And so I persecuted this movement to the death, arresting its followers, men and women alike, and committing them to prison, ⁵ as the high priest and the whole Council of Elders can testify. It was they who gave me letters to our fellow-Jews at Damascus, and I was on my way to make arrests there also and bring the prisoners to Jerusalem for punishment. ⁶ What happened to me on my journey was this: when I was nearing Damascus, about midday, a great light suddenly flashed from the sky all around me. ⁷ I fell to the ground, and heard a voice saying: "Saul, Saul, why do you persecute me?" ⁸ I answered, "Tell me, Lord, who you are." "I am Jesus of Nazareth, whom you are persecuting," he said. ⁹ My companions saw the light, but did not hear the voice that spoke to me. ¹⁰ "What shall I do, Lord?" I asked, and he replied, "Get up, and go on to Damascus; there you will be told all that

---

21:25 *from anything ... strangled: some witnesses omit.*

you are appointed to do." [11] As I had been blinded by the brilliance of that light, my companions led me by the hand, and so I came to Damascus.

[12] 'There a man called Ananias, a devout observer of the law and well spoken of by all the Jews who lived there, [13] came and stood beside me, and said, "Saul, my brother, receive your sight again!" Instantly I recovered my sight and saw him. [14] He went on: "The God of our fathers appointed you to know his will and to see the Righteous One and to hear him speak, [15] because you are to be his witness to tell the world what you have seen and heard. [16] Do not delay. Be baptized at once and wash away your sins, calling on his name."

[17] 'After my return to Jerusalem, as I was praying in the temple I fell into a trance [18] and saw him there, speaking to me. "Make haste", he said, "and leave Jerusalem quickly, for they will not accept your testimony about me." [19] "But surely, Lord," I answered, "they know that I imprisoned those who believe in you and flogged them in every synagogue; [20] when the blood of Stephen your witness was shed I stood by, approving, and I looked after the clothes of those who killed him." [21] He said to me, "Go, for I mean to send you far away to the Gentiles."'

[22] Up to this point the crowd had given him a hearing; but now they began to shout, 'Down with the scoundrel! He is not fit to be alive!' [23] And as they were yelling and waving their cloaks and flinging dust in the air, [24] the commandant ordered him to be brought into the barracks, and gave instructions that he should be examined under the lash, to find out what reason there was for such an outcry against him. [25] But when they tied him up for the flogging, Paul said to the centurion who was standing there, 'Does the law allow you to flog a Roman citizen, and an unconvicted one at that?' [26] When the centurion heard this, he went and reported to the commandant: 'What are you about? This man is a Roman citizen.' [27] The commandant came to Paul and asked, 'Tell me, are you a Roman citizen?' 'Yes,' said he. [28] The commandant rejoined, 'Citizenship cost me a large sum of money.' Paul said, 'It was mine by birth.' [29] Then those who were about to examine him promptly withdrew; and the commandant himself was alarmed when he realized that Paul was a Roman citizen and that he had put him in irons.

Paul's trials

[30] THE following day, wishing to be quite sure what charge the Jews were bringing against Paul, he released him and ordered the chief priests and the entire Council to assemble. He then brought Paul down to stand before them.

23 With his eyes steadily fixed on the Council, Paul said, 'My brothers, all my life to this day I have lived with a perfectly clear conscience before God.' [2] At this the high priest Ananias ordered his attendants to strike him on the mouth. [3] Paul retorted, 'God will strike you, you whitewashed wall! You sit there to judge me in accordance with the law; then, in defiance of the law, you order me to be struck!' [4] The attendants said, 'Would you insult God's high priest?' [5] 'Brothers,' said Paul, 'I had no idea he was high priest; scripture, I know, says: "You shall not abuse the ruler of your people."'

[6] Well aware that one section of them were Sadducees and the other Pharisees, Paul called out in the Council, 'My brothers, I am a Pharisee, a Pharisee born and bred; and the issue in this trial is our hope of the resurrection of the dead.' [7] At these words the Pharisees and Sadducees fell out among themselves, and the assembly was divided. [8] (The Sadducees deny that there is any resurrection or angel or spirit, but the Pharisees believe in all three.) [9] A great uproar ensued; and some of the scribes belonging to the Pharisaic party openly took sides and declared, 'We find no fault with this man; perhaps an angel or spirit has spoken to him.' [10] In the mounting dissension, the commandant was afraid that Paul would be torn to pieces, so he ordered the troops to go down, pull him out of the crowd, and bring him into the barracks.

[11] The following night the Lord appeared to him and said, 'Keep up your courage! You have affirmed the truth about me in Jerusalem, and you must do the same in Rome.'

[12] When day broke, the Jews banded together and took an oath not to eat or drink until they had killed Paul. [13] There were more than forty in the conspiracy;

¹⁴ they went to the chief priests and elders and said, 'We have bound ourselves by a solemn oath not to taste food until we have killed Paul. ¹⁵ It is now up to you and the rest of the Council to apply to the commandant to have him brought down to you on the pretext of a closer investigation of his case; we have arranged to make away with him before he reaches you.'

¹⁶ The son of Paul's sister, however, learnt of the plot and, going to the barracks, obtained entry, and reported it to Paul, ¹⁷ who called one of the centurions and said, 'Take this young man to the commandant; he has something to report.' ¹⁸ The centurion brought him to the commandant and explained, 'The prisoner Paul sent for me and asked me to bring this young man to you; he has something to tell you.' ¹⁹ The commandant took him by the arm, drew him aside, and asked him, 'What is it you have to report?' ²⁰ He replied, 'The Jews have agreed on a plan: they will request you to bring Paul down to the Council tomorrow on the pretext of obtaining more precise information about him. ²¹ Do not listen to them; for a party more than forty strong are lying in wait for him, and they have sworn not to eat or drink until they have done away with him. They are now ready, waiting only for your consent.' ²² The commandant dismissed the young man, with orders not to let anyone know that he had given him this information.

²³ He then summoned two of his centurions and gave them these orders: 'Have two hundred infantry ready to proceed to Caesarea, together with seventy cavalrymen and two hundred light-armed troops; parade them three hours after sunset, ²⁴ and provide mounts for Paul so that he may be conducted under safe escort to Felix the governor.' ²⁵ And he wrote a letter to this effect:

²⁶ From Claudius Lysias to His Excellency the Governor Felix. Greeting.
²⁷ This man was seized by the Jews and was on the point of being murdered when I intervened with the troops, and, on discovering that he was a Roman citizen, I removed him to safety. ²⁸ As I

wished to ascertain the ground of their charge against him, I brought him down to their Council. ²⁹ I found that their case had to do with controversial matters of their law, but there was no charge against him which merited death or imprisonment. ³⁰ Information, however, has now been brought to my notice of an attempt to be made on the man's life, so I am sending him to you without delay, and have instructed his accusers to state their case against him before you.

³¹ Acting on their orders, the infantry took custody of Paul and brought him by night to Antipatris. ³² Next day they returned to their barracks, leaving the cavalry to escort him the rest of the way. ³³ When the cavalry reached Caesarea, they delivered the letter to the governor, and handed Paul over to him. ³⁴ He read the letter, and asked him what province he was from; and learning that he was from Cilicia ³⁵ he said, 'I will hear your case when your accusers arrive.' He ordered him to be held in custody at his headquarters in Herod's palace.

24 Five days later the high priest Ananias came down, accompanied by some of the elders and an advocate named Tertullus, to lay before the governor their charge against Paul. ²⁻³ When the prisoner was called, Tertullus opened the case.

'Your excellency,' he said to Felix, 'we owe it to you that we enjoy unbroken peace, and it is due to your provident care that, in all kinds of ways and in all sorts of places, improvements are being made for the good of this nation. We appreciate this, and are most grateful to you. ⁴ And now, not to take up too much of your time, I crave your indulgence for a brief statement of our case. ⁵ We have found this man to be a pest, a fomenter of discord among the Jews all over the world, a ringleader of the sect of the Nazarenes. ⁶ He made an attempt to profane the temple and we arrested him. ⁸ If you examine him yourself you can ascertain the truth of all the charges we bring against him.' ⁹ The Jews supported the

24:6 **arrested him:** *some witnesses add* It was our intention to try him under our law; ⁷ but Lysias the commandant intervened and forcibly removed him out of our hands, ⁽⁸⁾ ordering his accusers to come before you.

charge, alleging that the facts were as he stated. [10] The governor then motioned to Paul to speak, and he replied as follows: 'Knowing as I do that for many years you have administered justice to this nation, I make my defence with confidence. [11] As you can ascertain for yourself, it is not more than twelve days since I went up to Jerusalem on a pilgrimage. [12] They did not find me in the temple arguing with anyone or collecting a crowd, or in the synagogues or anywhere else in the city; [13] and they cannot make good the charges they now bring against me. [14] But this much I will admit: I am a follower of the new way (the "sect" they speak of), and it is in that manner that I worship the God of our fathers; for I believe all that is written in the law and the prophets, [15] and in reliance on God I hold the hope, which my accusers too accept, that there is to be a resurrection of good and wicked alike. [16] Accordingly I, no less than they, train myself to keep at all times a clear conscience before God and man.

[17] 'After an absence of several years I came to bring charitable gifts to my nation and to offer sacrifices. [18] I was ritually purified and engaged in this service when they found me in the temple; I had no crowd with me, and there was no disturbance. But some Jews from the province of Asia were there, [19] and if they had any charge against me, it is they who ought to have been in court to state it. [20] Failing that, it is for these persons here present to say what crime they discovered when I was brought before the Council, [21] apart from this one declaration which I made as I stood there: "The issue in my trial before you today is the resurrection of the dead."'

[22] Then Felix, who was well informed about the new way, adjourned the hearing. 'I will decide your case when Lysias the commanding officer comes down,' he said. [23] He gave orders to the centurion to keep Paul under open arrest and not to prevent any of his friends from making themselves useful to him.

[24] Some days later Felix came with his wife Drusilla, who was a Jewess, and sent for Paul. He let him talk to him about faith in Christ Jesus, [25] but when the discourse turned to questions of morals, self-control, and the coming judgement, Felix became alarmed and exclaimed, 'Enough for now! When I find it convenient I will send for you again.' [26] He also had hopes of a bribe from Paul, so he sent for him frequently and talked with him. [27] When two years had passed, Felix was succeeded by Porcius Festus. Wishing to curry favour with the Jews, Felix left Paul in custody.

25 THREE days after taking up his appointment, Festus went up from Caesarea to Jerusalem, [2] where the chief priests and the Jewish leaders laid before him their charge against Paul. [3] They urged Festus to support them in their case and have Paul sent to Jerusalem, for they were plotting to kill him on the way. [4] Festus, however, replied, 'Paul is in safe custody at Caesarea, and I shall be leaving Jerusalem shortly myself; [5] so let your leading men come down with me, and if the man is at fault in any way, let them prosecute him.'

[6] After spending eight or ten days at most in Jerusalem, he went down to Caesarea, and next day he took his seat in court and ordered Paul to be brought before him. [7] When he appeared, the Jews who had come down from Jerusalem stood round bringing many grave charges, which they were unable to prove. [8] Paul protested: 'I have committed no offence against the Jewish law, or against the temple, or against the emperor.' [9] Festus, anxious to ingratiate himself with the Jews, turned to Paul and asked, 'Are you willing to go up to Jerusalem and stand trial on these charges before me there?' [10] But Paul said, 'I am now standing before the emperor's tribunal; that is where I ought to be tried. I have committed no offence against the Jews, as you very well know. [11] If I am guilty of any capital crime, I do not ask to escape the death penalty; if, however, there is no substance in the charges which these men bring against me, it is not open to anyone to hand me over to them. I appeal to Caesar!' [12] Then Festus, after conferring with his advisers, replied, 'You have appealed to Caesar: to Caesar you shall go!'

[13] Some days later King Agrippa and Bernice arrived at Caesarea on a courtesy visit to Festus. [14] They spent some time there, and during their stay Festus raised

Paul's case with the king. 'There is a man here', he said, 'left in custody by Felix; [15] and when I was in Jerusalem the chief priests and elders of the Jews brought a charge against him, demanding his condemnation. [16] I replied that it was not Roman practice to hand a man over before he had been confronted with his accusers and given an opportunity of answering the charge. [17] So when they had come here with me I lost no time, but took my seat in court the very next day and ordered the man to be brought before me. [18] When his accusers rose to speak, they brought none of the charges I was expecting; [19] they merely had certain points of disagreement with him about their religion, and about someone called Jesus, a dead man whom Paul alleged to be alive. [20] Finding myself out of my depth in such discussions, I asked if he was willing to go to Jerusalem and stand trial there on these issues. [21] But Paul appealed to be remanded in custody for his imperial majesty's decision, and I ordered him to be detained until I could send him to the emperor.' [22] Agrippa said to Festus, 'I should rather like to hear the man myself.' 'You shall hear him tomorrow,' he answered.

[23] Next day Agrippa and Bernice came in full state and entered the audience-chamber accompanied by high-ranking officers and prominent citizens; and on the orders of Festus, Paul was brought in. [24] Then Festus said, 'King Agrippa, and all you who are in attendance, you see this man: the whole body of the Jews approached me both in Jerusalem and here, loudly insisting that he had no right to remain alive. [25] It was clear to me, however, that he had committed no capital crime, and when he himself appealed to his imperial majesty, I decided to send him. [26] As I have nothing definite about him to put in writing for our sovereign, I have brought him before you all and particularly before you, King Agrippa, so that as a result of this preliminary enquiry I may have something to report. [27] There is no sense, it seems to me, in sending on a prisoner without indicating the charges against him.'

26 Agrippa said to Paul: 'You have our permission to give an account of yourself.' Then Paul stretched out his hand and began his defence.

[2] 'I consider myself fortunate, King Agrippa, that it is before you I am to make my defence today on all the charges brought against me by the Jews, [3] particularly as you are expert in all our Jewish customs and controversies. I beg you therefore to give me a patient hearing.

[4] 'My life from my youth up, a life spent from the first among my nation and in Jerusalem, is familiar to all Jews. [5] Indeed they have known me long enough to testify, if they would, that I belonged to the strictest group in our religion: I was a Pharisee. [6] It is the hope based on the promise God made to our forefathers that has led to my being on trial today. [7] Our twelve tribes worship with intense devotion night and day in the hope of seeing the fulfilment of that promise; and for this very hope I am accused, your majesty, and accused by Jews. [8] Why should Jews find it incredible that God should raise the dead?

[9] 'I myself once thought it my duty to work actively against the name of Jesus of Nazareth; [10] and I did so in Jerusalem. By authority obtained from the chief priests, I sent many of God's people to prison, and when they were condemned to death, my vote was cast against them. [11] In all the synagogues I tried by repeated punishment to make them commit blasphemy; indeed my fury rose to such a pitch that I extended my persecution to foreign cities.

[12] 'On one such occasion I was travelling to Damascus with authority and commission from the chief priests; [13] and as I was on my way, your majesty, at midday I saw a light from the sky, more brilliant than the sun, shining all around me and my companions. [14] We all fell to the ground, and I heard a voice saying to me in the Jewish language, "Saul, Saul, why do you persecute me? It hurts to kick like this against the goad." [15] I said, "Tell me, Lord, who you are," and the Lord replied, "I am Jesus, whom you are persecuting. [16] But now, get to your feet. I have appeared to you for a purpose: to appoint you my servant and witness, to tell what you have seen and what you shall yet see of me. [17] I will rescue you from your own people and from the Gentiles to whom I am sending you. [18] You are to open their eyes and to turn them from darkness to light, from the dominion of Satan to God, so that they

may obtain forgiveness of sins and a place among those whom God has made his own through faith in me."

[19] 'So, King Agrippa, I did not disobey the heavenly vision. [20] I preached first to the inhabitants of Damascus, and then to Jerusalem and all the country of Judaea, and to the Gentiles, calling on them to repent and turn to God, and to prove their repentance by their deeds. [21] That is why the Jews seized me in the temple and tried to do away with me. [22] But I have had God's help to this very day, and here I stand bearing witness to the great and to the lowly. I assert nothing beyond what was foretold by the prophets and by Moses: [23] that the Messiah would suffer and that, as the first to rise from the dead, he would announce the dawn both to the Jewish people and to the Gentiles.'

[24] While Paul was thus making his defence, Festus shouted at the top of his voice, 'Paul, you are raving; too much study is driving you mad.' [25] 'I am not mad, your excellency,' said Paul; 'what I am asserting is sober truth. [26] The king is well versed in these matters, and I can speak freely to him. I do not believe that he can be unaware of any of these facts, for this has been no hole-and-corner business. [27] King Agrippa, do you believe the prophets? I know you do.' [28] Agrippa said to Paul, 'With a little more of your persuasion you will make a Christian of me.' [29] 'Little or much,' said Paul, 'I wish to God that not only you, but all those who are listening to me today, might become what I am—apart from these chains!'

[30] With that the king rose, and with him the governor, Bernice, and the rest of the company, [31] and after they had withdrawn they talked it over. 'This man', they agreed, 'is doing nothing that deserves death or imprisonment.' [32] Agrippa said to Festus, 'The fellow could have been discharged, if he had not appealed to the emperor.'

Paul's journey to Rome

27 WHEN it was decided that we should sail for Italy, Paul and some other prisoners were handed over to a centurion named Julius, of the Augustan Cohort. [2] We embarked in a ship of Adramyttium, bound for ports in the province of Asia, and put out to sea. Aristarchus, a Macedonian from Thessalonica, came with us. [3] Next day we landed at Sidon, and Julius very considerately allowed Paul to go to his friends to be cared for. [4] Leaving Sidon we sailed under the lee of Cyprus because of the head winds, [5] then across the open sea off the coast of Cilicia and Pamphylia, and so reached Myra in Lycia.

[6] There the centurion found an Alexandrian vessel bound for Italy and put us on board. [7] For a good many days we made little headway, and we were hard put to it to reach Cnidus. Then, as the wind continued against us, off Salmone we began to sail under the lee of Crete, [8] and, hugging the coast, struggled on to a place called Fair Havens, not far from the town of Lasea.

[9] By now much time had been lost, and with the Fast already over, it was dangerous to go on with the voyage. So Paul gave them this warning: [10] 'I can see, gentlemen, that this voyage will be disastrous; it will mean heavy loss, not only of ship and cargo but also of life.' [11] But the centurion paid more attention to the captain and to the owner of the ship than to what Paul said; [12] and as the harbour was unsuitable for wintering, the majority were in favour of putting to sea, hoping, if they could get so far, to winter at Phoenix, a Cretan harbour facing south-west and north-west. [13] When a southerly breeze sprang up, they thought that their purpose was as good as achieved, and, weighing anchor, they sailed along the coast of Crete hugging the land. [14] But before very long a violent wind, the Northeaster as they call it, swept down from the landward side. [15] It caught the ship and, as it was impossible to keep head to wind, we had to give way and run before it. [16] As we passed under the lee of a small island called Cauda, we managed with a struggle to get the ship's boat under control. [17] When they had hoisted it on board, they made use of tackle to brace the ship. Then, afraid of running on to the sandbanks of Syrtis, they put out a sea-anchor and let her drift. [18] Next day, as we were making very heavy weather, they began to lighten the

27:17 **put ... sea-anchor:** *or* lowered the mainsail.

ship; 19 and on the third day they jettisoned the ship's gear with their own hands. 20 For days on end there was no sign of either sun or stars, the storm was raging unabated, and our last hopes of coming through alive began to fade.

21 When they had gone for a long time without food, Paul stood up among them and said, 'You should have taken my advice, gentlemen, not to put out from Crete: then you would have avoided this damage and loss. 22 But now I urge you not to lose heart; not a single life will be lost, only the ship. 23 Last night there stood by me an angel of the God whose I am and whom I worship. 24 "Do not be afraid, Paul," he said; "it is ordained that you shall appear before Caesar; and, be assured, God has granted you the lives of all who are sailing with you." 25 So take heart, men! I trust God: it will turn out as I have been told; 26 we are to be cast ashore on an island.'

27 The fourteenth night came and we were still drifting in the Adriatic Sea. At midnight the sailors felt that land was getting nearer, 28 so they took a sounding and found twenty fathoms. Sounding again after a short interval they found fifteen fathoms; 29 then, fearing that we might be cast ashore on a rugged coast, they let go four anchors from the stern and prayed for daylight to come. 30 The sailors tried to abandon ship; they had already lowered the ship's boat, pretending they were going to lay out anchors from the bows, 31 when Paul said to the centurion and the soldiers, 'Unless these men stay on board you cannot reach safety.' 32 At that the soldiers cut the ropes of the boat and let it drop away.

33 Shortly before daybreak Paul urged them all to take some food. 'For the last fourteen days,' he said, 'you have lived in suspense and gone hungry; you have eaten nothing. 34 So have something to eat, I beg you; your lives depend on it. Remember, not a hair of your heads will be lost.' 35 With these words, he took bread, gave thanks to God in front of them all, broke it, and began eating. 36 Then they plucked up courage, and began to take food themselves. 37 All told there were on board two hundred and seventy-six of us. 38 After they had eaten as much as they wanted, they lightened the ship by dumping the grain into the sea.

39 When day broke, they did not recognize the land, but they sighted a bay with a sandy beach, on which they decided, if possible, to run ashore. 40 So they slipped the anchors and let them go; at the same time they loosened the lashings of the steering-paddles, set the foresail to the wind, and let her drive to the beach. 41 But they found themselves caught between cross-currents and ran the ship aground, so that the bow stuck fast and remained immovable, while the stern was being pounded to pieces by the breakers. 42 The soldiers thought they had better kill the prisoners for fear that any should swim away and escape; 43 but the centurion was determined to bring Paul safely through, and prevented them from carrying out their plan. He gave orders that those who could swim should jump overboard first and get to land; 44 the rest were to follow, some on planks, some on parts of the ship. And thus it was that all came safely to land.

28 Once we had made our way to safety, we identified the island as Malta. 2 The natives treated us with uncommon kindness: because it had started to rain and was cold they lit a bonfire and made us all welcome. 3 Paul had got together an armful of sticks and put them on the fire, when a viper, driven out by the heat, fastened on his hand. 4 The natives, seeing the snake hanging on to his hand, said to one another, 'The man must be a murderer; he may have escaped from the sea, but divine justice would not let him live.' 5 Paul, however, shook off the snake into the fire and was none the worse. 6 They still expected him to swell up or suddenly drop down dead, but after waiting a long time without seeing anything out of the way happen to him, they changed their minds and said, 'He is a god.'

7 In that neighbourhood there were lands belonging to the chief magistrate of the island, whose name was Publius. He took us in and entertained us hospitably for three days. 8 It so happened that this man's father was in bed suffering from recurrent bouts of fever and dysentery. Paul visited him and, after prayer, laid his hands on him and healed him; 9 whereupon the other sick people on the island came and were cured. 10 They honoured us with many marks of respect, and when

we were leaving they put on board the supplies we needed.

¹¹ Three months had passed when we put to sea in a ship which had wintered in the island; she was the *Castor and Pollux* of Alexandria. ¹² We landed at Syracuse and spent three days there; ¹³ then we sailed up the coast and arrived at Rhegium. Next day a south wind sprang up and we reached Puteoli in two days. ¹⁴ There we found fellow-Christians and were invited to stay a week with them. And so to Rome. ¹⁵ The Christians there had had news of us and came out to meet us as far as Appii Forum and the Three Taverns, and when Paul saw them, he gave thanks to God and took courage.

¹⁶ WHEN we entered Rome Paul was allowed to lodge privately, with a soldier in charge of him. ¹⁷ Three days later he called together the local Jewish leaders, and when they were assembled, he said to them: 'My brothers, I never did anything against our people or against the customs of our forefathers; yet I was arrested in Jerusalem and handed over to the Romans. ¹⁸ They examined me and would have liked to release me because there was no capital charge against me; ¹⁹ but the Jews objected, and I had no option but to appeal to Caesar; not that I had any accusation to bring against my own people. ²⁰ This is why I have asked to see and talk to you; it is for loyalty to the hope of Israel that I am in these chains.' ²¹ They replied, 'We have had no communication about you from Judaea, nor has any countryman of ours arrived with any report or gossip to your discredit. ²² We should like to hear from you what your views are; all we know about this sect is that no one has a good word to say for it.'

²³ So they fixed a day, and came in large numbers to his lodging. From dawn to dusk he put his case to them; he spoke urgently of the kingdom of God and sought to convince them about Jesus by appealing to the law of Moses and the prophets. ²⁴ Some were won over by his arguments; others remained unconvinced. ²⁵ Without reaching any agreement among themselves they began to disperse, but not before Paul had spoken this final word: 'How well the Holy Spirit spoke to your fathers through the prophet Isaiah ²⁶ when he said, "Go to this people and say: You may listen and listen, but you will never understand; you may look and look, but you will never see. ²⁷ For this people's mind has become dull; they have stopped their ears and closed their eyes. Otherwise, their eyes might see, their ears hear, and their mind understand, and then they might turn again, and I would heal them." ²⁸ Therefore take note that this salvation of God has been sent to the Gentiles; the Gentiles will listen.'

³⁰ He stayed there two full years at his own expense, with a welcome for all who came to him; ³¹ he proclaimed the kingdom of God and taught the facts about the Lord Jesus Christ quite openly and without hindrance.

28:28 **listen**: *some witnesses add* ²⁹ After he had spoken, the Jews went away, arguing vigorously among themselves.

THE LETTER OF PAUL TO THE

ROMANS

The gospel of Christ

1 FROM Paul, servant of Christ Jesus, called by God to be an apostle and set apart for the service of his gospel.

[2] This gospel God announced beforehand in sacred scriptures through his prophets. [3-4] It is about his Son: on the human level he was a descendant of David, but on the level of the spirit—the Holy Spirit—he was proclaimed Son of God by an act of power that raised him from the dead: it is about Jesus Christ our Lord. [5] Through him I received the privilege of an apostolic commission to bring people of all nations to faith and obedience in his name, [6] including you who have heard the call and belong to Jesus Christ.

[7] I send greetings to all of you in Rome, who are loved by God and called to be his people. Grace and peace to you from God our Father and the Lord Jesus Christ.

[8] Let me begin by thanking my God, through Jesus Christ, for you all, because the story of your faith is being told all over the world. [9] God is my witness, to whom I offer the service of my spirit by preaching the gospel of his Son: God knows that I make mention of you in my prayers continually, [10] and am always asking that by his will I may, somehow or other, at long last succeed in coming to visit you. [11] For I long to see you; I want to bring you some spiritual gift to make you strong; [12] or rather, I want us to be encouraged by one another's faith when I am with you, I by yours and you by mine.

[13] Brothers and sisters, I should like you to know that I have often planned to come, though so far without success, in the hope of achieving something among you, as I have in the rest of the gentile world. [14] I have an obligation to Greek and non-Greek, to learned and simple; [15] hence my eagerness to declare the gospel to you in Rome as well. [16] For I am not ashamed of the gospel. It is the saving power of God for everyone who has faith—the Jew first, but the Greek also—[17] because in it the righteousness of God is seen at work, beginning in faith and ending in faith; as scripture says, 'Whoever is justified through faith shall gain life.'

God's judgement on sin

[18] DIVINE retribution is to be seen at work, falling from heaven on all the impiety and wickedness of men and women who in their wickedness suppress the truth. [19] For all that can be known of God lies plain before their eyes; indeed God himself has disclosed it to them. [20] Ever since the world began his invisible attributes, that is to say his everlasting power and deity, have been visible to the eye of reason, in the things he has made. Their conduct, therefore, is indefensible; [21] knowing God, they have refused to honour him as God, or to render him thanks. Hence all their thinking has ended in futility, and their misguided minds are plunged in darkness. [22] They boast of their wisdom, but they have made fools of themselves, [23] exchanging the glory of the immortal God for an image shaped like mortal man, even for images like birds, beasts, and reptiles.

[24] For this reason God has given them up to their own vile desires, and the consequent degradation of their bodies. [25] They have exchanged the truth of God for a lie, and have offered reverence and worship to created things instead of to the Creator. Blessed is he for ever, Amen. [26] As a result God has given them up to shameful passions. Among them women have exchanged natural intercourse for unnatural, [27] and men too, giving up natural relations with women, burn with lust for one another; males behave indecently with males, and are paid in their own persons the fitting wage of such perversion.

[28] Thus, because they have not seen fit

1:3-4 **Son of God ... dead**: *or* Son of God with full power at his resurrection from the dead.   1:17 **Whoever ... life**: *or* The righteous shall live by faith.

to acknowledge God, he has given them up to their own depraved way of thinking, and this leads them to break all rules of conduct. ²⁹ They are filled with every kind of wickedness, villainy, greed, and malice; they are one mass of envy, murder, rivalry, treachery, and malevolence; gossips ³⁰ and scandalmongers; and blasphemers, insolent, arrogant, and boastful; they invent new kinds of vice, they show no respect to parents, ³¹ they are without sense or fidelity, without natural affection or pity. ³² They know well enough the just decree of God, that those who behave like this deserve to die; yet they not only do these things themselves but approve such conduct in others.

2 You have no defence, then, whoever you may be, when you sit in judgement—for in judging others you condemn yourself, since in judging you, the judge, are equally guilty. ² We all know that God's judgement on those who commit such crimes is just; ³ and do you imagine—you that pass judgement on the guilty while committing the same crimes yourself—do you imagine that you, any more than they, will escape the judgement of God? ⁴ Or do you despise his wealth of kindness and tolerance and patience, failing to see that God's kindness is meant to lead you to repentance? ⁵ In the obstinate impenitence of your heart you are laying up for yourself a store of retribution against the day of retribution, when God's just judgement will be revealed, ⁶ and he will pay everyone for what he has done. ⁷ To those who pursue glory, honour, and immortality by steady persistence in well-doing, he will give eternal life; ⁸ but the retribution of his wrath awaits those who are governed by selfish ambition, who refuse obedience to truth and take evil for their guide. ⁹ There will be affliction and distress for every human being who is a wrongdoer, for the Jew first and for the Greek also; ¹⁰ but for everyone who does right there will be glory, honour, and peace, for the Jew first and also for the Greek. ¹¹ God has no favourites.

¹² Those who have sinned outside the pale of the law of Moses will perish outside the law, and all who have sinned under that law will be judged by it. ¹³ None will be justified before God by hearing the law, but by doing it. ¹⁴ When Gentiles who do not possess the law carry out its precepts by the light of nature, then, although they have no law, they are their own law; ¹⁵ they show that what the law requires is inscribed on their hearts, and to this their conscience gives supporting witness, since their own thoughts argue the case, sometimes against them, sometimes even for them. ¹⁶ So it will be on the day when, according to my gospel, God will judge the secrets of human hearts through Christ Jesus.

The Jews and their law

¹⁷ BUT as for you who bear the name of Jew and rely on the law: you take pride in your God; ¹⁸ you know his will; taught by the law, you know what really matters; ¹⁹ you are confident that you are a guide to the blind, a light to those in darkness, ²⁰ an instructor of the foolish, and a teacher of the immature, because you possess in the law the embodiment of knowledge and truth. ²¹ You teach others, then; do you not teach yourself? You proclaim, 'Do not steal'; but are you yourself a thief? ²² You say, 'Do not commit adultery'; but are you an adulterer? You abominate false gods; but do you rob shrines? ²³ While you take pride in the law, you dishonour God by breaking it. ²⁴ As scripture says, 'Because of you the name of God is profaned among the Gentiles.'

²⁵ Circumcision has value, provided you keep the law; but if you break the law, then your circumcision is as if it had never been. ²⁶ Equally, if an uncircumcised man keeps the precepts of the law, will he not count as circumcised? ²⁷ He may be physically uncircumcised, but by fulfilling the law he will pass judgement on you who break it, for all your written code and your circumcision. ²⁸ It is not externals that make a Jew, nor an external mark in the flesh that makes circumcision. ²⁹ The real Jew is one who is inwardly a Jew, and his circumcision is of the heart, spiritual not literal; he receives his commendation not from men but from God.

3 Then what advantage has the Jew? What is the value of circumcision? ² Great, in every way. In the first place, the Jews were entrusted with the oracles of God. ³ What if some of them were unfaithful? Will their faithlessness cancel the faithfulness of God? ⁴ Certainly not!

God must be true though all men be proved liars; for we read in scripture, 'When you speak you will be vindicated; when you are accused, you will win the case.'

⁵Another question: if our injustice serves to confirm God's justice, what are we to say? Is it unjust of God (I speak of him in human terms) to bring retribution upon us? ⁶Certainly not! If God were unjust, how could he judge the world?

⁷Again, if the truth of God is displayed to his greater glory through my falsehood, why should I any longer be condemned as a sinner? ⁸Why not indeed 'do evil that good may come', as some slanderously report me as saying? To condemn such men as these is surely just.

⁹Well then, are we Jews any better off? No, not at all! For we have already drawn up the indictment that all, Jews and Greeks alike, are under the power of sin. ¹⁰Scripture says:

There is no one righteous; no, not one;
¹¹no one who understands, no one who seeks God.
¹²All have swerved aside, all alike have become debased;
there is no one to show kindness: no, not one.

¹³Their throats are open tombs,
they use their tongues for treachery,
adders' venom is on their lips,
¹⁴and their mouths are full of bitter curses.

¹⁵Their feet hasten to shed blood,
¹⁶ruin and misery mark their tracks,
¹⁷they are strangers to the path of peace,
¹⁸and reverence for God does not enter their thoughts.

¹⁹Now all the words of the law are addressed, as we know, to those who are under the law, so that no one may have anything to say in self-defence, and the whole world may be exposed to God's judgement. ²⁰For no human being can be justified in the sight of God by keeping the law: law brings only the consciousness of sin.

²¹But now, quite independently of law, though with the law and the prophets bearing witness to it, the righteousness of God has been made known; ²²it is effective through faith in Christ for all who have such faith—all, without distinction. ²³For all alike have sinned, and are deprived of the divine glory; ²⁴and all are justified by God's free grace alone, through his act of liberation in the person of Christ Jesus. ²⁵For God designed him to be the means of expiating sin by his death, effective through faith. God meant by this to demonstrate his justice, because in his forbearance he had overlooked the sins of the past—²⁶to demonstrate his justice now in the present, showing that he is himself just and also justifies anyone who puts his faith in Jesus.

²⁷What room then is left for human pride? It is excluded. And on what principle? The keeping of the law would not exclude it, but faith does. ²⁸For our argument is that people are justified by faith quite apart from any question of keeping the law.

²⁹Do you suppose God is the God of the Jews alone? Is he not the God of Gentiles also? Certainly, of Gentiles also. ³⁰For if the Lord is indeed one, he will justify the circumcised by their faith and the uncircumcised through their faith. ³¹Does this mean that we are using faith to undermine the law? By no means: we are upholding the law.

Abraham's faith

4 WHAT, then, are we to say about Abraham, our ancestor by natural descent? ²If Abraham was justified by anything he did, then he has grounds for pride. But not in the eyes of God! ³For what does scripture say? 'Abraham put his faith in God, and that faith was counted to him as righteousness.'

⁴Now if someone does a piece of work, his wages are not 'counted' to be a gift; they are paid as his due. ⁵But if someone without any work to his credit simply puts his faith in him who acquits the wrongdoer, then his faith is indeed 'counted as righteousness'. ⁶In the same sense David speaks of the happiness of the man whom God 'counts' as righteous, apart from any good works: ⁷'Happy are they', he says, 'whose lawless deeds are forgiven, whose sins are blotted out; ⁸happy is the man

3:9 **No, not at all**: *or* Not altogether.   3:25 **designed him to be**: *or* set him forth as.

whose sin the Lord does not count against him.'

⁹ Is this happiness confined to the circumcised, or is it for the uncircumcised also? We have just been saying: 'Abraham's faith was counted as righteousness.' ¹⁰ In what circumstances was it so counted? Was he circumcised at the time, or not? He was not yet circumcised, but uncircumcised; ¹¹ he received circumcision later as the sign and hallmark of that righteousness which faith had given him while he was still uncircumcised. It follows that he is the father of all who have faith when uncircumcised, and so have righteousness 'counted' to them; ¹² and at the same time he is the father of the circumcised, provided they are not merely circumcised, but also follow that path of faith which our father Abraham trod while he was still uncircumcised.

¹³ It was not through law that Abraham and his descendants were given the promise that the world should be their inheritance, but through righteousness that came from faith. ¹⁴ If the heirs are those who hold by the law, then faith becomes pointless and the promise goes for nothing; ¹⁵ law can bring only retribution, and where there is no law there can be no breach of law. ¹⁶ The promise was made on the ground of faith in order that it might be a matter of sheer grace, and that it might be valid for all Abraham's descendants, not only for those who hold by the law, but also for those who have Abraham's faith. For he is the father of us all, ¹⁷ as scripture says: 'I have appointed you to be father of many nations.' In the presence of God, the God who makes the dead live and calls into being things that are not, Abraham had faith. ¹⁸ When hope seemed hopeless, his faith was such that he became 'father of many nations', in fulfilment of the promise, 'So shall your descendants be.' ¹⁹ His faith did not weaken when he considered his own body, which was as good as dead (for he was about a hundred years old), and the deadness of Sarah's womb; ²⁰ no distrust made him doubt God's promise, but, strong in faith, he gave glory to God, ²¹ convinced that what he had promised he was able to do. ²² And that is why

Abraham's faith was 'counted to him as righteousness'.

²³ The words 'counted to him' were meant to apply not only to Abraham ²⁴ but to us; our faith too is to be 'counted', the faith in the God who raised Jesus our Lord from the dead; ²⁵ for he was given up to death for our misdeeds, and raised to life for our justification.

Life in Christ

5 THEREFORE, now that we have been justified through faith, we are at peace with God through our Lord Jesus Christ, ² who has given us access to that grace in which we now live; and we exult in the hope of the divine glory that is to be ours. ³ More than this: we even exult in our present sufferings, because we know that suffering is a source of endurance, ⁴ endurance of approval, and approval of hope. ⁵ Such hope is no fantasy; through the Holy Spirit he has given us, God's love has flooded our hearts.

⁶ It was while we were still helpless that, at the appointed time, Christ died for the wicked. ⁷ Even for a just man one of us would hardly die, though perhaps for a good man one might actually brave death; ⁸ but Christ died for us while we were yet sinners, and that is God's proof of his love towards us. ⁹ And so, since we have now been justified by Christ's sacrificial death, we shall all the more certainly be saved through him from final retribution. ¹⁰ For if, when we were God's enemies, we were reconciled to him through the death of his Son, how much more, now that we have been reconciled, shall we be saved by his life! ¹¹ But that is not all: we also exult in God through our Lord Jesus, through whom we have now been granted reconciliation.

¹² What does this imply? It was through one man that sin entered the world, and through sin death, and thus death pervaded the whole human race, inasmuch as all have sinned. ¹³ For sin was already in the world before there was law; and although in the absence of law no reckoning is kept of sin, ¹⁴ death held sway from Adam to Moses, even over those who had not sinned as Adam did, by disobeying a direct command—and

---

5:1 **we are at peace**: *some witnesses read* let us continue at peace.   5:2 **we exult**: *or* let us exult.   5:3 **we even exult**: *or* let us even exult.

Adam foreshadows the man who was to come. [15] But God's act of grace is out of all proportion to Adam's wrongdoing. For if the wrongdoing of that one man brought death upon so many, its effect is vastly exceeded by the grace of God and the gift that came to so many by the grace of the one man, Jesus Christ. [16] And again, the gift of God is not to be compared in its effect with that one man's sin; for the judicial action, following on the one offence, resulted in a verdict of condemnation, but the act of grace, following on so many misdeeds, resulted in a verdict of acquittal. [17] If, by the wrongdoing of one man, death established its reign through that one man, much more shall those who in far greater measure receive grace and the gift of righteousness live and reign through the one man, Jesus Christ.

[18] It follows, then, that as the result of one misdeed was condemnation for all people, so the result of one righteous act is acquittal and life for all. [19] For as through the disobedience of one man many were made sinners, so through the obedience of one man many will be made righteous.

[20] Law intruded into this process to multiply law-breaking. But where sin was multiplied, grace immeasurably exceeded it, [21] in order that, as sin established its reign by way of death, so God's grace might establish its reign in righteousness, and result in eternal life through Jesus Christ our Lord.

Baptism into Christ

6 WHAT are we to say, then? Shall we persist in sin, so that there may be all the more grace? [2] Certainly not! We died to sin: how can we live in it any longer? [3] Have you forgotten that when we were baptized into union with Christ Jesus we were baptized into his death? [4] By that baptism into his death we were buried with him, in order that, as Christ was raised from the dead by the glorious power of the Father, so also we might set out on a new life.

[5] For if we have become identified with him in his death, we shall also be identified with him in his resurrection. [6] We know that our old humanity has been crucified with Christ, for the destruction of the sinful self, so that we may no longer be slaves to sin, [7] because death cancels the claims of sin. [8] But if we thus died with Christ, we believe that we shall also live with him, [9] knowing as we do that Christ, once raised from the dead, is never to die again: he is no longer under the dominion of death. [10] When he died, he died to sin, once for all, and now that he lives, he lives to God. [11] In the same way you must regard yourselves as dead to sin and alive to God, in union with Christ Jesus.

[12] Therefore sin must no longer reign in your mortal body, exacting obedience to the body's desires. [13] You must no longer put any part of it at sin's disposal, as an implement for doing wrong. Put yourselves instead at the disposal of God; think of yourselves as raised from death to life, and yield your bodies to God as implements for doing right. [14] Sin shall no longer be your master, for you are no longer under law, but under grace.

[15] What then? Are we to sin, because we are not under law but under grace? Of course not! [16] You know well enough that if you bind yourselves to obey a master, you are slaves of the master you obey; and this is true whether the master is sin and the outcome death, or obedience and the outcome righteousness. [17] Once you were slaves of sin, but now, thank God, you have yielded wholehearted obedience to that pattern of teaching to which you were made subject; [18] emancipated from sin, you have become slaves of righteousness [19] (to use language that suits your human weakness). As you once yielded your bodies to the service of impurity and lawlessness, making for moral anarchy, so now you must yield them to the service of righteousness, making for a holy life.

[20] When you were slaves of sin, you were free from the control of righteousness. [21] And what gain did that bring you? Things that now make you ashamed, for their end is death. [22] But now, freed from the commands of sin and bound to the service of God, you have gains that lead to holiness, and the end is eternal life. [23] For sin pays a wage, and the wage is death, but God gives freely, and his gift is eternal life in union with Christ Jesus our Lord.

The role of the law

7 YOU must be aware, my friends—I am sure you have some knowledge of law—that a person is subject to the law

6:17 **to which ... subject:** *or* which was handed on to you.

138

only so long as he is alive. [2] For example, a married woman is by law bound to her husband while he lives; but if the husband dies, she is released from the marriage bond. [3] If, therefore, in her husband's lifetime she gives herself to another man, she will be held to be an adulteress; but if the husband dies, she is free of the law and she does not commit adultery by giving herself to another man. [4] So too, my friends, through the body of Christ you died to the law and were set free to give yourselves to another, to him who rose from the dead so that we may bear fruit for God. [5] While we lived on the level of mere human nature, the sinful passions evoked by the law were active in our bodies, and bore fruit for death. [6] But now, having died to that which held us bound, we are released from the law, to serve God in a new way, the way of the spirit in contrast to the old way of a written code.

[7] What follows? Is the law identical with sin? Of course not! Yet had it not been for the law I should never have become acquainted with sin. For example, I should never have known what it was to covet, if the law had not said, 'You shall not covet.' [8] Through that commandment sin found its opportunity, and produced in me all kinds of wrong desires. In the absence of law, sin is devoid of life. [9] There was a time when, in the absence of law, I was fully alive; but when the commandment came, sin sprang to life and I died. [10] The commandment which should have led to life proved in my experience to lead to death, [11] because in the commandment sin found its opportunity to seduce me, and through the commandment killed me. [12] So then, the law in itself is holy and the commandment is holy and just and good.

[13] Are we therefore to say that this good thing caused my death? Of course not! It was sin that killed me, and thereby sin exposed its true character: it used a good thing to bring about my death, and so, through the commandment, sin became more sinful than ever. [14] We know that the law is spiritual; but I am not: I am unspiritual, sold as a slave to sin. [15] I do not even acknowledge my own actions as mine, for what I do is not what I want to do, but what I detest. [16] But if what I do is against my will, then clearly I agree with the law and hold it to be admirable. [17] This means that it is no longer I who perform the action, but sin that dwells in me. [18] For I know that nothing good dwells in me— my unspiritual self, I mean—for though the will to do good is there, the ability to effect it is not. [19] The good which I want to do, I fail to do; but what I do is the wrong which is against my will; [20] and if what I do is against my will, clearly it is no longer I who am the agent, but sin that has its dwelling in me.

[21] I discover this principle, then: that when I want to do right, only wrong is within my reach. [22] In my inmost self I delight in the law of God, [23] but I perceive in my outward actions a different law, fighting against the law that my mind approves, and making me a prisoner under the law of sin which controls my conduct. [24] Wretched creature that I am, who is there to rescue me from this state of death? [25] Who but God? Thanks be to him through Jesus Christ our Lord! To sum up then: left to myself I serve God's law with my mind, but with my unspiritual nature I serve the law of sin.

Life through the Spirit

8 It follows that there is now no condemnation for those who are united with Christ Jesus. [2] In Christ Jesus the life-giving law of the Spirit has set you free from the law of sin and death. [3] What the law could not do, because human weakness robbed it of all potency, God has done: by sending his own Son in the likeness of our sinful nature and to deal with sin, he has passed judgement against sin within that very nature, [4] so that the commandment of the law may find fulfilment in us, whose conduct is no longer controlled by the old nature, but by the Spirit.

[5-6] Those who live on the level of the old nature have their outlook formed by it, and that spells death; but those who live on the level of the spirit have the spiritual outlook, and that is life and peace. [7] For the outlook of the unspiritual nature is enmity with God; it is not subject to the law of God and indeed it

8:3 **and to deal with sin**: *or* and as a sacrifice for sin.

cannot be; [8] those who live under its control cannot please God.

[9] But you do not live like that. You live by the spirit, since God's Spirit dwells in you; and anyone who does not possess the Spirit of Christ does not belong to Christ. [10] But if Christ is in you, then although the body is dead because of sin, yet the Spirit is your life because you have been justified. [11] Moreover, if the Spirit of him who raised Jesus from the dead dwells in you, then the God who raised Christ Jesus from the dead will also give new life to your mortal bodies through his indwelling Spirit.

[12] It follows, my friends, that our old nature has no claim on us; we are not obliged to live in that way. [13] If you do so, you must die. But if by the Spirit you put to death the base pursuits of the body, then you will live.

[14] For all who are led by the Spirit of God are sons of God. [15] The Spirit you have received is not a spirit of slavery, leading you back into a life of fear, but a Spirit of adoption, enabling us to cry 'Abba! Father!' [16] The Spirit of God affirms to our spirit that we are God's children; [17] and if children, then heirs, heirs of God and fellow-heirs with Christ; but we must share his sufferings if we are also to share his glory.

[18] For I reckon that the sufferings we now endure bear no comparison with the glory, as yet unrevealed, which is in store for us. [19] The created universe is waiting with eager expectation for God's sons to be revealed. [20] It was made subject to frustration, not of its own choice but by the will of him who subjected it, yet with the hope [21] that the universe itself is to be freed from the shackles of mortality and is to enter upon the glorious liberty of the children of God. [22] Up to the present, as we know, the whole created universe in all its parts groans as if in the pangs of childbirth. [23] What is more, we also, to whom the Spirit is given as the firstfruits of the harvest to come, are groaning inwardly while we look forward eagerly to our adoption, our liberation from mortality. [24] It was with this hope that we were saved. Now to see something is no longer to hope: why hope for what is already seen? [25] But if we hope for something we

do not yet see, then we look forward to it eagerly and with patience.

[26] In the same way the Spirit comes to the aid of our weakness. We do not even know how we ought to pray, but through our inarticulate groans the Spirit himself is pleading for us, [27] and God who searches our inmost being knows what the Spirit means, because he pleads for God's people as God himself wills; [28] and in everything, as we know, he co-operates for good with those who love God and are called according to his purpose. [29] For those whom God knew before ever they were, he also ordained to share the likeness of his Son, so that he might be the eldest among a large family of brothers; [30] and those whom he foreordained, he also called, and those whom he called he also justified, and those whom he justified he also glorified.

[31] With all this in mind, what are we to say? If God is on our side, who is against us? [32] He did not spare his own Son, but gave him up for us all; how can he fail to lavish every other gift upon us? [33] Who will bring a charge against those whom God has chosen? Not God, who acquits! [34] Who will pronounce judgement? Not Christ, who died, or rather rose again; not Christ, who is at God's right hand and pleads our cause! [35] Then what can separate us from the love of Christ? Can affliction or hardship? Can persecution, hunger, nakedness, danger, or sword? [36] 'We are being done to death for your sake all day long,' as scripture says; 'we have been treated like sheep for slaughter' —[37] and yet, throughout it all, overwhelming victory is ours through him who loved us. [38] For I am convinced that there is nothing in death or life, in the realm of spirits or superhuman powers, in the world as it is or the world as it shall be, in the forces of the universe, [39] in heights or depths—nothing in all creation that can separate us from the love of God in Christ Jesus our Lord.

Israel and the Gentiles in God's plan

9 I AM speaking the truth as a Christian; my conscience, enlightened by the Holy Spirit, assures me that I do not lie when I tell you [2] that there is great grief

---

8:24 **why hope for:** *some witnesses read* why endure.   8:28 **and in everything ... God:** *or* and, as we know, all things work together for good for those who love God; *some witnesses read* and we know God himself co-operates for good with those who love God.

and unceasing sorrow in my heart. [3] I would even pray to be an outcast myself, cut off from Christ, if it would help my brothers, my kinsfolk by natural descent. [4] They are descendants of Israel, chosen to be God's sons; theirs is the glory of the divine presence, theirs the covenants, the law, the temple worship, and the promises. [5] The patriarchs are theirs, and from them by natural descent came the Messiah. May God, supreme above all, be blessed for ever! Amen.

[6] It cannot be that God's word has proved false. Not all the offspring of Israel are truly Israel, [7] nor does being Abraham's descendants make them all his true children; but, in the words of scripture, 'It is through the line of Isaac's descendants that your name will be traced.' [8] That is to say, it is not the children of Abraham by natural descent who are children of God; it is the children born through God's promise who are reckoned as Abraham's descendants. [9] For the promise runs: 'In due season I will come, and Sarah shall have a son.'

[10] And that is not all: Rebecca's children had one and the same father, our ancestor Isaac; [11] yet, even before they were born, when they as yet had done nothing, whether good or ill, in order that the purpose of God, which is a matter of his choice, might stand firm, based not on human deeds but on the call of God, [12] she was told, 'The elder shall be servant to the younger.' [13] That accords with the text of scripture, 'Jacob I loved and Esau I hated.'

[14] What shall we say to that? Is God to be charged with injustice? Certainly not! [15] He says to Moses, 'I will show mercy to whom I will show mercy, and have pity on whom I will have pity.' [16] Thus it does not depend on human will or effort, but on God's mercy. [17] For in scripture Pharaoh is told, 'I have raised you up for this very purpose, to exhibit my power in my dealings with you, and to spread my fame over all the earth.' [18] Thus he not only shows mercy as he chooses, but also makes stubborn as he chooses.

[19] You will say, 'Then why does God find fault, if no one can resist his will?' [20] Who do you think you are to answer God back? Can the pot say to the potter, 'Why did you make me like this?'? [21] Surely the potter can do what he likes with the clay. Is he not free to make two vessels out of the same lump, one to be treasured, the other for common use?

[22] But if it is indeed God's purpose to display his retribution and to make his power known, can it be that he has with great patience tolerated vessels that were objects of retribution due for destruction, [23] precisely in order to make known the full wealth of his glory on vessels that were objects of mercy, prepared from the first for glory?

[24] We are those objects of mercy, whom he has called from among Jews and Gentiles alike, [25] as he says in Hosea: 'Those who were not my people I will call my people, and the unloved I will call beloved. [26] In the very place where they were told, "You are no people of mine," they shall be called sons of the living God.' [27] But about Israel Isaiah makes this proclamation: 'Though the Israelites be countless as the sands of the sea, only a remnant shall be saved, [28] for the Lord's sentence on the land will be summary and final'; [29] as also he said previously, 'If the Lord of Hosts had not left us descendants, we should have become like Sodom, and no better than Gomorrah.'

[30] Then what are we to say? That Gentiles, who made no effort after righteousness, nevertheless achieved it, a righteousness based on faith; [31] whereas Israel made great efforts after a law of righteousness, but never attained to it. [32] Why was this? Because their efforts were not based on faith but, mistakenly, on deeds. They tripped over the 'stone' [33] mentioned in scripture: 'Here I lay in Zion a stone to trip over, a rock to stumble against; but he who has faith in it will not be put to shame.'

10 Friends, my heart's desire and my prayer to God is for their salvation. [2] To their zeal for God I can testify; but it is an ill-informed zeal. [3] For they ignore God's way of righteousness, and try to set up their own, and therefore they have not submitted themselves to God's righteousness; [4] for Christ is the end of the law and brings righteousness for everyone who has faith.

9:5 **Messiah**: *Gk* Christ. **Messiah ... for ever**: *or* Messiah, who is God, supreme above all and blessed for ever; *or* Messiah, who is supreme above all. Blessed be God for ever!   9:7 **all ... children**: *or* all children of God.

⁵ Of righteousness attained through the law Moses writes, 'Anyone who keeps it shall have life by it.' ⁶ But the righteousness that comes by faith says, 'Do not say to yourself, "Who can go up to heaven?"' (that is, to bring Christ down) ⁷ 'or, "Who can go down to the abyss?"' (to bring Christ up from the dead). ⁸ And what does it say next? 'The word is near you: it is on your lips and in your heart'; and that means the word of faith which we proclaim. ⁹ If the confession 'Jesus is Lord' is on your lips, and the faith that God raised him from the dead is in your heart, you will find salvation. ¹⁰ For faith in the heart leads to righteousness, and confession on the lips leads to salvation.

¹¹ Scripture says, 'No one who has faith in him will be put to shame': ¹² there is no distinction between Jew and Greek, because the same Lord is Lord of all, and has riches enough for all who call on him. ¹³ For 'Everyone who calls on the name of the Lord will be saved.' ¹⁴ But how could they call on him without having faith in him? And how could they have faith without having heard of him? And how could they hear without someone to spread the news? ¹⁵ And how could anyone spread the news without being sent? As scripture says, 'How welcome are the feet of the messengers of good news!' ¹⁶ It is true that not all have responded to the good news; as Isaiah says, 'Lord, who believed when they heard us?' ¹⁷ So then faith does come from hearing, and hearing through the word of Christ.

¹⁸ I ask, then: Can it be that they never heard? Of course they did: 'Their voice has sounded all over the world, and their words to the ends of the earth.' ¹⁹ I ask again: Can it be that Israel never understood? Listen first to Moses: 'I will use a nation that is no nation to stir you to envy, and a foolish nation to rouse your anger.' ²⁰ Isaiah is still more daring: 'I was found', he says, 'by those who were not looking for me; I revealed myself to those who never asked about me'; ²¹ while of Israel he says, 'All day long I have stretched out my hands to a disobedient and defiant people.'

11 I ASK, then: Has God rejected his people? Of course not! I am an Israelite myself, of the stock of Abraham, of the tribe of Benjamin. ² God has not rejected the people he acknowledged of old as his own. Surely you know what scripture says in the story of Elijah—how he pleads with God against Israel: ³ 'Lord, they have killed your prophets, they have torn down your altars, and I alone am left, and they are seeking my life.' ⁴ But what was the divine word to him? 'I have left myself seven thousand men who have not knelt to Baal.' ⁵ In just the same way at the present time a 'remnant' has come into being, chosen by the grace of God. ⁶ But if it is by grace, then it does not rest on deeds, or grace would cease to be grace.

⁷ What follows? What Israel sought, Israel has not attained, but the chosen few have attained it. The rest were hardened, ⁸ as it stands written: 'God has dulled their senses; he has given them blind eyes and deaf ears, and so it is to this day.' ⁹ Similarly David says:

May their table be a snare and a trap,
their downfall and their retribution!
¹⁰ May their eyes become darkened and blind!
Bow down their backs unceasingly!

¹¹ I ask, then: When they stumbled, was their fall final? Far from it! Through a false step on their part salvation has come to the Gentiles, and this in turn will stir them to envy. ¹² If their false step means the enrichment of the world, if their falling short means the enrichment of the Gentiles, how much more will their coming to full strength mean!

¹³ It is to you Gentiles that I am speaking. As an apostle to the Gentiles, I make much of that ministry, ¹⁴ yet always in the hope of stirring those of my own race to envy, and so saving some of them. ¹⁵ For if their rejection has meant the reconciliation of the world, what will their acceptance mean? Nothing less than life from the dead! ¹⁶ If the first loaf is holy, so is the whole batch. If the root is holy, so are the branches. ¹⁷ But if some of the branches have been lopped off, and you, a wild olive, have been grafted in among them, and have come to share the same root and sap as the olive, ¹⁸ do not make yourself superior to the branches. If you do, remember that you do not sustain the root: the root sustains you.

¹⁹ You will say, 'Branches were lopped

off so that I might be grafted in.' ²⁰ Very well: they were lopped off for lack of faith, and by faith you hold your place. Put away your pride, and be on your guard; ²¹ for if God did not spare the natural branches, no more will he spare you. ²² Observe the kindness and the severity of God—severity to those who fell away, divine kindness to you provided that you remain within its scope; otherwise you too will be cut off, ²³ whereas they, if they do not continue faithless, will be grafted in, since it is in God's power to graft them in again. ²⁴ For if you were cut from your native wild olive and against nature grafted into the cultivated olive, how much more readily will they, the natural olive branches, be grafted into their native stock!

²⁵ There is a divine secret here, my friends, which I want to share with you, to keep you from thinking yourselves wise: this partial hardening has come on Israel only until the Gentiles have been admitted in full strength; ²⁶ once that has happened, the whole of Israel will be saved, in accordance with scripture:

From Zion shall come the Deliverer;
he shall remove wickedness from
    Jacob.
²⁷ And this is the covenant I will grant
    them,
when I take away their sins.

²⁸ Judged by their response to the gospel, they are God's enemies for your sake; but judged by his choice, they are dear to him for the sake of the patriarchs; ²⁹ for the gracious gifts of God and his calling are irrevocable. ³⁰ Just as formerly you were disobedient to God, but now have received mercy because of their disobedience, ³¹ so now, because of the mercy shown to you, they have proved disobedient, but only in order that they too may receive mercy. ³² For in shutting all mankind in the prison of their disobedience, God's purpose was to show mercy to all mankind.

³³ How deep are the wealth
    and the wisdom and the knowledge
        of God!
How inscrutable his judgements,
    how unsearchable his ways!
³⁴ 'Who knows the mind of the Lord?
    Who has been his counsellor?'
³⁵ 'Who has made a gift to him first,

and earned a gift in return?'
³⁶ From him and through him and for
    him all things exist—
to him be glory for ever! Amen.

Christian service and the community

12 THEREFORE, my friends, I implore you by God's mercy to offer your very selves to him: a living sacrifice, dedicated and fit for his acceptance, the worship offered by mind and heart. ² Conform no longer to the pattern of this present world, but be transformed by the renewal of your minds. Then you will be able to discern the will of God, and to know what is good, acceptable, and perfect.

³ By authority of the grace God has given me I say to everyone among you: do not think too highly of yourself, but form a sober estimate based on the measure of faith that God has dealt to each of you. ⁴ For just as in a single human body there are many limbs and organs, all with different functions, ⁵ so we who are united with Christ, though many, form one body, and belong to one another as its limbs and organs.

⁶ Let us use the different gifts allotted to each of us by God's grace: the gift of inspired utterance, for example, let us use in proportion to our faith; ⁷ the gift of administration to administer, the gift of teaching to teach, ⁸ the gift of counselling to counsel. If you give to charity, give without grudging; if you are a leader, lead with enthusiasm; if you help others in distress, do it cheerfully.

⁹ Love in all sincerity, loathing evil and holding fast to the good. ¹⁰ Let love of the Christian community show itself in mutual affection. Esteem others more highly than yourself. ¹¹ With unflagging zeal, aglow with the Spirit, serve the Lord. ¹² Let hope keep you joyful; in trouble stand firm; persist in prayer; ¹³ contribute to the needs of God's people, and practise hospitality. ¹⁴ Call down blessings on your persecutors— blessings, not curses. ¹⁵ Rejoice with those who rejoice, weep with those who weep. ¹⁶ Live in agreement with one another. Do not be proud, but be ready to mix with humble people. Do not keep thinking how wise you are.

¹⁷ Never pay back evil for evil. Let your aims be such as all count honourable. ¹⁸ If

possible, so far as it lies with you, live at peace with all. ¹⁹ My dear friends, do not seek revenge, but leave a place for divine retribution; for there is a text which reads, 'Vengeance is mine, says the Lord, I will repay.' ²⁰ But there is another text: 'If your enemy is hungry, feed him; if he is thirsty, give him a drink; by doing this you will heap live coals on his head.' ²¹ Do not let evil conquer you, but use good to conquer evil.

13 Every person must submit to the authorities in power, for all authority comes from God, and the existing authorities are instituted by him. ² It follows that anyone who rebels against authority is resisting a divine institution, and those who resist have themselves to thank for the punishment they will receive. ³ Governments hold no terrors for the law-abiding but only for the criminal. You wish to have no fear of the authorities? Then continue to do right and you will have their approval, ⁴ for they are God's agents working for your good. But if you are doing wrong, then you will have cause to fear them; it is not for nothing that they hold the power of the sword, for they are God's agents of punishment bringing retribution on the offender. ⁵ That is why you are obliged to submit. It is an obligation imposed not merely by fear of retribution but by conscience. ⁶ That is also why you pay taxes. The authorities are in God's service and it is to this they devote their energies.

⁷ Discharge your obligations to everyone; pay tax and levy, reverence and respect, to those to whom they are due. ⁸ Leave no debt outstanding, but remember the debt of love you owe one another. He who loves his neighbour has met every requirement of the law. ⁹ The commandments, 'You shall not commit adultery, you shall not commit murder, you shall not steal, you shall not covet,' and any other commandment there may be, are all summed up in the one rule, 'Love your neighbour as yourself.' ¹⁰ Love cannot wrong a neighbour; therefore love is the fulfilment of the law.

¹¹ Always remember that this is the hour of crisis: it is high time for you to wake out of sleep, for deliverance is nearer to us now than it was when first we believed. ¹² It is far on in the night; day is near. Let us therefore throw off the deeds of darkness and put on the armour of light. ¹³ Let us behave with decency as befits the day: no drunken orgies, no debauchery or vice, no quarrels or jealousies! ¹⁴ Let Christ Jesus himself be the armour that you wear; give your unspiritual nature no opportunity to satisfy its desires.

14 ACCEPT anyone who is weak in faith without debate about his misgivings. ² For instance, one person may have faith strong enough to eat all kinds of food, while another who is weaker eats only vegetables. ³ Those who eat meat must not look down on those who do not, and those who do not eat meat must not pass judgement on those who do; for God has accepted them. ⁴ Who are you to pass judgement on someone else's servant? Whether he stands or falls is his own Master's business; and stand he will, because his Master has power to enable him to stand.

⁵ Again, some make a distinction between this day and that; others regard all days alike. Everyone must act on his own convictions. ⁶ Those who honour the day honour the Lord, and those who eat meat also honour the Lord, since when they eat they give thanks to God; and those who abstain have the Lord in mind when abstaining, since they too give thanks to God.

⁷ For none of us lives, and equally none of us dies, for himself alone. ⁸ If we live, we live for the Lord; and if we die, we die for the Lord. So whether we live or die, we belong to the Lord. ⁹ This is why Christ died and lived again, to establish his lordship over both dead and living. ¹⁰ You, then, why do you pass judgement on your fellow-Christian? And you, why do you look down on your fellow-Christian? We shall all stand before God's tribunal; ¹¹ for we read in scripture, 'As I live, says the Lord, to me every knee shall bow and every tongue acknowledge God.' ¹² So, you see, each of us will be answerable to God.

¹³ Let us therefore cease judging one another, but rather make up our minds to place no obstacle or stumbling block in a fellow-Christian's way. ¹⁴ All that I know

13:10 **the fulfilment of the law:** *or* the whole content of the law.

of the Lord Jesus convinces me that nothing is impure in itself; only, if anyone considers something impure, then for him it is impure. [15] If your fellow-Christian is outraged by what you eat, then you are no longer guided by love. Do not by your eating be the ruin of one for whom Christ died! [16] You must not let what you think good be brought into disrepute; [17] for the kingdom of God is not eating and drinking, but justice, peace, and joy, inspired by the Holy Spirit. [18] Everyone who shows himself a servant of Christ in this way is acceptable to God and approved by men.

[19] Let us, then, pursue the things that make for peace and build up the common life. [20] Do not destroy the work of God for the sake of food. Everything is pure in itself, but it is wrong to eat if by eating you cause another to stumble. [21] It is right to abstain from eating meat or drinking wine or from anything else which causes a fellow-Christian to stumble. [22] If you have some firm conviction, keep it between yourself and God. Anyone who can make his decision without misgivings is fortunate. [23] But anyone who has misgivings and yet eats is guilty, because his action does not arise from conviction, and anything which does not arise from conviction is sin.

15 [1] Those of us who are strong must accept as our own burden the tender scruples of the weak, and not just please ourselves. [2] Each of us must consider his neighbour and think what is for his good and will build up the common life. [3] Christ too did not please himself; to him apply the words of scripture, 'The reproaches of those who reproached you fell on me.' [4] The scriptures written long ago were all written for our instruction, in order that through the encouragement they give us we may maintain our hope with perseverance. [5] And may God, the source of all perseverance and all encouragement, grant that you may agree with one another after the manner of Christ Jesus, [6] and so with one mind and one voice may praise the God and Father of our Lord Jesus Christ.

[7] In a word, accept one another as Christ accepted us, to the glory of God. [8] Remember that Christ became a servant of the Jewish people to maintain the faithfulness of God by making good his promises to the patriarchs, [9] and by giving the Gentiles cause to glorify God for his mercy. As scripture says, 'Therefore I will praise you among the Gentiles and sing hymns to your name'; [10] and again, 'Gentiles, join in celebration with his people'; [11] and yet again, 'All Gentiles, praise the Lord; let all peoples praise him.' [12] Once again, Isaiah says, 'The Scion of Jesse shall come, a ruler who rises to govern the Gentiles; on him shall they set their hope.' [13] And may God, who is the ground of hope, fill you with all joy and peace as you lead the life of faith until, by the power of the Holy Spirit, you overflow with hope.

[14] My friends, I have no doubt in my own mind that you yourselves are full of goodness and equipped with knowledge of every kind, well able to give advice to one another; [15] nevertheless I have written to refresh your memory, and written somewhat boldly at times, in virtue of the gift I have from God. [16] His grace has made me a minister of Christ Jesus to the Gentiles; and in the service of the gospel of God it is my priestly task to offer the Gentiles to him as an acceptable sacrifice, consecrated by the Holy Spirit.

[17] In Christ Jesus I have indeed grounds for pride in the service of God. [18] I will venture to speak only of what Christ has done through me to bring the Gentiles into his allegiance, by word and deed, [19] by the power of signs and portents, and by the power of the Holy Spirit. I have completed the preaching of the gospel of Christ from Jerusalem as far round as Illyricum. [20] But I have always made a point of taking the gospel to places where the name of Christ has not been heard, not wanting to build on another man's foundation; [21] as scripture says,

Those who had no news of him shall see,
and those who never heard of him shall understand.

[22] That is why I have been prevented all this time from coming to you. [23] But now I have no further scope in these parts, and I

have been longing for many years to visit you [24] on my way to Spain; for I hope to see you in passing, and to be sent on my way there with your support after having enjoyed your company for a while. [25] But at the moment I am on my way to Jerusalem, on an errand to God's people there. [26] For Macedonia and Achaia have resolved to raise a fund for the benefit of the poor among God's people at Jerusalem. [27] They have resolved to do so, and indeed they are under an obligation to them. For if the Jewish Christians shared their spiritual treasures with the Gentiles, the Gentiles have a clear duty to contribute to their material needs. [28] So when I have finished this business and seen the proceeds safely delivered to them, I shall set out for Spain and visit you on the way; [29] I am sure that when I come it will be with a full measure of the blessing of Christ.

[30] I implore you by our Lord Jesus Christ and by the love that the Spirit inspires, be my allies in the fight; pray to God for me [31] that I may be saved from unbelievers in Judaea and that my errand to Jerusalem may find acceptance with God's people, [32] in order that by his will I may come to you in a happy frame of mind and enjoy a time of rest with you. [33] The God of peace be with you all. Amen.

Greetings

16 I commend to you Phoebe, a fellow-Christian who is a minister in the church at Cenchreae. [2] Give her, in the fellowship of the Lord, a welcome worthy of God's people, and support her in any business in which she may need your help, for she has herself been a good friend to many, including myself.

[3] Give my greetings to Prisca and Aquila, my fellow-workers in Christ Jesus. [4] They risked their necks to save my life, and not I alone but all the gentile churches are grateful to them. [5] Greet also the church that meets at their house.

Give my greetings to my dear friend Epaenetus, the first convert to Christ in Asia, [6] and to Mary, who worked so hard for you. [7] Greet Andronicus and Junia, my fellow-countrymen and comrades in captivity, who are eminent among the apostles and were Christians before I was.

[8] Greetings to Ampliatus, my dear friend in the fellowship of the Lord, [9] to Urban my comrade in Christ, and to my dear Stachys. [10] My greetings to Apelles, well proved in Christ's service, to the household of Aristobulus, [11] to my countryman Herodion, and to those of the household of Narcissus who are in the Lord's fellowship. [12] Greet Tryphaena and Tryphosa, who work hard in the Lord's service, and dear Persis who has worked hard in his service for so long. [13] Give my greetings to Rufus, an outstanding follower of the Lord, and to his mother, whom I call mother too. [14] Greet Asyncritus, Phlegon, Hermes, Patrobas, Hermas, and any other Christians who are with them. [15] Greet Philologus and Julia, Nereus and his sister, and Olympas, and all God's people who are with them.

[16] Greet one another with the kiss of peace. All Christ's churches send you their greetings.

[17] I implore you, my friends, keep an eye on those who stir up quarrels and lead others astray, contrary to the teaching you received. Avoid them; [18] such people are servants not of Christ our Lord but of their own appetites, and they seduce the minds of simple people with smooth and specious words. [19] The fame of your obedience has spread everywhere, and this makes me happy about you. I want you to be expert in goodness, but innocent of evil, [20] and the God of peace will soon crush Satan beneath your feet. The grace of our Lord Jesus be with you!

[21] Greetings to you from my colleague Timothy, and from Lucius, Jason, and Sosipater my fellow-countrymen. [22] (I Tertius, who took this letter down, add my Christian greetings.) [23] Greetings also from Gaius, my host and host of the whole congregation, and from Erastus, treasurer of this city, and our brother Quartus.

[25] To him who has power to make you stand firm, according to my gospel and the proclamation of Jesus Christ, according to the revelation of that divine secret kept in silence for long ages [26] but now

15:33 *See note on* 16:27.   16:1 **minister:** *or* deacon.   16:7 **Junia:** *or* Junias.   16:15 **Julia:** *or* Julias.   16:20 **The grace ... with you:** *These words are omitted at this point in some witnesses; in some, these or similar words are given as verse 24, and in some others after verse 27.*   16:23 *After this verse some witnesses add* [24] The grace of our Lord Jesus Christ be with you all! Amen.

disclosed, and by the eternal God's command made known to all nations through prophetic scriptures, to bring them to faith and obedience—27 to the only wise God through Jesus Christ be glory for endless ages! Amen.

16:27 *After this verse some witnesses add* The grace of our Lord Jesus Christ be with you! *Some witnesses place verses 25–27 at the end of chapter 14, one other places them at the end of chapter 15, and others omit them altogether.*

THE FIRST LETTER OF PAUL TO THE
CORINTHIANS

1 FROM Paul, apostle of Christ Jesus by God's call and by his will, together with our colleague Sosthenes, 2 to God's church at Corinth, dedicated to him in Christ Jesus, called to be his people, along with all who invoke the name of our Lord Jesus Christ wherever they may be—their Lord as well as ours.

3 Grace and peace to you from God our Father and the Lord Jesus Christ.

4 I am always thanking God for you. I thank him for his grace given to you in Christ Jesus; 5 I thank him for all the enrichment that has come to you in Christ. You possess full knowledge and you can give full expression to it, 6 because what we testified about Christ has been confirmed in your experience. 7 There is indeed no single gift you lack, while you wait expectantly for our Lord Jesus Christ to reveal himself. 8 He will keep you firm to the end, without reproach on the day of our Lord Jesus. 9 It is God himself who called you to share in the life of his Son Jesus Christ our Lord; and God keeps faith.

True and false wisdom

10 I APPEAL to you, my friends, in the name of our Lord Jesus Christ: agree among yourselves, and avoid divisions; let there be complete unity of mind and thought. 11 My friends, it has been brought to my notice by Chloe's people that there are quarrels among you. 12 What I mean is this: each of you is saying, 'I am for Paul,' or 'I am for Apollos'; 'I am for Cephas,' or 'I am for Christ.' 13 Surely Christ has not been divided! Was it Paul who was crucified for you? Was it in Paul's name that you were baptized? 14 Thank God, I never baptized any of you, except Crispus and Gaius; 15 no one can say you were baptized in my name. 16 I did of course baptize the household of Stephanas; I cannot think of anyone else. 17 Christ did not send me to baptize, but to proclaim the gospel; and to do it without recourse to the skills of rhetoric, lest the cross of Christ be robbed of its effect.

18 The message of the cross is sheer folly to those on the way to destruction, but to us, who are on the way to salvation, it is the power of God. 19 Scripture says, 'I will destroy the wisdom of the wise, and bring to nothing the cleverness of the clever.' 20 Where is your wise man now, your man of learning, your subtle debater of this present age? God has made the wisdom of this world look foolish! 21 As God in his wisdom ordained, the world failed to find him by its wisdom, and he chose by the folly of the gospel to save those who have faith. 22 Jews demand signs, Greeks look for wisdom, 23 but we proclaim Christ nailed to the cross; and though this is an offence to Jews and folly to Gentiles, 24 yet to those who are called, Jews and Greeks alike, he is the power of God and the wisdom of God.

25 The folly of God is wiser than human wisdom, and the weakness of God stronger than human strength. 26 My friends, think what sort of people you are, whom God has called. Few of you are wise by any human standard, few powerful or of noble birth. 27 Yet, to shame the wise, God has chosen what the world counts folly, and to shame what is strong, God has chosen what the world counts weakness. 28 He has chosen things without

rank or standing in the world, mere nothings, to overthrow the existing order. [29] So no place is left for any human pride in the presence of God. [30] By God's act you are in Christ Jesus; God has made him our wisdom, and in him we have our righteousness, our holiness, our liberation. [31] Therefore, in the words of scripture, 'If anyone must boast, let him boast of the Lord.'

2 So it was, my friends, that I came to you, without any pretensions to eloquence or wisdom in declaring the truth about God. [2] I resolved that while I was with you I would not claim to know anything but Jesus Christ—Christ nailed to the cross. [3] I came before you in weakness, in fear, in great trepidation. [4] The word I spoke, the gospel I proclaimed, did not sway you with clever arguments; it carried conviction by spiritual power, [5] so that your faith might be built not on human wisdom but on the power of God.

[6] Among the mature I do speak words of wisdom, though not a wisdom belonging to this present age or to its governing powers, already in decline; [7] I speak God's hidden wisdom, his secret purpose framed from the very beginning to bring us to our destined glory. [8] None of the powers that rule the world has known that wisdom; if they had, they would not have crucified the Lord of glory. [9] Scripture speaks of 'things beyond our seeing, things beyond our hearing, things beyond our imagining, all prepared by God for those who love him'; [10] and these are what God has revealed to us through the Spirit. For the Spirit explores everything, even the depths of God's own nature. [11] Who knows what a human being is but the human spirit within him? In the same way, only the Spirit of God knows what God is. [12] And we have received this Spirit from God, not the spirit of the world, so that we may know all that God has lavished on us; [13] and, because we are interpreting spiritual truths to those who have the Spirit, we speak of these gifts of God in words taught us not by our human wisdom but by the Spirit. [14] An unspiritual person refuses what belongs to the Spirit of God; it is folly to him; he cannot grasp it, because it needs to be judged in the light of the Spirit. [15] But a spiritual person can judge the worth of everything, yet is not himself subject to judgement by others. [16] Scripture indeed asks, 'Who can know the mind of the Lord or be his counsellor?' Yet we possess the mind of Christ.

Servants of Christ

3 But I could not talk to you, my friends, as people who have the Spirit; I had to deal with you on the natural plane, as infants in Christ. [2] I fed you on milk, instead of solid food, for which you were not yet ready. Indeed, you are still not ready for it; [3] you are still on the merely natural plane. Can you not see that as long as there is jealousy and strife among you, you are unspiritual, living on the purely human level? [4] When one declares, 'I am for Paul,' and another, 'I am for Apollos,' are you not all too human?

[5] After all, what is Apollos? What is Paul? Simply God's agents in bringing you to faith. Each of us performed the task which the Lord assigned to him: [6] I planted the seed, and Apollos watered it; but God made it grow. [7] It is not the gardeners with their planting and watering who count, but God who makes it grow. [8] Whether they plant or water, they work as a team, though each will get his own pay for his own labour. [9] We are fellow-workers in God's service; and you are God's garden.

Or again, you are God's building. [10] God gave me the privilege of laying the foundation like a skilled master builder; others put up the building. Let each take care how he builds. [11] There can be no other foundation than the one already laid: I mean Jesus Christ himself. [12] If anyone builds on that foundation with gold, silver, and precious stones, or with wood, hay, and straw, [13] the work that each does will at last be brought to light; the day of judgement will expose it. For that day dawns in fire, and the fire will test the worth of each person's work. [14] If anyone's building survives, he will be rewarded; [15] if it burns down, he will have to bear the loss; yet he will escape with his life, though only by passing through the

2:1 declaring ... God: *some witnesses read* declaring God's secret purpose.   3:9 We ... service: *or* We are God's fellow-workers.

fire. [16] Surely you know that you are God's temple, where the Spirit of God dwells. [17] Anyone who destroys God's temple will himself be destroyed by God, because the temple of God is holy; and you are that temple.

[18] Make no mistake about this: if there is anyone among you who fancies himself wise—wise, I mean, by the standards of this age—he must become a fool if he is to be truly wise. [19] For the wisdom of this world is folly in God's sight. Scripture says, 'He traps the wise in their own cunning,' [20] and again, 'The Lord knows that the arguments of the wise are futile.' [21] So never make any human being a cause for boasting. For everything belongs to you—[22] Paul, Apollos, and Cephas, the world, life, and death, the present and the future, all are yours—[23] and you belong to Christ, and Christ to God.

4 We are to be regarded as Christ's subordinates and as stewards of the secrets of God. [2] Now stewards are required to show themselves trustworthy. [3] To me it matters not at all if I am called to account by you or by any human court. Nor do I pass judgement on myself, [4] for I have nothing on my conscience; but that does not prove me innocent. My judge is the Lord. [5] So pass no premature judgement; wait until the Lord comes. He will bring to light what darkness hides and disclose our inward motives; then will be the time for each to receive commendation from God.

[6] My friends, I have applied all this to Apollos and myself for your benefit, so that you may take our case as an example, and learn the true meaning of 'nothing beyond what stands written', and may not be inflated with pride as you take sides in support of one against another. [7] My friend, who makes you so important? What do you possess that was not given you? And if you received it as a gift, why take the credit to yourself?

[8] No doubt you already have all you could desire; you have come into your fortune already! Without us you have come into your kingdom. How I wish you had indeed come into your kingdom; then you might share it with us! [9] For it seems to me God has made us apostles the last act in the show, like men condemned to death in the arena, a spectacle to the whole universe—to angels as well as men. [10] We are fools for Christ's sake, while you are sensible Christians! We are weak; you are powerful! You are honoured; we are in disgrace! [11] To this day we go hungry and thirsty and in rags; we are beaten up; we wander from place to place; [12] we wear ourselves out earning a living with our own hands. People curse us, and we bless; they persecute us, and we submit; [13] they slander us, and we try to be conciliatory. To this day we are treated as the scum of the earth, as the dregs of humanity.

[14] I am not writing this to shame you, but to bring you to reason; for you are my dear children. [15] You may have thousands of tutors in Christ, but you have only one father; for in Christ Jesus you are my offspring, and mine alone, through the preaching of the gospel. [16] I appeal to you therefore to follow my example. [17] That is why I have sent Timothy, who is a dear son to me and a trustworthy Christian, to remind you of my way of life in Christ, something I teach everywhere in all the churches. [18] There are certain persons who are filled with self-importance because they think I am not coming to Corinth. [19] I shall come very soon, if it is the Lord's will; and then I shall take the measure of these self-important people, not by what they say, but by what they can do, [20] for the kingdom of God is not a matter of words, but of power. [21] Choose, then: am I to come to you with a rod in my hand, or with love and a gentle spirit?

Sexual immorality

5 I ACTUALLY hear reports of sexual immorality among you, immorality such as even pagans do not tolerate: the union of a man with his stepmother. [2] And you are proud of yourselves! You ought to have gone into mourning; anyone who behaves like that should be turned out of your community. [3] For my part, though I am absent in body, I am present in spirit, and have already reached my judgement on the man who did this thing, as if I were indeed present: [4] when you are all assembled in the name of our Lord Jesus, and I am with you in spirit, through the power of our Lord Jesus you are [5] to consign this man to Satan for the destruction of his body, so that his spirit may be saved on the day of the Lord.

[6] Your self-satisfaction ill becomes you. Have you never heard the saying, 'A little leaven leavens all the dough'? [7] Get rid of the old leaven and then you will be a new batch of unleavened dough. Indeed you already are, because Christ our Passover lamb has been sacrificed. [8] So we who observe the festival must not use the old leaven, the leaven of depravity and wickedness, but only the unleavened bread which is sincerity and truth.

[9] In my letter I wrote that you must have nothing to do with those who are sexually immoral. [10] I was not, of course, referring to people in general who are immoral or extortioners or swindlers or idolaters; to avoid them you would have to withdraw from society altogether. [11] I meant that you must have nothing to do with any so-called Christian who leads an immoral life, or is extortionate, idolatrous, a slanderer, a drunkard, or a swindler; with anyone like that you should not even eat. [12-13] What business of mine is it to judge outsiders? God is their judge. But within the fellowship, you are the judges: 'Root out the wrongdoer from your community.'

Lawsuits among Christians

6 IF one of your number has a dispute with another, does he have the face to go to law before a pagan court instead of before God's people? [2] It is God's people who are to judge the world; surely you know that. And if the world is subject to your judgement, are you not competent to deal with these trifling cases? [3] Are you not aware that we are to judge angels, not to mention day to day affairs? [4] If therefore you have such everyday disputes, how can you entrust jurisdiction to outsiders with no standing in the church? [5] I write this to shame you. Can it be that there is not among you a single person wise enough to give a decision in a fellow-Christian's cause? [6] Must Christian go to law with Christian—and before unbelievers at that? [7] Indeed, you suffer defeat by going to law with one another at all. Why not rather submit to wrong? Why not let yourself be defrauded? [8] But instead, it is you who are wronging and defrauding, and fellow-Christians at that! [9] Surely you know that wrongdoers will never possess the kingdom of God. Make no mistake: no fornicator or idolater, no adulterer or sexual pervert, [10] no thief, extortioner, drunkard, slanderer, or swindler will possess the kingdom of God. [11] Such were some of you; but you have been washed clean, you have been dedicated to God, you have been justified through the name of the Lord Jesus and through the Spirit of our God.

[12] 'I am free to do anything,' you say. Yes, but not everything does good. No doubt I am free to do anything, but I for one will not let anything make free with me. [13] 'Food is for the belly and the belly for food,' you say. True; and one day God will put an end to both. But the body is not for fornication; it is for the Lord—and the Lord for the body. [14] God not only raised our Lord from the dead; he will also raise us by his power. [15] Do you not know that your bodies are limbs and organs of Christ? Shall I then take parts of Christ's body and make them over to a prostitute? Never! [16] You surely know that anyone who joins himself to a prostitute becomes physically one with her, for scripture says, 'The two shall become one flesh'; [17] but anyone who joins himself to the Lord is one with him spiritually. [18] Have nothing to do with fornication. Every other sin that one may commit is outside the body; but the fornicator sins against his own body. [19] Do you not know that your body is a temple of the indwelling Holy Spirit, and the Spirit is God's gift to you? You do not belong to yourselves; [20] you were bought at a price. Then honour God in your body.

Sex, marriage, and divorce

7 Now FOR the matters you wrote about. You say, 'It is a good thing for a man not to have intercourse with a woman.' [2] Rather, in the face of so much immorality, let each man have his own wife and each woman her own husband. [3] The husband must give the wife what is due to her, and equally the wife must give the husband his due. [4] The wife cannot claim her body as her own; it is her husband's. Equally, the husband cannot claim his body as his own; it is his wife's. [5] Do not deny yourselves to one another, except when you agree to devote yourselves to prayer for a time, and to come together again afterwards; otherwise, through lack of self-control, you may be tempted by Satan. [6] I say this by way of

concession, not command. ⁷I should like everyone to be as I myself am; but each person has the gift God has granted him, one this gift and another that.

⁸To the unmarried and to widows I say this: it is a good thing if like me they stay as they are; ⁹but if they do not have self-control, they should marry. It is better to be married than burn with desire.

¹⁰To the married I give this ruling, which is not mine but the Lord's: a wife must not separate herself from her husband—¹¹if she does, she must either remain unmarried or be reconciled to her husband—and the husband must not divorce his wife.

¹²To the rest I say this, as my own word, not as the Lord's: if a Christian has a wife who is not a believer, and she is willing to live with him, he must not divorce her; ¹³and if a woman has a husband who is not a believer, and he is willing to live with her, she must not divorce him. ¹⁴For the husband now belongs to God through his Christian wife, and the wife through her Christian husband. Otherwise your children would not belong to God, whereas in fact they do. ¹⁵If however the unbelieving partner wishes for a separation, it should be granted; in such cases the Christian husband or wife is not bound by the marriage. God's call is a call to live in peace. ¹⁶But remember: a wife may save her husband; and a husband may save his wife.

¹⁷However that may be, each one should accept the lot which the Lord has assigned him and continue as he was when God called him. That is the rule I give in all the churches. ¹⁸Was a man called with the marks of circumcision on him? Let him not remove them. Was he uncircumcised when he was called? Let him not be circumcised. ¹⁹Circumcision or uncircumcision is neither here nor there; what matters is to keep God's commands. ²⁰Everyone should remain in the condition in which he was called. ²¹Were you a slave when you were called? Do not let that trouble you; though if a chance of freedom should

come, by all means take it. ²²Anyone who received his call to be a Christian while a slave is the Lord's freedman, and, equally, every free man who has received the call is a slave in the service of Christ. ²³You were bought at a price; do not become slaves of men. ²⁴So, my friends, everyone is to remain before God in the condition in which he received his call.

²⁵About the unmarried, I have no instructions from the Lord, but I give my opinion as one who by the Lord's mercy is fit to be trusted. ²⁶I think the best way for a man to live in a time of stress like the present is this—to remain as he is. ²⁷Are you bound in marriage? Do not seek a dissolution. Has your marriage been dissolved? Do not seek a wife. ²⁸But if you do marry, you are not doing anything wrong, nor does a girl if she marries; it is only that those who marry will have hardships to endure, and my aim is to spare you.

²⁹What I mean, my friends, is this: the time we live in will not last long. While it lasts, married men should be as if they had no wives; ³⁰mourners should be as if they had nothing to grieve them, the joyful as if they did not rejoice; those who buy should be as if they possessed nothing, ³¹and those who use the world's wealth as if they did not have full use of it. For the world as we know it is passing away.

³²I want you to be free from anxious care. An unmarried man is concerned with the Lord's business; his aim is to please the Lord. ³³But a married man is concerned with worldly affairs; his aim is to please his wife, ³⁴and he is pulled in two directions. The unmarried woman or girl is concerned with the Lord's business; her aim is to be dedicated to him in body as in spirit. But the married woman is concerned with worldly affairs; her aim is to please her husband.

³⁵In saying this I am thinking simply of your own good. I have no wish to keep you on a tight rein; I only want you to be beyond criticism and be free from distraction in your devotion to the Lord. ³⁶But if

7:21 **though if ... take it:** *or* but even if a chance of freedom should come, choose rather to make good use of your servitude.   7:33–34 **his wife ... girl is concerned:** *some witnesses read* his wife. ³⁴There is this difference between the wife and the virgin; the unmarried woman is concerned.   7:36–38 **But if ... better:** *or* But if a man feels open to criticism about his daughter, because she has reached puberty and the normal course ought to be followed, he may do as he wishes: let the marriage take place; there is nothing wrong in it. ³⁷But if a man is steadfast in his purpose and under no obligation, if he is free to act at his own discretion, and has decided in his

a man feels that he is not behaving properly towards the girl to whom he is betrothed, if his passions are strong and something must be done, let him carry out his intention by getting married; there is nothing wrong in it. [37] But if a man is steadfast in his purpose and under no obligation, if he is free to act at his own discretion, and has decided in his own mind to respect her virginity, he will do well. [38] Thus he who marries his betrothed does well, and he who does not marry does better.

[39] A wife is bound to her husband as long as he lives. But if the husband dies, she is free to marry whom she will, provided the marriage is within the Lord's fellowship. [40] But she is better off as she is; that is my opinion, and I believe that I too have the Spirit of God.

Food offered to idols

8 Now ABOUT meat consecrated to heathen deities.

Of course 'We all have knowledge,' as you say. 'Knowledge' inflates a man, whereas love builds him up. [2] If anyone fancies that he has some kind of knowledge, he does not yet know in the true sense of knowing. [3] But if anyone loves God, he is known by God.

[4] Well then, about eating this consecrated meat: of course, as you say, 'A false god has no real existence, and there is no god but one.' [5] Even though there be so-called gods, whether in heaven or on earth—and indeed there are many such gods and many such lords—[6] yet for us there is one God, the Father, from whom are all things, and we exist for him; there is one Lord, Jesus Christ, through whom are all things, and we exist through him.

[7] But not everyone possesses this knowledge. There are some who have been so accustomed to idolatry that they still think of this meat as consecrated to the idol, and their conscience, being weak, is defiled by eating it. [8] Certainly food will not bring us into God's presence: if we do not eat, we are none the worse,

and if we do eat, we are none the better. [9] But be careful that this liberty of yours does not become a pitfall for the weak. [10] If one of them sees you sitting down to a meal in a heathen temple—you with your 'knowledge'—will not his conscience be emboldened to eat meat consecrated to the heathen deity? [11] This 'knowledge' of yours destroys the weak, the fellow-Christian for whom Christ died. [12] In sinning against your brothers and sisters in this way and wounding their conscience, weak as it is, you sin against Christ. [13] Therefore, if food be the downfall of a fellow-Christian, I will never eat meat again, for I will not be the cause of a fellow-Christian's downfall.

9 AM I not free? Am I not an apostle? Have I not seen Jesus our Lord? Are not you my own handiwork in the Lord? [2] If others do not accept me as an apostle, you at least are bound to do so, for in the Lord you are the very seal of my apostleship.

[3] To those who would call me to account, this is my defence: [4] Have I no right to eat and drink? [5] Have I not the right to take a Christian wife about with me, like the rest of the apostles and the Lord's brothers and Cephas? [6] Are only Barnabas and I bound to work for our living? [7] Did you ever hear of a man serving in the army at his own expense? Or planting a vineyard without eating the fruit? Or tending a flock without using the milk? [8] My case does not rest on these human analogies, for the law says the same; [9] in the law of Moses we read, 'You shall not muzzle an ox while it is treading out the grain.' Do you suppose God's concern is with oxen? [10] Must not the saying refer to us? Of course it does: the ploughman should plough and the thresher thresh in hope of sharing the produce. [11] If we have sown a spiritual crop for you, is it too much to expect from you a material harvest? [12] If you allow others those rights, have not we a stronger claim?

own mind to keep the girl unmarried, he will do well. [38] Thus he who gives his daughter in marriage does well, and he who does not does better. *Or* But if a man has a partner in celibacy and feels that he is not behaving properly towards her, if, that is, his instincts are too strong for him, and something must be done, let him do what he wishes: let them marry; there is nothing wrong in it. [37] But if a man is steadfast in his purpose and under no obligation, if he is free to act at his own discretion, and has decided in his own mind to keep his partner in her virginity, he will do well. [38] Thus he who marries his partner does well, and he who does not marry her does better.   8:12 *Some witnesses omit* weak as it is.

But I have never availed myself of any such right. On the contrary, I put up with all that comes my way rather than offer any hindrance to the gospel of Christ. [13] You must know that those who are engaged in temple service eat the temple offerings, and those who officiate at the altar claim their share of the sacrifice. [14] In the same way the Lord gave instructions that those who preach the gospel should get their living by the gospel. [15] But I have never taken advantage of any such right, nor do I intend to claim it in this letter. I had rather die! No one shall make my boast an empty boast. [16] Even if I preach the gospel, I can claim no credit for it; I cannot help myself; it would be agony for me not to preach. [17] If I did it of my own choice, I should be earning my pay; but since I have no choice, I am simply discharging a trust. [18] Then what is my pay? It is the satisfaction of preaching the gospel without expense to anyone; in other words, of waiving the rights my preaching gives me.

[19] I am free and own no master; but I have made myself everyone's servant, to win over as many as possible. [20] To Jews I behaved like a Jew, to win Jews; that is, to win those under the law I behaved as if under the law, though not myself subject to the law. [21] To win those outside the law, I behaved as if outside the law, though not myself outside God's law, but subject to the law of Christ. [22] To the weak I became weak, to win the weak. To them all I have become everything in turn, so that in one way or another I may save some. [23] All this I do for the sake of the gospel, to have a share in its blessings.

[24] At the games, as you know, all the runners take part, though only one wins the prize. [25] You also must run to win. Every athlete goes into strict training. They do it to win a fading garland; we, to win a garland that never fades. [26] For my part, I am no aimless runner; I am not a boxer who beats the air. [27] I do not spare my body, but bring it under strict control, for fear that after preaching to others I should find myself disqualified.

10 Let me remind you, my friends, that our ancestors were all under the cloud, and all of them passed through the Red Sea; [2] so they all received baptism into the fellowship of Moses in cloud and sea. [3] They all ate the same supernatural food, [4] and all drank the same supernatural drink; for they drank from the supernatural rock that accompanied their travels—and that rock was Christ. [5] Yet most of them were not accepted by God, for the wilderness was strewn with their corpses.

[6] These events happened as warnings to us not to set our desires on evil things as they did. [7] Do not be idolaters, like some of them; as scripture says, 'The people sat down to feast and rose up to revel.' [8] Let us not commit fornication; some of them did, and twenty-three thousand died in one day. [9] Let us not put the Lord to the test as some of them did; they were destroyed by the snakes. [10] Do not grumble as some of them did; they were destroyed by the Destroyer.

[11] All these things that happened to them were symbolic, and were recorded as a warning for us, upon whom the end of the ages has come. [12] If you think you are standing firm, take care, or you may fall. [13] So far you have faced no trial beyond human endurance; God keeps faith and will not let you be tested beyond your powers, but when the test comes he will at the same time provide a way out and so enable you to endure.

[14] SO THEN, my dear friends, have nothing to do with idolatry. [15] I appeal to you as sensible people; form your own judgement on what I say. [16] When we bless the cup of blessing, is it not a means of sharing in the blood of Christ? When we break the bread, is it not a means of sharing in the body of Christ? [17] Because there is one loaf, we, though many, are one body; for it is one loaf of which we all partake.

[18] Consider Jewish practice: are not those who eat the sacrificial meal partners in the altar? [19] What do I imply by this? That meat consecrated to an idol is anything more than meat, or that an idol is anything more than an idol? [20] No, I mean that pagan sacrifices are offered (in the words of scripture) 'to demons and to that which is not God'; and I will not have

10:9 **the Lord:** *some witnesses read* Christ.   10:17 **Because ... body:** *or* For we, many as we are, are one loaf, one body.

153

you become partners with demons. ²¹ You cannot drink the cup of the Lord and the cup of demons. You cannot partake of the Lord's table and the table of demons. ²² Are we to provoke the Lord? Are we stronger than he is?

²³ 'We are free to do anything,' you say. Yes, but not everything is good for us. We are free to do anything, but not everything builds up the community. ²⁴ You should each look after the interests of others, not your own.

²⁵ You may eat anything sold in the meat market without raising questions of conscience; ²⁶ 'for the earth is the Lord's and all that is in it'.

²⁷ If an unbeliever invites you to a meal and you accept, eat whatever is put before you, without raising questions of conscience. ²⁸ But if somebody says to you, 'This food has been offered in sacrifice,' then, out of consideration for him and for conscience' sake, do not eat it—²⁹ not your conscience, I mean, but his.

'What?' you say. 'Is my freedom to be called in question by another's conscience? ³⁰ If I partake with thankfulness, why am I blamed for eating food over which I have said grace?' ³¹ You may eat or drink, or do anything else, provided it is all done to the glory of God; ³² give no offence to Jews, or Greeks, or to the church of God. ³³ For my part I always try to be considerate to everyone, not seeking my own good but the good of the many, so

11 that they may be saved. ¹ Follow my example as I follow Christ's.

Public worship

² I COMMEND you for always keeping me in mind, and maintaining the tradition I handed on to you. ³ But I wish you to understand that, while every man has Christ for his head, a woman's head is man, as Christ's head is God. ⁴ A man who keeps his head covered when he prays or prophesies brings shame on his head; ⁵ but a woman brings shame on her head if she prays or prophesies bareheaded; it is as bad as if her head were shaved. ⁶ If a woman does not cover her head she might as well have her hair cut off; but if it is a disgrace for her to be cropped and shaved, then she should cover her head. ⁷ A man must not cover his head, because

man is the image of God, and the mirror of his glory, whereas a woman reflects the glory of man. ⁸ For man did not originally spring from woman, but woman was made out of man; ⁹ and man was not created for woman's sake, but woman for the sake of man; ¹⁰ and therefore a woman must have the sign of her authority on her head, out of regard for the angels. ¹¹ Yet in the Lord's fellowship woman is as essential to man as man to woman. ¹² If woman was made out of man, it is through woman that man now comes to be; and God is the source of all.

¹³ Judge for yourselves: is it fitting for a woman to pray to God bareheaded? ¹⁴ Does not nature herself teach you that while long hair disgraces a man, ¹⁵ it is a woman's glory? For her hair was given as a covering.

¹⁶ And if anyone still insists on arguing, there is no such custom among us, or in any of the congregations of God's people.

¹⁷ In giving you these instructions I come to something I cannot commend: your meetings tend to do more harm than good. ¹⁸ To begin with, I am told that when you meet as a congregation you fall into sharply divided groups. I believe there is some truth in it, ¹⁹ for divisions are bound to arise among you if only to show which of your members are genuine. ²⁰ The result is that when you meet as a congregation, it is not the Lord's Supper you eat; when it comes to eating, ²¹ each of you takes his own supper, one goes hungry and another has too much to drink. ²² Have you no homes of your own to eat and drink in? Or are you so contemptuous of the church of God that you shame its poorer members? What am I to say? Can I commend you? On this point, certainly not!

²³ For the tradition which I handed on to you came to me from the Lord himself: that on the night of his arrest the Lord Jesus took bread, ²⁴ and after giving thanks to God broke it and said: 'This is my body, which is for you; do this in memory of me.' ²⁵ In the same way, he took the cup after supper, and said: 'This cup is the new covenant sealed by my blood. Whenever you drink it, do this in memory of me.' ²⁶ For every time you eat this bread and drink the cup, you

11: 3 **is man**: *or* is her husband.   11: 7 **a woman … man**: *or* a woman reflects her husband's glory.

proclaim the death of the Lord, until he comes.

²⁷ It follows that anyone who eats the bread or drinks the cup of the Lord unworthily will be guilty of offending against the body and blood of the Lord. ²⁸ Everyone must test himself before eating from the bread and drinking from the cup. ²⁹ For he who eats and drinks eats and drinks judgement on himself if he does not discern the body. ³⁰ That is why many of you are feeble and sick, and a number have died. ³¹ But if we examined ourselves, we should not fall under judgement. ³² When, however, we do fall under the Lord's judgement, he is disciplining us to save us from being condemned with the rest of the world.

³³ Therefore, my friends, when you meet for this meal, wait for one another. ³⁴ If you are hungry, eat at home, so that in meeting together you may not fall under judgement. The other matters I will settle when I come.

Spiritual gifts

12 ABOUT gifts of the Spirit, my friends, I want there to be no misunderstanding.

² You know how, in the days when you were still pagan, you used to be carried away by some impulse or other to those dumb heathen gods. ³ For this reason I must impress upon you that no one who says 'A curse on Jesus!' can be speaking under the influence of the Spirit of God; and no one can say 'Jesus is Lord!' except under the influence of the Holy Spirit.

⁴ There are varieties of gifts, but the same Spirit. ⁵ There are varieties of service, but the same Lord. ⁶ There are varieties of activity, but in all of them and in everyone the same God is active. ⁷ In each of us the Spirit is seen to be at work for some useful purpose. ⁸ One, through the Spirit, has the gift of wise speech, while another, by the power of the same Spirit, can put the deepest knowledge into words. ⁹ Another, by the same Spirit, is granted faith; another, by the one Spirit, gifts of healing, ¹⁰ and another miraculous powers; another has the gift of prophecy, and another the ability to distinguish true spirits from false; yet another has the gift of tongues of various kinds, and another the ability to interpret them. ¹¹ But all these gifts are the activity of one and the same Spirit, distributing them to each individual at will.

¹² Christ is like a single body with its many limbs and organs, which, many as they are, together make up one body; ¹³ for in the one Spirit we were all brought into one body by baptism, whether Jews or Greeks, slaves or free; we were all given that one Spirit to drink.

¹⁴ A body is not a single organ, but many. ¹⁵ Suppose the foot were to say, 'Because I am not a hand, I do not belong to the body,' it belongs to the body none the less. ¹⁶ Suppose the ear were to say, 'Because I am not an eye, I do not belong to the body,' it still belongs to the body. ¹⁷ If the body were all eye, how could it hear? If the body were all ear, how could it smell? ¹⁸ But, in fact, God appointed each limb and organ to its own place in the body as he chose. ¹⁹ If the whole were a single organ, there would not be a body at all; ²⁰ in fact, however, there are many different organs, but one body. ²¹ The eye cannot say to the hand, 'I do not need you,' or the head to the feet, 'I do not need you.' ²² Quite the contrary: those parts of the body which seem to be more frail than others are indispensable, ²³ and those parts of the body which we regard as less honourable are treated with special honour. The parts we are modest about are treated with special respect, ²⁴ whereas our respectable parts have no such need. But God has combined the various parts of the body, giving special honour to the humbler parts, ²⁵ so that there might be no division in the body, but that all its parts might feel the same concern for one another. ²⁶ If one part suffers, all suffer together; if one flourishes, all rejoice together.

²⁷ Now you are Christ's body, and each of you a limb or organ of it. ²⁸ Within our community God has appointed in the first place apostles, in the second place prophets, thirdly teachers; then miracle-workers, then those who have gifts of healing, or ability to help others or power to guide them, or the gift of tongues of various kinds. ²⁹ Are all apostles? All prophets? All teachers? Do all work miracles? ³⁰ Do all have gifts of healing? Do all speak in tongues of ecstasy? Can all interpret them? ³¹ The higher gifts are those you should prize.

But I can show you an even better way.

13 I may speak in tongues of men or of angels, but if I have no love, I am a sounding gong or a clanging cymbal. ² I may have the gift of prophecy and the knowledge of every hidden truth; I may have faith enough to move mountains; but if I have no love, I am nothing. ³ I may give all I possess to the needy, I may give my body to be burnt, but if I have no love, I gain nothing by it.

⁴ Love is patient and kind. Love envies no one, is never boastful, never conceited, ⁵ never rude; love is never selfish, never quick to take offence. Love keeps no score of wrongs, ⁶ takes no pleasure in the sins of others, but delights in the truth. ⁷ There is nothing love cannot face; there is no limit to its faith, its hope, its endurance.

⁸ Love will never come to an end. Prophecies will cease; tongues of ecstasy will fall silent; knowledge will vanish. ⁹ For our knowledge and our prophecy alike are partial, ¹⁰ and the partial vanishes when wholeness comes. ¹¹ When I was a child I spoke like a child, thought like a child, reasoned like a child; but when I grew up I finished with childish things. ¹² At present we see only puzzling reflections in a mirror, but one day we shall see face to face. My knowledge now is partial; then it will be whole, like God's knowledge of me. ¹³ There are three things that last for ever: faith, hope, and love; and the greatest of the three is love.

14 Make love your aim; then be eager for the gifts of the Spirit, above all for prophecy. ² If anyone speaks in tongues he is talking with God, not with men and women; no one understands him, for he speaks divine mysteries in the Spirit. ³ On the other hand, if anyone prophesies, he is talking to men and women, and his words have power to build; they stimulate and they encourage. ⁴ Speaking in tongues may build up the speaker himself, but it is prophecy that builds up a Christian community. ⁵ I am happy for you all to speak in tongues, but happier still for you to prophesy. The prophet is worth more than one who speaks in tongues—unless indeed he can explain its meaning, and so help to build up the community. ⁶ Suppose, my friends, that when I come to you I speak in tongues: what good shall I do you unless what I say contains something by way of revelation, or enlightenment, or prophecy, or instruction?

⁷ Even with inanimate things that produce sounds—a flute, say, or a lyre—unless their notes are distinct, how can you tell what tune is being played? ⁸ Or again, if the trumpet-call is not clear, who will prepare for battle? ⁹ In the same way, if what you say in tongues yields no precise meaning, how can anyone tell what is being said? You will be talking to empty air. ¹⁰ There are any number of different languages in the world; nowhere is without language. ¹¹ If I do not know the speaker's language, his words will be gibberish to me, and mine to him. ¹² You are, I know, eager for gifts of the Spirit; then aspire above all to excel in those which build up the church.

¹³ Anyone who speaks in tongues should pray for the ability to interpret. ¹⁴ If I use such language in prayer, my spirit prays, but my mind is barren. ¹⁵ What then? I will pray with my spirit, but also with my mind; I will sing hymns with my spirit, but with my mind as well. ¹⁶ Suppose you are praising God with the spirit alone: how will an ordinary person who is present be able to say 'Amen' to your thanksgiving, when he does not know what you are saying? ¹⁷ Your prayer of thanksgiving may be splendid, but it is no help to the other person. ¹⁸ Thank God, I am more gifted in tongues than any of you, ¹⁹ but in the congregation I would rather speak five intelligible words, for the benefit of others as well as myself, than thousands of words in the language of ecstasy.

²⁰ Do not be children in your thinking, my friends; be infants in evil, but in your thinking be grown-up. ²¹ We read in the law: 'I will speak to this people through strange tongues, and by the lips of foreigners; and even so they will not heed me, says the Lord.' ²² Clearly then these 'strange tongues' are not intended as a sign for believers, but for unbelievers, whereas prophecy is designed not for unbelievers but for believers. ²³ So if the whole congregation is assembled and all are using the 'strange tongues' of ecstasy, and some uninstructed persons or unbelievers should enter, will they not think

---

13:3 **give my … burnt:** *some witnesses read* seek glory by self-sacrifice.

you are mad? ²⁴ But if all are uttering prophecies, the visitor, when he enters, hears from everyone something that searches his conscience and brings conviction, ²⁵ and the secrets of his heart are laid bare. So he will fall down and worship God, declaring, 'God is certainly among you!'

²⁶ To sum up, my friends: when you meet for worship, each of you contributing a hymn, some instruction, a revelation, an ecstatic utterance, or its interpretation, see that all of these aim to build up the church. ²⁷ If anyone speaks in tongues, only two should speak, or at most three, one at a time, and someone must interpret. ²⁸ If there is no interpreter, they should keep silent and speak to themselves and to God. ²⁹ Of the prophets, two or three may speak, while the rest exercise their judgement upon what is said. ³⁰ If someone else present receives a revelation, let the first speaker stop. ³¹ You can all prophesy, one at a time, so that all may receive instruction and encouragement. ³² It is for prophets to control prophetic inspiration, ³³ for God is not a God of disorder but of peace.

As in all congregations of God's people, ³⁴ women should keep silent at the meeting. They have no permission to talk, but should keep their place as the law directs. ³⁵ If there is something they want to know, they can ask their husbands at home. It is a shocking thing for a woman to talk at the meeting.

³⁶ Did the word of God originate with you? Or are you the only people to whom it came? ³⁷ If anyone claims to be inspired or a prophet, let him recognize that what I write has the Lord's authority. ³⁸ If he does not acknowledge this, his own claim cannot be acknowledged.

³⁹ In short, my friends, be eager to prophesy; do not forbid speaking in tongues; ⁴⁰ but let all be done decently and in order.

The resurrection of the dead

15 AND now, my friends, I must remind you of the gospel that I preached to you; the gospel which you received, on which you have taken your stand, ² and which is now bringing you salvation. Remember the terms in which I

preached the gospel to you—for I assume that you hold it fast and that your conversion was not in vain.

³ First and foremost, I handed on to you the tradition I had received: that Christ died for our sins, in accordance with the scriptures; ⁴ that he was buried; that he was raised to life on the third day, in accordance with the scriptures; ⁵ and that he appeared to Cephas, and afterwards to the Twelve. ⁶ Then he appeared to over five hundred of our brothers at once, most of whom are still alive, though some have died. ⁷ Then he appeared to James, and afterwards to all the apostles.

⁸ Last of all he appeared to me too; it was like a sudden, abnormal birth. ⁹ For I am the least of the apostles, indeed not fit to be called an apostle, because I had persecuted the church of God. ¹⁰ However, by God's grace I am what I am, and his grace to me has not proved vain; in my labours I have outdone them all—not I, indeed, but the grace of God working with me. ¹¹ But no matter whether it was I or they! This is what we all proclaim, and this is what you believed.

¹² Now if this is what we proclaim, that Christ was raised from the dead, how can some of you say there is no resurrection of the dead? ¹³ If there is no resurrection, then Christ was not raised; ¹⁴ and if Christ was not raised, then our gospel is null and void, and so too is your faith; ¹⁵ and we turn out to have given false evidence about God, because we bore witness that he raised Christ to life, whereas, if the dead are not raised, he did not raise him. ¹⁶ For if the dead are not raised, it follows that Christ was not raised; ¹⁷ and if Christ was not raised, your faith has nothing to it and you are still in your old state of sin. ¹⁸ It follows also that those who have died within Christ's fellowship are utterly lost. ¹⁹ If it is for this life only that Christ has given us hope, we of all people are most to be pitied.

²⁰ But the truth is, Christ was raised to life—the firstfruits of the harvest of the dead. ²¹ For since it was a man who brought death into the world, a man also brought resurrection of the dead. ²² As in Adam all die, so in Christ all will be brought to life; ²³ but each in proper order: Christ the firstfruits, and afterwards,

---

14:38 **If ... acknowledged:** *some witnesses read* If he refuses to recognize this, let him refuse!

at his coming, those who belong to Christ. [24] Then comes the end, when he delivers up the kingdom to God the Father, after deposing every sovereignty, authority, and power. [25] For he is destined to reign until God has put all enemies under his feet; [26] and the last enemy to be deposed is death. [27] Scripture says, 'He has put all things in subjection under his feet.' But in saying 'all things', it clearly means to exclude God who made all things subject to him; [28] and when all things are subject to him, then the Son himself will also be made subject to God who made all things subject to him, and thus God will be all in all.

[29] Again, there are those who receive baptism on behalf of the dead. What do you suppose they are doing? If the dead are not raised to life at all, what do they mean by being baptized on their behalf?

[30] And why do we ourselves face danger hour by hour? [31] Every day I die: I swear it by my pride in you, my friends—for in Christ Jesus our Lord I am proud of you. [32] With no more than human hopes, what would have been the point of my fighting those wild beasts at Ephesus? If the dead are never raised to life, 'Let us eat and drink, for tomorrow we die.'

[33] Make no mistake: 'Bad company ruins good character.' [34] Wake up, be sober, and stop sinning: some of you have no knowledge of God—to your shame I say it.

[35] But, you may ask, how are the dead raised? In what kind of body? [36] What stupid questions! The seed you sow does not come to life unless it has first died; [37] and what you sow is not the body that shall be, but a bare grain, of wheat perhaps, or something else; [38] and God gives it the body of his choice, each seed its own particular body. [39] All flesh is not the same: there is human flesh, flesh of beasts, of birds, and of fishes—all different. [40] There are heavenly bodies and earthly bodies; and the splendour of the heavenly bodies is one thing, the splendour of the earthly another. [41] The sun has a splendour of its own, the moon another splendour, and the stars yet another; and one star differs from another in brightness. [42] So it is with the resurrection of the dead: what is sown as

a perishable thing is raised imperishable. [43] Sown in humiliation, it is raised in glory; sown in weakness, it is raised in power; [44] sown a physical body, it is raised a spiritual body.

If there is such a thing as a physical body, there is also a spiritual body. [45] It is in this sense that scripture says, 'The first man, Adam, became a living creature,' whereas the last Adam has become a life-giving spirit. [46] Observe, the spiritual does not come first; the physical body comes first, and then the spiritual. [47] The first man is from earth, made of dust: the second man is from heaven. [48] The man made of dust is the pattern of all who are made of dust, and the heavenly man is the pattern of all the heavenly. [49] As we have worn the likeness of the man made of dust, so we shall wear the likeness of the heavenly man.

[50] What I mean, my friends, is this: flesh and blood can never possess the kingdom of God, the perishable cannot possess the imperishable. [51] Listen! I will unfold a mystery: we shall not all die, but we shall all be changed [52] in a flash, in the twinkling of an eye, at the last trumpet-call. For the trumpet will sound, and the dead will rise imperishable, and we shall be changed. [53] This perishable body must be clothed with the imperishable, and what is mortal with immortality. [54] And when this perishable body has been clothed with the imperishable and our mortality has been clothed with immortality, then the saying of scripture will come true: 'Death is swallowed up; victory is won!' [55] 'O Death, where is your victory? O Death, where is your sting?' [56] The sting of death is sin, and sin gains its power from the law. [57] But thanks be to God! He gives us victory through our Lord Jesus Christ.

[58] Therefore, my dear friends, stand firm and immovable, and work for the Lord always, work without limit, since you know that in the Lord your labour cannot be lost.

Plans and greetings

16 Now ABOUT the collection in aid of God's people: you should follow the instructions I gave to our churches in Galatia. [2] Every Sunday each of you is to

15:54 *Some witnesses omit* this perishable body has been clothed with the imperishable and.

put aside and keep by him whatever he can afford, so that there need be no collecting when I come. [3] When I arrive, I will give letters of introduction to persons approved by you, and send them to carry your gift to Jerusalem. [4] If it seems right for me to go as well, they can travel with me.

[5] I shall come to Corinth after passing through Macedonia—for I am travelling by way of Macedonia—[6] and I may stay some time with you, perhaps even for the whole winter; and then you can help me on my way wherever I go next. [7] I do not want this to be a flying visit; I hope to spend some time with you, if the Lord permits. [8] But I shall remain at Ephesus until Pentecost, [9] for a great opportunity has opened for effective work, and there is much opposition.

[10] If Timothy comes, see that you put him at his ease; for it is the Lord's work that he is engaged on, as I am myself; [11] so no one must slight him. Speed him on his way with your blessing; for he is to join me, and I am waiting for him with our friends. [12] As for our friend Apollos, I urged him strongly to go to Corinth with the others, but he was quite determined not to go at present; he will go when the time is right.

[13] Be on the alert; stand firm in the faith; be valiant, be strong. [14] Let everything you do be done in love.

[15] One thing more, my friends. You know that the Stephanas family were the first converts in Achaia, and have devoted themselves to the service of God's people. [16] I urge you to accept the leadership of people like them, of anyone who labours hard at our common task. [17] It is a great pleasure to me that Stephanas, Fortunatus, and Achaicus have arrived, because they have done what you had no chance to do; [18] they have raised my spirits—and no doubt yours too. Such people deserve recognition.

[19] Greetings from the churches of Asia. Many greetings in the Lord from Aquila and Prisca and the church that meets in their house. [20] Greetings from the whole brotherhood. Greet one another with the kiss of peace.

[21] This greeting is in my own hand— Paul.

[22] If anyone does not love the Lord, let him be outcast.

Marana tha—Come, Lord!

[23] The grace of the Lord Jesus be with you.

[24] My love to you all in Christ Jesus.

16:12 **but … not to go:** *or* but it was clearly not the will of God that he should go.

THE SECOND LETTER OF PAUL TO THE
CORINTHIANS

1 FROM Paul, apostle of Christ Jesus by God's will, and our colleague Timothy, to God's church at Corinth, together with all God's people throughout the whole of Achaia.

[2] Grace and peace to you from God our Father and the Lord Jesus Christ.

[3] Praise be to the God and Father of our Lord Jesus Christ, the all-merciful Father, the God whose consolation never fails us! [4] He consoles us in all our troubles, so that we in turn may be able to console others in any trouble of theirs and to share with them the consolation we ourselves receive from God. [5] As Christ's suffering exceeds all measure and extends to us, so too it is through Christ that our consolation has no limit. [6] If distress is our lot, it is the price we pay for your consolation and your salvation; if our lot is consolation, it is to help us to bring you consolation, and strength to face with fortitude the same sufferings we now endure. [7] And our hope for you is firmly grounded; for we know that if you share in the suffering, you share also in the consolation.

[8] In saying this, my friends, we should like you to know how serious was the trouble that came upon us in the province of Asia. The burden of it was far too heavy

for us to bear, so heavy that we even despaired of life. ⁹Indeed, we felt in our hearts that we had received a death sentence. This was meant to teach us to place reliance not on ourselves, but on God who raises the dead. ¹⁰From such mortal peril God delivered us; and he will deliver us again, he on whom our hope is fixed. Yes, he will continue to deliver us, ¹¹while you co-operate by praying for us. Then, with so many people praying for our deliverance, there will be many to give thanks on our behalf for God's gracious favour towards us.

Paul's concern for the church at Corinth

¹²THERE is one thing we are proud of: our conscience shows us that in our dealings with others, and above all in our dealings with you, our conduct has been governed by a devout and godly sincerity, by the grace of God and not by worldly wisdom. ^{13–14}There is nothing in our letters to you but what you can read and understand. You do understand us in some measure, but I hope you will come to understand fully that you have as much reason to be proud of us, as we of you, on the day of our Lord Jesus.

¹⁵It was because I felt so confident about all this that I had intended to come first of all to you and give you the benefit of a double visit: ¹⁶I meant to visit you on my way to Macedonia and, after leaving Macedonia, to return to you, and you could then have sent me on my way to Judaea. ¹⁷That was my intention; did I lightly change my mind? Or do I, when framing my plans, frame them as a worldly man might, first saying 'Yes, yes' and then 'No, no'? ¹⁸God is to be trusted, and therefore what we tell you is not a mixture of Yes and No. ¹⁹The Son of God, Christ Jesus, proclaimed among you by us (by Silvanus and Timothy, I mean, as well as myself), was not a mixture of Yes and No. With him it is always Yes; ²⁰for all the promises of God have their Yes in him. That is why, when we give glory to God, it is through Christ Jesus that we say 'Amen'. ²¹And if you and we belong to Christ, guaranteed as his and anointed, it is all God's doing; ²²it is God also who has set his seal upon us and, as a pledge of

what is to come, has given the Spirit to dwell in our hearts.

²³I appeal to God as my witness and stake my life upon it: it was out of consideration for you that I did not after all come to Corinth. ²⁴It is not that we have control of your faith; rather we are working with you for your happiness. For it is by that faith that you stand. ¹So I made up my mind that my next visit to you must not be another painful one. ²If I cause pain to you, who is left to cheer me up, except you whom I have offended? ³This is precisely the point I made in my letter: I did not want, I said, to come and be made miserable by the very people who ought to have made me happy; and I had sufficient confidence in you all to know that for me to be happy is for all of you to be happy. ⁴That letter I sent you came out of great distress and anxiety; how many tears I shed as I wrote it! Not because I wanted to cause you pain; rather I wanted you to know the love, the more than ordinary love, that I have for you.

⁵Any injury that has been done has not been done to me; to some extent (I do not want to make too much of it) it has been done to you all. ⁶The penalty on which the general meeting has agreed has met the offence well enough. ⁷Something very different is called for now: you must forgive the offender and put heart into him; the man's distress must not be made so severe as to overwhelm him. ⁸I urge you therefore to reassure him of your love for him. ⁹I wrote, I may say, to see how you stood the test, whether you fully accepted my authority. ¹⁰But anyone who has your forgiveness has mine too; and when I speak of forgiving (so far as there is anything for me to forgive), I mean that as the representative of Christ I have forgiven him for your sake. ¹¹For Satan must not be allowed to get the better of us; we know his wiles all too well.

¹²When I came to Troas, where I was to preach the gospel of Christ, and where an opening awaited me for serving the Lord, ¹³I still found no relief of mind, for my colleague Titus was not there to meet me; so I took leave of the people and went

---

1:12 **devout:** *some witnesses read* frank.   1:17 **That was … mind?:** *or* In forming this intention, did I act irresponsibly?   2:10 **as the representative:** *or* in the presence.

off to Macedonia. [14] But thanks be to God, who continually leads us as captives in Christ's triumphal procession, and uses us to spread abroad the fragrance of the knowledge of himself! [15] We are indeed the incense offered by Christ to God, both among those who are on the way to salvation, and among those who are on the way to destruction: [16] to the latter it is a deadly fume that kills, to the former a vital fragrance that brings life: Who is equal to such a calling? [17] We are not adulterating the word of God for profit as so many do; when we declare the word we do it in sincerity, as from God and in God's sight, as members of Christ.

Paul's commission as an apostle

3 ARE we beginning all over again to produce our credentials? Do we, like some people, need letters of introduction to you, or from you? [2] No, you are all the letter we need, a letter written on our heart; anyone can see it for what it is and read it for himself. [3] And as for you, it is plain that you are a letter that has come from Christ, given to us to deliver; a letter written not with ink but with the Spirit of the living God, written not on stone tablets but on the pages of the human heart.

[4] It is in full reliance upon God, through Christ, that we make such claims. [5] There is no question of our having sufficient power in ourselves: we cannot claim anything as our own. The power we have comes from God; [6] it is he who has empowered us as ministers of a new covenant, not written but spiritual; for the written law condemns to death, but the Spirit gives life.

[7] The ministry that brought death, and that was engraved in written form on stone, was inaugurated with such glory that the Israelites could not keep their eyes on Moses, even though the glory on his face was soon to fade. [8] How much greater, then, must be the glory of the ministry of the Spirit! [9] If glory accompanied the ministry that brought condemnation, how much richer in glory must be the ministry that brings acquittal! [10] Indeed, the glory that once was is now no glory at all; it is outshone by a still greater glory. [11] For if what was to fade away had

its glory, how much greater is the glory of what endures!

[12] With such a hope as this we speak out boldly; [13] it is not for us to do as Moses did: he put a veil over his face to keep the Israelites from gazing at the end of what was fading away. [14] In any case their minds had become closed, for that same veil is there to this very day when the lesson is read from the old covenant; and it is never lifted, because only in Christ is it taken away. [15] Indeed to this very day, every time the law of Moses is read, a veil lies over the mind of the hearer. [16] But (as scripture says) 'Whenever he turns to the Lord the veil is removed.' [17] Now the Lord of whom this passage speaks is the Spirit; and where the Spirit of the Lord is, there is liberty. [18] And because for us there is no veil over the face, we all see as in a mirror the glory of the Lord, and we are being transformed into his likeness with ever-increasing glory, through the power of the Lord who is the Spirit.

4 SINCE God in his mercy has given us this ministry, we never lose heart. [2] We have renounced the deeds that people hide for very shame; we do not practise cunning or distort the word of God. It is by declaring the truth openly that we recommend ourselves to the conscience of our fellow-men in the sight of God. [3] If our gospel is veiled at all, it is veiled only for those on the way to destruction; [4] their unbelieving minds are so blinded by the god of this passing age that the gospel of the glory of Christ, who is the image of God, cannot dawn upon them and bring them light. [5] It is not ourselves that we proclaim; we proclaim Christ Jesus as Lord, and ourselves as your servants for Jesus's sake. [6] For the God who said, 'Out of darkness light shall shine,' has caused his light to shine in our hearts, the light which is knowledge of the glory of God in the face of Jesus Christ.

[7] But we have only earthenware jars to hold this treasure, and this proves that such transcendent power does not come from us; it is God's alone. [8] We are hard pressed, but never cornered; bewildered, but never at our wits' end; [9] hunted, but never abandoned to our fate; struck down, but never killed. [10] Wherever we go

3:18 see ... mirror: *or* reflect like a mirror.

we carry with us in our body the death that Jesus died, so that in this body also the life that Jesus lives may be revealed. [11] For Jesus's sake we are all our life being handed over to death, so that the life of Jesus may be revealed in this mortal body of ours. [12] Thus death is at work in us, but life in you.

[13] But scripture says, 'I believed, and therefore I spoke out,' and we too, in the same spirit of faith, believe and therefore speak out; [14] for we know that he who raised the Lord Jesus to life will with Jesus raise us too, and bring us to his presence, and you with us. [15] Indeed, all this is for your sake, so that, as the abounding grace of God is shared by more and more, the greater may be the chorus of thanksgiving that rises to the glory of God.

[16] No wonder we do not lose heart! Though our outward humanity is in decay, yet day by day we are inwardly renewed. [17] Our troubles are slight and short-lived, and their outcome is an eternal glory which far outweighs them, [18] provided our eyes are fixed, not on the things that are seen, but on the things that are unseen; for what is seen is transient, what is unseen is eternal. 5 [1] We know that if the earthly frame that houses us today is demolished, we possess a building which God has provided—a house not made by human hands, eternal and in heaven. [2] In this present body we groan, yearning to be covered by our heavenly habitation put on over this one, [3] in the hope that, being thus clothed, we shall not find ourselves naked. [4] We groan indeed, we who are enclosed within this earthly frame; we are oppressed because we do not want to have the old body stripped off. What we want is to be covered by the new body put on over it, so that our mortality may be absorbed into life immortal. [5] It is for this destiny that God himself has been shaping us; and as a pledge of it he has given us the Spirit.

[6] Therefore we never cease to be confident. We know that so long as we are at home in the body we are exiles from the Lord; [7] faith is our guide, not sight. [8] We are confident, I say, and would rather be exiled from the body and make our home with the Lord. [9] That is why it is our ambition, wherever we are, at home or in exile, to be acceptable to him. [10] For we must all have our lives laid open before the tribunal of Christ, where each must receive what is due to him for his conduct in the body, good or bad.

The message of reconciliation

[11] WITH this fear of the Lord before our eyes we address our appeal to men and women. To God our lives lie open, and I hope that in your heart of hearts they lie open to you also. [12] This is not another attempt to recommend ourselves to you: we are rather giving you a chance to show yourselves proud of us; then you will have something to say to those whose pride is all in outward show and not in inward worth. [13] If these are mad words, take them as addressed to God; if sound sense, as addressed to you. [14] For the love of Christ controls us once we have reached the conclusion that one man died for all and therefore all mankind has died. [15] He died for all so that those who live should cease to live for themselves, and should live for him who for their sake died and was raised to life. [16] With us therefore worldly standards have ceased to count in our estimate of anyone; even if once they counted in our understanding of Christ, they do so now no longer. [17] For anyone united to Christ, there is a new creation: the old order has gone; a new order has already begun.

[18] All this has been the work of God. He has reconciled us to himself through Christ, and has enlisted us in this ministry of reconciliation: [19] God was in Christ reconciling the world to himself, no longer holding people's misdeeds against them, and has entrusted us with the message of reconciliation. [20] We are therefore Christ's ambassadors. It is as if God were appealing to you through us: we implore you in Christ's name, be reconciled to God! [21] Christ was innocent of sin, and yet for our sake God made him one with human sinfulness, so that in him we might be made one with the

---

5:13 **If these ... to you:** *or* If we speak in ecstasy, it is to God's glory; if we speak sober sense, it is to your advantage.   5:17 **For anyone ... begun:** *or* When anyone is united to Christ he is a new creature: his old life is over; a new life has already begun.   5:19 **God ... himself:** *or* God was reconciling the world to himself by Christ.

righteousness of God. [1] Sharing in God's work, we make this appeal: you have received the grace of God; do not let it come to nothing. [2] He has said:

In the hour of my favour I answered you;
on the day of deliverance I came to your aid.

This is the hour of favour, this the day of deliverance. [3] Lest our ministry be brought into discredit, we avoid giving any offence in anything. [4] As God's ministers, we try to recommend ourselves in all circumstances by our steadfast endurance: in affliction, hardship, and distress; [5] when flogged, imprisoned, mobbed; overworked, sleepless, starving. [6] We recommend ourselves by innocent behaviour and grasp of truth, by patience and kindliness, by gifts of the Holy Spirit, by unaffected love, [7] by declaring the truth, by the power of God. We wield the weapons of righteousness in right hand and left. [8] Honour and dishonour, praise and blame, are alike our lot: we are the impostors who speak the truth, [9] the unknown men whom all men know; dying we still live on; disciplined by suffering, we are not done to death; [10] in our sorrows we have always cause for joy; poor ourselves, we bring wealth to many; penniless, we own the world. [11] We have spoken very frankly to you, friends in Corinth; we have opened our heart to you. [12] There is no constraint on our part; any constraint there may be is in you. [13] In fair exchange then (if I may speak to you like a father) open your hearts to us.

Church life and discipline

[14] Do NOT team up with unbelievers. What partnership can righteousness have with wickedness? Can light associate with darkness? [15] Can Christ agree with Belial, or a believer join with an unbeliever? [16] Can there be a compact between the temple of God and idols? And the temple of the living God is what we are. God's own words are: 'I will live and move about among them; I will be their God, and they shall be my people.' [17] And therefore, 'Come away and leave them, separate yourselves, says the Lord; touch nothing unclean. Then I will accept you,

[18] says the Lord Almighty; I will be a father to you, and you shall be my sons and daughters.' [1] Such are the promises that have been made to us, dear friends. Let us therefore cleanse ourselves from all that can defile flesh or spirit and, in the fear of God, let us complete our consecration.

[2] MAKE a place for us in your hearts! We have wronged no one, ruined no one, exploited no one. [3] My words are no reflection on you. I have told you before that, come death, come life, your place in our hearts is secure. [4] I am speaking to you with great frankness, but my pride in you is just as great. In all our many troubles my cup is full of consolation and overflows with joy.

[5] Even when we reached Macedonia we still found no relief; instead trouble met us at every turn, fights without and fears within. [6] But God, who brings comfort to the downcast, has comforted us by the arrival of Titus, [7] and not merely by his arrival, but by his being so greatly encouraged about you. He has told us how you long for me, how sorry you are, and how eager to take my side; and that has made me happier still.

[8] Even if I did hurt you by the letter I sent, I do not now regret it. I did regret it; but now that I see the letter gave you pain, though only for a time, [9] I am happy—not because of the pain but because the pain led to a change of heart. You bore the pain as God would have you bear it, and so you came to no harm from what we did. [10] Pain borne in God's way brings no regrets but a change of heart leading to salvation; pain borne in the world's way brings death. [11] You bore your pain in God's way, and just look at the results: it made you take the matter seriously and vindicate yourselves; it made you indignant and apprehensive; it aroused your longing for me, your devotion, and your eagerness to see justice done! At every point you have cleared yourselves of blame. [12] And so, although I did send you that letter, it was not the offender or his victim that most concerned me. My aim in writing was to help to make plain to you, in the sight of God, how truly you are devoted to us. [13] That is why we have been so encouraged.

But besides being encouraged ourselves,

we have also been delighted beyond everything by seeing how happy Titus is: you have all helped to set his mind completely at rest. [14] Anything I may have said to him to show my pride in you has been justified. Every word we addressed to you bore the mark of truth, and the same holds of the proud boast we made in the presence of Titus; that also has proved true. [15] His heart warms all the more to you as he recalls how ready you all were to do what he asked, meeting him as you did in fear and trembling. [16] How happy I am now to have complete confidence in you!

The collection for the church in Jerusalem

8 WE must tell you, friends, about the grace that God has given to the churches in Macedonia. [2] The troubles they have been through have tried them hard, yet in all this they have been so exuberantly happy that from the depths of their poverty they have shown themselves lavishly open-handed. [3] Going to the limit of their resources, as I can testify, and even beyond that limit, [4] they begged us most insistently, and on their own initiative, to be allowed to share in this generous service to their fellow-Christians. [5] And their giving surpassed our expectations; for first of all they gave themselves to the Lord and, under God, to us. [6] The upshot is that we have asked Titus, since he has already made a beginning, to bring your share in this further work of generosity also to completion. [7] You are so rich in everything—in faith, speech, knowledge, and diligence of every kind, as well as in the love you have for us—that you should surely show yourselves equally lavish in this generous service! [8] This is not meant as an order; by telling you how keen others are I am putting your love to the test. [9] You know the generosity of our Lord Jesus Christ: he was rich, yet for your sake he became poor, so that through his poverty you might become rich.

[10] Here is my advice, and I have your interests at heart. You made a good beginning last year both in what you did and in your willingness to do it. [11] Now go on and finish it. Be as eager to complete the scheme as you were to adopt it, and give according to your means. [12] If we give eagerly according to our means, that is acceptable to God; he does not ask for what we do not have. [13] There is no question of relieving others at the cost of hardship to yourselves; [14] it is a question of equality. At the moment your surplus meets their need, but one day your need may be met from their surplus. The aim is equality; [15] as scripture has it, 'Those who gathered more did not have too much, and those who gathered less did not have too little.'

[16] I thank God that he has made Titus as keen on your behalf as we are! [17] So keen is he that he not only welcomed our request; it is by his own choice he is now leaving to come to you. [18] With him we are sending one of our company whose reputation for his services to the gospel among all the churches is high. [19] Moreover they have duly appointed him to travel with us and help in this beneficent work, by which we do honour to the Lord himself and show our own eagerness to serve. [20] We want to guard against any criticism of our handling of these large sums; [21] for our aims are entirely honourable, not only in the Lord's eyes, but also in the eyes of men and women.

[22] We are sending with them another of our company whose enthusiasm we have had repeated opportunities of testing, and who is now all the more keen because of the great confidence he has in you. [23] If there is any question about Titus, he is my partner and my fellow-worker in dealings with you; as for the others, they are delegates of the churches and bring honour to Christ. [24] So give them, and through them the churches, clear evidence of your love and justify our pride in you.

9 About this aid for God's people, it is superfluous for me to write to you. [2] I know how eager you are to help and I speak of it with pride to the Macedonians, telling them that Achaia had everything ready last year; and most of them have been fired by your zeal. [3] My purpose in sending these friends is to ensure that what we have said about you in this matter should not prove to be an empty

---

8:7 **the love ... us:** *some witnesses read* the love we have for you, *or* the love which we have kindled in your hearts.

boast. I want you to be prepared, as I told them you were; [4] for if I bring men from Macedonia with me and they find you are not prepared, what a disgrace it will be to us, let alone to you, after all the confidence we have shown! [5] I have accordingly thought it necessary to ask these friends to go on ahead to Corinth, to see that your promised bounty is in order before I come; it will then be awaiting me as genuine bounty, and not as an extortion.

[6] Remember: sow sparingly, and you will reap sparingly; sow bountifully, and you will reap bountifully. [7] Each person should give as he has decided for himself; there should be no reluctance, no sense of compulsion; God loves a cheerful giver. [8] And it is in God's power to provide you with all good gifts in abundance, so that, with every need always met to the full, you may have something to spare for every good cause; [9] as scripture says: 'He lavishes his gifts on the needy; his benevolence lasts for ever.' [10] Now he who provides seed for sowing and bread for food will provide the seed for you to sow; he will multiply it and swell the harvest of your benevolence, [11] and you will always be rich enough to be generous. Through our action such generosity will issue in thanksgiving to God, [12] for as a piece of willing service this is not only a contribution towards the needs of God's people; more than that, it overflows in a flood of thanksgiving to God. [13] For with the proof which this aid affords, those who receive it will give honour to God when they see how humbly you obey him and how faithfully you confess the gospel of Christ; and they will thank him for your liberal contribution to their need and to the general good. [14] And as they join in prayer on your behalf, their hearts will go out to you because of the richness of the grace which God has given you. [15] Thanks be to God for his gift which is beyond all praise!

The challenge to Paul's authority

10 I, PAUL, appeal to you by the gentleness and magnanimity of Christ—I who am so timid (you say) when face to face with you, so courageous when I am away from you. [2] Spare me when I come, I beg you, the need for that courage and self-assurance, which I reckon I could confidently display against those who assume my behaviour to be dictated by human weakness. [3] Weak and human we may be, but that does not dictate the way we fight our battles. [4] The weapons we wield are not merely human; they are strong enough with God's help to demolish strongholds. [5] We demolish sophistries and all that rears its proud head against the knowledge of God; we compel every human thought to surrender in obedience to Christ; [6] and we are prepared to punish any disobedience once your own obedience is complete.

[7] Look facts in the face. Is someone convinced that he belongs to Christ? Let him think again and reflect that we belong to Christ as much as he does. [8] Indeed, if I am boasting too much about our authority—an authority given by the Lord to build your faith, not pull it down—I shall make good my boast. [9] So you must not think of me as one who tries to scare you by the letters he writes. [10] 'His letters', so it is said, 'are weighty and powerful; but when he is present he is unimpressive, and as a speaker he is beneath contempt.' [11] People who talk in that way should reckon with this: my actions when I come will show the same man as my letters showed while I was absent.

[12] We should not dare to class ourselves or compare ourselves with any of those who commend themselves. What fools they are to measure themselves on their own, to find in themselves their standard of comparison! [13] As for us, our boasting will not go beyond the proper limits; and our sphere is determined by the limit God laid down for us, which permitted us to come as far as Corinth. [14] We are not overstretching our commission, as we would be if we had never come to you; but we were the first to reach as far as Corinth in the work of the gospel of Christ. [15] And we do not boast of work done where others have laboured, work beyond our proper sphere. Our hope is rather that, as your faith grows, we may attain a position among you greater than ever before, but still within the limits of our sphere. [16] Then we can carry the gospel to lands that lie beyond you, never priding ourselves on work already done in anyone else's sphere. [17] If anyone would boast, let him boast of the Lord. [18] For it is not the one who recommends himself, but the

one whom the Lord recommends, who is to be accepted.

Paul speaks as a fool

11 I SHOULD like you to bear with me in a little foolishness; please bear with me. ²I am jealous for you, with the jealousy of God; for I betrothed you to Christ, thinking to present you as a chaste virgin to her true and only husband. ³Now I am afraid that, as the serpent in his cunning seduced Eve, your thoughts may be corrupted and you may lose your single-hearted devotion to Christ. ⁴For if some newcomer proclaims another Jesus, not the Jesus whom we proclaimed, or if you receive a spirit different from the Spirit already given to you, or a gospel different from the gospel you have already accepted, you put up with that well enough. ⁵I am not aware of being in any way inferior to those super-apostles. ⁶I may be no speaker, but knowledge I do have; at all times we have made known to you the full truth.

⁷Or was this my offence, that I made no charge for preaching the gospel of God, humbling myself in order to exalt you? ⁸I robbed other churches—by accepting support from them to serve you. ⁹If I ran short while I was with you, I did not become a charge on anyone; my needs were fully met by friends from Macedonia; I made it a rule, as I always shall, never to be a burden to you. ¹⁰As surely as the truth of Christ is in me, nothing shall bar me from boasting about this throughout Achaia. ¹¹Why? Because I do not love you? God knows I do.

¹²And I shall go on doing as I am doing now, to cut the ground from under those who would seize any chance to put their vaunted apostleship on the same level as ours. ¹³Such people are sham apostles, confidence tricksters masquerading as apostles of Christ. ¹⁴And no wonder! Satan himself masquerades as an angel of light, ¹⁵so it is easy enough for his agents to masquerade as agents of good. But their fate will match their deeds.

¹⁶I repeat: let no one take me for a fool; but if you must, then give me the privilege of a fool, and let me have my little boast like others. ¹⁷In boasting so confidently I am not speaking like a Christian, but like

a fool. ¹⁸So many people brag of their earthly distinctions that I shall do so too. ¹⁹How gladly you put up with fools, being yourselves so wise! ²⁰If someone tyrannizes over you, exploits you, gets you in his clutches, puts on airs, and hits you in the face, you put up with it. ²¹And you call me a weakling! I admit the reproach.

But if there is to be bravado (and I am still speaking as a fool), I can indulge in it too. ²²Are they Hebrews? So am I. Israelites? So am I. Abraham's descendants? So am I. ²³Are they servants of Christ? I am mad to speak like this, but I can outdo them: more often overworked, more often imprisoned, scourged more severely, many a time face to face with death. ²⁴Five times the Jews have given me the thirty-nine strokes; ²⁵three times I have been beaten with rods; once I was stoned; three times I have been shipwrecked, and for twenty-four hours I was adrift on the open sea. ²⁶I have been constantly on the road; I have met dangers from rivers, dangers from robbers, dangers from my fellow-countrymen, dangers from foreigners, dangers in the town, dangers in the wilderness, dangers at sea, dangers from false Christians. ²⁷I have toiled and drudged and often gone without sleep; I have been hungry and thirsty and have often gone without food; I have suffered from cold and exposure.

²⁸Apart from these external things, there is the responsibility that weighs on me every day, my anxious concern for all the churches. ²⁹Is anyone weak? I share his weakness. If anyone brings about the downfall of another, does my heart not burn with anger? ³⁰If boasting there must be, I will boast of the things that show up my weakness. ³¹He who is blessed for ever, the God and Father of the Lord Jesus, knows that what I say is true. ³²When I was in Damascus, the commissioner of King Aretas kept the city under observation to have me arrested; ³³and I was let down in a basket, through a window in the wall, and so escaped his clutches.

12 IT may do no good, but I must go on with my boasting; I come now to visions and revelations granted by the Lord. ²I know a Christian man who

---

11:3 *lose … devotion: some witnesses read* lose your purity and single-hearted devotion.

fourteen years ago (whether in the body or out of the body, I do not know—God knows) was caught up as far as the third heaven. ³ And I know that this same man (whether in the body or apart from the body, I do not know—God knows) ⁴ was caught up into paradise, and heard words so secret that human lips may not repeat them. ⁵ About such a man I am ready to boast; but I will not boast on my own account, except of my weaknesses. ⁶ If I chose to boast, it would not be the boast of a fool, for I should be speaking the truth. But I refrain, because I do not want anyone to form an estimate of me which goes beyond the evidence of his own eyes and ears. ⁷ To keep me from being unduly elated by the magnificence of such revelations, I was given a thorn in my flesh, a messenger of Satan sent to buffet me; this was to save me from being unduly elated. ⁸ Three times I begged the Lord to rid me of it, ⁹ but his answer was: 'My grace is all you need; power is most fully seen in weakness.' I am therefore happy to boast of my weaknesses, because then the power of Christ will rest upon me. ¹⁰ So I am content with a life of weakness, insult, hardship, persecution, and distress, all for Christ's sake; for when I am weak, then I am strong.

Paul's final appeal

¹¹ I AM being very foolish, but it was you who drove me to it; my credentials should have come from you. In nothing did I prove inferior to those super-apostles, even if I am a nobody. ¹² The signs of an apostle were there in the work I did among you, marked by unfailing endurance, by signs, portents, and miracles. ¹³ Is there any way in which you were treated worse than the other churches—except this, that I was never a charge on you? Forgive me for being so unfair!

¹⁴ I am now getting ready to pay you a third visit; and I am not going to be a charge on you. It is you I want, not your money; parents should make provision for their children, not children for their parents. ¹⁵ I would gladly spend everything for you—yes, and spend myself to the limit. If I love you overmuch, am I to be loved the less? ¹⁶ All very well, you say;

I did not myself prove a burden to you, but I did use a confidence trick to take you in. ¹⁷ Was it one of the men I sent to you that I used to exploit you? ¹⁸ I begged Titus to visit you, and I sent our friend with him. Did Titus exploit you? Have we not both been guided by the same Spirit, and followed the same course?

¹⁹ Perhaps you have been thinking all this time that it is to you we are addressing our defence. No; we are speaking in God's sight, and as Christians. Our whole aim, dear friends, is to build you up. ²⁰ I fear that when I come I may find you different from what I wish, and you may find me to be what you do not wish. I fear I may find quarrelling and jealousy, angry tempers and personal rivalries, backbiting and gossip, arrogance and general disorder. ²¹ I am afraid that when I come my God may humiliate me again in your presence, that I may have cause to grieve over many who were sinning before and have not repented of their unclean lives, their fornication and sensuality.

13 This will be my third visit to you. As scripture says, 'Every charge must be established on the evidence of two or three witnesses': ² to those who sinned before, and to everyone else, I repeat the warning I gave last time; on my second visit I gave it in person, and now I give it while absent. It is that when I come this time, I will show no leniency. ³ Then you will have the proof you seek of the Christ who speaks through me, the Christ who, far from being weak with you, makes his power felt among you. ⁴ True, he died on the cross in weakness, but he lives by the power of God; so you will find that we who share his weakness shall live with him by the power of God.

⁵ Examine yourselves: are you living the life of faith? Put yourselves to the test. Surely you recognize that Jesus Christ is among you? If not, you have failed the test. ⁶ I hope you will come to see that we have not failed. ⁷ Our prayer to God is that you may do no wrong, not that we should win approval; we want you to do what is right, even if we should seem failures. ⁸ We have no power to act against the truth, but only for it. ⁹ We are happy to be weak at any time if only you are strong.

12:6–7 **ears...given:** *some witnesses read* ears, ⁷ and because of the magnificence of the revelations themselves. Therefore to keep me from being unduly elated I was given.

Our prayer, then, is for your amendment. [10] In writing this letter before I come, my aim is to spare myself, when I do come, any sharp exercise of authority—authority which the Lord gave me for building up and not for pulling down.

[11] And now, my friends, farewell. Mend your ways; take our appeal to heart; agree with one another; live in peace; and the God of love and peace will be with you. [12] Greet one another with the kiss of peace. [13] All God's people send you greetings.

[14] The grace of the Lord Jesus Christ, and the love of God, and the fellowship of the Holy Spirit, be with you all.

THE LETTER OF PAUL TO THE
GALATIANS

1 FROM Paul, an apostle commissioned not by any human authority or human act, but by Jesus Christ and God the Father who raised him from the dead. [2] I and all the friends now with me send greetings to the churches of Galatia.

[3] Grace to you and peace from God the Father and our Lord Jesus Christ, [4] who gave himself for our sins, to rescue us out of the present wicked age as our God and Father willed; [5] to him be glory for ever and ever! Amen.

One gospel for all

[6] I AM astonished to find you turning away so quickly from him who called you by grace, and following a different gospel. [7] Not that it is in fact another gospel; only there are some who unsettle your minds by trying to distort the gospel of Christ. [8] But should anyone, even I myself or an angel from heaven, preach a gospel other than the gospel I preached to you, let him be banned! [9] I warned you in the past and now I warn you again: if anyone preaches a gospel other than the gospel you received, let him be banned!

[10] Now do I sound as if I were asking for human approval and not for God's alone? Am I currying favour with men? If I were still seeking human favour, I should be no servant of Christ.

[11] I must make it clear to you, my friends, that the gospel you heard me preach is not of human origin. [12] I did not take it over from anyone; no one taught it me; I received it through a revelation of Jesus Christ.

[13] You have heard what my manner of life was when I was still a practising Jew: how savagely I persecuted the church of God and tried to destroy it; [14] and how in the practice of our national religion I outstripped most of my Jewish contemporaries by my boundless devotion to the traditions of my ancestors. [15] But then in his good pleasure God, who from my birth had set me apart, and who had called me through his grace, chose [16] to reveal his Son in and through me, in order that I might proclaim him among the Gentiles. Immediately, without consulting a single person, [17] without going up to Jerusalem to see those who were apostles before me, I went off to Arabia, and afterwards returned to Damascus.

[18] Three years later I did go up to Jerusalem to get to know Cephas, and I stayed two weeks with him. [19] I saw none of the other apostles, except James, the Lord's brother. [20] What I write is plain truth; God knows I am not lying!

[21] Then I left for the regions of Syria and Cilicia. [22] I was still unknown by sight to the Christian congregations in Judaea; [23] they had simply heard it said, 'Our former persecutor is preaching the good news of the faith which once he tried to destroy,' [24] and they praised God for what had happened to me.

2 Fourteen years later, I went up again to Jerusalem with Barnabas, and we took Titus with us. [2] I went in response to a revelation from God; I explained, at a private interview with those of repute, the gospel which I preach to the Gentiles, to

1:3 **God ... Christ:** *some witnesses read* God our Father and the Lord Jesus Christ.   1:6 **from him ... grace:** *some witnesses read* from Christ who called you by grace, *or* from him who called you by the grace of Christ.

168

make sure that the race I had run and was running should not be in vain. ³ Not even my companion Titus, Greek though he is, was compelled to be circumcised. ⁴ That course was urged only as a concession to certain sham Christians, intruders who had sneaked in to spy on the liberty we enjoy in the fellowship of Christ Jesus. These men wanted to bring us into bondage, ⁵ but not for one moment did I yield to their dictation; I was determined that the full truth of the gospel should be maintained for you.

⁶ As for those reputed to be something (not that their importance matters to me: God does not recognize these personal distinctions)—these men of repute, I say, imparted nothing further to me. ⁷ On the contrary, they saw that I had been entrusted to take the gospel to the Gentiles as surely as Peter had been entrusted to take it to the Jews; ⁸ for the same God who was at work in Peter's mission to the Jews was also at work in mine to the Gentiles.

⁹ Recognizing, then, the privilege bestowed on me, those who are reputed to be pillars of the community, James, Cephas, and John, accepted Barnabas and myself as partners and shook hands on it: the agreement was that we should go to the Gentiles, while they went to the Jews. ¹⁰ All they asked was that we should keep in mind the poor, the very thing I have always made it my business to do.

¹¹ But when Cephas came to Antioch, I opposed him to his face, because he was clearly in the wrong. ¹² For until some messengers came from James, he was taking his meals with gentile Christians; but after they came he drew back and began to hold aloof, because he was afraid of the Jews. ¹³ The other Jewish Christians showed the same lack of principle; even Barnabas was carried away and played false like the rest. ¹⁴ But when I saw that their conduct did not square with the truth of the gospel, I said to Cephas in front of the whole congregation, 'If you, a Jew born and bred, live like a Gentile, and not like a Jew, how can you insist that Gentiles must live like Jews?'

¹⁵ We ourselves are Jews by birth, not gentile sinners; ¹⁶ yet we know that no one is ever justified by doing what the law

requires, but only through faith in Christ Jesus. So we too have put our faith in Jesus Christ, in order that we might be justified through this faith, and not through actions dictated by law; for no human being can be justified by keeping the law.

¹⁷ If then, in seeking to be justified in Christ, we ourselves no less than the Gentiles turn out to be sinners, does that mean that Christ is a promoter of sin? Of course not! ¹⁸ On the contrary, it is only if I start building up again all I have pulled down that I prove to be one who breaks the law. ¹⁹ For through the law I died to law—to live for God. ²⁰ I have been crucified with Christ: the life I now live is not my life, but the life which Christ lives in me; and my present mortal life is lived by faith in the Son of God, who loved me and gave himself up for me. ²¹ I will not nullify the grace of God; if righteousness comes by law, then Christ died for nothing.

The freedom of faith

3 YOU STUPID Galatians! You must have been bewitched—you before whose eyes Jesus Christ was openly displayed on the cross! ² Answer me one question: did you receive the Spirit by keeping the law or by believing the gospel message? ³ Can you really be so stupid? You started with the spiritual; do you now look to the material to make you perfect? ⁴ Is all you have experienced to come to nothing—surely not! ⁵ When God gives you the Spirit and works miracles among you, is it because you keep the law, or is it because you have faith in the gospel message?

⁶ Look at Abraham: he put his faith in God, and that faith was counted to him as righteousness. ⁷ You may take it, then, that it is those who have faith who are Abraham's sons. ⁸ And scripture, foreseeing that God would justify the Gentiles through faith, declared the gospel to Abraham beforehand: 'In you all nations shall find blessing.' ⁹ Thus it is those with faith who share the blessing with faithful Abraham.

¹⁰ On the other hand, those who rely on obedience to the law are under a curse; for scripture says, 'Cursed is everyone who does not persevere in doing everything

2:4–5 **bondage ... for you**: *or, following some witnesses,* bondage; ⁵ I yielded to their demand for the moment, to ensure that gospel truth should not be prevented from reaching you.   2:12 **the Jews**: *or* the advocates of circumcision.

that is written in the book of the law.' [11] It is evident that no one is ever justified before God by means of the law, because we read, 'He shall gain life who is justified through faith.' [12] Now the law does not operate on the basis of faith, for we read, 'He who does this shall gain life by what he does.' [13] Christ bought us freedom from the curse of the law by coming under the curse for our sake; for scripture says, 'Cursed is everyone who is hanged on a gibbet.' [14] The purpose of this was that the blessing of Abraham should in Jesus Christ be extended to the Gentiles, so that we might receive the promised Spirit through faith.

[15] My friends, let me give you an illustration. When a man's will and testament has been duly executed, no one else can set it aside or add a codicil. [16] Now, the promises were pronounced to Abraham and to his 'issue'. It does not say 'issues' in the plural, but 'your issue' in the singular; and by 'issue' is meant Christ. [17] My point is this: a testament, or covenant, had already been validated by God; a law made four hundred and thirty years later cannot invalidate it and so render its promises ineffective. [18] If the inheritance is by legal right, then it is not by promise; but it was by promise that God bestowed it as a free gift on Abraham.

[19] Then what of the law? It was added to make wrongdoing a legal offence; it was an interim measure pending the arrival of the 'issue' to whom the promise was made. It was promulgated through angels, and there was an intermediary; [20] but an intermediary is not needed for one party acting alone, and God is one.

[21] Does the law, then, contradict the promises? Of course not! If a law had been given which had power to bestow life, then righteousness would indeed have come from keeping the law. [22] But scripture has declared the whole world to be prisoners in subjection to sin, so that faith in Jesus Christ should be the ground on which the promised blessing is given to those who believe.

[23] Before this faith came, we were close prisoners in the custody of law, pending the revelation of faith. [24] The law was thus put in charge of us until Christ should come, when we should be justified through faith; [25] and now that faith has come, its charge is at an end.

[26] It is through faith that you are all sons of God in union with Christ Jesus. [27] Baptized into union with him, you have all put on Christ like a garment. [28] There is no such thing as Jew and Greek, slave and freeman, male and female; for you are all one person in Christ Jesus. [29] So if you belong to Christ, you are the 'issue' of Abraham and heirs by virtue of the promise.

Life under the law

4 THIS is what I mean: so long as the heir is a minor, he is no better off than a slave, even though the whole estate is his; [2] he is subject to guardians and trustees until the date set by his father. [3] So it was with us: during our minority we were slaves, subject to the elemental spirits of the universe, [4] but when the appointed time came, God sent his Son, born of a woman, born under the law, [5] to buy freedom for those who were under the law, in order that we might attain the status of sons.

[6] To prove that you are sons, God has sent into our hearts the Spirit of his Son, crying 'Abba, Father!' [7] You are therefore no longer a slave but a son, and if a son, an heir by God's own act.

[8] Formerly, when you did not know God, you were slaves to gods who are not gods at all. [9] But now that you do acknowledge God—or rather, now that he has acknowledged you—how can you turn back to those feeble and bankrupt elemental spirits? Why do you propose to enter their service all over again? [10] You keep special days and months and seasons and years. [11] I am afraid that all my hard work on you may have been wasted.

[12] PUT yourselves in my place, my friends, I beg you, as I put myself in yours. You never did me any wrong: [13] it was bodily illness, as you will remember, that originally led to my bringing you the gospel, [14] and you resisted any temptation to show scorn or disgust at my physical condition; on the contrary you welcomed me as if I were an angel of God, as you might have

---

3:19 **added ... offence:** *or* added to restrain offences. belonging to this world.   4:9 **bankrupt ... spirits:** *or* threadbare elementary notions.   4:3 **to ... universe:** *or* to elementary notions.

welcomed Christ Jesus himself. ¹⁵What has become of the happiness you felt then? I believe you would have torn out your eyes and given them to me, had that been possible! ¹⁶ Have I now made myself your enemy by being frank with you?

¹⁷ Others are lavishing attention on you, but without sincerity: what they really want is to isolate you so that you may lavish attention on them. ¹⁸ To be the object of sincere attentions is always good, and not just when I am with you. ¹⁹ You are my own children, and I am in labour with you all over again until you come to have the form of Christ. ²⁰ How I wish I could be with you now, for then I could modify my tone; as it is, I am at my wits' end about you.

Freedom through Christ

²¹ TELL me now, you that are so anxious to be under law, will you not listen to what the law says? ²² It is written there that Abraham had two sons, the one by a slave, the other by a free-born woman. ²³ The slave's son was born in the ordinary course of nature, but the free woman's through God's promise. ²⁴ This is an allegory: the two women stand for two covenants. The one covenant comes from Mount Sinai; that is Hagar, and her children are born into slavery. ²⁵ Sinai is a mountain in Arabia and represents the Jerusalem of today, for she and her children are in slavery. ²⁶ But the heavenly Jerusalem is the free woman; she is our mother. ²⁷ For scripture says, 'Rejoice, O barren woman who never bore a child; break into a shout of joy, you who have never been in labour; for the deserted wife will have more children than she who lives with her husband.'

²⁸ Now you, my friends, like Isaac, are children of God's promise, ²⁹ but just as in those days the natural-born son persecuted the spiritual son, so it is today. ³⁰ Yet what does scripture say? 'Drive out the slave and her son, for the son of the slave shall not share the inheritance with the son of the free woman.' ³¹ You see, then, my friends, we are no slave's children; our mother is the free woman. ¹ It is for freedom that Christ set us free. Stand firm, therefore, and refuse to submit again to the yoke of slavery.

² Mark my words: I, Paul, say to you that if you get yourself circumcised Christ will benefit you no more. ³ I impress on you once again that every man who accepts circumcision is under obligation to keep the entire law. ⁴ When you seek to be justified by way of law, you are cut off from Christ: you have put yourselves outside God's grace. ⁵ For it is by the Spirit and through faith that we hope to attain that righteousness which we eagerly await. ⁶ If we are in union with Christ Jesus, circumcision makes no difference at all, nor does the lack of it; the only thing that counts is faith expressing itself through love.

⁷ You were running well; who was it hindered you from following the truth? ⁸ Whatever persuasion was used, it did not come from God who called you. ⁹ 'A little leaven', remember, 'leavens all the dough.' ¹⁰ The Lord gives me confidence that you will not adopt the wrong view; but whoever it is who is unsettling your minds must bear God's judgement. ¹¹ As for me, my friends, if I am still advocating circumcision, then why am I still being persecuted? To do that would be to strip the cross of all offence. ¹² Those agitators had better go the whole way and make eunuchs of themselves!

Guidance by the Spirit

¹³ YOU, MY friends, were called to be free; only beware of turning your freedom into licence for your unspiritual nature. Instead, serve one another in love; ¹⁴ for the whole law is summed up in a single commandment: 'Love your neighbour as yourself.' ¹⁵ But if you go on fighting one another, tooth and nail, all you can expect is mutual destruction.

¹⁶ What I mean is this: be guided by the Spirit and you will not gratify the desires of your unspiritual nature. ¹⁷ That nature sets its desires against the Spirit, while the Spirit fights against it. They are in conflict with one another so that you cannot do what you want. ¹⁸ But if you are led by the Spirit, you are not subject to law.

¹⁹Anyone can see the behaviour that belongs to the unspiritual nature: fornication, indecency, and debauchery; ²⁰idolatry and sorcery; quarrels, a contentious temper, envy, fits of rage, selfish ambitions, dissensions, party intrigues, ²¹ and jealousies; drinking bouts, orgies, and the like. I warn you, as I warned you before, that no one who behaves like that will ever inherit the kingdom of God.

²² But the harvest of the Spirit is love, joy, peace, patience, kindness, goodness, fidelity, ²³ gentleness, and self-control. Against such things there is no law. ²⁴ Those who belong to Christ Jesus have crucified the old nature with its passions and desires. ²⁵ If the Spirit is the source of our life, let the Spirit also direct its course.

²⁶ We must not be conceited, inciting one another to rivalry, jealous of one another. ¹ If anyone is caught doing something wrong, you, my friends, who live by the Spirit must gently set him right. Look to yourself, each one of you: you also may be tempted. ² Carry one another's burdens, and in this way you will fulfil the law of Christ.

³ If anyone imagines himself to be somebody when he is nothing, he is deluding himself. ⁴ Each of you should examine his own conduct, and then he can measure his achievement by comparing himself with himself and not with anyone else; ⁵ for everyone has his own burden to bear.

⁶ When anyone is under instruction in the faith, he should give his teacher a share of whatever good things he has.

⁷ Make no mistake about this: God is not to be fooled; everyone reaps what he sows. ⁸ If he sows in the field of his unspiritual nature, he will reap from it a harvest of corruption; but if he sows in the field of the Spirit, he will reap from it a harvest of eternal life. ⁹ Let us never tire of doing good, for if we do not slacken our efforts we shall in due time reap our harvest. ¹⁰ Therefore, as opportunity offers, let us work for the good of all, especially members of the household of the faith.

¹¹ LOOK how big the letters are, now that I am writing to you in my own hand. ¹² It is those who want to be outwardly in good standing who are trying to force circumcision on you; their sole object is to escape persecution for the cross of Christ. ¹³ Even those who do accept circumcision are not thoroughgoing observers of the law; they want you to be circumcised just in order to boast of your submission to that outward rite. ¹⁴ God forbid that I should boast of anything but the cross of our Lord Jesus Christ, through which the world is crucified to me and I to the world! ¹⁵ Circumcision is nothing; uncircumcision is nothing; the only thing that counts is new creation! ¹⁶ All who take this principle for their guide, peace and mercy be upon them, the Israel of God!

¹⁷ In future let no one make trouble for me, for I bear the marks of Jesus branded on my body. ¹⁸ The grace of our Lord Jesus Christ be with you, my friends. Amen.

6:14 **which**: *or* whom.   6:16 **the ... God**: *or* and upon the whole Israel of God.

THE LETTER OF PAUL TO THE
EPHESIANS

1 FROM Paul, by the will of God apostle of Christ Jesus, to God's people at Ephesus, to the faithful, incorporate in Christ Jesus.

² Grace to you and peace from God our Father and the Lord Jesus Christ.

The glory of Christ in the church

³ BLESSED be the God and Father of our Lord Jesus Christ, who has conferred on us in Christ every spiritual blessing in the heavenly realms. ⁴ Before the foundation of the world he chose us in Christ to be his people, to be without blemish in his sight, to be full of love; ⁵ and he predestined us to be adopted as his children through Jesus Christ. This was his will and pleasure ⁶ in order that the glory of his gracious gift, so graciously conferred on us in his Beloved, might redound to his praise. ⁷ In Christ our release is secured and our sins forgiven through the shedding of his blood. In the richness of his grace ⁸ God has lavished on us all wisdom and insight.

1:1 **at Ephesus**: *some witnesses omit*.   1:4–5 **sight ... he**: *or* sight. In his love ⁵ he.

[9] He has made known to us his secret purpose, in accordance with the plan which he determined beforehand in Christ, [10] to be put into effect when the time was ripe: namely, that the universe, everything in heaven and on earth, might be brought into a unity in Christ.

[11] In Christ indeed we have been given our share in the heritage, as was decreed in his design whose purpose is everywhere at work; for it was his will [12] that we, who were the first to set our hope on Christ, should cause his glory to be praised. [13] And in Christ you also—once you had heard the message of the truth, the good news of your salvation, and had believed it—in him you were stamped with the seal of the promised Holy Spirit; [14] and that Spirit is a pledge of the inheritance which will be ours when God has redeemed what is his own, to his glory and praise.

[15] Because of all this, now that I have heard of your faith in the Lord Jesus and the love you bear towards all God's people, [16] I never cease to give thanks for you when I mention you in my prayers. [17] I pray that the God of our Lord Jesus Christ, the all-glorious Father, may confer on you the spiritual gifts of wisdom and vision, with the knowledge of him that they bring. [18] I pray that your inward eyes may be enlightened, so that you may know what is the hope to which he calls you, how rich and glorious is the share he offers you among his people in their inheritance, [19] and how vast are the resources of his power open to us who have faith. His mighty strength was seen at work [20] when he raised Christ from the dead, and enthroned him at his right hand in the heavenly realms, [21] far above all government and authority, all power and dominion, and any title of sovereignty that commands allegiance, not only in this age but also in the age to come. [22] He put all things in subjection beneath his feet, and gave him as head over all things to the church [23] which is his body, the fullness of him who is filling the universe in all its parts.

God's grace to Gentiles

2 YOU ONCE were dead because of your sins and wickedness; [2] you followed the ways of this present world order, obeying the commander of the spiritual powers of the air, the spirit now at work among God's rebel subjects. [3] We too were once of their number: we were ruled by our physical desires, and did what instinct and evil imagination suggested. In our natural condition we lay under the condemnation of God like the rest of mankind. [4] But God is rich in mercy, and because of his great love for us, [5] he brought us to life with Christ when we were dead because of our sins; it is by grace you are saved. [6] And he raised us up in union with Christ Jesus and enthroned us with him in the heavenly realms, [7] so that he might display in the ages to come how immense are the resources of his grace, and how great his kindness to us in Christ Jesus. [8] For it is by grace you are saved through faith; it is not your own doing. It is God's gift, [9] not a reward for work done. There is nothing for anyone to boast of; [10] we are God's handiwork, created in Christ Jesus for the life of good deeds which God designed for us.

[11] Remember then your former condition, Gentiles as you are by birth, 'the uncircumcised' as you are called by those who call themselves 'the circumcised' because of a physical rite. [12] You were at that time separate from Christ, excluded from the community of Israel, strangers to God's covenants and the promise that goes with them. Yours was a world without hope and without God. [13] Once you were far off, but now in union with Christ Jesus you have been brought near through the shedding of Christ's blood. [14] For he is himself our peace. Gentiles and Jews, he has made the two one, and in his own body of flesh and blood has broken down the barrier of enmity which separated them; [15] for he annulled the law with its rules and regulations, so as to create out of the two a single new humanity in himself, thereby making peace. [16] This was his purpose, to reconcile the two in a single body to God through the cross, by which he killed the enmity. [17] So he came and proclaimed the good news: peace to you who were far off, and peace to those who were near; [18] for through him we both alike have access to the Father in the one Spirit.

1:12 who ... Christ: *or* who already looked forward in hope to Christ.   1:23 body ... parts: *or* body, filled as he is with the full being of God, who is imparting to all things that same fullness.   2:16 cross ... enmity: *or* cross. Thus in his own person he put to death the enmity.

¹⁹Thus you are no longer aliens in a foreign land, but fellow-citizens with God's people, members of God's household. ²⁰You are built on the foundation of the apostles and prophets, with Christ Jesus himself as the corner-stone. ²¹In him the whole building is bonded together and grows into a holy temple in the Lord. ²²In him you also are being built with all the others into a spiritual dwelling for God.

Paul's prayer

3 WITH this in mind I pray for you, I, Paul, who for the sake of you Gentiles am now the prisoner of Christ Jesus—²for surely you have heard how God's gift of grace to me was designed for your benefit. ³It was by a revelation that his secret purpose was made known to me. I have already written you a brief account of this, ⁴and by reading it you can see that I understand the secret purpose of Christ. ⁵In former generations that secret was not disclosed to mankind; but now by inspiration it has been revealed to his holy apostles and prophets, ⁶that through the gospel the Gentiles are joint heirs with the Jews, part of the same body, sharers together in the promise made in Christ Jesus. ⁷Such is the gospel of which I was made a minister by God's unmerited gift, so powerfully at work in me. ⁸To me, who am less than the least of all God's people, he has granted the privilege of proclaiming to the Gentiles the good news of the unfathomable riches of Christ, ⁹and of bringing to light how this hidden purpose was to be put into effect. It lay concealed for long ages with God the Creator of the universe, ¹⁰in order that now, through the church, the wisdom of God in its infinite variety might be made known to the rulers and authorities in the heavenly realms. ¹¹This accords with his age-long purpose, which he accomplished in Christ Jesus our Lord, ¹²in whom we have freedom of access to God, with the confidence born of trust in him. ¹³I beg you, then, not to lose heart over my sufferings for you; indeed, they are your glory.

¹⁴With this in mind, then, I kneel in prayer to the Father, ¹⁵from whom every family in heaven and on earth takes its name, ¹⁶that out of the treasures of his glory he may grant you inward strength and power through his Spirit, ¹⁷that through faith Christ may dwell in your hearts in love. With deep roots and firm foundations ¹⁸may you, in company with all God's people, be strong to grasp what is the breadth and length and height and depth ¹⁹of Christ's love, and to know it, though it is beyond knowledge. So may you be filled with the very fullness of God.

²⁰Now to him who is able through the power which is at work among us to do immeasurably more than all we can ask or conceive, ²¹to him be glory in the church and in Christ Jesus from generation to generation for evermore! Amen.

Christian conduct

4 I IMPLORE you then—I, a prisoner for the Lord's sake: as God has called you, live up to your calling. ²Be humble always and gentle, and patient too, putting up with one another's failings in the spirit of love. ³Spare no effort to make fast with bonds of peace the unity which the Spirit gives. ⁴There is one body and one Spirit, just as there is one hope held out in God's call to you; ⁵one Lord, one faith, one baptism; ⁶one God and Father of all, who is over all and through all and in all.

⁷But each of us has been given a special gift, a particular share in the bounty of Christ. ⁸That is why scripture says:

He ascended into the heights;
he took captives into captivity;
he gave gifts to men.

⁹Now, the word 'ascended' implies that he also descended to the lowest level, down to the very earth. ¹⁰He who descended is none other than he who ascended far above all heavens, so that he might fill the universe. ¹¹And it is he who has given some to be apostles, some prophets, some evangelists, some pastors and teachers, ¹²to equip God's people for work in his service, for the building up of the body of Christ, ¹³until we all attain to the unity inherent in our faith and in our knowledge of the Son of God—to mature manhood, measured by nothing less than the full stature of Christ. ¹⁴We are no longer to be children, tossed about by the waves and whirled around by every fresh gust of teaching, dupes of cunning rogues

4:9 **descended ... earth:** *or* descended to the regions beneath the earth.

and their deceitful schemes. ¹⁵ Rather we are to maintain the truth in a spirit of love; so shall we fully grow up into Christ. He is the head, ¹⁶ and on him the whole body depends. Bonded and held together by every constituent joint, the whole frame grows through the proper functioning of each part, and builds itself up in love.

¹⁷ Here then is my word to you, and I urge it on you in the Lord's name: give up living as pagans do with their futile notions. ¹⁸ Their minds are closed, they are alienated from the life that is in God, because ignorance prevails among them and their hearts have grown hard as stone. ¹⁹ Dead to all feeling, they have abandoned themselves to vice, and there is no indecency that they do not practise. ²⁰ But that is not how you learned Christ. ²¹ For were you not told about him, were you not as Christians taught the truth as it is in Jesus? ²² Renouncing your former way of life, you must lay aside the old human nature which, deluded by its desires, is in process of decay: ²³ you must be renewed in mind and spirit, ²⁴ and put on the new nature created in God's likeness, which shows itself in the upright and devout life called for by the truth.

²⁵ Then have done with falsehood and speak the truth to each other, for we belong to one another as parts of one body.

²⁶ If you are angry, do not be led into sin; do not let sunset find you nursing your anger; ²⁷ and give no foothold to the devil. ²⁸ The thief must give up stealing, and work hard with his hands to earn an honest living, so that he may have something to share with the needy.

²⁹ Let no offensive talk pass your lips, only what is good and helpful to the occasion, so that it brings a blessing to those who hear it. ³⁰ Do not grieve the Holy Spirit of God, for that Spirit is the seal with which you were marked for the day of final liberation. ³¹ Have done with all spite and bad temper, with rage, insults, and slander, with evil of any kind. ³² Be generous to one another, tender-hearted, forgiving one another as God in Christ forgave you.

5 In a word, as God's dear children, you must be like him. ² Live in love as Christ loved you and gave himself up on your behalf, an offering and sacrifice whose fragrance is pleasing to God.

³ Fornication and indecency of any kind, or ruthless greed, must not be so much as mentioned among you, as befits the people of God. ⁴ No coarse, stupid, or flippant talk: these things are out of place; you should rather be thanking God. ⁵ For be very sure of this: no one given to fornication or vice, or the greed which makes an idol of gain, has any share in the kingdom of Christ and of God. ⁶ Let no one deceive you with shallow arguments; it is for these things that divine retribution falls on God's rebel subjects. ⁷ Have nothing to do with them. ⁸ Though you once were darkness, now as Christians you are light. Prove yourselves at home in the light, ⁹ for where light is, there is a harvest of goodness, righteousness, and truth. ¹⁰ Learn to judge for yourselves what is pleasing to the Lord; ¹¹ take no part in the barren deeds of darkness, but show them up for what they are. ¹² It would be shameful even to mention what is done in secret. ¹³ But everything is shown up by being exposed to the light, and whatever is exposed to the light itself becomes light. ¹⁴ That is why it is said:

Awake, sleeper,
rise from the dead,
and Christ will shine upon you.

¹⁵ Take great care, then, how you behave: act sensibly, not like simpletons. ¹⁶ Use the present opportunity to the full, for these are evil days. ¹⁷ Do not be foolish, but understand what the will of the Lord is. ¹⁸ Do not give way to drunkenness and the ruin that goes with it, but let the Holy Spirit fill you: ¹⁹ speak to one another in psalms, hymns, and songs; sing and make music from your heart to the Lord; ²⁰ and in the name of our Lord Jesus Christ give thanks every day for everything to our God and Father.

Christian relationships

²¹ BE subject to one another out of reverence for Christ.

²² Wives, be subject to your husbands as though to the Lord; ²³ for the man is the head of the woman, just as Christ is the head of the church. Christ is, indeed, the saviour of that body; ²⁴ but just as

5:19 hymns, and: *some witnesses add* spiritual.

the church is subject to Christ, so must women be subject to their husbands in everything. ²⁵ Husbands, love your wives, as Christ loved the church and gave himself up for it, ²⁶ to consecrate and cleanse it by water and word, ²⁷ so that he might present the church to himself all glorious, with no stain or wrinkle or anything of the sort, but holy and without blemish. ²⁸ In the same way men ought to love their wives, as they love their own bodies. In loving his wife a man loves himself. ²⁹ For no one ever hated his own body; on the contrary, he keeps it nourished and warm, and that is how Christ treats the church, ³⁰ because it is his body, of which we are living parts. ³¹ 'This is why' (in the words of scripture) 'a man shall leave his father and mother and be united to his wife, and the two shall become one flesh.' ³² There is hidden here a great truth, which I take to refer to Christ and to the church. ³³ But it applies also to each one of you: the husband must love his wife as his very self, and the wife must show reverence for her husband.

6 Children, obey your parents; for it is only right that you should. ² 'Honour your father and your mother' is the first commandment to carry a promise with it: ³ 'that it may be well with you and that you may live long on the earth.'

⁴ Fathers, do not goad your children to resentment, but bring them up in the discipline and instruction of the Lord.

⁵ Slaves, give single-minded obedience to your earthly masters with fear and trembling, as if to Christ. ⁶ Do it not merely to catch their eye or curry favour with them, but as slaves of Christ do the will of God wholeheartedly. ⁷ Give cheerful service, as slaves of the Lord rather than of men. ⁸ You know that whatever good anyone may do, slave or free, will be repaid by the Lord.

⁹ Masters, treat your slaves in the same spirit: give up using threats, and remember that you both have the same Master

in heaven; there is no favouritism with him.

The Christian's armoury

¹⁰ FINALLY, find your strength in the Lord, in his mighty power. ¹¹ Put on the full armour provided by God, so that you may be able to stand firm against the stratagems of the devil. ¹² For our struggle is not against human foes, but against cosmic powers, against the authorities and potentates of this dark age, against the superhuman forces of evil in the heavenly realms. ¹³ Therefore, take up the armour of God; then you will be able to withstand them on the evil day and, after doing your utmost, to stand your ground. ¹⁴ Stand fast, I say. Fasten on the belt of truth; for a breastplate put on integrity; ¹⁵ let the shoes on your feet be the gospel of peace, to give you firm footing; ¹⁶ and, with all these, take up the great shield of faith, with which you will be able to quench all the burning arrows of the evil one. ¹⁷ Accept salvation as your helmet, and the sword which the Spirit gives you, the word of God. ¹⁸ Constantly ask God's help in prayer, and pray always in the power of the Spirit. To this end keep watch and persevere, always interceding for all God's people. ¹⁹ Pray also for me, that I may be granted the right words when I speak, and may boldly and freely make known the hidden purpose of the gospel, ²⁰ for which I am an ambassador—in chains. Pray that I may speak of it boldly, as is my duty.

²¹ YOU WILL want to know how I am and what I am doing; Tychicus will give you all the news. He is our dear brother and trustworthy helper in the Lord's work. ²² I am sending him to you on purpose to let you have news of us and to put fresh heart into you.

²³ Peace to the community and love with faith, from God the Father and the Lord Jesus Christ. ²⁴ God's grace be with all who love our Lord Jesus Christ with undying love.

6:24 **Christ ... love:** *or* Christ, grace and immortality.

THE LETTER OF PAUL TO THE
PHILIPPIANS

1 FROM Paul and Timothy, servants of Christ Jesus, to all God's people at Philippi, who are incorporate in Christ Jesus, with the bishops and deacons. ² Grace to you and peace from God our Father and the Lord Jesus Christ.

³ I thank my God every time I think of you; ⁴ whenever I pray for you all, my prayers are always joyful, ⁵ because of the part you have taken in the work of the gospel from the first day until now. ⁶ Of this I am confident, that he who started the good work in you will bring it to completion by the day of Christ Jesus. ⁷ It is only natural that I should feel like this about you all, because I have great affection for you, knowing that, both while I am kept in prison and when I am called on to defend the truth of the gospel, you all share in this privilege of mine. ⁸ God knows how I long for you all with the deep yearning of Christ Jesus himself. ⁹ And this is my prayer, that your love may grow ever richer in knowledge and insight of every kind, ¹⁰ enabling you to learn by experience what things really matter. Then on the day of Christ you will be flawless and without blame, ¹¹ yielding the full harvest of righteousness that comes through Jesus Christ, to the glory and praise of God.

Paul in prison

¹² My friends, I want you to understand that the progress of the gospel has actually been helped by what has happened to me. ¹³ It has become common knowledge throughout the imperial guard, and indeed among the public at large, that my imprisonment is in Christ's cause; ¹⁴ and my being in prison has given most of our fellow-Christians confidence to speak the word of God fearlessly and with extraordinary courage.

¹⁵ Some, it is true, proclaim Christ in a jealous and quarrelsome spirit, but some do it in goodwill. ¹⁶ These are moved by love, knowing that it is to defend the gospel that I am where I am; ¹⁷ the others are moved by selfish ambition and present Christ from mixed motives, meaning to cause me distress as I lie in prison. ¹⁸ What does it matter? One way or another, whether sincerely or not, Christ is proclaimed; and for that I rejoice.

Yes, and I shall go on rejoicing; ¹⁹ for I know well that the issue will be my deliverance, because you are praying for me and the Spirit of Jesus Christ is given me for support. ²⁰ It is my confident hope that nothing will daunt me or prevent me from speaking boldly; and that now as always Christ will display his greatness in me, whether the verdict be life or death. ²¹ For to me life is Christ, and death is gain. ²² If I am to go on living in the body there is fruitful work for me to do. Which then am I to choose? I cannot tell. ²³ I am pulled two ways: my own desire is to depart and be with Christ—that is better by far; ²⁴ but for your sake the greater need is for me to remain in the body. ²⁵ This convinces me: I am sure I shall remain, and stand by you all to ensure your progress and joy in the faith, ²⁶ so that on my account you may have even more cause for pride in Christ Jesus—through seeing me restored to you.

Unity and witness

²⁷ WHATEVER happens, let your conduct be worthy of the gospel of Christ, so that whether or not I come and see you for myself I may hear that you are standing firm, united in spirit and in mind, side by side in the struggle to advance the gospel faith, ²⁸ meeting your opponents without so much as a tremor. This is a sure sign to them that destruction is in store for them and salvation for you, a sign from God himself; ²⁹ for you have been granted the privilege not only of believing in Christ but also of suffering for him. ³⁰ Your conflict is the same as mine; once you saw me in it, and now you hear I am in it still.

1:1 **bishops and deacons**: *or* overseers and assistants.   1:13 **the imperial guard:** *or* the Residency.

2 If then our common life in Christ yields anything to stir the heart, any consolation of love, any participation in the Spirit, any warmth of affection or compassion, ²fill up my cup of happiness by thinking and feeling alike, with the same love for one another and a common attitude of mind. ³Leave no room for selfish ambition and vanity, but humbly reckon others better than yourselves. ⁴Look to each other's interests and not merely to your own.

⁵Take to heart among yourselves what you find in Christ Jesus: ⁶'He was in the form of God; yet he laid no claim to equality with God, ⁷but made himself nothing, assuming the form of a slave. Bearing the human likeness, ⁸sharing the human lot, he humbled himself, and was obedient, even to the point of death, death on a cross! ⁹Therefore God raised him to the heights and bestowed on him the name above all names, ¹⁰that at the name of Jesus every knee should bow—in heaven, on earth, and in the depths— ¹¹and every tongue acclaim, "Jesus Christ is Lord," to the glory of God the Father.'

¹²So you too, my friends, must be obedient, as always; even more, now that I am absent, than when I was with you. You must work out your own salvation in fear and trembling; ¹³for it is God who works in you, inspiring both the will and the deed, for his own chosen purpose.

¹⁴Do everything without grumbling or argument. ¹⁵Show yourselves innocent and above reproach, faultless children of God in a crooked and depraved generation, in which you shine like stars in a dark world ¹⁶and proffer the word of life. Then you will be my pride on the day of Christ, proof that I did not run my race in vain or labour in vain. ¹⁷But if my life-blood is to be poured out to complete the sacrifice and offering up of your faith, I rejoice and share my joy with you all. ¹⁸You too must rejoice and share your joy with me.

Paul's plans

¹⁹I HOPE, in the Lord Jesus, to send Timothy to you soon; it will cheer me up to have news of you. ²⁰I have no one else here like him, who has a genuine concern for your affairs; ²¹they are all bent on their own interests, not on those of Christ Jesus. ²²But Timothy's record is known to you: you know that he has been at my side in the service of the gospel like a son working under his father. ²³So he is the one I mean to send as soon as I see how things go with me; ²⁴and I am confident, in the Lord, that I shall be coming myself before long.

²⁵I have decided I must also send our brother Epaphroditus, my fellow-worker and comrade, whom you commissioned to attend to my needs. ²⁶He has been missing you all, and was upset because you heard he was ill. ²⁷Indeed he was dangerously ill, but God was merciful to him; and not only to him but to me, to spare me one sorrow on top of another. ²⁸For this reason I am all the more eager to send him and give you the happiness of seeing him again; that will relieve my anxiety as well. ²⁹Welcome him then in the fellowship of the Lord with whole-hearted delight. You should honour people like him; ³⁰in Christ's cause he came near to death, risking his life to render me the service you could not give.

3 And now, my friends, I wish you joy in the Lord.

The Christian's goal

To REPEAT what I have written to you before is no trouble to me, and it is a safeguard for you. ²Be on your guard against those dogs, those who do nothing but harm and who insist on mutilation— 'circumcision' I will not call it; ³we are the circumcision, we who worship by the Spirit of God, whose pride is in Christ Jesus, and who put no confidence in the physical. ⁴It is not that I am myself without grounds for such confidence. If anyone makes claims of that kind, I can make a stronger case for myself: ⁵circumcised on my eighth day, Israelite by race, of the tribe of Benjamin, a Hebrew born and bred; in my practice of the law a Pharisee, ⁶in zeal for religion a persecutor of the church, by the law's standard of righteousness without fault. ⁷But all such assets I have written off because of Christ. ⁸More than that, I count everything

---

2:20 no one ... who has: *or* no one else here who sees things as I do, and has.   3:3 who worship ... God: *some witnesses read* who worship God in the spirit; *one reads* whose worship is spiritual.

sheer loss, far outweighed by the gain of knowing Christ Jesus my Lord, for whose sake I did in fact forfeit everything. I count it so much rubbish, for the sake of gaining Christ [9] and finding myself in union with him, with no righteousness of my own based on the law, nothing but the righteousness which comes from faith in Christ, given by God in response to faith. [10] My one desire is to know Christ and the power of his resurrection, and to share his sufferings in growing conformity with his death, [11] in hope of somehow attaining the resurrection from the dead.

[12] It is not that I have already achieved this. I have not yet reached perfection, but I press on, hoping to take hold of that for which Christ once took hold of me. [13] My friends, I do not claim to have hold of it yet. What I do say is this: forgetting what is behind and straining towards what lies ahead, [14] I press towards the finishing line, to win the heavenly prize to which God has called me in Christ Jesus.

[15] We who are mature should keep to this way of thinking. If on any point you think differently, this also God will make plain to you. [16] Only let our conduct be consistent with what we have already attained.

[17] Join together, my friends, in following my example. You have us for a model; imitate those whose way of life conforms to it. [18] As I have often told you, and now tell you with tears, there are many whose way of life makes them enemies of the cross of Christ. [19] They are heading for destruction, they make appetite their god, they take pride in what should bring shame; their minds are set on earthly things. [20] We, by contrast, are citizens of heaven, and from heaven we expect our deliverer to come, the Lord Jesus Christ. [21] He will transfigure our humble bodies, and give them a form like that of his own glorious body, by that power which enables him to make all things subject to himself. [1] This, my dear friends, whom I love and long for, my joy and crown, this is what it means to stand firm in the Lord.

[2] Euodia and Syntyche, I appeal to you both: agree together in the Lord. [3] Yes, and you too, my loyal comrade, I ask you to help these women, who shared my struggles in the cause of the gospel, with Clement and my other fellow-workers, who are enrolled in the book of life.

[4] I wish you joy in the Lord always. Again I say: all joy be yours. [5] Be known to everyone for your consideration of others.

The Lord is near; [6] do not be anxious, but in everything make your requests known to God in prayer and petition with thanksgiving. [7] Then the peace of God, which is beyond all understanding, will guard your hearts and your thoughts in Christ Jesus.

[8] And now, my friends, all that is true, all that is noble, all that is just and pure, all that is lovable and attractive, whatever is excellent and admirable—fill your thoughts with these things. [9] Put into practice the lessons I taught you, the tradition I have passed on, all that you heard me say or saw me do; and the God of peace will be with you.

Thanks and greetings

[10] It is a great joy to me in the Lord that after so long your care for me has now revived. I know you always cared; it was opportunity you lacked. [11] Not that I am speaking of want, for I have learned to be self-sufficient whatever my circumstances. [12] I know what it is to have nothing, and I know what it is to have plenty. I have been thoroughly initiated into fullness and hunger, plenty and poverty. [13] I am able to face anything through him who gives me strength. [14] All the same, it was kind of you to share the burden of my troubles.

[15] You Philippians are aware that, when I set out from Macedonia in the early days of my mission, yours was the only church to share with me in the giving and receiving; [16] more than once you contributed to my needs, even at Thessalonica. [17] Do not think I set my heart on the gift; all I care for is the interest mounting up in your account. [18] I have been paid in full; I have all I need and more, now that I have received from Epaphroditus what you sent. It is a fragrant offering, an acceptable sacrifice, pleasing to God. [19] And my God will supply all your needs out of the magnificence of his riches in Christ Jesus. [20] To our God

and Father be glory for ever and ever! Amen.

²¹ Give my greetings, in the fellowship of Christ Jesus, to each one of God's people. My colleagues send their greetings to you, ²² and so do all God's people here, particularly those in the emperor's service.

²³ The grace of our Lord Jesus Christ be with your spirit.

THE LETTER OF PAUL TO THE

COLOSSIANS

1 FROM Paul, by the will of God apostle of Christ Jesus, and our colleague Timothy, ² to God's people at Colossae, our fellow-believers in Christ.

Grace to you and peace from God our Father.

³ In all our prayers to God, the Father of our Lord Jesus Christ, we thank him for you, ⁴ because we have heard of your faith in Christ Jesus and the love you bear towards all God's people; ⁵ both spring from that hope stored up for you in heaven of which you learned when the message of the true gospel first ⁶ came to you. That same gospel is bearing fruit and making new growth the whole world over, as it does among you and has done since the day when you heard of God's grace and learned what it truly is. ⁷ It was Epaphras, our dear fellow-servant and a trusted worker for Christ on our behalf, who taught you this, ⁸ and it is he who has brought us news of the love the Spirit has awakened in you.

The supremacy of Christ

⁹ THIS is why, ever since we first heard about you, we have not ceased to pray for you. We ask God that you may receive from him full insight into his will, all wisdom and spiritual understanding, ¹⁰ so that your manner of life may be worthy of the Lord and entirely pleasing to him. We pray that you may bear fruit in active goodness of every kind, and grow in knowledge of God. ¹¹ In his glorious might may he give you ample strength to meet with fortitude and patience whatever comes; ¹² and to give joyful thanks to the Father who has made you fit to share the heritage of God's people in the realm of light.

¹³ He rescued us from the domain of darkness and brought us into the kingdom of his dear Son, ¹⁴ through whom our release is secured and our sins are forgiven. ¹⁵ He is the image of the invisible God; his is the primacy over all creation. ¹⁶ In him everything in heaven and on earth was created, not only things visible but also the invisible orders of thrones, sovereignties, authorities, and powers: the whole universe has been created through him and for him. ¹⁷ He exists before all things, and all things are held together in him. ¹⁸ He is the head of the body, the church. He is its origin, the first to return from the dead, to become in all things supreme. ¹⁹ For in him God in all his fullness chose to dwell, ²⁰ and through him to reconcile all things to himself, making peace through the shedding of his blood on the cross—all things, whether on earth or in heaven.

²¹⁻²² Formerly you yourselves were alienated from God, his enemies in heart and mind, as your evil deeds showed. But now by Christ's death in his body of flesh and blood God has reconciled you to himself, so that he may bring you into his own presence, holy and without blame or blemish. ²³ Yet you must persevere in faith, firm on your foundations and never to be dislodged from the hope offered in the gospel you accepted. This is the gospel which has been proclaimed in the whole creation under heaven, the gospel of which I, Paul, became a minister.

1:7 **our behalf:** *some witnesses read* your behalf. whatever comes; ¹² and to give thanks.   1:16 **for him:** *or* with him as its goal.   1:11–12 **patience ... thanks:** *or* patience, and joy   1:20 **to himself:** *or* to their goal in him.

²⁴ It is now my joy to suffer for you; for the sake of Christ's body, the church, I am completing what still remains for Christ to suffer in my own person. ²⁵ I became a servant of the church by virtue of the task assigned to me by God for your benefit: to put God's word into full effect, ²⁶ that secret purpose hidden for long ages and through many generations, but now disclosed to God's people. ²⁷ To them he chose to make known what a wealth of glory is offered to the Gentiles in this secret purpose: Christ in you, the hope of glory.

²⁸ He it is whom we proclaim. We teach everyone and instruct everyone in all the ways of wisdom, so as to present each one of you as a mature member of Christ's body. ²⁹ To this end I am toiling strenuously with all the energy and power of Christ at work in me. ¹ I want you to know how strenuous are my exertions for you and the Laodiceans, and for all who have never set eyes on me. ² My aim is to keep them in good heart and united in love, so that they may come to the full wealth of conviction which understanding brings, and grasp God's secret, which is Christ himself, ³ in whom lie hidden all the treasures of wisdom and knowledge. ⁴ I tell you this to make sure no one talks you into error by specious arguments. ⁵ I may be absent in body, but in spirit I am with you, and rejoice to see your unbroken ranks and the solid front which your faith in Christ presents.

True and false teaching

⁶ THEREFORE, since you have accepted Christ Jesus as Lord, live in union with him. ⁷ Be rooted in him, be built in him, grow strong in the faith as you were taught; let your hearts overflow with thankfulness. ⁸ Be on your guard; let no one capture your minds with hollow and delusive speculations, based on traditions of human teaching and centred on the elemental spirits of the universe and not on Christ.

⁹ For it is in Christ that the Godhead in all its fullness dwells embodied, ¹⁰ it is in him you have been brought to fulfilment. Every power and authority in the universe is subject to him as head. ¹¹ In him also you were circumcised, not in a physical sense, but by the stripping away of the old nature, which is Christ's way of circumcision. ¹² For you were buried with him in baptism, and in that baptism you were also raised to life with him through your faith in the active power of God, who raised him from the dead. ¹³ And although you were dead because of your sins and your uncircumcision, he has brought you to life with Christ. For he has forgiven us all our sins; ¹⁴ he has cancelled the bond which was outstanding against us with its legal demands; he has set it aside, nailing it to the cross. ¹⁵ There he disarmed the cosmic powers and authorities and made a public spectacle of them, leading them as captives in his triumphal procession.

¹⁶ ALLOW no one, therefore, to take you to task about what you eat or drink, or over the observance of festival, new moon, or sabbath. ¹⁷ These are no more than a shadow of what was to come; the reality is Christ's. ¹⁸ You are not to be disqualified by the decision of people who go in for self-mortification and angel-worship and access to some visionary world. Such people, bursting with the futile conceit of worldly minds, ¹⁹ lose their hold upon the head; yet it is from the head that the whole body, with all its joints and ligaments, has its needs supplied, and thus knit together grows according to God's design.

²⁰ Did you not die with Christ and pass beyond reach of the elemental spirits of the universe? Then why behave as though you were still living the life of the world? Why let people dictate to you: ²¹ 'Do not handle this, do not taste that, do not touch the other'—²² referring to things that must all perish as they are used? That is to follow human rules and regulations. ²³ Such conduct may have an air of wisdom, with its forced piety, its self-mortification, and its severity to the body; but it is of no use at all in combating sensuality.

³ Were you not raised to life with Christ? Then aspire to the realm above, where Christ is, seated at God's right hand, ² and fix your thoughts on

---

2:8 **and centred ... universe:** *or* and elementary ideas belonging to this world.   2:15 **he disarmed ... of them:** *or* he stripped himself of his physical body, and thereby made a public spectacle of the cosmic powers and authorities.   2:20 **elemental ... universe:** *or* elementary ideas belonging to this world.

that higher realm, not on this earthly life. [3] You died; and now your life lies hidden with Christ in God. [4] When Christ, who is our life, is revealed, then you too will be revealed with him in glory.

Christian conduct

[5] So PUT to death those parts of you which belong to the earth—fornication, indecency, lust, evil desires, and the ruthless greed which is nothing less than idolatry; [6] on these divine retribution falls. [7] This is the way you yourselves once lived; [8] but now have done with rage, bad temper, malice, slander, filthy talk—banish them all from your lips! [9] Do not lie to one another, now that you have discarded the old human nature and the conduct that goes with it, [10] and have put on the new nature which is constantly being renewed in the image of its Creator and brought to know God. [11] There is no question here of Greek and Jew, circumcised and uncircumcised, barbarian, Scythian, slave and freeman; but Christ is all, and is in all. [12] Put on, then, garments that suit God's chosen and beloved people: compassion, kindness, humility, gentleness, patience. [13] Be tolerant with one another and forgiving, if any of you has cause for complaint: you must forgive as the Lord forgave you. [14] Finally, to bind everything together and complete the whole, there must be love. [15] Let Christ's peace be arbiter in your decisions, the peace to which you were called as members of a single body. Always be thankful. [16] Let the gospel of Christ dwell among you in all its richness; teach and instruct one another with all the wisdom it gives you. With psalms and hymns and spiritual songs, sing from the heart in gratitude to God. [17] Let every word and action, everything you do, be in the name of the Lord Jesus, and give thanks through him to God the Father.

[18] WIVES, be subject to your husbands; that is your Christian duty. [19] Husbands, love your wives and do not be harsh with them. [20] Children, obey your parents in everything, for that is pleasing to God and is the Christian way. [21] Fathers, do not exasperate your children, in case they lose heart. [22] Slaves, give entire obedience to your earthly masters, not merely to catch their eye or curry favour with them, but with single-mindedness, out of reverence for the Lord. [23] Whatever you are doing, put your whole heart into it, as if you were doing it for the Lord and not for men, [24] knowing that there is a master who will give you an inheritance as a reward for your service. Christ is the master you must serve. [25] Wrongdoers will pay for the wrong they do; there will 4 be no favouritism. [1] Masters, be just and fair to your slaves, knowing that you too have a master in heaven.

[2] Persevere in prayer, with minds alert and with thankful hearts; [3] and include us in your prayers, asking God to provide an opening for the gospel, that we may proclaim the secret of Christ, for which indeed I am in prison. [4] Pray that I may make the secret plain, as it is my duty to do.

[5] Be wise in your dealings with outsiders, but use your opportunities to the full. [6] Let your words always be gracious, never insipid; learn how best to respond to each person you meet.

News and greetings

[7] YOU WILL hear all my news from Tychicus, our dear brother and trustworthy helper and fellow-servant in the Lord's work. [8] I am sending him to you for this purpose, to let you know how we are and to put fresh heart into you. [9] With him comes Onesimus, our trustworthy and dear brother, who is one of yourselves. They will tell you all that has happened here.

[10] Aristarchus, Christ's captive like myself, sends his greetings; so does Mark, the cousin of Barnabas (you have had instructions about him; if he comes, make him welcome), [11] and Jesus Justus. Of the Jewish Christians, these are the only ones working with me for the kingdom of God, and they have been a great comfort to me. [12] Greetings from Epaphras, servant of Christ, who is one of yourselves. He prays hard for you all the time, that you may stand fast, as mature Christians, fully determined to do the will of God. [13] I can vouch for him, that he works tirelessly for you and the people at Laodicea and Hierapolis. [14] Greetings to you from our dear friend Luke, the doctor, and from Demas. [15] Give our greetings to the

4:15 **Nympha ... her house:** *some witnesses read* Nymphas ... his house.

Christians at Laodicea, and to Nympha and the congregation that meets at her house. ¹⁶ Once this letter has been read among you, see that it is read also to the church at Laodicea, and that you in turn read my letter to Laodicea. ¹⁷ Give Archip-pus this message: 'See that you carry out fully the duty entrusted to you in the Lord's service.'

¹⁸ I add this greeting in my own hand— Paul. Remember I am in prison. Grace be with you.

THE FIRST LETTER OF PAUL TO THE
THESSALONIANS

1 From Paul, Silvanus, and Timothy to the church of the Thessalonians who belong to God the Father and the Lord Jesus Christ.

Grace to you and peace.

² We always thank God for you all, and mention you in our prayers. ³ We continually call to mind, before our God and Father, how your faith has shown itself in action, your love in labour, and your hope of our Lord Jesus Christ in perseverance. ⁴ My dear friends, beloved by God, we are certain that he has chosen you, ⁵ because when we brought you the gospel we did not bring it in mere words but in the power of the Holy Spirit and with strong conviction. You know what we were like for your sake when we were with you.

⁶ You, in turn, followed the example set by us and by the Lord; the welcome you gave the message meant grave suffering for you, yet you rejoiced in the Holy Spirit; ⁷ and so you have become a model for all believers in Macedonia and in Achaia. ⁸ From you the word of the Lord rang out; and not in Macedonia and Achaia alone, but everywhere your faith in God has become common knowledge. No words of ours are needed; ⁹ everyone is spreading the story of our visit to you: how you turned from idols to be servants of the true and living God, ¹⁰ and to wait expectantly for his Son from heaven, whom he raised from the dead, Jesus our deliverer from the retribution to come.

Paul and the church at Thessalonica

2 You know for yourselves, my friends, that our visit to you was not fruitless. ² Far from it! After all the injury and outrage which as you know we had suffered at Philippi, by the help of our God we declared the gospel of God to you frankly and fearlessly in face of great opposition. ³ The appeal we make does not spring from delusion or sordid motive or from any attempt to deceive; ⁴ but God has approved us as fit to be entrusted with the gospel. So when we preach, we do not curry favour with men; we seek only the favour of God, who is continually testing our hearts. ⁵ We have never resorted to flattery, as you have cause to know; nor, as God is our witness, have our words ever been a cloak for greed. ⁶ We have never sought honour from men, not from you or from anyone else, ⁷ although as Christ's own envoys we might have made our weight felt; but we were as gentle with you as a nurse caring for her children. ⁸ Our affection was so deep that we were determined to share with you not only the gospel of God but our very selves; that is how dear you had become to us! ⁹ You remember, my friends, our toil and drudgery; night and day we worked for a living, rather than be a burden to any of you while we proclaimed to you the good news of God.

¹⁰ We call you to witness, yes and God himself, how devout and just and blameless was our conduct towards you who are believers. ¹¹ As you well know, we dealt with each one of you as a father deals with his children; ¹² we appealed to you, we encouraged you, we urged you, to live lives worthy of the God who calls you into his kingdom and glory.

¹³ We have reason to thank God continually because, when we handed on God's message, you accepted it, not as the word of men, but as what it truly is, the very word of God at work in you who are

believers. [14] You, my friends, have followed the example of the Christians in the churches of God in Judaea: you have been treated by your own countrymen as they were treated by the Jews, [15] who killed the Lord Jesus and the prophets and drove us out, and are so heedless of God's will and such enemies of their fellow-men [16] that they hinder us from telling the Gentiles how they may be saved. All this time they have been making up the full measure of their guilt. But now retribution has overtaken them for good and all!

[17] My friends, when for a short spell you were lost to us—out of sight but not out of mind—we were exceedingly anxious to see you again. [18] So we made up our minds to visit you—I, Paul, more than once—but Satan thwarted us. [19] For what hope or joy or triumphal crown is there for us when we stand before our Lord Jesus at his coming? What indeed but you? [20] You are our glory and our joy.

3 So when we could bear it no longer, we decided to stay on alone at Athens, [2] and sent Timothy, our colleague and a fellow-worker with God in the service of the gospel of Christ, to encourage you to stand firm for the faith [3] and under all these hardships remain unshaken. You know that this is our appointed lot, [4] for when we were with you we warned you that we were bound to suffer hardship; and so it has turned out, as you have found. [5] This was why I could bear it no longer and sent to find out about your faith; I was afraid that the tempter might have tempted you and our labour might be wasted.

[6] But now Timothy has just returned from his visit to you, bringing good news of your faith and love. He tells us that you always think kindly of us, and are as anxious to see us as we are to see you. [7] So amid all our difficulties and hardships we are reassured, my friends, by the news of your faith. [8] It is the breath of life to us to know that you stand firm in the Lord. [9] What thanks can we give to God in return for you? What thanks for all the joy you have brought us, making us rejoice before our God [10] while we pray most earnestly night and day to be allowed to see you again and to make good whatever is lacking in your faith? [11] May our God and Father himself, and

our Lord Jesus, open the way for us to come to you; [12] and may the Lord make your love increase and overflow to one another and to everyone, as our love does to you. [13] May he make your hearts firm, so that you may stand before our God and Father holy and faultless when our Lord Jesus comes with all those who are his own.

Christian conduct

4 AND now, friends, we have one thing to ask of you, as fellow-Christians. We passed on to you the tradition of the way we must live if we are to please God; you are indeed already following it, but we beg you to do so yet more thoroughly. [2] You know the rules we gave you in the name of the Lord Jesus. [3] This is the will of God, that you should be holy: you must abstain from fornication; [4] each one of you must learn to gain mastery over his body, to hallow and honour it, [5] not giving way to lust like the pagans who know nothing of God; [6] no one must do his fellow-Christian wrong in this matter, or infringe his rights. As we impressed on you before, the Lord punishes all such offences. [7] For God called us to holiness, not to impurity. [8] Anyone therefore who flouts these rules is flouting not man but the God who bestows on you his Holy Spirit.

[9] About love of the brotherhood you need no words of mine, for you are yourselves taught by God to love one another, [10] and you are in fact practising this rule of love towards all your fellow-Christians throughout Macedonia. Yet we appeal to you, friends, to do better still. [11] Let it be your ambition to live quietly and attend to your own business; and to work with your hands, as we told you, [12] so that you may command the respect of those outside your own number, and at the same time never be in want.

Christ's return

[13] WE wish you not to remain in ignorance, friends, about those who sleep in death; you should not grieve like the rest of mankind, who have no hope. [14] We believe that Jesus died and rose again; so too will God bring those who died as Christians to be with Jesus.

[15] This we tell you as a word from the Lord: those of us who are still alive when the Lord comes will have no advantage

over those who have died; ¹⁶ when the command is given, when the archangel's voice is heard, when God's trumpet sounds, then the Lord himself will descend from heaven; first the Christian dead will rise, ¹⁷ then we who are still alive shall join them, caught up in clouds to meet the Lord in the air. Thus we shall always be with the Lord. ¹⁸ Console one another, then, with these words.

5 About dates and times, my friends, there is no need to write to you, ² for you yourselves know perfectly well that the day of the Lord comes like a thief in the night. ³ While they are saying, 'All is peaceful, all secure,' destruction is upon them, sudden as the pangs that come on a woman in childbirth; and there will be no escape. ⁴ But you, friends, are not in the dark; the day will not come upon you like a thief. ⁵ You are all children of light, children of day. We do not belong to night and darkness, ⁶ and we must not sleep like the rest, but keep awake and sober. ⁷ Sleepers sleep at night, and drunkards get drunk at night, ⁸ but we, who belong to the daylight, must keep sober, armed with the breastplate of faith and love, and the hope of salvation for a helmet. ⁹ God has not destined us for retribution, but for the full attainment of salvation through our Lord Jesus Christ. ¹⁰ He died for us so that awake or asleep we might live in company with him. ¹¹ Therefore encourage one another, build one another up— as indeed you do.

Final instructions and greetings

¹² WE beg you, friends, to acknowledge those who are working so hard among you, and are your leaders and counsellors in the Lord's fellowship. ¹³ Hold them in the highest esteem and affection for the work they do.

Live at peace among yourselves. ¹⁴ We urge you, friends, to rebuke the idle, encourage the faint-hearted, support the weak, and be patient with everyone.

¹⁵ See to it that no one pays back wrong for wrong, but always aim at what is best for each other and for all.

¹⁶ Always be joyful; ¹⁷ pray continually; ¹⁸ give thanks whatever happens; for this is what God wills for you in Christ Jesus.

¹⁹ Do not stifle inspiration ²⁰ or despise prophetic utterances, ²¹ but test them all; keep hold of what is good ²² and avoid all forms of evil.

²³ May God himself, the God of peace, make you holy through and through, and keep you sound in spirit, soul, and body, free of any fault when our Lord Jesus Christ comes. ²⁴ He who calls you keeps faith; he will do it.

²⁵ Friends, pray for us also.

²⁶ Greet all our fellow-Christians with the kiss of peace.

²⁷ I adjure you by the Lord to have this letter read to them all.

²⁸ The grace of our Lord Jesus Christ be with you!

THE SECOND LETTER OF PAUL TO THE
THESSALONIANS

1 FROM Paul, Silvanus, and Timothy to the church of the Thessalonians who belong to God our Father and the Lord Jesus Christ.

² Grace to you and peace from God the Father and the Lord Jesus Christ.

³ Friends, we are always bound to thank God for you, and it is right that we should, because your faith keeps on increasing and the love you all have for each other grows ever greater. ⁴ Indeed we boast about you among the churches

of God, because your faith remains so steadfast under all the persecutions and troubles you endure. ⁵ This points to the justice of God's judgement; you will be proved worthy of the kingdom of God, for which indeed you are suffering. ⁶ It is just that God should balance the account by sending affliction to those who afflict you, ⁷ and relief to you who are afflicted, and to us as well, when the Lord Jesus is revealed from heaven with his mighty angels ⁸ in blazing fire. Then he will mete out punishment to those who refuse to acknowledge God and who will not obey the gospel of our Lord Jesus. [9] They will suffer the penalty of eternal destruction, cut off from the presence of the Lord and the splendour of his might, [10] when on the great day he comes to reveal his glory among his own and his majesty among all believers; and therefore among you, since you believed the testimony we brought you.

[11] With this in mind we pray for you always, that our God may count you worthy of your calling, and that his power may bring to fulfilment every good purpose and every act inspired by faith, [12] so that the name of our Lord Jesus may be glorified in you, and you in him, according to the grace of our God and the Lord Jesus Christ.

Christ's return

2 Now ABOUT the coming of our Lord Jesus Christ, when he is to gather us to himself: I beg you, my friends, [2] do not suddenly lose your heads, do not be alarmed by any prophetic utterance, any pronouncement, or any letter purporting to come from us, alleging that the day of the Lord is already here. [3] Let no one deceive you in any way. That day cannot come before the final rebellion against God, when wickedness will be revealed in human form, the man doomed to destruction. [4] He is the adversary who raises himself up against every so-called god or object of worship, and even enthrones himself in God's temple claiming to be God. [5] Do you not remember that I told you this while I was still with you? [6] You know, too, about the restraining power which ensures that he will be revealed only at his appointed time; [7] for already the secret forces of wickedness are at work, secret only for the present until the restraining hand is removed from the scene. [8] Then he will be revealed, the wicked one whom the Lord Jesus will destroy with the breath of his mouth and annihilate by the radiance of his presence. [9] The coming of the wicked one is the work of Satan; it will be attended by all the powerful signs and miracles that falsehood can devise, [10] all the deception that sinfulness can impose on those

doomed to destruction, because they did not open their minds to love of the truth and so find salvation. [11] That is why God puts them under a compelling delusion, which makes them believe what is false, [12] so that all who have not believed the truth but made sinfulness their choice may be brought to judgement.

[13] WE are always bound to thank God for you, my friends beloved by the Lord. From the beginning of time God chose you to find salvation in the Spirit who consecrates you and in the truth you believe. [14] It was for this that he called you through the gospel we brought, so that you might come to possess the splendour of our Lord Jesus Christ.

[15] Stand firm then, my friends, and hold fast to the traditions which you have learned from us by word or by letter. [16] And may our Lord Jesus Christ himself and God our Father, who has shown us such love, and in his grace has given us such unfailing encouragement and so sure a hope, [17] still encourage and strengthen you in every good deed and word.

Christian conduct

3 AND now, friends, pray for us, that the word of the Lord may have everywhere the swift and glorious success it has had among you, [2] and that we may be rescued from wrong-headed and wicked people; for not all have faith. [3] But the Lord keeps faith, and he will strengthen you and guard you from the evil one; [4] and in the Lord we have confidence about you, that you are doing and will continue to do what we tell you. [5] May the Lord direct your hearts towards God's love and the steadfastness of Christ.

[6] These are our instructions to you, friends, in the name of our Lord Jesus Christ: hold aloof from every Christian who falls into idle habits, and disregards the tradition you received from us. [7] You yourselves know how you ought to follow our example: you never saw us idling; [8] we did not accept free hospitality from anyone; night and day in toil and drudgery we worked for a living, rather than be a burden to any of you—[9] not because we do not have the right to maintenance, but to set an example for you to follow.

2:13 From ... chose you: *some witnesses read* God chose you as his firstfruits.

[10] Already during our stay with you we laid down this rule: anyone who will not work shall not eat. [11] We mention this because we hear that some of you are idling their time away, minding everybody's business but their own. [12] We instruct and urge such people in the name of the Lord Jesus Christ to settle down to work and earn a living.

[13] My friends, you must never tire of doing right. [14] If anyone disobeys the instructions given in my letter, single him out, and have nothing to do with him until he is ashamed of himself. [15] I do not mean treat him as an enemy, but admonish him as one of the family.

[16] May the Lord of peace himself give you peace at all times and in all ways. The Lord be with you all.

[17] This greeting is in my own handwriting; all genuine letters of mine bear the same signature—Paul.

[18] The grace of our Lord Jesus Christ be with you all.

THE FIRST LETTER OF PAUL TO

TIMOTHY

1 FROM Paul, apostle of Christ Jesus by command of God our Saviour and Christ Jesus our hope, [2] to Timothy his true-born son in the faith.

Grace, mercy, and peace to you from God the Father and Christ Jesus our Lord.

Paul's charge to Timothy

[3] WHEN I was starting for Macedonia, I urged you to stay on at Ephesus. You were to instruct certain people to give up teaching erroneous doctrines [4] and devoting themselves to interminable myths and genealogies, which give rise to mere speculation, and do not further God's plan for us, which works through faith.

[5] This instruction has love as its goal, the love which springs from a pure heart, a good conscience, and a genuine faith. [6] Through lack of these some people have gone astray into a wilderness of words. [7] They set out to be teachers of the law, although they do not understand either the words they use or the subjects about which they are so dogmatic.

[8] We all know that the law is an admirable thing, provided we treat it as law, [9] recognizing that it is designed not for good citizens, but for the lawless and unruly, the impious and sinful, the irreligious and worldly, for parricides and matricides, murderers [10] and fornicators, perverts, kidnappers, liars, perjurers—in fact all whose behaviour flouts the sound teaching [11] which conforms with the gospel entrusted to me, the gospel which tells of the glory of the ever-blessed God.

[12] I give thanks to Christ Jesus our Lord, who has made me equal to the task; I thank him for judging me worthy of trust and appointing me to his service— [13] although in the past I had met him with abuse and persecution and outrage. But because I acted in the ignorance of unbelief I was dealt with mercifully; [14] the grace of our Lord was lavished upon me, along with the faith and love which are ours in Christ Jesus.

[15] Here is a saying you may trust, one that merits full acceptance: 'Christ Jesus came into the world to save sinners'; and among them I stand first. [16] But I was mercifully dealt with for this very purpose, that Jesus Christ might find in me the first occasion for displaying his inexhaustible patience, and that I might be typical of all who were in future to have faith in him and gain eternal life. [17] To the King eternal, immortal, invisible, the only God, be honour and glory for ever and ever! Amen.

[18] In laying this charge upon you, Timothy my son, I am guided by those prophetic utterances which first directed me to you. Encouraged by them, fight the good fight [19] with faith and a clear conscience. It was through spurning conscience that certain persons made

1:4 do not ... faith: or do not promote the faithful discharge of God's stewardship.

shipwreck of their faith, [20] among them Hymenaeus and Alexander, whom I consigned to Satan, in the hope that through this discipline they might learn not to be blasphemous.

Christian conduct

2 FIRST of all, then, I urge that petitions, prayers, intercessions, and thanksgivings be offered for everyone, [2] for sovereigns and for all in high office so that we may lead a tranquil and quiet life, free to practise our religion with dignity. [3] Such prayer is right, and approved by God our Saviour, [4] whose will it is that all should find salvation and come to know the truth. [5] For there is one God, and there is one mediator between God and man, Christ Jesus, himself man, [6] who sacrificed himself to win freedom for all mankind, revealing God's purpose at God's good time; [7] of this I was appointed herald and apostle (this is no lie, it is the truth), to instruct the Gentiles in the true faith.

[8] It is my desire, therefore, that everywhere prayers be said by the men of the congregation, who shall lift up their hands with a pure intention, without anger or argument. [9] Women must dress in becoming manner, modestly and soberly, not with elaborate hair-styles, not adorned with gold or pearls or expensive clothes, [10] but with good deeds, as befits women who claim to be religious. [11] Their role is to learn, listening quietly and with due submission. [12] I do not permit women to teach or dictate to the men; they should keep quiet. [13] For Adam was created first, and Eve afterwards; [14] moreover it was not Adam who was deceived; it was the woman who, yielding to deception, fell into sin. [15] But salvation for the woman will be in the bearing of children, provided she continues in faith, love, and holiness, with modesty.

3 Here is a saying you may trust: 'To aspire to leadership is an honourable ambition.' [2] A bishop, therefore, must be above reproach, husband of one wife, sober, temperate, courteous, hospitable, and a good teacher; [3] he must not be given to drink or brawling, but be of a forbearing disposition, avoiding quarrels,

and not avaricious. [4] He must be one who manages his own household well and controls his children without losing his dignity, [5] for if a man does not know how to manage his own family, how can he take charge of a congregation of God's people? [6] He should not be a recent convert; conceit might bring on him the devil's punishment. [7] He must moreover have a good reputation with the outside world, so that he may not be exposed to scandal and be caught in the devil's snare.

[8] Deacons, likewise, must be dignified, not indulging in double talk, given neither to excessive drinking nor to money-grubbing. [9] They must be men who combine a clear conscience with a firm hold on the mystery of the faith. [10] And they too must first undergo scrutiny, and only if they are of unimpeachable character may they serve as deacons. [11] Women in this office must likewise be dignified, not scandalmongers, but sober, and trustworthy in every way. [12] A deacon must be the husband of one wife, and good at managing his children and his own household. [13] For deacons with a good record of service are entitled to high standing and the right to be heard on matters of the Christian faith.

[14] I am hoping to come to you before long, but I write this [15] in case I am delayed, to let you know what is proper conduct in God's household, that is, the church of the living God, the pillar and bulwark of the truth. [16] And great beyond all question is the mystery of our religion:

He was manifested in flesh,
vindicated in spirit,
seen by angels;
he was proclaimed among the
    nations,
believed in throughout the world,
raised to heavenly glory.

False teaching

4 THE Spirit explicitly warns us that in time to come some will forsake the faith and surrender their minds to subversive spirits and demon-inspired doctrines, [2] through the plausible falsehoods of those whose consciences have been permanently branded. [3] They will forbid marriage, and insist on abstinence from foods

---

3:1 **Here ... trust:** *some witnesses read* There is a popular saying.   3:11 **Women ... office:** *or* Their wives.
4:1 **in time to come:** *or* in the last times.   4:2 **branded:** *or* seared.

which God created to be enjoyed with thanksgiving by believers who have come to knowledge of the truth. ⁴Everything that God has created is good, and nothing is to be rejected provided it is accepted with thanksgiving, ⁵for it is then made holy by God's word and by prayer.

⁶By offering such advice as this to the brotherhood you will prove to be a good servant of Christ Jesus, nurtured in the precepts of our faith and of the sound instruction which you have followed. ⁷Have nothing to do with superstitious myths, mere old wives' tales. Keep yourself in training for the practice of religion; ⁸for while the training of the body brings limited benefit, the benefits of religion are without limit, since it holds out promise not only for this life but also for the life to come. ⁹Here is a saying you may trust, one that merits full acceptance. ¹⁰'This is why we labour and struggle, because we have set our hope on the living God, who is the Saviour of all'—the Saviour, above all, of believers.

¹¹Insist on these things in your teaching. ¹²Let no one underrate you because you are young, but be to believers an example in speech and behaviour, in love, fidelity, and purity. ¹³Until I arrive devote yourself to the public reading of the scriptures, to exhortation, and to teaching. ¹⁴Do not neglect the spiritual endowment given you when, under the guidance of prophecy, the elders laid their hands on you.

¹⁵Make these matters your business, make them your absorbing interest, so that your progress may be plain to all. ¹⁶Persevere in them, keeping close watch on yourself and on your teaching; by doing so you will save both yourself and your hearers.

Church discipline

5 Never be harsh with an older man; appeal to him as if he were your father. Treat the younger men as brothers, ²the older women as mothers, and the younger as your sisters, in all purity. ³Enrol as widows only those who are widows in the fullest sense. ⁴If a widow

has children or grandchildren, they should learn as their first duty to show loyalty to the family and so repay what they owe to their parents and grandparents; for that has God's approval. ⁵But a widow in the full sense, one who is alone in the world, puts all her trust in God, and regularly, night and day, attends the meetings for prayer and worship. ⁶A widow given to self-indulgence, however, is as good as dead. ⁷Add these instructions to the rest, so that the widows may be above reproach. ⁸And if anyone does not make provision for his relations, and especially for members of his own household, he has denied the faith and is worse than an unbeliever.

⁹A widow under sixty years of age should not be put on the roll. An enrolled widow must have been the wife of one husband, ¹⁰and must have gained a reputation for good deeds, by taking care of children, by showing hospitality, by washing the feet of God's people, by supporting those in distress—in short, by doing good at every opportunity.

¹¹Do not admit younger widows to the roll; for if they let their passions distract them from Christ's service they will want to marry again, ¹²and so be guilty of breaking their earlier vow to him. ¹³Besides, in going round from house to house they would learn to be idle, indeed worse than idle, gossips and busybodies, speaking of things better left unspoken. ¹⁴For that reason it is my wish that young widows should marry again, have children, and manage a household; then they will give the enemy no occasion for scandal. ¹⁵For there have in fact been some who have taken the wrong turning and gone over to Satan.

¹⁶If a Christian woman has widows in her family, she must support them; the congregation must be relieved of the burden, so that it may be free to support those who are widows in the full sense.

¹⁷Elders who give good service as leaders should be reckoned worthy of a double stipend, in particular those who work hard at preaching and teaching. ¹⁸For scripture says, 'You shall not muzzle an

---

4:8–10 **for while ... Saviour of all'**: *or* for 'While the training of the body brings limited benefit, the benefits of religion are without limit, since it holds out promise not only for this life but also for the life to come.' ⁹That is a saying you may trust, one that merits full acceptance. ¹⁰This is why we labour and struggle, because we have set our hope on the living God, who is the Saviour of all.   4:14 **prophecy ... on you**: *or* prophecy, you were ordained as an elder.

ox while it is treading out the grain';
besides, 'The worker earns his pay.'

[19] Do not entertain a charge against an
elder unless it is supported by two or three
witnesses. [20] Those who do commit sins
you must rebuke in public, to put fear into
the others. [21] Before God and Christ Jesus
and the angels who are his chosen, I
solemnly charge you: maintain these
rules, never prejudging the issue, but
acting with strict impartiality. [22] Do not be
over-hasty in the laying on of hands, or
you may find yourself implicated in other
people's misdeeds; keep yourself above
reproach.

[23] Stop drinking only water; in view of
your frequent ailments take a little wine
to help your digestion.

[24] There are people whose offences are
so obvious that they precede them into
court, and others whose offences have not
yet caught up with them. [25] So too with
good deeds; they may be obvious, but,
even if they are not, they cannot be concealed for ever.

6 All who wear the yoke of slavery
must consider their masters worthy
of all respect, so that the name of God and
the Christian teaching are not brought
into disrepute. [2] Slaves of Christian
masters must not take liberties with them
just because they are their brothers. Quite
the contrary: they must do their work all
the better because those who receive the
benefit of their service are one with them
in faith and love.

Final instructions

THIS is what you are to teach and preach.
[3] Anyone who teaches otherwise, and
does not devote himself to sound precepts—that is, those of our Lord Jesus
Christ—and to good religious teaching,
[4] is a pompous ignoramus with a morbid
enthusiasm for mere speculations and
quibbles. These give rise to jealousy, quarrelling, slander, base suspicions, [5] and
endless wrangles—all typical of those
whose minds are corrupted and who have
lost their grip of the truth. They think
religion should yield dividends; [6] and of
course religion does yield high dividends,
but only to those who are content with
what they have. [7] We brought nothing
into this world, and we can take nothing
out; [8] if we have food and clothing let us
rest content. [9] Those who want to be rich
fall into temptations and snares and into
many foolish and harmful desires which
plunge people into ruin and destruction.
[10] The love of money is the root of all evil,
and in pursuit of it some have wandered
from the faith and spiked themselves on
many a painful thorn.

[11] But you, man of God, must shun all
that, and pursue justice, piety, integrity,
love, fortitude, and gentleness. [12] Run the
great race of faith and take hold of eternal
life, for to this you were called, when you
confessed your faith nobly before many
witnesses. [13] Now in the presence of God,
who gives life to all things, and of Jesus
Christ, who himself made that noble
confession in his testimony before Pontius
Pilate, I charge you [14] to obey your orders
without fault or failure until the appearance of our Lord Jesus Christ [15] which God
will bring about in his own good time. He
is the blessed and only Sovereign, King
of kings and Lord of lords; [16] he alone
possesses immortality, dwelling in unap-
proachable light; him no one has ever
seen or can ever see; to him be honour
and dominion for ever! Amen.

[17] Instruct those who are rich in this
world's goods not to be proud, and to fix
their hopes not on so uncertain a thing as
money, but on God, who richly provides
all things for us to enjoy. [18] They are to do
good and to be rich in well-doing, to be
ready to give generously and to share
with others, [19] and so acquire a treasure
which will form a good foundation for the
future. Then they will grasp the life that is
life indeed.

[20] Timothy, keep safe what has been
entrusted to you. Turn a deaf ear to empty
and irreligious chatter, and the contra-
dictions of 'knowledge' so-called, [21] for by
laying claim to it some have strayed far
from the faith.

Grace be with you all!

THE SECOND LETTER OF PAUL TO
TIMOTHY

1 FROM Paul, apostle of Christ Jesus by the will of God, whose promise of life is fulfilled in Christ Jesus, ² to Timothy his dear son.

Grace, mercy, and peace to you from God the Father and Christ Jesus our Lord.

³ I give thanks to the God of my forefathers, whom I worship with a clear conscience, when I mention you in my prayers as I do constantly night and day; ⁴ when I remember the tears you shed, I long to see you again and so make my happiness complete. ⁵ I am reminded of the sincerity of your faith, a faith which was alive in Lois your grandmother and Eunice your mother before you, and which, I am confident, now lives in you.

The gospel of Jesus Christ

⁶ THAT is why I remind you to stir into flame the gift from God which is yours through the laying on of my hands. ⁷ For the spirit that God gave us is no cowardly spirit, but one to inspire power, love, and self-discipline. ⁸ So never be ashamed of your testimony to our Lord, nor of me imprisoned for his sake, but through the power that comes from God accept your share of suffering for the sake of the gospel. ⁹ It is he who has brought us salvation and called us to a dedicated life, not for any merit of ours but for his own purpose and of his own grace, granted to us in Christ Jesus from all eternity, ¹⁰ and now at length disclosed by the appearance on earth of our Saviour Jesus Christ. He has broken the power of death and brought life and immortality to light through the gospel.

¹¹ Of this gospel I have been appointed herald, apostle, and teacher. ¹² That is the reason for my present plight; but I am not ashamed of it, because I know whom I have trusted, and am confident of his power to keep safe what he has put into my charge until the great day. ¹³ Hold to the outline of sound teaching which you heard from me, living by the faith and love which are ours in Christ Jesus. ¹⁴ Keep safe the treasure put into our charge, with the help of the Holy Spirit dwelling within us.

¹⁵ As you are aware, everyone in the province of Asia deserted me, including Phygelus and Hermogenes. ¹⁶ But may the Lord's mercy rest on the house of Onesiphorus! He has often relieved me in my troubles; he was not ashamed to visit a prisoner, ¹⁷ but when he came to Rome took pains to search me out until he found me. ¹⁸ The Lord grant that he find mercy from the Lord on the great day! You know as well as anyone the many services he rendered at Ephesus.

Charge to Timothy

2 TAKE strength, my son, from the grace of God which is ours in Christ Jesus. ² You heard my teaching in the presence of many witnesses; hand on that teaching to reliable men who in turn will be qualified to teach others.

³ Take your share of hardship, like a good soldier of Christ Jesus. ⁴ A soldier on active service must not let himself be involved in the affairs of everyday life if he is to give satisfaction to his commanding officer. ⁵ Again, no athlete wins a prize unless he abides by the rules. ⁶ The farmer who does the work has first claim on the crop. ⁷ Reflect on what I am saying, and the Lord will help you to full understanding.

⁸ Remember the theme of my gospel: Jesus Christ, risen from the dead, born of David's line. ⁹ For preaching this I am exposed to hardship, even to the point of being fettered like a criminal; but the word of God is not fettered. ¹⁰ All this I endure for the sake of God's chosen ones, in the hope that they too may attain the glorious and eternal salvation which is in Christ Jesus.

¹¹ Here is a saying you may trust:

1:12 **what ... charge**: *or* what I have put into his charge. 1:13 **Hold ... teaching**: *or* Take as your model the sound teaching.

191

If we died with him, we shall live
  with him;
[12] if we endure, we shall reign with him;
  if we disown him, he will disown us;
[13] if we are faithless, he remains
  faithful,
for he cannot disown himself.

[14] Keep on reminding people of this, and charge them solemnly before God to stop disputing about mere words; it does no good, and only ruins those who listen. [15] Try hard to show yourself worthy of God's approval, as a worker with no cause for shame; keep strictly to the true gospel, [16] avoiding empty and irreligious chatter; those who indulge in it will stray farther and farther into godless ways, [17] and the infection of their teaching will spread like gangrene. Such are Hymenaeus and Philetus; [18] in saying that our resurrection has already taken place they are wide of the truth and undermine people's faith. [19] But God has laid a foundation-stone, and it stands firm, bearing this inscription: 'The Lord knows his own' and 'Everyone who takes the Lord's name upon his lips must forsake wickedness.' [20] Now in any great house there are not only utensils of gold and silver, but also others of wood or earthenware; the former are valued, the latter held cheap. [21] Anyone who cleanses himself from all this wickedness will be a vessel valued and dedicated, a thing useful to the master of the house, and fit for any honourable purpose.

[22] Turn from the wayward passions of youth, and pursue justice, integrity, love, and peace together with all who worship the Lord in singleness of mind; [23] have nothing to do with foolish and wild speculations. You know they breed quarrels, [24] and a servant of the Lord must not be quarrelsome; he must be kindly towards all. He should be a good teacher, tolerant, [25] and gentle when he must discipline those who oppose him. God may then grant them a change of heart and lead them to recognize the truth; [26] thus they may come to their senses and escape from the devil's snare in which they have been trapped and held at his will.

3 Remember, the final age of this world is to be a time of turmoil! [2] People will love nothing but self and money; they will be boastful, arrogant, and abusive; disobedient to parents, devoid of gratitude, piety, [3] and natural affection; they will be implacable in their hatreds, scandalmongers, uncontrolled and violent, hostile to all goodness, [4] perfidious, foolhardy, swollen with self-importance. They will love their pleasures more than their God. [5] While preserving the outward form of religion, they are a standing denial of its power. Keep clear of them. [6] They are the sort that insinuate themselves into private houses and there get silly women into their clutches, women burdened with sins and carried away by all kinds of desires, [7] always wanting to be taught but incapable of attaining to a knowledge of the truth. [8] As Jannes and Jambres opposed Moses, so these men oppose the truth; their warped minds disqualify them from grasping the faith. [9] Their successes will be short-lived; like those opponents of Moses, they will come to be recognized by everyone for the fools they are.

[10] But you, my son, have observed closely my teaching and manner of life, my resolution, my faithfulness, patience, and spirit of love, and my fortitude [11] under persecution and suffering—all I went through at Antioch, at Iconium, at Lystra, and the persecutions I endured; and from all of them the Lord rescued me. [12] Persecution will indeed come to everyone who wants to live a godly life as a follower of Christ Jesus, [13] whereas evildoers and charlatans will progress from bad to worse, deceiving and deceived. [14] But for your part, stand by the truths you have learned and are assured of. Remember from whom you learned them; [15] remember that from early childhood you have been familiar with the sacred writings which have power to make you wise and lead you to salvation through faith in Christ Jesus. [16] All inspired scripture has its use for teaching the truth and refuting error, or for reformation of manners and discipline in right living, [17] so that the man of God may be capable and equipped for good work of every kind.

4 Before God, and before Christ Jesus who is to judge the living and the dead, I charge you solemnly by his coming

---

2:26 trapped ... will: *or* trapped, and be made subject to God's will.

appearance and his reign, [2] proclaim the message, press it home in season and out of season, use argument, reproof, and appeal, with all the patience that teaching requires. [3] For the time will come when people will not stand sound teaching, but each will follow his own whim and gather a crowd of teachers to tickle his fancy. [4] They will stop their ears to the truth and turn to fables. [5] But you must keep your head whatever happens; put up with hardship, work to spread the gospel, discharge all the duties of your calling.

[6] As for me, my life is already being poured out on the altar, and the hour for my departure is upon me. [7] I have run the great race, I have finished the course, I have kept the faith. [8] And now there awaits me the garland of righteousness which the Lord, the righteous Judge, will award to me on the great day, and not to me alone, but to all who have set their hearts on his coming appearance.

Final instructions

[9] Do YOUR best to join me soon. [10] Demas, his heart set on this present world, has deserted me and gone to Thessalonica; Crescens is away in Galatia, Titus in Dalmatia; apart from Luke [11] I have no one with me. Get hold of Mark and bring him with you; he is a great help to me.

[12] Tychicus I have sent to Ephesus. [13] When you come, bring the cloak I left with Carpus at Troas, and the books, particularly my notebooks.

[14] Alexander the coppersmith did me a great deal of harm. The Lord will deal with him as he deserves, [15] but you had better be on your guard against him, for he is bitterly opposed to everything we teach. [16] At the first hearing of my case no one came into court to support me; they all left me in the lurch; I pray that it may not be counted against them. [17] But the Lord stood by me and lent me strength, so that I might be his instrument in making the full proclamation of the gospel for the whole pagan world to hear; and thus I was rescued from the lion's jaws. [18] The Lord will rescue me from every attempt to do me harm, and bring me safely into his heavenly kingdom. Glory to him for ever and ever! Amen.

[19] Greetings to Prisca and Aquila, and the household of Onesiphorus. [20] Erastus stayed behind at Corinth, and Trophimus I left ill at Miletus. [21] Do try to get here before winter.

Greetings from Eubulus, Pudens, Linus, and Claudia, and from all the brotherhood here. [22] The Lord be with your spirit. Grace be with you all!

4:10 **Galatia:** *or* Gaul.

THE LETTER OF PAUL TO

TITUS

1 FROM Paul, servant of God and apostle of Jesus Christ, marked as such by the faith of God's chosen people and the knowledge of the truth enshrined in our religion [2] with its hope of eternal life, which God, who does not lie, promised long ages ago, [3] and now in his own good time has openly declared in the proclamation entrusted to me by command of God our Saviour.

[4] To Titus, my true-born son in the faith which we share. Grace and peace to you from God the Father and Jesus Christ our Saviour.

Christian discipline

[5] MY intention in leaving you behind in Crete was that you should deal with any outstanding matters, and in particular should appoint elders in each town in accordance with the principles I have laid down: [6] Are they men of unimpeachable character? Is each the husband of one wife? Are their children believers, not

1:1 **apostle ... knowledge:** *or* apostle of Jesus Christ, to bring God's chosen people to faith and to knowledge.

open to any charge of dissipation or indiscipline? [7] For as God's steward a bishop must be a man of unimpeachable character. He must not be overbearing or short-tempered or given to drink; no brawler, no money-grubber, [8] but hospitable, right-minded, temperate, just, devout, and self-controlled. [9] He must keep firm hold of the true doctrine, so that he may be well able both to appeal to his hearers with sound teaching and to refute those who raise objections.

[10] There are many, especially among Jewish converts, who are undisciplined, who talk wildly and lead others astray. [11] Such men must be muzzled, because they are ruining whole families by teaching what they should not, and all for sordid gain. [12] It was a Cretan prophet, one of their own countrymen, who said, 'Cretans were ever liars, vicious brutes, lazy gluttons'—[13] and how truly he spoke! All the more reason why you should rebuke them sharply, so that they may be restored to a sound faith, [14] instead of paying heed to Jewish myths and to human commandments, the work of those who turn their backs on the truth.

[15] To the pure all things are pure; but nothing is pure to tainted disbelievers, tainted both in reason and in conscience. [16] They profess to know God but by their actions deny him; they are detestable and disobedient, disqualified for any good work.

2 For your part, what you say must be in keeping with sound doctrine. [2] The older men should be sober, dignified, and temperate, sound in faith, love, and fortitude. [3] The older women, similarly, should be reverent in their demeanour, not scandalmongers or slaves to excessive drinking; they must set a high standard, [4] and so teach the younger women to be loving wives and mothers, [5] to be temperate, chaste, busy at home, and kind, respecting the authority of their husbands. Then the gospel will not be brought into disrepute.

[6] Urge the younger men, similarly, to be temperate [7] in all things, and set them an example of good conduct yourself. In your teaching you must show integrity and seriousness, [8] and offer sound instruction to which none can take exception. Any opponent will be at a loss when he finds nothing to say to our discredit.

[9] Slaves are to respect their masters' authority in everything and to give them satisfaction; they are not to answer back, [10] nor to pilfer, but are to show themselves absolutely trustworthy. In all this they will add lustre to the doctrine of God our Saviour.

[11] For the grace of God has dawned upon the world with healing for all mankind; [12] and by it we are disciplined to renounce godless ways and worldly desires, and to live a life of temperance, honesty, and godliness in the present age, [13] looking forward to the happy fulfilment of our hope when the splendour of our great God and Saviour Christ Jesus will appear. [14] He it is who sacrificed himself for us, to set us free from all wickedness and to make us his own people, pure and eager to do good.

[15] These are your themes; urge them and argue them with an authority which no one can disregard.

3 Remind everyone to be submissive to the government and the authorities, and to obey them; to be ready for any honourable work; [2] to slander no one, to avoid quarrels, and always to show forbearance and a gentle disposition to all.

[3] There was a time when we too were lost in folly and disobedience and were slaves to passions and pleasures of every kind. Our days were passed in malice and envy; hateful ourselves, we loathed one another. [4] 'But when the kindness and generosity of God our Saviour dawned upon the world, [5] then, not for any good deeds of our own, but because he was merciful, he saved us through the water of rebirth and the renewing power of the Holy Spirit, [6] which he lavished upon us through Jesus Christ our Saviour, [7] so that, justified by his grace, we might in hope become heirs to eternal life.' [8] That is a saying you may trust.

Final instructions

SUCH are the points I want you to insist on, so that those who have come to believe in God may be sure to devote themselves to good works. These precepts

---

2:13 **of our great ... Saviour:** *or* of the great God and our Saviour.   3:5 **water ... power of:** *or* water of rebirth and of renewal by.   3:8 **devote ... good in themselves:** *or* engage in honest employment. This is good in itself.

are good in themselves and also useful to society. ⁹ But avoid foolish speculations, genealogies, quarrels, and controversies over the law; they are unprofitable and futile.

¹⁰ If someone is contentious, he should be allowed a second warning; after that, have nothing more to do with him, ¹¹ recognizing that anyone like that has a distorted mind and stands self-condemned in his sin.

¹² Once I have sent Artemas or Tychi-cus to you, join me at Nicopolis as soon as you can, for that is where I have decided to spend the winter. ¹³ Do your utmost to help Zenas the lawyer and Apollos on their travels, and see that they are not short of anything. ¹⁴ And our own people must be taught to devote themselves to good works to meet urgent needs; they must not be unproductive.

¹⁵ All who are with me send you greetings. My greetings to our friends in the faith. Grace be with you all!

3:14 **devote ... needs:** *or* engage in honest employment to produce the necessities of life.

THE LETTER OF PAUL TO
PHILEMON

FROM Paul, a prisoner of Christ Jesus, and our colleague Timothy, to Philemon our dear friend and fellow-worker, ² together with Apphia our sister, and Archippus our comrade-in-arms, and the church that meets at your house.

³ Grace to you and peace from God our Father and the Lord Jesus Christ.

⁴ I thank my God always when I mention you in my prayers, ⁵ for I hear of your love and faith towards the Lord Jesus and for all God's people. ⁶ My prayer is that the faith you hold in common with us may deepen your understanding of all the blessings which belong to us as we are brought closer to Christ. ⁷ Your love has brought me much joy and encouragement; through you God's people have been much refreshed.

A runaway slave

⁸ ACCORDINGLY, although in Christ I might feel free to dictate where your duty lies, ⁹ yet, because of that same love, I would rather appeal to you. Ambassador as I am of Christ Jesus, and now his prisoner, ¹⁰ I, Paul, appeal to you about my child, whose father I have become in this prison. I mean Onesimus, ¹¹ once so useless to you, but now useful indeed, both to you and to me. ¹² In sending him back to you I am sending my heart. ¹³ I should have liked to keep him with me, to look after me on your behalf, here in prison for the gospel, ¹⁴ but I did not want to do anything without your consent, so that your kindness might be a matter not of compulsion, but of your own free will. ¹⁵ Perhaps this is why you lost him for a time to receive him back for good—¹⁶ no longer as a slave, but as more than a slave: as a dear brother, very dear to me, and still dearer to you, both as a man and as a Christian.

¹⁷ If, then, you think of me as your partner in the faith, welcome him as you would welcome me. ¹⁸ If he did you any wrong and owes you anything, put it down to my account. ¹⁹ Here is my signature: Paul. I will repay you—not to mention that you owe me your very self. ²⁰ Yes, brother, I am asking this favour of you as a fellow-Christian; set my mind at rest.

²¹ I write to you confident that you will meet my wishes; I know that you will in fact do more than I ask. ²² And one last thing: have a room ready for me, for I hope through the prayers of you all to be restored to you.

²³ Epaphras, a captive of Christ Jesus like myself, sends you greetings. ²⁴ So do my fellow-workers Mark, Aristarchus, Demas, and Luke.

²⁵ The grace of the Lord Jesus Christ be with your spirit!

A LETTER TO
HEBREWS

Jesus, divine and human

1 WHEN in times past God spoke to our forefathers, he spoke in many and varied ways through the prophets. ² But in this the final age he has spoken to us in his Son, whom he has appointed heir of all things; and through him he created the universe. ³ He is the radiance of God's glory, the stamp of God's very being, and he sustains the universe by his word of power. When he had brought about purification from sins, he took his seat at the right hand of God's Majesty on high, ⁴ raised as far above the angels as the title he has inherited is superior to theirs.

⁵ To which of the angels did God ever say, 'You are my son; today I have become your father,' or again, 'I shall be his father, and he will be my son'? ⁶ Again, when he presents the firstborn to the world, he says, 'Let all God's angels pay him homage.' ⁷ Of the angels he says:

He makes his angels winds,
and his ministers flames of fire;

⁸ but of the Son:

Your throne, O God, is for ever and
ever,
and the sceptre of his kingdom is the
sceptre of justice.
⁹ You have loved right and hated
wrong;
therefore, O God, your God has set
you above your fellows
by anointing you with oil, the token
of joy.

¹⁰ And again:

By you, Lord, were earth's
foundations laid of old,
and the heavens are the work of
your hands.
¹¹ They will perish, but you remain;
like clothes they will all wear out.
¹² You will fold them up like a cloak,
they will be changed like any
garment.

But you are the same, and your years will have no end.

¹³ To which of the angels has he ever said, 'Sit at my right hand until I make your enemies your footstool'? ¹⁴ Are they not all ministering spirits sent out in God's service, for the sake of those destined to receive salvation?

2 That is why we are bound to pay all the more heed to what we have been told, for fear of drifting from our course. ² For if God's word spoken through angels had such force that any violation of it, or any disobedience, met with its proper penalty, ³ what escape can there be for us if we ignore so great a deliverance? This deliverance was first announced through the Lord, and those who heard him confirmed it to us, ⁴ God himself adding his testimony by signs and wonders, by miracles of many kinds, and by gifts of the Holy Spirit distributed at his own will.

⁵ For it is not to angels that he has subjected the world to come, which is our theme. ⁶ There is somewhere this solemn assurance:

What is man, that you should
remember him,
a man, that you should care for
him?
⁷ You made him for a short while
subordinate to the angels;
with glory and honour you crowned
him;
⁸ you put everything in subjection
beneath his feet.

For in subjecting everything to him, God left nothing that is not made subject. But in fact we do not yet see everything in subjection to man. ⁹ What we do see is Jesus, who for a short while was made subordinate to the angels, crowned now with glory and honour because he suffered death, so that, by God's gracious will, he should experience death for all mankind.

1:6 **Again ... presents:** *or* And when he again presents. 1:9 **therefore ... your God:** *or* therefore God who is your God. 2:9 **so that ... will:** *some witnesses read* so that, apart from God.

196

¹⁰ In bringing many sons to glory it was fitting that God, for whom and through whom all things exist, should make the pioneer of their salvation perfect through sufferings; ¹¹ for he who consecrates and those who are consecrated are all of one stock. That is why he does not shrink from calling men his brothers, ¹² when he says, 'I will make your fame known to my brothers; in the midst of the assembly I will praise you'; ¹³ and again, 'I will keep my trust fixed on him'; and again, 'Here am I, and the children whom God has given me.' ¹⁴ Since the children share in flesh and blood, he too shared in them, so that by dying he might break the power of him who had death at his command, that is, the devil, ¹⁵ and might liberate those who all their life had been in servitude through fear of death. ¹⁶ Clearly they are not angels whom he helps, but the descendants of Abraham. ¹⁷ Therefore he had to be made like his brothers in every way, so that he might be merciful and faithful as their high priest before God, to make expiation for the sins of the people. ¹⁸ Because he himself has passed through the test of suffering, he is able to help those who are in the midst of their test.

Jesus, the faithful high priest

3 THEREFORE, brothers in the family of God, partners in a heavenly calling, think of Jesus, the apostle and high priest of the faith we profess: ² he was faithful to God who appointed him, as Moses also was faithful in God's household; ³ but Jesus has been counted worthy of greater honour than Moses, as the founder of a house enjoys more honour than his household. ⁴ Every house has its founder; and the founder of all is God. ⁵ Moses indeed was faithful as a servant in God's whole household; his task was to bear witness to the words that God would speak; ⁶ but Christ is faithful as a son, set over the household. And we are that household, if only we are fearless and keep our hope high.

⁷ 'TODAY', therefore, as the Holy Spirit says—

Today if you hear his voice,
⁸ do not grow stubborn as in the
    rebellion,
at the time of testing in the desert,

⁹ where your forefathers tried me and
    tested me,
though for forty years they saw the
    things I did.
¹⁰ Therefore I was incensed with that
    generation
and said, Their hearts are for ever
    astray;
they would not discern my ways;
¹¹ so I vowed in my anger,
they shall never enter my rest.

¹² See to it, my friends, that no one among you has the wicked and faithless heart of a deserter from the living God. ¹³ Rather, day by day, as long as that word 'today' sounds in your ears, encourage one another, so that no one of you is made stubborn by the wiles of sin. ¹⁴ For we have become partners with Christ, if only we keep our initial confidence firm to the end. ¹⁵ When scripture says, 'Today if you hear his voice, do not grow stubborn as in the rebellion,' ¹⁶ who was it that heard and yet rebelled? All those, surely, whom Moses had led out of Egypt. ¹⁷ And with whom was God indignant for forty years? With those, surely, who had sinned, whose bodies lay where they fell in the desert. ¹⁸ And to whom did he vow that they should not enter his rest, if not to those who had refused to believe? ¹⁹ We see, then, it was unbelief that prevented their entering.

4 What we must fear, therefore, is that, while the promise of entering his rest remains open, any one of you should be found to have missed his opportunity. ² For indeed we have had the good news preached to us, just as they had. But the message they heard did them no good, for it was not combined with faith in those who heard it. ³ Because we have faith, it is we who enter that rest of which he has said: 'As I vowed in my anger, they shall never enter my rest.' Yet God's work had been finished ever since the world was created. ⁴ Scripture somewhere says of the seventh day: 'God rested from all his work on the seventh day'—⁵ and in the passage above we read: 'They shall never enter my rest.' ⁶ This implies that some are to enter it, and since those who first heard the good news failed to enter through unbelief, ⁷ once more God sets a day. 'Today', he says, speaking so many years later in the words already quoted from the

Psalms: 'Today if you hear his voice, do not grow stubborn.' [8] If Joshua had given them rest, God would not have spoken afterwards of another day. [9] Therefore, a sabbath rest still awaits the people of God; [10] anyone who enters God's rest, rests from his own work, as God did from his. [11] Let us, then, make every effort to enter that rest, so that no one may fall by following the old example of unbelief.

[12] The word of God is alive and active. It cuts more keenly than any two-edged sword, piercing so deeply that it divides soul and spirit, joints and marrow; it discriminates among the purposes and thoughts of the heart. [13] Nothing in creation can hide from him; everything lies bare and exposed to the eyes of him to whom we must render account.

[14] Since therefore we have a great high priest who has passed through the heavens, Jesus the Son of God, let us hold fast to the faith we profess. [15] Ours is not a high priest unable to sympathize with our weaknesses, but one who has been tested in every way as we are, only without sinning. [16] Let us therefore boldly approach the throne of grace, in order that we may receive mercy and find grace to give us timely help.

5 FOR every high priest is taken from among men and appointed their representative before God, to offer gifts and sacrifices for sins. [2] He is able to bear patiently with the ignorant and erring, since he too is beset by weakness; [3] and because of this he is bound to make sin-offerings for himself as well as for the people. [4] Moreover nobody assumes the office on his own authority: he is called by God, just as Aaron was. [5] So it is with Christ: he did not confer on himself the glory of becoming high priest; it was granted by God, who said to him, 'You are my son; today I have become your father'; [6] as also in another place he says, 'You are a priest for ever, in the order of Melchizedek.' [7] In the course of his earthly life he offered up prayers and petitions, with loud cries and tears, to God who was able to deliver him from death. Because of his devotion his prayer was heard: [8] son though he was, he learned obedience through his sufferings, [9] and, once per-

fected, he became the source of eternal salvation for all who obey him, [10] and by God he was designated high priest in the order of Melchizedek.

Jesus and Melchizedek

[11] ABOUT Melchizedek we have much to say, much that is difficult to explain to you, now that you have proved so slow to learn. [12] By this time you ought to be teachers, but instead you need someone to teach you the ABC of God's oracles over again. It comes to this: you need milk instead of solid food. [13] Anyone who lives on milk is still an infant, with no experience of what is right. [14] Solid food is for adults, whose perceptions have been trained by long use to discriminate between good and evil.

6 [1-2] Let us stop discussing the rudiments of Christianity. We ought not to be laying the foundation all over again: repentance from the deadness of our former ways and faith in God, by means of instruction about cleansing rites and the laying on of hands, the resurrection of the dead and eternal judgement. Instead, let us advance towards maturity; [3] and so we shall, if God permits. [4] For when people have once been enlightened, when they have tasted the heavenly gift and have shared in the Holy Spirit, [5] when they have experienced the goodness of God's word and the spiritual power of the age to come, [6] and then after all this have fallen away, it is impossible to bring them afresh to repentance; for they are crucifying to their own hurt the Son of God and holding him up to mockery. [7] When the soil drinks in the rain that falls often upon it, and yields a crop for the use of those who cultivate it, it receives its blessing from God; [8] but if it bears thorns and thistles, it is worthless and a curse hangs over it; it ends by being burnt.

[9] Yet although we speak as we do, we are convinced that you, dear friends, are in a better state, which makes for your salvation. [10] For God is not so unjust as to forget what you have done for love of his name in rendering service to his people, as you still do. [11] But we should dearly like each one of you to show the same keenness to the end, until your hope is fully realized. [12] We want you not to be lax, but

---

6:6 **crucifying**: *or* crucifying again.

to imitate those who, through faith and patience, receive the promised inheritance.

[13] When God made his promise to Abraham, because he had no one greater to swear by he swore by himself: [14] 'I vow that I will bless you abundantly and multiply your descendants.' [15] Thus it was that Abraham, after patient waiting, obtained the promise. [16] People swear by what is greater than themselves, and making a statement on oath sets a limit to what can be called in question; [17] and so, since God desired to show even more clearly to the heirs of his promise how immutable was his purpose, he guaranteed it by an oath. [18] Here, then, are two irrevocable acts in which God could not possibly play us false. They give powerful encouragement to us, who have laid claim to his protection by grasping the hope set before us. [19] We have that hope as an anchor for our lives, safe and secure. It enters the sanctuary behind the curtain, [20] where Jesus has entered on our behalf as forerunner, having become high priest for ever in the order of Melchizedek.

7 THIS Melchizedek, king of Salem, priest of God Most High, met Abraham returning from the defeat of the kings and blessed him; [2] and Abraham gave him a tithe of everything as his share. His name, in the first place, means 'king of righteousness'; next he is king of Salem, that is, 'king of peace'. [3] He has no father, no mother, no ancestors; his life has no beginning and no end. Bearing the likeness of the Son of God, he remains a priest for all time.

[4] Consider now how great he must be for the patriarch Abraham to give him his tithe from the finest of the spoil. [5] The descendants of Levi who succeed to the priestly office are required by the law to tithe the people, that is, their fellow-countrymen, although they too are descendants of Abraham. [6] But Melchizedek, though he does not share their ancestry, tithed Abraham himself and gave his blessing to the man who had been given the promises; [7] and, beyond all dispute, it is always the lesser who is blessed by the greater. [8] Moreover, in the one instance tithes are received by men who must die; but in the other, by one whom scripture affirms to be alive. [9] It might even be said that Levi, the receiver of tithes, was himself tithed through Abraham; [10] for he was still in his ancestor's loins when Melchizedek met him.

[11] Now if perfection had been attainable through the levitical priesthood (on the basis of which the people were given the law), there would have been no need for another kind of priest to arise, described as being in the order of Melchizedek, instead of in the order of Aaron. [12] But a change of priesthood must mean a change of law; [13] for he who is spoken of here belongs to a different tribe, no member of which has ever served at the altar. [14] It is beyond all doubt that our Lord is sprung from Judah, a tribe to which Moses made no reference in speaking of priests.

[15] What makes this still clearer is that a new priest has arisen, one like Melchizedek; [16] he owes his priesthood not to a system of rules relating to descent but to the power of a life that cannot be destroyed. [17] For here is the testimony: 'You are a priest for ever, in the order of Melchizedek.' [18] The earlier rules are repealed as ineffective and useless, [19] since the law brought nothing to perfection; and a better hope is introduced, through which we draw near to God.

[20-22] Notice also that no oath was sworn when the other men were made priests; but for this priest an oath was sworn in the words addressed to him: 'The Lord has sworn and will not go back on his word, "You are a priest for ever."' In the same way, God's oath shows how superior is the covenant which Jesus guarantees. [23] There have been many levitical priests, because death prevents them from continuing in office; [24] but Jesus holds a perpetual priesthood, because he remains for ever. [25] That is why he is able to save completely those who approach God through him, since he is always alive to plead on their behalf.

[26] Such a high priest is indeed suited to our need: he is holy, innocent, undefiled, set apart from sinners, and raised high above the heavens. [27] He has no need to

---

6:18 **They give ... grasping**: *or* They give to us, who have laid claim to his protection, a powerful encouragement to grasp.   7:25 **completely**: *or* for all time.

offer sacrifices daily, as the high priests do, first for their own sins and then for those of the people; he did this once for all when he offered up himself. [28] The high priests appointed by the law are men in all their weakness; but the priest appointed by the words of the oath which supersedes the law is the Son, who has been made perfect for ever.

8 My main point is: this is the kind of high priest we have, and he has taken his seat at the right hand of the throne of Majesty in heaven, [2] a minister in the real sanctuary, the tent set up by the Lord, not by man. [3] Every high priest is appointed to offer gifts and sacrifices; hence, of necessity, this one too had something to offer. [4] If he were on earth, he would not be a priest at all, since there are already priests to offer the gifts prescribed by the law, [5] although the sanctuary in which they minister is only a shadowy symbol of the heavenly one. This is why Moses, when he was about to put up the tent, was instructed by God: 'See to it that you make everything according to the pattern shown you on the mountain.' [6] But in fact the ministry which Jesus has been given is superior to theirs, for he is the mediator of a better covenant, established on better promises.

[7] Had that first covenant been faultless, there would have been no occasion to look for a second to replace it. [8] But God finds fault with his people when he says, 'The time is coming, says the Lord, when I shall conclude a new covenant with the house of Israel and the house of Judah. [9] It will not be like the covenant I made with their forefathers when I took them by the hand to lead them out of Egypt; because they did not abide by the terms of that covenant, and so I abandoned them, says the Lord. [10] For this is the covenant I shall make with Israel after those days, says the Lord: I shall set my laws in their understanding and write them on their hearts; I shall be their God, and they will be my people. [11] They will not teach one another, each saying to his fellow-citizen and his brother, "Know the Lord!" For all of them will know me, high and low alike; [12] I shall pardon their wicked deeds, and their sins I shall remember no more.' [13] By speaking of a new covenant, he has

pronounced the first one obsolete; and anything that is becoming obsolete and growing old will shortly disappear.

9 The first covenant had its ordinances governing divine service and its sanctuary, but it was an earthly sanctuary. [2] An outer tent, called the Holy Place, was set up to contain the lampstand, the table, and the Bread of the Presence. [3] Beyond the second curtain was the tent called the Most Holy Place. [4] Here were a gold incense-altar and the Ark of the Covenant plated all over with gold, in which were kept a gold jar containing the manna, and Aaron's staff which once budded, and the tablets of the covenant; [5] and above the Ark were the cherubim of God's glory, overshadowing the place of expiation. These we need not discuss in detail now. [6] Under this arrangement, the priests are continually entering the first tent in the performance of their duties; [7] but the second tent is entered by the high priest alone, and that only once a year. He takes with him the blood which he offers for himself and for the people's inadvertent sins. [8] By this the Holy Spirit indicates that so long as the outer tent still stands, the way into the sanctuary has not been opened up. [9] All this is symbolic, pointing to the present time. It means that the prescribed offerings and sacrifices cannot give the worshipper a clear conscience and so bring him to perfection; [10] they are concerned only with food and drink and various rites of cleansing—external ordinances in force until the coming of the new order.

[11] But now Christ has come, high priest of good things already in being. The tent of his priesthood is a greater and more perfect one, not made by human hands, that is, not belonging to this created world; [12] the blood of his sacrifice is his own blood, not the blood of goats and calves; and thus he has entered the sanctuary once for all and secured an eternal liberation. [13] If sprinkling the blood of goats and bulls and the ashes of a heifer consecrates those who have been defiled and restores their ritual purity, [14] how much greater is the power of the blood of Christ; through the eternal Spirit he offered himself without blemish to God. His blood will cleanse our conscience from the deadness of our former ways to serve the living God.

9:11 **things … being:** *some witnesses read* things to be.

¹⁵ That is why the new covenant or testament of which he is mediator took effect once a death had occurred, to bring liberation from sins committed under the former covenant; its purpose is to enable those whom God has called to receive the eternal inheritance he has promised them. ¹⁶ Now where there is a testament it is necessary for the death of the testator to be established; ¹⁷ for a testament takes effect only when a death has occurred: it has no force while the testator is still alive. ¹⁸ Even the former covenant itself was not inaugurated without blood, ¹⁹ for when Moses had told the assembled people all the commandments as set forth in the law, he took the blood of calves, with water, scarlet wool, and marjoram, and sprinkled the law book itself and all the people, ²⁰ saying, 'This is the blood of the covenant which God commanded you to keep.' ²¹ In the same way he sprinkled the blood over the tent and all the vessels of divine service. ²² Indeed, under the law, it might almost be said that everything is cleansed by blood, and without the shedding of blood there is no forgiveness.

Jesus, the final sacrifice

²³ IF, then, the symbols of heavenly things required those sacrifices to cleanse them, the heavenly things themselves required still better sacrifices; ²⁴ for Christ has not entered a sanctuary made by human hands which is only a pointer to the reality; he has entered heaven itself, to appear now before God on our behalf. ²⁵ It was not his purpose to offer himself again and again, as the high priest enters the sanctuary year after year with blood not his own; ²⁶ for then he would have had to suffer repeatedly since the world was created. But as it is, he has appeared once for all at the climax of history to abolish sin by the sacrifice of himself. ²⁷ Just as it is our human lot to die once, with judgement to follow, ²⁸ so Christ was offered once to bear the sins of mankind, and will appear a second time, not to deal with sin, but to bring salvation to those who eagerly await him.

10 THE law contains but a shadow of the good things to come, not the true picture. With the same sacrifices offered year after year for all time, it can never bring the worshippers to perfection. ² If it could, these sacrifices would surely have ceased to be offered, because the worshippers, cleansed once for all, would no longer have any sense of sin. ³ Instead, by these sacrifices sins are brought to mind year after year, ⁴ because they can never be removed by the blood of bulls and goats.

⁵ That is why, at Christ's coming into the world, he says:

Sacrifice and offering you did not desire,
but you have prepared a body for me.
⁶ Whole-offerings and sin-offerings you did not delight in.
⁷ Then I said, 'Here I am: as it is written of me in the scroll,
I have come, O God, to do your will.'

⁸ First he says, 'Sacrifices and offerings, whole-offerings and sin-offerings, you did not desire or delight in,' although the law prescribes them. ⁹ Then he adds, 'Here I am: I have come to do your will.' He thus abolishes the former to establish the latter. ¹⁰ And it is by the will of God that we have been consecrated, through the offering of the body of Jesus Christ once for all.

¹¹ Daily every priest stands performing his service and time after time offering the same sacrifices, which can never remove sins. ¹² Christ, having offered for all time a single sacrifice for sins, took his seat at God's right hand, ¹³ where he now waits until his enemies are made his footstool. ¹⁴ So by one offering he has perfected for ever those who are consecrated by it. ¹⁵ To this the Holy Spirit also adds his witness. First he says, ¹⁶ 'This is the covenant which I will make with them after those days, says the Lord: I will set my laws in their hearts and write them on their understanding'; ¹⁷ then he adds, 'and their sins and wicked deeds I will remember no more.' ¹⁸ And where these have been forgiven, there are no further offerings for sin.

¹⁹ So NOW, my friends, the blood of Jesus makes us free to enter the sanctuary with

9:28 **to bear the sins:** *or* to remove the sins.   10:1 **sacrifices ... perfection:** *or* sacrifices offered year after year it can never bring the worshippers to perfection for all time.   10:12 **for all time ... seat:** *or* a single sacrifice for sins, took his seat for all time.

201

confidence ²⁰ by the new and living way which he has opened for us through the curtain, the way of his flesh. ²¹ We have a great priest set over the household of God; ²² so let us make our approach in sincerity of heart and the full assurance of faith, inwardly cleansed from a guilty conscience, and outwardly washed with pure water. ²³ Let us be firm and unswerving in the confession of our hope, for the giver of the promise is to be trusted. ²⁴ We ought to see how each of us may best arouse others to love and active goodness. ²⁵ We should not stay away from our meetings, as some do, but rather encourage one another, all the more because we see the day of the Lord drawing near.

²⁶ For if we deliberately persist in sin after receiving the knowledge of the truth, there can be no further sacrifice for sins; there remains ²⁷ only a terrifying expectation of judgement, of a fierce fire which will consume God's enemies. ²⁸ Anyone who flouts the law of Moses is put to death without mercy on the evidence of two or three witnesses. ²⁹ Think how much more severe a penalty will be deserved by anyone who has trampled underfoot the Son of God, profaned the blood of the covenant by which he was consecrated, and insulted God's gracious Spirit! ³⁰ For we know who it is that said, 'Justice is mine: I will repay'; and again, 'The Lord will judge his people.' ³¹ It is a terrifying thing to fall into the hands of the living God.

³² Remember those early days when, newly enlightened, you met the test of great suffering and held firm. ³³ Some of you were publicly exposed to abuse and tormented, while others stood loyally by those who were so treated. ³⁴ For indeed you shared the sufferings of those who were in prison, and you cheerfully accepted the seizure of your possessions, knowing that you had a better, more lasting possession. ³⁵ Do not, therefore, throw away your confidence, for it carries a great reward. ³⁶ You need endurance in order to do God's will and win what he has promised. ³⁷ For, in the words of scripture,

> very soon he who is to come will come;

he will not delay;
³⁸ and by faith my righteous servant
> shall find life;
but if anyone shrinks back,
I take no pleasure in him.

³⁹ But we are not among those who shrink back and are lost; we have the faith to preserve our life.

Faith in times past

11 FAITH gives substance to our hopes and convinces us of realities we do not see.

² It was for their faith that the people of old won God's approval.

³ By faith we understand that the universe was formed by God's command, so that the visible came forth from the invisible.

⁴ By faith Abel offered a greater sacrifice than Cain's; because of his faith God approved his offerings and attested his goodness; and through his faith, though he is dead, he continues to speak.

⁵ By faith Enoch was taken up to another life without passing through death; he was not to be found, because God had taken him, and it is the testimony of scripture that before he was taken he had pleased God. ⁶ But without faith it is impossible to please him, for whoever comes to God must believe that he exists and rewards those who seek him.

⁷ By faith Noah took good heed of the divine warning about the unseen future, and built an ark to save his household. Through his faith he put the whole world in the wrong, and made good his own claim to the righteousness which comes of faith.

⁸ By faith Abraham obeyed the call to leave his home for a land which he was to receive as a possession; he went away without knowing where he was to go. ⁹ By faith he settled as an alien in the land which had been promised him, living in tents with Isaac and Jacob, who were heirs with him to the same promise. ¹⁰ For he was looking forward to a city with firm foundations, whose architect and builder is God.

¹¹ By faith even Sarah herself was enabled to conceive, though she was past the age, because she judged that God who

---

10:20 **curtain ... flesh**: *or* curtain of his flesh. **was**: *some witnesses add* barren and.

11:1 **substance**: *or* assurance.   11:11 **though she**

had promised would keep faith. ¹² Therefore from one man, a man as good as dead, there sprang descendants as numerous as the stars in the heavens or the countless grains of sand on the seashore.

¹³ All these died in faith. Although they had not received the things promised, yet they had seen them far ahead and welcomed them, and acknowledged themselves to be strangers and aliens without fixed abode on earth. ¹⁴ Those who speak in that way show plainly that they are looking for a country of their own. ¹⁵ If their thoughts had been with the country they had left, they could have found opportunity to return. ¹⁶ Instead, we find them longing for a better country, a heavenly one. That is why God is not ashamed to be called their God; for he has a city ready for them.

¹⁷ By faith Abraham, when put to the test, offered up Isaac: he had received the promises, and yet he was ready to offer his only son, ¹⁸ of whom he had been told, 'Through the line of Isaac your descendants shall be traced.' ¹⁹ For he reckoned that God had power even to raise from the dead—and it was from the dead, in a sense, that he received him back.

²⁰ By faith Isaac blessed Jacob and Esau and spoke of things to come. ²¹ By faith Jacob, as he was dying, blessed each of Joseph's sons, and bowed in worship over the top of his staff.

²² By faith Joseph, at the end of his life, spoke of the departure of Israel from Egypt, and gave instructions about his burial.

²³ By faith, when Moses was born, his parents hid him for three months, because they saw what a fine child he was; they were not intimidated by the king's edict. ²⁴ By faith Moses, when he grew up, refused to be called a son of Pharaoh's daughter, ²⁵ preferring to share hardship with God's people rather than enjoy the transient pleasures of sin. ²⁶ He considered the stigma that rests on God's Anointed greater wealth than the treasures of Egypt, for his eyes were fixed on the coming reward. ²⁷ By faith he left Egypt, with no fear of the king's anger; for he was resolute, as one who saw the invisible God. ²⁸ By faith he celebrated the Passover

and the sprinkling of blood, so that the destroying angel might not touch the firstborn of Israel. ²⁹ By faith they crossed the Red Sea as though it were dry land, whereas the Egyptians, when they attempted the crossing, were engulfed.

³⁰ By faith the walls of Jericho were made to fall after they had been encircled on seven successive days. ³¹ By faith the prostitute Rahab escaped the fate of the unbelievers, because she had given the spies a kindly welcome.

³² Need I say more? Time is too short for me to tell the stories of Gideon, Barak, Samson, and Jephthah, of David and Samuel and the prophets. ³³ Through faith they overthrew kingdoms, established justice, saw God's promises fulfilled. They shut the mouths of lions, ³⁴ quenched the fury of fire, escaped death by the sword. Their weakness was turned to strength, they grew powerful in war, they put foreign armies to rout. ³⁵ Women received back their dead raised to life. Others were tortured to death, refusing release, to win resurrection to a better life. ³⁶ Others, again, had to face jeers and flogging, even fetters and prison bars. ³⁷ They were stoned to death, they were sawn in two, they were put to the sword, they went about clothed in skins of sheep or goats, deprived, oppressed, ill-treated. ³⁸ The world was not worthy of them. They were refugees in deserts and on the mountains, hiding in caves and holes in the ground. ³⁹ All these won God's approval because of their faith; and yet they did not receive what was promised, ⁴⁰ because, with us in mind, God had made a better plan, that only with us should they reach perfection.

Faith today

12 WITH this great cloud of witnesses around us, therefore, we too must throw off every encumbrance and the sin that all too readily restricts us, and run with resolution the race which lies ahead of us, ² our eyes fixed on Jesus, the pioneer and perfecter of faith. For the sake of the joy that lay ahead of him, he endured the cross, ignoring its disgrace, and has taken his seat at the right hand of the throne of God. ³ Think of him who submitted to such

11:37 **stoned to death:** *some witnesses add* they were tested.   12:1 **restricts:** *some witnesses read* distracts.
12:2 **For the sake ... him:** *or* In place of the joy that was open to him.

opposition from sinners: that will help you not to lose heart and grow faint. [4] In the struggle against sin, you have not yet resisted to the point of shedding your blood. [5] You have forgotten the exhortation which addresses you as sons:

My son, do not think lightly of the
    Lord's discipline,
or be discouraged when he corrects
    you;
[6] for whom the Lord loves he
    disciplines;
he chastises every son whom he
    acknowledges.

[7] You must endure it as discipline: God is treating you as sons. Can anyone be a son and not be disciplined by his father? [8] If you escape the discipline in which all sons share, you must be illegitimate and not true sons. [9] Again, we paid due respect to our human fathers who disciplined us; should we not submit even more readily to our spiritual Father, and so attain life? [10] They disciplined us for a short time as they thought best; but he does so for our true welfare, so that we may share his holiness. [11] Discipline, to be sure, is never pleasant; at the time it seems painful, but afterwards those who have been trained by it reap the harvest of a peaceful and upright life. [12] So brace your drooping arms and shaking knees, [13] and keep to a straight path; then the weakened limb will not be put out of joint, but will regain its former powers.

The fruit of righteousness

[14] AIM at peace with everyone and a holy life, for without that no one will see the Lord. [15] Take heed that there is no one among you who forfeits the grace of God, no bitter, noxious weed growing up to contaminate the rest, [16] no immoral person, no one worldly-minded like Esau. He sold his birthright for a single meal, [17] and you know that afterwards, although he wanted to claim the blessing, he was rejected; though he begged for it to the point of tears, he found no way open for a change of mind.

[18] IT is not to the tangible, blazing fire of Sinai that you have come, with its darkness, gloom, and whirlwind, [19] its trumpet-blast and oracular voice, which the people heard and begged to hear no more; [20] for they could not bear the command, 'If even an animal touches the mountain, it must be stoned to death.' [21] So appalling was the sight that Moses said, 'I shudder with fear.'

[22] No, you have come to Mount Zion, the city of the living God, the heavenly Jerusalem, to myriads of angels, [23] to the full concourse and assembly of the firstborn who are enrolled in heaven, and to God the judge of all, and to the spirits of good men made perfect, [24] and to Jesus the mediator of a new covenant, whose sprinkled blood has better things to say than the blood of Abel. [25] See that you do not refuse to hear the voice that speaks. Those who refused to hear the oracle speaking on earth found no escape; still less shall we escape if we reject him who speaks from heaven. [26] Then indeed his voice shook the earth, but now he has promised, 'Once again I will shake not only the earth, but the heavens also.' [27] The words 'once again' point to the removal of all created things, of all that is shaken, so that what cannot be shaken may remain. [28] The kingdom we are given is unshakeable; let us therefore give thanks to God for it, and so worship God as he would be worshipped, with reverence and awe; [29] for our God is a devouring fire.

13 NEVER cease to love your fellow-Christians. [2] Do not neglect to show hospitality; by doing this, some have entertained angels unawares. [3] Remember those in prison, as if you were there with them, and those who are being maltreated, for you are vulnerable too.

[4] Marriage must be honoured by all, and the marriage bond be kept inviolate; for God's judgement will fall on fornicators and adulterers.

[5] Do not live for money; be content with what you have, for God has said, 'I will never leave you or desert you.' [6] So we can take courage and say, 'The Lord is my helper, I will not fear; what can man do to me?'

[7] Remember your leaders, who spoke God's message to you. Keep before you the outcome of their life and follow the example of their faith.

[8] Jesus Christ is the same yesterday, today, and for ever. [9] So do not be swept off your course by all sorts of outlandish

teachings; it is good that we should gain inner strength from the grace of God, and not from rules about food, which have never benefited those who observed them. [10] Our altar is one from which the priests of the sacred tent have no right to eat. [11] As you know, the animals whose blood is brought by the high priest into the sanctuary as a sin-offering have their bodies burnt outside the camp. [12] Therefore, to consecrate the people by his own blood, Jesus also suffered outside the gate. [13] Let us then go to him outside the camp, bearing the stigma that he bore. [14] For here we have no lasting city, but we are seekers after the city which is to come. [15] Through Jesus let us continually offer up to God a sacrifice of praise, that is, the tribute of lips which acknowledge his name.

[16] Never neglect to show kindness and to share what you have with others; for such are the sacrifices which God approves.

[17] Obey your leaders and submit to their authority; for they are tireless in their care for you, as those who must render an account. See that their work brings them happiness, not pain and grief, for that would be no advantage to you.

[18] Pray for us. We are sure that our conscience is clear, and our desire is always to do what is right. [19] I specially ask for your prayers, so that I may be restored to you the sooner.

[20] May the God of peace, who brought back from the dead our Lord Jesus, the great Shepherd of the sheep, through the blood of an eternal covenant, [21] make you perfect in all goodness so that you may do his will; and may he create in us what is pleasing to him, through Jesus Christ, to whom be glory for ever and ever! Amen.

[22] I beg you, friends, bear with my appeal; for this is after all a short letter. [23] I have news for you: our friend Timothy has been released; and if he comes in time he will be with me when I see you.

[24] Greet all your leaders and all God's people. Greetings to you from our Italian friends.

[25] God's grace be with you all!

A LETTER OF

JAMES

1 FROM James, a servant of God and the Lord Jesus Christ. Greetings to the twelve tribes dispersed throughout the world.

Faith under trial

[2] MY friends, whenever you have to face all sorts of trials, count yourselves supremely happy [3] in the knowledge that such testing of your faith makes for strength to endure. [4] Let endurance perfect its work in you that you may become perfected, sound throughout, lacking in nothing. [5] If any of you lacks wisdom, he should ask God and it will be given him, for God is a generous giver who neither grudges nor reproaches anyone. [6] But he who asks must ask in faith, with never a doubt in his mind; for the doubter is like a wave of the sea tossed hither and thither by the wind. [7] A man like that should not think he will receive anything from the Lord. [8] He is always in two minds and unstable in all he does.

[9] The church member in humble circumstances does well to take pride in being exalted; [10] the wealthy member must find his pride in being brought low, for the rich man will disappear like a wild flower; [11] once the sun is up with its scorching heat, it parches the plant, its flower withers, and what was lovely to look at is lost for ever. So shall the rich man fade away as he goes about his business.

[12] Happy is the man who stands up to trial! Having passed that test he will receive in reward the life which God has promised to those who love him. [13] No one when tempted should say, 'I am being tempted by God'; for God cannot be tempted by evil and does not himself tempt anyone. [14] Temptation comes when anyone is lured and dragged away by his own desires; [15] then desire conceives and gives birth to sin, and sin when it is full-grown breeds death.

[16] Make no mistake, my dear friends. [17] Every good and generous action and every perfect gift come from above, from the Father who created the lights of heaven. With him there is no variation, no play of passing shadows. [18] Of his own choice, he brought us to birth by the word of truth to be a kind of firstfruits of his creation.

[19] Of that you may be certain, my dear friends. But everyone should be quick to listen, slow to speak, and slow to be angry. [20] For human anger does not promote God's justice. [21] Then discard everything sordid, and every wicked excess, and meekly accept the message planted in your hearts, with its power to save you.

[22] Only be sure you act on the message, and do not merely listen and so deceive yourselves. [23] Anyone who listens to the message but does not act on it is like somebody looking in a mirror at the face nature gave him; [24] he glances at himself and goes his way, and promptly forgets what he looked like. [25] But he who looks into the perfect law, the law that makes us free, and does not turn away, remembers what he hears; he acts on it, and by so acting he will find happiness.

[26] If anyone thinks he is religious but does not bridle his tongue, he is deceiving himself; that man's religion is futile. [27] A pure and faultless religion in the sight of God the Father is this: to look after orphans and widows in trouble and to keep oneself untarnished by the world.

Love your neighbour as yourself

2 MY friends, you believe in our Lord Jesus Christ who reigns in glory and you must always be impartial. [2] For instance, two visitors may enter your meeting, one a well-dressed man with gold rings, and the other a poor man in grimy clothes. [3] Suppose you pay special attention to the well-dressed man and say to him, 'Please take this seat,' while to the

---

1:17 **no variation ... shadows:** *some witnesses read* no variation, or shadow caused by change.   1:21 **Then discard ... and meekly accept:** *or* Then meekly discard ... and accept.   2:3 **Please ... seat:** *or* Do take this comfortable seat.

poor man you say, 'You stand over there, or sit here on the floor by my footstool,' [4] do you not see that you are discriminating among your members and judging by wrong standards? [5] Listen, my dear friends: has not God chosen those who are poor in the eyes of the world to be rich in faith and to possess the kingdom he has promised to those who love him? [6] And yet you have humiliated the poor man. Moreover, are not the rich your oppressors? Is it not they who drag you into court [7] and pour contempt on the honoured name by which God has claimed you?

[8] If, however, you are observing the sovereign law laid down in scripture, 'Love your neighbour as yourself,' that is excellent. [9] But if you show partiality, you are committing a sin and you stand convicted by the law as offenders. [10] For if a man breaks just one commandment and keeps all the others, he is guilty of breaking all of them. [11] For he who said, 'You shall not commit adultery,' said also, 'You shall not commit murder.' If you commit murder you are a breaker of the law, even if you do not commit adultery as well. [12] Always speak and act as men who are to be judged under a law which makes them free. [13] In that judgement there will be no mercy for the man who has shown none. Mercy triumphs over judgement.

[14] WHAT good is it, my friends, for someone to say he has faith when his actions do nothing to show it? Can that faith save him? [15] Suppose a fellow-Christian, whether man or woman, is in rags with not enough food for the day, [16] and one of you says, 'Goodbye, keep warm, and have a good meal,' but does nothing to supply their bodily needs, what good is that? [17] So with faith; if it does not lead to action, it is by itself a lifeless thing.

[18] But someone may say: 'One chooses faith, another action.' To which I reply: 'Show me this faith you speak of with no actions to prove it, while I by my actions will prove to you my faith.' [19] You have faith and believe that there is one God. Excellent! Even demons have faith like that, and it makes them tremble. [20] Do you have to be told, you fool, that faith divorced from action is futile? [21] Was it not by his action, in offering his son Isaac

upon the altar, that our father Abraham was justified? [22] Surely you can see faith was at work in his actions, and by these actions his faith was perfected? [23] Here was fulfilment of the words of scripture: 'Abraham put his faith in God, and that faith was counted to him as righteousness,' and he was called 'God's friend'. [24] You see then it is by action and not by faith alone that a man is justified. [25] The same is true also of the prostitute Rahab. Was she not justified by her action in welcoming the messengers into her house and sending them away by a different route? [26] As the body is dead when there is no breath left in it, so faith divorced from action is dead.

Christian speaking

3 My friends, not many of you should become teachers, for you may be certain that we who teach will ourselves face severer judgement. [2] All of us go wrong again and again; a man who never says anything wrong is perfect and is capable of controlling every part of his body. [3] When we put a bit into a horse's mouth to make it obey our will, we can direct the whole animal. [4] Or think of a ship: large though it may be and driven by gales, it can be steered by a very small rudder on whatever course the helmsman chooses. [5] So with the tongue; it is small, but its pretensions are great.

What a vast amount of timber can be set ablaze by the tiniest spark! [6] And the tongue is a fire, representing in our body the whole wicked world. It pollutes our whole being, it sets the whole course of our existence alight, and its flames are fed by hell. [7] Beasts and birds of every kind, creatures that crawl on the ground or swim in the sea, can be subdued and have been subdued by man; [8] but no one can subdue the tongue. It is an evil thing, restless and charged with deadly venom. [9] We use it to praise our Lord and Father; then we use it to invoke curses on our fellow-men, though they are made in God's likeness. [10] Out of the same mouth come praise and curses. This should not be so, my friends. [11] Does a fountain flow with both fresh and brackish water from the same outlet? [12] My friends, can a fig tree produce olives, or a grape vine produce figs? No more can salt water produce fresh.

The sin of envy

[13] WHICH of you is wise or learned? Let him give practical proof of it by his right conduct, with the modesty that comes of wisdom. [14] But if you are harbouring bitter jealousy and the spirit of rivalry in your hearts, stop making false claims in defiance of the truth. [15] This is not the wisdom that comes from above; it is earth-bound, sensual, demonic. [16] For with jealousy and rivalry come disorder and the practice of every kind of evil. [17] But the wisdom from above is in the first place pure; and then peace-loving, considerate, and open-minded; it is straightforward and sincere, rich in compassion and in deeds of kindness that are its fruit. [18] Peace is the seed-bed of righteousness, and the peacemakers will reap its harvest.

4 What causes fighting and quarrels among you? Is not their origin the appetites that war in your bodies? [2] You want what you cannot have, so you murder; you are envious, and cannot attain your ambition, so you quarrel and fight. You do not get what you want, because you do not pray for it. [3] Or, if you do, your requests are not granted, because you pray from wrong motives, in order to squander what you get on your pleasures. [4] Unfaithful creatures! Surely you know that love of the world means enmity to God? Whoever chooses to be the world's friend makes himself God's enemy. [5] Or do you suppose that scripture has no point when it says that the spirit which God implanted in us is filled with envious longings? [6] But the grace he gives is stronger; thus scripture says, 'God opposes the arrogant and gives grace to the humble.' [7] Submit then to God. Stand up to the devil, and he will turn and run. [8] Come close to God, and he will draw close to you. Sinners, make your hands clean; you whose motives are mixed, see that your hearts are pure. [9] Be sorrowful, mourn, and weep. Turn your laughter into mourning and your gaiety into gloom. [10] Humble yourselves before the Lord, and he will exalt you.

[11] Friends, you must never speak ill of one another. He who speaks ill of a brother or passes judgement on him speaks ill of the law and judges the law. But if you judge the law, you are not keeping it but sitting in judgement upon

it. [12] There is only one lawgiver and judge: he who is able to save life or destroy it. So who are you to judge your neighbour?

The danger of wealth

[13] Now a word with all who say, 'Today or the next day we will go off to such and such a town and spend a year there trading and making money.' [14] Yet you have no idea what tomorrow will bring. What is your life after all? You are no more than a mist, seen for a little while and then disappearing. [15] What you ought to say is: 'If it be the Lord's will, we shall live to do so and so.' [16] But instead, you boast and brag, and all such boasting is wrong. [17] What it comes to is that anyone who knows the right thing to do and does not do it is a sinner.

5 Next a word to you who are rich. Weep and wail over the miserable fate overtaking you: [2] your riches have rotted away; your fine clothes are motheaten; [3] your silver and gold have corroded, and their corrosion will be evidence against you and consume your flesh like fire. You have piled up wealth in an age that is near its close. [4] The wages you never paid to the men who mowed your fields are crying aloud against you, and the outcry of the reapers has reached the ears of the Lord of Hosts. [5] You have lived on the land in wanton luxury, gorging yourselves—and that on the day appointed for your slaughter. [6] You have condemned and murdered the innocent one, who offers no resistance.

Patience and prayer

[7] You MUST be patient, my friends, until the Lord comes. Consider: the farmer looking for the precious crop from his land can only wait in patience until the early and late rains have fallen. [8] You too must be patient and stout-hearted, for the coming of the Lord is near. [9] My friends, do not blame your troubles on one another, or you will fall under judgement; and there at the door stands the Judge. [10] As a pattern of patience under ill-treatment, take the prophets who spoke in the name of the Lord. [11] We count those happy who stood firm. You have heard how Job stood firm, and you have seen how the Lord treated him in the end, for the Lord is merciful and compassionate.

¹² ABOVE all things, my friends, do not use oaths, whether 'by heaven' or 'by earth' or by anything else. When you say 'Yes' or 'No', let it be plain Yes or No, for fear you draw down judgement on yourselves.

¹³ Is anyone among you in trouble? Let him pray. Is anyone in good heart? Let him sing praises. ¹⁴ Is one of you ill? Let him send for the elders of the church to pray over him and anoint him with oil in the name of the Lord; ¹⁵ the prayer offered in faith will heal the sick man, the Lord will restore him to health, and if he has committed sins they will be forgiven. ¹⁶ Therefore confess your sins to one another, and pray for one another, that you may be healed. A good man's prayer is very powerful and effective. ¹⁷ Elijah was a man just like us; yet when he prayed fervently that there should be no rain, the land had no rain for three and a half years; ¹⁸ when he prayed again, the rain poured down and the land bore crops once more.

¹⁹ My friends, if one of you strays from the truth and another succeeds in bringing him back, ²⁰ you may be sure of this: the one who brings a sinner back from his erring ways will be rescuing a soul from death and cancelling a multitude of sins.

THE FIRST LETTER OF

PETER

1 FROM Peter, apostle of Jesus Christ, to the scattered people of God now living as aliens in Pontus, Galatia, Cappadocia, Asia, and Bithynia, [2] chosen in the foreknowledge of God the Father, by the consecrating work of the Holy Spirit, for obedience to Jesus Christ and sprinkling with his blood.

Grace and peace to you in fullest measure.

Peter gives thanks

[3] PRAISED be the God and Father of our Lord Jesus Christ! In his great mercy by the resurrection of Jesus Christ from the dead, he gave us new birth into a living hope, [4] the hope of an inheritance, reserved in heaven for you, which nothing can destroy or spoil or wither. [5] Because you put your faith in God, you are under the protection of his power until the salvation now in readiness is revealed at the end of time.

[6] This is cause for great joy, even though for a little while you may have had to suffer trials of many kinds. [7] Even gold passes through the assayer's fire, and much more precious than perishable gold is faith which stands the test. These trials come so that your faith may prove itself worthy of all praise, glory, and honour when Jesus Christ is revealed.

[8] You have not seen him, yet you love him; and trusting in him now without seeing him, you are filled with a glorious joy too great for words, [9] while you are reaping the harvest of your faith, that is, salvation for your souls.

The calling of a Christian

[10] THIS salvation was the subject of intense search by the prophets who prophesied about the grace of God awaiting you. [11] They tried to find out the time and the circumstances to which the spirit of Christ in them pointed, when it foretold the sufferings in Christ's cause and the glories to follow. [12] It was disclosed to them that these matters were not for their benefit but for yours. Now they have been openly announced to you through preachers who brought you the gospel in the power of the Holy Spirit sent from heaven. These are things that angels long to glimpse.

[13] Your minds must therefore be stripped for action and fully alert. Fix your hopes on the grace which is to be yours when Jesus Christ is revealed. [14] Be obedient to God your Father, and do not let your characters be shaped any longer by the desires you cherished in your days of ignorance. [15] He who called you is holy; like him, be holy in all your conduct. [16] Does not scripture say, 'You shall be holy, for I am holy'?

[17] If you say 'Father' to him who judges everyone impartially on the basis of what they have done, you must live in awe of him during your time on earth. [18] You know well that it was nothing of passing value, like silver or gold, that bought your freedom from the futility of your traditional ways. [19] You were set free by Christ's precious blood, blood like that of a lamb without mark or blemish. [20] He was predestined before the foundation of the world, but in this last period of time he has been revealed for your sake. [21] Through him you have come to trust in God who raised him from the dead and gave him glory, and so your faith and hope are fixed on God.

[22] Now that you have purified your souls by obedience to the truth until you feel sincere affection towards your fellow-Christians, love one another wholeheartedly with all your strength. [23] You have been born again, not of mortal but of immortal parentage, through the living and enduring word of God. [24] As scripture says:

All mortals are like grass;
all their glory like the flower of the
    field;
the grass withers, the flower falls;
[25] but the word of the Lord endures for
    evermore.

1:11 *the time: or* the person.

And this 'word' is the gospel which was preached to you.

2 Then away with all wickedness and deceit, hypocrisy and jealousy and malicious talk of any kind! ² Like the new-born infants you are, you should be craving for pure spiritual milk so that you may thrive on it and be saved; for ³ surely you have tasted that the Lord is good.

⁴ So come to him, to the living stone which was rejected by men but chosen by God and of great worth to him. ⁵ You also, as living stones, must be built up into a spiritual temple, and form a holy priesthood to offer spiritual sacrifices acceptable to God through Jesus Christ. ⁶ For you will find in scripture:

I am laying in Zion a chosen corner-stone of great worth.
Whoever has faith in it will not be put to shame.

⁷ So for you who have faith it has great worth; but for those who have no faith 'the stone which the builders rejected has become the corner-stone', ⁸ and also 'a stone to trip over, a rock to stumble against'. They trip because they refuse to believe the word; this is the fate appointed for them.

⁹ But you are a chosen race, a royal priesthood, a dedicated nation, a people claimed by God for his own, to proclaim the glorious deeds of him who has called you out of darkness into his marvellous light. ¹⁰ Once you were not a people at all; but now you are God's people. Once you were outside his mercy; but now you are outside no longer.

The Christian household

¹¹ DEAR friends, I appeal to you, as aliens in a foreign land, to avoid bodily desires which make war on the soul. ¹² Let your conduct among unbelievers be so good that, although they now malign you as wrongdoers, reflection on your good deeds will lead them to give glory to God on the day when he comes in judgement.

¹³ Submit yourselves for the sake of the Lord to every human authority, whether to the emperor as supreme, ¹⁴ or to governors as his deputies for the punishment of those who do wrong and the commenda-

tion of those who do right. ¹⁵ For it is God's will that by doing right you should silence ignorance and stupidity.

¹⁶ Live as those who are free; not however as though your freedom provided a cloak for wrongdoing, but as slaves in God's service. ¹⁷ Give due honour to everyone: love your fellow-Christians, reverence God, honour the emperor.

¹⁸ Servants, submit to your masters with all due respect, not only to those who are kind and forbearing, but even to those who are unjust. ¹⁹ It is a sign of grace if, because God is in his thoughts, someone endures the pain of undeserved suffering. ²⁰ What credit is there in enduring the beating you deserve when you have done wrong? On the other hand, when you have behaved well and endured suffering for it, that is a sign of grace in the sight of God. ²¹ It is your vocation because Christ himself suffered on your behalf, and left you an example in order that you should follow in his steps. ²² 'He committed no sin, he was guilty of no falsehood.' ²³ When he was abused he did not retaliate, when he suffered he uttered no threats, but delivered himself up to him who judges justly. ²⁴ He carried our sins in his own person on the gibbet, so that we might cease to live for sin and begin to live for righteousness. By his wounds you have been healed. ²⁵ You were straying like sheep, but now you have turned towards the Shepherd and Guardian of your souls.

3 In the same way you women must submit to your husbands, so that if there are any of them who disbelieve the gospel they may be won over without a word being said, ² by observing your chaste and respectful behaviour. ³ Your beauty should lie, not in outward adornment—braiding the hair, wearing gold ornaments, or dressing up in fine clothes—⁴ but in the inmost self, with its imperishable quality of a gentle, quiet spirit, which is of high value in the sight of God. ⁵ This is how in past days the women of God's people, whose hope was in him, used to make themselves attractive, submitting to their husbands. ⁶ Such was Sarah, who obeyed Abraham and called him master. By doing good and

---

2:19, 20 **a sign of grace**: *or* creditable.   2:21 **suffered**: *some witnesses read* died.   2:24 **on the gibbet**: *or* to the gibbet.

showing no fear, you have become her daughters.

⁷ In the same way, you husbands must show understanding in your married life: treat your wives with respect, not only because they are physically weaker, but also because God's gift of life is something you share together. Then your prayers will not be impeded.

⁸ Finally, be united, all of you, in thought and feeling; be full of brotherly affection, kindly and humble. ⁹ Do not repay wrong with wrong, or abuse with abuse; on the contrary, respond with blessing, for a blessing is what God intends you to receive. As scripture says:

¹⁰ If anyone wants to love life
     and see good days
     he must restrain his tongue from evil
     and his lips from deceit;
¹¹ he must turn from wrong and do good,
     seek peace and pursue it.
¹² The Lord has eyes for the righteous,
     and ears open to their prayers;
     but the face of the Lord is set against
     wrongdoers.

¹³ Who is going to do you harm if you are devoted to what is good? ¹⁴ Yet if you should suffer for doing right you may count yourselves happy. Have no fear of other people: do not be perturbed, ¹⁵ but hold Christ in your hearts in reverence as Lord. Always be ready to make your defence when anyone challenges you to justify the hope which is in you. But do so with courtesy and respect, ¹⁶ keeping your conscience clear, so that when you are abused, those who malign your Christian conduct may be put to shame. ¹⁷ It is better to suffer for doing right, if such should be the will of God, than for doing wrong.

¹⁸ Christ too suffered for our sins once and for all, the just for the unjust, that he might bring us to God; put to death in the body, he was brought to life in the spirit. ¹⁹ In the spirit also he went and made his proclamation to the imprisoned spirits, ²⁰ those who had refused to obey in the past, while God waited patiently in the days when Noah was building the ark; in

it a few people, eight in all, were brought to safety through the water. ²¹ This water symbolized baptism, through which you are now brought to safety. Baptism is not the washing away of bodily impurities but the appeal made to God from a good conscience; and it brings salvation through the resurrection of Jesus Christ, ²² who is now at the right hand of God, having entered heaven and received the submission of angels, authorities, and powers.

The final testing

4 SINCE Christ endured bodily suffering, you also must arm yourselves with the same disposition. When anyone has endured bodily suffering he has finished with sin, ² so that for the rest of his days on earth he may live, not to satisfy human appetites, but to do what God wills. ³ You have spent time enough in the past doing what pagans like to do. You lived then in licence and debauchery, drunkenness, orgies and carousal, and the forbidden worship of idols. ⁴ Now, when you no longer plunge with the pagans into all this reckless dissipation, they cannot understand it and start abusing you; ⁵ but they will have to give account of themselves to him who is ready to pass judgement on the living and the dead. ⁶ That was why the gospel was preached even to the dead: in order that, although in the body they were condemned to die as everyone dies, yet in the spirit they might live as God lives.

⁷ The end of all things is upon us; therefore to help you to pray you must lead self-controlled and sober lives. ⁸ Above all, maintain the fervour of your love for one another, because love cancels a host of sins. ⁹ Be hospitable to one another without grumbling. ¹⁰ As good stewards of the varied gifts given you by God, let each use the gift he has received in service to others. ¹¹ Are you a speaker? Speak as one who utters God's oracles. Do you give service? Give it in the strength which God supplies. In all things let God be glorified through Jesus Christ; to him belong glory and power for ever and ever. Amen.

3:14 Have ... people: *or* Do not fear what other people fear.   3:18 suffered: *some witnesses read* died. for our sins: *some witnesses read* for sins.   3:21 from a good conscience: *or* for a good conscience.   4:6 although ... lives: *or* although in the body they suffered judgement by human standards, in the spirit they might be given life in accordance with God's purpose.

¹² DEAR friends, do not be taken aback by the fiery ordeal which has come to test you, as though it were something extraordinary. ¹³ On the contrary, in so far as it gives you a share in Christ's sufferings, you should rejoice; and then when his glory is revealed, your joy will be unbounded. ¹⁴ If you are reviled for being Christians, count yourselves happy, because the Spirit of God in all his glory rests upon you. ¹⁵ If you do suffer, it must not be for murder, theft, or any other crime, nor should it be for meddling in other people's business. ¹⁶ But if anyone suffers as a Christian, he should feel it no disgrace, but confess that name to the honour of God.

¹⁷ The time has come for the judgement to begin; it is beginning with God's own household. And if it is starting with us, how will it end for those who refuse to obey the gospel of God? ¹⁸ Scripture says: 'It is hard enough for the righteous to be saved; what then will become of the impious and sinful?' ¹⁹ So let those who suffer according to God's will entrust their souls to him while continuing to do good; their Maker will not fail them.

The Christian community

5 Now I APPEAL to the elders of your community, as a fellow-elder and a witness to Christ's sufferings, and as one who has shared in the glory to be revealed: ² look after the flock of God whose shepherds you are; do it, not under compulsion, but willingly, as God would have it; not for gain but out of sheer devotion; ³ not lording it over your charges, but setting an example to the flock. ⁴ So when the chief shepherd appears, you will receive glory, a crown that never fades.

⁵ In the same way the younger men should submit to the older. You should all clothe yourselves with humility towards one another, because 'God sets his face against the arrogant but shows favour to the humble.' ⁶ Humble yourselves, then, under God's mighty hand, and in due time he will lift you up. ⁷ He cares for you, so cast all your anxiety on him.

⁸ Be on the alert! Wake up! Your enemy the devil, like a roaring lion, prowls around looking for someone to devour. ⁹ Stand up to him, firm in your faith, and remember that your fellow-Christians in this world are going through the same kinds of suffering. ¹⁰ After your brief suffering, the God of all grace, who called you to his eternal glory in Christ, will himself restore, establish, and strengthen you on a firm foundation. ¹¹ All power belongs to him for ever and ever! Amen.

Final greetings

¹² I WRITE you this brief letter through Silvanus, whom I know to be a trustworthy colleague, to encourage you and to testify that this is the true grace of God; in this stand fast.

¹³ Greetings from your sister church in Babylon, and from my son Mark. ¹⁴ Greet one another with a loving kiss.

Peace to you all who belong to Christ!

THE SECOND LETTER OF
PETER

1 FROM Simeon Peter, servant and apostle of Jesus Christ, to those who share equally with us in the privileges of faith through the righteousness of our God and Saviour Jesus Christ. ² Grace and peace be yours in fullest measure, through knowledge of God and of Jesus our Lord.

Living in the last days

³ GOD's divine power has bestowed on us everything that makes for life and true religion, through our knowledge of him who called us by his own glory and goodness. ⁴ In this way he has given us his promises, great beyond all price, so that through them you may escape the corruption with which lust has infected the world, and may come to share in the very being of God.

⁵ With all this in view, you should make every effort to add virtue to your faith, knowledge to virtue, ⁶ self-control to knowledge, fortitude to self-control, piety

to fortitude, ⁷ brotherly affection to piety, and love to brotherly affection.

⁸ If you possess and develop these gifts, you will grow actively and effectively in knowledge of our Lord Jesus Christ. ⁹ Whoever lacks them is wilfully blind; he has forgotten that his past sins were washed away. ¹⁰ All the more then, my friends, do your utmost to establish that God has called and chosen you. If you do this, you will never stumble, ¹¹ and there will be rich provision for your entry into the eternal kingdom of our Lord and Saviour Jesus Christ.

¹² I shall keep reminding you of all this, although you know it and are well grounded in the truth you possess; ¹³ yet I think it right to keep on reminding you as long as I still lodge in this body. ¹⁴ I know I must soon leave it, as our Lord Jesus Christ told me. ¹⁵ But I will do my utmost to ensure that after I am gone you will always be able to call these things to mind.

¹⁶ It was not on tales, however cleverly concocted, that we relied when we told you about the power of our Lord Jesus Christ and his coming; rather with our own eyes we had witnessed his majesty. ¹⁷ He was invested with honour and glory by God the Father, and there came to him from the sublime Presence a voice which said: 'This is my Son, my Beloved, on whom my favour rests.' ¹⁸ We ourselves heard this voice when it came from heaven, for we were with him on the sacred mountain.

¹⁹ All this confirms for us the message of the prophets, to which you will do well to attend; it will go on shining like a lamp in a murky place, until day breaks and the morning star rises to illuminate your minds.

²⁰ But first note this: no prophetic writing is a matter for private interpretation. ²¹ It was not on any human initiative that prophecy came; rather, it was under the compulsion of the Holy Spirit that people spoke as messengers of God.

God's judgement on false teaching

2 In the past there were also false prophets among the people, just as you also will have false teachers among you. They will introduce their destructive views, disowning the very Master who redeemed them, and bringing swift destruction on their own heads. ² They will gain many adherents to their dissolute practices, through whom the way of truth will be brought into disrepute. ³ In their greed for money they will trade on your credulity with sheer fabrications.

But judgement has long been in preparation for them; destruction waits for them with unsleeping eyes. ⁴ God did not spare the angels who sinned, but consigned them to the dark pits of hell, where they are held for judgement. ⁵ Nor did he spare the world in ancient times (except for Noah, who proclaimed righteousness, and was preserved with seven others), but brought the flood upon that world with its godless people. ⁶ God reduced the cities of Sodom and Gomorrah to ashes, condemning them to total ruin as an object-lesson for the ungodly in future days. ⁷ But he rescued Lot, a good man distressed by the dissolute habits of the lawless society in which he lived; ⁸ day after day every sight and sound of their evil ways tortured that good man's heart. ⁹ The Lord knows how to rescue the godly from their trials, and to keep the wicked under punishment until the day of judgement.

¹⁰ Above all he will punish those who follow their abominable lusts and flout authority. Reckless and headstrong, they are not afraid to insult celestial beings, ¹¹ whereas angels, for all their superior strength and power, employ no insults in seeking judgement against them before the Lord.

¹² These men are like brute beasts, mere creatures of instinct, born to be caught and killed. They pour abuse upon things they do not understand; they will perish like the beasts, ¹³ suffering hurt for the hurt they have inflicted. To carouse in broad daylight is their idea of pleasure; while they sit with you at table they are an ugly blot on your company, because they revel in their deceits. ¹⁴ They have eyes for nothing but loose women, eyes never resting from sin. They lure the unstable to their ruin; experts in mercenary greed, God's curse is on them!

1:17 *This...Beloved: or* This is my only Son.   2:4 *consigned...hell: some witnesses read* consigned them to darkness and chains in hell.

¹⁵ They have abandoned the straight road and gone astray. They have followed in the steps of Balaam son of Bosor, who eagerly accepted payment for doing wrong, ¹⁶ but had his offence brought home to him when a dumb beast spoke with a human voice and checked the prophet's madness.

¹⁷ These men are springs that give no water, mists driven by a storm; the place reserved for them is blackest darkness. ¹⁸ They utter empty bombast; they use sensual lusts and debauchery as a bait to catch people who have only just begun to escape from their pagan associates. ¹⁹ They promise them freedom, but are themselves slaves of corruption; for people are the slaves of whatever has mastered them. ²⁰ If they escaped the world's defilements through coming to know our Lord and Saviour Jesus Christ and entangled themselves in them again, and were mastered by them, their last state would be worse than the first. ²¹ Better for them never to have known the right way, than, having known it, to turn back and abandon the sacred commandment entrusted to them! ²² In their case the proverb has proved true: 'The dog returns to its vomit,' and 'The washed sow wallows in the mud again.'

The coming end

3 THIS, dear friends, is now my second letter to you. In both I have been recalling to you what you already know, to rouse you to honest thought. ² Remember the predictions made by God's own prophets, and the commandment given by the Lord and Saviour through your apostles.

³ First of all, note this: in the last days there will come scoffers who live self-indulgent lives; they will mock you and say: ⁴ 'What has happened to his promised coming? Our fathers have been laid to rest, but still everything goes on exactly as it always has done since the world began.'

⁵ In maintaining this they forget that there were heavens and earth long ago, created by God's word out of water and with water; ⁶ and that the first world was destroyed by water, the water of the flood. ⁷ By God's word the present heavens and earth are being reserved for burning; they are being kept until the day of judgement when the godless will be destroyed.

⁸ Here is something, dear friends, which you must not forget: in the Lord's sight one day is like a thousand years and a thousand years like one day. ⁹ It is not that the Lord is slow in keeping his promise, as some suppose, but that he is patient with you. It is not his will that any should be lost, but that all should come to repentance.

¹⁰ But the day of the Lord will come like a thief. On that day the heavens will disappear with a great rushing sound, the elements will be dissolved in flames, and the earth with all that is in it will be brought to judgement.

¹¹ Since the whole universe is to dissolve in this way, think what sort of people you ought to be, what devout and dedicated lives you should live! ¹² Look forward to the coming of the day of God, and work to hasten it on; that day will set the heavens ablaze until they fall apart, and will melt the elements in flames. ¹³ Relying on his promise we look forward to new heavens and a new earth, in which justice will be established.

¹⁴ In expectation of all this, my friends, do your utmost to be found at peace with him, unblemished and above reproach. ¹⁵ Bear in mind that our Lord's patience is an opportunity for salvation, as Paul, our dear friend and brother, said when he wrote to you with the wisdom God gave him. ¹⁶ He does the same in all his other letters, wherever he speaks about this, though they contain some obscure passages, which the ignorant and unstable misinterpret to their own ruin, as they do the other scriptures.

¹⁷ So, dear friends, you have been forewarned. Take care not to let these unprincipled people seduce you with their errors; do not lose your own safe foothold. ¹⁸ But grow in grace and in the knowledge of our Lord and Saviour Jesus Christ. To him be glory both now and for all eternity!

2:15 **Bosor:** *some witnesses read* Beor.   3:10 **will be brought to judgement:** *lit.* will be found.

THE FIRST LETTER OF

JOHN

1 It was there from the beginning; we have heard it; we have seen it with our own eyes; we looked upon it, and felt it with our own hands: our theme is the Word which gives life. ² This life was made visible; we have seen it and bear our testimony; we declare to you the eternal life which was with the Father and was made visible to us. ³ It is this which we have seen and heard that we declare to you also, in order that you may share with us in a common life, that life which we share with the Father and his Son Jesus Christ. ⁴ We are writing this in order that our joy may be complete.

Fellowship, obedience, and forgiveness

⁵ HERE is the message we have heard from him and pass on to you: God is light, and in him there is no darkness at all. ⁶ If we claim to be sharing in his life while we go on living in darkness, our words and our lives are a lie. ⁷ But if we live in the light as he himself is in the light, then we share a common life, and the blood of Jesus his Son cleanses us from all sin.

⁸ If we claim to be sinless, we are self-deceived and the truth is not in us. ⁹ If we confess our sins, he is just and may be trusted to forgive our sins and cleanse us from every kind of wrongdoing. ¹⁰ If we say we have committed no sin, we make him out to be a liar and his word has no place in us.

2 My children, I am writing this to you so that you should not commit sin. But if anybody does, we have in Jesus Christ one who is acceptable to God and will plead our cause with the Father. ² He is himself a sacrifice to atone for our sins, and not ours only but the sins of the whole world.

³ It is by keeping God's commands that we can be sure we know him. ⁴ Whoever says, 'I know him,' but does not obey his commands, is a liar and the truth is not in him; ⁵ but whoever is obedient to his word, in him the love of God is truly made

perfect. This is how we can be sure that we are in him: ⁶ whoever claims to be dwelling in him must live as Christ himself lived.

⁷ Dear friends, it is no new command that I am sending you, but an old command which you have had from the beginning; the old command is the instruction which you have already received. ⁸ Yet because the darkness is passing away and the true light already shining, it is a new command that I write and it is true in Christ's life and in yours.

⁹ Whoever says, 'I am in the light,' but hates his fellow-Christian, is still in darkness. ¹⁰ He who loves his fellow-Christian dwells in light: there is no cause of stumbling in him. ¹¹ But anyone who hates his fellow is in darkness; he walks in the dark and has no idea where he is going, because the darkness has made him blind.

¹² I write to you, children, because your
     sins have been forgiven for his
     sake.
¹³ I write to you, fathers, because you
     know him who is and has been
     from the beginning.
   I write to you, young men, because
     you have conquered the evil one.

   I have written to you, children,
     because you know the Father.
¹⁴ I have written to you, fathers,
     because you know him who is and
     has been from the beginning.
   I have written to you, young men,
     because you are strong; God's
     word remains in you, and you
     have conquered the evil one.

¹⁵ Do not set your hearts on the world or what is in it. Anyone who loves the world does not love the Father. ¹⁶ Everything in the world, all that panders to the appetites or entices the eyes, all the arrogance based on wealth, these spring not from the Father but from the world. ¹⁷ That

2:9 fellow-Christian: *lit.* brother.

216

world with all its allurements is passing away, but those who do God's will remain for ever.

The danger of false teaching

[18] CHILDREN, this is the last hour! You were told that an antichrist was to come. Well, many antichrists have already appeared, proof to us that this is indeed the last hour. [19] They left our ranks, but never really belonged to us; if they had, they would have stayed with us. They left so that it might be clear that none of them belong to us.

[20] What is more, you have been anointed by the Holy One, and so you all have knowledge. [21] It is not because you are ignorant of the truth that I have written to you, but because you do know it, and know that lies never come from the truth.

[22] Anyone who denies that Jesus is the Christ is nothing but a liar. He is the antichrist, for he denies both the Father and the Son: [23] to deny the Son is to be without the Father; to acknowledge the Son is to have the Father too. [24] You must therefore keep hold of what you heard at the beginning; if what you heard then still dwells in you, you will yourselves dwell both in the Son and in the Father. [25] And this is the promise that he himself gave us, the promise of eternal life.

[26] So much for those who would mislead you. [27] But as for you, the anointing which you received from him remains with you; you need no other teacher, but you learn all you need to know from his anointing, which is true and no lie. Dwell in him as he taught you to do.

[28] Even now, children, dwell in him, so that when he appears we may be confident and unashamed before him at his coming. [29] You know that God is righteous; then recognize that everyone who does what is right is his child.

How Christians live together

3 CONSIDER how great is the love which the Father has bestowed on us in calling us his children! For that is what we are. The reason why the world does not recognize us is that it has not known

him. [2] Dear friends, we are now God's children; what we shall be has not yet been disclosed, but we know that when Christ appears we shall be like him, because we shall see him as he is. [3] As he is pure, everyone who has grasped this hope makes himself pure.

[4] To commit sin is to break God's law: for sin is lawlessness. [5] You know that Christ appeared in order to take away sins, and in him there is no sin. [6] No one who dwells in him sins any more; the sinner has neither seen him nor known him.

[7] Children, do not be misled: anyone who does what is right is righteous, just as Christ is righteous; [8] anyone who sins is a child of the devil, for the devil has been a sinner from the first; and the Son of God appeared for the very purpose of undoing the devil's work. [9] No child of God commits sin, because the divine seed remains in him; indeed because he is God's child he cannot sin. [10] This is what shows who are God's children and who are the devil's: anyone who fails to do what is right or love his fellow-Christians is not a child of God.

[11] The message you have heard from the beginning is that we should love one another. [12] Do not be like Cain, who was a child of the evil one and murdered his brother. And why did he murder him? Because his own actions were wrong, and his brother's were right.

[13] Friends, do not be surprised if the world hates you. [14] We know we have crossed over from death to life, because we love our fellow-Christians. Anyone who does not love is still in the realm of death, [15] for everyone who hates a fellow-Christian is a murderer, and murderers, as you know, do not have eternal life dwelling within them. [16] This is how we know what love is: Christ gave his life for us. And we in our turn must give our lives for our fellow-Christians. [17] But if someone who possesses the good things of this world sees a fellow-Christian in need and withholds compassion from him, how can it be said that the love of God dwells in him?

[18] Children, love must not be a matter of theory or talk; it must be true love which

---

2:19 **none of them**: *or* not all of them.   2:20 **you all have knowledge**: *some witnesses read* you have all knowledge.   3:2 **we are ... like him**: *or* we are God's children, though he has not yet appeared; what we shall be we know, for when he does appear we shall be like him. **when Christ appears**: *or* when it is disclosed.

shows itself in action. [19] This is how we shall know that we belong to the realm of truth, and reassure ourselves in his sight [20] where conscience condemns us; for God is greater than our conscience and knows all.

[21] My dear friends, if our conscience does not condemn us, then we can approach God with confidence, [22] and obtain from him whatever we ask, because we are keeping his commands and doing what he approves. [23] His command is that we should give our allegiance to his Son Jesus Christ and love one another, as Christ commanded us. [24] Those who keep his commands dwell in him and he dwells in them. And our certainty that he dwells in us comes from the Spirit he has given us.

Spirits of truth and error

4 MY dear friends, do not trust every spirit, but test the spirits, to see whether they are from God; for there are many false prophets about in the world. [2] The way to recognize the Spirit of God is this: every spirit which acknowledges that Jesus Christ has come in the flesh is from God, [3] and no spirit is from God which does not acknowledge Jesus. This is the spirit of antichrist; you have been warned that it was to come, and now here it is, in the world already!

[4] Children, you belong to God's family, and you have the mastery over these false prophets, because God who inspires you is greater than the one who inspires the world. [5] They belong to that world, and so does their teaching; that is why the world listens to them. [6] But we belong to God and whoever knows God listens to us, while whoever does not belong to God refuses to listen to us. That is how we can distinguish the spirit of truth from the spirit of error.

Love one another

[7] MY dear friends, let us love one another, because the source of love is God. Everyone who loves is a child of God and knows God, [8] but the unloving know nothing of God, for God is love. [9] This is how he showed his love among us: he sent his only Son into the world that we might

have life through him. [10] This is what love really is: not that we have loved God, but that he loved us and sent his Son as a sacrifice to atone for our sins. [11] If God thus loved us, my dear friends, we also must love one another. [12] God has never been seen by anyone, but if we love one another, he himself dwells in us; his love is brought to perfection within us.

[13] This is how we know that we dwell in him and he dwells in us: he has imparted his Spirit to us. [14] Moreover, we have seen for ourselves, and we are witnesses, that the Father has sent the Son to be the Saviour of the world. [15] If anyone acknowledges that Jesus is God's Son, God dwells in him and he in God. [16] Thus we have come to know and believe in the love which God has for us.

God is love; he who dwells in love is dwelling in God, and God in him. [17] This is how love has reached its perfection among us, so that we may have confidence on the day of judgement; and this we can have, because in this world we are as he is. [18] In love there is no room for fear; indeed perfect love banishes fear. For fear has to do with punishment, and anyone who is afraid has not attained to love in its perfection. [19] We love because he loved us first. [20] But if someone says, 'I love God,' while at the same time hating his fellow-Christian, he is a liar. If he does not love a fellow-Christian whom he has seen, he is incapable of loving God whom he has not seen. [21] We have this command from Christ: whoever loves God must love his fellow-Christian too.

Obedience to the truth

5 EVERYONE who believes that Jesus is the Christ is a child of God. To love the parent means to love his child. [2] It follows that when we love God and obey his commands we love his children too. [3] For to love God is to keep his commands; and these are not burdensome, [4] because every child of God overcomes the world. Now, the victory by which the world is overcome is our faith, [5] for who is victor over the world but he who believes that Jesus is the Son of God?

[6] This is he whose coming was with water and blood: Jesus Christ. He came,

---

3:19–20 **reassure ... than our conscience:** *or* convince ourselves in his sight that even if our conscience condemns us, God is greater than our conscience.

not by the water alone, but both by the water and by the blood; and to this the Spirit bears witness, because the Spirit is truth. [7-8] In fact there are three witnesses, the Spirit, the water, and the blood, and these three are in agreement. [9] We accept human testimony, but surely the testimony of God is stronger, and the testimony of God is the witness he has borne to his Son. [10] He who believes in the Son of God has the testimony in his own heart, but he who does not believe God makes him out to be a liar by refusing to accept God's witness to his Son. [11] This is the witness: God has given us eternal life, and this life is found in his Son. [12] He who possesses the Son possesses life; he who does not possess the Son of God does not possess life.

Final instructions and encouragement

[13] YOU HAVE given your allegiance to the Son of God; this letter is to assure you that you have eternal life. [14] We can approach God with this confidence: if we make requests which accord with his will, he listens to us; [15] and if we know that our requests are heard, we also know that all we ask of him is ours.

[16] If anyone sees a fellow-Christian committing a sin which is not a deadly sin, he should intercede for him, and God will grant him life—that is, to those who are not guilty of deadly sin. There is such a thing as deadly sin, and I do not suggest that he should pray about that. [17] Although all wrongdoing is sin, not all sin is deadly sin.

[18] We know that no child of God commits sin; he is kept safe by the Son of God, and the evil one cannot touch him.

[19] We know that we are of God's family, but that the whole world lies in the power of the evil one.

[20] We know that the Son of God has come and given us understanding to know the true God; indeed we are in him who is true, since we are in his Son Jesus Christ. He is the true God and eternal life. [21] Children, be on your guard against idols.

THE SECOND LETTER OF
JOHN

Truth and love

THE Elder to the Lady chosen by God and to her children whom I love in the truth, and not I alone but all who know the truth. [2] We love you for the sake of the truth that dwells among us and will be with us for ever.

[3] Grace, mercy, and peace will be with us from God the Father and from Jesus Christ the Son of the Father, in truth and love.

[4] I was very glad to find that some of your children are living by the truth, in accordance with the command we have received from the Father. [5] And now, Lady, I have a request to make of you. Do not think I am sending a new command; I am recalling the one we have had from the beginning: I ask that we love one another. [6] What love means is to live according to the commands of God. This is the command that was given you from the beginning, to be your rule of life.

[7] Many deceivers have gone out into the world, people who do not acknowledge Jesus Christ as coming in the flesh. Any such person is the deceiver and antichrist. [8] See to it that you do not lose what we have worked for, but receive your reward in full.

[9] Anyone who does not stand by the teaching about Christ, but goes beyond it, does not possess God; he who stands by it possesses both the Father and the Son. [10] If anyone comes to you who does not bring this teaching, do not admit him to your house or give him any greeting; [11] for he who greets him becomes an accomplice in his evil deeds.

[12] I have much to write to you, but I do not care to put it down on paper. Rather, I hope to visit you and talk with you face to face, so that our joy may be complete. [13] The children of your Sister, chosen by God, send you greetings.

THE THIRD LETTER OF
JOHN

Trouble in the church

THE Elder to dear Gaius, whom I love in the truth.

² Dear friend, above all I pray that things go well with you, and that you may enjoy good health: I know it is well with your soul. ³ I was very glad when some fellow-Christians arrived and told me of your faithfulness to the truth; indeed you live by the truth. ⁴ Nothing gives me greater joy than to hear that my children are living by the truth.

⁵ Dear friend, you show a fine loyalty in what you do for our fellow-Christians, though they are strangers to you. ⁶ They have testified to your kindness before the congregation here. Please help them on their journey in a manner worthy of the God we serve. ⁷ It was for love of Christ's name that they went out; and they would accept nothing from unbelievers. ⁸ Therefore we ought to support such people, and so play our part in spreading the truth.

⁹ I wrote to the congregation, but Diotrephes, who enjoys taking the lead, will have nothing to do with us. ¹⁰ So when I come, I will draw attention to the things he is doing: he lays nonsensical and spiteful charges against us; not content with that, he refuses to receive fellow-Christians himself, and interferes with those who would receive them, and tries to expel them from the congregation.

¹¹ Dear friend, follow good examples, not bad ones. The well-doer is a child of God; the evildoer has never seen God.

¹² Demetrius is well spoken of by everyone, and even by the truth itself. I add my testimony, and you know that my testimony is true.

¹³ I had much to write to you, but I do not care to set it down with pen and ink. ¹⁴ I hope to see you very soon, when we will talk face to face. Peace be with you. Your friends here send you greetings. Greet each of our friends by name.

A LETTER OF
JUDE

The danger of false belief

FROM Jude, servant of Jesus Christ and brother of James, to those whom God has called, who live in the love of God the Father and are kept safe for the coming of Jesus Christ.

² Mercy, peace, and love be yours in fullest measure.

³ My friends, I was fully intending to write to you about the salvation we share, when I found it necessary to take up my pen and urge you to join in the struggle for that faith which God entrusted to his people once for all. ⁴ Certain individuals have wormed their way in, the very

people whom scripture long ago marked down for the sentence they are now incurring. They are enemies of religion; they pervert the free favour of our God into licentiousness, disowning Jesus Christ, our only Master and Lord.

⁵ You already know all this, but let me remind you how the Lord, having once for all delivered his people out of Egypt, later destroyed those who did not believe. ⁶ Remember too those angels who were not content to maintain the dominion assigned to them, but abandoned their proper dwelling-place; God is holding them, bound in darkness with everlasting

---

1 kept . . . coming: *or* in the safe keeping.   4 disowning . . . Lord: *or* disowning our one and only Master, and Jesus Christ our Lord.   5 the Lord: *some witnesses read* Jesus; *others read* God.

chains, for judgement on the great day. [7] Remember Sodom and Gomorrah and the neighbouring towns; like the angels, they committed fornication and indulged in unnatural lusts; and in eternal fire they paid the penalty, a warning for all.

[8] In the same way these deluded dreamers continue to defile their bodies, flout authority, and insult celestial beings. [9] Not even the archangel Michael, when he was disputing with the devil for possession of Moses' body, presumed to condemn him in insulting words, but said, 'May the Lord rebuke you!'

[10] But these people pour abuse on whatever they do not understand; the things that, like brute beasts, they do understand by their senses prove their undoing. [11] Alas for them! They have followed the way of Cain; for profit they have plunged into Balaam's error; they have rebelled like Korah, and they share his fate.

[12] These people are a danger at your love-feasts with their shameless carousals. They are shepherds who take care only of themselves. They are clouds carried along by a wind without giving rain, trees fruitless in autumn, dead twice over and pulled up by the roots. [13] They are wild sea waves, foaming with disgraceful deeds; they are stars that have wandered from their courses, and the place reserved for them is an eternity of blackest darkness.

[14] It was against them that Enoch, the seventh in descent from Adam, prophesied when he said: 'I saw the Lord come with his myriads of angels, [15] to bring all mankind to judgement and to convict all the godless of every godless deed they had committed, and of every defiant word they had spoken against him, godless sinners that they are.'

[16] They are a set of grumblers and malcontents. They follow their lusts. Bombast comes rolling from their lips, and they court favour to gain their ends. [17] But you, my friends, should remember the predictions made by the apostles of our Lord Jesus Christ. [18] They said to you: 'In the final age there will be those who mock at religion and follow their own ungodly lusts.'

[19] These people create divisions; they are worldly and unspiritual. [20] But you, my friends, must make your most sacred faith the foundation of your lives. Continue to pray in the power of the Holy Spirit. [21] Keep yourselves in the love of God, and look forward to the day when our Lord Jesus Christ in his mercy will give eternal life.

[22] There are some doubting souls who need your pity. [23] Others you should save by snatching them from the flames. For others your pity must be mixed with fear; hate the very clothing that is contaminated with sensuality.

[24] Now to the One who can keep you from falling and set you in the presence of his glory, jubilant and above reproach, [25] to the only God our Saviour, be glory and majesty, power and authority, through Jesus Christ our Lord, before all time, now, and for evermore. Amen.

---

9 **to condemn ... words:** *or* to charge him with blasphemy.   19 **These ... unspiritual:** *or* These people draw a line between spiritual and unspiritual persons, although they themselves are unspiritual, not spiritual.
23 **Others you ... fear:** *some witnesses read* There are some whom you should snatch from the flames. Show pity to doubting souls with fear.

THE
REVELATION
OF JOHN

1 THIS is the revelation of Jesus Christ, which God gave him so that he might show his servants what must soon take place. He made it known by sending his angel to his servant John, [2] who in telling all that he saw has borne witness to the word of God and to the testimony of Jesus Christ.

[3] Happy is the one who reads aloud the words of this prophecy, and happy those who listen if they take to heart what is here written; for the time of fulfilment is near.

Christ's messages to seven churches

[4] JOHN, to the seven churches in the province of Asia.

Grace be to you and peace, from him who is, who was, and who is to come, from the seven spirits before his throne, [5] and from Jesus Christ, the faithful witness, the firstborn from the dead and ruler of the kings of the earth.

To him who loves us and has set us free from our sins with his blood, [6] who has made of us a royal house to serve as the priests of his God and Father—to him be glory and dominion for ever! Amen.

[7] Look, he is coming with the clouds; everyone shall see him, including those who pierced him; and all the peoples of the world shall lament in remorse. So it shall be. Amen.

[8] 'I am the Alpha and the Omega,' says the Lord God, who is, who was, and who is to come, the sovereign Lord of all.

[9] I, John, your brother, who share with you in the suffering, the sovereignty, and the endurance which are ours in Jesus, was on the island called Patmos because I had preached God's word and borne my testimony to Jesus. [10] On the Lord's day the Spirit came upon me; and I heard behind me a loud voice, like the sound of a trumpet, [11] which said, 'Write down in a book what you see and send it to the seven churches: to Ephesus, Smyrna, Pergamum, Thyatira, Sardis, Philadelphia, and Laodicea.' [12] I turned to see whose voice it was that spoke to me; and when I turned I saw seven lampstands of gold. [13] Among the lamps was a figure like a man, in a robe that came to his feet, with a golden girdle round his breast. [14] His hair was as white as snow-white wool, and his eyes flamed like fire; [15] his feet were like burnished bronze refined in a furnace, and his voice was like the sound of a mighty torrent. [16] In his right hand he held seven stars, and from his mouth came a sharp, two-edged sword; his face shone like the sun in full strength.

[17] When I saw him, I fell at his feet as though I were dead. But he laid his right hand on me and said, 'Do not be afraid. I am the first and the last, [18] and I am the living One; I was dead and now I am alive for evermore, and I hold the keys of death and Hades. [19] Write down therefore what you have seen, what is now, and what is to take place hereafter.

[20] 'This is the secret meaning of the seven stars you saw in my right hand, and of the seven gold lamps: the seven stars are the angels of the seven churches, and the seven lamps are the seven churches themselves.

2 'To THE angel of the church at Ephesus write:
' "These are the words of the One who holds the seven stars in his right hand, who walks among the seven gold lamps: [2] I know what you are doing, how you toil and endure. I know you cannot abide wicked people; you have put to the test those who claim to be apostles but are not, and you have found them to be false. [3] Endurance you have; you have borne up in my cause and have never become weary. [4] However, I have this against you: the love you felt at first you have now lost. [5] Think from what a height you have fallen; repent, and do as once you did. If you do not, I will come to you and remove your lamp from its place. [6] Yet

you have this much in your favour: you detest as I do the practices of the Nicolaitans. [7] You have ears, so hear what the Spirit says to the churches! To those who are victorious I will give the right to eat from the tree of life that stands in the garden of God."

[8] 'To the angel of the church at Smyrna write:

' "These are the words of the First and the Last, who was dead and came to life again: [9] I know how hard pressed and poor you are, but in reality you are rich. I know how you are slandered by those who claim to be Jews but are not; they are really a synagogue of Satan. [10] Do not be afraid of the sufferings to come. The devil will throw some of you into prison, to be put to the test, and for ten days you will be hard pressed. Be faithful till death, and I will give you the crown of life. [11] You have ears, so hear what the Spirit says to the churches! Those who are victorious cannot be harmed by the second death."

[12] 'To the angel of the church at Pergamum write:

' "These are the words of the One who has the sharp, two-edged sword: [13] I know where you live; it is where Satan is enthroned. Yet you are holding fast to my cause, and did not deny your faith in me even at the time when Antipas, my faithful witness, was put to death in your city, where Satan has his home. [14] But I have a few matters to bring against you. You have in Pergamum some that hold to the teaching of Balaam, who taught Balak to put temptation in the way of the Israelites; he encouraged them to eat food sacrificed to idols and to commit fornication. [15] In the same way you also have some who hold to the teaching of the Nicolaitans. [16] So repent! If you do not, I will come to you quickly and make war on them with the sword that comes out of my mouth. [17] You have ears, so hear what the Spirit says to the churches! To anyone who is victorious I will give some of the hidden manna; I will also give him a white stone, and on it will be written a new name, known only to him who receives it."

[18] 'To the angel of the church at Thyatira write:

' "These are the words of the Son of God, whose eyes flame like fire, and whose feet are like burnished bronze: [19] I know

what you are doing, your love and faithfulness, your service and your endurance; indeed of late you have done even better than you did at first. [20] But I have this against you: you tolerate that Jezebel, the woman who claims to be a prophetess, whose teaching lures my servants into fornication and into eating food sacrificed to idols. [21] I have given her time to repent, but she refuses to repent of her fornication. [22] So I will throw her on a bed of pain, and I will plunge her lovers into terrible suffering, unless they renounce what she is doing; [23] and her children I will kill with pestilence. This will teach all the churches that I am the searcher of men's hearts and minds, and that I will give to each of you what his deeds deserve. [24] And now I speak to the rest of you in Thyatira, all who do not accept this teaching and have had no experience of what they call the deep secrets of Satan. On you I impose no further burden; [25] only hold fast to what you have, until I come. [26] To him who is victorious, to him who perseveres in doing my will to the end, I will give authority over the nations—[27] that same authority which I received from my Father—and he will rule them with a rod of iron, smashing them to pieces like earthenware; [28] and I will give him the star of dawn. [29] You have ears, so hear what the Spirit says to the churches!"

3 'To the angel of the church at Sardis write:

' "These are the words of the One who has the seven spirits of God and the seven stars: I know what you are doing; people say you are alive, but in fact you are dead. [2] Wake up, and put some strength into what you still have, because otherwise it must die! For I have not found any work of yours brought to completion in the sight of my God. [3] Remember therefore the teaching you received; observe it, and repent. If you do not wake up, I will come upon you like a thief, and you will not know the moment of my coming. [4] Yet you have a few people in Sardis who have not polluted their clothing, and they will walk with me in white, for so they deserve. [5] Anyone who is victorious will be robed in white like them, and I shall never strike his name off the roll of the living; in the presence of my Father and his angels I shall acknowledge him as mine. [6] You have ears, so hear what the Spirit says to the churches!"

[7] 'To the angel of the church at Philadelphia write:

'"These are the words of the Holy One, the True One, who has David's key, so that when he opens the door, no one can shut it, and when he shuts it, no one can open it: [8] I know what you are doing. I have set before you an open door which no one can shut. I know your strength is small, yet you have observed my command and have not disowned my name. [9] As for those of Satan's synagogue, who falsely claim to be Jews, I will make them come and fall at your feet; and they will know that you are my beloved people. [10] Because you have kept my command to stand firm, I will also keep you from the ordeal that is to fall upon the whole world to test its inhabitants. [11] I am coming soon; hold fast to what you have, and let no one rob you of your crown. [12] Those who are victorious I shall make pillars in the temple of my God; they will remain there for ever. I shall write on them the name of my God, and the name of the city of my God, that new Jerusalem which is coming down out of heaven from my God, and my own new name. [13] You have ears, so hear what the Spirit says to the churches!"

[14] 'To the angel of the church at Laodicea write:

'"These are the words of the Amen, the faithful and true witness, the source of God's creation: [15] I know what you are doing; you are neither cold nor hot. How I wish you were either cold or hot! [16] Because you are neither one nor the other, but just lukewarm, I will spit you out of my mouth. [17] You say, 'How rich I am! What a fortune I have made! I have everything I want.' In fact, though you do not realize it, you are a pitiful wretch, poor, blind, and naked. [18] I advise you to buy from me gold refined in the fire to make you truly rich, and white robes to put on to hide the shame of your nakedness, and ointment for your eyes so that you may see. [19] All whom I love I reprove and discipline. Be wholehearted therefore in your repentance. [20] Here I stand knocking at the door; if anyone hears my voice and opens the door, I will come in and he and I will eat together. [21] To anyone who is victorious I will grant

a place beside me on my throne, as I myself was victorious and sat down with my Father on his throne. [22] You have ears, so hear what the Spirit says to the churches!"'

Visions of heaven

4 AFTER this I had a vision: a door stood open in heaven, and the voice that I had first heard speaking to me like a trumpet said, 'Come up here, and I will show you what must take place hereafter.' [2] At once the Spirit came upon me. There in heaven stood a throne. On it sat One [3] whose appearance was like jasper or cornelian, and round it was a rainbow, bright as an emerald. [4] In a circle about this throne were twenty-four other thrones, and on them were seated twenty-four elders, robed in white and wearing gold crowns. [5] From the throne came flashes of lightning and peals of thunder. Burning before the throne were seven flaming torches, the seven spirits of God, [6] and in front of it stretched what looked like a sea of glass or a sheet of ice.

In the centre, round the throne itself, were four living creatures, covered with eyes in front and behind. [7] The first creature was like a lion, the second like an ox, the third had a human face, and the fourth was like an eagle in flight. [8] Each of the four living creatures had six wings, and eyes all round and inside them. Day and night unceasingly they sing:

'Holy, holy, holy is God the sovereign Lord of all, who was, and is, and is to come!'

[9] Whenever the living creatures give glory and honour and thanks to the One who sits on the throne, who lives for ever and ever, [10] the twenty-four elders prostrate themselves before the One who sits on the throne and they worship him who lives for ever and ever. As they lay their crowns before the throne they cry:

[11] 'You are worthy, O Lord our God, to receive glory and honour and power, because you created all things; by your will they were created and have their being!'

5 I saw in the right hand of the One who sat on the throne a scroll with writing on both sides, and sealed with seven seals. [2] And I saw a mighty angel

proclaiming in a loud voice, 'Who is worthy to break the seals and open the scroll?' ³ But there was no one in heaven or on earth or under the earth able to open the scroll to look inside it. ⁴ And because no one was found worthy to open the scroll and look inside, I wept bitterly. ⁵ One of the elders said to me: 'Do not weep; the Lion from the tribe of Judah, the shoot growing from David's stock, has won the right to open the scroll and its seven seals.'

⁶ Then I saw a Lamb with the marks of sacrifice on him, standing with the four living creatures between the throne and the elders. He had seven horns and seven eyes, the eyes which are the seven spirits of God sent to every part of the world. ⁷ The Lamb came and received the scroll from the right hand of the One who sat on the throne. ⁸ As he did so, the four living creatures and the twenty-four elders prostrated themselves before the Lamb. Each of the elders had a harp; they held golden bowls full of incense, the prayers of God's people, ⁹ and they were singing a new song:

'You are worthy to receive the scroll and break its seals, for you were slain and by your blood you bought for God people of every tribe and language, nation and race. ¹⁰ You have made them a royal house of priests for our God, and they shall reign on earth.'

¹¹ As I looked I heard, all round the throne and the living creatures and the elders, the voices of many angels, thousands on thousands, myriads on myriads. ¹² They proclaimed with loud voices:

'Worthy is the Lamb who was slain, to receive power and wealth, wisdom and might, honour and glory and praise!'

¹³ Then I heard all created things, in heaven, on earth, under the earth, and in the sea, crying:

'Praise and honour, glory and might, to him who sits on the throne and to the Lamb for ever!'

¹⁴ The four living creatures said, 'Amen,' and the elders prostrated themselves in worship.

The seven seals

6 I WATCHED as the Lamb broke the first of the seven seals, and I heard one of the four living creatures say in a voice like thunder, 'Come!' ² There before my eyes was a white horse, and its rider held a bow. He was given a crown, and he rode forth, conquering and to conquer.

³ The Lamb broke the second seal, and I heard the second creature say, 'Come!' ⁴ Out came another horse, which was red. Its rider was given power to take away peace from the earth that men might slaughter one another; and he was given a great sword.

⁵ He broke the third seal, and I heard the third creature say, 'Come!' There, as I looked, was a black horse, and its rider was holding in his hand a pair of scales. ⁶ I heard what sounded like a voice from among the four living creatures; it said, 'A day's wage for a quart of flour, a day's wage for three quarts of barley-meal! But do not damage the olive and the vine!'

⁷ He broke the fourth seal, and I heard the fourth creature say, 'Come!' ⁸ There, as I looked, was another horse, sickly pale; its rider's name was Death, and Hades followed close behind. To them was given power over a quarter of the earth, power to kill by sword and famine, by pestilence and wild beasts.

⁹ He broke the fifth seal, and I saw beneath the altar the souls of those who had been slaughtered for God's word and for the testimony they bore. ¹⁰ They gave a great cry: 'How long, sovereign Lord, holy and true, must it be before you will vindicate us and avenge our death on the inhabitants of the earth?' ¹¹ They were each given a white robe, and told to rest a little longer, until the number should be complete of all their brothers in Christ's service who were to be put to death, as they themselves had been.

¹² I watched as the Lamb broke the sixth seal. There was a violent earthquake; the sun turned black as a funeral pall and the moon all red as blood; ¹³ the stars in the sky fell to the earth, like figs blown off a tree in a gale; ¹⁴ the sky vanished like a scroll being rolled up, and every mountain and island was dislodged from its place. ¹⁵ The kings of the earth,

5:6 **standing** ... **elders:** *or* standing in the middle of the throne, inside the circle of living creatures and the circle of elders.   6:9 **beneath:** *or* at the foot of.

the nobles and the commanders, the rich and the powerful, and all men, slave or free, hid themselves in caves and under mountain crags; [16] and they called out to the mountains and the crags, 'Fall on us, hide us from the One who sits on the throne and from the wrath of the Lamb, [17] for the great day of their wrath has come, and who can stand?'

7 After that I saw four angels stationed at the four corners of the earth, holding back its four winds so that no wind should blow on land or sea or on any tree. [2] I saw another angel rising from the east, bearing the seal of the living God. To the four angels who had been given the power to ravage land and sea, he cried out: [3] 'Do no damage to land or sea or to the trees until we have set the seal of our God upon the foreheads of his servants.' [4] I heard how many had been marked with the seal—a hundred and forty-four thousand from all the tribes of Israel: [5] twelve thousand from the tribe of Judah, twelve thousand from the tribe of Reuben, twelve thousand from the tribe of Gad, [6] twelve thousand from the tribe of Asher, twelve thousand from the tribe of Naphtali, twelve thousand from the tribe of Manasseh, [7] twelve thousand from the tribe of Simeon, twelve thousand from the tribe of Levi, twelve thousand from the tribe of Issachar, [8] twelve thousand from the tribe of Zebulun, twelve thousand from the tribe of Joseph, and twelve thousand from the tribe of Benjamin.

[9] After that I looked and saw a vast throng, which no one could count, from all races and tribes, nations and languages, standing before the throne and the Lamb. They were robed in white and had palm branches in their hands, [10] and they shouted aloud:

'Victory to our God who sits on the throne, and to the Lamb!'

[11] All the angels who stood round the throne and round the elders and the four living creatures prostrated themselves before the throne and worshipped God, [12] crying:

'Amen! Praise and glory and wisdom, thanksgiving and honour, power and might, be to our God for ever! Amen.'

[13] One of the elders turned to me and asked, 'Who are these all robed in white, and where do they come from?' [14] I answered, 'My lord, it is you who know.' He said to me, 'They are those who have passed through the great ordeal; they have washed their robes and made them white in the blood of the Lamb. [15] That is why they stand before the throne of God and worship him day and night in his temple; and he who sits on the throne will protect them with his presence. [16] Never again shall they feel hunger or thirst; never again shall the sun beat on them or any scorching heat, [17] because the Lamb who is at the centre of the throne will be their shepherd and will guide them to springs of the water of life; and God will wipe every tear from their eyes.'

8 Now when the Lamb broke the seventh seal, there was silence in heaven for about half an hour.

The seven trumpets

[2] I SAW the seven angels who stand in the presence of God: they were given seven trumpets.

[3] Another angel came and stood at the altar, holding a golden censer. He was given much incense to offer with the prayers of all God's people on the golden altar in front of the throne, [4] and the smoke of the incense from the angel's hand went up before God with his people's prayers. [5] The angel took the censer, filled it with fire from the altar, and threw it down on the earth; and there came peals of thunder, lightning-flashes, and an earthquake.

[6] THE seven angels who held the seven trumpets prepared to blow them.

[7] The first angel blew his trumpet. There came hail and fire mingled with blood, and this was hurled upon the earth; a third of the earth was burnt, a third of the trees, and all the green grass.

[8] The second angel blew his trumpet. What looked like a great mountain flaming with fire was hurled into the sea; a third of the sea was turned to blood, [9] a third of the living creatures in it died, and a third of the ships on it were destroyed.

[10] The third angel blew his trumpet. A great star shot from the sky, flaming like a torch, and fell on a third of the rivers and springs; [11] the name of the star was Wormwood. A third of the water turned

to wormwood, and great numbers of people died from drinking the water because it had been made bitter.

¹² The fourth angel blew his trumpet. A third part of the sun was struck, a third of the moon, and a third of the stars, so that a third part of them turned dark and a third of the light failed to appear by day or by night.

¹³ As I looked, I heard an eagle calling with a loud cry as it flew in mid-heaven: 'Woe, woe, woe to the inhabitants of the earth at the sound of the other trumpets which the next three angels must now blow!'

9 The fifth angel blew his trumpet. I saw a star that had fallen from heaven to earth, and the star was given the key to the shaft of the abyss. ² He opened it, and smoke came up from it like smoke from a great furnace and darkened the sun and the air. ³ Out of the smoke came locusts over the earth, and they were given the powers of scorpions. ⁴ They were told not to do damage to the grass or to any plant or tree, but only to those people who had not received God's seal on their foreheads. ⁵ They were given permission to torment them for five months with torment like a scorpion's sting; but they were not to kill them. ⁶ During that time people will seek death, but will not find it; they will long to die, but death will elude them.

⁷ In appearance the locusts were like horses equipped for battle. On their heads were what looked like gold crowns; their faces were like human faces ⁸ and their hair like women's hair; they had teeth like lions' teeth ⁹ and chests like iron breastplates; the sound of their wings was like the noise of many horses and chariots charging into battle; ¹⁰ they had tails like scorpions, with stings in them, and in their tails lay their power to injure people for five months. ¹¹ They had for their king the angel of the abyss, whose name in Hebrew is Abaddon, and in Greek Apollyon, the Destroyer.

¹² The first woe has now passed; but there are still two more to come.

¹³ The sixth angel blew his trumpet. I heard a voice coming from the horns of the golden altar that stood in the presence of God. ¹⁴ To the sixth angel, who held the trumpet, the voice said: 'Release the four angels held bound at the Great River, the Euphrates!' ¹⁵ So the four angels were let loose, to kill a third of mankind; they had been held in readiness for this very year, month, day, and hour. ¹⁶ And their squadrons of cavalry numbered twice ten thousand times ten thousand; this was the number I heard.

¹⁷ This was how I saw the horses and their riders in my vision: they wore breastplates, fiery red, turquoise, and sulphur-yellow; the horses had heads like lions' heads, and from their mouths issued fire, smoke, and sulphur. ¹⁸ By these three plagues, the fire, the smoke, and the sulphur that came from their mouths, a third of mankind was killed. ¹⁹ The power of the horses lay in their mouths and in their tails; for their tails had heads like serpents, and with them they inflicted injuries.

²⁰ The rest of mankind who survived these plagues still did not renounce the gods their hands had made, or cease their worship of demons and of idols fashioned from gold, silver, bronze, stone, and wood, which cannot see or hear or walk; ²¹ nor did they repent of their murders, their sorcery, their fornication, or their robberies.

10 I saw another mighty angel coming down from heaven. He was wrapped in cloud, with a rainbow over his head; his face shone like the sun and his legs were like pillars of fire. ² In his hand he held a little scroll which had been opened. He planted his right foot on the sea and his left on the land, ³ and gave a great shout like the roar of a lion; when he shouted, the seven thunders spoke. ⁴ I was about to write down what the seven thunders had said, but I heard a voice from heaven saying, 'Put under seal what the seven thunders have said; do not write it down.' ⁵ Then the angel whom I saw standing on the sea and the land raised his right hand towards heaven ⁶ and swore by him who lives for ever, who created heaven and earth and the sea and everything in them: 'There shall be no more delay; ⁷ when the time comes for the seventh angel to sound his trumpet, the hidden purpose of God will have been fulfilled, as he promised to his servants the prophets.'

⁸ The voice which I had heard from heaven began speaking to me again; it

said, 'Go and take the scroll which is open in the hand of the angel who stands on the sea and the land.' [9] I went to the angel and asked him to give me the little scroll. He answered, 'Take it, and eat it. It will turn your stomach sour, but in your mouth it will taste as sweet as honey.' [10] I took the scroll from the angel's hand and ate it, and in my mouth it did taste as sweet as honey, but when I swallowed it my stomach turned sour. [11] Then I was told, 'Once again you must utter prophecies over many nations, races, languages, and kings.'

11 I was given a long cane to use as a measuring rod, and was told: 'Go and measure the temple of God and the altar, and count the worshippers. [2] But leave the outer court of the temple out of your measurements; it has been given over to the Gentiles, and for forty-two months they will trample the Holy City underfoot. [3] I will give my two witnesses authority to prophesy, dressed in sackcloth, for those twelve hundred and sixty days.' [4] They are the two olive trees and the two lamps that stand in the presence of the Lord of the earth. [5] If anyone tries to injure them, fire issues from their mouths and consumes their enemies; so shall anyone die who tries to do them injury. [6] These two have the power to shut up the sky, so that no rain falls during the time of their prophesying; and they have power to turn water into blood and to afflict the earth with every kind of plague whenever they like. [7] But when they have completed their testimony, the beast that comes up from the abyss will wage war on them and will overcome and kill them. [8] Their bodies will lie in the street of the great city, whose name in prophetic language is Sodom, or Egypt, where also their Lord was crucified. [9] For three and a half days people from every nation and tribe, language, and race, gaze on their corpses and refuse them burial. [10] The earth's inhabitants gloat over them; they celebrate and exchange presents, for these two prophets were a torment to them. [11] But at the end of the three and a half days the breath of life from God came into their bodies, and they rose to their feet, to the terror of those who saw them. [12] A loud voice from heaven was heard saying to them, 'Come up here!' and they ascended to heaven in a cloud, in full view of their enemies. [13] At that moment there was a violent earthquake, and a tenth of the city collapsed. Seven thousand people were killed in the earthquake; the rest, filled with fear, did homage to the God of heaven.

[14] The second woe has now passed; but the third is soon to come.

[15] Then the seventh angel blew his trumpet. Voices in heaven were heard crying aloud:

'Sovereignty over the world has passed to our Lord and his Christ, and he shall reign for ever!'

[16] The twenty-four elders, who sit on their thrones before God, prostrated themselves before him in adoration, [17] saying:

'O Lord God, sovereign over all, you are and you were; we give you thanks because you have assumed full power and entered upon your reign. [18] The nations rose in wrath, but your day of wrath has come. Now is the time for the dead to be judged; now is the time for rewards to be given to your servants the prophets, to your own people, and to all who honour your name, both small and great; now is the time to destroy those who destroy the earth.'

[19] God's sanctuary in heaven was opened, and within his sanctuary was seen the ark of his covenant. There came flashes of lightning and peals of thunder, an earthquake, and a violent hailstorm.

Seven visions

12 AFTER that there appeared a great sign in heaven: a woman robed with the sun, beneath her feet the moon, and on her head a crown of twelve stars. [2] She was about to bear a child, and in the anguish of her labour she cried out to be delivered. [3] Then a second sign appeared in heaven: a great, fiery red dragon with seven heads and ten horns. On his heads were seven diadems, [4] and with his tail he swept down a third of the stars in the sky and hurled them to the earth. The dragon stood in front of the woman who was about to give birth, so that when her child was born he might devour it. [5] But when she gave birth to a male child, who is destined to rule all nations with a rod of iron, the child was snatched up to God and to his throne. [6] The woman herself

fled into the wilderness, where she was to be looked after for twelve hundred and sixty days in a place prepared for her by God.

⁷ Then war broke out in heaven; Michael and his angels fought against the dragon. The dragon with his angels fought back, ⁸ but he was too weak, and they lost their place in heaven. ⁹ The great dragon was thrown down, that ancient serpent who led the whole world astray, whose name is the Devil, or Satan; he was thrown down to the earth, and his angels with him.

¹⁰ I heard a loud voice in heaven proclaim: 'This is the time of victory for our God, the time of his power and sovereignty, when his Christ comes to his rightful rule! For the accuser of our brothers, he who day and night accused them before our God, is overthrown. ¹¹ By the sacrifice of the Lamb and by the witness they bore, they have conquered him; faced with death they did not cling to life. ¹² Therefore rejoice, you heavens and you that dwell in them! But woe to you, earth and sea, for the Devil has come down to you in great fury, knowing that his time is short!'

¹³ When the dragon saw that he had been thrown down to the earth, he went in pursuit of the woman who had given birth to the male child. ¹⁴ But she was given the wings of a mighty eagle, so that she could fly to her place in the wilderness where she was to be looked after for three and a half years, out of reach of the serpent. ¹⁵ From his mouth the serpent spewed a flood of water after the woman to sweep her away with its spate. ¹⁶ But the earth came to her rescue: it opened its mouth and drank up the river which the dragon spewed from his mouth. ¹⁷ Furious with the woman, the dragon went off to wage war on the rest of her offspring, those who keep God's commandments and maintain their witness to

13 Jesus. ¹ He took his stand on the seashore.

Then I saw a beast rising out of the sea. It had ten horns and seven heads; on the horns were ten diadems, and on each head was a blasphemous name. ² The beast I saw resembled a leopard, but its

feet were like a bear's and its mouth like a lion's. The dragon conferred on it his own power, his throne, and great authority. ³ One of the heads seemed to have been given a death blow, yet its mortal wound was healed. The whole world went after the beast in wondering admiration, ⁴ and worshipped the dragon because he had conferred his authority on the beast; they worshipped the beast also. 'Who is like the beast?' they said. 'Who can fight against it?'

⁵ The beast was allowed to mouth bombast and blasphemy, and was granted permission to continue for forty-two months. ⁶ It uttered blasphemies against God, reviling his name and his dwelling-place, that is, those who dwell in heaven. ⁷ It was also allowed to wage war on God's people and to defeat them, and it was granted authority over every tribe, nation, language, and race. ⁸ All the inhabitants of the earth will worship it, all whose names have not been written in the book of life of the Lamb, slain since the foundation of the world.

⁹ You have ears, so hear! ¹⁰ Whoever is to be made prisoner, to prison he shall go; whoever is to be slain by the sword, by the sword he must be slain. This calls for the endurance and faithfulness of God's people.

¹¹ Then I saw another beast; it came up out of the earth, and had two horns like a lamb's, but spoke like a dragon. ¹² It wielded all the authority of the first beast in its presence, and made the earth and its inhabitants worship this first beast, whose mortal wound had been healed. ¹³ It worked great miracles, even making fire come down from heaven to earth, where people could see it. ¹⁴ By the miracles it was allowed to perform in the presence of the beast it deluded the inhabitants of the earth, and persuaded them to erect an image in honour of the beast which had been wounded by the sword and yet lived. ¹⁵ It was allowed to give breath to the image of the beast, so that it could even speak and cause all who would not worship the image to be put to death. ¹⁶ It caused everyone, small and great, rich and poor, free man and slave, to have a mark put on his right hand or

12:11 **the witness they bore:** *or* the word of God to which they bore witness. 13:8 **written ... world:** *or* written, since the foundation of the world, in the book of life of the slain Lamb. 13:10 **whoever ... slain by the sword:** *or* whoever takes the sword to slay.

his forehead, ¹⁷ and no one was allowed to buy or sell unless he bore this beast's mark, either name or number. ¹⁸ (This calls for skill; let anyone who has intelligence work out the number of the beast, for the number represents a man's name, and the numerical value of its letters is six hundred and sixty-six.)

14 I LOOKED, and there on Mount Zion stood the Lamb, and with him were a hundred and forty-four thousand who had his name and the name of his Father written on their foreheads. ² I heard a sound from heaven like a mighty torrent or a great peal of thunder; what I heard was like harpists playing on their harps. ³ They were singing a new song before the throne and the four living creatures and the elders, and no one could learn it except the hundred and forty-four thousand ransomed from the earth. ⁴ These are men who have kept themselves chaste and have not defiled themselves with women; these follow the Lamb wherever he goes. They have been ransomed as the firstfruits of mankind for God and the Lamb. ⁵ No lie was found on their lips; they are without fault.

⁶ Then I saw an angel flying in midheaven, with an eternal gospel to proclaim to those on earth, to every race, tribe, language, and nation. ⁷ He spoke in a loud voice: 'Fear God and pay him homage, for the hour of his judgement has come! Worship him who made heaven and earth, the sea and the springs of water!'

⁸ A second angel followed, saying, 'Fallen, fallen is Babylon the great, who has made all nations drink the wine of God's anger roused by her fornication!'

⁹ A third angel followed, saying in a loud voice, 'Whoever worships the beast and its image and receives its mark on his forehead or hand, ¹⁰ he too shall drink the wine of God's anger, poured undiluted into the cup of his wrath. He shall be tormented in sulphurous flames in the sight of the holy angels and the Lamb. ¹¹ The smoke of their torment will rise for ever; there will be no respite day or night for those who worship the beast and its image, or for anyone who receives the mark of its name.' ¹² This calls for the endurance of God's people, all those who keep his commands and remain loyal to Jesus.

¹³ I heard a voice from heaven say, 'Write this: "Happy are the dead who henceforth die in the faith of the Lord!" "Yes," says the Spirit, "let them rest from their labours, for the record of their deeds goes with them."'

¹⁴ As I looked there appeared a white cloud, on which was seated a figure like a man; he had a gold crown on his head and a sharp sickle in his hand. ¹⁵ Another angel came out of the temple and called in a loud voice to him who sat on the cloud: 'Put in your sickle and reap, for harvest time has come and earth's crop is fully ripe.' ¹⁶ So the one who sat on the cloud swept over the earth with his sickle and the harvest was reaped.

¹⁷ Another angel came out of the heavenly sanctuary, and he also had a sharp sickle. ¹⁸ Then from the altar came yet another, the angel who has authority over fire, and he called aloud to the one with the sharp sickle: 'Put in your sharp sickle, and gather in earth's grape harvest, for its clusters are ripe.' ¹⁹ So the angel swept over the earth with his sickle and gathered in its grapes, and threw them into the great winepress of God's wrath. ²⁰ The winepress was trodden outside the city, and for a distance of two hundred miles blood flowed from the press to the height of horses' bridles.

The seven bowls

15 THEN I saw in heaven another great and astonishing sign: seven angels with seven plagues, the last plagues of all, for with them the wrath of God was completed.

² I saw what looked like a sea of glass shot through with fire. Standing beside it and holding the harps which God had given them were those who had been victorious against the beast, its image, and the number of its name.

³ They were singing the song of Moses, the servant of God, and the song of the Lamb:

'Great and marvellous are your
    deeds,

13: 18 **the numerical … letters:** *lit.* his number.   14: 13 **the dead … the Spirit:** *some witnesses read* the dead who die trusting in the Lord! Henceforth", says the Spirit.

O Lord God, sovereign over all;
just and true are your ways,
O King of the ages.
4 Who shall not fear you, Lord,
and do homage to your name?
For you alone are holy.
All nations shall come and worship
before you,
for your just decrees stand revealed.'

5 After this, as I looked, the sanctuary of the heavenly Tent of Testimony was opened, 6 and from it came the seven angels with the seven plagues. They were robed in fine linen, pure and shining, and had golden girdles round their breasts. 7 One of the four living creatures gave to the seven angels seven golden bowls full of the wrath of God who lives for ever. 8 The sanctuary was filled with smoke from the glory of God and from his power, so that no one could enter it until the seven plagues of the seven angels were completed.

16 I heard a loud voice from the sanctuary say to the seven angels, 'Go and pour out the seven bowls of God's wrath on the earth.'

2 The first angel went and poured out his bowl on the earth; and foul malignant sores appeared on the men that wore the mark of the beast and worshipped its image.

3 The second angel poured out his bowl on the sea; and the sea turned to blood like the blood from a dead body, and every living thing in it died.

4 The third angel poured out his bowl on the rivers and springs, and they turned to blood.

5 And I heard the angel of the waters say, 'You are just in these your judgements, you who are, and were, O Holy One; 6 for they shed the blood of your people and your prophets, and blood you have given them to drink. They have what they deserve!' 7 I heard a voice from the altar cry, 'Yes, Lord God, sovereign over all, true and just are your judgements!'

8 The fourth angel poured out his bowl on the sun; and it was allowed to burn people with its flames. 9 They were severely burned, and cursed the name of God who had the power to inflict such plagues, but they did not repent and do him homage.

10 The fifth angel poured out his bowl on the throne of the beast; and its kingdom was plunged into darkness. Men gnawed their tongues in agony, 11 and cursed the God of heaven for their pain and sores, but they would not repent of what they had done.

12 The sixth angel poured out his bowl on the Great River, the Euphrates; and its water was dried up to prepare a way for the kings from the east.

13 I saw three foul spirits like frogs coming from the mouths of the dragon, the beast, and the false prophet. 14 These are demonic spirits with power to work miracles, sent out to muster all the kings of the world for the battle on the great day of God the sovereign Lord. 15 ('See, I am coming like a thief! Happy the man who stays awake, and keeps his clothes at hand so that he will not have to go naked and ashamed for all to see!') 16 These spirits assembled the kings at the place called in Hebrew Armageddon.

17 The seventh angel poured out his bowl on the air; and out of the sanctuary came a loud voice from the throne, which said, 'It is over!' 18 There followed flashes of lightning and peals of thunder, and a violent earthquake, so violent that nothing like it had ever happened in human history.

The destruction of Babylon

19 THE great city was split in three, and the cities of the nations collapsed in ruin. God did not forget Babylon the great, but made her drink the cup which was filled with the fierce wine of his wrath. 20 Every island vanished, and not a mountain was to be seen. 21 Huge hailstones, weighing as much as a hundredweight, crashed down from the sky on the people; and they cursed God because the plague of hail was so severe.

17 ONE of the seven angels who held the seven bowls came and spoke to me; 'Come,' he said, 'I will show you the verdict on the great whore, she who is enthroned over many waters. 2 The kings of the earth have committed fornication with her, and people the world over have made themselves drunk on the wine of her fornication.' 3 He carried me in spirit into the wilderness, and I saw a woman mounted on a scarlet beast which was

covered with blasphemous names and had seven heads and ten horns. [4] The woman was clothed in purple and scarlet, and decked out with gold and precious stones and pearls. In her hand she held a gold cup full of obscenities and the foulness of her fornication. [5] Written on her forehead was a name with a secret meaning: 'Babylon the great, the mother of whores and of every obscenity on earth.' [6] I saw that the woman was drunk with the blood of God's people, and with the blood of those who had borne their testimony to Jesus.

At the sight of her I was greatly astonished. [7] But the angel said to me, 'Why are you astonished? I will tell you the secret of the woman and of the beast she rides, with the seven heads and the ten horns. [8] The beast you saw was once alive, and is alive no longer, but has yet to ascend out of the abyss before going to be destroyed. All the inhabitants of the earth whose names have not been written in the book of life since the foundation of the world will be astonished to see the beast, which once was alive, and is alive no longer, and has still to appear.

[9] 'This calls for a mind with insight. The seven heads are seven hills on which the woman sits enthroned. [10] They also represent seven kings: five have already fallen, one is now reigning, and the other has yet to come. When he does come, he is to last for only a little while. [11] As for the beast that once was alive and is alive no longer, he is an eighth—and yet he is one of the seven, and he is going to destruction. [12] The ten horns you saw are ten kings who have not yet begun to reign, but who for a brief hour will share royal authority with the beast. [13] They have a single purpose and will confer their power and authority on the beast. [14] They will wage war on the Lamb, but the Lamb will conquer them, for he is Lord of lords and King of kings, and those who are with him are called and chosen and faithful.'

[15] He continued: 'The waters you saw, where the great whore sat enthroned, represent nations, populations, races, and languages. [16] As for the ten horns you saw, and the beast, they will come to hate the whore. They will strip her naked and leave her destitute; they will devour her flesh and burn her up. [17] For God has put it into their minds to carry out his purpose, by making common cause and conferring their sovereignty on the beast until God's words are fulfilled. [18] The woman you saw is the great city that holds sway over the kings of the earth.'

18 After this I saw another angel coming down from heaven; he possessed great authority and the earth shone with his splendour. [2] In a mighty voice he proclaimed, 'Fallen, fallen is Babylon the great! She has become a dwelling for demons, a haunt for every unclean spirit, for every unclean and loathsome bird. [3] All the nations have drunk the wine of God's anger roused by her fornication; the kings of the earth have committed fornication with her, and merchants the world over have grown rich on her wealth and luxury.'

[4] I heard another voice from heaven saying: 'Come out from her, my people, lest you have any part in her sins and you share in her plagues, [5] for her sins are piled high as heaven, and God has not forgotten her crimes. [6] Pay her back in her own coin, repay her twice over for her deeds! Give her a potion twice as strong as the one she mixed! [7] Measure out torment and grief to match her pomp and luxury! "I am a queen on my throne!" she says to herself. "No widow's weeds for me, no mourning!" [8] That is why plagues shall strike her in a single day, pestilence, bereavement, and famine, and she shall perish in flames; for mighty is the Lord God who has pronounced her doom!'

[9] The kings of the earth who committed fornication with her and wallowed in her luxury will weep and wail over her, as they see the smoke of her burning. [10] In terror at her torment they will keep their distance and say, 'Alas, alas for you great city, mighty city of Babylon! In a moment your doom has come upon you!'

[11] The merchants of the world will weep and mourn for her, because no one buys their cargoes any more, [12] cargoes of gold and silver, precious stones and pearls, purple and scarlet cloth, silks and fine linens; all sorts of fragrant wood, and all kinds of objects made of ivory or of costly woods, bronze, iron, or marble; [13] cinnamon and spice, incense, perfumes, and

17:10 **kings:** *or* emperors.

frankincense; wine, oil, flour and wheat, cattle and sheep, horses, chariots, slaves, and human lives. ¹⁴ 'The harvest you longed for', they will say, 'is gone from you; all the glitter and glamour are lost, never to be found again!' ¹⁵ The traders in all these goods, who grew rich on her, will keep their distance in terror at her torment; weeping and mourning ¹⁶ they will say: 'Alas, alas for the great city that was clothed in fine linen and purple and scarlet, decked out with gold and precious stones and pearls! ¹⁷ So much wealth laid waste in a moment!'

All the sea-captains and voyagers, the sailors and those who made a living on the sea, stayed at a distance; ¹⁸ as they saw the smoke of her burning, they cried out, 'Was there ever a city like the great city?' ¹⁹ They threw dust on their heads and, weeping and mourning, they cried aloud: 'Alas, alas for the great city, where all who had ships at sea grew rich from her prosperity! In a single hour she has been laid waste!'

²⁰ But let heaven exult over her; exult, God's people, apostles and prophets, for he has imposed on her the sentence she passed on you!

²¹ Then a mighty angel picked up a stone like a great millstone and hurled it into the sea, saying, 'Thus shall Babylon, the great city, be sent hurtling down, never to be seen again! ²² The sound of harpists and minstrels, flute-players and trumpeters, shall no more be heard in you; no more shall craftsmen of any trade be found in you, or the sound of the mill be heard in you; ²³ no more shall the light of the lamp appear in you, no more the voices of the bridegroom and bride be heard in you! Your traders were once the merchant princes of the world, and with your sorcery you deceived all the nations.' ²⁴ The blood of the prophets and of God's people was found in her, the blood of all who had been slain on earth.

19 After this I heard what sounded like a vast throng in heaven shouting:

'Hallelujah! Victory and glory and power belong to our God, ² for true and just are his judgements! He has condemned the great whore who corrupted the earth with her fornication; he has taken vengeance on her for the blood of his servants.'

³ Once more they shouted:

'Hallelujah! The smoke from her burning will rise for ever!'

⁴ The twenty-four elders and the four living creatures bowed down and worshipped God who sits on the throne; they cried: 'Amen! Hallelujah!'

⁵ THERE came a voice from the throne saying: 'Praise our God, all you his servants, you that fear him, both small and great!' ⁶ And I heard what sounded like a vast throng, like the sound of a mighty torrent or of great peals of thunder, and they cried:

'Hallelujah! The Lord our God, sovereign over all, has entered on his reign! ⁷ Let us rejoice and shout for joy and pay homage to him, for the wedding day of the Lamb has come! His bride has made herself ready, ⁸ and she has been given fine linen, shining and clean, to wear.'

(The fine linen signifies the righteous deeds of God's people.)

⁹ THE angel said to me, 'Write this: "Happy are those who are invited to the wedding banquet of the Lamb!"' He added, 'These are the very words of God.' ¹⁰ I prostrated myself to worship him, but he said, 'You must not do that! I am a fellow-servant with you and your brothers who bear their witness to Jesus. It is God you must worship. For those who bear witness to Jesus have the spirit of prophecy.'

More visions

¹¹ I SAW heaven wide open, and a white horse appeared; its rider's name was Faithful and True, for he is just in judgement and just in war. ¹² His eyes flamed like fire, and on his head were many diadems. Written on him was a name known to none but himself; ¹³ he was robed in a garment dyed in blood, and he was called the Word of God. ¹⁴ The armies of heaven followed him, riding on white horses and clothed in fine linen, white and clean. ¹⁵ Out of his mouth came a sharp sword to smite the nations; for it is he who will rule them with a rod of iron, and tread the winepress of the fierce wrath of God the sovereign Lord.

¹⁶ On his robe and on his thigh was written the title: 'King of kings and Lord of lords'.

¹⁷ I saw an angel standing in the sun. He cried aloud to all the birds flying in mid-heaven: 'Come, gather together for God's great banquet, ¹⁸ to eat the flesh of kings, commanders, and warriors, the flesh of horses and their riders, the flesh of all, the free and the slave, the small and the great!' ¹⁹ I saw the beast and the kings of the earth with their armies mustered to do battle against the rider and his army. ²⁰ The beast was taken prisoner, along with the false prophet who had worked miracles in its presence and deluded those who had received the mark of the beast and worshipped its image. The two of them were thrown alive into the lake of fire with its sulphurous flames. ²¹ The rest were killed by the sword which came out of the rider's mouth, and the birds all gorged themselves on their flesh.

20 I saw an angel coming down from heaven with the key to the abyss and a great chain in his hand. ² He seized the dragon, that ancient serpent who is the Devil, or Satan, and chained him up for a thousand years; ³ he threw him into the abyss, shutting and sealing it over him, so that he might not seduce the nations again till the thousand years were ended. After that he must be let loose for a little while.

⁴ I saw thrones, and on them sat those to whom judgement was committed. I saw the souls of those who, for the sake of God's word and their witness to Jesus, had been beheaded, those who had not worshipped the beast and its image or received its mark on forehead or hand. They came to life again and reigned with Christ for a thousand years, ⁵ though the rest of the dead did not come to life until the thousand years were ended. This is the first resurrection. ⁶ Blessed and holy are those who share in this first resurrection! Over them the second death has no power; but they shall be priests of God and of Christ, and shall reign with him for the thousand years.

⁷ When the thousand years are ended, Satan will be let loose from his prison, ⁸ and he will come out to seduce the nations in the four quarters of the earth. He will muster them for war, the hosts of Gog and Magog, countless as the sands of the sea. ⁹ They marched over the breadth of the land and laid siege to the camp of God's people and the city that he loves. But fire came down on them from heaven and consumed them. ¹⁰ Their seducer, the Devil, was flung into the lake of fire and sulphur, where the beast and the false prophet had been flung to be tormented day and night for ever.

¹¹ I saw a great, white throne, and the One who sits upon it. From his presence earth and heaven fled away, and there was no room for them any more. ¹² I saw the dead, great and small, standing before the throne; and books were opened. Then another book, the book of life, was opened. The dead were judged by what they had done, as recorded in these books. ¹³ The sea gave up the dead that were in it, and Death and Hades gave up the dead in their keeping. Everyone was judged on the record of his deeds. ¹⁴ Then Death and Hades were flung into the lake of fire. This lake of fire is the second death; ¹⁵ into it were flung any whose names were not to be found in the book of life.

21 I SAW a new heaven and a new earth, for the first heaven and the first earth had vanished, and there was no longer any sea. ² I saw the Holy City, new Jerusalem, coming down out of heaven from God, made ready like a bride adorned for her husband. ³ I heard a loud voice proclaiming from the throne: 'Now God has his dwelling with mankind! He will dwell among them and they shall be his people, and God himself will be with them. ⁴ He will wipe every tear from their eyes. There shall be an end to death, and to mourning and crying and pain, for the old order has passed away!'

⁵ The One who sat on the throne said, 'I am making all things new!' ('Write this down,' he said, 'for these words are trustworthy and true.') ⁶ Then he said to me, 'It is done! I am the Alpha and the Omega, the beginning and the end. To the thirsty I will give water from the spring of life as a gift. ⁷ This is the victors' heritage; and I will be their God and they will be my children. ⁸ But as for the cowardly, the faithless, and the obscene, the murderers, fornicators, sorcerers, idolaters, and liars of every kind, the lake that burns with sulphurous flames will be their portion, and that is the second death.'

The new Jerusalem

[9] ONE of the seven angels who held the seven bowls full of the seven last plagues came and spoke to me. 'Come,' he said, 'and I will show you the bride, the wife of the Lamb.' [10] So in the spirit he carried me away to a great and lofty mountain, and showed me Jerusalem, the Holy City, coming down out of heaven from God. [11] It shone with the glory of God; it had the radiance of some priceless jewel, like a jasper, clear as crystal. [12] It had a great and lofty wall with twelve gates, at which were stationed twelve angels; on the gates were inscribed the names of the twelve tribes of Israel. [13] There were three gates to the east, three to the north, three to the south, and three to the west. [14] The city wall had twelve foundation-stones, and on them were the names of the twelve apostles of the Lamb.

[15] The angel who spoke with me carried a gold measuring rod to measure the city, its gates, and its wall. [16] The city had four sides, and it was as wide as it was long. Measured by his rod, it was twelve thousand furlongs, its length and breadth and height being equal. [17] Its wall was one hundred and forty-four cubits high, by human measurements, which the angel used. [18] The wall was built of jasper, while the city itself was of pure gold, bright as clear glass. [19] The foundations of the city wall were adorned with precious stones of every kind, the first of the foundation-stones being jasper, the second lapis lazuli, the third chalcedony, the fourth emerald, [20] the fifth sardonyx, the sixth cornelian, the seventh chrysolite, the eighth beryl, the ninth topaz, the tenth chrysoprase, the eleventh turquoise, and the twelfth amethyst. [21] The twelve gates were twelve pearls, each gate fashioned from a single pearl. The great street of the city was of pure gold, like translucent glass.

[22] I saw no temple in the city, for its temple was the sovereign Lord God and the Lamb. [23] The city did not need the sun or the moon to shine on it, for the glory of God gave it light, and its lamp was the Lamb. [24] By its light shall the nations walk, and to it the kings of the earth shall bring their splendour. [25] The gates of the city shall never be shut by day, nor will there be any night there. [26] The splendour and wealth of the nations shall be brought into it, [27] but nothing unclean shall enter, nor anyone whose ways are foul or false; only those shall enter whose names are inscribed in the Lamb's book of life.

22 Then the angel showed me the river of the water of life, sparkling like crystal, flowing from the throne of God and of the Lamb [2] down the middle of the city's street. On either side of the river stood a tree of life, which yields twelve crops of fruit, one for each month of the year. The leaves of the trees are for the healing of the nations. [3] Every accursed thing shall disappear. The throne of God and of the Lamb will be there, and his servants shall worship him; [4] they shall see him face to face and bear his name on their foreheads. [5] There shall be no more night, nor will they need the light of lamp or sun, for the Lord God will give them light; and they shall reign for ever.

Conclusion

[6] HE said to me, 'These words are trustworthy and true. The Lord God who inspires the prophets has sent his angel to show his servants what must soon take place. [7] And remember, I am coming soon!'

Happy is the man who takes to heart the words of prophecy contained in this book! [8] It was I, John, who heard and saw these things. When I had heard and seen them, I prostrated myself to worship the angel who had shown them to me. [9] But he said, 'You must not do that! I am a fellow-servant with you and your brothers the prophets and with those who take to heart the words of this book. It is God you must worship.' [10] He told me, 'Do not seal up the words of the prophecy that are in this book, for the time of fulfilment is near. [11] Meanwhile, let the evildoers persist in doing evil and the filthy-minded continue in their filth, but let the good persevere in their goodness and the holy continue in holiness.'

[12] 'I am coming soon, and bringing with me my recompense to repay everyone according to what he has done! [13] I am the Alpha and the Omega, the first and the last, the beginning and the end.'

[14] Happy are those who wash their robes clean! They shall be free to eat from the tree of life and may enter the city by

the gates. [15] Outside are the perverts, the sorcerers and fornicators, the murderers and idolaters, and all who love and practise deceit.

[16] 'I, Jesus, have sent my angel to you with this testimony for the churches. I am the offspring of David, the shoot growing from his stock, the bright star of dawn.'

[17] 'Come!' say the Spirit and the bride. 'Come!' let each hearer reply.

Let the thirsty come; let whoever wishes accept the water of life as a gift.

[18] I, John, give this warning to everyone who is listening to the words of prophecy in this book: if anyone adds to them, God will add to him the plagues described in this book; [19] if anyone takes away from the words in this book of prophecy, God will take away from him his share in the tree of life and in the Holy City, which are described in this book.

[20] He who gives this testimony says: 'Yes, I am coming soon!'

Amen. Come, Lord Jesus!

[21] The grace of the Lord Jesus be with all.

22:15 **perverts:** *lit.* dogs.

236